New Perspectives on
Microsoft® Excel for Windows®

ADVANCED

The **New Perspectives Series**

The New Perspectives Series consists of texts and technology that teach computer concepts and the programs listed below. Both Windows 3.1 and Windows 95 versions of these programs are available. You can order these New Perspectives texts in many different lengths, software releases, custom-bound combinations, CourseKits™, and Custom Editions®. Contact your CTI sales representative or customer service representative for the most up-to-date details.

The New Perspectives Series

Computer Concepts

dBASE®

Internet Using Netscape Navigator™

Lotus® 1-2-3®

Microsoft® Access

Microsoft® Excel

Microsoft® Office Professional

Microsoft® PowerPoint®

Microsoft® Windows® 3.1

Microsoft® Windows® 95

Microsoft® Word

Microsoft® Works

Novell® Perfect Office™

Paradox®

Presentations™

Quattro Pro®

WordPerfect®

New Perspectives on
Microsoft® Excel for Windows®

ADVANCED

Roy Ageloff
University of Rhode Island

Roger Hayen
Central Michigan University

A DIVISION OF COURSE TECHNOLOGY
ONE MAIN STREET, CAMBRIDGE, MA 02142

an International Thomson Publishing company I(T)P

Albany • Bonn • Boston • Cincinnati • London • Madrid • Melbourne • Mexico City
New York • Paris • San Francisco • Singapore • Tokyo • Toronto • Washington

New Perspectives on Microsoft Excel for Windows — Advanced is published by CTI.

Managing Editor	Mac Mendelsohn
Series Consulting Editor	Susan Solomon
Developmental Editor/Product Manager	Kim Crowley
Production Editor	Nancy Ray
Text and Cover Designer	Ella Hanna
Cover Illustrator	Nancy Nash

© 1996 by CTI.
A Division of Course Technology – I(T)P

For more information contact:

Course Technology
One Main Street
Cambridge, MA 02142

International Thomson Publishing Europe
Berkshire House 168-173
High Holborn
London WCIV 7AA
England

Thomas Nelson Australia
102 Dodds Street
South Melbourne, 3205
Victoria, Australia

Nelson Canada
1120 Birchmount Road
Scarborough, Ontario
Canada M1K 5G4

International Thomson Editores
Campos Eliseos 385, Piso 7
Col. Polanco
11560 Mexico D.F. Mexico

International Thomson Publishing GmbH
Kônigswinterer Strasse 418
53227 Bonn
Germany

International Thomson Publishing Asia
211 Henderson Road
#05-10 Henderson Building
Singapore 0315

International Thomson Publishing Japan
Hirakawacho Kyowa Building, 3F
2-2-1 Hirakawacho
Chiyoda-ku, Tokyo 102
Japan

All rights reserved. This publication is protected by federal copyright law. No part of this publication may be reproduced, stored in a retrieval system, or transmitted in any form or by any means, electronic, mechanical, photocopying, recording, or otherwise, or be used to make a derivative work (such as translation or adaptation), without prior permission in writing from Course Technology.

Trademarks
Course Technology and the open book logo are registered trademarks of Course Technology.
I(T)P the ITP logo is a trademark under license.
Custom Edition is a registered trademark of International Thomson Publishing, Inc.
Microsoft and Windows are registered trademarks of Microsoft Corporation.

Some of the product names and company names used in this book have been used for identification purposes only and may be trademarks or registered trademarks of their respective manufacturers and sellers.

Disclaimer
CTI reserves the right to revise this publication and make changes from time to time in its content without notice.

ISBN 0-7600-3533-4

Printed in the United States of America

10 9 8 7 6 5 4 3 2

From the New Perspectives Series Team

At Course Technology we have one foot in education and the other in technology. We believe that technology is transforming the way people teach and learn, and we are excited about providing instructors and students with materials that use technology to teach about technology.

Our development process is unparalleled in the higher education publishing industry. Every product we create goes through an exacting process of design, development, review, and testing.

Reviewers give us direction and insight that shape our manuscripts and bring them up to the latest standards. Every manuscript is quality tested. Students whose backgrounds match the intended audience work through every keystroke, carefully checking for clarity and pointing out errors in logic and sequence. Together with our own technical reviewers, these testers help us ensure that everything that carries our name is error-free and easy to use.

We show both *how* and *why* technology is critical to solving problems in college and in whatever field you choose to teach or pursue. Our time-tested, step-by-step instructions provide unparalleled clarity. Examples and applications are chosen and crafted to motivate students.

As the New Perspectives Series team at Course Technology, our goal is to produce the most timely, accurate, creative, and technologically sound product in the entire college publishing industry. We strive for consistent high quality. This takes a lot of communication, coordination, and hard work. But we love what we do. We are determined to be the best. Write us and let us know what you think. You can also e-mail us at info@course.com.

The New Perspectives Series Team

Joseph J. Adamski	Kathy Finnegan	June Parsons
Judy Adamski	Robin Geller	Sandra Poindexter
Roy Ageloff	Chris Greacen	Mark Reimold
David Auer	Roger Hayen	Ann Shaffer
Rachel Bunin	Charles Hommel	Susan Solomon
Joan Carey	Chris Kelly	Christine Spillett
Patrick Carey	Mary Kemper	Susanne Walker
Barbara Clemens	Terry Ann Kremer	Christie Williams
Kim Crowley	Melissa Lima	John Zeanchock
Kristin Duerr	Mac Mendelsohn	Beverly Zimmerman
Jessica Evans	Dan Oja	Scott Zimmerman

Preface The New Perspectives Series

What is the New Perspectives Series?

Course Technology's **New Perspectives Series** combines text and technology products that teach computer concepts and microcomputer applications. Users consistently praise this series for innovative pedagogy, creativity, supportive and engaging style, accuracy, and use of interactive technology. The first New Perspectives text was published in January of 1993. Since then, the series has grown to more than thirty titles and has become the best-selling series on computer concepts and microcomputer applications. Others have imitated the New Perspectives features, design, and technologies, but none have replicated its quality and its ability to consistently anticipate and meet the needs of instructors and students.

How is the New Perspectives Series different from other microcomputer applications series?

The **New Perspectives Series** distinguishes itself from other series in at least four substantial ways: sound instructional design, consistent quality, innovative technology, and proven pedagogy. The texts in this series consist of two or more tutorials, which are based on sound instructional design. Each tutorial is motivated by a realistic case that is meaningful to students. Rather than learn a laundry list of features, students learn the features in the context of solving a problem. This process motivates all concepts and skills by demonstrating to students why they would want to know them.

Instructors and students have come to rely on the high quality of the **New Perspectives Series** and to consistently praise its accuracy. This accuracy is a result of Course Technology's unique multi-step quality assurance process that incorporates student testing at three stages of development, using hardware and software configurations appropriate to the product. All solutions, test questions, and other Course Tools (see below) are tested using similar procedures. Instructors who adopt this series report that students can work through the tutorials independently, with a minimum of intervention or "damage control" by instructors or staff. This consistent quality has meant that if instructors are pleased with one product from the series, they can rely on the same quality with any other New Perspectives product.

The **New Perspectives Series** also distinguishes itself by its innovative technology. This series innovated Course Labs, truly *interactive* learning applications. These have set the standard for interactive learning.

How do I know that the New Perspectives Series will work?

Some instructors who use this series report a significant difference between how much their students learn and retain with this series as compared to other series. With other series, instructors often find that students can work through the book and do well on homework and tests, but still not demonstrate competency when asked to perform particular tasks outside the context of the text's sample case or project. With the **New Perspectives Series**, however, instructors report that students have a complete, integrative learning experience that stays with them. They credit this high retention and competency to the fact that this series incorporates critical thinking and problem solving with computer skills mastery.

How does this book I'm holding fit into the New Perspectives Series?

New Perspectives microcomputer applications books are available in the following categories:

Brief books are about 100 pages long and are intended to teach only the essentials of the particular-microcomputer application.

Introductory books are about 300 pages long and consist of 6 or 7 tutorials. An Introductory book is designed for a short course on a particular application or for a one-term course to be used in combination with other Introductory books.

Four-in-One books and **Five-in-One** books combine a Brief book on Windows with 3 or 4 Introductory books. An Essential Computer Concepts section is also included.

Comprehensive books consist of all of the tutorials in the Introductory book, plus 3 or 4 more tutorials on more advanced topics. They also include Brief Windows tutorials, 3 or 4 Additional Cases, and a Reference Section.

Intermediate books take the 3 or 4 tutorials at the end of 3 or 4 Comprehensive books and combine them. Additional Cases and Reference Sections are also included.

Advanced books begin by covering topics similar to those in the Comprehensive books, but cover them in more depth. Advanced books then go on to present the most high-level coverage in the series. Additional Cases and Reference Sections are also included.

Concepts and Applications books combine the *New Perspectives on Computer Concepts* book with various Brief and Introductory microcomputer applications books.

Custom Books Course Technology offers you two ways to customize a text to fit your course exactly: **CourseKits**™, 2 or more texts packaged together in a box, and **Custom Editions**®, your choice of New Perspectives books bound together. Both options offer significant price discounts.

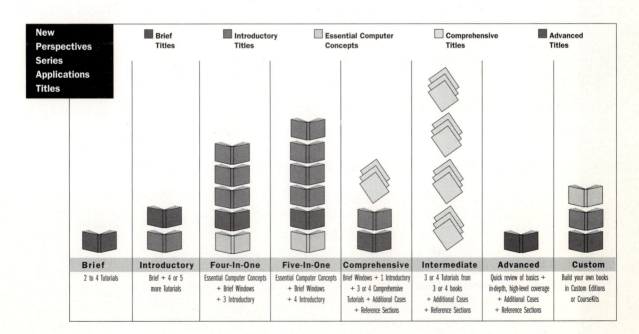

What is unique about the Advanced New Perspectives books?

The Advanced New Perspectives books are designed to fit a need not addressed by other books in that they cover concepts and skills required of advanced students. Research indicates that students in upper-division courses need a higher level of coverage. In the past, professors have had to use trade books to attain this level of coverage, but these books do not provide the pedagogical foundations for advanced learning. For example, trade books typically do not have end of chapter questions and exercises by which students can test and measure their understanding of the material. The Advanced New Perspectives books combine the high level coverage with reinforcing pedagogical features.

In what kind of course could I use this book?

This book can be used in any course in which you want students to learn all the most important topics of Microsoft Excel for Windows. This book is written primarily for use with Excel Version 7 for Windows 95, but can also be used with Excel Version 5 for Windows 3.1. (For more information, see the *Excel 5 and 3.1 Notes* section later in this preface.)

In this book, students plan, create, format, and edit a spreadsheet. Students also create and run macros, perform what-if analyses, and create charts, tables, and lists. Students also are introduced to more advanced topics, such as using Excel to perform regression analysis, solve linear programming problems, and create custom applications using Visual Basic for Applications (VBA). This book assumes students have taken an introductory spreadsheet course, and learned basic Windows navigation and file management skills from Course Technology's *New Perspectives on Microsoft Windows 95 Brief*, *New Perspectives on Microsoft Windows 3.1 Brief*, or an *equivalent* book.

What features are contained in Advanced Windows 95 editions of the New Perspectives series?

Large Page Size If you've used a *New Perspectives* text before, you'll immediately notice that the book you are holding is larger than the Windows 3.1 series books. We've responded to user requests for a larger page, which allows for larger screen shots and associated callouts. Look on page ADVEX 18 for an example of how we've made the screen shots easy to read.

Design We have designed this book to help students easily differentiate between what they are to *do* and what they are to *read*. The steps are easily identified by their shaded background and numbered steps. Furthermore, this design presents steps and screen shots in a large, easy to read format. Some good examples of our design are pages ADVEX 20 and ADVEX 21, and ADVEX 166 and ADVEX 167.

"Read this Before You Begin" Page This page is consistent with Course Technology's unequaled commitment to helping instructors introduce technology into the classroom. Technical considerations and assumptions about hardware and software are listed in one place to help instructors save time and eliminate unnecessary aggravation. The "Read This Before You Begin" page for this book is on page 2.

Tutorial Case Each tutorial begins with a problem presented in a running case that is meaningful to students. The problem turns the task of learning how to use an application into a problem-solving process. The problems increase in complexity with each tutorial. The running case touches on multicultural, international, and ethical issues—so important to today's business curriculum.

Step-by-Step Methodology This unique Course Technology methodology keeps students on track. They click or press keys always within the context of solving the problem posed in the tutorial case. The text constantly guides students, letting them know where they are in the course of solving the problem. In addition, the numerous screen shots include callouts that direct students' attention to what they should look at on the screen. On almost every page in this book, you can find an example of how steps, screen shots, and callouts work together.

TROUBLE? Paragraphs TROUBLE? paragraphs anticipate the mistakes that students are likely to make and help them recover from these mistakes. By putting these paragraphs in the book, rather than in the instructor's manual, we facilitate independent learning and free the instructor to focus on substantive conceptual issues rather than on common procedural errors. Two representative examples of TROUBLE? are on pages ADVEX 38 and ADVEX 133.

Excel 5 Notes and 3.1 Notes Excel 5 Notes and 3.1 Notes provide information specific to those students using Excel 5 and Windows 3.1. For example, these notes appear whenever a task requires a particular action in Excel 5 or Windows 3.1, or when a screen element appears differently in these environments.

Reference Windows Reference Windows appear throughout the text. They are short, succinct summaries of the most important tasks covered in the tutorials. Reference Windows are specially designed and written so students can use them for their reference value when doing the Tutorial Exercises, Case Problems, and Comprehensive Applications, and after completing the course. Page ADVEX 27 contains the Reference Window for Building Formulas By Pointing.

Help Desks The Help Desk feature encourages students to use on-line Help to explore additional methods for completing a task. The more exposure the students have to the on-line Help system, the more comfortable they will be getting help for tasks that are new to them. Each Help Desk includes instructions for starting Help and accessing the correct Help tab. It provides the keyword they should enter, and then names the topic that contains the information. Although the Help Desks do not replace the Step by Step tutorial, students can explore the Help Desk topics while they are working through the tutorial, or they can come back to them later during review.

Task Reference The Task Reference is a summary of how to perform common tasks using the most efficient method, as well as helpful shortcuts. It appears as a table at the end of the book. In this book, the Task Reference is on pages ADVEX 625 through ADVEX 632.

Tutorial Exercises, Case Problems, and Comprehensive Applications Each tutorial concludes with Tutorial Exercises, which provide students with additional hands-on practice of the skills they learned in the tutorial. The Tutorial Exercises are followed by two Case Problems that have approximately the same scope as the tutorial case. Two Comprehensive Applications follow the Case Problems. These Comprehensive Applications require students' to solve a case problem from scratch by utilizing skills they have developed in the current and preceding tutorials. Some of the Comprehensive Applications continue through several tutorials, giving students the opportunity to plan and build a complete workbook in response to a complex business problem.

Additional Cases The Additional Cases are four to five cases problems that encompass all the skills and concepts related to full workbook development and analysis needed to solve intricate business problems. Each case is designed as a semester-long project to be completed by each student individually, or by a group of students working together.

What Course Tools are available with this Text?

Instructor's Manual The Instructor's Manual is written by the authors and is quality assurance tested. It contains answers and solutions to all of the Tutorial Exercises, Case Problems, Comprehensive Applications, and Additional Cases. This is available in hard copy and electronic form.

Student Disk Files Student Files disks contain all of the datafiles that students will use for the Tutorials, Tutorial Exercises, Case Problems, and Comprehensive Applications. A README file includes technical tips for lab management. These files are also available on-line. See the inside cover of this book and the "Read This Before You Begin" page before Tutorial 1 for more information on student files.

Acknowledgments

Our appreciation goes to our reviewers, whose comments and suggestions helped shape this book: Don Hoggan, Solano Community College; Joe Schopfer, College of Great Falls; and John Zales, Harrisburg Area Community College. Also, thanks to Hilda Allred, Al Della Bitta, Dennis McLeavey, and Adam Naftalin for their input on case material.

We would also like to thank all the members of the New Perspectives team who helped in the development and production of this book. Special thanks to Kim Crowley for her valuable suggestions on the development and writing of the material, and her exceptional managerial skills. Additional thanks go to the unequaled quality assurance and technology support from Jim Valente and the QA testers, Gina Griffiths and Tia McCarthy; to the excellent production work of Nancy Ray, and the staff at Gex; and the editorial support of Mac Mendelsohn, Susan Solomon, and Barbara Clemens.

Roy Ageloff expresses his special thanks to his wife, Hilda, for her support and encouragement.

Roger Hayen thanks his family. During this project, the book overshadowed many family activities, but their encouragement, support, and most of all, perseverance, enabled him to complete his work on this book.

Brief Contents

From the New Perspectives Team ... v

Preface ... vi

Advanced Microsoft Excel for Windows Tutorials ... ADVEX 1

TUTORIAL 1	Creating Worksheets Using Excel for Windows	ADVEX 3
TUTORIAL 2	Developing Effective Worksheets	ADVEX 63
TUTORIAL 3	Creating and Printing Charts	ADVEX 125
TUTORIAL 4	Automating Tasks Using Macros	ADVEX 177
TUTORIAL 5	Preparing and Examining What-If Alternative	ADVEX 211
TUTORIAL 6	Analyzing Data and Preparing Forecasts	ADVEX 271
TUTORIAL 7	Consolidating Workbook Results	ADVEX 333
TUTORIAL 8	Working with Excel Lists	ADVEX 387
TUTORIAL 9	Integrating Excel With Other Windows Programs	ADVEX 431
TUTORIAL 10	Introduction to Visual Basic for Applications	ADVEX 473
TUTORIAL 11	Creating a Custom Application Using VBA	ADVEX 537

ADDITIONAL CASES ... ADVEX 597

INDEX ... ADVEX 617

TASK REFERENCE ... ADVEX 625

Table of Contents

From the New Perspectives Team	**v**
Preface	**vi**
Advanced Microsoft Excel for Windows Tutorials	**ADVEX 1**
Read This Before You Begin	**ADVEX 2**

TUTORIAL 1

Creating Worksheets Using Excel for Windows

Preparing an Operating Budget	**ADVEX 3**
Introducing Excel	**ADVEX 4**
Using the Tutorials Effectively	**ADVEX 6**
Launching Excel	**ADVEX 7**
Examining the Excel Window	**ADVEX 8**
Menu Bar	ADVEX 9
Title Bar	ADVEX 9
Toolbars	ADVEX 10
Formula Bar	ADVEX 10
Worksheet Window	ADVEX 10
Cell Pointer	ADVEX 10
Sheet Tabs	ADVEX 10
Reference Area	ADVEX 10
Mouse Pointer	ADVEX 11
Status Bar	ADVEX 11
Navigating Through the Worksheet	**ADVEX 11**
Scrolling Using the Keyboard and the Mouse	ADVEX 11
Scrolling Using Special Keys	ADVEX 13
Introduction to Creating a Worksheet	**ADVEX 13**
Developing Worksheets	**ADVEX 13**
Analyzing the Problem	ADVEX 13
Designing the Worksheet	ADVEX 15
Building the Worksheet	**ADVEX 16**
Entering Text Labels	ADVEX 17
Entering Values	ADVEX 19
Entering Formulas	ADVEX 21
Entering Functions	ADVEX 25
Building Formulas by Pointing	**ADVEX 25**
Using Save As to Save a Workbook File	**ADVEX 28**
Workbook Filenames for the Tutorials	**ADVEX 29**
Reviewing the Worksheet	**ADVEX 30**
Editing Cell Contents	ADVEX 30
Clearing Cell Contents	ADVEX 31
Spell Checking the Worksheet	ADVEX 32
Help Desk for the Tutorials	**ADVEX 33**
Changing Column Width	**ADVEX 35**
Specifying Cell Ranges	**ADVEX 36**
Changing Appearance with Formatting	**ADVEX 37**

Using Boldface, Italics, and Underlining	ADVEX 39
Using Fonts and Font Sizes	ADVEX 40
Using Save to Save a Workbook	**ADVEX 41**
Printing a Worksheet	**ADVEX 41**
Closing the Workbook	**ADVEX 44**
Opening the Workbook	**ADVEX 44**
Performing a What-If Analysis	**ADVEX 46**
Exiting Excel	**ADVEX 47**
Tutorial Exercises	**ADVEX 48**
Case Problems	**ADVEX 49**
Comprehensive Applications	**ADVEX 56**

TUTORIAL 2

Developing Effective Worksheets

Expanding the Operating Budget	**ADVEX 63**
Introduction to Worksheet Design	**ADVEX 64**
Expanding the Basic Worksheet	**ADVEX 64**
Retrieving the Worksheet	**ADVEX 67**
Using AutoFill to Create a Series	**ADVEX 67**
Using the Format Painter to Copy Cell Formats	**ADVEX 69**
Copying Formulas	**ADVEX 69**
Relative and Absolute References	ADVEX 70
Using the Clipboard to Copy Cells	ADVEX 72
Creating a Total Column with SUM	**ADVEX 74**
Arranging Worksheets in Sections	**ADVEX 75**
Using Absolute References	**ADVEX 77**
Rounding Results	ADVEX 79
Reviewing the Worksheet	**ADVEX 82**
Revising a Worksheet	**ADVEX 84**
Splitting the Worksheet Window	ADVEX 84
Inserting Rows in a Worksheet	ADVEX 86
Moving Cell Contents	ADVEX 90
Deleting Rows from the Worksheet	ADVEX 90
Using Range Names	**ADVEX 91**
Printing a Selected Range	ADVEX 93
Using Range Names in Formulas	ADVEX 93
Designing a Presentation-Quality Report	**ADVEX 96**
Including the Date Using the TODAY Function	ADVEX 97
Aligning Text Headings	ADVEX 98
Using Borders and Patterns	ADVEX 98
Using Page Setup to Print the Worksheet	**ADVEX 100**
Using Page Breaks	ADVEX 102
Hiding Data	**ADVEX 103**
Using Multiple Sheets	**ADVEX 104**
Using Graphic Objects	**ADVEX 109**
Protecting the Worksheet	**ADVEX 112**
Tutorial Exercises	**ADVEX 114**
Case Problems	**ADVEX 116**
Comprehensive Applications	**ADVEX 120**

CONTENTS NEW PERSPECTIVES SERIES **XIII**

TUTORIAL 3

Creating and Printing Charts

Adding Charts to the Budget **ADVEX 125**

Introduction to Charts	**ADVEX 126**
Excel Charts	ADVEX 128
Examining an Excel Chart	ADVEX 129
Arranging Data Series for Charts	**ADVEX 130**
Creating a Column Chart	**ADVEX 131**
Selecting Nonadjacent Ranges	**ADVEX 132**
Using the ChartWizard	**ADVEX 133**
Resizing a Chart	**ADVEX 135**
Activating a Chart for Editing	**ADVEX 136**
Adding and Deleting Chart Data Series	**ADVEX 137**
Selecting a Different Chart Type and Format	**ADVEX 139**
Saving and Printing Charts	**ADVEX 142**
Reviewing the Chart	**ADVEX 143**
Adding and Changing Titles	ADVEX 144
Changing Axis Number Formats	ADVEX 145
Changing the Axis Scale	ADVEX 145
Controlling Colors and Fill Patterns	**ADVEX 146**
Adding Graphic Objects to Charts	ADVEX 147
Creating a Pie Chart	**ADVEX 148**
Performing a What-If Analysis with Charts	**ADVEX 151**
Creating a 3-D Column Chart	**ADVEX 153**
Preparing a Combination Chart	**ADVEX 156**
Creating a Picture Chart	**ADVEX 157**
Integrating Windows Programs	**ADVEX 159**
Introduction to Maps	**ADVEX 162**
Creating a Map	**ADVEX 164**
Modifying a Map	**ADVEX 168**
Tutorial Exercises	**ADVEX 170**
Case Problems	**ADVEX 172**
Comprehensive Applications	**ADVEX 175**

TUTORIAL 4

Automating Tasks Using Macros

Making the Operating Budget Workbook Easier to Use **ADVEX 177**

Introduction to Macros	**ADVEX 178**
Running a Sample Macro	**ADVEX 178**
Creating Macros	**ADVEX 179**
Planning Macros	**ADVEX 180**
Recording the GotoAssumptions Macro	**ADVEX 180**
Running the GotoAssumptions Macro	ADVEX 182
Assigning the GotoAssumptions Macro to a Button Object	**ADVEX 183**
Viewing the GoToAssumptions Macro	ADVEX 186
Visual Basic Toolbar	**ADVEX 187**
Visual Basic Code	**ADVEX 188**
Recording the ResetData Macro	**ADVEX 188**
Setting Recording Options	**ADVEX 190**
Assigning Macros	ADVEX 190
Macro Storage Locations	ADVEX 190
Macro Language	ADVEX 191
Assigning the ResetData Macro to a Button Object	**ADVEX 192**
Running the ResetData Macro	ADVEX 193
Viewing the ResetData Macro	ADVEX 194
Recording the PrintBudget Macro	**ADVEX 195**
Viewing the PrintReport and InputAssumptions Macro	ADVEX 197
Running a Macro Automatically	**ADVEX 198**
Recording and Running the Auto_Open Macro	ADVEX 199
Printing Macros	**ADVEX 200**
Related Macro Topics	**ADVEX 203**
Editing a Macro by Recording at a Particular Location	ADVEX 203
Deleting Macros	ADVEX 205
Stopping a Macro During Execution	ADVEX 205
Tutorial Exercises	**ADVEX 205**
Case Problems	**ADVEX 206**
Comprehensive Applications	**ADVEX 207**

XIV CONTENTS NEW PERSPECTIVES SERIES

TUTORIAL 5

Preparing and Examining What-If Alternatives

Developing the Best Operating Plan **ADVEX 211**

Retrieving the Worksheet	**ADVEX 214**
Examining Alternatives with Goal Seeking	**ADVEX 215**
Using the Trial-and-Error Method to Perform Goal Seeking	**ADVEX 215**
Using Goal Seek to Find a Solution	**ADVEX 217**
Exploring Alternatives with Data Tables	**ADVEX 219**
One-Input Data Table	ADVEX 219
Two-Input Data Table	ADVEX 225
Charting Data Table Results	ADVEX 229
Performing a What-If Analysis on a Data Table	ADVEX 230
Understanding Scenarios	**ADVEX 231**
Naming Changing Cells	ADVEX 232
Creating Scenarios	ADVEX 233
Creating a Scenario Summary	ADVEX 237
Using Solver to Find the Best Solution	**ADVEX 238**
Formulating the Problem	ADVEX 239
Setting Up the Optimization Worksheet	ADVEX 242
Finding the Optimal Solution	ADVEX 244
Changing Constraints	ADVEX 247
Using Integer Constraints	ADVEX 249
Printing Solver Reports	ADVEX 251
Understanding the Results	ADVEX 253
Using Macros with What-If Alternatives	**ADVEX 255**
Tutorial Exercises	**ADVEX 259**
Case Problems	**ADVEX 260**
Comprehensive Applications	**ADVEX 266**

TUTORIAL 6

Analyzing Data and Preparing Forecasts

Controlling Costs and Forecasting Sales **ADVEX 271**

Introduction to Applying Functions	**ADVEX 272**
Describing Data with Functions	**ADVEX 275**
Retrieving the Workbook	ADVEX 275
Using the MAX and MIN Functions	ADVEX 276
Using the AVERAGE, MEDIAN, and STDEV Functions	**ADVEX 278**

Using Functions for Financial Analysis	**ADVEX 279**
Calculating a Loan Payment with PMT	ADVEX 279
Calculating a Lease Payment with PMT	ADVEX 282
Calculating a Bond Interest Rate with YIELD	**ADVEX 284**
Building in Decisions	**ADVEX 287**
Using the IF Function	**ADVEX 287**
Using a Table Lookup	**ADVEX 292**
Using Logical Functions	**ADVEX 295**
Forecasting with Regression Analysis	**ADVEX 298**
Performing Regression Analysis	ADVEX 299
Preparing a Growth Rate Forecast	ADVEX 308
Creating and Using a Template Workbook	**ADVEX 318**
Using Macros with Template Workbooks	**ADVEX 322**
Tutorial Exercises	**ADVEX 326**
Case Problems	**ADVEX 328**
Comprehensive Applications	**ADVEX 331**

TUTORIAL 7

Consolidating Workbook Results

Providing Executive Information **ADVEX 333**

Introduction to Workbook Consolidation	**ADVEX 334**
Retrieving the Workbooks	**ADVEX 339**
Consolidating Multiple Workbook Files	**ADVEX 342**
Updating Consolidated Results	**ADVEX 346**
Linking Workbook Files	**ADVEX 347**
Consolidating with 3-D Formulas	ADVEX 347
Using the Group Edit Mode	ADVEX 349
Using Formulas to Link Workbooks	ADVEX 351
Using Arrays to Link Workbooks	ADVEX 358
Working with Outline Groups	**ADVEX 364**
Using Groups to Consolidate Data	ADVEX 367
Auditing the Workbook	**ADVEX 370**
Expanding the Consolidation	**ADVEX 374**
Using Macros to Automate Consolidations	**ADVEX 377**
Tutorial Exercises	**ADVEX 379**
Case Problems	**ADVEX 381**
Comprehensive Applications	**ADVEX 383**

TUTORIAL 8

Working with Excel Lists

Managing Human Resources Data **ADVEX 387**

Introduction to Lists	**ADVEX 388**
Planning and Creating a List	**ADVEX 388**
Sorting Data	**ADVEX 390**
Sorting a List Using One Sort Field	ADVEX 390
Sorting a List Using More than One Sort Field	ADVEX 391
Maintaining a List Using the Data Form	**ADVEX 394**
Using the Data Form to Search for Records	ADVEX 396
Using the Data Form to Delete a Record	ADVEX 397
Filtering a List Using AutoFilters	**ADVEX 398**
Using Custom AutoFilters to Specify More Complex Criteria	**ADVEX 402**
Inserting Subtotals in a List	**ADVEX 404**
Using Macros to Automate the Departmental Salary Report	**ADVEX 406**
Creating and Using Pivot Tables to Summarize a List	**ADVEX 408**
Creating a Pivot Table	**ADVEX 409**
Defining the Layout of the Pivot Table	ADVEX 410
Changing the Layout of the Pivot Table	**ADVEX 414**
Repositioning a Field on the Pivot Table	ADVEX 414
Rearranging Items Within the Pivot Table	ADVEX 415
Formatting Numbers in the Pivot Table	ADVEX 416
Adding a Field to the Pivot Table	**ADVEX 417**
Removing a Field from the Pivot Table	ADVEX 418
Hiding and Showing Items in the Pivot Table	ADVEX 419
Refreshing the Pivot Table	**ADVEX 420**
Grouping Data in the Pivot Table	**ADVEX 421**
Creating Charts from a Pivot Table	ADVEX 424
Tutorial Exercises	**ADVEX 425**
Case Problems	**ADVEX 425**
Comprehensive Applications	**ADVEX 427**

TUTORIAL 9

Integrating Excel with Other Windows Programs

Retrieving and Sharing Data with Other Programs **ADVEX 431**

External Databases and Queries	**ADVEX 432**
Using Microsoft Query	**ADVEX 433**
The Microsoft Query Window	**ADVEX 434**
Selecting a Data Source	**ADVEX 435**
Querying Only One Table	**ADVEX 438**
Using the Criteria Pane	**ADVEX 439**
Querying More Than One Table	**ADVEX 443**
Transferring and Sharing Data Among Windows Programs	**ADVEX 447**
Pasting Data	ADVEX 448
Embedding Data	ADVEX 448
Linking Data	ADVEX 449
Linking an Excel Worksheet to a Word Processor Document	ADVEX 449
Opening Multiple Programs	ADVEX 451
Updating the Linked Object	ADVEX 454
Linking Versus Embedding	**ADVEX 456**
Embedding an Excel Object in a Word Processor Document	ADVEX 457
Updating the Embedded Object	ADVEX 459
Working with Text Files	**ADVEX 460**
Importing Text Files	**ADVEX 460**
Tutorial Exercises	**ADVEX 465**
Case Problems	**ADVEX 467**
Comprehensive Applications	**ADVEX 469**

TUTORIAL 10

Introduction to Visual Basic for Applications

Building Complex Macros Using VBA **ADVEX 473**

Overview of VBA	**ADVEX 475**
Why VBA?	ADVEX 476
Macros Versus Procedures	ADVEX 476
Storing VBA Code	ADVEX 477
VBA Objects, Properties, and Methods	**ADVEX 478**
Hierarchy of Objects	ADVEX 478
Collections	ADVEX 479
Using VBA to Refer to Objects in Collections	ADVEX 480
Using VBA to Reference Objects in the Object Hierarchy	ADVEX 480
Properties of Excel Objects	ADVEX 481
Methods of Excel Objects	ADVEX 482
Changing Properties of Objects	ADVEX 483

Entering a Simple VBA Macro	**ADVEX 483**
Entering a Macro in a Module Sheet	**ADVEX 485**
Examining Property Settings of Objects	**ADVEX 487**
Using VBA to Access an Object's Method	**ADVEX 491**
Working with Worksheet Objects	**ADVEX 493**
Working with Variables	**ADVEX 496**
Declaring a Variable	ADVEX 496
Getting Information from the User	**ADVEX 497**
Visual Basic Control Structures	**ADVEX 501**
Using the If-Then-Else Statement	ADVEX 501
Using the Select Case Statement to Make Multiple Decisions	**ADVEX 508**
Using the For...Next Loop Control Structure	ADVEX 509
Using Select Case and For...Next Statements in a Macro	ADVEX 510
Using the Do...Loop Control Structure	ADVEX 513
Tutorial Exercises	**ADVEX 518**
Case Problems	**ADVEX 518**
Comprehensive Applications	**ADVEX 520**

TUTORIAL 10 APPENDIX	**ADVEX 523**
On-line Help, Types of Errors, and Debugging Tools	**ADVEX 523**

Using On-line Help	**ADVEX 524**
Getting Help Using the Object Browser	**ADVEX 524**
Getting Help Using the Macro Recorder	ADVEX 527
Encountering Errors in VBA Procedures	**ADVEX 527**
Syntax Errors	ADVEX 527
Run-time Errors	ADVEX 529
Logic Errors	ADVEX 531
Debugging Macros	**ADVEX 532**
Establishing Breakpoints	ADVEX 532
Using the Debug Window to Debug a Macro	ADVEX 532
Establishing Watch Expressions	ADVEX 533
Stepping Through a Macro	ADVEX 534

TUTORIAL 11

Creating a Custom Application Using VBA

Tracking Rotary Club Sponsorship	**ADVEX 537**
Running a Completed Application	**ADVEX 538**
Planning the Application	**ADVEX 541**

Creating a Custom Dialog Box	**ADVEX 543**
An Overview of Dialog Box Controls	ADVEX 543
Building the Sponsor Data Entry Custom Dialog Box	**ADVEX 545**
Placing Controls in the Dialog Box	**ADVEX 547**
Placing Descriptive Labels in the Dialog Box	ADVEX 547
Creating the Edit Boxes	ADVEX 549
Viewing the Custom Dialog Box	ADVEX 551
Creating a Group Box and Option Buttons	ADVEX 552
Creating a Combination Drop-Down Edit Box	ADVEX 555
Testing the Completed Custom Dialog Box	**ADVEX 558**
Creating Macros to Update the Sponsor List	**ADVEX 559**
Displaying the Custom Dialog Box	ADVEX 559
Returning Data from a Control to the Worksheet	ADVEX 561
Recording a Macro to Add the Sponsor to the Sponsor List	**ADVEX 567**
Entering a Macro to Update a Range Name	**ADVEX 571**
Tying the Data Entry Steps Together	**ADVEX 572**
Preparing the Other Macros	**ADVEX 575**
Creating the Summary—How Paid Report	**ADVEX 577**
Creating the Summary— Members Report	**ADVEX 578**
Recording the Report Macros	**ADVEX 579**
Recording a Macro to Print the Unpaid Sponsors Report	ADVEX 581
Creating a Custom Menu	**ADVEX 582**
Understanding Menu Terms	**ADVEX 583**
Displaying the Menu Editor	**ADVEX 584**
Adding a New Menu to an Existing Menu Bar	**ADVEX 585**
Adding Menu Items to a Custom Menu	**ADVEX 587**
Creating a New Submenu	**ADVEX 588**
Testing the FundRaising Menu	**ADVEX 591**
Tutorial Exercises	**ADVEX 592**
Case Problems	**ADVEX 593**
Comprehensive Applications	**ADVEX 594**
Additional Cases	**ADVEX 597**
Index	**ADVEX 617**
Task Reference	**ADVEX 625**

Microsoft® Excel for Windows®

ADVANCED TUTORIALS

TUTORIAL 1 Creating Worksheets Using Excel for Windows	ADVEX 3
TUTORIAL 2 Developing Effective Worksheets	ADVEX 63
TUTORIAL 3 Creating and Printing Charts	ADVEX 125
TUTORIAL 4 Automating Tasks Using Macros	ADVEX 177
TUTORIAL 5 Preparing and Examining What-If Alternatives	ADVEX 211
TUTORIAL 6 Analyzing Data and Preparing Forecasts	ADVEX 271
TUTORIAL 7 Consolidating Workbook Results	ADVEX 333
TUTORIAL 8 Working with Excel Lists	ADVEX 387
TUTORIAL 9 Integrating Excel with Other Windows Programs	ADVEX 431
TUTORIAL 10 Introduction to Visual Basic for Applications	ADVEX 473
TUTORIAL 10 Appendix	ADVEX 523
TUTORIAL 11 Creating a Custom Application Using VBA	ADVEX 537

Read This **Before You Begin**

TO THE STUDENT

STUDENT DISKS

To complete the tutorials, Tutorial Exercises, Case Problems, and Comprehensive Applications in this book, you need ten Student Disks. Your instructor will either provide you with Student Disks or ask you to make your own.

If you are suppose to make your own Student Disks, you will need ten blank, formatted disks. You will need to copy a set of folders from a file server or standalone computer onto your disks. Your instructor will tell you which computer, drive letter, and folders contain the folders you need. The following table shows you which folders go on each of your disks, so that you will have enough disk space to complete all the tutorials, Tutorial Exercises, Case Problems, and Comprehensive Applications:

Disk	Write on this disk label	Put these folders on the disk
1	Student Disk 1: Tutorials 1 & 2	Tut01, Tut02
2	Student Disk 2: Tutorial 3	Tut03
3	Student Disk 3: Tutorial 4	Tut04
4	Student Disk 4: Tutorial 5	Tut05
5	Student Disk 5: Tutorial 6	Tut06
6	Student Disk 6: Tutorial 7	Tut07
7	Student Disk 7: Tutorial 8	Tut08
8	Student Disk 8: Tutorial 9	Tut09
9	Student Disk 9: Tutorials 10 & 11	Tut10, Tut11
10	Student Disk 10: Additional Cases	X_Case1, X_Case2, X_Case3, X_Case4, X_Case5

When you begin each tutorial, be sure you are using the correct Student Disk. See the inside front or inside back cover of this book for more information on Student Disks, or ask your instructor or technical support person for assistance.

USING YOUR OWN COMPUTER

If you are going to work through this book using your own computer, you need:

■ **Computer System** Microsoft Windows 95 and Microsoft Excel 7 for Windows 95; or Microsoft Windows 3.1 and Microsoft Excel 5 for Windows 3.1; or Microsoft Windows 95 and Microsoft Excel 5 for Windows 3.1 must be installed on your computer. This book assumes a complete installation of Excel.

■ **Student Disks** Ask your instructor or technical support person for details on how to get the Student Disks. You will not be able to complete the tutorials or exercises in this book using your won computer until you have Student Disks.

TO THE INSTRUCTOR

To complete the tutorials in this book, your students must use a set of Student Files. These files are stored on the Student Files Disk(s) that is included with the Instructor's Manual. Follow the instructions on the disk label(s) and the Readme.doc file to copy them to your server or standalone computer. You can view the Readme.doc file using WordPad or Write.

Once the files are copied, you can make Student Disks for the students yourself, or tell students where to find the files so they can make their own Student Disks. Make sure the files get correctly copied by following the instructions in the Student Disks section above, which will ensure that students have enough disk space to complete all the tutorials, Tutorial Exercises, Case Problems, and Comprehensive Applications.

CTI DATA FILES

You are granted a license to copy the Student Files to any computer or computer network used by students who have purchased this book. The files are included with the Instructor's Manual and may also be obtained electronically over the Internet. See the inside front or inside back cover of this book for more details.

TUTORIAL 1

Creating Worksheets Using Excel for Windows

Preparing an Operating Budget

OBJECTIVES

In this tutorial you will learn how to:

- Launch and exit Excel

- Examine the Excel program window

- Plan, design, build, and review a worksheet

- Enter and edit text labels, values, formulas, and functions

- Build formulas by pointing

- Check the spelling in a worksheet

- Save, preview, and print a worksheet

- Use on-line Help

- Specify a cell range

- Format the data in a worksheet

- Perform a what-if analysis

CASE

Sunny Morning Products

Sunny Morning Products is an international bottler and distributor of the Olympic Gold brand of fresh orange juice and sports Thirst Quencher. While orange juice is the mainstay of the breakfast of many champions, the Olympic Gold Thirst Quencher delivers the fluids, electrolytes, and carbohydrate energy that the human body needs for peak performance in athletic competition. Olympic Gold has provided the company with significant growth and increased profitability during the past ten years. Sunny Morning Products, located in Garden Grove, California, was established in 1909 by Edwin Towle. The business remains family owned and operated. Edwin's grandson, Matthew Towle, now serves as the chairman of the board of Sunny Morning Products, while his granddaughter, Kimberly Scott-Martin, is the president and chief executive officer (CEO). In addition to Matt and Kim, other officers of Sunny Morning Products include Travis Towle as the vice president and general manager, Carmen Martin-Rivera as the chief financial officer (CFO), and Kristin Towle-Hertz as the secretary.

Ann Trego has been working for Sunny Morning Products for almost two years as a budget analyst. Last month Ann was promoted to assistant budget manager. In her new job she assists Carmen, the CFO. One of Ann's first responsibilities is working with Carmen to create next year's operating budget. They estimated first-quarter sales of $898,300 (that is, 276,400 bottles of Olympic Gold at $3.25 per bottle) and Travis provided the other assumptions included in the initial operating budget shown in Figure 1-1. You will work along with the staff at Sunny Morning Products throughout these tutorials as you learn how to use Excel to solve the business problems they encounter.

Figure 1-1
Printout of projected Operating Budget for Sunny Morning Products

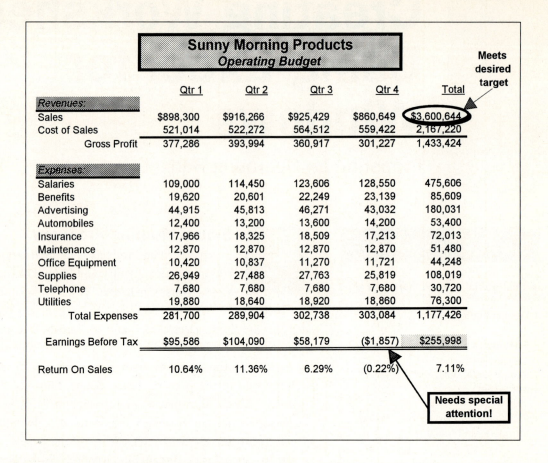

Introducing Excel

Excel is a software tool known as an **electronic spreadsheet**, which helps computer users like you produce reports similar to an accountant's paper spreadsheet, like the one shown in Figure 1-2. A spreadsheet, or **worksheet**, is a grid of intersecting vertical columns and horizontal rows that organizes data as a table. With this grid arrangement, you enter data into cells, which are located at the intersections of the rows and columns. A **cell** is the basic unit of a worksheet. Compared to an accountant's spreadsheet, an Excel worksheet is huge, with 256 columns and 16,384 rows.

Figure 1-2
Accountant's spreadsheet

cell →

row →

column →

	Qtr 1	Qtr 2	Qtr 3	Qtr 4	Total	
		Sunny Morning Products				
		Operating Budget				
	Qtr 1	Qtr 2	Qtr 3	Qtr 4	Total	
Revenues:						
Sales	$898,300	$916,266	$925,429	$860,649	$3,600,644	
Cost of Sales	521,014	522,272	564,512	559,422	2,167,220	
Gross Profit	377,286	393,994	360,917	301,227	1,433,424	
Expenses:						
Salaries	109,000	114,450	123,606	128,550	475,606	
Benefits	19,620	20,601	22,249	23,139	85,609	
Advertising	44,915	45,813	46,271	43,032	180,031	
Automobiles	12,400	13,200	13,600	14,200	53,400	
Insurance	17,966	18,325	18,509	17,213	72,013	
Maintenance	12,870	12,870	12,870	12,870	51,480	
Office Equipment	10,420	10,837	11,270	11,721	44,248	
Supplies	26,949	27,488	27,763	25,819	108,019	
Telephone	7,680	7,680	7,680	7,680	30,720	
Utilities	19,880	18,640	18,920	18,860	76,300	
Total Expenses	281,700	289,904	302,738	303,084	1,177,426	
Earnings Before Tax	$95,586	$104,090	$58,179	($1,857)	$255,998	
Return On Sales	10.64%	11.36%	6.29%	(0.22%)	7.11%	

Each cell in a worksheet is identified by a **cell reference**, **cell name**, or **cell address** that consists of the column letter and row number of its location. For example, the cell reference D8 indicates the cell at the intersection of column D and row 8. Excel also provides an *alternative method* of referencing a cell by its row number (R) and column number (C). For example, the cell D8 could also be referenced as R8C4, where "R" designates the row and "C" specifies the column. Throughout these tutorials, cell references are usually specified using the column letter and row number method, although you will encounter several situations in which the R8C4 notation is used. Also, a complete cell reference includes the name of the worksheet. Because cell D8 is located on the first, or Sheet1, worksheet, the complete cell reference is Sheet1!D8. However, Excel does not require the use of a worksheet name with every cell reference, so when a worksheet name does not appear, the cell reference specifies a cell in the active worksheet.

With a paper worksheet, you use a calculator and pencil to calculate values and write them in the proper cells. Then, if just one number changes, you have to recalculate and rewrite the entire worksheet. With Excel, the computer automatically recalculates the values for you and displays the revised numbers.

Ann used Excel to create the initial Sunny Morning Products Operating Budget shown in Figure 1-1. A **budget** is a plan for managing resources and/or expenditures for a specific amount of time. Many of the numbers in a budget are **projected**, or estimated for the future, so they may change as the budget is finalized. Making these types of changes to the budget will be easy for Ann because she created the budget using Excel.

Excel is not only effective at summarizing numerical data and keeping records—it is also a powerful decision-making tool used for business modeling. A **business model** is a mathematical description of a business problem that usually states the assumptions and relationships among the variables that make up the model.

The spreadsheet's ability to answer the question "What if?" helps business people make better decisions. For example, what if Ann needs to increase Carmen's initial estimate of Salaries for the first quarter to $112,000? Then how much are the Total Expenses? A **what-if analysis** is performed whenever you revise an input data value in order to see the effect on the results. The *entire spreadsheet is recalculated*. You can do a series of different what-if alternatives quickly and easily once you create your spreadsheet.

With Excel, you can prepare information that supports decision-making for a wide variety of business and government situations in accounting, finance, marketing, manufacturing, and human resources management. These tutorials and problems provide examples of how you can use Excel in some of the more common applications. The applications of a spreadsheet software tool like Excel for solving business problems are nearly limitless.

Using the Tutorials Effectively

These tutorials will help you learn about Excel. They are designed to be used at your computer. First, read the text that explains the concepts. When you come to the numbered steps, follow them as you work at your computer. *Read each step carefully and completely before you try it.*

In the steps of these tutorials, the commands you select or keys you press appear in boldface. Key names separated by a plus sign (+) indicate that you hold down the first key, press the second key, and then release both keys; for example, Ctrl + O. Key names separated by a space indicate that you press the first key and release it, and then press the second key and release it; for example, End Home. Some of the more common mouse actions that you use in completing the steps are described in Figure 1-3.

Figure 1-3 ◀
Common
mouse actions
used in tutorials

Action	Meaning
Click	Quickly press and release the left mouse button
Right-click	Quickly press and release the right mouse button
Double-click	Click the left mouse button twice in rapid succession
Click and drag	Hold down the left mouse button while you move the mouse
Point	Move the mouse until the mouse pointer on the screen is on top of the specified item

As you work, compare your screen with the figures in the tutorial to verify your results. Don't worry if parts of your screen display are somewhat different from the figures. The important parts of the screen display are labeled in each figure. Just be sure these parts are on your screen. Some parts of your screen will be different if you are using Windows 3.1 rather than Windows 95, and if you are using Excel Version 5.0 rather than Version 7.0. Special callouts are used in the figures to point out the differences in Windows 3.1 and Excel Version 5.0.

Don't worry about making mistakes—that's part of the learning process. TROUBLE? paragraphs identify common problems and explain how to get back on track. Perform the activities in the TROUBLE? paragraph *only* if you are having the problem described.

After you have read each tutorial and completed the steps, you can do the exercises. The exercises are carefully structured so you will review what you have learned and then apply your knowledge to new situations. When you are doing the exercises, refer to the Reference Windows, which provide you with short summaries of the frequently used procedures presented in the tutorial, including alternative methods for executing commands.

Launching Excel

Launching, or starting, Excel is similar to starting other Windows programs. You can launch Excel from a shortcut icon, from the Programs selection on the Start menu, from the Excel folder, or from the Microsoft Office shortcut bar. When you launch Excel, the Book1 workbook window appears on the screen. In Excel, the file that contains your spreadsheet is called a **workbook** and it has the initial, or default, name "Book1." You can use the Book1 window to create a new document, or you can open a workbook that has already been created. In this tutorial you will learn how Ann designed and created the Sunny Morning Products Operating Budget shown in Figure 1-1. You are ready to begin by launching Excel.

To launch Excel:

1. Launch Windows 95. (If you are using a different operating system, then start it now.)

2. Look for an icon or folder titled "Excel" or "Excel.exe." See Figure 1-4.

   Look for an icon or window for Microsoft Office; if you see the Microsoft Office group icon, double-click the Microsoft Office group icon to open it.

   TROUBLE? If you don't see anything called Excel, click the Start button, click Programs, then point to Microsoft Office; look for Excel and click it. If you still can't find anything called Excel, use Find on the Start menu to search for Excel.exe and click it.

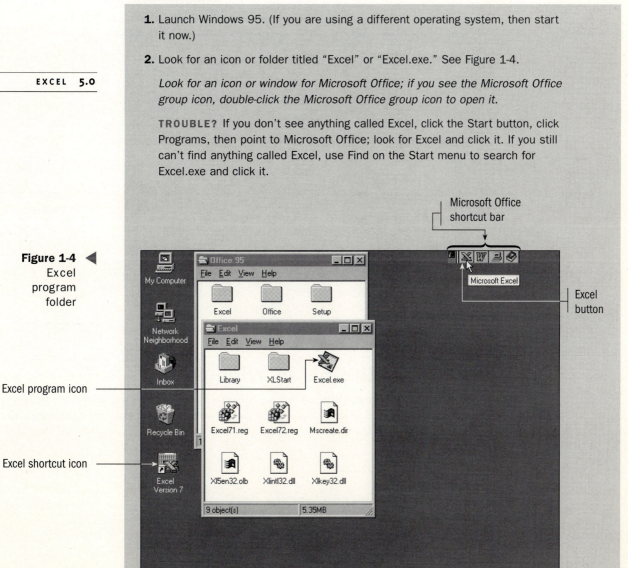

Figure 1-4 Excel program folder

3. Double-click the **Excel program** box, or click the **Excel shortcut** button, or click the **Excel** button on the Microsoft Office shortcut bar. After a brief pause, the Excel copyright information appears in a box and remains on the screen until Excel is ready for you to use.

4. Click the **program window Maximize** button if your Excel program window is not maximized.

5. Click the **worksheet window Maximize** button to maximize the Book1 worksheet window, if it's not already maximized. See Figure 1-5.

   TROUBLE? Your screen might display more or less of the grid shown in Figure 1-5. Don't worry if your screen doesn't match exactly; this should not be a problem as you continue with the tutorials.

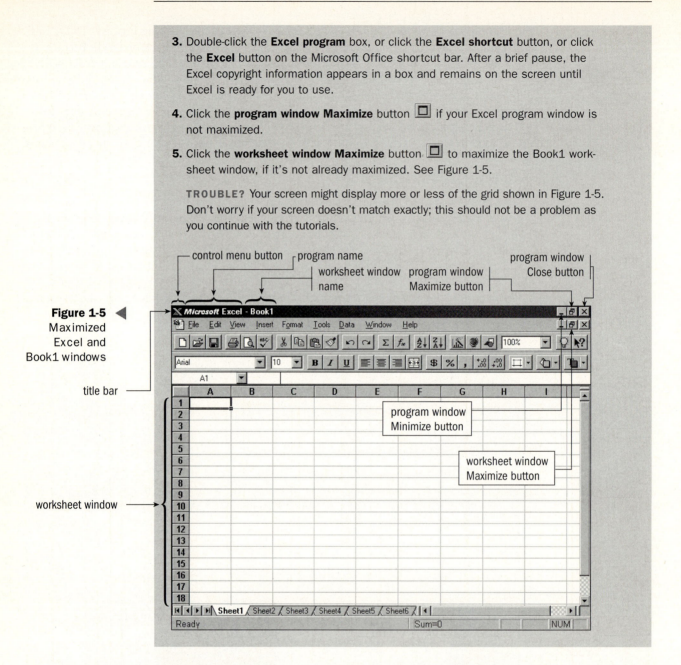

Figure 1-5 Maximized Excel and Book1 windows

You have successfully launched Excel. Now you can review the components and features of the Excel window.

Examining the Excel Window

Examining Excel's program window introduces you to some of its components. Take a look at Figure 1-6 and review these components so you are familiar with their location.

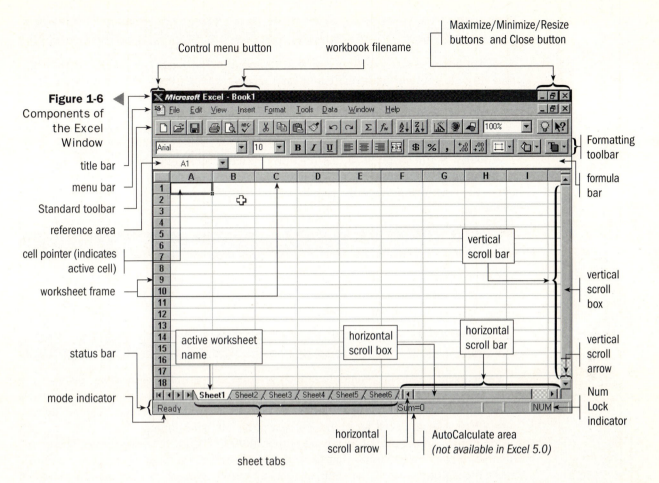

Figure 1-6 Components of the Excel Window

Notice that the Excel window contains components common to all Windows programs. Some examples are the Control menu button, the menu bar, the status bar, the Minimize and Resize/Maximize and Close buttons, the scroll bars and arrows, and the title bar.

EXCEL 5.0

In Excel 5.0, the Resize button is referred to as the Restore button.

Menu Bar

The Excel **menu bar**, located at the top of the screen, is similar to that of other Windows programs, but it contains commands specific to Excel. Each menu choice on the menu bar contains a list of commands.

You select commands on the menu bar by using the mouse or the keyboard, including shortcut keys, in the same way as you would for other Windows programs. Because using the mouse is often the most efficient method for choosing commands in Excel, that method is emphasized in these tutorials.

Title Bar

The **title bar** at the top of the window identifies the Excel window in the same manner as in other Windows programs. The title bar indicates the name of the active workbook file. In Figure 1-6, the title bar displays "Microsoft Excel - Book1." Book1 is a default workbook filename that is assigned automatically by Excel until you change it.

Toolbars

A **toolbar button** is a small picture or icon representing an Excel command. Toolbar buttons provide you with immediate and easy access to many of the commonly used Excel commands, allowing you to perform tasks more quickly. The **Standard toolbar** and the **Formatting toolbar** are located below the menu bar and are usually displayed when Excel is launched. Excel has several other toolbars and you can also create your own custom arrangement of tools on a toolbar.

A **tooltip** is a description of the function of each toolbar button. When you move the mouse pointer over the top of the toolbar button, its name displays in a floating text box under the button and the tooltip appears on the status bar at the bottom of the program window.

Formula Bar

The **formula bar**, located immediately below the toolbars, displays the content of the active cell. A **cell's content** is the data that you enter into it. As you enter or edit data, the changes appear in the formula bar.

Worksheet Window

The document window, commonly known in Excel as the **worksheet window**, displays the active sheet you are creating, editing, or using. The worksheet window consists of the rows and columns of your spreadsheet. The **worksheet frame** contains the column letters and row numbers that identify cell locations. These are the letters beginning with A across the top of the frame and the numbers starting with 1 along the left side of the frame. The actual number of rows and columns that appear depends on the size of your computer monitor.

At the bottom and to the right of the worksheet window are the **scroll bars**, **scroll arrows**, and **scroll boxes**, which you can use to display different areas of your active worksheet. You use these controls in the same manner as with other Windows programs.

Cell Pointer

The **cell pointer** indicates the active cell. The cell pointer is identified by the rectangular highlight surrounding the cell. The **active cell** is where the cell pointer is and where data you enter is stored. When you first opened the worksheet, the cell pointer was located in cell A1, so A1 is the active cell.

Sheet Tabs

The **sheet tabs** at the bottom of the worksheet window identify the worksheets contained in a single workbook file. Excel automatically names each tab Sheet1, Sheet2, Sheet3, etc. The **active sheet** is the worksheet in which you are entering data or performing other activities. The sheet tabs allow you to move quickly between active sheets simply by clicking the desired sheet tab. When you open a new workbook, Excel automatically assigns 16 sheets, although not all the tabs are visible. You can include additional sheets up to a maximum of 255, and you can give each sheet a more meaningful name.

Reference Area

The **reference area**, which is located immediately above the worksheet frame to the left of the formula bar, displays the cell reference or name of the currently active selection. This is the cell reference of the active cell, or the name of an Excel object, such as a chart. The location of the cell pointer at the active cell is confirmed by the cell reference that appears in this reference area.

Mouse Pointer

The mouse pointer can be one of 14 different shapes, depending on the task you are performing in Excel and the pointer's location in the program window. The mouse pointer in Figure 1-6 is the shape of a block plus sign ✚. Other common mouse pointer shapes are the block arrow ↖ and the I-beam I. The block arrow appears when you move the mouse pointer outside the worksheet window; the mouse pointer changes to the I-beam when it is positioned on a text box, such as the formula bar, where you can type or edit data. The other mouse pointer shapes are described when they appear throughout these tutorials.

Status Bar

The **status bar**, located at the very bottom of the Excel window, contains several status indicators that advise you of conditions concerning the operation of Excel. The left side of the status bar acts like an on-line Help function and provides a brief description of the current command selected (or highlighted) on the menu, the action of the tool button the mouse is pointing to, or the current activity (or mode). **Mode indicators**, such as Enter or Ready, specify the **mode**, or state, that Excel is currently in. When the mode is Ready, Excel is waiting for you to select the next command or enter data. When the mode is Enter, Excel is in the process of accepting data for the active cell.

The **AutoCalculate** area in the status bar provides a quick-check total for selected cells containing numbers in the worksheet. As you select different cells, the total changes. This is like using your pocket calculator to compute a temporary total before entering a calculation in a cell. You can also have the selected numbers averaged or counted by right clicking the AutoCalculate area to display a menu for changing the method of calculation. If you are using Excel Version 5.0, the status bar does not have an AutoCalculate area.

The right side of the status bar shows the status of important keys, such as CAPS (Caps Lock) and NUM (Num Lock). In Figure 1-6, the status bar shows that the Num Lock is engaged, which means you can use your numeric keypad to enter numbers.

Navigating Through the Worksheet

A potentially football-field-size worksheet with 256 columns and 16,384 rows is impossible for you to view on your screen all at one time. Therefore, your screen becomes a window that allows you to look at a small area of the worksheet. The number of visible rows and columns depends on your particular display screen. Because you can view only one small area of the worksheet at a time, you need to navigate through the worksheet to see other areas of it. You do this by clicking specific cells, and using the scroll arrows and bars, the cursor movement keys, and the reference area.

Scrolling Using the Keyboard and the Mouse

You can view different areas of the worksheet that aren't visible by scrolling the worksheet window. You scroll by using the mouse with the vertical and horizontal scroll bars or by using the cursor movement keys. Figure 1-7 lists the most commonly used cursor movement keys.

Figure 1-7
Commonly used cursor movement keys

Key	Moves cell pointer
[→] or Tab	Right one cell
[←] or Shift + Tab	Left one cell
[↓] or Enter	Down one cell
[↑] or Shift + Enter	Up one cell
Home	To column A of the current row
Ctrl + Home	To cell A1
Ctrl + End	To the cell in the lower-right corner of the used portion of the worksheet
Ctrl + Backspace	To redisplay the active cell when not visible on the screen
Page Down	Down one screen
Page up	Up one screen

When you scroll the worksheet window using the scroll bars, you do not change the location of the active cell. As a result, your active cell may disappear from the window. If you want to see the active cell, press Ctrl + Backspace to scroll the window so the active cell is visible. Figure 1-8 summarizes the most commonly used scroll bar movements. When you drag the scroll box, a floating text box appears to indicate the row number that will be at the top of the worksheet window or the column letter that will be at the left side of the worksheet window when you release the mouse button. If you are using Excel Version 5.0, this page indicator feature is not available.

Figure 1-8
Commonly used scroll bar movements

To move worksheet display	Do this
Up or down one row	Click up or down scroll arrow
Left or right one column	Click left or right scroll arrow
Left or right one full screen	Click the horizontal scroll bar to the left or right of the scroll box
Up or down one full screen	Click the vertical scroll bar above or below the scroll box
Left or right to any position	Drag the scroll box in the horizontal scroll bar with the floating text box displayed
Up or down to any position	Drag the scroll box in the vertical scroll bar with the floating text box displayed

DEVELOPING WORKSHEETS **ADVEX 13**

Scrolling Using Special Keys

You can quickly move the cell pointer around the worksheet area by using the reference area, F5 (Go To key), or End keys, as summarized in Figure 1-9.

Figure 1-9 ◀
Special
cell pointer
movement keys

Keys	Moves cell pointer
F5 (Go To key)	Directly to a cell reference you specify
End [↑]	Up the current column to the cell in the first or last row that contains data
End [↓]	Down the current column to the cell in the first or last row that contains data
End [→]	Right in the current row to the cell in the first or last column that contains data
End [←]	Left in the current row to the cell in the first or last column that contains data
End Home	To the cell in the lower right corner of the worksheet's active area

Now that you are familiar with the elements of the Excel window, and you understand how to navigate through the spreadsheet, you are ready to learn how Ann created the Sunny Morning Products Operating Budget.

Introduction to Creating a Worksheet

Before Ann could begin creating the Sunny Morning Products Operating Budget, she needed to collect some basic information. So, Tuesday morning, Ann met with Carmen and Travis to talk over the requirements of the budget. Carmen helped Ann determine the expected sales for the first quarter. Then they reviewed last year's data and discussed the company's plan with Travis. Because they were just beginning the budget's development, Carmen suggested that Ann should build a budget worksheet for just the first quarter of next year. Once this was completed and approved by Travis and Kim, then they would expand the budget for the four quarters of next year's plan.

After you explore how Ann created her first draft of the worksheet for review with Carmen, you will continue to work with Ann as she improves her worksheet by enhancing its appearance and updating the data.

Developing Worksheets

The process of developing a worksheet can be divided into four major tasks: (1) analyze/define the problem, (2) design the worksheet, (3) build the worksheet, and (4) review/test the worksheet. This is a good process to follow when solving nearly any business problem. Ann is ready to begin the first step in this process—analysis.

Analyzing the Problem

Although Ann is anxious to launch Excel and begin typing, she knows that the first step in creating a professional worksheet is analyzing the problem you are trying to solve. You do this by defining the problem and determining what type of information needs to be included in the worksheet. Then you need to collect the necessary data.

Ann's task, as she learned in her initial meeting with Carmen and Travis, is to develop an operating budget for the first quarter of next year, with the intent of further developing it into a budget for the full year. Ann took notes as they discussed their budget for the first quarter and now she has all the information she needs to begin creating their operating budget, as illustrated in Figure 1-10.

Figure 1-10
Ann's notes for the budget

Using this preliminary information, Ann has created a planning analysis sheet. A **planning analysis sheet** contains answers to the following four questions:

1. **What is the goal of your worksheet?** The goal defines the problem you want to solve.

2. **What results do you want to see?** This information describes your **output**, the information required to help solve your problem.

3. **What data do you need to calculate the results you want to see?** This information is your **input**, which you enter into the worksheet to solve your problem.

4. **What calculations do you need to produce the desired output results?** These calculations specify the formulas used in your worksheet.

Ann's completed planning analysis sheet is shown in Figure 1-11.

DEVELOPING WORKSHEETS **ADVEX 15**

Figure 1-11 ◀
Ann's planning
analysis sheet

Planning Analysis Sheet

My goal:

Develop a worksheet of the operating budget for the first quarter of next year

What results do I want to see?

Revenues and expenses for the quarter

What information do I need?

Column is Qtr 1

Sales = 898300

Salaries = 109000

Office Equipment = 10420

Telephone = 7680

What calculations will I perform?

Cost of Sales = Sales * 0.61

Gross Profit = Sales — Cost of Sales

Benefits = Salaries * 18%

Advertising = Sales * 5%

Supplies = Sales * 3%

Total Exp = Add expense planning items

Earnings Before Tax = Gross Profit — Total Expenses

Return On Sales = Earnings Before Tax / Sales

Designing the Worksheet

Next, Ann needs to design the worksheet. On a piece of paper she prepares a rough sketch of her worksheet. First, she enters the headings, the column titles, and the revenue and expense item names, as shown in Figure 1-12. Then, she adds the data values and formulas to complete her worksheet design. Finally, she examines her rough sketch to make sure she has included all the required information. She is now ready to enter the data into Excel and build her worksheet.

ADVEX 16 **TUTORIAL 1** **CREATING WORKSHEETS USING EXCEL FOR WINDOWS**

Figure 1-12 ◄
Ann's sketch of
her worksheet

		A	B				
		WORKSHEET DESIGN SKETCH					
		A	B				
1		Sunny Morning Products					
2		Operating Budget					
3							
4			Qtr 1				
5		Revenues:					
6		Sales	898300				
7		Cost of Sales	=B6*0.61				
8		Gross Profit	=B6-B7				
9							
10		Expenses:					
11		Salaries	109000				
12		Benefits	=B11*18%				
13		Advertising	=B6*5%				
14		Office Equipment	10420				
15		Supplies	=B6*3%				
16		Telephone	7680				
17		Total Exp	=SUM(B11:B16)				
18							
19		Earnings Before Tax	=B8-B17				
20							
21		Return On Sales	=B19/B6				

Building the Worksheet

Ann will use her rough sketch in Figure 1-12 to create the Operating Budget worksheet shown in Figure 1-13. As you work with Ann, you will learn how to enter and revise text labels, values, and formulas into worksheet cells.

Figure 1-13 ◄
Ann's completed
Operating Budget
for Qtr 1

Sunny Morning Products
Operating Budget

	Qtr 1
Revenues:	
Sales	$898,300
Cost of Sales	521,014
Gross Profit	377,286
Expenses:	
Salaries	109,000
Benefits	19,620
Advertising	44,915
Office Equipment	10,420
Supplies	26,949
Telephone	7,680
Total Exp	218,584
Earnings Before Tax	$158,702
Return On Sales	**17.67%**

A **cell's content** is what you see displayed in the formula bar for your active cell, while the **cell's display** is what actually appears in your worksheet. The cells in Ann's worksheet contain text, values, formulas, and functions. **Text** is any descriptive title or information, such as a name or address, that is used to label a row or column in the worksheet. A **value** is a number, formula, or function. A **formula** is the arithmetic used to calculate numbers displayed in the worksheet. A **function** is a predefined formula that is built into Excel as a calculation tool. Functions save you the trouble of creating your own formulas to perform various mathematical tasks. While a cell's content and display are the same for text, they are usually different for formulas and functions. For numbers, a cell's content and display may be the same or different, depending on the formatting applied to the cell.

When you create an Excel worksheet, you enter text labels and data values into the cells of your worksheet to produce a report that you can either view on your screen or print as a paper copy. During this process, you type the worksheet contents arranged as they are to be printed or viewed. This is known as the **WYSIWYG** approach to creating a report. **WYSIWYG** (pronounced wiz-ee-wig) stands for "what you see is what you get." This approach is used with a number of different Windows programs, including many word-processing programs, as well as spreadsheet programs like Excel.

Entering Text Labels

Ann's worksheet contains an assortment of text labels. These labels describe the rest of the data in the worksheet. You cannot use text entries for calculations. If you accidentally use a cell that contains text in calculating a formula, an error occurs. Some data you commonly refer to as numbers is actually treated as text by Excel. For example, a telephone number such as 555-1234 or a social security number such as 123-45-6789 is treated as text and cannot be used for calculations.

It is good practice to enter identifying text labels before any other data. These labels help you identify the data values and formulas as you enter them into the rest of your worksheet. This helps to ensure that you are building correct formulas in the desired cells. When you enter a text label into a cell, you have four ways to complete your entry: you can click the Enter button ☑, you can press the Enter key, you can click another cell, or you can press a cursor movement key. If you make a mistake, you can click the Cancel button ☒ or press the Escape key to cancel your entry and try again. Notice that these buttons appear in the formula bar only while you are entering data. Now you can enter the text labels for Ann's worksheet by following her design sketch in Figure 1-12.

To enter the Sunny Morning Products main report heading:

1. Make sure that the cell pointer is located at cell A1. If it is not at that location, click **A1**.

2. Type **Sunny Morning Products**.
   Note that the mode indicator displays "Enter" as you type this text label and that "Sunny Morning Products" appears both in the formula bar and in cell A1. Also notice that the Cancel button ☒ and Enter button ☑ appear to the left of the formula bar. See Figure 1-14. Excel automatically detects that you are entering a text label, because the data value is not a number.

Figure 1-14
Entering the Sunny Morning Products heading

Enter button

Cancel button

text label appears in cell A1

mode indicator displays Enter

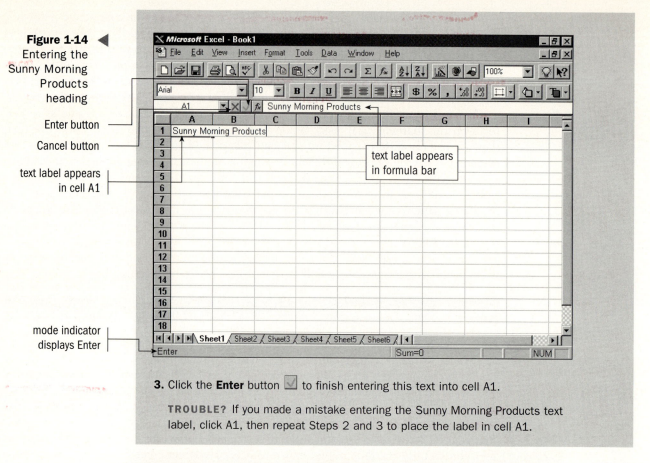

3. Click the **Enter** button to finish entering this text into cell A1.

   TROUBLE? If you made a mistake entering the Sunny Morning Products text label, click A1, then repeat Steps 2 and 3 to place the label in cell A1.

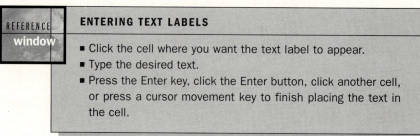

ENTERING TEXT LABELS

- Click the cell where you want the text label to appear.
- Type the desired text.
- Press the Enter key, click the Enter button, click another cell, or press a cursor movement key to finish placing the text in the cell.

Now you are ready to enter the other worksheet headings and all the revenue and expense item text labels for Ann's worksheet.

To continue entering the text labels into the operating budget worksheet:

1. Click **A2** or press [↓] to select the active cell for the next text label, the heading.

2. Type **Operating Budget**, then press the Enter key.

   TROUBLE? If you make a mistake in typing the Operating Budget text label and you notice your error before you finish entering the label, use the Backspace key to remove the unwanted characters. Type the desired characters, then click the Enter button to finish your correction.

3. Refer to Figure 1-12 and enter the text labels in cells A5 through A21 to continue to build the worksheet. Make sure your text labels match those shown in Figure 1-15.

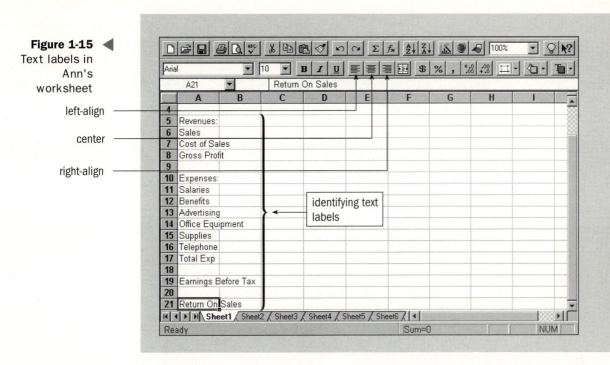

Figure 1-15
Text labels in Ann's worksheet

According to Ann's sketch, her worksheet contains a "Qtr 1" column heading, which is flush right in the column. The Formatting toolbar contains the buttons that control the **alignment** of text in a cell. The text can be left-aligned, right-aligned, or centered. Next, enter the column heading for the first quarter and right-align it.

To enter the column heading for the first quarter and right-align it:

1. Click **B4**, the location of the column heading.

2. Type **Qtr 1** and click the **Enter** button ☑ to finish entering this text and identify the data that goes in this column of Ann's worksheet.

3. Click the **Align Right** button to right-align this column heading.

Now you are ready to enter the values and formulas for the first quarter.

Entering Values

Values can be numbers, formulas, or functions. You use numbers in formulas that you create to calculate a displayed value. These values can, in turn, be used in formulas in other cells. In this way, the numbers you enter in just a few cells often control all the values displayed in your worksheet. Excel lets you include special **data editing characters**, like the comma (,) and the currency symbol ($) to control how a value is displayed in the worksheet. The way a number is displayed is called the cell's **format**.

The next step in building the worksheet is entering the values into the appropriate cells. In this set of steps, you will enter all of the numbers, or numeric values. In the next set of steps you will enter the values that are formulas. Begin by entering the value for Sales.

To enter the value for Sales for Qtr 1:

1. Click **B6**, if necessary, to make it the active cell.

2. Type **898300** and note that the mode indicator displays "Enter." Be sure to type the number zero and not the letter O.

3. Click the **Enter** button to finish entering this value in cell B6. Note that Excel automatically right-aligns a number in its worksheet cell. See Figure 1-16.

Figure 1-16
Entering a numeric value

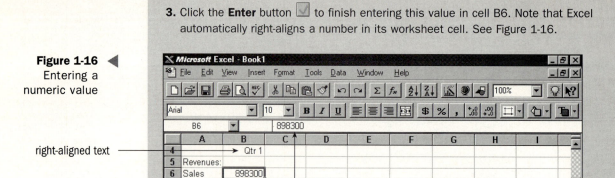

right-aligned text

numeric data value

Now, continue by entering the data value for Salaries.

4. Enter the value **109000** for Salaries in cell **B11** according to Ann's sketch, as shown in Figure 1-12. Observe the mode indicator as you enter this data.

5. Enter the remaining data values for Office Equipment and Telephone, as shown in Figure 1-12. When you enter the value for Office Equipment in cell B14, the Office Equipment text label is cut off in its cell in the worksheet. This is because the text "Office Equipment" is wider than the cell and there is now a value in the cell *immediately to the right*, so the text label can't spill over into the adjacent cell. You will correct this situation, and the others where text labels are cut off, later in the tutorial when you review the worksheet. See Figure 1-17.

Figure 1-17
Numeric values in Ann's worksheet

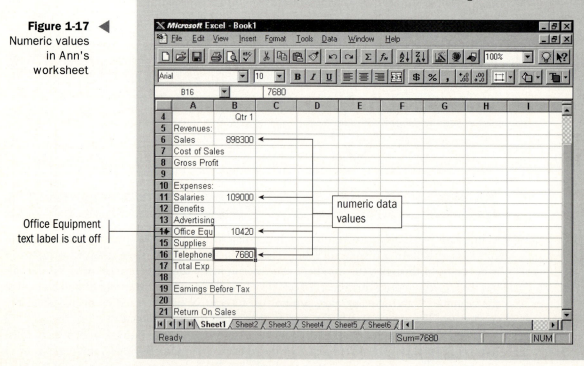

Office Equipment text label is cut off

numeric data values

REFERENCE window

ENTERING VALUES

- Click the cell where you want the value to be located.
- Type the value, including any desired formatting for its display.
- Press the Enter key, click the Enter button, click another cell, or press a cursor movement key to finish placing the data value in the cell as a numeric constant.

You are finished entering the numeric values for Ann's worksheet. All of the remaining values to be entered are formulas.

Entering Formulas

In many ways, Ann's Operating Budget is similar to a report or table that you might just create using your word processor. A major difference between using Excel and a word processor is the *use of formulas to calculate data values* that are displayed in the cells that make up the budget table. In fact, one way to think about Excel is that it is a big calculator, displaying the results of many different formulas arranged as a presentation-quality report, like Ann's budget. Recall that a **formula** is the arithmetic used to calculate values displayed in a worksheet. You can take advantage of the power of Excel by using formulas in worksheets. If you change one number in the worksheet, Excel recalculates any formula affected by the change. This saves you time reentering calculated values and reduces the possibility of errors. For example, in Ann's budget, Benefits are 18% of Salaries; that is, Benefits are Salaries multiplied by .18. She can enter this as a formula in her spreadsheet. Then, when the amount budgeted for Salaries changes, as she prepares several revisions of her plan, the amount for Benefits is recalculated automatically from the new amount for Salaries, using Ann's formula.

Formulas are constructed by combining numbers, cell references, and arithmetic operators, such as the plus sign (+) and the minus sign (−), to define your calculation. Figure 1-18 displays the complete list of arithmetic operators. These operators are the same as those used with a variety of other software programs used for arithmetic calculations.

Figure 1-18 ◀
Arithmetic operators used in formulas

Symbol	Operation
+	Add
−	Subtract
*	Multiply
/	Divide
%	Percentage
^	Exponentiation
( )	Group calculations

A formula must begin with the equal sign or one of the other arithmetic operators shown in Figure 1-19. Otherwise, Excel will treat it as a text label and your worksheet will not calculate correctly.

ADVEX 22 **TUTORIAL 1** CREATING WORKSHEETS USING EXCEL FOR WINDOWS

Figure 1-19 ◀
First characters
that begin a cell
formula entry

First Character:	Example:	Explanation:
= (equal sign)	=27*C14	Multiply the value in cell C14 by 27
+ (plus sign)	+D5*0.62	Multiply the positive value in cell D5 by .62
− (minus sign)	−C11+52	Add the negative value in cell C11 to 52

For example, Ann knows that at Sunny Morning Products the Benefits expenses for each employee are 18% of Salaries. She has already entered the value of Salaries for Qtr 1 in cell B11. To calculate the value for Benefits and display it in the worksheet area, she uses the formula =B11*0.18. This formula instructs Excel to take the value in cell B11, multiply it by 0.18, and display the result in cell B12. Ann decides to use a formula instead of calculating the result herself, because she knows that the Salaries value might change. By using a formula to calculate Benefits, she ensures that this data value is *recalculated automatically* by Excel whenever the data value for Salaries changes.

When you construct a formula, the formula bar displays the formula, but the result calculated by the formula is displayed in the cell. This feature of formulas makes them different from text labels and numeric constants, which have the same value displayed both in the formula bar and in the worksheet cell. See Figure 1-20.

Figure 1-20 ◀
Summary of
selected cell
contents and
use in Ann's
budget

Cell Reference	Cell Content	Cell Display	Cell Use
A11	Salaries	Salaries	Text label
B4	Qtr 1	Qtr 1	Text label
B11	109000	109,000	Value — Number
B6	898300	$898,300	Value — Number
B21	=B19/B6	0.1467	Value — Formula

Now that you understand formulas and how to construct them, you are ready to enter the formula for calculating the Cost of Sales. In analyzing her problem, Ann determined that the Cost of Sales is 61% of Sales, or in other words, the result of multiplying the value in cell B6 by .61.

To enter the Cost of Sales formula:

1. Click **B7** to make it the active cell.

2. Type the formula **=B6*.61** and click the **Enter** button ☑. Be sure to type the formula exactly as it appears. Note that 547963 is displayed in cell B7. See Figure 1-21. Remember that when a formula is used to calculate a value, the result of the calculation is displayed in the worksheet area, while the formula is displayed in the formula bar. Again, when you enter the formula for Cost of Sales in cell B7, the Cost of Sales text label in cell A7 is cut off, because the text is wider than the cell and there is now a value in the cell immediately to the right.

Figure 1-21
Entering the formula for Cost of Sales

formula as entered

text label cut off

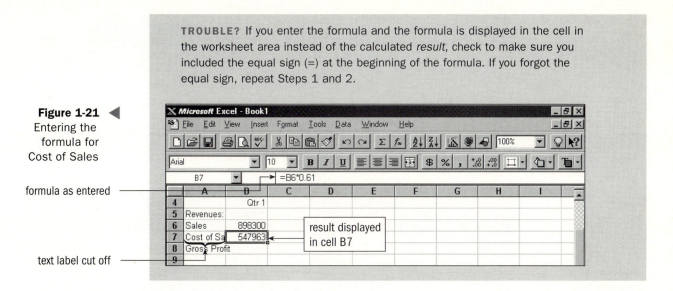

Now, enter the formula for Gross Profit, which is calculated by subtracting Sales from the Cost of Sales.

To enter the formula for Gross Profit:

1. Click **B8**, if necessary, to make it the active cell.

2. Type **=B6-B7** and press the **Enter** key. The desired calculated value, 350337, appears in cell B8. Numbers calculated by a formula initially appear using the general format. The **general format** is Excel's default format and displays numbers without any commas or other special characters. Integer numbers are displayed without decimals, while fractional numbers are displayed with a varying number of decimals that depend on the value being displayed. A minus sign appears to the left of a negative number. Excel has many other number formats that you will learn about when you enhance the appearance of the Operating Budget.

Next, you are ready to enter the Benefits formula into Ann's worksheet. Benefits are calculated as 18% of Salaries.

To enter the Benefits formula:

1. Click **B12** to make this the active cell.

2. Enter the formula **=B11*18%** for Benefits.

The formulas you have entered thus far into Ann's worksheet have been fairly basic; they required only one arithmetic operator. When calculating a formula, Excel can perform only one operation at a time. If a formula contains two or more arithmetic operators, for example 1+.8*50/5, the calculation is performed in a particular sequence. This sequence, shown in Figure 1-22, is called the **order of precedence**.

ADVEX 24 **TUTORIAL 1** CREATING WORKSHEETS USING EXCEL FOR WINDOWS

Figure 1-22
Order of
precedence

Order	Operator	Description
1	( )	parentheses
2	−	negation or unary minus (as in −11)
3	%	percent
4	^	exponentiation
5	* /	multiplication or division
6	+ −	addition or subtraction
7	&	text joining or concatenation
8	= <> > < >= <=	comparison

When a formula contains two or more arithmetic operators that have equal precedence, Excel uses the **left-to-right rule**, calculating the operators with the same precedence in order from left to right. For example, Excel would calculate the formula 1+.8*50/5 by first multiplying .8*50 to get 40. This result is then divided by 5, yielding 8. Finally, 1 is then added to 8 to produce the result, 9.

Sometimes you want the arithmetic operations in your formulas done in a sequence different from that determined by the precedence and left-to-right rules. By using **parentheses**, you can override the rules of precedence and the left-to-right rule. The arithmetic operations *inside* parentheses are calculated before operations *outside* the parentheses. If you are not sure of the sequence in which the arithmetic operations will be carried out within a formula, use parentheses to control the desired sequence of calculation. If you include parentheses that are not required, no harm is done.

One of the key features of Excel in calculating formulas is that it is **nonprocedural**, meaning that Excel uses the natural order of calculation in computing your formulas in a worksheet. The **natural order of calculation** means that you can enter formulas in any cell you want without concern for which cell's value is calculated first. As a result, you are free to organize the formulas in your worksheet as you want them displayed, rather than arranging them in the sequence in which you would calculate them with your calculator. If this sequence happens to be different than the sequence in which they are calculated, Excel determines the necessary computation sequence and then calculates your formulas in that sequence. That is, if a formula in cell F43 needs to be calculated so its result can be used in cell B22, Excel detects this situation and calculates the value for the formula in F43 first. In this manner, the natural order, or nonprocedural, feature of Excel becomes your "silent partner" that makes it much easier for you to enter formulas and numbers arranged in your worksheet *as you want them to be displayed*, the WYSIWYG approach.

Computer tools like Excel that are nonprocedural are known as a **fourth-generation language** (4GL). In general, with a 4GL you should expect to develop a computer solution to your business problem in about one-tenth the time that would be required to produce the same solution using a third-generation language (3GL), such as BASIC, Pascal, C++, or COBOL. For this reason, when you encounter a problem that looks like an accountant's spreadsheet, you should consider using Excel as the most appropriate software tool for developing your solution.

BUILDING FORMULAS BY POINTING **ADVEX 25**

Entering Functions

The last type of value you need to enter is a function. **Functions** are predefined formulas that are built into Excel as a shortcut for performing mathematical calculations. A function takes one or more input values, performs the predefined calculation, and returns a *single value* that is displayed in the cell. All functions begin with a name and include the arguments enclosed in parentheses after the function name. The **function name** briefly describes the function's action. The **arguments** represent the required information that the function needs to do its task.

For example, Ann could use the formula B11+B12+B13+B14+B15+B16 to calculate the Total Exp in Qtr 1, but this would be tedious and the possibility of errors increases. When you want to add several adjacent cells together, the Excel SUM function is the best choice. The function SUM(B11:B16) adds all the numbers in the cell range B11 through B16; the colon (:) specifies "through." In this example, the function name is SUM and the argument is B11:B16. A cell **range** is a rectangular block of cells specified by the cell references of its upper-left and lower-right corners.

Because a function performs a calculation, you must enter it as an Excel formula, using the equal sign (=) to indicate that the cell contains a formula. Although you can enter the SUM function by typing it, the **AutoSum button** on the Standard toolbar automatically creates a formula with the SUM function that adds a specified range of cells. Next, use the AutoSum button to create the formula for the Total Exp in Qtr 1.

To enter the SUM function using the AutoSum button:

1. Click and drag the cell pointer from cell **B11** to cell **B17** to select this cell range. The selection includes both the cells you want summed and the cell where you want the formula to be (the last cell selected, B17).

2. Click the **AutoSum** button $\boxed{\Sigma}$ to place a formula that consists of the SUM function in cell B17.

3. Click **B17** and confirm that the function SUM(B11:B16) displays in the formula bar, and the value 146,720 displays in the cell.

REFERENCE window

USING THE AUTOSUM BUTTON

- Select the cells you want to add by dragging the cell pointer over the cells row by row and/or column by column, including a blank cell to the right or below those to be added.
- Click the AutoSum button to place the SUM function in the blank cell.

  or

  If there are no blanks or non-numeric cells in the group of cells you want to sum, but there is a blank cell to the right of or above the group, then click the cell where you want the sum, click the AutoSum button, and press the Enter key.

You can enter the remaining formulas into Ann's worksheet by pointing, a more convenient method of creating formulas.

Building Formulas by Pointing

Excel allows you to create formulas either by typing them, as you have done so far, or by pointing to the cell references you want to include in the formulas. With **pointing**, you click the cell whose reference you want included in the formula you are entering. *Pointing* *is the preferred method of building formulas* because it is quicker and reduces your chances of making a mistake. For example, it is very easy to type F41 when you mean F14. You can enter Ann's remaining formulas by using the pointing method.

To enter the formula for Advertising by pointing:

1. Click **B13** to make it the active cell. Before entering a formula using pointing, make sure the cell where you want the completed formula is active.

2. Type = (the equal sign) to begin the formula.

3. Click **B6**. This is pointing to cell B6. Notice that the mode indicator in the status bar displays "Point." The cell reference appears in the formula you are entering in cell B13 and in the formula bar. Also, a dashed box appears around cell B6. See Figure 1-23. Note that instead of clicking cell B6, you could also use the cursor movement keys to point to the cell reference. However, using the mouse is usually more efficient.

   TROUBLE? If you happen to click the wrong cell, then simply click the desired cell, B6, to place the correct cell reference in the formula.

Figure 1-23
Cell reference specified by pointing

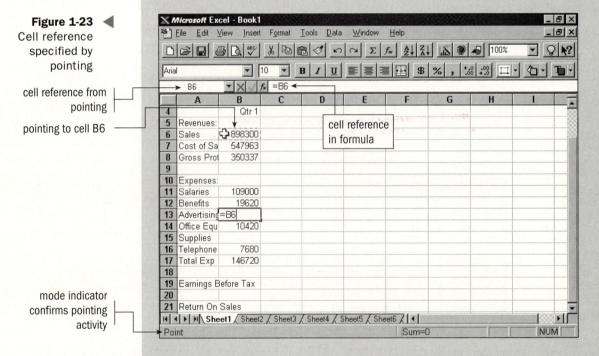

4. Type * (an asterisk) to specify the multiplication arithmetic operator.

5. Type **5%** to include this numeric constant in the formula with an arithmetic operator. You can include as many cell references and numeric constants separated by arithmetic operators in a formula as you like, as long as the total number of characters is 255 or less.

6. Click the **Enter** button to complete the formula. When you use pointing to build a formula, you need to press the Enter key or click the Enter button to complete it; otherwise, you may change the last cell reference you specified by pointing. The formula is displayed in the formula bar while the result, 44915, is displayed in the worksheet at cell B13. See Figure 1-24.

Figure 1-24
Completed formula for Advertising

desired formula

calculated result of formula

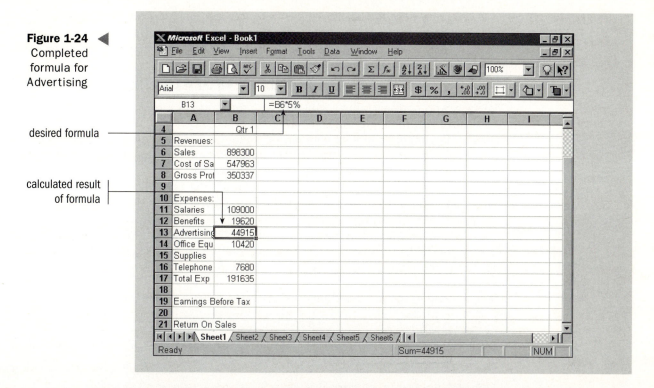

Next, enter the formulas for Supplies, Earnings Before Tax, and Return on Sales according to Ann's sketch in Figure 1-12, using the pointing method.

To enter the additional formulas by pointing:

1. Make the cell for Supplies in Qtr 1 your active cell and use pointing to enter the formula **B6*3%**.

2. Use pointing to enter the formula **B19/B6** into the cell for Return On Sales in Qtr 1. Notice that a zero is used for the value for B19 because that cell is empty and does not contain a formula yet. As soon as you enter a value in cell B19, Excel will calculate the correct result for the formula in cell B21. This demonstrates the nonprocedural aspect of Excel; you do not need to enter formulas in the sequence in which they are either calculated or referenced from one formula to the next.

3. Make the cell for Earnings Before Tax in Qtr 1 the active cell and use pointing to enter the formula **B8-B17**. Return On Sales is calculated as 0.146669.

   TROUBLE? Be sure to place the formula in column B, even though the Earnings Before Tax text label spills over into this column and covers the entire cell.

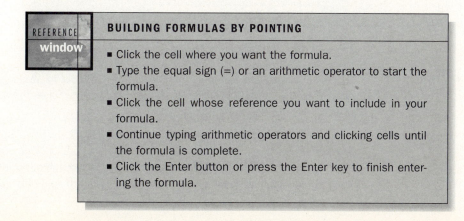

REFERENCE window

BUILDING FORMULAS BY POINTING

- Click the cell where you want the formula.
- Type the equal sign (=) or an arithmetic operator to start the formula.
- Click the cell whose reference you want to include in your formula.
- Continue typing arithmetic operators and clicking cells until the formula is complete.
- Click the Enter button or press the Enter key to finish entering the formula.

By entering all of the labels, values, formulas, and functions for Ann's worksheet, you have implemented her design as specified by her planning analysis sheet. You have successfully built a worksheet! Your next step is to save the worksheet to your Student Disk.

Using Save As to Save a Workbook File

Saving a workbook file allows you access to the workbook even after you end your session with Excel. It is important to save your work *frequently*. When you are building a workbook, it is stored in your computer's random access memory (RAM). Until you save your workbook, if your computer system crashes for any reason, you might lose all of the information you included since the last time you saved.

There are two commands to save a workbook—the Save command and the Save As command. If the worksheet does not have a filename, or if you want to give it a *different* filename, you must use the Save As command. Because you created the worksheet in the Book1 default workbook window, you need to give this workbook a different filename. Once you give the workbook a filename, you can use the Save command, which you will do later in this tutorial. Now you want to name and save your workbook file.

To name and save your workbook file using the Save As command:

1. Click **File** on the menu bar to display the File menu.

2. Click **Save As** to display the Save As dialog box for specifying a filename for this workbook file.

3. Click the **Save in** list arrow, then click the disk drive containing your Student Disk.

   Click the Drives list arrow, then click the disk drive containing your Student Disk.

4. Double-click the **Tut01 folder** to select it as the destination for your workbook file.

   Double-click the Tut01 directory in the Directories text box.

5. Double-click the **File name** text box, and type **S_SMP1**. See Figure 1-25. You'll learn why we use this name for the file in the next section, "Workbook Filenames for the Tutorials."

Figure 1-25 ◀
Using Save As to save your workbook file

a different dialog box appears with a Directories list box

files already saved in the Tut01 folder

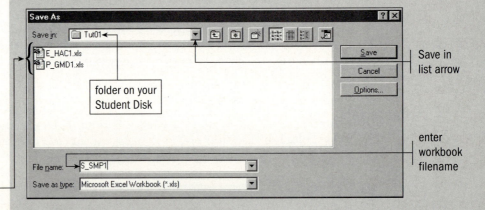

6. Click **Save** to save the file to your Student Disk.

   Click OK to display the Summary Info dialog box. Enter Sunny Morning Products as the title, Operating Budget as the subject, and your name as the author, then click OK. The file is saved to your Student Disk.

7. Examine the Excel program window. Notice that S_SMP1.xls now displays as the filename at the top of the workbook window. See Figure 1-26. Remember that Excel automatically adds the .xls file extension to the filename, but depending on your Excel installation, the file extension .XLS may or may not display.

Figure 1-26
New filename displayed in title bar of workbook window

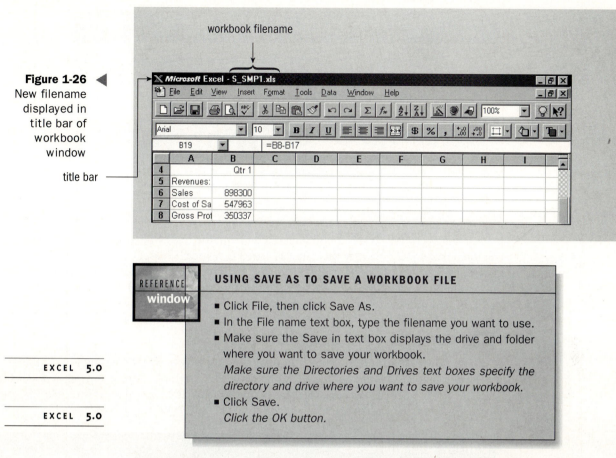

EXCEL 5.0

EXCEL 5.0

Workbook Filenames for the Tutorials

When saving files, you should use descriptive names that help you identify the contents of your workbook files. Windows 95 supports long filenames of up to 255 characters. To ensure backward compatibility with MS-DOS, the 8.3 naming convention is still used with Windows 95, but it is hidden from view with a long filename. To avoid possible conflicts, workbook filenames for these tutorials are limited to eight characters, with the .xls extension assigned automatically by Excel. These characters can be letters, numbers, and all symbols except for spaces, commas, colons, and asterisks. Although eight characters do not often allow you to use descriptive names, you can create meaningful abbreviations. For example, the Student Disk for Excel contains several dozen files. The files for each tutorial are stored in a separate folder or directory. The folder Tut01 contains the files for Tutorial 1, and similarly for the other tutorials. The files in each tutorial folder or directory, have a one-letter abbreviation that tells you what kind of files they are, as shown in Figure 1-27.

ADVEX 30 **TUTORIAL 1** CREATING WORKSHEETS USING EXCEL FOR WINDOWS

Figure 1-27 ◀

Naming convention for files on your Student Disk

First Letter	File Category	Description of File Category
C	Tutorial Cases	The files that contain the workbook you need to complete some of the tutorial steps
E	Tutorial Exercises	The files that contain the workbook you need to complete the Tutorial Exercises at the end of each tutorial
P	Case Problems	The files that contain the workbook you need to complete the Case Problems and Comprehensive Applications at the end of each tutorial
S	Saved Worksheet	Any workbook file that you have saved

An underscore separates the first character from the rest of the filename. The next three characters uniquely identify the name assigned to a specific case, exercise, or problem, for example, SMP for **S**unny **M**orning **P**roducts. The last number indicates a version number; for example, a file named S_SMP3 is the third version of a saved file. This naming convention continues throughout these tutorials.

Reviewing the Worksheet

You are now ready for the fourth and final step in the process of creating a worksheet—reviewing and testing the worksheet. This is when you look closely at your worksheet. Are all of the calculations correct? Is anything misspelled? How does it look? In the following sections you will correct the errors in Ann's worksheet.

Editing Cell Contents

Travis is negotiating a new contract with the Orange Growers Association that is expected to reduce their costs, and he just informed Ann of this new value. As Carmen and Ann review the worksheet results, they decide that the Cost of Sales percent of 61% is too high, given the terms of the new contract Travis is working on. They feel that 58% is more appropriate. Ann decides to make this revision to her worksheet.

You can change the content of a cell by either replacing or editing it. In this section you will learn how to edit a cell's content. Excel uses a method of entering and revising a cell's content known as "editing within a cell." When you are **editing within a cell**, the edit cursor appears in the cell, and any changes you make are displayed both in the worksheet cell and in the formula bar. Remember that before you can edit a cell's content, you need to be sure that the cell you want to edit is the active cell. You will use editing to revise the Cost of Sales percent in Ann's worksheet.

To revise the cell's content by editing:

1. Click **B7** to make it the active cell.

2. Double-click **B7** or press **F2** to activate the Edit mode. Notice that the mode indicator now displays "Edit" and the edit cursor appears as a vertical bar (I), indicating that Excel is ready for editing within a cell. The mouse pointer changes to I, which you can drag to highlight the characters you want to delete or replace. See Figure 1-28.

Figure 1-28
Editing within a cell

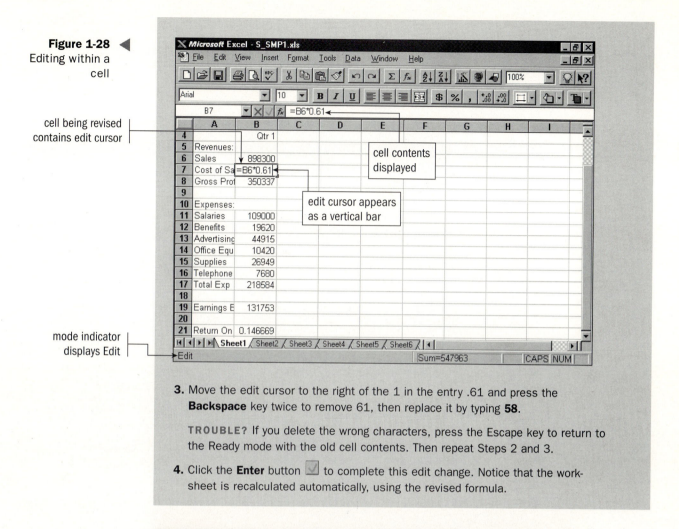

3. Move the edit cursor to the right of the 1 in the entry .61 and press the **Backspace** key twice to remove 61, then replace it by typing **58**.

   TROUBLE? If you delete the wrong characters, press the Escape key to return to the Ready mode with the old cell contents. Then repeat Steps 2 and 3.

4. Click the **Enter** button to complete this edit change. Notice that the worksheet is recalculated automatically, using the revised formula.

REFERENCE window

EDITING CELL CONTENTS

- Click the cell containing the label or value you want to change to make it the active cell.
- Double-click the cell or press F2 to initiate the edit process.
- Within the cell containing the label or value, move the edit cursor to where you want to either remove or insert characters.
- Use either the Backspace or Delete key to remove unwanted characters, then type any desired new characters to insert them.
- Press the Enter key or click the Enter button to complete the edit change to the cell.

Clearing Cell Contents

As you are building and editing your worksheets, you may occasionally find that you have entered a label or value in a cell that you want to be empty. An **empty cell** is one that does *not* contain a label or a value—it has no cell contents. When you first launch Excel, all worksheets in the Book1 workbook have empty cells. An empty cell is different from a cell that contains a blank space. If you use the Spacebar key and the Enter key to make a cell *appear* blank, it contains a text label, the space character. Cells that look empty but contain space characters can cause unwanted results when they are included in some calculations. If you want to make a cell appear blank, the preferred method is to erase the cell's content so the cell is truly empty. You do this by selecting the cell and using the

Delete key to erase its content. Ann is considering adding a ratio of the Salaries and Benefits to Sales, that is, a ratio that is a measure of the proportion of sales revenue that goes to people costs. She adds this calculation to her worksheet as she considers its importance in analyzing the operating budget.

To include the ratio calculation in the worksheet:

1. Scroll the worksheet window and click **B23** to make it the active cell.

2. Enter the formula **(B11+B12)/B6**, which is a ratio of Salaries and Benefits to Sales. The calculated value, 0.143182 displays.

Ann reviews the ratio. Although it is interesting, she decides it is not as important as she thought, so this cell's content needs to be cleared.

To clear the cell's content:

1. Click **B23**, if necessary, to make it the active cell.

2. Press the **Delete** key to delete the cell's content.

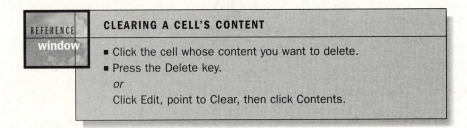

REFERENCE window

CLEARING A CELL'S CONTENT

- Click the cell whose content you want to delete.
- Press the Delete key.

or

Click Edit, point to Clear, then click Contents.

Ann's calculations are complete. Her next step in reviewing the worksheet is to check the spelling.

Spell Checking the Worksheet

Ann knows that spelling errors make a worksheet look very unprofessional. It is a good practice to always spell check your worksheet as part of the review process.

To spell check the worksheet:

1. Press **Ctrl + Home** to make cell A1 the active cell, because you want to begin the spelling check at the top of the worksheet.

2. Click the **Spelling** button on the Standard toolbar.

3. When the Spelling dialog box appears with the word "Exp," which is not in the dictionary, type **Expenses** in the Change To text box as the desired spelling for this word, then click the **Change** button to correct this spelling error in the worksheet.

    See Figure 1-29. If the word *was* spelled correctly, but was not in the dictionary, you would click the Ignore button. This is often the situation when you use abbreviations.

Figure 1-29
Spelling dialog box with unknown word

list of suggested alternatives

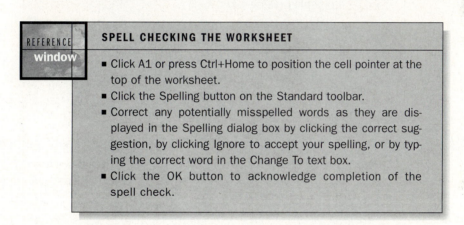

> **TROUBLE?** If you encounter any misspelled words in your worksheet before "Exp," go to Step 4 and correct them. When you get to "Exp," correct it as described in Step 3.
>
> 4. If any other misspelled words are detected and displayed in the dialog box, select the correct suggestion or edit the word in the Change To text box.
>
> 5. Click the **OK** button when prompted with the "Finished spell checking entire sheet" message.

REFERENCE window

SPELL CHECKING THE WORKSHEET

- Click A1 or press Ctrl+Home to position the cell pointer at the top of the worksheet.
- Click the Spelling button on the Standard toolbar.
- Correct any potentially misspelled words as they are displayed in the Spelling dialog box by clicking the correct suggestion, by clicking Ignore to accept your spelling, or by typing the correct word in the Change To text box.
- Click the OK button to acknowledge completion of the spell check.

As she is reviewing the worksheet Ann notices that column A is too narrow. She needs to widen the column but cannot remember how to do this in Excel. She decides to use Excel's Help feature to refresh her memory.

Help Desk for the Tutorials

Excel's on-line Help feature displays information in a separate Help window describing the various commands and activities available for creating worksheets and charts. By double-clicking the Help button , you can display the Help Topics dialog box and then type a keyword for a topic on which you want additional instructions. But what if the question you have is what keyword provides the topic you need help with? The Help Desk feature in these tutorials indicates the keywords and topics you should select when you want additional on-line Help from Excel. The following Help Desk is an example of those you'll find used throughout these tutorials.

ADVEX 34 **TUTORIAL 1** CREATING WORKSHEETS USING EXCEL FOR WINDOWS

HELP DESK

EXCEL **5.0**

Index

CHANGING COLUMN WIDTH

Double-click the Help button to display the Help Topics dialog box, then click the Index tab.

Keywords	**Topic**
adjusting row height and column width	Adjust column width and row height
adjusting column width	*Adjusting column width*

You can use Help to find more information about any topic. Frequently, the keywords in Excel Version 7.0 are slightly different from those in Version 5.0. However, as you can see from the Help window example, they are very similar. When the keywords are different, you can frequently type just the first few letters of the keyword and then scroll the keyword list to search for a similar entry. After you get the information you need, you can exit from Help and return to Ready mode.

Ann doesn't remember the options for widening a column in her worksheet, so she wants to look them up using Help. Apply the keyword procedure to learn how to use the step-by-step keyword reference to obtain the on-line Help that describes how to widen a column.

To obtain on-line Help for widening a column using keywords:

1. Double-click the **Help** button 🔍 on the Standard toolbar to display the Help Topics dialog box.

   TROUBLE? If you just click the Help button, the mouse pointer changes to ↳?, which lets you click a command or screen element to obtain help with that item. To display the Help Topics window, click the Help button again to return to the regular mouse pointer, then repeat Step 1.

2. Click the **Index** tab, if necessary, to display that sheet, then type **adjust** in the Type a word text box.

   Type adjust in the Type the first few letters of the word you are looking for text box.

EXCEL **5.0**

3. Click **Display** to display a list of topics for selection. As you type the keyword, Excel automatically scrolls the list of topics; you do not need to type the entire keyword.

   Click the Show Topics button to display a list of topics for selection.

EXCEL **5.0**

4. Click **Adjusting column width and row height** in the Topics Found dialog box, then click **Display**.

   Click Adjust column width in the Topics Found dialog box, then click the Go To button.

EXCEL **5.0**

5. Click the **Adjust column width** button to display that Help description.

   The desired description appears; you do not need to click the button.

EXCEL **5.0**

   The Help window displays instructions on how to adjust the column width. Read them by scrolling the Help window.

6. Click the Help window **Close** button ☒ to close the Help window and return to the worksheet window.

EXCEL **5.0**

   Click Close, then double-click the Microsoft Excel Help window control menu box to return to the worksheet window.

Thanks to the on-line Help feature, Ann now recalls how to widen a column and is ready to do so to enhance the display of data in her worksheet.

Changing Column Width

Changing column width is one way to improve the appearance of the worksheet, making it easier to read and interpret data. In Ann's worksheet you need to increase the width of column A so the entire text label "Earnings Before Tax" appears in the cell. You can change the width of column A using **AutoFit**, which adjusts the column to accommodate the longest text label in the column.

To change the width of column A to match the widest label in the column using AutoFit:

1. Move the mouse pointer to the line that separates column A from column B in the worksheet border. The pointer changes to ✥.

2. Double-click the **right boundary of column A** in the worksheet border to resize the column to fit its longest text. See Figure 1-30.

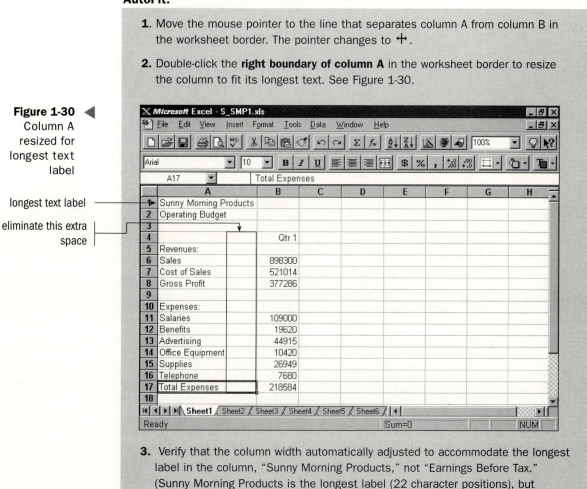

Figure 1-30 ◀ Column A resized for longest text label

longest text label

eliminate this extra space

3. Verify that the column width automatically adjusted to accommodate the longest label in the column, "Sunny Morning Products," not "Earnings Before Tax." (Sunny Morning Products is the longest label (22 character positions), but because there isn't anything in the column next to it, it spills over into the adjacent cell and doesn't appear cut off.)

Now there is too much space between the labels in column A and the values in column B. Ann wants to adjust the column width to reduce the white space between the expense items and the data for Qtr 1. Column A needs to be resized so that it is only 17 character spaces wide.

To resize Column A to the desired width:

1. Move the mouse pointer to the line that separates column A from column B in the worksheet border. Again, the pointer changes to ✥.

2. Click and drag the **resize arrow** ✥ to the left, thereby decreasing the width of the column to 17 characters, as indicated in the reference area. Notice that you can set the column width to any number of characters, including fractional characters.

> **REFERENCE window**
>
> **CHANGING COLUMN WIDTH**
>
> *Method 1*
> - Double-click the right boundary of the column in the worksheet border to size the column to accommodate its longest text.
>
> *Method 2*
> - Click the column letter in the worksheet border to select the column to size it so it accommodates its longest text.
>   or
>   Click the individual cell whose content is to be used to determine the column width.
> - Click Format, point to Column, and click AutoFit Selection.
> - Click any worksheet cell to unselect the column, if necessary.
>
> *Method 3*
> - Move the pointer to the worksheet frame until it is on top of the line that separates the column you want to change from the next column to the right. The pointer changes to a double-headed arrow.
> - Click and drag the pointer to the left to reduce the column's width, or to the right to increase the width.
> - Release the mouse button when the column width is correct.

With column A adjusted to an acceptable width, Ann wants to add formatting to the text labels and data values displayed in her worksheet. Before you do that, you need to know how to specify cell ranges so you can work with a group of several cells at one time.

Specifying Cell Ranges

Recall that a **cell range** is a rectangular group of cells. Ranges are used with various tasks in Excel when you want to specify a group of cells for formatting, printing, or use in a chart. When using ranges, you must follow two simple rules. First, ranges must be *rectangular*. Second, you identify a range of cells by specifying its upper-left corner and lower-right corner. Excel automatically includes the colon (:) to separate the cell references. For example, range A10:C20 specifies cells A10 through C20. Now that you know more about ranges, you can select the range of cells to format.

To select the range A4:B21:

1. Click **A4**. This will be the upper-left corner of the cell range.

2. With the cell pointer in the shape of the block plus ✛, drag the cell pointer to **B21** to specify the range A4:B21. *If your cell pointer changes to the shape of a bold plus ✚, do not drag the cell pointer to B21.* Note that when you select a range, the first cell in that range, cell A4 in this example, remains white and the other cells in the range are highlighted. See Figure 1-31.

   TROUBLE? If the mouse pointer changes to the shape of a bold plus ✚, you will accidentally copy the cell's content rather than select a cell range. Release the mouse button and click the Undo button. Then repeat the selection, beginning with Step 1.

Figure 1-31
Cell range selection

active cell of range is outlined

specified range highlighted

Now, you can practice unselecting this cell range.

3. Click **A4** to select this single cell as a range, which also unselects the previously selected range, A4:B21. Selecting any cell causes a previously selected range to be unselected.

> **REFERENCE window**
>
> **SELECTING A CELL RANGE**
> - Click the cell that is to be the upper-left corner of your range to make it the active cell.
> - Drag the cell pointer to the lower-right corner of the cell range and release the mouse button to finish specifying the cell range.

Changing Appearance with Formatting

The way a text label or number is displayed in a cell is called the cell's **format**. The format affects only the display of the cell's content. It does not change the actual content of the cell in any way. You can change how Excel displays text and numbers by using the buttons and lists on the Formatting toolbar. In addition, you can specify the format of a number by typing special data editing characters, such as commas and currency symbols, as you enter the number.

Unless you specify otherwise, Excel displays numbers with the **general format**, which uses a minus sign for negative values, no thousands separators, and no trailing zeros to the right of the decimal point. The number of decimal places displayed in a number is determined by Excel and depends on the value in a cell and the column width.

You can change the format of the numbers in Ann's worksheet by using the Currency Style, Percent Style, Comma Style, Increase Decimal, and Decrease Decimal buttons on the Formatting toolbar. You are ready to apply number formats to the Operating Budget to enhance its appearance.

To apply the currency style to sales:

1. Click **B6** to make it the active cell.

2. Click the **Currency Style** button $ to apply the currency style to this cell. The cell is filled with a series of pound signs (#) that indicate that the width of the cell is too narrow to display the cell's current value and editing characters. See Figure 1-32. The default for the Currency Style is to display numbers with two places to the right of the decimal. This made the number wider than the column. Although you could increase the width of the column, you can also correct this condition by decreasing the number of decimal places displayed by the Currency Style for Ann's Operating Budget.

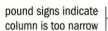

Figure 1-32
Column too narrow to display number with editing characters

pound signs indicate column is too narrow

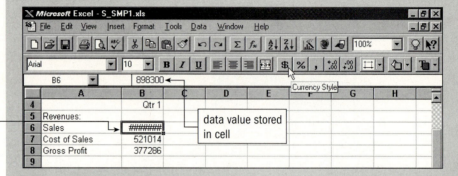

3. Click the **Decrease Decimal** button twice to display the number with no decimal places.

   TROUBLE? If you click the Decrease Decimal button twice and the pound signs still appear, then the default column width is too narrow for your font. Increase the column width by dragging the right boundary of the column in the worksheet border so the number $898,300 appears.

4. Click **B19**, then apply the Currency Style with no decimals to this cell.

For the Operating Budget, the number format desired for cells B7 through B17 is the comma style with no decimals. You can apply this format to all the cells in this range at the same time.

To apply the comma format to the cell range:

1. Select the range where the format is to be changed, in this case, **B7:B17**.

2. Click the **Comma Style** button to apply this format to the selected range and display the numbers with commas and two places to the right of the decimal, which is the Excel default. This format is applied to all cells in the selected range, even the blank cells. If you later entered a number in one of the blank cells, it would appear with the comma style. This allows you to apply a format to a cell before you enter data into it.

3. Click the **Decrease Decimal** button twice to remove the unwanted decimal places.

The final number format is for the Return On Sales. Ann wants this to be displayed as a percent with two places to the right of the decimal.

To apply the Percent Style to the Return On Sales:

1. Click **B21** to make it the active cell.

2. Click the **Percent Style** button % to apply this style, which appears without any decimals.

3. Click the **Increase Decimal** button twice to obtain two decimal places. Return On Sales displays as 17.67%.

Ann has all her numbers formatted. Now she is ready to improve the display of her Operating Budget report by changing the font style for some of the cells in the worksheet.

Using Boldface, Italics, and Underlining

A **font** is a set of letters, numbers, and symbols that are distinguished by their typeface, point size, and styles. A font can have one of the following **font styles**: regular, italic, bold, or bold italic. In addition, you can apply underlining to any of these font styles. You can also toggle the application of these styles to a cell's display on and off. That is, if the style is not applied, then selecting the style applies it; if the style is applied, then selecting the style removes it. The appearance of Ann's Operating Budget is improved by applying some of these styles.

To apply boldface to the report title:

1. Click **A1** to make it the active cell.

2. Click the **Bold** button B to apply boldface to this text label. Note that when a style like boldface is applied to the display of a cell's content, the toolbar button appears depressed to indicate that this style is applied to the active cell. See Figure 1-33.

   TROUBLE? If you click the Bold button twice, the text will not appear in boldface, because this button acts as a toggle to turn the boldface style on and off. Click the Bold button one more time to toggle the boldface style on.

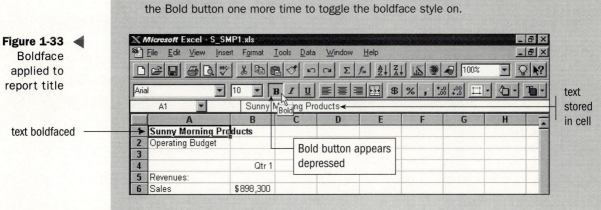

Figure 1-33 Boldface applied to report title

Ann wants the subtitle to display in italics, so you need to make that change next.

To apply italics to the subtitle:

1. Click **A2** to make it the active cell.

2. Click the **Italics** button *I* to change the appearance of the text label.

Now, underline the column title for Qtr 1, using underlining within a cell.

To underline characters within a cell:

1. Click **B4** to make it the active cell.

2. Click the **Underline** button to underline the text. The underline appears only under the characters displayed in the cell and does not extend across the entire cell.

In a similar manner, you can apply these styles to any of the cells that display numbers. Next, boldface both the text and value for the Return On Sales.

To boldface the Return On Sales values and text:

1. Select **A21:B21** as the desired cell range.

2. Click the **Bold** button to boldface the data displayed in these cells.

You can also apply boldface, italics, and underlines using the shortcut keys Ctrl + B, Ctrl + I, and Ctrl + U, respectively.

Using Fonts and Font Sizes

A **typeface** or **font** is a group of letters, numbers, punctuation marks, and symbols sharing a specific graphical design. Arial is the Excel default font, but you can select a different typeface by choosing another font in the Font box on the Formatting toolbar. Change the title to the Times New Roman font.

To change the font:

1. Click **A1** to make it the active cell.

2. Click the **Font** list arrow to display a list of available fonts. See Figure 1-34. Your list may be different, depending on the fonts available on your computer.

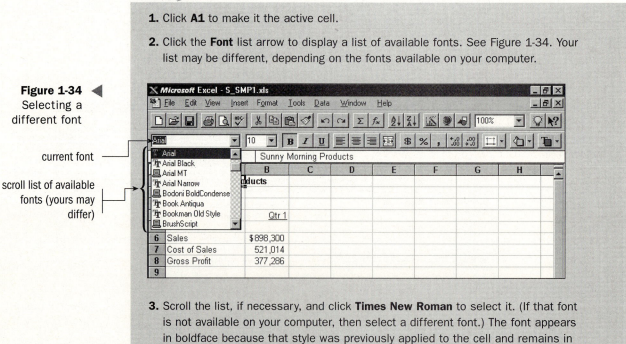

Figure 1-34 Selecting a different font

current font

scroll list of available fonts (yours may differ)

3. Scroll the list, if necessary, and click **Times New Roman** to select it. (If that font is not available on your computer, then select a different font.) The font appears in boldface because that style was previously applied to the cell and remains in effect until you change it, even when you change the font.

Ann notices that the title appears smaller in the new font. She wants to increase the point size of the font. **Point size** is the measurement of the height of a character. You need to use the Font Size box to increase the point size of the title.

PRINTING A WORKSHEET **ADVEX 41**

To change the font point size:

1. Click **A1**, if necessary, to make it the active cell.

2. Click the **Font Size** list arrow to display the available point sizes for the currently selected font. Not all fonts are available in all font sizes; it depends on the fonts available for your particular computer.

3. Click **14** to select this font size for the title.

REFERENCE window

FORMATTING CELL CONTENTS

- Select the cell range you want to format.
- Click Bold, Italics, Underline, or another format button on the Formatting toolbar to apply the style to the selected range.

HELP DESK

EXCEL 5.0

Index

FORMATTING CELL CONTENTS

Double-click the Help button to display the Help Topics dialog box, then click the Index tab.

Keywords
formatting cells, overview
formatting, cell contents

Topic
Font, Size, and Style
Formatting cell contents

In reviewing the worksheet, you have made important changes since you last saved. You edited a formula, performed a spell check, widened a column, and changed the appearance of several cells. You are ready to save these changes.

Using Save to Save a Workbook

As mentioned earlier, you can use the Save command or the Save button on the Standard toolbar to save the changes you have made to your workbook, using the same filename. Saving the new, edited version of your workbook *replaces* the old version. Use the Save command if you do *not* want to keep a copy of the old version of your workbook.

To save a workbook using the Save button:

1. Check to be sure you are in Ready mode.

2. Click the **Save** button 🖫 on the Standard toolbar. Note that "Saving S_SMP1" displays in the status bar as the mode indicator while the file is being saved to your Student Disk, and it returns to Ready mode when the save is complete.

Ann has completed the four steps in creating a worksheet—planning, designing, building, and reviewing. She is happy with her work and wants to print the Operating Budget so she can present it to Carmen for her approval.

Printing a Worksheet

Before Ann prints her worksheet, she wants to preview it on the screen to check its overall layout. If it isn't what she wants, she can change the worksheet before she prints it. You need to preview and then print Ann's worksheet.

ADVEX 42 **TUTORIAL 1** CREATING WORKSHEETS USING EXCEL FOR WINDOWS

To preview and print the Operating Budget worksheet:

1. Click the **Print Preview** button 🔍 on the Standard toolbar to display a preview of the worksheet. Don't worry that the preview isn't completely readable. It's only supposed to show you the overall layout of the worksheet and how it will fit on a piece of paper.

2. Move the pointer on top of the preview page. The pointer changes to 🔍. See Figure 1-35.

Your worksheet may be displayed with gridlines, because this is the Version 5.0 default.

EXCEL 5.0

Figure 1-35 ◀
Preview of
worksheet

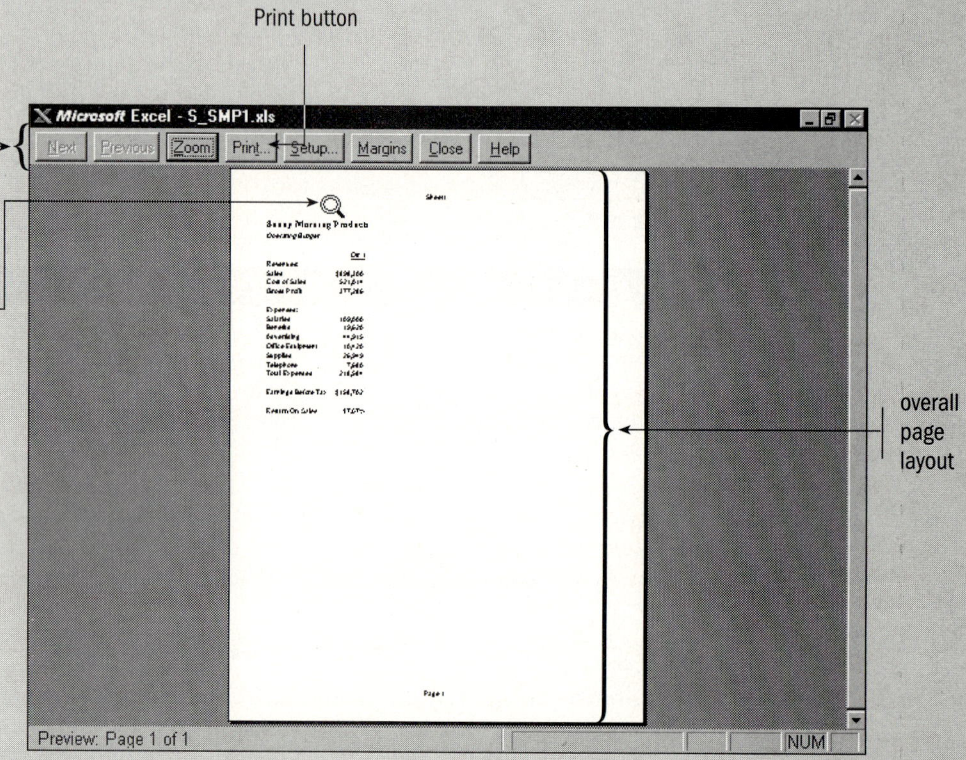

toolbar displayed with
Print Preview

mouse pointer

Print button

overall
page
layout

3. Click anywhere on the preview page to zoom to an enlargement of the print preview. The area where the pointer was located appears on your screen; you can scroll to examine other areas of the preview page.

The layout of the worksheet is acceptable, and ready for printing.

4. Check to make sure that your printer is turned on, and has paper.

5. Click the **Print** button to display the Print dialog box. You want to print Selected Sheets, which is the default option.

6. Click the **OK** button. Notice that a Printing dialog box appears. In Excel, you can cancel printing at any time, if necessary. Your printout should look like Figure 1-36. Your worksheet may be printed with gridlines, depending on the settings for your page setup. The default setting in Version 7.0 is not to print the worksheet gridlines; the default in Version 5.0 is to print them.

PRINTING A WORKSHEET **ADVEX 43**

Figure 1-36
Printout of the Operating Budget

Sunny Morning Products
Operating Budget

	Qtr 1
Revenues:	
Sales	$898,300
Cost of Sales	521,014
Gross Profit	377,286
Expenses:	
Salaries	109,000
Benefits	19,620
Advertising	44,915
Office Equipment	10,420
Supplies	26,949
Telephone	7,680
Total Expenses	218,584
Earnings Before Tax	$158,702
Return On Sales	**17.67%**

REFERENCE window | PRINTING A WORKSHEET

Method 1
- Click the Print button to print your active worksheet immediately, without previewing it.

Method 2
- Click the Print Preview button to preview your active worksheet, then click the Print button from the Print Preview window.

Method 3
- Click File, then click Print to display the Print dialog box.
  or
  Press Ctrl + P to display the Print dialog box.
- Adjust any settings in the Print dialog box.
- Click the OK button.

HELP DESK

Index

PRINTING WORKSHEET GRIDLINES

Double-click the Help button to display the Help Topics dialog box, then click the Index tab:

Keywords
sheets, printing
printing gridlines

Topic
Setting up a worksheet for printing
Printing gridlines and row and column headings

EXCEL 5.0

Ann removes her printed worksheet from the printer and meets with Carmen to review it. They are both happy to see that the Earnings Before Tax for Qtr 1 of 158,702, is acceptable. Now they know they are on target for the quarter. Carmen is impressed with the layout and design of Ann's worksheet.

Closing the Workbook

Congratulations on successfully building and printing your Excel workbook. Now that you have finished printing Ann's worksheet, you can close it. This removes it from the RAM, but the file remains stored on your Student Disk. You are ready to close the S_SMP1.xls worksheet file containing Ann's Operating Budget.

To close Ann's Sunny Morning Products Operating Budget workbook file:

1. Click the **Control menu** button ![X] located at the left side of the menu bar.

2. Click **Close** to display the Microsoft Excel message box. See Figure 1-37.

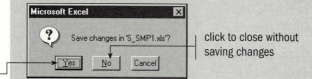

Figure 1-37
Closing Ann's S_SMP1.xls workbook file

click to save changes

click to close without saving changes

TROUBLE? If the Microsoft Excel dialog box does not display, the automatic save option is turned on for your installation of Excel. In this situation, you are returned to an empty Excel program window.

3. Click the **Yes** button to save your changes to the workbook.

CLOSING A WORKBOOK

Method 1
- Click the Control menu box located at the left side of the menu bar or on the worksheet window title bar, depending on whether the worksheet is maximized.
  or
  Click File.
- Click Close to display the Microsoft Excel dialog box.
- Select the desired action for saving the file before closing it.

Method 2
- Double-click the Control menu button located at the left side of the menu bar to display the Microsoft Excel dialog box.
- Select the desired action for saving the file before closing it.

Opening the Workbook

After Ann and Carmen review the Operating Budget, they decide to perform a what-if analysis to obtain additional information for Carmen's budget meeting. Once a workbook has been created, saved, and closed, you need to open it before you can begin using it. You are ready to open Ann's S_SMP1 workbook in the Tut01 folder in preparation for doing the what-if analysis.

OPENING THE WORKBOOK **ADVEX 45**

To open the S_SMP1 workbook:

1. Make sure your Student Disk is still in the disk drive.

2. Click the **Open** button to display the Open dialog box. See Figure 1-38.

   The Open dialog box is different than the one for Version 7.0. These differences are described in the steps that follow.

EXCEL 5.0

Figure 1-38 ◄
Open dialog box

Select workbook file from list

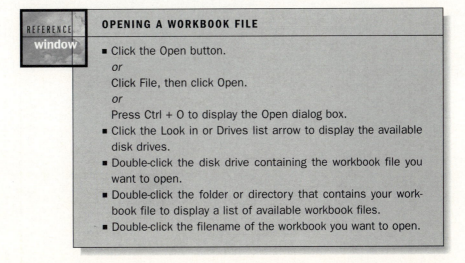

3. If the desired disk drive does not appear in the Look in text box, click the **Look in** list arrow and click the disk drive that contains your Student Disk to select it.

   If the desired disk drive does not appear in the Drives text box, click the Drives list arrow, then click the desired disk drive.

EXCEL 5.0

4. Double-click the **Tut01 folder** to open it and display the available files, if necessary.

   Double-click Tut01 in the Directories list box to select it.

EXCEL 5.0

5. Double-click the **S_SMP1.xls** filename to select and open the workbook.

REFERENCE window

OPENING A WORKBOOK FILE

- Click the Open button.
  or
  Click File, then click Open.
  or
  Press Ctrl + O to display the Open dialog box.
- Click the Look in or Drives list arrow to display the available disk drives.
- Double-click the disk drive containing the workbook file you want to open.
- Double-click the folder or directory that contains your workbook file to display a list of available workbook files.
- Double-click the filename of the workbook you want to open.

Performing a What-If Analysis

With the S_SMP1.xls file re-opened, Ann is ready to exploit another powerful feature of Excel. As noted earlier in this tutorial, a **what-if analysis** is performed when you revise the content of one or more cells in a worksheet and observe the effect this change has on all the other cells in the worksheet. What-if analysis is used to make better business decisions.

Ann can change the values in her worksheet to see how new values would affect the results. For example, what if the Sales for Qtr 1 increased? How would this affect the Earnings Before Tax? Because Ann set up her worksheet using formulas to calculate many of the numeric values, she knows that if she enters a new amount for Sales, Excel will automatically recalculate her entire worksheet.

If Ann had created her worksheet by merely typing the data value displayed in each cell as a numeric constant, she would not be able to perform this what-if analysis. You *must set up your worksheets using formulas* to calculate many of your data values if you want to be able to do a what-if analysis. If Travis is successful in his negotiations with the Orange Growers Association, they will be able to buy more oranges and increase the amount of Olympic Gold they produce and sell. Travis and Carmen want to know the answer to this what-if: If the number of bottles of Olympic Gold sold increases so their Sales in Qtr 1 are 940,550 (that is, 289,400 bottles of Olympic Gold at $3.25), what are the expected Earnings Before Tax and the Return on Sales? This what-if analysis is evaluated by entering the new value 940,550 in cell B6 for Sales in Qtr 1 and observing the recalculation of many of the data values in Ann's budget worksheet.

To perform the what-if analysis:

1. Click **B6**. This is the value you want to change for the what-if. *Your cell pointer must be located at the cell whose value you want to change.*

2. Type **940550** then press the **Enter** key. This is the new value for the what-if analysis. Notice that the mode indicator displays "Enter" while you are entering the number.

   TROUBLE? If you enter the wrong value or place the value in the wrong cell, then click the Undo button and repeat Steps 1 and 2.

3. Position the displayed worksheet area so you can view the Earnings Before Tax in cell B19 and notice how this data value was recalculated for this what-if analysis. See Figure 1-39.

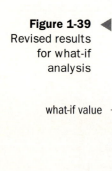

Figure 1-39
Revised results for what-if analysis

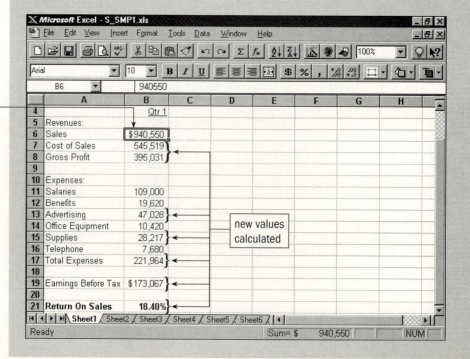

At this point Ann could make a decision about this what-if analysis. She could determine whether this seems to be an acceptable change in the Earnings Before Tax. If it is not, she can easily change the worksheet back to the way it was. She could also decide to print this version of her worksheet so she could review the results of this alternative with Carmen.

PERFORMING A WHAT-IF ANALYSIS

- Position the cell pointer at the cell that contains the value you want to change.
- Enter the new value for the what-if analysis.
- Review the automatically recalculated results.

Exiting Excel

You have successfully completed your introduction to Excel. You can now exit from Excel and, if you want, turn off your computer. When you want to complete the exercises at the end of this tutorial, you will need to launch Excel again.

To exit from Excel:

1. Click the **Close** button ⊠ in the upper-right corner of the Excel window to display the Microsoft Excel message box, asking if you would like to save the changes to S_SMP1.xls.

   Click the Control menu box located at the left side of the title bar, then click the Close button.

2. Click the **No** button because you do not want to save the what-if analysis change. You return to the Windows desktop.

3. From the desktop, proceed as desired to any other Windows programs.

EXITING EXCEL

- Click the Close button in the upper-right corner of the Excel window.
  Click the Control menu box, then click the Close button.
  or
  Double-click the Control menu box.

You now have a better understanding of Excel and have examined a number of its important features. Ann and Carmen are ready for tomorrow afternoon's review meeting with the Sunny Morning Products board of directors, as they continue to work on finalizing next year's Operating Budget.

ADVEX 48 TUTORIAL 1 CREATING WORKSHEETS USING EXCEL FOR WINDOWS

Tutorial Exercises

For these exercises, launch Excel, if necessary, and insert your Student Disk into the disk drive. Open E_HAC1.xls in the Tut01 folder or directory, the partially completed Recruitment Planning worksheet for Holiday Adventure Cruises (HAC). Immediately save it under the filename S_HAC1.xls in the Tut01 folder or directory.

Holiday Adventure's Human Resource (HR) Department recruits employees for its fun ships from four sources: newspapers, radio, walk-ins, and referrals. All recruits are interviewed and a hiring decision is made. Brenda Carranza, the HR Department's recruiting coordinator, monitors the number of interviews conducted by each recruitment source. She wants to know which source yields the most hires and the average cost per hire to assist her in planning future recruiting activities. Brenda has sketched a design of her worksheet, as shown in Figure 1-40.

Figure 1-40 ◀

WORKSHEET DESIGN SKETCH

	A	B	C	D	E
1		Recruitment Planning Report			
2					
3		Newspaper	Radio	Walk-ins	Referrals
4	Interviews	1620	1140	290	810
5	Offers	412	173	76	321
6	Hires	286	101	29	252
7	Total Cost	93070	101360	12560	26900
8					
9	Percent Offers	B5/B4	C5/C4	D5/D4	E5/E4
10	Yield Ratio	B6/B4	C6/C4	D6/D4	E6/E4
11	Cost/Interview	B7/B4	C7/C4	D7/D4	E7/E4
12	Cost/Hire	B7/B6	C7/C6	D7/D6	E7/E6

1. Review Brenda's partially completed worksheet. Don't be concerned about the appearance of the zeros and of the "#DIV/0!" error value that indicates division by zero. These will change to the desired calculated values when you finish entering the data. For now, just verify that these cells contain the formulas specified by Brenda's design.
2. Enter the missing text labels that identify the data values that will reside in the worksheet. Then enter the missing numeric data values from Brenda's design. The #DIV/0! error value should now be replaced by the appropriate calculations.
3. Enter the missing formulas in the worksheet by using pointing.
4. Format the numbers for the Interviews, Offers, Hires, and Total Cost using the Comma Style with no decimals.
5. Format the numbers for the Percent Offers using the Percent Style with two decimal places.
6. Format the number for the Yield Ratio using the Comma Style with four decimal places.
7. Format the Cost/Interview and Cost/Hire numbers using the Currency Style with two decimal places. Adjust the column width as necessary.
8. Underline the column headings.

9. Add boldface to the report title, change the font to Times New Roman (if this is not available on your computer, select a different font), and change the font size to 14.

10. Save the workbook file as S_HAC1.xls in the Tut01 folder or directory, then preview and print the worksheet.

11. Brenda wants to create a Total column in column F of the worksheet that contains the sum of the four recruitment sources for each of the planning items, Interviews, Offers, Hires, and Total Cost. Add "Total" as the heading for this column, then use the SUM function to calculate these totals in this new column.

12. Enter formulas that calculate the totals of the Percent Offers, Yield Ratio, Cost/Interview, and Cost/Hire in the Total column. These formulas are similar to those used for each of the four recruitment sources, but are calculated using the totals values. Format the numbers and the column heading in this Total column to match those for the four recruitment sources. Save this as the S_HAC1.xls workbook in the Tut01 folder or directory, then preview and print it.

13. Perform a what-if analysis by changing Newspaper Interviews to 1596. Preview and print this what-if analysis.

14. Use Excel Help to learn about the AutoFormat feature, which you can use to improve the appearance of a table of data arranged like Brenda's report. Select the range A3:F13, which is Brenda's table with the Total column you added to it. Apply an AutoFormat of your choice to this table. If you don't like the appearance of your first choice, then try a different one.

15. Save the workbook as file S_HAC2.xls in the Tut01 folder or directory, then preview and print the worksheet with your AutoFormat.

Case Problems

1. Conducting an Audit for Barrett Morris & Wright PC Barrett Morris & Wright (BMW) is an international public accounting firm with offices in most major metropolitan areas. One of the primary business services provided by BMW is conducting accounting audits for their clients. These audits are an independent examination of the client's business records, which provide an impartial expert opinion about the reliability of the client's financial statements, and determine whether they have been presented to shareholders and other concerned parties in accordance with generally accepted accounting principles.

Charlie Cameron is the BMW manager in the Nashville office; he is in charge of the audit team conducting an audit at Tennessee Valley Energy (TVE). TVE is a pioneer in the independent power industry, specializing in "clean coal" gasification and gas turbine-powered cogeneration of electrical and steam energy. Gas-fired cogeneration is highly efficient because it uses waste energy and saves fuel, while it is environmentally friendly and operationally flexible. TVE has a total capacity of approximately 1,040 megawatts of electricity and two million pounds per hour of steam. This is a uniquely vertically integrated company with all the skills necessary to manage power plants for the long term, from initial development to ownership and operation.

Charlie's responsibilities include reviewing and approving the information his team collects during the audit, commonly called workpapers. Workpapers serve as the means of recording the field work performed in obtaining the audit evidence. Charlie has assigned Lindsay Torres, an audit associate, the task of developing the workpapers that summarize TVE's operations.

Lindsay uses Excel to produce the necessary financial statement workpapers. As she examines a client's records, the evidence she collects, such as Net Sales and Marketing Expenses, is entered in her worksheet. If further examination should produce a different value than the one initially entered, she can easily revise her Excel worksheet.

In preparing for the TVE audit, Lindsay has obtained the layout of a Statement of Earnings from the illustrative financial statements in BMW's *Accounting and Auditing Manual*. Although she has participated in a number of audits, BMW procedures require this review to ensure that their audit standards are being followed. She has selected an appropriate report layout with Charlie's assistance for use with the TVE audit (Figure 1-41).

Figure 1-41 ◀

REPORT LAYOUT SKETCH			
Example Company, Inc.			
STATEMENT OF EARNINGS			
(Dollars in thousands)			
	This Year	Last Year	Increase
Net Sales	XXXXX	XXXXX	XXXXX
Cost of Sales	XXXXX	XXXXX	XXXXX
Gross Profit	XXXXX	XXXXX	XXXXX
Operating Expenses	XXXXX	XXXXX	XXXXX
Marketing	XXXXX	XXXXX	XXXXX
Research and Development	XXXXX	XXXXX	XXXXX
Administrative	XXXXX	XXXXX	XXXXX
Operating Profit	XXXXX	XXXXX	XXXXX
Other Income	XXXXX	XXXXX	XXXXX
Earnings Before Tax	XXXXX	XXXXX	XXXXX
Income Tax	XXXXX	XXXXX	XXXXX
NET EARNINGS	XXXXX	XXXXX	XXXXX

During the past several weeks, Lindsay has been collecting evidential matter through inspection, observation, and inquiry about the company's operations. Tomorrow she will meet with Charlie to review the first draft of her workspapers. Using the TVE preferred report layout, she has prepared to develop the Statement of Earnings by creating her planning analysis sheet (Figure 1-42).

Figure 1-42 ◀

Planning Analysis Sheet

My goal:

Develop a worksheet of the statement of earnings that compares this year with last year using a standard report layout

What results do I want to see?

Sales and expenses for each year with a comparison between the two years

What information do I need?

Columns are This Year, Last Year, Increase

Net Sales = 969098, 801132

Cost of Sales = 662950, 560180

Marketing = 129299, 109477

Research and Development = 38700, 27162

Administrative = 70246, 59670

Other Income = 16264, 8229

Income Tax = 24630, 21386

(Note that each pair of numbers is for This Year and Last Year, respectively)

What calculations will I perform?

Gross Profit = Sales - Cost of Sales

Operating Profit = Gross Profit - (Marketing + Research and Development +Administrative)

Earnings Before Tax = Operating Profit + Other Income

NET EARNINGS = Earnings Before Tax - Income Tax

Increase = This Year - Last Year

(Note that the increase is calculated for each line item)

In this planning analysis sheet, the dollar amounts are data that Lindsay has collected as part of her audit activities; the formulas are those generally accepted accounting equations applied in calculating the other financial statement accounts. She is ready to complete her worksheet design sketch so she can build her Excel worksheet in preparation for her progress meeting with Charlie.

ADVEX 52   TUTORIAL 1   CREATING WORKSHEETS USING EXCEL FOR WINDOWS

1. Prepare a worksheet design sketch, beginning with the partially completed sketch shown in Figure 1-43. Use Lindsay's report layout sketch and planning analysis sheet in preparing your sketch.

Figure 1-43 ◀

WORKSHEET DESIGN SKETCH

	A	B	C	D
		This Year	Last Year	Increase

Tennessee Valley Energy
STATEMENT OF EARNINGS
(Dollars in thousands)

	A	B	C	D
1		Tennessee Valley Energy		
2		STATEMENT OF EARNINGS		
3		(Dollars in thousands)		
4				
5		This Year	Last Year	Increase
6		--------	--------	--------
7	Net Sales			
8	Cost of Sales			
9		--------	--------	--------
10	Gross Profit			
11	Operating Expenses			
12	Marketing			
13	Research and Development			
14	Administrative			
15		--------	--------	--------
16	Operating Profit			
17	Other Income			
18	Earnings Before Tax			
19	Income Tax			
20				
21	NET EARNINGS	--------	--------	--------

2. Launch Excel and make sure that a new workbook is displayed for creating the worksheet.

3. Build Lindsay's audit worksheet by entering the identifying text labels from her sketch. Resize column A to a width of 25 characters so all the account names will fit. Then enter the numbers and formulas for the calculations. (*Hint*: If Net Earnings [Increase] equals 28051, you have entered the data and formulas correctly.) You can use underlining within a cell or a text label of '-------------------- to create the underlining in a separate cell that matches the worksheet design sketch. You'll learn more about underlining in the next tutorial. Or, if you want, use Excel Help to learn more about underlining, then use another method that you like better.

4. Spell check the worksheet. Did you skip any unknown words? Which ones? Save this worksheet as file S_TVE1.xls in the Tut01 folder or directory. Preview and print it.

5. Format the numbers for Net Sales, Gross Profit, and NET EARNINGS using the Currency Style with no decimals. Format all other numbers using the Comma Style with no decimals. Resize the columns as necessary.

6. Enhance the appearance of the report title by selecting appropriate fonts and attributes. Use both boldface and italics. Why did you select these enhancements? Save this worksheet, using the same filename, then preview and print it.

7. Review your printed audit report and, with a pen or pencil, draw a circle around the Operating Expense that increased the most.

8. Lindsay just received a change for this year's marketing expenses. Based on her further investigation, this value should now be 132767. Make this change to the worksheet, then preview and print it. Save the worksheet using the same workbook filename.

9. Write a paragraph describing why you think Excel is an appropriate tool for preparing accounting audit workpaper reports like this one for TVE.

10. Write a short narrative describing how you might improve the audit report by adding one or more columns to determine where the most significant changes occurred.

2. Analyzing Financial Ratios for General Micro Devices General Micro Devices (GMD) manufactures and markets a variety of microelectronic equipment that includes cellular phones, two-way radios, beepers, citizen-band radios, radar detectors, and remote-keyless entry systems. Founded in 1968 by Kevin Lee, GMD recently moved its cellular phone manufacturing into a new plant near its Clarksville headquarters in the Executive Plaza. Kevin still serves as the company's president and chief executive officer. Corey Trujillo was recently hired as a junior financial analyst by Justin Rhodes, the vice president of finance. Corey assists Justin in regularly monitoring the financial health of GMD, with review meetings scheduled monthly with Kevin and other senior managers.

GMD's accountants just finished closing the company's books for last year. Corey needs to prepare a comparison of GMD's performance with that of other companies in the same industry for the next review meeting. She knows that this can be done by comparing financial ratios for GMD against others in the same industry segment. Corey recently received an updated report from the Electronic Manufacturers Association with this comparative information.

In preparing for her monthly review meeting, Corey has assembled GMD's income statement and balance sheet (or statement of financial position) data and entered it into a worksheet along with the ratio data from the Electronic Manufacturers Association.

An income statement, or statement of operations, details revenues and expenditures, such as sales, cost of goods sold, administrative expenses, and marketing expenses. This statement shows the net income or earnings of the organization for a specified period of time. These earnings may be distributed to shareholders or owners as a dividend, or they may be retained by the firm for investment in other business activities.

A balance sheet, or statement of financial position, indicates the assets and liabilities of an organization at a particular time, such as the end of a quarter or year. Liabilities represent the proportion of the business financed by a firm's suppliers and creditors. The difference between a firm's assets and its liabilities is the owners' equity, or the owners' share of the firm.

Corey knows that a performance ratio report of GMD's overall business assists in monitoring and controlling its operations. These performance ratios can be measured against an external industry standard. The ratios are computed using data from the general ledger and other accounting systems. Some of the more popular ratios, and those used by GMD, are as follows:

1. *Liquidity ratios.* These ratios describe the ability of an organization to pay its financial obligations when they are due.
   - *Current ratio*, a measure of the ability of a firm to cover its short-term obligations with assets readily converted to cash:
   Current ratio = Total current assets / Total current liabilities
   (A ratio greater than 1.0 is usually desired.)
   - *Quick ratio*, a measure of the ability of a firm to pay off its short-term obligations without relying on the sales of its inventories:
   Quick ratio = (Total current assets - Inventories) / Total current liabilities
2. *Asset management ratios.* These ratios indicate how effectively a firm is managing its assets.
   - *Inventory turnover*, a measure of how rapidly goods are being purchased and sold as they move through inventory:
   Inventory turnover = Cost of goods sold / Inventory
   - *Average collection period*, a measure of the level of accounts receivable:
   Average collection period = Accounts receivable / Average sales per day
   where Average sales per day = Sales / 360
   - *Total asset turnover*, a measure of the utilization of all the assets of a firm:
   Total asset turnover = Sales / Total assets

3. *Debt management ratios.* These ratios indicate the extent to which a firm uses debt financing. Debt financing allows owners to maintain control of a firm with a limited investment. When a firm earns more with borrowed funds than it pays in interest, the return to the owners is greater than if no borrowing had been used.

   - *Debt ratio*, a measure of the total funds provided by creditors:
     Debt ratio = Total debt / Total assets
     where Total debt = Notes payable + Long-term debt
   - *Times-interest-earned (TIE) ratio*, a measure of a firm's ability to meet interest payments when they are due:
     TIE ratio = Earnings before interest and taxes / Interest expense

4. *Profitability ratios.* These ratios supply information about a firm's overall operating performance, which reflects the effectiveness of the firm's management.

   - *Return on sales (ROS)*, a measure of the amount of profit generated from each dollar of sales, also known as the profit margin:
     ROS = Net income / Sales
   - *Return on total assets (ROA)*, a measure of the profit generated by the assets of the company:
     ROA = Net income / Total assets
   - *Return on equity (ROE)*, a measure of the amount of profit generated by the investment of the owners:
     ROE = Net income / Total stockholders' equity

5. *Market value ratios.* These ratios indicate a company's past accomplishments and its investors' outlook for future performance.

   - *Earnings per share (EPS)*, a measure of the earnings for each share of common stock:
     EPS = Net income / Number of common stock shares
   - *Price/Earnings (P/E) ratio*, a measure comparing the price of a share of common stock to the earnings for a share:
     Price/earnings ratio = Price per share / Earnings per share

Corey has begun to create her planning analysis sheet to be used in building a spreadsheet illustrating the comparison of GMD's performance with the rest of the industry (Figure 1-44). She needs to complete this analysis and finish her worksheet design.

CASE PROBLEMS **ADVEX 55**

Figure 1-44 ◀

Planning Analysis Sheet

My goal:

Develop a worksheet of financial ratios that are compared to industry ratios

What results do I want to see?

Balance sheet and income statement for the year with key financial ratios that
are compared with the industry ratios

What information do I need?

Column is Last Year

Cash = 230

Accounts receivable = 1948

Inventory = 1602

Net plant and equipment = 1640

Accounts payable = 727

Notes payable = 480

Other current liabilities = 579

Long-term debt = 1550

Common stock = 1200

Retained earnings = 884

Sales = 9060

Cost of goods sold = 7800

Marketing expenses = 640

General and admin expenses = 168

Interest expense = 127

Shares of common stock = 24

Stock price = 96

What calculations will I perform?

Total current assets = Cash + Accounts receivable + Inventory

Total assets = Total current assets + Net plant and equipment

Total current liabilities = Accounts payable + Notes payable + Other current liabilities

Total stockholder's equity = Common stock + Retained earnings

Total liabilities and equity = Total current liabilities + Long-term debt
        + Total stockholder's equity

Gross profit = Sales − Cost of goods sold

Earnings before interest and taxes = Gross profit − (Marketing expenses
        + General and admin expenses)

Net income before tax = Earnings before interest and taxes − Interest expense

Federal and state income taxes = Net income before taxes * 0.4

Net income = Net income before taxes − Federal and state income taxes

---

She has already entered the desired text labels in the P_GMD1.xls workbook, located
in the Tut01 folder or directory, together with the balance sheet data. To complete her
worksheet, she needs to enter the remaining data values and all the formulas; then the
worksheet will be ready for the review meeting with Kevin and Justin.

1. Complete Corey's planning analysis sheet by including the liquidity, asset management, debt management, profitability, and market value ratios used by GMD.
2. Launch Excel and open the P_GMD1.xls workbook file. Save it immediately as
   S_GMD1.xls in the Tut01 folder or directory. Examine the contents of this file,
   then print the worksheet. All dollar amounts and the number of shares of common stock are entered in thousands, except the stock price, which is entered in
   dollars. Notice that Corey has already entered the industry ratios that are a
   standard for comparison. Use this printout and your completed planning
   analysis sheet to prepare a worksheet design sketch by writing the missing data
   values and the cell formulas on the printout.

3. Complete building Corey's worksheet by entering the remaining data values and all the formulas using your worksheet design sketch.
4. Spell check the worksheet. Did you skip any unknown words? Which ones?
5. Select and apply appropriate number formats to the income statement and the balance sheet, using the Currency Style and the Comma Style. Display these dollar amounts with no decimal places. Increase column widths as necessary.
6. Improve the appearance of the report title by selecting appropriate fonts and attributes. Use both boldface and italics. Save this as the S_GMD1.xls workbook file in the Tut01 folder or directory, then preview and print this report.
7. The COMMENT column of the ratio analysis provides an indication of the possible evaluation from comparing GMD's ratios to those of the industry— OK, LOW, HIGH, POOR, and GOOD. Make your own comparison for these ratios, then select the indicator *that you feel best describes the comparison* and enter it in the COMMENT column, replacing the list of choices.
8. Save this as the S_GMD1.xls workbook, then preview and print the report.
9. Review your printed report and determine the one or two ratios that appear as areas of concern, where GMD's management should focus their attention. Write a short narrative describing your analysis of the ratios and the area of most concern.
10. Corey just received a change in sales and marketing expenses from accounting. These values should now be Sales of 9243 and Marketing expenses of 521. Make this change to the worksheet, then preview and print it. Does this change your evaluation of the area of most concern? Why or why not? Save the workbook with this change in the S_GMD1.xls file.
11. Review GMD's financial ratio analysis. Write a paragraph describing at least two changes that you would like to make in this worksheet to improve its usefulness, and indicate how each change would be helpful.

Comprehensive Applications

The Comprehensive Applications that start in this tutorial are continued into several of the following tutorials. The problems in those tutorials build on the solution you develop in this tutorial and the subsequent tutorials.

1. Production Planning for Oak World Furniture Oak World Furniture is an established manufacturer of home furniture. Oak World, founded in 1947, is located in the heart of the hardwood forest country. Originally, the company's market was local; it has since expanded into a 12-state regional market. Oak World's president, Todd Newberry, an MBA from Central State University, has positioned the company among the top ten furniture makers in the region. Todd has achieved this remarkable accomplishment in his four-year tenure at Oak World. He attributes his success to his fine staff and their proactive management style. To further improve operations, you were recently hired to coordinate their planning and budgeting activities. Todd has asked you to prepare a plan for next month's operations by creating a flexible business model.

Oak World's product line includes tables, chairs, and sofas. Robin Tameko, the director of marketing, has compiled the results of her market research for next month. She expects 1,060 tables to be sold. For each table, on the average, six chairs are sold. She expects the sale of 707 sofas. The price schedule for each unit is as follows:

Product	Price
Tables	$640
Chairs	120
Sofas	850

Robin has planned an advertising expenditure of 10 percent of total sales.

Sam Sherwood, production manager, expects to produce these units with 143 production line employees at an average salary of $17.70 per hour. For the same month last year, the average hours worked per employee were 170. Sam expects the same number of hours next month. A check of Sam's records indicates that the raw material cost is 26 percent of total sales. The factory overhead charge is 18 percent of the cost of raw materials.

After meeting with Todd and reviewing last year's monthly financial statements, you gather the following estimates:

1. Insurance expense is 4 percent of total sales.
2. Management salaries will be $47,600.
3. General and administrative expenses will be $31,000.

In your meeting with Todd, you settled on the report layout shown in Figure 1-45. In this design, the X's are used to indicate where an input or calculated value will appear.

Figure 1-45 ◄

REPORT LAYOUT SKETCH

Oak World Furniture
Projected Statement of Operations

	July
Production (in units):	
Tables sold	XXXXX
Chairs sold	XXXXX
Sofas sold	XXXXX
Sales revenues:	
Table Sales	XXXXX
Chair Sales	XXXXX
Sofa Sales	XXXXX
Total Sales	XXXXX
Cost of sales:	
Raw Materials	XXXXX
Labor	XXXXX
Overhead	XXXXX
Cost of Sales	XXXXX
Gross Profit	XXXXX
Operating expenses:	
Advertising	XXXXX
Insurance	XXXXX
Management Salaries	XXXXX
General and Administrative	XXXXX
Operating Expenses	XXXXX
Operating Profit	XXXXX
Return on Sales	XXXXX

You have all of the preliminary data required to prepare a projection for next month. In preparation for creating this worksheet, you list these useful accounting identities, or formulas:

Gross Profit = Total Sales − Cost of Sales
Operating Profit = Gross Profit − Operating Expenses
Return on Sales = Operating Profit / Total Sales

Your first step is to organize the input data values and formulas that you will be using on the planning analysis sheet in Figure 1-46. By organizing your worksheet like this, you will have the formulas needed for entry into Excel. In the Information/ Calculation column, write the equation in English or the input data value. This will simplify your preparation of a worksheet design sketch.

ADVEX 58 TUTORIAL 1 CREATING WORKSHEETS USING EXCEL FOR WINDOWS

Figure 1-46 ◄

Planning Analysis Sheet

Account Name	Information/Calculation
Tables Sold	= 1060
Chairs Sold	= 1060*6
Sofas Sold	= 707
4 Table Sales	= 1060*640
5 Chair Sales	= (1060*6)*120
6 Sofa Sales	= 707*850
7 Total Sales	= (4+5+6)
8 Raw Materials	= 7*.26
9 Labor	= 143*(7.20*170)
10 Overhead	= (8)×18%
11 Cost of Sales	= (8+9+10)
12 Gross Profit	= (7-11)
13 Advertising	= (7*10%)
14 Insurance	= (7*4%)
15 Management Salaries	= 47,600
16 General and Administrative	= 31,000
17 Operating Expenses	= (Sum 13:16)
18 Operating Profit	= 12-17
Return on Sales	= 18/7

After your last visit with Todd, you are ready to prepare Oak World's statement of operation.

1. Complete the planning analysis sheet in Figure 1-46, then use it to prepare a worksheet design sketch that follows the report layout sketch in Figure 1-45.
2. Launch Excel and make sure that a new workbook is displayed for creating the worksheet, then enter the text labels to identify the results that appear in the worksheet.
3. Enter all the numeric data values in the worksheet from your design, then enter the formulas.
4. Save the workbook file as S_OWF1.xls in the Tut01 folder or directory, then preview and print the worksheet.
5. Format Table Sales, Gross Profit, and Operating Profit using the Currency Style with no decimals. Format all other numbers, except Return on Sales, using the Comma Style with no decimals. Format Return on Sales using the Percent Style with two decimals.
6. Enhance the appearance of the report title by selecting appropriate fonts and attributes. Use both boldface and italics. Save this workbook as the S_OWF1.xls file, then preview and print the worksheet.
7. Perform a what-if analysis by changing the production in units as follows:

Product	Units
Tables	1,107
Sofas	930

Preview and print this what-if analysis. Close the workbook, but do not save this what-if change.

2. Profit Planning for Valley Gas Alliance Valley Gas Alliance (VGA) is a diversified energy company servicing the needs of business and industry throughout its tri-state market area. Recently, the company has experienced a shift in demand for natural gas. This is partly due to changing economic activity and energy conservation. The director of VGA's gas division, Amanda Barclay, has just called you to her office. Amanda is concerned that her division's after-tax return on investment for the quarter might fall below

4 percent (or 16 percent annually). She instructs you to coordinate the compilation of next quarter's projected income statement for the gas division, with all dollar amounts stated in thousands.

Your first task is to establish a demand forecast of natural gas in VGA's markets for next quarter. Martin Simmons, the director of marketing, said that production and sales for the same quarter last year were 210 billion cubic feet (BCF). He also reported that this year's demand has decreased because of economic and conservation activities. Martin believes that, given the proper budget, his department will be able to add several additional accounts to the 64 communities currently being served. In the past several years, marketing and selling expenses have been between 10 and 14 percent of sales. Martin asked for an increased level of 15 percent of sales to support a more aggressive marketing effort. In addition to the anticipated new accounts, Martin expects an expansion in industrial accounts. After considering all these factors, he expects next quarter's volume of gas sales to be 232 BCF. Based on an analysis of prior years' sales, he expects revenues to be generated in this manner:

Volume Sold	Rate *
23% Residential	$350 per BCF
77% Industrial	$286 per BCF

* In thousands of dollars

Given this forecast of demand for next quarter, you decide to check with the production department to ensure VGA's ability to meet the demand. Mark Perez reports no problem in satisfying this demand and that the company has sufficient pipeline capacity to transport the gas. Mark discusses a variety of sources and costs for next quarter's production with you. Mark finally indicates that he expects the average cost of gas to be 61 percent of total sales revenue.

Having secured the demand and production forecast, your next encounter is with Dennis Corbin, the division controller. Dennis reviews the operating budget and concludes that with anticipated salary increases and other price adjustments, next quarter's administrative expenses will be $4,250 (dollars in thousands). Also, Dennis expects to be able to charge off 3 percent of the division's investments in plant and equipment as depreciation for the quarter (that is, 12 percent annually). With the adjustment for new plants and equipment, the total division investments will total $102,800 (dollars in thousands). VGA has $43,000 (dollars in thousands) in debt, borrowing at an average annual interest rate of 10 percent (that is, 2.5% quarterly). Dennis expects federal, state, and local taxes to be at an overall rate of 46 percent. He works with you in laying out the report format shown in Figure 1-47.

ADVEX 60 TUTORIAL 1 CREATING WORKSHEETS USING EXCEL FOR WINDOWS

Figure 1-47 ◀

REPORT LAYOUT SKETCH

Valley Gas Alliance
Projected Income Statement
(Dollars in thousands)

	Quarter 1
Production (in BCF):	
Residential Gas	XXXXX
Industrial Gas	XXXXX
Total Gas Sold	XXXXX
Sales Revenues:	
Residential Sales	XXXXX
Industrial Sales	XXXXX
Total Sales	XXXXX
Cost of Sales	XXXXX
Gross Profit	XXXXX
Expenses:	
Marketing and Selling	XXXXX
General and Administrative	XXXXX
Depreciation	XXXXX
Total Expenses	XXXXX
Operating Income	XXXXX
Interest Expense	XXXXX
Income Before Taxes	XXXXX
Income Taxes	XXXXX
Net Income	XXXXX
Return on Investment	XXXXX
Supporting Balance Sheet Items:	
Investments	XXXXX
Debt	XXXXX

You now have all of the preliminary data required to prepare the first quarter's forecast. Remember, the projected income statement is in dollars in thousands, and all the dollar amounts provided are already in thousands of dollars, so no additional adjustment is necessary. In preparation for constructing this worksheet, you refer to your list of useful accounting identities and financial ratios:

Gross Profit = Total Sales − Cost of Sales
Depreciation = Investments * Depreciation Rate
Operating Income = Gross Profit − Total Expenses
Interest Expense = Debt * Interest Rate
Income Before Taxes = Operating Income − Interest Expense

Income Taxes = Income Before Taxes * Tax Rate
Net Income = Income Before Taxes − Income Taxes
Return on Investments = Net Income / Investments

Your first step is to organize the input data values and formulas that you will be using on the planning analysis sheet in Figure 1-48. By organizing your worksheet like this, you will have the formulas needed for entry into Excel. Under the Information/Calculation column, write out the equation in English, or the input data value. This will simplify your preparation of a worksheet design sketch.

Figure 1-48 ◀

Planning Analysis Sheet

Account Name	Information/Calculation
Residential Gas	=
Industrial Gas	=
Total Gas Sold	=
Residential Sales	=
Industrial Sales	=
Total Sales	=
Cost of Sales	=
Gross Profit	=
Marketing and Selling	=
General and Administrative	=
Depreciation	=
Total Expenses	=
Operating Income	=
Interest Expense	=
Income Before Taxes	=
Income Taxes	=
Net Income	=
Return on Investment	=
Investments	=
Debt	=

After your visit with Dennis, you are ready to prepare VGA's projected income statement for the next quarter.

1. Complete the planning analysis sheet in Figure 1-48, then use it to prepare a worksheet design sketch that follows the report layout sketch in Figure 1-47.
2. Launch Excel and make sure that a new workbook is displayed for creating the worksheet, then enter the text labels that will identify the results you want to appear in the worksheet.
3. Enter all the numeric data values in the worksheet from your design, then enter the formulas. Make sure the formulas refer to the data values you have entered. Do not reenter a data value in a formula, but create a formula that refers to any data values you need.
4. Save the workbook as S_VGA1.xls in the Tut01 folder or directory, then preview and print the worksheet.
5. Apply appropriate formats to the numbers displayed in the worksheet.
6. Enhance the appearance of the worksheet by selecting and applying appropriate fonts and attributes. Save this as the S_VGA1.xls workbook, then preview and print it.

7. Perform a what-if analysis by changing the Total Gas Sold to 243 BCF. This change should cause the sales revenues to be recalculated, together with all the other planning items that use sales revenues in their calculations. If the Net Income and Return on Sales are not recalculated, then you need to revise the formulas in your worksheet so they are recalculated when this what-if data value is entered. Preview and print this what-if analysis. Close the workbook, but do not save this what-if change unless you needed to revise your formulas in order to calculate the what-if results; then save the worksheet with the original Total Gas Sold value of 232 BCF.

TUTORIAL 2

Developing Effective Worksheets

Expanding the Operating Budget

OBJECTIVES

In this tutorial you will learn how to:

- Create a series with AutoFill
- Copy formulas and cell formats
- Apply relative and absolute cell references
- Use the SUM, ROUND, and TODAY functions
- Arrange worksheets in sections and add documentation to workbooks
- Split the worksheet window
- Insert, delete, move, and hide rows and columns
- Assign and use range names
- Apply borders, patterns, and colors
- Set up a page for printing, including headers and footers
- Create and place graphic objects in worksheets
- Protect worksheets

CASE

Sunny Morning Products

Travis and Carmen are pleased with the Operating Budget for Sunny Morning Products that Ann developed for the first quarter. It includes the desired planning items for their evaluation. As they discuss their information requirements, they agree that the one-quarter budget is a good start and should now be expanded to include all four quarters of next year. Travis also suggests the division of the worksheet into sections that emphasize critical information. These changes will provide better information to support decision-making by the management of Sunny Morning Products.

In this tutorial, you will explore how Ann expands her one-quarter report into a worksheet for next year's budget with four quarters and a total for the year, creating a much larger, more complex spreadsheet. You will learn how to organize and format the data in the worksheet to make it easy to view, interpret, navigate, and revise.

Introduction to Worksheet Design

Worksheet design involves presenting a business model that provides immediate access to important information. A well-designed worksheet blends the features of Excel with the techniques of business modeling to produce information that supports decision-making. The worksheet design must allow you to easily understand, enter, and update input data values and assumptions so that you can quickly perform what-if analyses.

Worksheets are often shared by people in the same department. Frequently a worksheet is used by a number of other people in addition to the individual who created it. One person builds a worksheet and a number of people use it to perform their job functions. For example, the Operating Budget Ann has been creating for Sunny Morning Products will be used by Carmen and Travis to make business decisions. Therefore, a primary consideration in worksheet design is that output is easy for people to use. There are both aesthetic and content considerations involved in designing effective and easy-to-use worksheets.

Aesthetic considerations mean that the worksheet should be

- Attractive—it is visually pleasing. You should avoid highlighting too much information, or using too many colors; highlighting and color are most effective when they are subtle.

- Readable—the information is clearly understood. The readability of a worksheet should be carefully evaluated. All information appearing in the worksheet and printed documents must be fully explained. Abbreviations should be kept to a minimum. Descriptive words should be used for report titles and column headings. Terminology should match the normal words, phrases, or terms that are natural to the user and should be standardized throughout the business model. Adequate spacing should separate columns to make information easy to read, and as a general rule, the normal reading sequence—top to bottom and left to right—should be followed.

- Organized—the information that belongs together is placed in a common area in the worksheet and printed output documents. For example, your worksheet should include a Summary section that extracts the pertinent details from your business model. Data items in the report should be in a logical order based on user requirements. Typically, more important data items usually appear first, and totals appear either on the far right or at the bottom of the report. Spacing should enhance user recognition and understanding, with logical groupings of data separated by blank lines and appropriate underlining.

Content considerations mean that a printed document is

- Brief—it contains only necessary information. The amount of data presented to a user at any given time should be considered, so the user is not overloaded to a level that inhibits recognition and understanding.

- Comprehensive—it contains all necessary information. The emphasis should be on delivering what is needed, not all that is known.

- Accurate—the information that it contains can be trusted to be correct. Therefore, testing the worksheet before it is used in the decision-making process is critical.

In general, the purpose of a worksheet is to convey the needed information in the simplest form possible. Carefully planned worksheets present this information with a professional appearance. This tutorial blends Excel features and commands with business modeling techniques to build professional worksheets that accomplish these objectives.

Expanding the Basic Worksheet

Ann is ready to expand her worksheet. This task is two-fold. First, she needs to include the budget data for the next four quarters. Then, she needs to organize the larger worksheet to emphasize important information by dividing the worksheet into sections.

EXPANDING THE BASIC WORKSHEET **ADVEX 65**

Carmen and Ann assemble the necessary data by reviewing last year's data and discussing the company's plan for next year with the budget committee. As part of their review, they determine that some values and expenditures will increase over the four quarters, and they will need to estimate the growth rate for these items. The **growth rate** is the expected amount of increase in a value from a prior period, and is usually expressed as a percentage. For example, the sales growth rate is the amount of increase in sales from a prior time period, such as the previous quarter. The general formula for a growth rate is

*prior value * (1 + growth rate as a decimal)*

Because the growth rate is an increase in a prior amount, the 1 is required in the formula to obtain the prior amount and is then increased by the growth rate. A growth rate can also be negative if a decrease occurs from one time period to the next.

In Ann's Operating Budget, three items are expected to increase over the next three quarters: Sales, Salaries, and Office Equipment. She estimates the Sales growth rate to be 2%, the Salaries growth rate to be 5%, and the Office Equipment growth rate to be 4%. She includes this information in her planning analysis sheet. Once the necessary data is collected, Ann begins the process of modifying the budget worksheet for Sunny Morning Products by revising her planning analysis sheet (Figure 2-1) and her worksheet design (Figure 2-2) to include the information on all four quarters.

Figure 2-1 ◄
Ann's revised
planning
analysis sheet

Planning Analysis Sheet

My goal:

Develop a worksheet of the Operating Budget for next year

What results do I want to see?

Revenues and expenses for the next year by quarter with an annual total

What information do I need?

Columns are Qtr 1, Qtr 2, Qtr 3, Qtr 4, Total

Sales [Qtr 1] = 898300

Sales growth rate = 2% for next three quarters

Cost of Sales percent = 58% for each quarter

Salaries [Qtr 1] = 109000

Salaries growth rate = 5% for next three quarters

Benefit rate = 18% for each quarter

Advertising percent = 5% for each quarter

Office Equipment [Qtr 1] = 10420

Office growth rate = 4% for next three quarters

Supplies percent = 3% for each quarter

Telephone [Qtr 1] = 7680

What calculations will I perform?

Sales = 898300, previous Sales * (1 + Sales growth rate) for three quarters

Cost of Sales = Sales * Cost of Sales percent for four quarters

Gross Profit = Sales - Cost of Sales for four quarters

Salaries = 109000, previous Salaries * (1 + Salaries growth rate) for three quarters

Benefits = Salaries * Benefit rate for four quarters

Advertising = Sales * Advertising percent for four quarters

Office Equipment = 10420, previous Office Equipment * (1 + Office growth rate)

Supplies = Sales * Supplies percent for four quarters

Telephone = 7680, previous Telephone for three quarters

Total Expenses = SUM(Salaries thru Telephone) for four quarters

Earnings Before Tax = Gross Profit - Total Expenses for four quarters

Total column = SUM(Qtr 1 thru Qtr 4) for each planning item

Return On Sales = Earnings Before Tax / Sales for four quarters and year

ADVEX 66 **TUTORIAL 2** DEVELOPING EFFECTIVE WORKSHEETS

Figure 2-2 ◀
Ann's modified
sketch of her
worksheet

	WORKSHEET DESIGN SKETCH				
	A	B	C	D	E	F
1	Sunny Morning Products					
2	Operating Budget					
3						
4		Qtr 1	Qtr 2	Qtr 3	Qtr 4	Total
5	Revenues:					
6	Sales	898300	B6*(1+.02)	C6*(1+.02)	D6*(1+.02)	SUM(B6:E6)
7	Cost of Sales	B6*58%	C6*58%	D6*58%	E6*58%	SUM(B7:E7)
8	Gross Profit	B6-B7	C6-C7	D6-D7	E6-E7	SUM(B8:E8)
9						
10	Expenses:					
11	Salaries	109000	B11*(1+.05)	C11*(1+.05)	D11*(1+.05)	SUM(B11:E11)
12	Benefits	B11*18%	C11*18%	D11*18%	E11*18%	SUM(B12:E12)
13	Advertising	B6*.05	C6*.05	D6*.05	E6*.05	SUM(B13:E13)
14	Office Equipment	10420	B14*(1+.04)	C14*(1+.04)	D14*(1+.04)	SUM(B14:E14)
15	Supplies	B6*.03	C6*.03	D6*.03	E6*.03	SUM(B15:E15)
16	Telephone	7680	B16	C16	D16	SUM(B16:E16)
17	Total Expenses	SUM(B11:B16)	SUM(C11:C16)	SUM(D11:D16)	SUM(E11:E16)	SUM(B17:E17)
18						
19	Earnings Before Tax	B8-B17	C8-C17	D8-D17	E8-E17	SUM(B19:E19)
20						
21	Return On Sales	B19/B6	C19/C6	D19/D6	E19/D6	F19/F6

When Ann finishes these modifications to the Operating Budget for Sunny Morning Products, her completed worksheet will look similar to Figure 2-3.

Figure 2-3 ◀
Ann's modified
annual
Operating
Budget

Sunny Morning Products
Operating Budget

	Qtr 1	Qtr 2	Qtr 3	Qtr 4	Total
Revenues:					
Sales	$898,300	$916,266	$934,591	$953,283	$3,702,440
Cost of Sales	521,014	531,434	542,063	552,904	2,147,415
Gross Profit	377,286	384,832	392,528	400,379	1,555,025
Expenses:					
Salaries	109,000	114,450	120,173	126,181	469,804
Benefits	19,620	20,601	21,631	22,713	84,565
Advertising	44,915	45,813	46,730	47,664	185,122
Office Equipment	10,420	10,837	11,270	11,721	44,248
Supplies	26,949	27,488	28,038	28,598	111,073
Telephone	7,680	7,680	7,680	7,680	30,720
Total Expenses	218,584	226,869	235,521	244,557	925,532
Earnings Before Tax	$158,702	$157,963	$157,007	$155,821	$629,493
Return On Sales	**17.67%**	**17.24%**	**16.80%**	**16.35%**	**17.00%**

Retrieving the Worksheet

Before you can begin modifying the budget, you need to retrieve the workbook containing Ann's first-quarter Operating Budget.

To launch Excel and open the C_SMP1.xls workbook:

1. Launch Excel and open the C_SMP1.xls workbook in the Tut02 folder in your Student Disk.

2. Save the workbook as S_SMP1.xls in the Tut02 folder in case you want to restart this tutorial.

You learned in Tutorial 1 that the first step in building a worksheet is entering all of the identifying labels. According to Ann's expanded plan, the additional column headings are missing. You will begin expanding the initial worksheet by entering these headings.

Using AutoFill to Create a Series

Before Ann enters the formulas for calculating the Operating Budget for the four quarters, she wants to enter the column headings to help her identify where data values are entered. Although Ann could type the column headings for the second, third, and fourth quarters, Excel provides a convenient method of completing a series of data values in a specified cell range, **AutoFill**. The series can be numbered quarters like Ann's, or it can be a numeric or alphabetical series. For example, if you have the headings January and February in your worksheet, you can use AutoFill to create the series of month names for the entire year, with January as the starting value for the series. All you have to do is start the series by entering the beginning data, which serves as the starting value, in the first cell of the range of cells to be filled. When you use AutoFill, you drag the fill handle to outline your initial entry *and* the cells you want to fill. The **fill handle**, shown in Figure 2-4, is the small black square in the lower-right corner of the active cell's border.

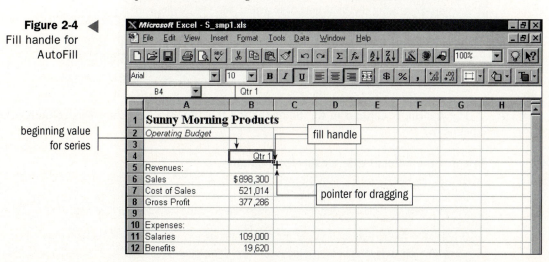

Figure 2-4
Fill handle for AutoFill

Enter the column headings for the second, third, and fourth quarters of Ann's report by using AutoFill to create a series in adjacent cells.

To complete a series of column headings using AutoFill:

1. Click **B4** to make it the active cell that contains the starting value for the series. Look closely at the cell's border and notice the fill handle in the lower-right corner.

2. Move the mouse pointer over the fill handle until the pointer changes to ✛.

3. Click and drag the pointer across the worksheet to select the cell range **B4:E4**. See Figure 2-5. Note that this range includes the initial value in the series in the leftmost cell in the range.

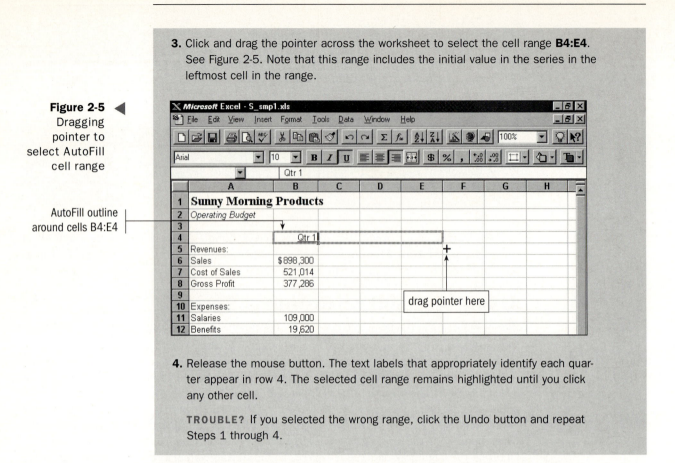

Figure 2-5
Dragging pointer to select AutoFill cell range

AutoFill outline around cells B4:E4

4. Release the mouse button. The text labels that appropriately identify each quarter appear in row 4. The selected cell range remains highlighted until you click any other cell.

   TROUBLE? If you selected the wrong range, click the Undo button and repeat Steps 1 through 4.

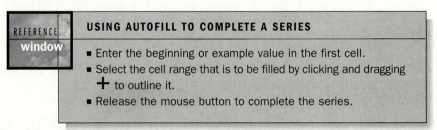

REFERENCE window

USING AUTOFILL TO COMPLETE A SERIES

- Enter the beginning or example value in the first cell.
- Select the cell range that is to be filled by clicking and dragging ✛ to outline it.
- Release the mouse button to complete the series.

The rightmost column in the budget is for the annual total. Enter this column's text label next.

To enter the column title for the Total column:

1. Click **F4** to make it the active cell.

2. Type **Total** and click the **Enter** button ✓ to place the desired column title in this cell.

3. Click the **Align Right** button on the Formatting toolbar, then click the **Underline** button to finish specifying the format for this column title.

Now Ann has all the rows and columns in the worksheet identified. She is ready to enter the formulas for calculating the second, third, and fourth quarters. Begin by entering the formulas in the second quarter that are calculated using a growth rate.

To enter the formulas in Qtr 2 that are calculated with a growth rate:

1. Click **C6** to make it the active cell and use pointing to enter the formula **B6*(1+0.02)**. Notice that the value 916266 is displayed using the default general format without the currency symbol or comma.

2. Click **C11** to make it the active cell and enter the formula **B11*(1+0.05)**. The result, 114450, is also displayed with the general format.

3. Click **C14** and enter the formula **B14*(1+0.04)**, which displays the value 10836.8.

Besides the growth rate formulas, Ann also uses a formula that repeats the value from Qtr 1 in the other three quarters, because the same value is always used for all four quarters. This formula makes it easier to revise the value in column B and have the desired values appear in the other three columns. Enter this formula next.

To enter a formula for repeating a data value in subsequent columns:

1. Click **C16** to make it the active cell.

2. Enter the formula **B16** to display a result of 7680 in Qtr 2 and set up this formula to use the same data value in all four quarters.

The results of these new formulas are displayed using the default format. The formats for these four formulas in the second quarter need to be changed to match those for Qtr 1.

Using the Format Painter to Copy Cell Formats

In Excel, the **Format Painter button** lets you apply the format you have already specified for one cell to other cells. This allows the formats from Qtr 1 to be used with the newly entered formulas for Qtr 2. Change the formats for these four cells in Qtr 2 to match the formats used in Qtr 1.

To apply an existing cell format to other cells:

1. Click **B6**, which contains the format you want to apply to cell C6.

2. Click the **Format Painter** button on the Standard toolbar to select the format. The pointer changes to indicate that a format is selected that can be pasted into other cells.

3. Click **C6** to apply the format to this cell. Notice that the pound signs (#) appear in this column.

4. Increase the column width so the number is displayed with the desired format.

5. Apply the format from cell B11 to cells **C11:C16**.

Next, you will continue to build the annual Operating Budget by copying the remaining formulas for the second, third, and fourth quarters in Ann's worksheet.

Copying Formulas

Although you could enter the remaining formulas by either typing or pointing, a more efficient solution is to copy them. Copying cell formulas is the preferred method of placing formulas in a worksheet because it reduces the possibility of entering a wrong formula. You should copy formulas when you want the same calculations carried out in other rows and columns, which use different data. This situation occurs frequently with worksheets like Ann's budget where the same accounting formula is used for each quarter.

All the formulas in the first quarter are similar to those in the other three quarters, except those for Sales, Salaries, and Office Equipment, which make use of a growth rate, and the one for Telephone, which uses the first-quarter value in all other quarters. This similarity allows these formulas in Ann's Operating Budget to be copied for use in other cells, as shown in Figure 2-6. From Ann's sketch (Figure 2-2), you can see that the formulas to be copied are nearly identical to the formulas already entered in each row and their cell references have the same pattern—the only difference is the column letters. You should examine your planning analysis sheet to look for this pattern of cell references to identify formulas that can be copied.

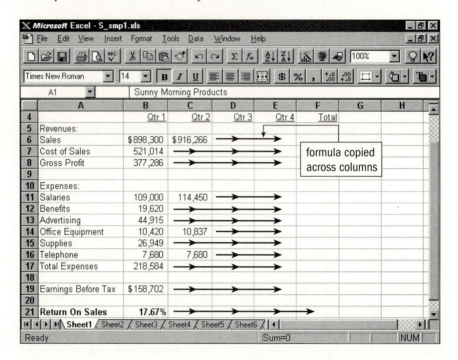

Figure 2-6
Arrangement for copying formulas in Ann's worksheet

When you copy a formula from one cell to another, Excel automatically *adjusts* the column letters or row numbers in cell references to keep the same pattern. This is called **relative referencing**. However, when you copy text labels and numeric constants, *exact duplicates* are placed in the other cells.

Relative and Absolute References

A relative reference tells Excel which cell to use, based on its location relative to the cell containing the formula. When you copy a formula that contains a relative reference, Excel changes the cell references so that they refer to cells located in the same position relative to the cell that contains the new copy of the formula. That is, Excel maintains the same pattern of cell references.

Relative references are the Excel default. All references in formulas are relative references unless you specify otherwise. In creating many business models, you will want to use relative references because you can then copy formulas easily for use in different cells in your worksheet.

From time to time, you might need to create a formula that refers to a cell in a fixed location in the worksheet. A reference that always specifies the same cell when it is copied is an **absolute reference**. Absolute references contain a dollar sign before the column letter and/or the row number. Examples of absolute references include $C$14 and $B$27. When you copy absolute references to other cells, Excel copies the specific cell references with no adjustments to the column letters or row numbers. Relative and absolute references *only make a difference when formulas are copied to different cells*. You will use absolute references later in this tutorial. For now, you will learn several methods for copying formulas containing relative references.

Excel provides several methods for copying, depending on the number of cells you want to copy at one time and whether the range you are copying from is adjacent to the range you want to copy to. The Excel AutoFill feature allows you to copy formulas, as well as to complete series. Excel automatically detects whether the cell contains a constant value of a series or a formula. Copy the formulas in Ann's worksheet for Qtr 2, Qtr 3, and Qtr 4 using AutoFill.

To copy a single formula using AutoFill:

1. Click **C6** to make it the active cell. The formula for Sales in the single cell C6 will be copied into the range D6:E6.

2. Move the mouse pointer over the fill handle until the pointer changes to +.

3. Click and drag the pointer across the row to select the range **C6:E6**. Release the mouse button to complete the AutoFill copy. Excel detects that a formula resides in cell C6 and that it should copy that formula, rather than completing an AutoFill series. When a copy is performed, both the cell's formula *and* its format are copied. Notice that the pound sign (#) fills any cell when you perform the copy. This means that the column is too narrow for the number with its format.

4. Select both **column D and column E** in the worksheet frame and increase the width of column D. This increases the width of column E at the same time.

5. Inspect the formulas in cells D6 and E6 by moving the cell pointer to each cell. Notice that the column letters adjusted automatically as the copies were performed. See Figure 2-7.

Figure 2-7
Column letters in formula adjusted automatically by Excel

TROUBLE? If you copied a formula to the wrong cells, click the Undo button and repeat the copy.

COPYING CELLS TO AN ADJACENT RANGE USING AUTOFILL

- Select the cell range for copying.
- Position the mouse pointer over the fill handle until the pointer changes to +.
- Click and drag the mouse pointer to outline the cell range for the desired location.
- Release the mouse button to copy the cell contents to this location.

ADVEX 72 **TUTORIAL 2** DEVELOPING EFFECTIVE WORKSHEETS

You can also copy several *adjacent* cells in one range at the same time, using the AutoFill copy. For Ann's budget, the formulas in the range B7:B8 for Cost of Sales and Gross Profit can be copied at the same time. However, they could not be copied with the Sales formula because the three formulas do not reside in a single rectangular cell range. Use AutoFill to copy the formulas for Cost of Sales and Gross Profit, and then complete copying the remaining formulas in Ann's worksheet.

To copy the other formulas for the Operating Budget using AutoFill:

1. Select the cell range **B7:B8**, which contains the formulas to be copied at one time.

2. Move the pointer over the fill handle until the pointer changes to **+**.

3. Click and drag the pointer across the worksheet to select the cells **B7:E8**.

4. Release the mouse button to complete the copy.

5. Copy the Salaries formula for Qtr 2 to Qtr 3 and Qtr 4, then copy the Office Equipment and Telephone formulas in the same manner. These formulas need to be copied separately because they are copied from Qtr 2, rather than Qtr 1.

6. Copy all the other formulas from Qtr 1 to Qtr 2, Qtr 3, and Qtr 4.

The last formula to be copied for Ann's Operating Budget is the one for Return On Sales in the Total column. We will use the clipboard to complete this copy.

Using the Clipboard to Copy Cells

Although the Return On Sales formula in the Total column could be copied using the fill handle, you can also copy Ann's formula for Return On Sales in Qtr 4 to the Total column using the Excel clipboard. The **clipboard** is a Windows area used to temporarily store data that you copy so that you can paste that same data elsewhere. You need to use the clipboard when you copy from a range that is *not* adjacent to the destination range that you are copying to.

When you copy a range of cells, you select the entire range you want copied, but you do not have to select the entire destination range. To paste a copied column, you specify only the top row of the destination range. Similarly, to paste a copied row you specify only the leftmost column of the destination range.

You can use the Copy and Paste buttons or you can use the Excel Shortcut menu or shortcut keys to copy several cells at a time to the clipboard. Use the Copy and Paste buttons to copy the Return On Sales formula from Qtr 4 to the Total column.

To copy a range of cells using the clipboard and the Copy and Paste buttons:

1. Click **E21** to select it as the source for the copy. This can be any size cell range, including a single cell.

2. Click the **Copy** button on the Standard toolbar to place a copy of the cell content, including format, on the clipboard.

3. Click **F21** to select it as the cell range of the destination for the cell formula.

4. Click the **Paste** button on the Standard toolbar to perform the copy operation. The error value "#DIV/0!" appears to indicate a division by zero. This will be corrected when the other formulas are placed in the Total column. Error values such

as #DIV/0! appear when a formula cannot be properly calculated for a cell. When they occur, you need to be sure you understand them so they can be corrected. Other error values are described when they are encountered in these tutorials. The worksheet with all the formulas copied appears, as shown in Figure 2-8.

Figure 2-8
Copying of cell formula complete

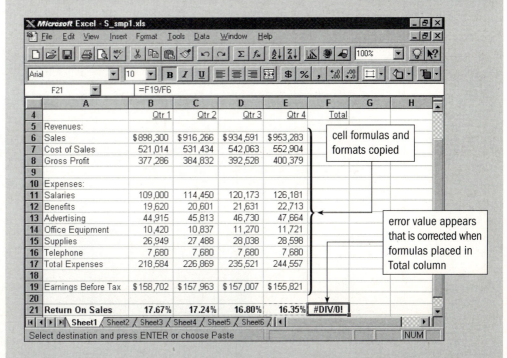

5. Inspect the cell where you copied the formula to verify that the column letter was adjusted in the formula.

6. Click the **Save** button to save the changes you have made to your worksheet.

REFERENCE window

COPYING A CELL RANGE USING THE CLIPBOARD

- Select the range of cells to copy.
- Click the Copy button to copy the cell content, including format, to the clipboard.
  or
  Right-click the selected range to display the Shortcut menu and click Copy on this menu to copy the contents to the clipboard.
  or
  Hold down the Ctrl key and press C to copy the contents to the clipboard.
- Select the cell range *for the destination range*, where the clipboard content is to be copied.
- Click the Paste button to place the cell contents in the selected range.
  or
  Right-click to redisplay the Shortcut menu and click Paste on this menu to place the cell contents in the selected range.
  or
  Hold down the Ctrl key and press V to paste the cell contents into the selected range.

Creating a Total Column with SUM

The final step in building Ann's Operating Budget is entering the remaining formulas for the Total column. Do that next, using the AutoSum button explored in Tutorial 1.

To total the values in each row of the Operating Budget except Return On Sales:

1. Select the cell range **B6:F19**. This range includes all the rows to be summed, and a column of blank cells in which the results of the SUM function will appear. See Figure 2-9.

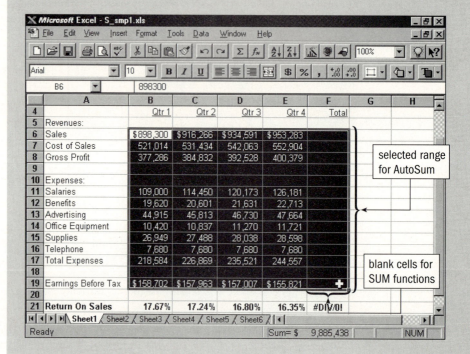

Figure 2-9 ◀ Range selected to sum quarters for the year

2. Click the **AutoSum** button ∑ on the Standard toolbar to create a SUM function for each of the rows in the selected range that contain data values.

3. Increase the width of column F as needed to display the numbers with the desired format. Excel automatically applies the same format used in the other cells in the rows. See Figure 2-10. Notice that the error value for Return On Sales is now replaced with a correct result of 17.00% and that Earnings Before Tax is $629,493.

Figure 2-10
Completed totals for the year

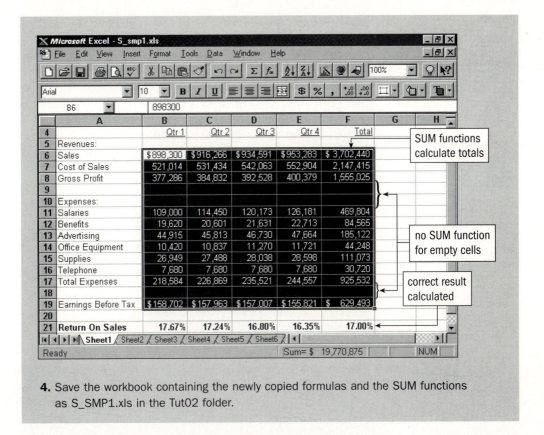

4. Save the workbook containing the newly copied formulas and the SUM functions as S_SMP1.xls in the Tut02 folder.

Arranging Worksheets in Sections

After printing the updated Operating Budget, Ann shows it to Carmen. They both review it to make sure that the formulas and all corresponding results are correct, that there aren't any spelling errors, and that all the information Carmen and Travis wanted is included. Carmen asks Ann to make one other change to the worksheet. She reminds Ann that several people will be using this worksheet to make critical business decisions. Therefore, she wants three sections added to the worksheet that will summarize pertinent information for users of this spreadsheet. The first section she would like to see added is a section listing the key assumptions used in carrying out the calculations. The **Key Input Assumptions section** contains constant data values that are referenced in formulas, so that the constant data value does not need to be included directly in the formula. For example, the growth rates and ratios included in Ann's formulas in the last draft of the Operating Budget are key input assumptions. Carmen and Travis may want to adjust these assumptions as they perform what-if analyses or receive new information from other functional areas of Sunny Morning Products. These key assumptions will be easier to review and change if they are listed in a separate section of the worksheet. As they consider the number of rows they have used in the worksheet, their preference is to place the assumptions at the bottom of the worksheet. That way when the worksheet is viewed the main report appears in the upper-left corner and is easily accessed with the Ctrl + Home keys. This arrangement of the worksheet divides it into two sections, the main calculated report and the key input assumptions.

The second section Carmen recommends adding is a Summary section. A **Summary section** uses formulas to reference information in the worksheet and to summarize that information in a report layout that is immediately understandable. The Summary section of a well-designed worksheet allows you to get at the "bottom line" quickly. The **bottom line** is the single most important planning item that provides the information necessary to evaluate a plan.

The third and final section Carmen would like added to the workbook is a Documentation sheet that will describe her workbook's contents and use. That way, if other associates at Sunny Morning Products use the workbook once Ann has completed its development, they can quickly determine whether they are using the appropriate workbook for their analysis and can easily find out how the workbook is organized. A **Documentation sheet** tells you what you will find in each sheet in the workbook and is a separate worksheet that you use for this purpose.

In Excel, you can place each section in a separate worksheet in your workbook, or you can place them all in the same worksheet. For larger workbooks, each section is often located in a separate worksheet. Considering the overall size of their worksheet, Carmen wants Ann to include a Key Input Assumptions section for their Operating Budget in the same worksheet; then it can be printed as a single one-page report for presentation to the Sunny Morning Products board of directors. The other two sections will be added as separate sheets in the workbook. Ann revises her worksheet design sketch to include the Key Input Assumptions section (Figure 2-11). Usually, you would include this section with your initial worksheet design.

Figure 2-11 ◀
Ann's revised worksheet design sketch with a Key Input Assumptions section

	A	B	C	D	E	F
			WORKSHEET DESIGN SKETCH			
1	Sunny Morning Products					
2	Operating Budget					
3						
4		Qtr 1	Qtr 2	Qtr 3	Qtr 4	Total
5	Revenues:					
6	Sales	898300	B6*(1+B25)	C6*(1+B25)	D6*(1+B25)	SUM(B6:E6)
7	Cost of Sales	B6*B26	C6*B26	D6*B26	E5*B26	SUM(B7:E7)
8	Gross Profit	B6-B7	C6-C7	D6-D7	E6-E7	SUM(B8:E8)
9						
10	Expenses:					
11	Salaries	109000	B11*(1+B27)	C11*(1+B27)	D11*(1+B27)	SUM(B11:E11)
12	Benefits	B11*B28	C11*B28	D11*B28	E11*B28	SUM(B12:E12)
13	Advertising	B6*B29	C6*B29	D6*B29	E6*B29	SUM(B13:E13)
14	Office Equipment	10420	B14*(1+B30)	C14*(1+B30)	D14*(1+B30)	SUM(B14:E14)
15	Supplies	B6*B31	C6*B31	D6*B31	E6*B31	SUM(B15:E15)
16	Telephone	7680	B16	C16	D16	SUM(B16:E16)
17	Total Expenses	SUM(B11:B16)	SUM(C11:C16)	SUM(D11:D16)	SUM(E11:E16)	SUM(B17:E17)
18						
19	Earnings Before Tax	B8-B17	C8-C17	D8-D17	E8-E17	SUM(B19:E19)
20						
21	Return On Sales	B19/B6	C19/C6	D19/D6	E19/D6	F19/F6
22						
23						
24	Key Input Assumptions:					
25	Sales Growth Rate	2%				
26	Cost of Sales Percent	58%				
27	Salary Growth Rate	5%				
28	Benefit Rate	18%				
29	Advertising Percent	5%				
30	Office Growth Rate	4%				
31	Supplies Percent	3%				

Note that the inclusion of the Key Input Assumptions section in Ann's worksheet design does not change her planning analysis. She is still using the same input data and calculations. They are just arranged more conveniently for input, printing, and review. Add the Key Input Assumptions section to Ann's worksheet.

To include a Key Input Assumptions section in a worksheet:

1. Scroll the worksheet as needed and click **A24** to make it the active cell.

2. Enter the text label **Key Input Assumptions:** to identify this section of the worksheet.

3. Enter the labels for the assumptions in column A as shown in Figure 2-11.

4. Enter the data values in column B as shown in Figure 2-11.

5. Format the cells as percents, with no decimal.

Once the Key Input Assumptions section is set up, Ann still needs to reference these values in the formulas in her worksheet. Remember, one of the main reasons for including a Key Input Assumptions section in the worksheet is to make it easier for Ann to conduct a what-if analysis. If she were to perform a what-if analysis by changing a value in the Key Input Assumptions section, *no* changes would be made to her current worksheet because she included these assumptions directly in her formulas. Therefore, the formulas need to be revised to reference the cells that contain the key input assumptions. Then when she changes a key input assumption, the formulas in the worksheet will automatically recalculate with the new assumption. However, many of the formulas in her worksheet were created by copying. Once a formula is placed in a cell, Excel does *not* remember how it got there. As a result, if you revise a formula that was copied into a cell, then you need to perform the copy again in order to change those formulas created by copying.

Using Absolute References

The formula for Sales shown in Ann's planning analysis sheet as "previous Sales * (1 + Sales Growth Rate)" references the *same* value for the Sales Growth Rate in cell B25 for the second, third, and fourth quarters. For this reason you don't want the cell reference for the growth rate to be adjusted for each column when the formula is copied. For example, the formula you need to enter in cell C6 is B6*(1+B25). If you copy this formula to cell D6 using relative referencing, the formula will automatically adjust to C6*(1+C25). This formula is incorrect—there is no value in cell C25. The correct formula would be C6*(1 + B25).

To copy the formula correctly, you need to include an absolute reference. An **absolute reference** is a cell address that is *not* adjusted automatically when it is copied to another location in the worksheet—it always references the same cell no matter where it is copied to. You indicate an absolute reference by preceding the column letter and/or row number with a dollar sign. For example, $B$25 is an absolute reference, whereas B25 is a relative reference. In some situations, a cell might have a **mixed reference**, such as $B25; in this case, when the formula is copied, the row number changes but the column letter does not. Similarly, copying B$25 changes the column letter but not the row number. Absolute references, mixed references, and relative references only make a difference when formulas are copied to different cells. Modify the formulas that include key input assumptions to include absolute references so they can be copied.

To create formulas that reference key input assumptions using absolute references:

1. Double-click **C6** to make it the active cell in Edit mode.

2. Change the constant value of 0.02 to **B25**.

ADVEX 78 **TUTORIAL 2** DEVELOPING EFFECTIVE WORKSHEETS

3. Place the edit cursor (I) anywhere in the cell reference B25 in the formula and press the **F4** key to insert the dollar signs for the absolute reference. If you know that you want an absolute reference to a cell in a formula, you can use the F4 key to insert the dollar signs as you create the formula initially.

4. Click the **Enter** button ☑ to complete the revision to the formula.

5. Edit each of the formulas in cells B7, C11, B12, B13, C14, and B15 in order to change the assumption to its corresponding absolute cell reference in the Key Input Assumptions section.

6. Copy the revised formulas to Qtr 2, Qtr 3, and Qtr 4 as appropriate for each of the planning items. The Return On Sales value in the Total column should still be 17.00%.

   TROUBLE? If your Return On Sales value is different, compare your formulas to those in Figure 2-11. Keep in mind the formulas you have copied will have absolute referencing. Edit your worksheet and change any formulas that are different.

7. Save the S_SMP1.xls workbook in the Tut02 folder.

Once you have created the formulas that reference the key input assumptions, you can test the worksheet to make sure the formulas properly reference the assumptions by performing a what-if analysis. If you change the data values in the Key Input Assumptions section, then formulas in the spreadsheet should recalculate and a different result should display. Test the worksheet by changing Cost of Sales Percent.

To test the worksheet to verify that a key assumption is referenced by the formulas:

1. Click **B26**, which contains the Cost of Sales Percent assumption, to make it the active cell.

2. Type **61%** and click the **Enter** button ☑ to replace the value in cell B26.

3. Inspect the worksheet results. Revised values should appear for Cost of Sales and all other planning items calculated using these results, including Earnings Before Tax and Return On Sales. Return On Sales in the Total column should now be 14.00%.

   TROUBLE? If the results did not change, then the Cost of Sales formulas do not reference the input assumptions. Revise these formulas so that they reference the Cost of Sales Percent in the Key Input Assumptions section, then repeat Steps 1 through 3.

4. Preview and print the worksheet with the Key Input Assumptions section.

As Ann reviews her revised report with the key input assumptions, she notices that several numbers *appear* to calculate incorrectly (Figure 2-12). For example, Gross Profit for Qtr 3 appears as 364,491, when it should appear 364,490. Recall that these numbers in Ann's worksheet are displayed as integers with the Comma format and no decimals. The apparent errors are from rounding the decimals when displaying the integer values, not from calculating incorrectly.

Figure 2-12
Apparent errors due to rounding

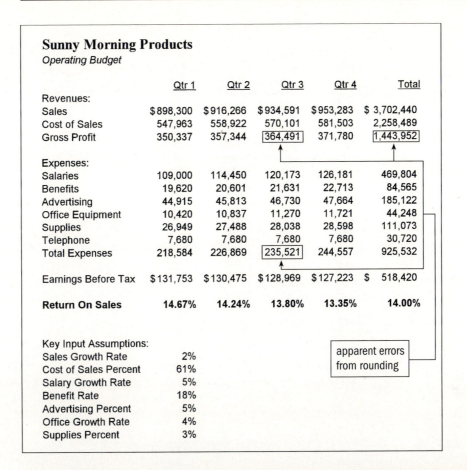

Rounding Results

The rounding problem Ann experienced is not unique to Excel and spreadsheet programs. It occurs throughout all computing programs. The ROUND function in Excel is a convenient method for approaching this situation, *so that the displayed results are the same as those used in other calculations.* That is, the ROUND function coordinates the calculated value with the displayed value controlled by its cell format. The **syntax**, or structure to use in entering the ROUND function, is

ROUND(*formula to be calculated, places to right of decimal*)

In general, the ROUND function has two arguments—a formula to be calculated and a formula specifying the number of decimal places.

You should consider using the ROUND function with a formula whenever you want to control the calculated number of decimal places and the formula contains (1) multiplication by a fraction, (2) a division, (3) an exponentiation, or (4) use of another function that may calculate a fractional result.

The apparent errors from rounding in Ann's worksheet can be "fixed" by adding the ROUND function to the formulas in cells C6:E6, B7:E7, and C11:E11. You can include the ROUND function in a cell formula by entering it when you initially create the formula or by editing an existing formula to add it. You specify the ROUND function either by typing the function name or by using the Function Wizard. In Excel, a **Wizard** is a series of dialog boxes that simplifies a task by guiding you through the process step by step, for example the steps for specifying a function or creating a chart. The **Function Wizard** guides you through two dialog boxes to specify a function in a formula. Reenter the formula in cell C6 so it includes rounding.

To reenter a formula with the ROUND function:

1. Click **C6**, which is the cell where you want to enter the formula with the ROUND function.

2. Click the **Function Wizard** button to display the Function Wizard - Step 1 of 2 dialog box. See Figure 2-13.

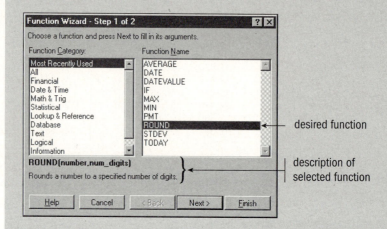

Figure 2-13 ◀
Function Wizard - Step 1 of 2 dialog box

3. Look for the ROUND function in the Function Name list. If it doesn't appear, click **Math & Trig** in the Function Category list and scroll the Function Name list again. Click **ROUND** in the Function Name list to select it. Then click the **Next>** button to display the Function Wizard - Step 2 of 2 dialog box. See Figure 2-14.

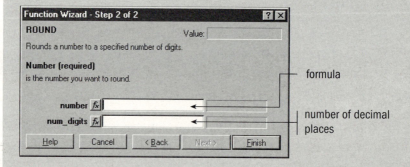

Figure 2-14 ◀
Function Wizard - Step 2 of 2 dialog box

4. Type the formula **B6*(1+$B$25)** in the number text box and press the **Tab** key. Because this formula is *not* being entered into a cell, you do not use an equal sign (=). You could also enter this formula using pointing, but you may need to reposition the dialog box in order to point to the desired cells. (You reposition a dialog box by dragging it by its title bar.)

5. Type **0** (zero) in the num_digits text box to specify rounding as an integer with no places to the right of the decimal.

6. Click the **Finish** button to finish specifying the ROUND function. The formula now appears in the formula bar as =ROUND(B6*(1+$B$25),0).

You may wonder whether the rounding for cell C6 is automatically applied to the formulas in cells D6 and E6 that were previously copied from cell C6. No. Recall that once a copy is complete, Excel does *not* remember that a formula was copied to a cell. As a result, Ann's formula with rounding needs to be copied from cell C6 into cells D6 and E6. Apply rounding to the other formulas for Sales by performing the same copy activities used previously with these cells.

USING ABSOLUTE REFERENCES **ADVEX 81**

To copy a formula with rounding into other cells:

1. Click **C6** to make it the active cell, if necessary.

2. Move the pointer over the fill handle until the pointer changes to ✛, click and drag the pointer across the worksheet to select cells **C6:E6**, then release the mouse button to complete the copy, which replaces the previous formulas with those that now contain the ROUND function.

If you anticipate the need to use rounding *before* you begin to build your worksheet, you can include the ROUND function in the formulas as you initially enter them, which is usually the best strategy. However, when you already have a formula entered in a worksheet and then decide you want to use the ROUND function, editing the formula is more convenient and less error-prone than reentering it. Since Ann's worksheet was built without initially including the appropriate use of the ROUND function, editing the existing formulas is the best approach. The Cost of Sales formula in B7 should include rounding because it is calculated by multiplication by a fraction. Edit the Cost of Sales formula to include the ROUND function.

To include the ROUND function by editing a previously entered formula:

1. Click **B7**, which contains the existing formula without the ROUND function.

2. Double-click **B7** or click the **formula in the formula bar** to begin editing the formula.

3. Place the edit cursor immediately to the right of the equal sign (=) and type **ROUND(**

4. Move the cursor to the right end of the formula and type **,0**) You can use the End and Home keys to quickly move the edit cursor to the right or left end of the cell's contents, respectively.

5. Click the **Enter** button ✓ to complete the edit change to this formula.

6. Copy the formula from cell B7 to cells **C7:E7**. The apparent errors from rounding that appeared for Gross Profit should now be fixed.

Several of the formulas that are used to calculate the expenses in Ann's worksheet include arithmetic that involves multiplication by a fraction. These formulas also need to be modified to include the ROUND function.

To include the ROUND function in the appropriate expense formulas:

1. Edit the formulas in cells C11, B12, B13, C14, and B15 to include the ROUND function with no decimal places.

2. Copy the edited formulas into the appropriate cells in Qtr 2, Qtr 3, and Qtr 4. When you perform your copies, be careful not to copy the formulas into column F, the Total column, because this column contains a SUM function and you do not want to change this formula. See Figure 2-15.

Figure 2-15
Results displayed using ROUND function

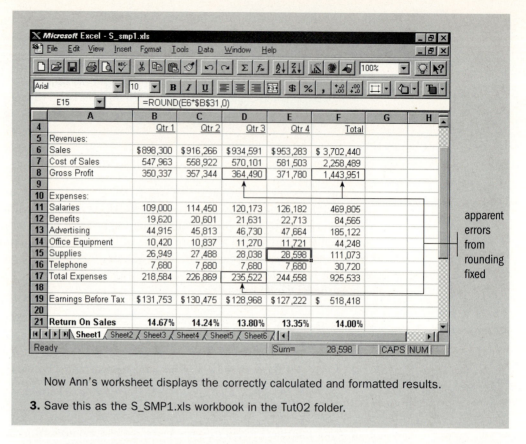

Now Ann's worksheet displays the correctly calculated and formatted results.

3. Save this as the S_SMP1.xls workbook in the Tut02 folder.

Ann has the results she wants. The formulas properly reference the key input assumptions, and she has fixed the rounding problem so that the numbers displayed are the ones actually used in the other calculations.

If you want to take a break and resume the tutorial at a later time, you can do so now. Close the workbook and exit Excel. If you are on a network, leave Windows running. If you are using your own computer, you may exit Windows and shut down the computer. When you resume the tutorial, place your Student Disk in the disk drive, launch Excel, then continue with the tutorial.

● ● ●

Reviewing the Worksheet

Carmen and Travis are pleased with the Operating Budget worksheet that Ann has created for next year. As they review the workbook, they realize that several additional expenses need to be included in their budget, for Automobiles, Insurance, Maintenance and Utilities. In the current version of the budget, all growth rates and ratios are assumed to be the same for each quarter, or constant. In their review, Carmen and Travis believe that several of the growth rates and ratios should vary from quarter to quarter in order to more clearly represent their expected operations.

After their review, Ann edits her original planning analysis sheet (Figure 2-16) and includes the new information in a revised worksheet sketch (Figure 2-17). A rough sketch is useful in showing the general layout of the rows and columns of a worksheet without entering all the formulas, which remain essentially the same for Ann's worksheet. In her planning analysis sheet, she uses "na" to indicate a column where a growth rate is not applicable because this column is not calculated from a previous column.

Figure 2-16 ◀
Ann's revised planning analysis sheet

Planning Analysis Sheet

My goal:

Develop a worksheet of the Operating Budget for next year

What results do I want to see?

Revenues and expenses for the next year by quarter with an annual total

What information do I need?

Columns are Qtr 1, Qtr 2, Qtr 3, Qtr 4, Total
Sales [Qtr 1] = 898300
Sales growth rate = na, 2%, 1%, -7%
Cost of Sales percent = 58%, 57%, 61%, 65%
Salaries [Qtr 1] = 109000
Salaries growth rate = na, 5%, 8%, 4%
Benefit rate = 18% for each quarter
Advertising percent = 5% for each quarter
Office Equipment [Qtr 1] = 10420
Office growth rate = 4% for next three quarters
Supplies percent = 3% for each quarter
Auto Increase = na, 800, 400, 600
Insurance percent = 2% for each quarter
Maintenance [each quarter] = 12870
Telephone [Qtr 1] = 7680
Utilities = 19800, 19640, 18920, 18860

What calculations will I perform?

Sales = 898300, previous Sales * (1 + Sales growth rate) for three quarters
Cost of Sales = Sales * Cost of Sales percent for four quarters
Gross Profit = Sales - Cost of Sales for four quarters
Salaries = 109000, previous Salaries * (1 + Salaries growth rate) for three quarters
Benefits = Salaries * Benefit rate for four quarters
Advertising = Sales * Advertising percent for four quarters
Office Equipment = 10420, previous Office Equipment * (1 + Office growth rate)
Supplies = Sales * Supplies percent for four quarters
Automobiles = 12400, previous Automobiles + Auto Increase for three quarters
Insurance = Sales * Insurance percent for four quarters
Telephone = 7680, previous Telephone for three quarters
Total Expenses = SUM(Salaries thru Telephone) for four quarters
Earnings Before Tax = Gross Profit - Total Expenses for four quarters

Figure 2-17
Ann's modified rough sketch of her worksheet

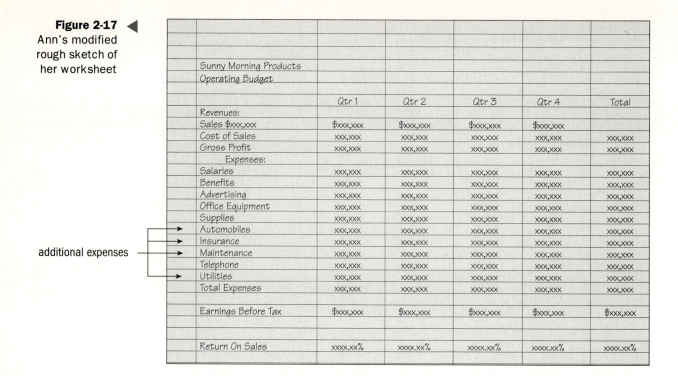

additional expenses

With her revised design finished, Ann is ready to include these changes in her budget worksheet as she prepares for the next meeting of the Sunny Morning Products board of directors.

Revising a Worksheet

Ann needs to include the additional planning items in her budget together with several new and revised input assumptions. Because she cannot view all of her expense items and their input assumptions in the same window, Ann needs to split the worksheet window before she can begin revising the worksheet. This will make it easier for her to create these new and revised formulas.

Splitting the Worksheet Window

Splitting a worksheet window allows you to view two separate areas, or **panes**, of the same worksheet at one time. You can split the worksheet window either horizontally or vertically by using the horizontal or vertical splitter. After you split the worksheet, you have two windows, which means two sets of scroll bars and buttons, and two sets of row numbers or column letters. You also have to make sure you select the section of the worksheet you want to work with. When you want to unsplit the window, you move the splitter back to its original position. Split the worksheet window horizontally so that the expenses are displayed in the top pane of the worksheet and the key input assumptions are displayed in the bottom pane.

REVISING A WORKSHEET **ADVEX 85**

To split a worksheet window horizontally:

1. Position the worksheet so A10 is in the upper-left corner and all the expense planning items are visible.

2. Point to the top of the vertical scroll bar and notice that the pointer changes to the horizontal splitter ⇳.

3. Click and drag the horizontal splitter ⇳ to the bottom of row 18. When you release the mouse button, the worksheet window is split into two panes.

4. Click any cell in the bottom pane and scroll the window to display the Key Input Assumptions section. See Figure 2-18. You can unsplit the window by dragging the horizontal or vertical splitter back to its original position.

Figure 2-18
Worksheet split to view two separate areas

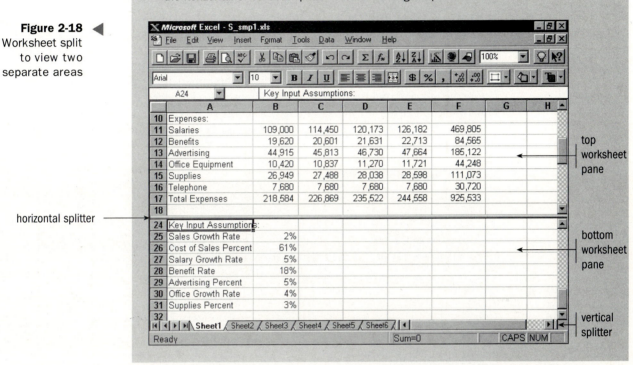

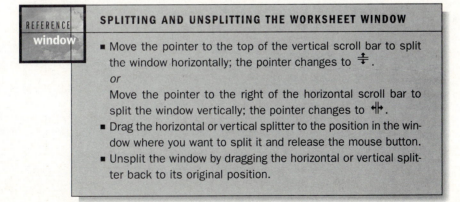

SPLITTING AND UNSPLITTING THE WORKSHEET WINDOW

REFERENCE window

- Move the pointer to the top of the vertical scroll bar to split the window horizontally; the pointer changes to ⇳.
  or
  Move the pointer to the right of the horizontal scroll bar to split the window vertically; the pointer changes to ⇿.
- Drag the horizontal or vertical splitter to the position in the window where you want to split it and release the mouse button.
- Unsplit the window by dragging the horizontal or vertical splitter back to its original position.

You are now ready to make the desired revisions to Ann's budget. She needs to begin by including several new planning items and their corresponding key input assumptions. This is accomplished by inserting additional rows into the current worksheet for these new items and creating their formulas. First, the new key input assumptions need to be added to the worksheet.

Inserting Rows in a Worksheet

Autos Increase and Insurance Percent are key assumptions that Ann needs to add to her worksheet. Although she could just place them at the bottom of the Assumptions section, she wants to position them where they are easier for her to work with. Of course, it makes no difference to Excel, because its nonprocedural feature will reference the cell in a formula regardless of its location in the worksheet. She needs to insert rows for each of her new input assumptions. To insert rows into a worksheet, you select a range of cells that specifies the number of rows to be inserted. The rows are inserted immediately *above* the selected range. By clicking a single cell, you select a range that is just one row. When you insert rows, Excel automatically adjusts the row numbers in formulas that reference cells *below* the inserted row for both relative and absolute cell references. However, it is important to check existing formulas in the worksheet to make sure they are adjusted for the newly inserted rows the way you want them to be adjusted. Insert the rows for Auto Increase and Insurance Percent.

To insert rows into a worksheet:

1. Click row number **28** in the worksheet frame to select the entire row in the worksheet.

2. Hold down the **Ctrl** key and press **+** (on the numeric keypad) to insert a row above the row that contains Benefit Rate. See Figure 2-19.

Figure 2-19 ◀
Blank row inserted in worksheet

inserted row ⎯⎯⎯

rows moved down ⎯⎯⎯

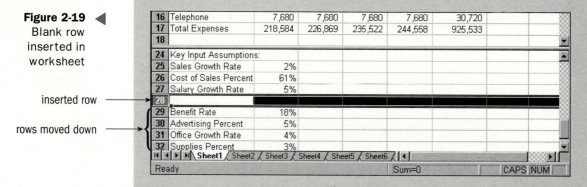

3. Click **C12** and review the formula in that cell to verify that the cell reference to Benefit Rate was automatically changed to $B$29.

4. Inspect other cells for Benefits to verify that their cell references were automatically adjusted when the row was inserted.

5. Click row number **31** in the worksheet frame and insert a second row.

>
> **INSERTING ROWS AND COLUMNS**
> - Click the row number in the worksheet frame or any cell above which you want to insert rows, or click the column letter in the worksheet frame or any cell to the left of where you want to insert columns.
> - Select a range of cells to specify the number of rows or columns to be inserted.
> - Hold down the Ctrl key and press + (on the numeric keypad).
> *or*
> Click Insert, then click Row or Column to insert either rows or columns.

Now enter the text labels and values in the inserted rows.

To add text labels and values in inserted rows:

1. Click **A28** and enter the text label **Auto Increase**.

2. Click **A31** and enter the text label **Insurance Percent**.

3. Enter values for these two planning items from Ann's revised planning analysis sheet (Figure 2-16).

   Next, enter the new values for the revised key input assumptions.

4. Enter the revised values for Sales Growth Rate, Cost of Sales Percent, and Salary Growth Rate from Ann's planning analysis sheet. For these assumptions, you want a different value in each quarter, rather than using a single assumption for all four quarters. When you enter "na" for Sales Growth Rate for Qtr 1, Excel displays the error value "#VALUE!" in all the cells whose calculation depends on this cell. This warns you that a text label such as "na" cannot be used in these calculations. This situation will be corrected when these formulas are revised.

Ann doesn't feel comfortable with the error values displayed in her worksheet and wants to fix this before she inserts her new expense items. That way she can see the results as the formulas are entered for the new expense planning items, rather than the error values. When you revise your worksheets, you will encounter similar situations with error values and you will usually want to fix them before you make other changes. Ann needs to revise the formulas for Sales, Cost of Sales, and Salaries, which use growth rates and ratios that now change in each quarter. When she completes these revisions, the desired results will be displayed in place of the #VALUE! error values. The formulas for these planning items were initially created using absolute referencing to a single cell with the same assumption value applied to each quarter. When a different assumption is applied to each quarter, there is no need to use absolute references to the key input assumptions. When you create a business model, you need to analyze your particular situation to determine whether it makes the best business sense to use the same or different growth rates and ratios in each column. Make these changes to Ann's budget to remove the error values.

To create formulas with different key assumptions applied to each time period:

1. Edit the formulas for Sales in column C, for Cost of Sales in column B, and for Salaries in column C to remove the absolute references to the key input assumptions. With the edit cursor on the cell reference, pressing the F4 key three times changes the reference to relative.

> 2. For Sales and Salaries, change the column letter of the cell containing the assumption value to correspond to that of the quarter that is calculated.
>
> 3. Copy the revised formulas from columns B and C into the other quarters as appropriate for each of the planning items changed in Step 1. Return On Sales should now be 14.14% with Earnings Before Tax of $509,191.

With the error values fixed and the data values of the key assumptions entered in her report, Ann is ready to include the expense planning items in the worksheet. First, she will add the Automobiles, Insurance, and Maintenance planning items, because they are in one range; then she will include Utilities, which is in a separate range. Insert the first range in the worksheet above Telephone, as shown in Ann's sketch in Figure 2-17, which is in the middle of the expense items.

To insert rows in the middle of a range of existing items:

> 1. Click the row number **16** to select it. The inserted rows will appear above row 16, which shows the Telephone expenses.
>
> 2. Click and drag the mouse pointer from row 16 to row 18 in the worksheet frame to select the cell range that includes all cells in the three rows, then insert three rows.
>
> 3. Enter the text labels in column A for these three new expense items.
>
> 4. Enter the data values for the Automobiles and Maintenance expenses, which are specified on the planning analysis sheet. Note that Automobiles is specified for Qtr 1 only, whereas Maintenance is specified as a constant value for each quarter. For Automobiles, a formula will have be used for Qtr 2, Qtr 3, and Qtr 4.
>
> 5. Use pointing to create the formulas for Automobiles in column C and Insurance in column B. Include rounding with the Insurance formula. Be careful in using absolute and relative referencing with these formulas.
>
> 6. Copy the formulas for Insurance and Automobiles into the other quarters.
>
> 7. Use the AutoSum tool to create the SUM functions for these expenses in the Total column.
>
> 8. Inspect the SUM function that calculates the Total Expenses in each of the four quarters. Verify that these *formulas were adjusted* to include the rows inserted in the middle of this range in the SUM function. Your results should be the same as those shown in Figure 2-20.

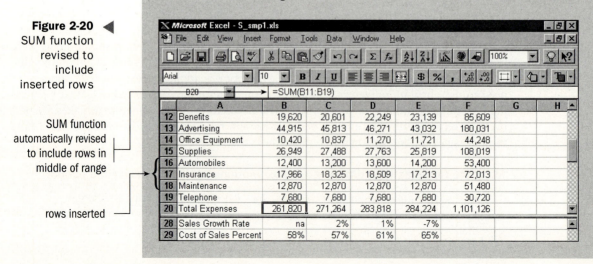

Figure 2-20
SUM function revised to include inserted rows

SUM function automatically revised to include rows in middle of range

rows inserted

Next, insert the row for Utilities.

To insert the Utilities expenses at the bottom of a range of values already added with a SUM function:

1. Insert a single row above row 20, which currently contains the Total Expenses planning item.

2. Enter the Utilities expenses, using Ann's revised planning analysis sheet (Figure 2-16), and place a SUM function for these quarterly expenses in the Total column.

3. Inspect the Total Expense formulas for each quarter. The Total Expenses in Qtr 1 remain unchanged at $261,820. The formula SUM(B11:B19) in cell B21 does *not* include the amount for Utilities in the new row 20, and similarly for the other formulas in columns C, D, and E.

Because the new row was inserted below the last row of the range specified in the SUM function, the range does *not* include the new row. Therefore, the Utilities expenses are not included in the Total Expenses. Whenever you insert a row at the *end* of a range specified in a SUM function, Excel does *not* automatically include it in the corresponding function. If you insert a row or column in the *middle* of a range, Excel *does* automatically include it in the corresponding range specifications. Correct this error.

To revise the formula with the SUM function in row 21 to include the newly inserted row:

1. Edit the formula in B21 to include row 20.

2. Copy the formula from cell B21 into the cells for the other quarters so they also include row 20 in calculating Total Expenses in their SUM functions. See Figure 2-21.

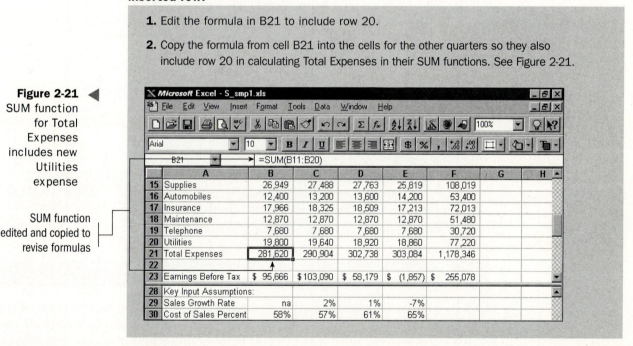

Figure 2-21
SUM function for Total Expenses includes new Utilities expense

SUM function edited and copied to revise formulas

Ann's budget includes all the new planning items and their appropriate calculations. However, as she reviews this version of her worksheet, she decides that she would like the Automobiles, Insurance, and Maintenance expense items to appear in her report immediately after the Advertising expense and before the Office Equipment expense. Then all her expense items other than Salaries and Benefits will be in alphabetical order, which is preferred by Travis for SMP's financial reports.

Moving Cell Contents

You move the contents of a single cell or a range of cells to a new location using **drag and drop**. You simply select the cell range you want to move and use the pointer to move the contents to the desired location. If the cells that you are moving to are *not* blank, then the contents being moved replace the existing cell contents. In order for Ann to relocate these expense items, she needs to first insert three blank rows at the location to which she wants to move the cell contents.

To move cell contents to a destination that already contains data:

1. Insert three blank rows above row 14, which contains the Office Equipment expenses.

2. Select the cell range **A19:F21**, which contains the desired expense items.

3. Move the mouse pointer to the edge of the selected range until it changes to the block arrow, which lets you drag the cell range to another location.

4. Click and drag the cell range so the outline is on top of **A14:F16**, which is the destination for the cells' contents. When you release the mouse button, the cell contents are placed at that location.

REFERENCE window

MOVING CELL CONTENTS

- If the destination cells are not blank and you do not want to replace the contents of the destination cells, then insert blank rows or columns for the cell contents you will move.
- Select the range to be moved.
- Move the pointer to the edge of the selected range until it changes to , then click and drag the range outline to the new location and release the mouse button.
  or
  Click the Cut button, click the upper-left corner of the destination, then click the Paste button.
  or
  Hold down the Ctrl key and press X to cut the contents to the clipboard, click the upper-left corner of the destination, then hold down the Ctrl key and press V to paste the clipboard's content.

Deleting Rows from the Worksheet

Now that you have moved the expense items to the desired location in the worksheet, you can delete the rows that no longer contain data. The procedure for deleting rows is similar to that for inserting rows. You select the range you want to delete, indicating the number of rows to be deleted. The rows that you delete can contain data or they can be blank. Be careful not to include any rows that contain values you want. Delete the unwanted rows from Ann's worksheet.

To delete rows from a worksheet:

1. Select rows **19**, **20**, and **21** by dragging the mouse pointer in the worksheet frame.

2. Hold down the **Ctrl** key and press – (on the numeric keypad) to delete the rows from the worksheet.

3. Verify that the absolute and relative references in the formulas for calculating Automobiles and Insurance were adjusted to reflect the new cell addresses. See Figure 2-22.

Figure 2-22 ◀
Cell references adjusted automatically when rows are deleted

cell reference automatically adjusted for deleted rows

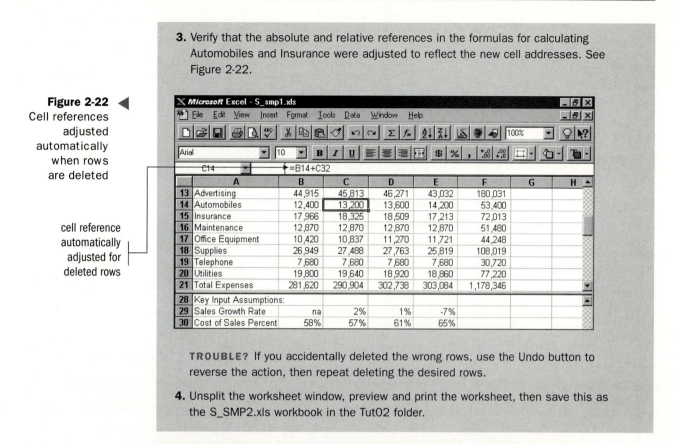

TROUBLE? If you accidentally deleted the wrong rows, use the Undo button to reverse the action, then repeat deleting the desired rows.

4. Unsplit the worksheet window, preview and print the worksheet, then save this as the S_SMP2.xls workbook in the Tut02 folder.

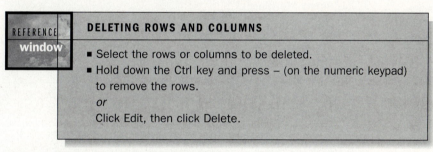

REFERENCE window

DELETING ROWS AND COLUMNS

- Select the rows or columns to be deleted.
- Hold down the Ctrl key and press – (on the numeric keypad) to remove the rows.
  or
  Click Edit, then click Delete.

Using Range Names

As Ann continues to develop the Sunny Morning Products Operating Budget, she finds herself scrolling the worksheet between the Key Input Assumptions and her calculations. Although she could split the window, she would like a way to easily reference these areas of her worksheet. Ann plans to name these ranges so that they will be easier to reference. A **range name** is a word or phrase that you substitute for a cell reference like A5 or a cell range like A5:F14. Anywhere that you would use a cell reference or cell range you can use the range name instead. Range names describe the data contained in the cells and are easier to remember. When you insert or delete rows and columns from a named range, Excel automatically adjusts the range specification. This makes it easier to review the formulas in a worksheet because the same formula appears even if you have inserted a row and changed the actual cell range. For example, you could specify the key assumptions with a range name; then these names would appear in the formulas that reference these assumptions.

You name ranges either by typing the name or by using a label in an adjacent cell. Range names can be up to 255 characters long and can include letters, numbers, underscores (_), and periods (.), but no other special characters. Do not use a space in a range name; instead, use an underscore or a period. Because formulas are also limited to 255 characters, long names in a formula leave you less room for the rest of the formula, and the full name does not show in a dialog box. Names of as many as 15 characters display in most list boxes, so

15 characters is a more practical limit to follow. You should *not* begin a range name with a number or try to create names that look like cell addresses, such as Q4 for Quarter 4 or FY98 for Fiscal Year 1998. This can be confusing in formulas.

Once a range is named, you can use that name in formulas, reports, and charts. Using range names instead of cell references is quicker for building formulas, selecting data, and printing specific areas of a worksheet. Range names reduce the need to modify worksheet formulas and help to avoid errors when you specify a range of cells. Range names are saved automatically with the workbook when you save it, but they do not alter the appearance of cell contents. Assign range names to the Operating Budget and the Key Input Assumptions so Ann can reference these areas more easily and print them individually.

To assign range names to selected areas of a worksheet:

1. Select the cell range **A1:G27**, which contains Ann's budget and an extra blank column on the right side. This column is included for displaying comments on the budget, which you'll add later in this tutorial.

2. Click the **Name** box in the left side of the formula bar to edit the value displayed.

3. Type **BUDGET** and press the **Enter** key to complete the range name specification. See Figure 2-23.

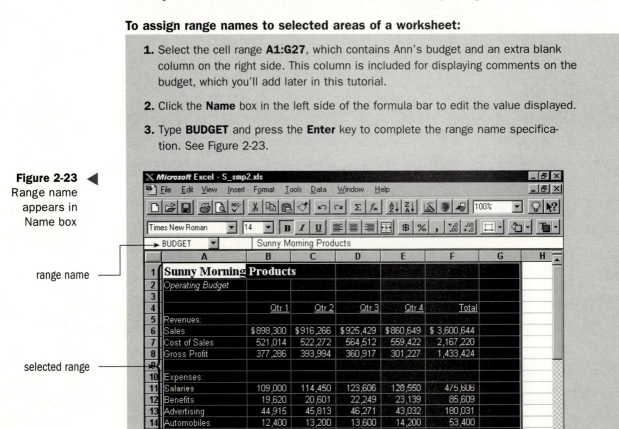

Figure 2-23
Range name appears in Name box

range name

selected range

Next, assign a range name to the Key Input Assumptions.

4. Select the cell range **A28:E37**, which contains the Key Input Assumptions.

5. Click the **Name** box, type **KEY_ASSUMPTIONS** as the desired range name, and press the **Enter** key.

6. Click any cell to unselect the KEY_ASSUMPTIONS range.

With these ranges named, Ann can easily select one range or the other. Select the BUDGET range and print it.

Printing a Selected Range

Range names are particularly useful in selecting a range for printing. With Ann's worksheet, the BUDGET and KEY_ASSUMPTIONS ranges are easily selected for viewing and printing. Of course, you could manually select a cell range for printing. But once a range is named, using its range name is easier and faster. Select a range and print it.

To select and print a defined range:

1. Click the **Name** box list arrow to display the list of defined names. See Figure 2-24.

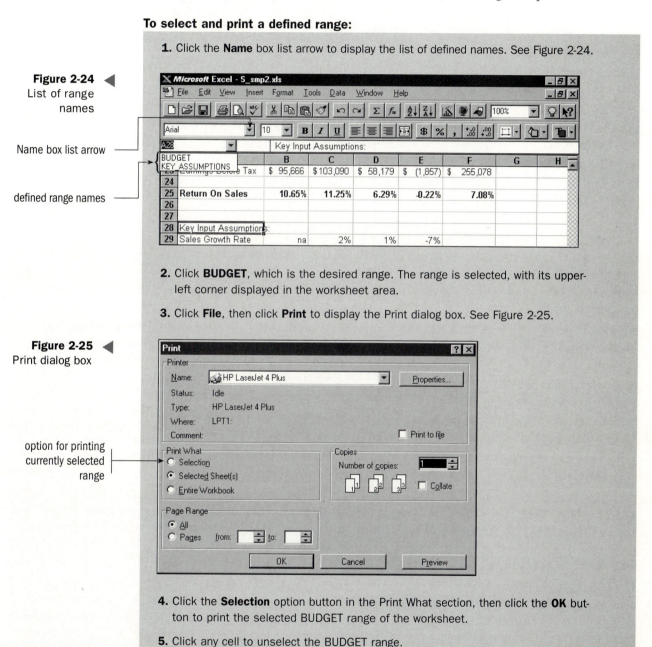

Figure 2-24 ◄ List of range names

Name box list arrow

defined range names

Figure 2-25 ◄ Print dialog box

option for printing currently selected range

2. Click **BUDGET**, which is the desired range. The range is selected, with its upper-left corner displayed in the worksheet area.

3. Click **File**, then click **Print** to display the Print dialog box. See Figure 2-25.

4. Click the **Selection** option button in the Print What section, then click the **OK** button to print the selected BUDGET range of the worksheet.

5. Click any cell to unselect the BUDGET range.

Using Range Names in Formulas

Range names reduce the chances of making errors in formulas. You are more likely to notice that you mistyped "Cost of Sales" than you are to detect an error when you type "B19:B24." When you enter an unrecognizable or undefined name, Excel displays the #NAME? error value.

Names are easier to remember than cell references. After you name cells or ranges, you can look at a list of names and paste the name you want into formulas. Ann wants to improve the readability of her formulas by using range names for the key input assumptions. This is accomplished by assigning the planning item names in column A to the data values in column B.

To assign text labels to range names for individual cells:

1. Select the cell range **A29:B37**, which contains the names of the key assumptions that are to be assigned to the cells in the column immediately to the right.

2. Click **Insert**, point to **Name**, then click **Create** to display the Create Names dialog box. See Figure 2-26.

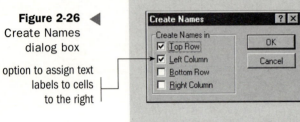

Figure 2-26
Create Names dialog box

option to assign text labels to cells to the right

3. Click the **Left Column** check box to select it. If any other selections are checked, uncheck them.

4. Click the **OK** button to assign the text labels in column A as names to the cells in column B. Then click any cell to unselect this range.

After these range names are created, they can be applied to the worksheet formulas. Applying a range name to a worksheet formula *permanently replaces* the cell reference with the range name. Once a range name is applied, you must continue to use the name in the formula. If you delete the range name, a #NAME? error value appears in the cell containing the range name because Excel *does not automatically replace the deleted range name with the original cell reference*. Although you can manually replace the cell reference, this is not very convenient. Therefore, once you apply a range name to a cell reference, you should always use the range name in the formula rather than the cell reference. Apply the range names that you created for the key input assumptions to the formulas.

To apply range names to formulas:

1. Click **Insert**, point to **Name**, then click **Apply** to display the Apply Names dialog box. See Figure 2-27.

Figure 2-27
Apply Names dialog box

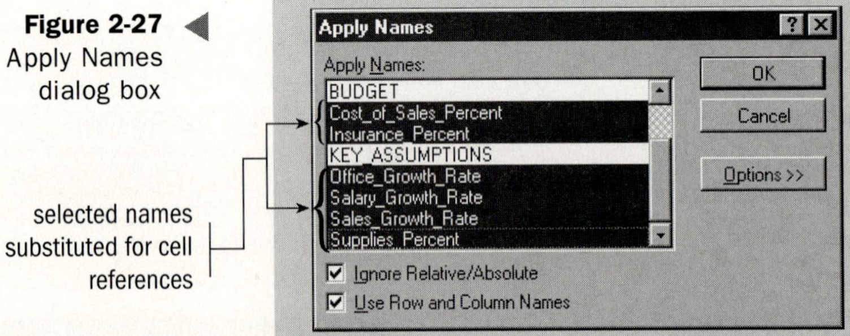

selected names substituted for cell references

2. Click the **OK** button to complete the substitution of the range names for the cell references.

Now review the formulas in the worksheet.

3. Click **B7** and confirm that the cell reference to Cost of Sales Percent is replaced by the range name. Then click several other cells and inspect the substitution of the range name for the cell reference.

4. Click **C7** and notice the appearance of the cell reference for Cost of Sales Percent in Qtr 2 rather than the range name. This occurs because a different percentage is desired for each column, rather than one value for use in all four quarters.

When you use range names with formulas where different values are used in different columns, then you need to set up the range names to include the column names. This is the situation with the assumptions for Sales Growth Rate, Cost of Sales Percent, Salary Growth Rate, and Autos Increase. Also, you can change the cell references for the planning items to range names using the other planning item names. Because the formulas for the planning items reference some cells in the same column and some in different columns, it is appropriate to use both the row name and the column name in assigning a range name to each of these cells. Assign the range names to the cells and then apply them to the formulas.

To assign range names to rows with multiple columns:

1. Select the cell range **A4:F32**, which contains the planning item names in the left-most column and the column titles in the topmost column.

2. Click **Insert**, point to **Name**, then click **Create** to display the Create Names dialog box.

3. If necessary, click the **Top Row** and **Left Column** check boxes to select these options. If any other selections are checked, uncheck them.

4. Click the **OK** button to create these range names. When requested to replace the existing definitions for the key input assumptions that were defined for only column B, click the **Yes** button. Then click any cell to unselect the range.

Next, apply these range names to the formulas in the worksheet.

5. Click **Insert**, point to **Name**, then click **Apply** to display the Apply Names dialog box.

6. Click the **Options>>** button, then uncheck the Omit Column Name if Same Column and the Omit Row Name if Same Row check boxes. This ensures that the entire range name is displayed in the formula.

7. Click the **OK** button to substitute the range names for the cell references in the formulas.

8. Inspect the formulas in the worksheet. All the formulas should now reference cells using the range names. See Figure 2-28.

Figure 2-28
Formula with range names

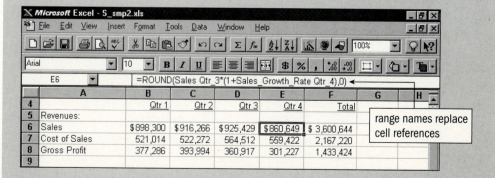

9. Save this as the S_SMP2.xls workbook in the Tut02 folder.

ADVEX 96 **TUTORIAL 2** DEVELOPING EFFECTIVE WORKSHEETS

If Ann encountered any difficulties in understanding the formulas as she reviewed her worksheet, she could have the formulas displayed in place of the calculated results in each cell. When you need to look at several formulas at one time in order to understand your calculations, you might want to consider using this view option for your worksheet.

HELP DESK

EXCEL 5.0

Index

DISPLAYING FORMULAS IN WORKSHEET CELLS

Double-click the Help button to display the Help Topics dialog box, then click the Index tab.

Keyword	Topic
formulas, displaying in cells	Display formulas and values on a worksheet
view options	*View Tab, Options Command (Tools Menu)*

If you want to take a break and resume the tutorial at a later time, you can do so now. Close the workbook and exit Excel. If you are on a network, leave Windows running. If you are using your own computer, you may exit Windows and shut down the computer. When you resume the tutorial, place your Student Disk in the disk drive, launch Excel, then continue with the tutorial.

● ● ●

Designing a Presentation-Quality Report

After she prints the updated Operating Budget, Ann shows it to Carmen and Travis. They review it to make sure the formulas and all corresponding results are correct, that there aren't any spelling errors, and that all the necessary information is included. Carmen asks Ann to enhance the report's aesthetic appearance before presenting it to the board of directors. She suggests centering the report and the heading, including the date and time, and applying spreadsheet publishing features such as outlines, shading, colors, and graphic objects. Also, she wants specific information printed at the top and bottom of the page with the report centered on the page. Carmen's suggestions for improving the worksheet appear in Figure 2-29.

DESIGNING A PRESENTATION-QUALITY REPORT   ADVEX 97

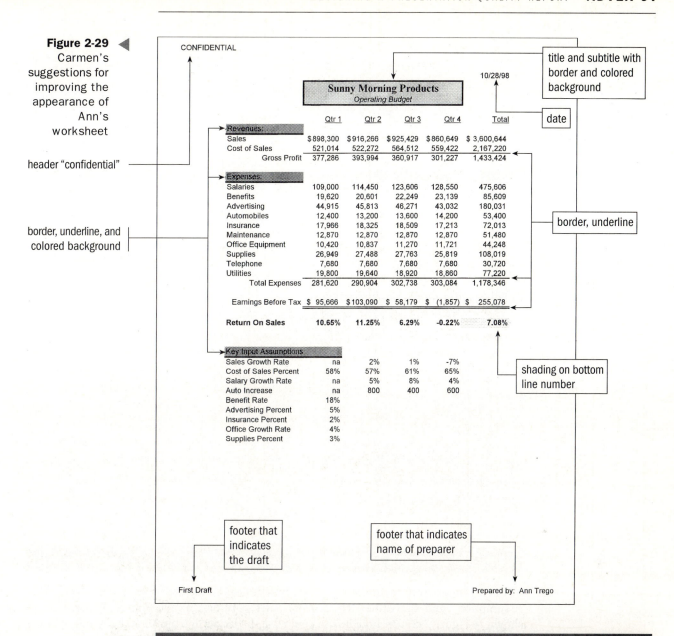

Figure 2-29
Carmen's suggestions for improving the appearance of Ann's worksheet

Including the Date Using the TODAY Function

Carmen wants the date on the report so that when she and Ann revise it they will know which report is the most current. In Excel, you use the TODAY function to obtain the current date from your computer's clock. The date is automatically displayed in the format month/day/year (mm/dd/yy), but you can change this to one of several other date formats. Add the current date to Ann's worksheet using the TODAY function.

To add the current date to a report using the TODAY function:

1. Click **A1**, then insert a row above that row that will contain the date, since the date is displayed above the report title.

2. Click **F1**, which is the desired location for the date, then click the **Function Wizard** button on the Standard toolbar to display the Function Wizard - Step 1 of 2 dialog box.

ADVEX 98 **TUTORIAL 2** DEVELOPING EFFECTIVE WORKSHEETS

---

3. Look for the TODAY function in the Function Name list. If it doesn't appear, then click **Date & Time** in the Function Category list and scroll the Function Name list again and click **TODAY** to select this function.

4. Click the **Finish** button because this function has no arguments for you to enter. The current date appears in its default format.

Aligning Text Headings

Carmen wants the report heading centered over the columns for the four quarters before it is outlined. That is, the report heading is to be **centered across columns** B through E. When Ann initially created the budget worksheet, she placed these text labels in column A. Next, align these text labels so they are centered across the columns.

To center text labels across columns:

1. Select the range **A2:A3**, which contains the report heading, and move that range to B2:B3. When you center text across columns, you place the text to be centered in the leftmost column of the range where it is centered.

2. Select the range **B2:E3** to specify the columns across which you want to center this text.

3. Click the **Center Across Columns** button on the Formatting toolbar to center the text as desired.

   Also, Carmen wants several labels for planning items to be right-aligned.

4. Right-align the planning item names for Gross Profit, Total Expenses, and Earnings Before Tax.

Using Borders and Patterns

Carmen wants Ann to underline the labels for Revenues, Expenses, and Key Input Assumptions and the values for Cost of Sales, Utilities, and Earnings Before Tax, as shown in Figure 2-29. Although Ann could use the Underline button like she did with the column titles, she wants a solid line under the *entire* cell. This is achieved by adding a border to the cell. A **border** is a line that you place on any one or all edges of a cell. For Carmen's desired underlines, she uses a border at the bottom of the cell. Add these borders to Ann's budget worksheet.

To add borders to a cell:

1. Click **A6**, which is the cell with the Revenues text that is to have the border.

2. Click the **Borders** button list arrow on the Formatting toolbar to display the palette of buttons for the most common border arrangements. See Figure 2-30.

Figure 2-30 ◄
Palette of border buttons

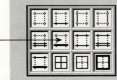

wide single-border selection

DESIGNING A PRESENTATION-QUALITY REPORT **ADVEX 99**

> **TROUBLE?** If you clicked the Borders button itself instead of its list arrow, you placed the current default border on the selected cells. Click the Undo button, then click the Borders button list arrow.
>
> 3. Click the Borders button for the wide single-border selection to apply that border to the selected cell range.
>
> 4. Place the wide single-line border on the Expenses and Key Input Assumptions text labels. For Key Input Assumptions, include the border for the cells in both column A and column B, because this is a *long text label* that spills over into the blank column B.
>
> 5. Select the cell range **B8:F8** and apply the narrow single-line border to it. Then apply the same border to the cell range B21:F21.
>
> 6. Select the cell range **B24:F24** and apply the double-line border to it.
>
>   Next, place a border around the report title.
>
> 7. Select the cell range **B2:E3** and apply a wide outline border to the range. Do not outline each cell in the range, but only place a border at the edges of the selected range, as shown in Ann's finished report in Figure 2-29.

Ann knows that she can draw a reader's attention even closer to important data by applying color or shading to a range of cells. **Shading** is a background pattern that you add to a cell range. Figure 2-31 shows the shading patterns available in Excel.

Figure 2-31
Excel shading patterns

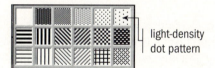 light-density dot pattern

Add shading to the Return On Sales value in the Total column to draw the reader's attention to this bottom-line item in the budget.

> **To shade a cell range:**
>
> 1. Click **F26** to select it, then right-click **F26** to display the Shortcut menu. See Figure 2-32.

Figure 2-32
Shortcut menu for cells

>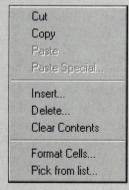
>
> 2. Click **Format Cells** to display the Format Cells dialog box, which contains six setting sheets. See Figure 2-33.

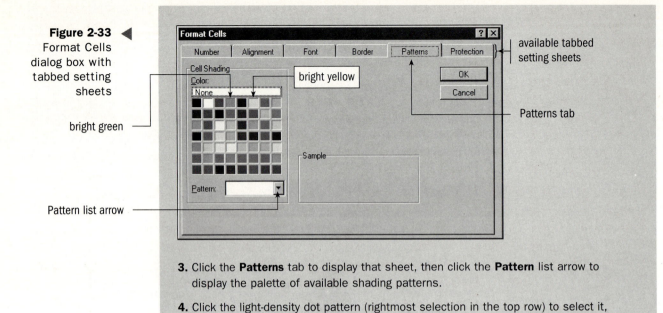

Figure 2-33
Format Cells dialog box with tabbed setting sheets

3. Click the **Patterns** tab to display that sheet, then click the **Pattern** list arrow to display the palette of available shading patterns.

4. Click the light-density dot pattern (rightmost selection in the top row) to select it, then click the **OK** button to apply that pattern to the selected cell range. When applying patterns to data in the worksheet, you need to be careful to choose a pattern that makes the data readable. Sometime this is a trial-and-error process as you experiment with different patterns. The sample box allows you to see how the pattern will look when applied.

Carmen is pleased with the shading pattern. The next enhancement she wants is to color the report title and the text labels for Revenues, Expenses, and Key Input Assumptions. They will appear in color on her computer's display, but will be printed as gray shades on a black-and-white printer.

To add a color background to cells:

1. Select the cell range **B2:E3**, which contains the report title that will have a background color applied to it.

2. Click the **Color** button list arrow on the Formatting toolbar to display the color palette.

3. Click bright yellow (the sixth color from the left in the top row of the palette) to apply that color to the background. Then click any cell outside the B2:E3 cell range, so you can see the color applied to those cells.

4. Select the cells that contain the Revenues, Expenses, and Key Input Assumptions labels, which you placed a border on the bottom of, and give them a bright green background (fourth button from the left in the top row of the color palette).

Ann has the report she wants. Now she is ready to set up her overall page arrangement for printing.

Using Page Setup to Print the Worksheet

Ann can add identifying information to the top and bottom of the page by specifying a header and a footer. A **header** is text that is printed at the top of every page. A **footer** is text that is printed at the bottom of every page. You do not add these enhancements to the cells in the worksheet; you specify this information in a setting sheet of the Page Setup dialog box when you prepare to print the report.

You can also use the Page Setup dialog box to specify the **orientation**—how the worksheet will be printed on a page—as either portrait or landscape. The **portrait** orientation prints the worksheet upright on the page, whereas the **landscape** orientation prints the worksheet sideways on the page. The **scaling** factor in this setting sheet allows you to reduce or enlarge the size of your worksheet for printing. The **center on page option** causes the output to be centered on the page within the margins you specify with the options for the Margins settings. You can also have the worksheet frame and grid lines printed on each page by selecting these options for the Sheet settings. If you want, you can explore these characteristics by selecting them and previewing the worksheet. You need to add a header and footer to Ann's report and then center them horizontally on the printed page.

To include a header and footer:

1. Click **File**, then click **Page Setup** to display the Page Setup dialog box. See Figure 2-34. The setting sheet that appears may be different than the one shown in the figure because Excel automatically displays the last setting sheet that was used with the dialog box.

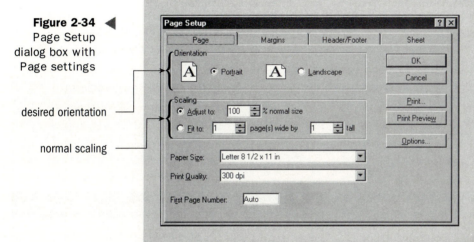

Figure 2-34
Page Setup dialog box with Page settings

desired orientation

normal scaling

2. Click the **Header/Footer** tab to display that setting sheet, which indicates the current default header for the worksheet. Then click the **Header** list arrow and scroll to the top of the list and click **(none)**. The Header list contains recently used headers for your active workbooks and includes several different standard arrangements that depend on your particular computer. If you wanted to use one of these headers, you would just select it.

3. Click the **Custom Header** button to display the Header dialog box. A custom header is required because Ann wants to use one that is not already defined in the Header list.

4. Type **CONFIDENTIAL** in the Left Section text box. The Center Section and Right Section text boxes should be empty. If they are not, delete their contents because you don't want to use these with the header for the budget. See Figure 2-35.

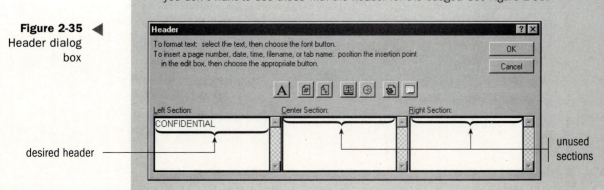

Figure 2-35
Header dialog box

desired header

unused sections

ADVEX 102 **TUTORIAL 2** DEVELOPING EFFECTIVE WORKSHEETS

5. Click the **OK** button to return to the Header/Footer setting sheet.

6. Click the **Custom Footer** button, then enter **First Draft** in the Left Section text box and **Prepared by: Ann Trego** in the Right Section text box for the footer. If an entry appears in the Center Section text box, delete it. Click the **OK** button to complete this specification.

Next, center Ann's report horizontally on the page.

To center a report horizontally on a page:

1. With the Page Setup dialog box still displayed, click the **Margins tab** to display that setting sheet.

2. Click the **Horizontally** check box to select that arrangement for the Center on Page options and verify the choice in the Preview box in the Margins setting sheet.

   Next, verify the page orientation.

3. Click the **Page** tab to display that setting sheet, then click the **Portrait** option button to select it, if necessary.

4. Click the **Print Preview** button to preview the completed report. When you finish your preview, click the **Print** button to display the Print dialog box, then click the **OK** button to actually print this worksheet.

5. Save this as the S_SMP3.xls workbook in the Tut02 folder on your Student Disk.

Using Page Breaks

Ann checks over her Operating Budget report and reviews it with Carmen. For her presentation, Carmen now thinks it would be better to print the Key Input Assumptions on a separate page from the rest of the budget. This will allow her to more easily discuss them individually. Excel uses **page breaks** to divide a worksheet into physical pages for printing. If a worksheet is longer than one printed page, Excel divides it into multiple pages for printing by inserting **automatic page breaks** that are based on the paper size, margin settings, and scaling options in the Page Setup dialog box. You can insert **manual page breaks** anywhere you want in a worksheet to obtain the paging arrangement you desire. A manual page break stays at the location that you set until you remove it. When you set a manual page break, Excel adjusts the automatic page breaks for the rest of the worksheet. Insert a manual page break above the Key Input Assumptions so that they will appear on a separate page.

To insert a manual page break:

1. Click **A29** to select row 29 and column A as the location of the manual page break. A break will be inserted immediately above and to the left of the selected cell. However, because the selected cell is at the left edge of the worksheet, no page break is inserted to the left of cell A29. If you selected cell C29, then columns A and B would be on one page, with column C starting on a new page.

2. Click **Insert**, then click **Page Break** to insert the page break between rows 28 and 29. See Figure 2-36.

Figure 2-36
Manual page break inserted in worksheet for printing

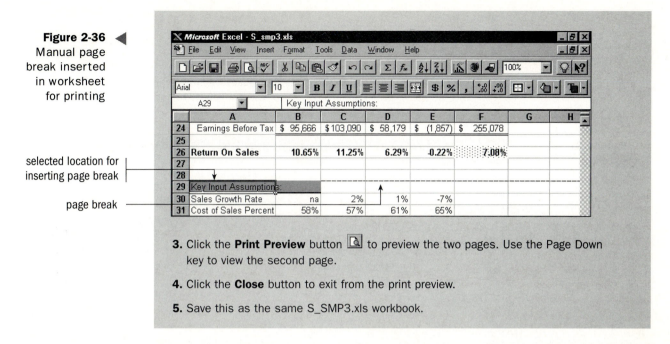

selected location for inserting page break

page break

3. Click the **Print Preview** button to preview the two pages. Use the Page Down key to view the second page.

4. Click the **Close** button to exit from the print preview.

5. Save this as the same S_SMP3.xls workbook.

Once Ann has her report set up, she could save this as a view using the **View Manager**, which allows you to look at the same worksheet displayed with different page setup settings and worksheet options. Then she could easily switch among her various views. However, for now, she decides that her current worksheet options are all that she needs.

HELP DESK

EXCEL 5.0

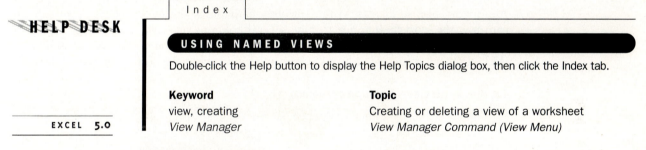

Index

USING NAMED VIEWS

Double-click the Help button to display the Help Topics dialog box, then click the Index tab.

Keyword	Topic
view, creating	Creating or deleting a view of a worksheet
View Manager	View Manager Command (View Menu)

Hiding Data

Travis asks Ann to prepare a special version of their report for his review with Matt and Kim, the senior executives of Sunny Morning Products. He wants a report that displays only the Qtr 1 and Total columns. The other three quarters are still calculated, but he doesn't want them displayed as a means of focusing their discussion on only the first quarter and the total for the year. You **hide** data to make an entire column, row, or worksheet disappear from the worksheet display. When data is hidden, the attention of the worksheet users is focused only on what you want them to see and not on distracting or confidential data. Formulas that refer to hidden data continue to work correctly. A hidden column, row, or worksheet can be redisplayed at any time, unless the worksheet is protected after the data is hidden. (Protecting a worksheet will be covered later in the tutorial.) Then the worksheet protection needs to be turned off before the hidden data can be redisplayed. Hide the columns for Qtr 2, Qtr 3, and Qtr 4 in Ann's worksheet to produce the special version of the report that Travis wants.

ADVEX 104   TUTORIAL 2   DEVELOPING EFFECTIVE WORKSHEETS

To hide columns:

1. Move the pointer to the line that separates column E from column F in the worksheet frame. The pointer changes to ↔.

2. Click and drag the pointer left to the line between columns B and C. As you drag the pointer, the columns disappear and they remain hidden when you release the mouse button. See Figure 2-37.

Figure 2-37 ◂
Hiding columns C, D, and E

columns C, D, and E hidden

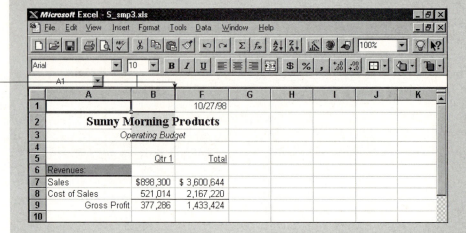

3. Select and print the BUDGET range to produce the special report for Travis.

With the special report printed, you can **unhide**, or redisplay, columns C, D, and E in Ann's worksheet so they are visible for other activities with the worksheet. Although you can drag the worksheet frame to hide several columns or rows at one time, when you unhide them using the mouse pointer, you need to do each column individually. Redisplay the columns in Ann's worksheet so she can continue working on the complete budget.

To unhide previously hidden columns:

1. Move the pointer to the right of the line that separates column B from column F in the worksheet frame. The pointer changes to ↔. Notice that this pointer is different from the pointer used to hide columns or to change their width.

2. Click and drag the pointer to the right until column E is displayed and its width matches that of column B.

3. Repeat Steps 1 and 2 to unhide the other two columns.

All the columns in Ann's worksheet are displayed. Now she is ready to add the second section that Carmen requested to the workbook, the Summary section. She decides to create this section in a separate worksheet.

Using Multiple Sheets

As mentioned previously, an Excel workbook can have up to 255 worksheets. So far Ann has only used one worksheet for the Sunny Morning Products Operating Budget. One use of another worksheet is for the Summary section of a workbook. After discussing the summary with Carmen and Travis, Ann decides to display these six critical planning items in her summary report—Sales, Cost of Sales, Gross Profit, Total Expenses, Earnings Before Tax, and Return On Sales. When Ann's summary is complete, it appears as shown in Figure 2-38.

Figure 2-38
Summary worksheet for the Operating Budget

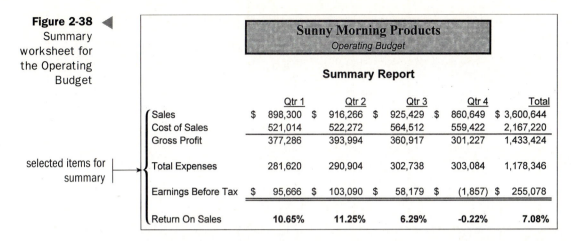

selected items for summary

Except for the report title and column headings, Ann wants all the information in the Summary sheet to be displayed by referencing its corresponding cell in Sheet1, which contains her budget. That way if she changes any planning item names or formulas in Sheet1, the correct results will automatically be displayed in Sheet2, which contains her summary. Referencing values for the summary in this manner reduces the chances of displaying different values for the same planning items. Your first step is to set up Sheet2 with appropriate column widths, the report title, and the column title.

To set up a Summary sheet:

1. Click the **Sheet2 worksheet** tab to display that worksheet and note that the column widths are set to the Excel default. Set column A to a width of 18 and each of the columns B through F to a width of 11. When you know the column widths you want to use, you can establish them as your first step in creating a worksheet, so the labels are not cut off. Then if they are still not appropriate, you can adjust them later.

2. Click the **Sheet1 worksheet** tab, select the range **B2:F5**, which contains the report title and column headings, then click the **Copy** button on the Standard toolbar to copy it to the clipboard.

3. Click the **Sheet2 worksheet** tab, click **B4** to specify the upper-left corner of the destination range, then click the **Paste** button on the Standard toolbar.

4. Enter **Summary Report** in cell B5. Change the point size to 12 and boldface this identifying text.

Next, include the formulas that reference the text labels and the calculated data values in Sheet1 in Ann's summary report. Create these formulas using pointing.

To create formulas that just reference values in other cells contained in other sheets in the workbook:

1. Make sure Sheet 2 is still displayed, click **A8**, then type **=** to begin entering the formula.

2. Click the **Sheet1** worksheet tab, click **A7** to place that cell reference in the formula, then press the **Enter** key to finish specifying the formula. Sales appears at the desired location in Sheet2. The formula you want in Sheet2 merely references a single cell in Sheet1.

3. In Sheet2, copy the formula from A8 to the range **A9:A10**. Then copy the formulas from the range A8:A10 to the range **B8:F10**. Because these cells are all located together in Sheet1, the relative references are changed appropriately in Sheet2 when you complete this copy. However, you can't copy the formulas for the other three planning items included in the summary report with this one copy activity because their formulas are from a different relative location in Sheet1. So you need to set up the other summary formulas separately.

4. Click **A12**, which is the location for the next planning item name in Ann's summary report, then type **=** to begin entering the formula.

5. Click the **Sheet1 worksheet** tab, click **A22** to place that cell name in the formula, then press the **Enter** key to finish specifying the formula.

6. Copy the formula from cell A12 to the range **A13:A16**, then delete the unwanted formulas from A13 and A15. Now copy the formulas from the range A12:A16 to the range **B12:F16**.

   Next, change the formats to match those in Sheet1.

7. Click the **Sheet1 worksheet** tab, click cell **B7**, which contains the desired format, click the **Format Painter** button on the Standard toolbar, click the **Sheet2 worksheet** tab, then click and drag the format mouse pointer over the range B8:F8 to apply the selected format to that range.

8. Apply the format from each of the corresponding planning items in Sheet1 to those in Sheet2.

9. Inspect the cells that contain the planning item names and data values displayed in Sheet2 to confirm that they all reference their corresponding cells in Sheet1. With this arrangement, any changes to the values in Sheet1 are *automatically* displayed in Sheet2.

Ann thinks that "Sheet1" and "Sheet2" are not very descriptive names for her worksheets. She wants to change these to more descriptive names that indicate the content of the worksheet. Change Ann's sheets to the more meaningful names "Budget" and "Summary."

To change a worksheet name:

1. Double-click the **Sheet1 worksheet** tab to open the Rename Sheet dialog box. See Figure 2-39.

Figure 2-39 ◀
Rename Sheet dialog box for changing worksheet tab name

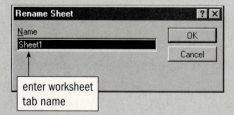

2. Type **Budget** and click the **OK** button to finish changing the tab name.

3. Double-click the **Sheet2 worksheet** tab, type **Summary**, then click the **OK** button to rename that worksheet.

4. Inspect the cell formulas in the Summary sheet and notice that the sheet name is changed to match the name you specified for the worksheet tab.

5. Save this as the same S_SMP3.xls workbook.

USING MULTIPLE SHEETS   **ADVEX 107**

When you plan your workbook, if you know you will be using several different worksheets, you may want to immediately give them more meaningful names. This is useful in helping you identify how the worksheets are being used as you enter text labels and formulas. However, as you can see from these steps, Excel permits you to change the name of a worksheet whenever you have the need.

CHANGING A SHEET NAME

- Double-click the tab of the worksheet whose name you want to change.
- Type a name of up to 31 characters.
- Click the OK button or press the Enter key to finish specifying the tab name.

The final section to be added to Ann's workbook, the Documentation section, can also be added as a separate worksheet. Placing this information in a separate worksheet makes it easier to access and review. Ann wants to include the documentation shown in Figure 2-40.

Figure 2-40 ◄
Operating Budget workbook documentation

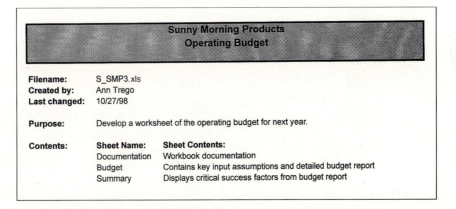

Add a separate sheet that contains her documentation to Ann's workbook.

To create a Documentation worksheet:

1. Click the **Sheet3** worksheet tab to make it the active worksheet.

2. Set columns A and B to a width of 14 and columns C through H to a width of 9, because they work well and you won't need to be concerned with truncating the display of any text labels. When you create your own Documentation sheet you may want to use different column widths, but these work well for Ann's workbook.

3. Enter the text from Figure 2-40 as the documentation and apply boldface as shown in the figure. Center the title across columns A through G. Change the point size of the title to 12. Place a border around A1:H3 and give this range a bright yellow background.

4. Change the name of the worksheet to **Documentation**.

Ann prefers to have the Documentation sheet as the first sheet in her workbook, because this makes it easier to reference when the workbook is initially opened. She wants to move the worksheet so it appears first in her workbook.

To move a worksheet within a workbook:

1. Point to the **Documentation worksheet** tab.

2. Click and drag the worksheet tab to the left until it is at the leftmost position. The pointer changes to ▧ while you drag the worksheet tab. The worksheet is relocated. See Figure 2-41.

Figure 2-41
Worksheet relocated within the workbook

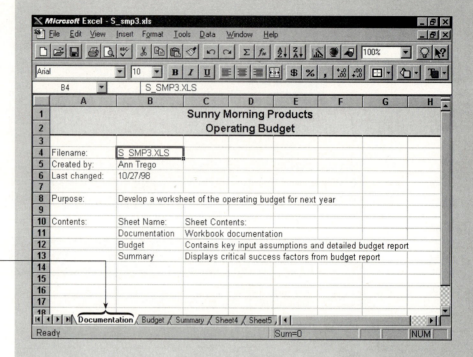

worksheet moved to desired location

3. Save this as the same S_SMP3.xls workbook.

REFERENCE window

MOVING A WORKSHEET WITHIN A WORKBOOK

- Point to the worksheet's tab.
- Click and drag the worksheet tab from its initial position to the desired destination. The pointer changes to ▧ while you drag the worksheet tab.

In addition to creating a Documentation worksheet like Ann's, Excel lets you include information about the workbook that is stored in its file, but does not appear in any of the worksheets. You use a Properties dialog box, accessed from the File menu, to input and view this information.

HELP DESK

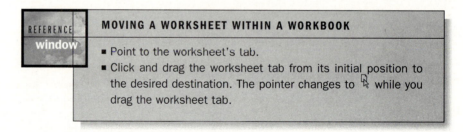

Index

USING WORKBOOK PROPERTIES

Double-click the Help button to display the Help Topics dialog box, then click the Index tab.

Keyword	Topic
properties (document properties), setting	Set file properties
Summary Info command (File menu)	*Summary Info Command (File menu)*

EXCEL 5.0

Ann is pleased with her worksheet and its documentation. However, she wants to place comment notes in her Budget worksheet that point out several critical numbers. She can do this best with graphics.

Using Graphic Objects

Ann suggests to Carmen and Travis that they should add notes to the worksheet that point out two of the key results of special interest to the board of directors. She can do this by adding graphic objects, such as lines, arrows, shapes, and text blocks, to enhance the worksheet report. Figure 2-42 shows a variety of graphic objects. However, you need to position these graphics objects carefully to avoid covering important information. Graphic objects are *placed on top* of the worksheet, which means they can sometimes cover important information unless they are carefully positioned in the worksheet.

Figure 2-42 ◀
Common graphic objects

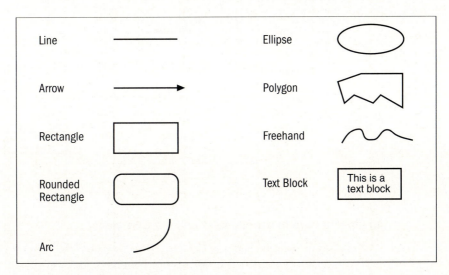

Ann needs to include the graphic object for the Return On Sales comment, as shown in her completed report in Figure 2-43. These objects include an arrow, a rectangle, and a text box. A text box is like a note you stick on a page to add comments or emphasize important information. When you add a note using a text box, the text is automatically surrounded by a box, which serves as a frame. You can remove this frame or change its attributes.

Figure 2-43
Ann's budget with graphic objects for emphasis

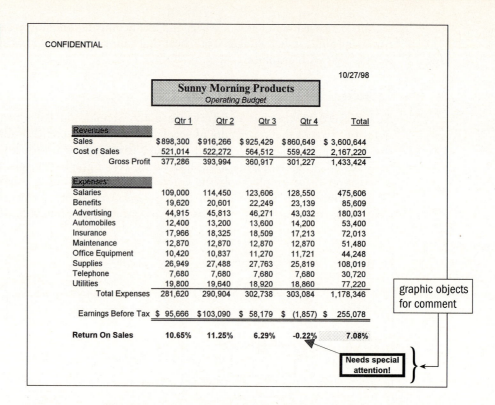

Add the note "Needs special attention!" as a text block:

To place a note in a worksheet using a text block:

1. Select the Budget worksheet and scroll it so that the cell range B22:G32 is displayed. Then click the **Drawing** button on the Standard toolbar to display the Drawing tool bar. See Figure 2-44.

Figure 2-44
Drawing toolbar as dialog box

floating Drawing toolbar

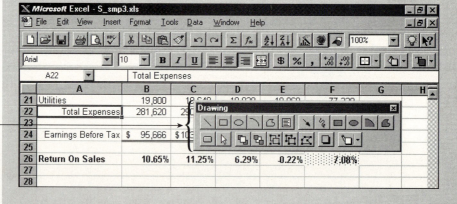

2. Insert two rows above row 28 so there is ample space for the notes on this printed page.

3. Click the **Text Box** button . The pointer changes to ✛ to indicate that you can specify the location and size of the text box.

4. Point to the middle of cell F28 and click and drag the pointer to the middle of cell G30. When you release the mouse button, the outline of the text box appears.

USING GRAPHIC OBJECTS **ADVEX 111**

5. Type **Needs special attention!**, which is the desired text. Then click the **Center** button on the Formatting toolbar to finished entering and centering the text. Don't worry if you can't see all of the text; the text box can easily be resized. If you didn't want to change the alignment of the text, you could just click anywhere in the worksheet outside the text box to finish entering the text.

6. Click the edge of the text box to select it. A heavy dashed line surrounds the object and handles appear on its border. You use these handles to resize the object by dragging a handle in the desired direction to increase or decrease the object's size.

7. Click the **Bold** button on the Formatting toolbar to boldface the text in the text box.

   TROUBLE? If the text is too big to fit in the text box when you apply the bold-face, then drag the handle in the middle of the right side of the text box to the right to increase its size and display all the text.

8. Right-click the text box to display the Shortcut menu for graphic objects, then click **Format Object** to display the Format Object dialog box.

9. Click the **Patterns** tab, click the **Weight** list arrow, click the widest weight at the bottom of the list, click the **Color** list arrow in the Border options, click red (third button from the left in the top row), then click the **OK** button to apply this line width and color to the outline border of the text box.

10. Click **Needs special attention!** in the text box to display the edit cursor I, click and drag the edit cursor to select all the text in the text box, click the text **Font Color** button list arrow in the Formatting toolbar to display the font color settings, then click red (third button from the left in the top row). Click anywhere in the worksheet outside the text box to unselect it so you can see the border and text.

Next, Ann wants an arrow that points from the text box to the value for Return On Sales in Qtr 4. An arrow is a separate graphic object. Place the arrow in Ann's worksheet.

To add an arrow object to a worksheet:

1. Click the **Arrow** button on the Drawing toolbar to change the pointer to **+** for specifying the location of the arrow.

2. Point to the upper-left corner of the border that surrounds the text box.

3. Click and drag the pointer to the value for Return On Sales in Qtr 4, as shown previously in Ann's printed report. As you drag the pointer, Excel displays a dotted line to indicate the location of the arrow. When you release the mouse button, the arrow appears. See Figure 2-45. Note that Excel assigns the default name "Line 2" to this drawn object, as shown in the Name box.

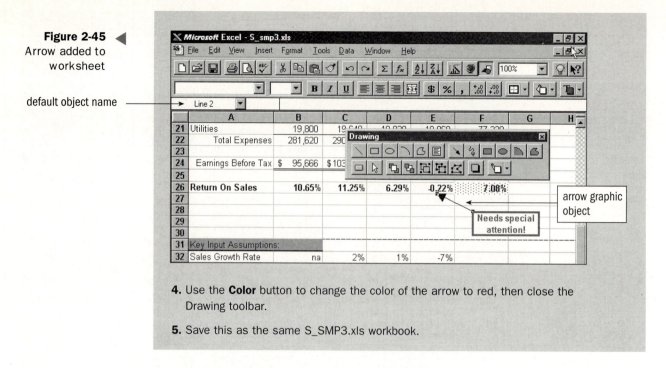

Figure 2-45
Arrow added to worksheet

default object name

4. Use the **Color** button to change the color of the arrow to red, then close the Drawing toolbar.

5. Save this as the same S_SMP3.xls workbook.

Protecting the Worksheet

Ann realizes that when she and Carmen explore different what-if alternatives, they are going to be changing values in various cells, and she doesn't want any of her formulas to be inadvertently deleted. She decides to protect the worksheet so that only the cells with the key input assumptions can be changed.

When you **protect** a worksheet, data in it cannot be changed except in the cell ranges you specifically *unlock* before protection is turned on. Once a worksheet is protected, you cannot insert or delete rows or columns, and you can't change cell formats or attributes, column widths, row heights, or graphic objects. Only the data values or text labels in the unlocked cells can be changed.

Using protection is a two-step process. First you need to identify the cells that are *not* to be locked or protected, then you turn on protection for the worksheet. Protect Ann's worksheet so only the key input assumption values can be changed.

To specify unlocked or unprotected cells:

1. Make sure the Budget sheet is displayed, select the cell range **B32:E35**, then press and hold down the **Ctrl** key while you select the cell range **B36:B40**. This use of the Ctrl key allows you to select several nonadjacent cell ranges at one time.

2. Right-click the selected range to display the Shortcut menu, then click **Format Cells** to display the Format Cells dialog box.

3. Click the **Protection** tab, click the **Locked** check box to deselect it, then click the **OK** button to finish specifying the cells you want to remain unlocked.

    Now you can turn on the worksheet protection.

4. Click **Tools**, point to **Protection**, then click **Protect Sheet** to display the Protect Sheet dialog box, where you have the option of entering a password for protecting the worksheet.

5. Click the **OK** button to turn on protection without using a password. When you protect your own worksheets you may want to use a password to prevent someone else from turning off protection, but that is not necessary for Ann's budget.

Figure 2-46
Locked cells message box

6. Click cell **C12**, then type **117000**. The locked cells message box appears. See Figure 2-46. Click the **OK** button to close this message box.

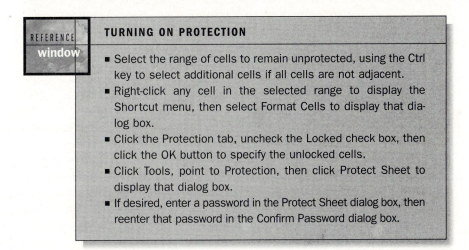

7. Click cell **B37** for Advertising Percent and enter **6%** as a new data value. The value is accepted because this cell is unlocked. Return On Sales is now 6.08%.

8. Click the **Undo** button on the Standard toolbar to remove this what-if value and redisplay the previous results.

> **REFERENCE window**
>
> **TURNING ON PROTECTION**
>
> - Select the range of cells to remain unprotected, using the Ctrl key to select additional cells if all cells are not adjacent.
> - Right-click any cell in the selected range to display the Shortcut menu, then select Format Cells to display that dialog box.
> - Click the Protection tab, uncheck the Locked check box, then click the OK button to specify the unlocked cells.
> - Click Tools, point to Protection, then click Protect Sheet to display that dialog box.
> - If desired, enter a password in the Protect Sheet dialog box, then reenter that password in the Confirm Password dialog box.

You will need to make some additional modifications to Ann's worksheet in the next tutorial. In order to make any changes except to the unlocked cells, you need to turn the protection off.

To turn off protection:

1. Click **Tools**, point to **Protection**, then click **Unprotect Sheet**. If you had password-protected the worksheet, the Unprotect Sheet dialog box would display so you could enter the password.

2. Save this as the S_SMP3.xls workbook in the Tut02 folder.

3. Close the workbook and exit Excel.

   Now Ann can continue to modify and improve her budget workbook in the next tutorial.

> **TURNING OFF PROTECTION**
>
> - Click Tools, point to Protection, then click Unprotect Sheet to display that dialog box.
> - If necessary, enter the password in the Unprotect Sheet dialog box.

Ann has completed her development of a professional workbook for the Sunny Morning Products Operating Budget for next year. The budget worksheet meets the requirements of Carmen and Travis. It contains the information they need and its design is attractive and well-organized. They are confident that the workbook will help them create a better business plan for their company.

Tutorial Exercises

For these exercises launch Excel, if necessary, and insert your Student Disk into the disk drive. Open E_RMC1.xls in the Tut02 folder or directory and save the file immediately as S_RMC1.xls. This workbook contains the partially completed projected income statement for next year for Riverwood Medical Center (RMC). Carrie Grant, an accounting intern in the hospital administrator's office, is responsible for completing this projection for tomorrow's planning meeting. Review her partially completed workbook and do the following:

1. Read through all the questions for this exercise and develop a planning analysis sheet in preparation for modifying the workbook. Use your planning analysis sheet to guide the development of your Excel solution.
2. Complete the series of column titles for the four quarters of the year in row 5.
3. A "Patient day" represents one patient in the hospital for one day. For example, ten patients in the hospital for ten days amounts to 100 patient days. Patient days are expected to remain constant each quarter. Using the pointing method, enter a formula that places patient days from the first quarter into the second quarter.
4. The revenue per patient day is expected to increase by $20 per quarter. Include a Key Input Assumptions section that contains this increase per quarter and all other assumptions for this plan. Use pointing to enter the formula that calculates the revenue per patient day for the second quarter.
5. The professional revenue is expected to grow by 7% per quarter. Using the pointing method, enter the formula that calculates the professional revenue for the second quarter.
6. The formulas that calculate In-patient revenue, Total revenue, Staff expense, Other expense, Total expense, and Gross profit are

   In-patient revenue = Patient days * Revenue per patient day
   Total revenue = In-patient revenue + Professional revenue
   Staff expense = In-patient revenue * In-patient ratio +
        Professional revenue * Professional ratio
   Other expense = Total revenue * Other expense ratio
   Total expense = Staff expense + Other expense
   Gross profit = Total revenue − Total expense

   where

   In-patient ratio = .73
   Professional ratio = .81
   Other expense ratio = .17

   Use pointing to enter these formulas for the first quarter and include the ROUND function in calculating each expense that uses a ratio. Why is it a good idea to use rounding for these expense calculations?

TUTORIAL EXCERCISES **ADVEX 115**

7. Copy the formulas for Patient days, Revenue per patient day, and Professional revenue from the second quarter to the other two quarters. Then copy the formulas for In-patient revenue, Total revenue, Staff expense, Other expense, Total expense, and Gross profit from the first quarter to the other three quarters.

8. Place a formula in the Total column that sums each of the planning items except the revenue per patient day. (*Hint*: If the total gross profit is $1,241,623, you have entered the formulas correctly.)

9. Enter a formula that calculates the average Revenue per patient day in the Total column. You want the average instead of the sum of the data for four quarters because summing the revenue per patient day has little meaning and a different revenue per patient day occurs each quarter. The average is calculated by dividing the total in-patient revenue by the total patient days. (*Hint*: If the average total revenue per patient day equals $410, you have entered the formula correctly.)

10. Format the planning item data values in the Comma format with no decimal places, except for In-patient revenue and Gross profit, which are formatted as currency with no decimals.

11. Use a border to underline each row *above* the patient days, total revenue, total expense, and gross profit amounts.

12. Apply shading to the Gross profit value in the Total column. Select a pattern so that the value is readable.

13. Insert a row above the report title. Use a function to place the current date in cell F1.

14. Surround the report title with a wide border. Color the background of your report title. Select a color that you feel is appropriate.

15. Apply shading, patterns, and colors to at least three other areas of your worksheet. Preview and print this Projected Income report. Write a short paragraph indicating why you selected these areas and the attributes you applied.

16. Protect the entire worksheet, other than the data values for the key input assumptions. Save this as the S_RMC1.xls workbook in the Tut02 folder. Test the protected worksheet. Write a short paragraph describing your test of this protection.

17. What if the number of patient days in the first quarter increases to 7218 while the revenue per patient day goes up to $454? What is the total gross profit? Use a graphic object to draw an ellipse around the total gross profit amount. Include a note as a graphic object in the worksheet that indicates whether this is a significant change in gross profit. (*Hint:* If necessary, turn off worksheet protection to change number of patient days.) Preview and print a copy of this what-if analysis. Write a short paragraph explaining your comment.

18. Create a summary on a separate sheet. Use the same report heading on this sheet. Include only these planning items in your summary—Patient days, Total revenue, Total expense, and Gross profit. Apply appropriate formats to the planning items. Name this the Summary sheet. Preview and print this sheet. Save it as the S_RMC1.xls workbook in the Tut02 folder.

19. Document the workbook using a separate sheet that appears as the first sheet in the workbook. Create the documentation following the example shown in Figure 2-40. Name it the Documentation sheet. Preview and print it. Save it as the S_RMC1.xls workbook.

Case Problems

1. Budget Variance Analysis for Safety-Lite Industries Safety-Lite Industries (SLI) is a leading manufacturer of automotive sealed-beam head lamps, tail-lamp assemblies, and related plastic molded parts. One of SLI's products is the rear deck stop and turn signal for the Ford Escort.

Jeff Walker, vice president of marketing for SLI, is concerned with monitoring SLI's marketing expenses. He received a worksheet from SLI's Accounting Department that contains the budget and actual expenses for last year. The Accounting Department prepared the special worksheet by extracting the data from its general ledger system and creating the Excel worksheet file. Jeff wants a variance analysis included as part of the expense report to determine which accounts require further investigation. A **variance analysis** is the difference between the estimated budget costs and the recorded actual costs. He asks Bridget Sheehan, a newly hired marketing analyst in his department, to prepare the variance report from the worksheet received from the Accounting Department. Bridget is familiar with using Excel to prepare special reports like the one Jeff wants. She discusses the details of the report with Jeff. For each account he wants to see the variance as a dollar amount and as a percent of budget. These are calculated as follows:

Variance = Budget – Actual

Variance Percent = Variance/Budget

Your task is to complete the variance report for Jeff using the formulas specified by Bridget.

1. Launch Excel and open P_SLI1.xls in the Tut02 folder or directory and immediately save it as S_SLI1.xls. This workbook contains the data obtained from the Accounting Department. Review the content and arrangement of data in this worksheet.
2. Read through all the questions for this case problem and develop a planning analysis sheet to guide the development of your Excel solution.
3. Use pointing to enter the formulas to calculate the variance and percent variance for the first expense in the worksheet, which is located in row 9. Remember that since the variance is a calculated ratio, you do not need to use rounding in its calculation.
4. Copy these formulas *down* the rows for each of the other expense items, including the Total Marketing Expenses. Any rows that do not contain an expense item should not include a formula. If you happen to copy formulas to these rows, delete the unwanted formulas.
5. Use the SUM function and pointing to enter formulas for each of the expense category totals of Total Salaries, Total Other Expenses, and Total Taxes. Enter these formulas in the Budget column and then copy them into the Actual and Variance columns.
6. Use pointing to enter the formula for Total Marketing Expenses, which is the sum of the Total Salaries, Total Other Expenses, and Total Taxes. Why can't you use the SUM function with a cell range for this calculation?
7. Format the Budget, Actual, and Variance columns in the Comma format with no decimals.
8. Format the first expense item and Total Marketing Expenses in the Currency format with no decimal places in the Budget, Actual, and Variance columns. Now the currency symbol appears that Jeff requested.
9. Format the Variance Percent column as percent with one decimal place for all expense items.
10. Place an underline in the row between Total Taxes and Total Marketing Expenses.

11. Add a row above the report titles; then place the date from the computer's clock in the upper-right corner of the report. Select a format that displays only the month and day.
12. Add a shading pattern of your choice to Total Marketing Expenses in the Variance and Percent Variance columns.
13. Enhance the appearance of report title by surrounding it with a border and applying an appropriate background color.
14. Consider other aesthetic enhancement features to further improve the appearance of the report. Apply at least three enhancements of your choice to the worksheet. Write a short paragraph and explain why you selected these enhancements.
15. Using the planning item names and the column titles, create range names for the worksheet cells that display numeric data values. Apply these range names to the worksheet formulas.
16. Protect all the cells in the worksheet except those that contain the numeric data values. That is, all the text labels and formulas are protected from change. Test this protection of your worksheet and write a short paragraph that describes your test of this protection.
17. Select at least three other cells and change their attributes to draw the reader's attention to these items. Use a border and shading pattern for at least one cell. (*Hint:* If necessary, turn off worksheet protection to change desired cells.)
18. Create an appropriate header and footer for this report. Include your name somewhere in the footer as the preparer and use at least one of the buttons in the Footer dialog box to insert this feature into your footer.
19. Create a summary on a separate sheet. Use the same report heading on it as on the initial worksheet. Include only Total Salaries, Total Other Expenses, Total Taxes, and Total Marketing Expenses in this summary. Give this sheet the name Summary. Preview and print this worksheet. Save it as the S_SLI1.xls workbook in the Tut02 folder.
20. Document the workbook, using a separate sheet that appears as the first sheet in the workbook. Create the documentation following the example provided in this tutorial. Name this the Documentation sheet. Preview and print this sheet. Save it as the S_SLI1.xls workbook in the Tut02 folder.
21. Mary Lou from the Accounting Department just phoned to advise you of an adjustment in the actual amount of Advertising and Promotion. This value should be 81932. Perform a what-if by changing this value. Print the revised worksheet. Were all the cells affected by the adjusted Advertising and Promotion expense? What effect does this change have on the Marketing Expense Variance and Variance Percent?
22. Review the variance report. Which three accounts have the largest variance and which have the largest percent variance? Use graphics objects to circle these six values in the worksheet.

2. Capacity Planning for Mobile One Products Mobile One Products (MOP) manufactures technologically enhanced wheelchairs for the mobility-impaired. MOP manufactures three different models that are ergonomically designed to provide the best mobility and comfort:

- Generalwheels — a basic utility model designed for all-around use
- Execuwheels — a luxury model designed for office use
- Sportswheels — a lightweight, stripped-down model designed for road-race competition

MOP produces all three models in a manufacturing plant that is designed to accommodate the needs of the physically challenged workers the company employs.

ADVEX 118 **TUTORIAL 2** DEVELOPING EFFECTIVE WORKSHEETS

MOP is experiencing explosive growth as the number of orders increases each quarter. Melissa Pei, manager of Manufacturing Operations, is concerned with MOP's ability to handle the increasing number of orders. She is responsible for organizing the company's operations into two manufacturing cells—fabrication and assembly. A manufacturing cell consists of a work team that turns out complete production units. The fabrication cell does plastic molding and metal shaping, and the assembly cell does the final assembly of each chair. Melissa needs to know when the design capacity of the current manufacturing cells will be exceeded so she can plan to upgrade their production equipment.

Gary Shibata just completed his first year with MOP as an intern in the Human Resources Department, where he gained experience with Excel, and accepted the job assignment as a production planner. While working with Melissa, Gary made notes on the definitions of their planning items (Figure 2-47). Then he sketched their manufacturing capacity planning worksheet (Figure 2-48). In Figure 2-48, columns E, F, G, and H are calculated using formulas that do the same arithmetic as those for columns C, D, and I.

Figure 2-47 ◄

Assoc hours per month — 8 hours per day, 22 days per month, 25% allowance for personal time.

Standard hours per order — the usual number of hours to complete the production operations in the manufacturing work cell.

Design capacity — the number of orders the manufacturing work cell is designed to produce under normal circumstances.

Capacity used — the current number of orders produced by the manufacturing work cell.

Capacity cushion — the unused capacity of the manufacturing work cell, calculated as the difference between the design capacity and the capacity used.

Capacity utilization — a measure of the extent to which the capacity is actually used, calculated by dividing the capacity used by the design capacity.

Associates — the number of employees needed to staff the manufacturing work cell with monthly hours converted to the number of hours per employee per quarter.

Figure 2-48 ◄

	A	B	C	D	I	J
4	ASSUMPTIONS					
5	Order growth rate	0.06	B5	C5	H5	
6	Assoc hours per month	8*22*0.75	B6	C6	H6	
7						
8	PROJECTIONS		Year 1			
9		Qtr 1	Qtr 2	Qtr 3	Qtr 4	Total
10						
11	Number of orders	1800	B11*(1+C5)	C11*(1+D5)	H11*(1+I5)	SUM(B11..I11)
12						
13	Fabrication (Mfg cell 1)					
14	Standard hours per order	3.5	B14	C14	H14	
15	Design capacity	2100	2100	2100	2100	
16	Capacity used	B11	C11	D11	I11	
17	Capacity cushion	B15-B16	C15-C16	D15-D16	I15-I16	
18	Capacity utilization	B16/B15	C16/C15	D16/D15	I16/I15	
19	Associates	B16/(B6*3/B14)	C16/(C6*3/C14)	D16/(D6*3/D14)	I16/(I6*3/I14)	I19
20						
21	Assembly (Mfg cell 2)					
22	Standard hours per order	1.2	B22	C22	H22	
23	Design capacity	2500	2500	2500	2500	
24	Capacity used	B11	C11	D11	I11	
25	Capacity cushion	B23-B24	C23-C24	D23-D24	I23-I24	
26	Capacity utilization	B24/B23	C24/C23	D24/D23	I24/I23	
27	Associates	B24/(B6*3/B22)	C24/(C6*3/C22)	D24/(D6*3/D22)	I24/(I6*3/I22)	I27
28						
29	Total Associates	B19+B27	C19+C27	D19+D27	I19+I27	I29
30						

With Melissa's approval, Gary started creating the P_MOP1.xls worksheet, which is arranged with separate areas for Assumptions and Projections. Gary entered the labels and data values for the eight-quarter plan. Your task is to complete the capacity planning worksheet for Melissa.

1. Access Excel and open P_MOP1.xls in the Tut02 folder or directory and immediately save it as S_MOP1.xls. This workbook contains the Manufacturing Capacity Plan. Review the content and organization of the data in this worksheet.

2. Read through all the questions for this case problem and prepare a planning analysis sheet for revising this workbook. Use your planning analysis sheet to make the revisions of your Excel solution.

3. Plan the work you need to do. On a piece of paper, list the cell addresses of the formulas you will enter by pointing. Then list the cell addresses of the formulas you will place in the worksheet by copying.

4. Complete the series of column titles for the eight quarters in row 9. What titles appear for the second year?

5. Use pointing to enter the formulas you listed in Task 3.

6. Copy the formulas listed in Task 3 into the appropriate cells. (*Hint*: Total Associates for the Total column is 32.123.)

7. Enter the SUM function in the Total column for the number of orders.

8. Use the ROUND function with no decimals in calculating the number of orders using the order growth rate. Use the ROUNDUP function with no decimals to calculate the associates for each manufacturing cell, because a person is either employed or not. The ROUNDUP function has the same arguments as the ROUND function. If you want to know more about the ROUNDUP function, use the Excel Help feature. With this rounding, Total Associates for the Total column is 33.

9. Format the planning item data values in the Comma style with no decimals, except for Order Growth Rate and Capacity Utilization, which are formatted as percent with no decimals.

10. When Gary started his worksheet, he placed his key input assumptions at the top of his sheet. Now that he considers his reporting requirements, he thinks it would be best to move these assumptions below Total Associates. Move the assumptions, including their subheading, and then remove the resulting blank rows from the worksheet.

11. Add a manual page break so that the assumptions are printed on a separate page.

12. Place the following title and subtitle at the top of the worksheet in column A:

    Mobile One Products
    Manufacturing Capacity Plan

    After entering these titles, specify their alignment as centered across columns A through J. Enhance the appearance of the report title by using the attributes and fonts you think give the report a professional appearance.

13. At the top of the report, in a separate line above the title, add the date from the computer's clock, then select a month and date format.

14. Select at least three other cells and change their attributes to draw the reader's attention to these items. Use a border and shading pattern for at least one cell.

15. Underline each column title, using underlining within the cells.

16. Assign the range name PRODUCTION to the area of the worksheet that contains that data, then assign the range name ASSUMPTIONS to the area that contains the assumptions data.

17. Include an appropriate header and footer in the report. Center the report on the page. Preview and print this Manufacturing Capacity Plan report by using the PRODUCTION range. Save this as the S_MOP1.xls workbook in the Tut02 folder.
18. Review the results and write out the answers to these questions.
    a. Is additional production capacity required?
    b. How do you know that additional capacity is needed?
    c. In which manufacturing cell is additional capacity needed? When will it be needed?
    Then add graphic objects that circle Capacity Cushion and Capacity Utilization in the quarter in which additional capacity is required. Add appropriate notes with arrows that point to the circled values. Preview and print this report.
19. Create a summary in a separate sheet. Use the same report heading as in the initial worksheet. Include only Number of orders, Fabrication Capacity Utilization, Fabrication Associates, Assembly Capacity Utilization, Assembly Associates, and Total Associates. Format the sheet as necessary. Rename this the Summary sheet, and name Sheet1 the Plan sheet. Preview and print this worksheet.
20. Document the workbook, using a separate sheet that appears as the first sheet in the workbook. Use the documentation sheet in this tutorial as an example for the sheet. Name it Documentation. Preview and print it. Save it as the S_MOP1.xls workbook.
21. Hide the columns for Year 2 in the Plan sheet. Preview and print this report with the Year 1 and Total columns. After printing this special report, redisplay the columns for Year 2 before continuing with the next question.
22. Protect all the cells in the worksheet except those that contain the numeric data values. That is, all the text labels and formulas are protected from change. Test this protection of your worksheet and write a short paragraph that describes your test of the protection.
23. Prepare a what-if analysis where Order Growth Rate is changed to 9%. In this worksheet, when you change the growth rate percent in column B, it is changed automatically in the other seven quarters. Why? Now, when is additional capacity needed in each of the manufacturing cells? Move the graphic objects that circle the results. Preview and print a copy of this what-if analysis. Save this as the S_MOP2.xls workbook in the Tut02 folder.

Comprehensive Applications

The Comprehensive Applications in this tutorial continue from the preceding tutorials.

1. Profit Planning for Valley Gas Alliance The first-quarter projection for Valley Gas Alliance (VGA) met Amanda's expectation of at least a 4 percent return on investment. She is very satisfied with the report you prepared, since it included the desired planning items. Now she wants this extended to a four-quarter plan for next year that shows the seasonal fluctuation in the demand for natural gas. This will provide better information for decision-making. In extending VGA's projected income statement, Amanda wants you to include a Total column for the year. Only those planning items that make business sense to add should be summed for the Total column. Recalculate those planning items that don't make business sense to add, using the summed values in the Total column.

After additional meetings and discussions, Martin, Mark, and Dennis provide the following data for next year:

	Quarter 1	Quarter 2	Quarter 3	Quarter 4
Total Gas Sold	232	221	94	243
General and Administrative	4,250	4,250	4,250	4,250

with amounts in thousands of dollars, in the same manner as provided in Tutorial 1.

COMPREHENSIVE APPLICATIONS **ADVEX 121**

The percents and ratios used to determine the Residential Gas, Industrial Gas, Cost of Sales, Marketing and Selling, Depreciation, Interest Expense, and Income taxes are the same for this four-quarter annual plan as they were for the first-quarter plan. After your review meetings, you are ready to extend VGA's projected income statement.

1. Prepare a planning analysis sheet for making these modifications to the worksheet. Include rounding as appropriate for all planning items except Return on Investment, which is a calculated ratio. You usually want to round units sold and dollar amounts, but not calculated ratios used to evaluate the acceptability of a plan. Which planning items need to be calculated, rather than summed, in the Total column?

2. Open the P_VGA1.xls workbook in the Tut02 folder as the beginning point for extending the time horizon of this worksheet. Save this file immediately as S_VGA1.xls in the same folder.

3. When added together, the percent of residential gas sold and industrial gas sold sum to a total of 100%. If each of these percents are included in the worksheet model, if you change one value, you must also remember to change the other value. Any time you have this type of allocation, a better business modeling technique is to input one percent and use a formula to calculate the other percent. Design your worksheet so you input the Residential Percent and then calculate the Industrial Percent by the formula (1 – Residential Percent).

4. Create a Key Input Assumptions section for the worksheet. This should include at least the assumptions of the Retail Percent, Residential Rate, Industrial Rate, Cost of Sales Percent, Depreciation Percent, Interest Rate, and Income Tax Rate. Enter appropriate planning item names for these assumptions. Revise the formulas in your worksheet model so they reference these assumptions. If the same assumption is used in all four quarters, then you should enter its value only once in your assumption section.

5. Use AutoFill, pointing, and copying to enter the revised formulas in the worksheet by following your planning analysis sheet from Question 1. The planning items should use the same formatting as those used previously for the first-quarter plan. The supporting balance sheet items should display their balances for each quarter and the Total column. The balance in the Total column is exactly the same as that for the fourth quarter, because the end of the fourth quarter is the same time as the end of the year. Set the column widths for the four quarters and Total columns as appropriate. If Return on Investment is 12.28% for the year, you have entered all your formulas correctly.

6. Center the report title across the width of the report, then enhance its appearance with an appropriate border and background color.

7. Consider other aesthetic enhancement features to further improve the appearance of the report. Apply these to the worksheet. Write out a list of the enhancements you used, indicating where they were applied.

8. Protect those cells in the worksheet that contain text labels or formulas that should not be changed when data values are revised. Test this protection and write a short paragraph describing your test.

9. Create range names for the Projected Income Statement Report section, the Key Input Assumptions section, and all the cells for planning item values. Apply these range names to the formulas in the worksheet.

10. Create an appropriate header and footer for your printed reports. Include your name somewhere in the footer as the preparer. Preview and print the worksheet.

11. Design a Summary sheet by selecting the planning items you feel are appropriate for the summary. Write a short paragraph explaining why you selected these planning items. Give your Summary sheet an appropriate name. Print it.

12. Document the workbook, using a separate sheet that appears as the first sheet in your workbook. Save this as the S_VGA1.xls workbook in the Tut02 folder. Print this Documentation sheet.

13. Perform a what-if evaluation by changing Residential Percent to 25%. Print the projected income statement. What is Return on Investment for the year? Now, formulate another what-if situation by selecting those input assumptions and data values that you feel should be revised. Write a short paragraph describing why you feel this what-if should be evaluated. Carry out the what-if analysis. Use graphic objects to indicate the what-if values you changed and include a text box with a brief note about the change. Use arrows to connect your text box to the revised data values. Preview and print this report. Save it as the S_VGA2.xls workbook in the Tut02 folder.

14. Create two additional operating expense planning items and include them in the worksheet under the Expense subheading. Use a growth rate for one expense item and a ratio for the other one. Include these growth rates and ratios in your Key Input Assumptions section. If the annual Return on Investment is less than 10%, adjust the values for these expense items so you have a Return on Investment of at least 10%. Write a short paragraph describing why you picked these expense items. Print this revised statement of operations, the Key Input Assumptions section, and the Summary sheet. Save this as the S_VG2.xls workbook in the Tut02 folder.

2. Production Planning for Oak World Furniture Todd and Robin are pleased with the production plan for July. It includes the desired planning items for their evaluation. They agree that their plan should be expanded to include all three months of the quarter. This will give them better information for their decision-making. In extending the Oak World worksheet, they want you to be certain to calculate a quarterly sum for only those planning items that make business sense to add. Recalculate those planning items that don't make business sense to add, using the summed values in the quarterly total column.

Todd, Robin, and Sam provide the following data for the quarter:

	July	August	September
Table Price	$640	$640	$670
Chair Price	120	125	125
Sofa Price	850	870	890
Employees	143	146	149
Hourly Rate	17.70	17.70	17.70
Hours Worked	170	170	170
Tables Sold	1,060	3% percent growth each month	
Sofas Sold	707	5% percent growth each month	
Management Salaries	47,600	47,600	47,600
General and Administrative	31,000	1,000 increase each month	

The percents and ratios used to determine Cost of Sales, Overhead, Advertising, and Insurance are the same for this quarterly plan as they were for the one-month plan. After your review meeting, you are ready to extend Oak World's statement of operation.

1. Prepare a planning analysis sheet for making these modifications to the worksheet. Include rounding as appropriate for all planning items except Return On Sales, which is a calculated ratio. Which planning items are calculated by a weighted average in the quarterly total column?

2. Open your S_OWF1.xls workbook in the Tut01 folder as the starting point for extending the time horizon of this worksheet. If you did not create this worksheet in Tutorial 1, see your instructor to receive the file you will need to complete this case application. Save this as the S_OWF1.xls workbook in the Tut02 folder before you start your revisions.

3. Use AutoFill, pointing, and copying to enter the revised formulas in the worksheet by following your planning analysis sheet from Question 1. The planning items should use the same formatting as you used previously for the one-month plan. Set the column widths for the three months and quarterly Total columns as appropriate.

4. Center the report title across the width of the report, then enhance its appearance with an appropriate border and background color.

5. Consider other aesthetic enhancement features to further improve the appearance of the report. Apply these to the worksheet. Write out a list of the enhancements you used, indicating where they were applied.

6. Create a Key Input Assumptions section for the worksheet. Enter appropriate planning item names for these assumptions. Enter the values for the assumptions. Revise the formulas in your worksheet model so they reference these assumptions. If the same assumption is used in all three months, then you should enter its value only once in your assumptions section.

7. Protect those cells in the worksheet that contain text labels or formulas that should not be changed when data values are revised. Test this protection and write a short paragraph describing your test. Unprotect the worksheet before you continue with the next question.

8. Create range names for the statement of operations Report section, the Key Input Assumptions section, and all the cells for planning item values. When asked if you want to replace the existing definitions of Cost_of_Sales and Operating_Expenses, select Yes because you need to replace the subheading references with the planning item references. Now substitute the planning item value range names in the worksheet formulas.

9. Complete the Properties Summary sheet (Version 5.0 Summary Info sheet) that is saved with the workbook in order to include this documentation.

10. Create an appropriate header and footer for your printed reports. Include your name somewhere in the footer as the preparer.

11. Design a Summary sheet by selecting the planning items you feel are appropriate for the summary. Write a short paragraph explaining why you selected those planning items. Give your Summary sheet an appropriate name. Print it.

12. Document the workbook, using a separate sheet that appears as the first sheet in your workbook. Save this as the S_OWF1.xls workbook in the Tut02 folder. Print this Documentation sheet.

ADVEX 124 TUTORIAL 2 DEVELOPING EFFECTIVE WORKSHEETS

13. Formulate a what-if situation by selecting those input assumptions and data values that you feel should be revised. Write a short paragraph describing why you feel that this what-if should be evaluated. Carry out the what-if analysis. Use graphic objects to indicate the what-if values you changed and include a text box with a brief note about the change. Use arrows to connect your text box to the revised data values. Preview and print this report. Save it as the S_0WF2.xls workbook in the Tut02 folder.

14. Create two additional operating expense planning items and include them in the worksheet under the Operating_Expenses subheading. Use a growth rate for one expense item and a ratio for the other one. Include these growth rates and ratios in your Key Input Assumptions section. If the quarterly Return On Sales is less than 17%, adjust the values for these expense items so you have a Return On Sales of at least 17%. Write a short paragraph describing why you picked these expense items. Print this revised statement of operations, the Key Input Assumptions section, and the Summary sheet. Save this as the S_0WF2.xls workbook.

TUTORIAL 3

Creating and Printing Charts

Adding Charts to the Budget

OBJECTIVES

In this tutorial you will learn how to:

- Select a chart type to support visual communication
- Create a stacked column and pie chart
- Select nonadjacent ranges
- Specify titles and axis labels
- Preview and print charts
- Enhance the appearance of charts
- Add graphic objects to charts
- Perform what-if analyses with charts
- Prepare combination charts
- Add pictures to column charts
- Integrate programs with a client and server relationship
- Create maps

CASE

Sunny Morning Products

Carmen has an upcoming meeting scheduled with the Sunny Morning Products management committee to review next year's Operating Budget. She is concerned that some people on the committee may find the numbers and data in the worksheet too complex. Ann suggests that they add some charts to help clarify the data.

Ann and Carmen discuss the different types of charts they could use, and agree that the charts should be accurate, clearly labeled, and attractive. Charts with these characteristics have a significant impact on the viewer.

They talk about several charts that Ann could create for Carmen's presentation. First, Carmen would like to see a chart comparing Cost of Sales and Gross Profit by quarter because she believes that the management committee will be interested in the overall profitability of selling Olympic Gold.

Second, Carmen recommends that Ann create a chart that summarizes the total expenses for next year. The management committee will be very interested in what it will cost to run the business next year. Carmen also realizes that if the budget is not accepted and she is asked to cut corners, she will need to have an idea of where those cuts could occur. She intends to be prepared for this possibility, so she wants a third chart with which she can perform some what-if alternatives to determine how changes in different operating expenses over the four quarters will affect the overall budget.

Carmen also suggests a chart that summarizes the high points of the budget, which will correspond directly to the Summary sheet in the budget. Perhaps she could include this chart in her memo to the committee confirming the meeting. She hopes this chart will pique their interest, and demonstrate the extensive time and thought that has gone into developing the budget. They agree that Ann should start by creating the charts that illustrate the overall profitability of Olympic Gold sales and that summarize the total expenses for next year. Once these charts are complete, they can review them to ensure that they appropriately present the data before Ann creates the other charts. Ann is excited about this assignment and returns to her desk to begin planning the first two charts.

Introduction to Charts

A chart is an effective way to convey the abstract data in a worksheet, and helps the audience visualize relationships between that data. A chart can convert a boring table of numeric data from your Excel worksheet into an attention-getting display. Presentations that include charts can be more effective and persuasive than presentations without charts. A chart can

- Make your message more powerful, clear, and persuasive.
- Help viewers grasp your point of view faster and remember it longer.
- Summarize large quantities of complex data.
- Discover new relationships among data.

Once you create a worksheet, you can chart any data that it contains. Each single set of data that you chart is a **data series**. For example, the data for Sales in Qtr 1 through Qtr 4 of the Sunny Morning Products operating budget is a data series. In a chart, a data series can be represented by graphical objects such as lines, columns, bars, or slices of a pie.

Once you know what data you want to chart, you have to determine the relationships you want to see among the various data series. The charts used in business often deal with three basic situations:

- showing trends (How do conditions change over time?)
- comparing components and relative amounts (What proportion is each individual component to the total amount?)
- showing the relationship between two variables (How are the two variables related?)

There are many different types of charts: column charts, line charts, stacked column charts, pie charts, XY charts, and combination charts. Each chart type is designed to illustrate a particular type of relationship between data. The type of relationship you want your chart to illustrate determines the chart type you need to use. Figure 3-1 summarizes the application of charts to typical situations.

Figure 3-1 ◀
Selecting a
chart type

Situation	Chart Type
Showing trends	Line chart, column chart, bar chart, combination chart
Comparing components	Pie chart, stacked column or bar chart
Showing relationships	XY chart

HELP DESK

EXCEL 5.0

Index

SELECTING A CHART TYPE OR FORMAT

Double-click the Help button to display the Help Topics dialog box, then click the Index tab.

Keyword
charts in Excel, chart type
not available

Topic
The best chart type for my data

After looking over her notes on the budget, Ann develops a planning analysis sheet for creating the charts (Figure 3-2). She then sketches the two charts that Carmen thinks would be most effective in representing the data (Figure 3-3). Ann decides to create a pie chart because it can effectively display the data for a single time period of the Total column to summarize their annual plan.

INTRODUCTION TO CHARTS **ADVEX 127**

Figure 3-2 ◀
Ann's planning
analysis sheet

Planning Analysis Sheet

My goal:

Prepare charts showing revenues and expenses for next year's budget

What results do I want to see?

Stacked column of Cost of Sales and Gross Profit by quarter where the entire column height represents Sales

Pie chart of overall expenses for the year from the annual total

What information do I need?

Expected revenues and expenses for next year by quarter and with an annual total

Figure 3-3 ◀
Ann's sketch of
the charts

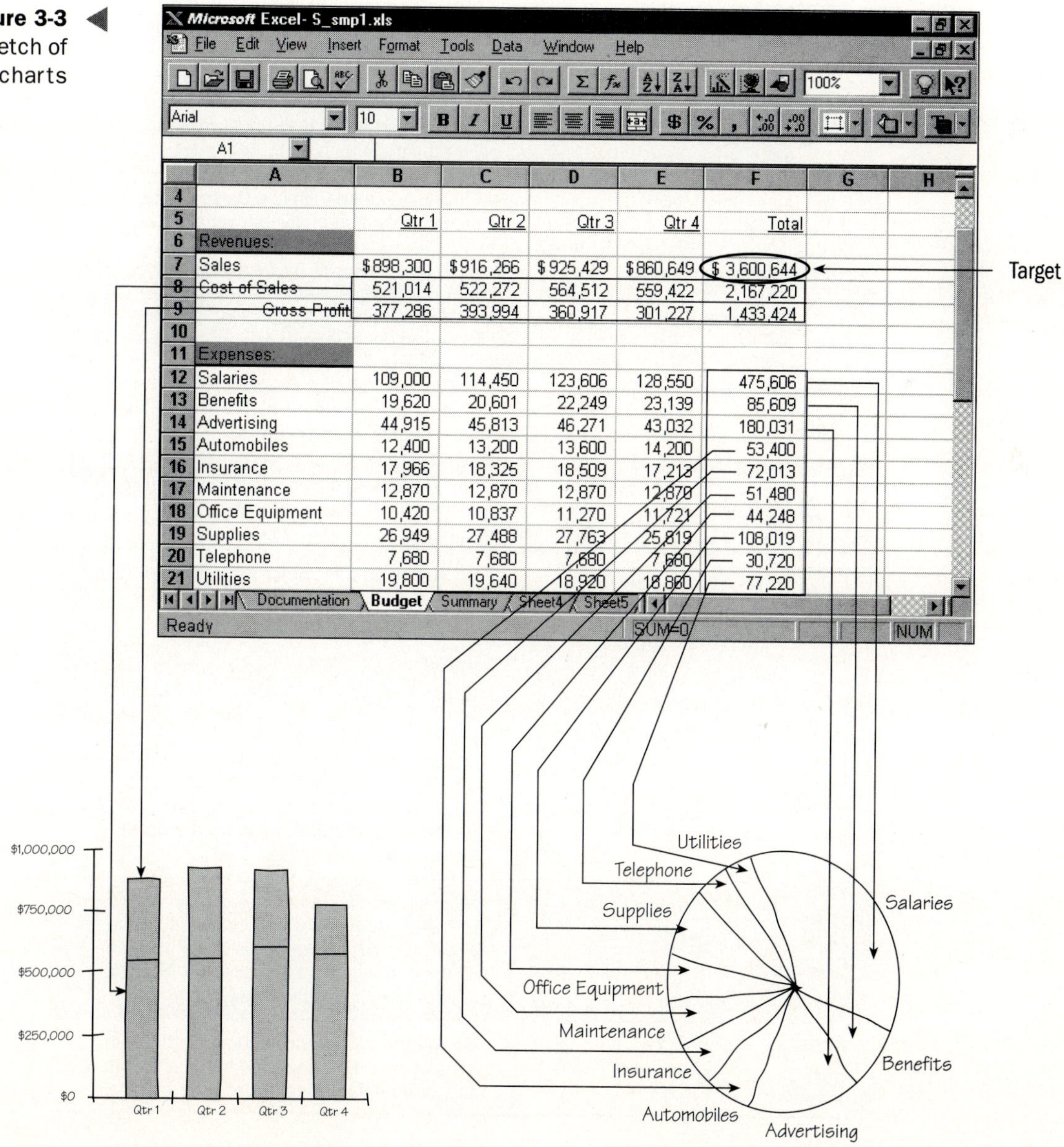

X Microsoft Excel- S_smp1.xls

File Edit View Insert Format Tools Data Window Help

Arial   10   B I U

A1

	A	B	C	D	E	F	G	H
4								
5		Qtr 1	Qtr 2	Qtr 3	Qtr 4	Total		
6	Revenues:							
7	Sales	$898,300	$916,266	$925,429	$860,649	$ 3,600,644			← Target
8	Cost of Sales	521,014	522,272	564,512	559,422	2,167,220		
9	Gross Profit	377,286	393,994	360,917	301,227	1,433,424		
10								
11	Expenses:							
12	Salaries	109,000	114,450	123,606	128,550	475,606		
13	Benefits	19,620	20,601	22,249	23,139	85,609		
14	Advertising	44,915	45,813	46,271	43,032	180,031		
15	Automobiles	12,400	13,200	13,600	14,200	53,400		
16	Insurance	17,966	18,325	18,509	17,213	72,013		
17	Maintenance	12,870	12,870	12,870	12,870	51,480		
18	Office Equipment	10,420	10,837	11,270	11,721	44,248		
19	Supplies	26,949	27,488	27,763	25,819	108,019		
20	Telephone	7,680	7,680	7,680	7,680	30,720		
21	Utilities	19,800	19,640	18,920	18,860	77,220		

Documentation / **Budget** / Summary / Sheet4 / Sheet5

Ready   SUM=0   NUM

$1,000,000

$750,000

$500,000

$250,000

$0

Qtr 1   Qtr 2   Qtr 3   Qtr 4

Utilities
Telephone
Supplies
Office Equipment
Maintenance
Insurance
Automobiles
Advertising
Salaries
Benefits

ADVEX 128 **TUTORIAL 3** CREATING AND PRINTING CHARTS

In this tutorial you will create Ann's charts for Carmen's presentation to the SMP management committee. You will learn how to construct charts and determine the type of chart that is best suited to communicate your data.

Excel Charts

Figure 3-4 shows the **chart types** you can use with Excel to represent your worksheet data. Each of these chart types has at least one **subtype**, or variation of its format. A chart's **format** is the specific arrangement and display of data on the chart. Of the 15 different major chart types, nine produce two-dimensional (2-D) charts and six produce three-dimensional (3-D) charts.

Figure 3-4 ◀
Excel chart types

Button	Chart Type	Purpose
	Area	Shows the magnitude of change over time.
	Bar	Shows comparisons among the data series represented by horizontal bars. Most useful with a limited number of data series.
	Column	Shows comparisons among the data series represented by vertical bars. Most useful with a limited number of data series.
	OHLC	Shows the Open-High-Low-Close of stock market data that changes over time.
	Line	Shows trends or changes over time. Most useful for showing trends with many data values in each series.
	Combination	Shows how one set of data corresponds to another set by combining parts from line, bar, column, or area charts.
	Pie	Shows the proportion of parts to a whole for a single data series.
	Doughnut	Shows the proportion of parts to a whole for *more than one* data series.
	Radar	Shows the symmetry or uniformity of data as a function of distance from a central point.
	Stacked Column	Shows totals in addition to comparing individual data values for each vertical bar segment. Overall height of bar shows the total of the components that make up the data series. Variant of column chart.
	Stacked Bar	Shows totals in addition to comparing individual data values for each horizontal bar segment. Overall length of bar shows the total of the components that make up the data series. Variant of bar chart.
	XY	Shows the pattern or relationship between sets of (x,y) data points. Most useful when the x-axis data series is *not* units of time.

Figure 3-4
Excel chart types (cont'd)

Button	Chart Type	Purpose
3-D Area	3-D Area	Shows the magnitude of each data series as a solid three-dimensional shape.
3-D Bar	3-D Bar	Similar to a 2-D bar chart, but bars appear three-dimensional.
3-D Column	3-D Column	Similar to a 2-D column chart, but columns appear three-dimensional and some formats show data on x-, y-, and z-axes.
3-D Line	3-D Line	Shows each line as a ribbon within a three-dimensional space.
3-D Pie	3-D Pie	Shows the proportion of parts to a whole, with emphasis on the data values in the front wedges, for a single data series.
3-D Surface	3-D Surface	Shows the interrelationships between large amounts of data.

Each chart type has several predefined or built-in chart **Autoformats**, or subtypes, that specify such format characteristics as the arrangement of data displayed on the chart. The side-by-side or stacked arrangement, like that for the column and bar charts, is a format selection. For example, the format arrangements for column charts are displayed in the ChartWizard - Step 3 of 5 dialog box shown in Figure 3-5. You can find out more about the different chart types and formats in the Microsoft Excel *User's Guide*, the Excel on-line Help facility, or by accessing the ChartWizard.

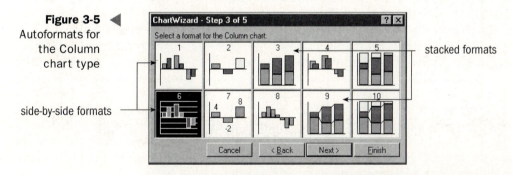

Figure 3-5
Autoformats for the Column chart type

side-by-side formats

stacked formats

Examining an Excel Chart

Figure 3-6 shows the elements of a typical Excel chart. It is particularly important to understand Excel chart terminology so you can successfully construct and edit charts. Examine the elements of Ann's completed stacked column chart.

Figure 3-6
Elements of an Excel chart

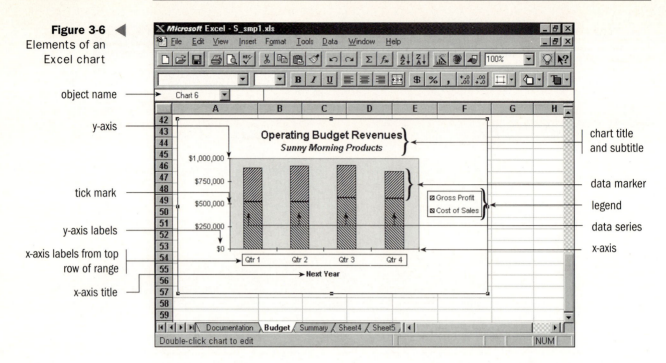

The **chart title** identifies the chart. You can expand it to include a **subtitle** when two or more descriptive lines are needed for identification. The horizontal axis of the chart is the **category axis** or **x-axis**. The vertical axis is the **value axis** or **y-axis**. Each axis on a chart can have a title that identifies the scale or categories of the chart data; in Figure 3-6 the x-axis title is "Next Year."

The **value labels** on the y-axis show the scale for the y-axis with a **tick mark** indicating the location for each value. Excel automatically generates this scale based on the values selected for the chart. The **category names** or **category labels** on the x-axis correspond to the labels you use for the worksheet data.

A **data point** is a single value in a cell in the worksheet. A **data marker** is a column, bar, area, slice, or symbol that marks a single data point on a chart. For example, the value 521,014 in cell B8 of the worksheet is a data point. Each segment of a column in Figure 3-6 is a data marker. With a line chart a symbol such as a small square is used as a data marker, while a data marker for a pie chart is a slice of the pie.

A **data series** is a group of related data points from a single cell range, such as the Gross Profit shown in cells B9 through E9 in Ann's worksheet. On a chart such as the one in Figure 3-6, a data series is shown as a set of data markers for one segment of each stacked column. In Excel each data series is a range for the chart. A chart can contain a number of different data series, with one data series usually used to specify values for the x-axis, such as A5:E5, which contains the column titles.

When you have more than one data series, your chart will contain more than one set of data markers. For example, each stacked column in Figure 3-6 has two segments, each representing one of the two data series shown on the chart. When you show more than one data series on a chart, it is a good idea to use a **legend** to identify which data markers represent each data series.

Arranging Data Series for Charts

Data series for Excel charts are located in data ranges that are organized either *by rows* or *by columns*, with the same number of data values in each data series. All the data series on one chart should have the same row or column arrangement, with each individual data series located in only one row or column. When you initially create a chart, Excel automatically organizes the data series the way the data is arranged as rows and columns in the worksheet. When Ann creates her chart, she will select the ranges A5:E5 and A8:E9, as shown in Figure 3-7. Because this data range contains *more columns of data than rows of data*, the data series will be *plotted by rows*. The topmost row of data values in the range A5:E5 is assigned to the x-axis data series.

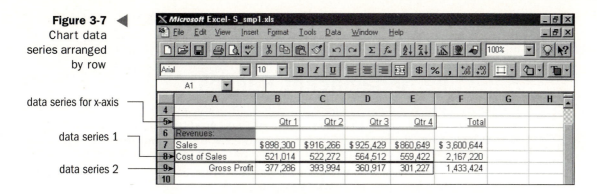

Figure 3-7
Chart data series arranged by row

data series for x-axis
data series 1
data series 2

If the selected data range for the chart contains *more rows of data than columns of data*, then the Excel Autoformat suggests that the data series be *plotted by columns* with the x-axis labels residing in the leftmost column of the selected range. You change whether data is arranged *by rows* or *by columns* in the ChartWizard - Step 3 of 5 dialog box.

Creating a Column Chart

Ann plans to create the column chart and then the pie chart. Retrieve Ann's worksheet containing the operating budget data for next year in preparation for creating her stacked column chart.

To open the workbook:

1. Launch Excel.

2. Open Ann's workbook, C_SMP1.xls, located in the Tut03 folder or directory on your Student Disk. Then save the workbook as S_SMP1.xls in the Tut03 folder in case you want to restart this tutorial.

3. Review the Budget worksheet. Observe the row arrangement of the data series for Cost of Sales and Gross Profit. Since these data series are located adjacent to one another, they are in a single worksheet range.

Notice the additional graphic that Ann has added to point out where Sales will meet the desired target in the 4th quarter. Travis wanted to ensure that the members of the committee noticed that the aggressive sales goals for next year would be met. According to Ann's sketch in Figure 3-3, one of the charts she wants to create is a stacked column chart comparing Cost of Sales and Gross Profit by quarter for next year. She chose this type of chart because it is useful for showing comparisons. The height of the stacked columns shows the total for each time period, which represents the Sales by quarter in Ann's chart. As a result, Ann's chart will show Sales, Cost of Sales, and Gross Profit, although she includes only the Cost of Sales and Gross Profit data series on the chart. This is one of the advantages of using a stacked column chart.

Ann wants to use an **embedded chart** that is placed in the same worksheet as her data. This way her chart is close to the data so she can more easily review and print both the worksheet and the chart. Excel provides a second alternative: placing a chart in a separate **chart sheet** in the workbook that contains only that chart. You view a chart sheet by selecting that workbook sheet. Whether you create an embedded chart or a chart sheet, your data is automatically linked to the associated worksheet data. When your worksheet data changes, the chart is automatically updated to reflect the change.

When you create a chart, you select the range of data you want to chart and then specify where you want the chart to appear in the worksheet. The ChartWizard is the easiest way to create an embedded Excel chart with an Autoformat. The **ChartWizard** is a series of dialog boxes that guides you through the steps required to create or modify settings for a chart. When creating a chart with the ChartWizard, you specify the worksheet range, select a chart type and format, and specify how you want your data to be plotted. You can also add a legend, a chart title, and a title to each axis. After you create a chart, you can use the ChartWizard to add or modify headings, titles, fonts, and attributes. Use the ChartWizard to create Ann's column chart after the data series are selected.

Selecting Nonadjacent Ranges

Frequently when you create a chart like Ann's, the data series and data labels are not next to each other in the spreadsheet. Therefore, you need to make a nonadjacent selection. **Nonadjacent selections** are cells or ranges of cells that are not next to, or adjacent to, one another. A nonadjacent selection is two or more separate cell ranges that you select at the same time, with each data series consisting of the same number of cells. When you select nonadjacent ranges, all the selected cells are highlighted. You can then apply formats to the cells, clear them, or use them to create a chart. A nonadjacent selection is needed for Ann's worksheet because all her data series are not adjacent to one another. She wants the column titles from a data series in row 5 and her other data series from rows 8 and 9. You make a nonadjacent selection by selecting the first cell or range in the usual manner by clicking and dragging, then adding each additional cell or range to the selection by holding down the Ctrl key while you click and drag the ranges to select them.

To select nonadjacent ranges for creating a chart:

1. Make sure the Budget sheet is active, then select the cell range **A5:E5**, which contains the column titles. Although cell A5 is empty, its selection is required to form the rectangular shape for the completed range specification.

2. Hold down the **Ctrl** key and select the cell range **A8:E9**, which contains the two data series for the chart arranged by row. This completes the selection of the cell ranges for the chart. See Figure 3-8.

Figure 3-8 ◀
Selected ranges for Ann's stacked column chart

nonadjacent ranges for data series

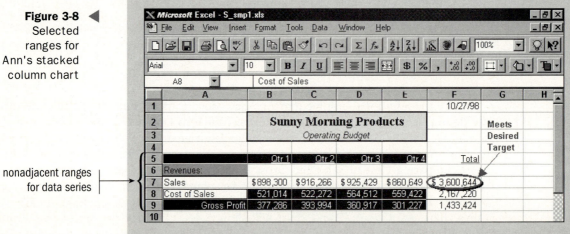

TROUBLE? If only the cell range A8:E9 was selected, then you did *not* specify nonadjacent ranges. Hold down the Ctrl key and select the range A5:E5 to specify the desired nonadjacent ranges.

REFERENCE window

SELECTING NONADJACENT RANGES

- Select the first cell range.
- Move the mouse pointer to the next cell range.
- Press and hold the Ctrl key while you select the second cell range.
- Continue selecting ranges with the Ctrl key for as many additional cell ranges as you want.

With the data series selected, the next step in creating Ann's chart is to use the ChartWizard to actually create it.

Using the ChartWizard

Once you select the cells for a column chart, you use the ChartWizard to specify the chart type, chart format, and chart titles. Specify these characteristics of Ann's chart.

To create a column chart using the ChartWizard:

1. Scroll the worksheet until A42 is positioned in the upper-left corner of the worksheet window. This is the desired location for the upper-left corner of the chart. Do *not* click the mouse or you will unselect the range you want to chart.

   TROUBLE? If you clicked A42 by mistake, select the column titles, Cost of Sales, and Gross Profit in columns A through E as nonadjacent ranges, then scroll the worksheet to the desired chart location.

2. Click the **ChartWizard** button on the Standard toolbar. The mouse pointer changes to + to indicate that Excel is ready for you to select the location and size of your new chart.

3. Move the pointer to cell **A42** where the upper-left corner of the column chart will be located, but *do not* click cell A42.

4. Click and drag the pointer over the area **A42:D52** to indicate the size and location of the chart. As you drag the mouse pointer, a dotted outline indicates the area the chart will fill. When you release the mouse button, the ChartWizard - Step 1 of 5 dialog box opens. See Figure 3-9.

Figure 3-9
ChartWizard - Step 1 of 5 dialog box

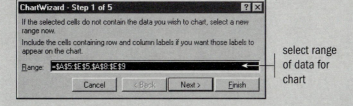

select range of data for chart

TROUBLE? If you selected the wrong data series for your chart, you can change it by editing the Range text box in the ChartWizard - Step 1 of 5 dialog box.

5. Inspect the Range text box to verify that the desired nonadjacent ranges **=$A$5:$E$5, $A$8:$E$9** are specified, then click the **Next >** button to display the ChartWizard - Step 2 of 5 dialog box, which shows the available built-in Autoformats for creating a chart. See Figure 3-10.

Figure 3-10
Built-in Autoformats for charts

available chart types

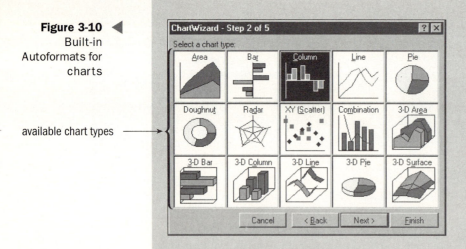

6. If necessary, click the **Column chart** type to select it, then click the **Next>** button to display the ChartWizard - Step 3 of 5 dialog box, which shows the available Autoformat variants or subtypes of the Column chart type. See Figure 3-11.

Figure 3-11
Column chart built-in Autoformat variants

available chart variants

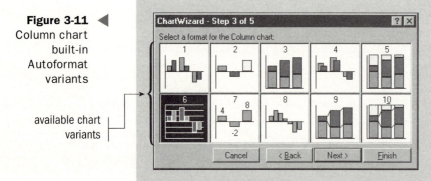

7. Click Column chart variant **1** to select that arrangement for the column chart, then click the **Next >** button to display the ChartWizard - Step 4 of 5 dialog box, which shows a sample preview of the chart's appearance. See Figure 3-12.

Figure 3-12
ChartWizard - Step 4 of 5 dialog box

preview of chart

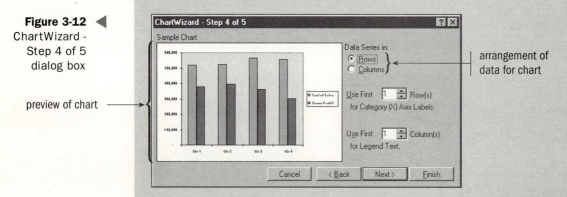

arrangement of data for chart

8. Verify that the **Rows** option button is selected for the Data Series in, the Use First **1** Row for Category (X) Axis Labels is specified, and the Use First **1** Column for Legend Text is specified, then click the **Next >** button to display the ChartWizard - Step 5 of 5 dialog box. The x-axis and legend labels are always located in the topmost rows and leftmost columns, although they may occupy more than one row or column.

9. Verify that the **Add a Legend? Yes** option button is selected, type **Operating Budget Revenues** in the Chart Title text box, and type **Next Year** in the Category (X) Axis Title box. Leave the Value (Y) text box blank. Then click the **Finish** button to finish specifying the chart format and display it in the worksheet. See Figure 3-13.

Figure 3-13
Ann's column chart embedded in the worksheet

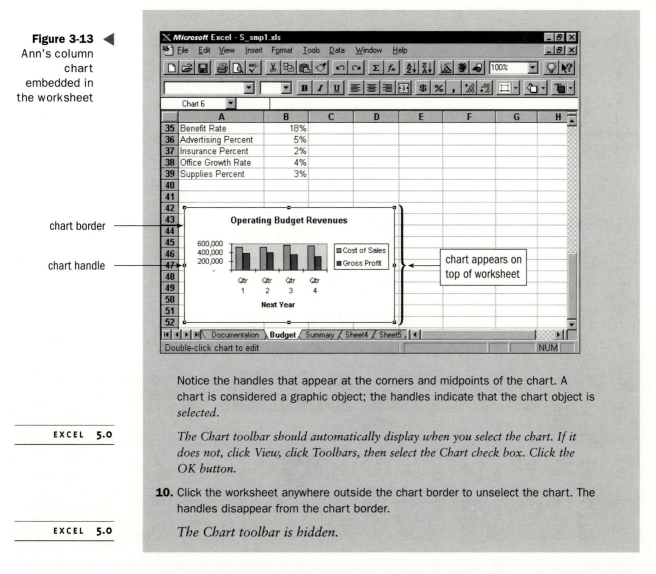

Notice the handles that appear at the corners and midpoints of the chart. A chart is considered a graphic object; the handles indicate that the chart object is *selected*.

The Chart toolbar should automatically display when you select the chart. If it does not, click View, click Toolbars, then select the Chart check box. Click the OK button.

10. Click the worksheet anywhere outside the chart border to unselect the chart. The handles disappear from the chart border.

The Chart toolbar is hidden.

EXCEL 5.0

Like other graphic objects, you can resize, move, copy, or delete a selected chart. After seeing the actual chart, Ann thinks she should increase its size.

Resizing a Chart

When you use the ChartWizard to create an embedded chart, you drag the pointer to outline the area of the worksheet where you want the chart to appear. If the area is too small, the chart may not appear as you would like. To resize an object, you select the object by clicking it, and then drag a handle to change the object's size. When you resize an object, you can change both its size and its proportions, as indicated in Figure 3-14.

Figure 3-14
Common resizing activities

To resize an object	Do this
Change its width	Drag a middle handle on the left or right side of the object
Change its height	Drag a middle handle on the top or bottom of the object
Change both its height and width	Drag a corner handle
Change its size *without* changing its proportions	Drag a corner handle while holding down the Shift key

Increase the size of Ann's chart to improve its appearance.

To resize a stacked column chart:

1. Click anywhere inside the chart border to select the chart. The handles appear on the chart border to indicate that it is selected.

2. Move the mouse pointer over the handle at the lower-right corner of the chart border until the pointer changes to ↘, then click and drag the handle to cell **F57**. A dotted line indicates the new size of the chart as you drag the handle. When you release the mouse button, the chart appears at its new size. See Figure 3-15.

Figure 3-15 ◀
Ann's resized column chart

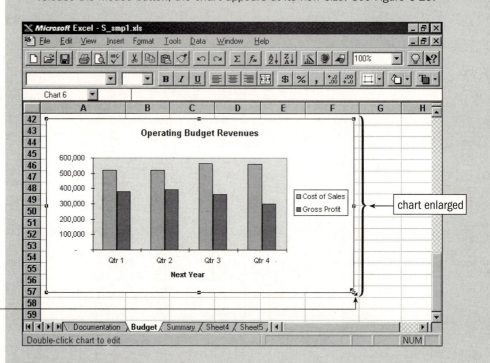

handle for resizing width and height

3. Click the worksheet anywhere outside of the chart border to unselect the chart.

Activating a Chart for Editing

An activated chart is different from a selected chart. A **selected chart** appears with eight handles and you can resize, move, copy, or delete it. An **activated chart** appears surrounded by a thicker gray border that covers the graphic object handles and you can edit its contents and elements.

You activate a chart by double-clicking anywhere within its borders. When a chart is activated, the menu bar displays the commands for working with charts. You can then change the chart type or format and insert items such as titles and gridlines.

If the chart is too big to be displayed on the screen without scrolling, the entire activated chart is displayed in a special chart window, with its own title bar. You can modify a chart displayed in a chart window just as you would an activated chart surrounded by a thick gray border. Select and then activate Ann's chart so it is ready for modification.

To activate a stacked column chart for modifications:

1. Click anywhere within the chart border to select the chart. The resize handles appear and the worksheet menu remains displayed.

2. Double-click anywhere within the chart border to activate the chart. The thick gray border surrounds the chart, the chart menu replaces the worksheet menu, and the pointer appears as the block arrow ⇗ for selecting chart objects. The horizontal and vertical scroll bars disappear from the worksheet window and the chart is ready for making changes. See Figure 3-16.

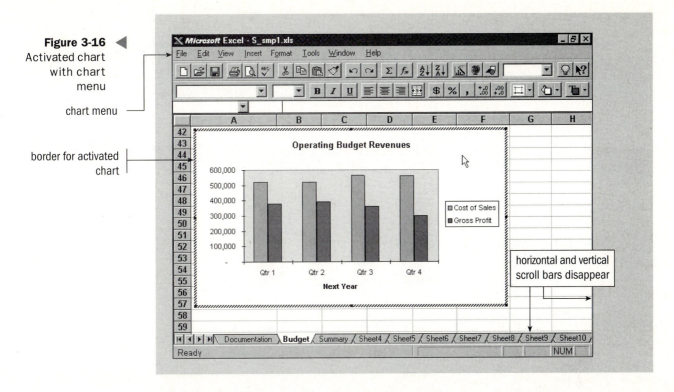

Figure 3-16 Activated chart with chart menu

chart menu

border for activated chart

horizontal and vertical scroll bars disappear

Adding and Deleting Chart Data Series

Ann reviews her column chart and wonders what it would look like if she included the Sales data values on her chart as a separate data series. She could re-create the chart using the ChartWizard, but a more expedient method would be to add the Sales data to the existing chart.

To add a data series to an existing embedded chart:

1. Click the worksheet anywhere outside the chart to deactivate it. The scroll bars appear so you can scroll the worksheet to locate the data that you want to add to the chart.

2. Scroll the worksheet and select the range **A7:E7**, which contains the data for Sales.

3. Move the mouse pointer to the edge of the selected range until it changes to the block arrow, then click and drag the **data series** until the block arrow is on top of the embedded chart. The worksheet window scrolls down when you move the pointer below the last row displayed in the window. Continue scrolling until the pointer is on top of the chart. The pointer changes to the block arrow with a plus to indicate that the data series will be added to the chart, and the chart is activated as indicated by the thick gray border.

4. Release the mouse button to complete the drag-and-drop that adds the data series to the chart. Scroll the worksheet as necessary to view the entire chart. See Figure 3-17.

Figure 3-17
Sales data series added to chart

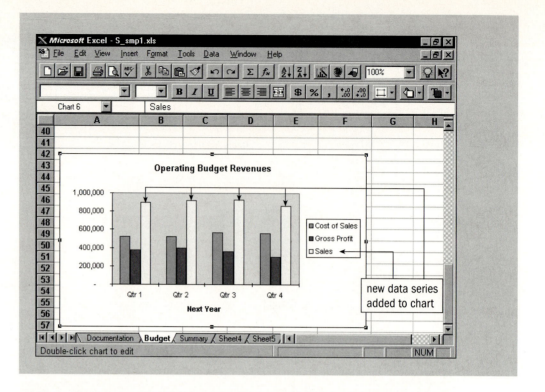

REFERENCE window	**ADDING A DATA SERIES TO A CHART**
	■ Select the data series in the worksheet. ■ Move the pointer to the edge of the selected range until it changes to ⇖. ■ Click and drag the selected range until the pointer is on top of the chart and changes to ⇖⁺, then release the mouse button.

As Ann inspects her revised chart, she decides it would really look better without the Sales data series. She wants to delete that data series from her chart. When you delete a data series from a chart, the data is no longer displayed on the chart, but remains in the worksheet. Remove the Sales data series from Ann's chart.

To delete a data series from a chart:

1. Double-click anywhere on the chart to activate it.

2. Click the **Sales** data series in any one of the four columns to select that data series.

3. Press the **Delete** key to remove the data series from the chart.

REFERENCE window	**DELETING A DATA SERIES FROM A CHART**
	■ Double-click the chart to activate it (as indicated by a thick gray border). ■ Click any of the data markers in the data series to select it. ■ Press the Delete key to remove the selected data series.

Ann is convinced that her initial design is the best arrangement for displaying this data for Sunny Morning Products and decides to continue with her original plan. Like Ann, as you create a chart, you might want to add or remove one or more data series to determine whether your revision provides an even clearer understanding of the message conveyed by the chart.

Selecting a Different Chart Type and Format

After Excel plots the data you want using your initial chart type selection, you can select another chart type from the Chart Type dialog box, or a specific format for your selected chart type from the Subtype setting sheet. You might have to experiment with different chart types and formats to find the one that best represents your data. Sometimes the chart you planned isn't the right chart type for the information you want to plot. As you work through this tutorial, you will find that changing from one built-in Autoformat chart type to another is easy.

HELP DESK

CHANGING CHART TYPE OR FORMAT — Index

Double-click the Help button to display the Help Topics dialog box, then click the Index tab.

Keyword
charts in Excel, chart type
chart types

Topic
Change the chart type
Changing the chart type of an entire chart

EXCEL 5.0

Ann needs to change her initial column chart from a side-by-side format to the stacked column format required for Carmen's presentation.

To change a chart's format:

1. If necessary, double-click the **chart** to activate it, then right-click anywhere on the chart to display the chart shortcut menu. This menu includes the Format Column Group menu item because Excel recognizes this particular chart as a chart group of the Column type. See Figure 3-18.

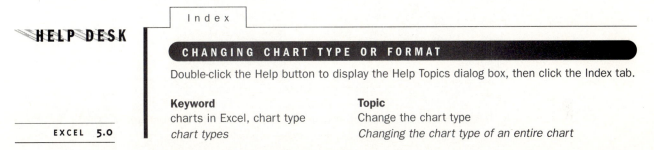

◀ **Figure 3-18**
Chart shortcut menu with menu item for chart group

menu choice for Column Group

2. Click **Format Column Group** to display the Format Column Group dialog box, then click the **Subtype** tab to display that setting sheet. See Figure 3-19. Notice that the Subtype setting sheet displays several of the available chart formats for this chart type; however, not all of the available formats are shown, only those that Excel determines to be most closely associated with the already selected format.

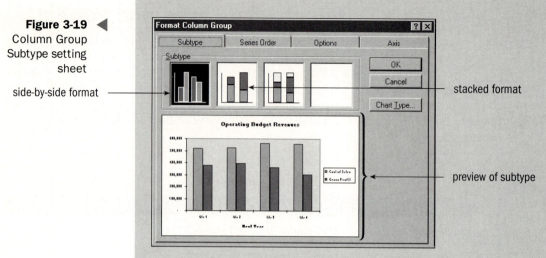

Figure 3-19
Column Group Subtype setting sheet

side-by-side format

stacked format

preview of subtype

3. Click the **stacked column** subtype, the second subtype from the left, to display that arrangement in the preview window of the setting sheet.

4. Click the **OK** button to finish specifying the change in the chart subtype and to return to the display of the embedded chart in the worksheet. See Figure 3-20. Note that double-clicking the stacked column subtype button is equivalent to clicking it once, and then clicking the OK button. You can use either method.

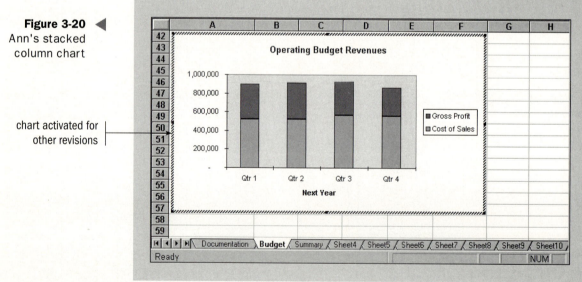

Figure 3-20
Ann's stacked column chart

chart activated for other revisions

SELECTING A DIFFERENT CHART TYPE AND FORMAT ADVEX 141

SELECTING A DIFFERENT CHART FORMAT

- Double-click the chart to activate it, as indicated by a thick gray border.
- Right-click the chart to display the chart shortcut menu.
  or
  Click Format.
- Click the Format Group selection for your chart type, which appears at the bottom of the menu. Notice that the Format Group selection changes to the one appropriate for the currently selected chart type group. A format dialog box appears for your chart's type group.
- Click the Subtype tab to display that setting sheet, click the desired subtype, then click the OK button to complete the selection.

Ann thinks her chart looks good but, now that she sees all of the other chart type options, she is curious how the data would look as a line chart and wonders if that would provide a better comparison. Change Ann's column chart to a line chart to see what that arrangement of the data looks like.

To change a chart type using the chart shortcut menu:

1. Make sure the chart is activated, and right-click anywhere on it to display the chart shortcut menu.

2. Click **Chart Type** to display the Chart Type dialog box, then double-click **Line** to select that chart type and display the data as a line chart. See Figure 3-21.

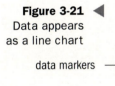

Figure 3-21
Data appears as a line chart

data markers

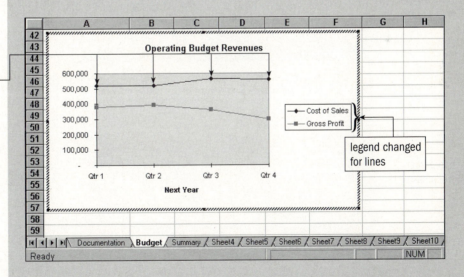

legend changed for lines

TROUBLE? If you picked the wrong chart type, repeat Steps 1 and 2.

Although this line chart is effective in showing the trend from quarter to quarter, it is not as good as the stacked column chart in showing the comparison between the two different components.

Now change it back to the stacked column chart.

3. Make sure the chart is still activated and right-click it to display the chart shortcut menu, then click **Chart Type** to display that dialog box.

> 4. Click **Column** to select that type, click the **Options** button to display the Format Column Group dialog box, click the **Subtype** tab, click the stacked column subtype (second from the left), then click the **OK** button to display the chart with a y-axis with a maximum value of 1,000,000.
>
> **TROUBLE?** If you double-clicked Column to redisplay the stacked column chart, the chart is displayed with Cost of Sales behind the Gross Profit data series with the same y-axis scale that was displayed with the line chart. Repeat Steps 3 and 4.

Ann's stacked column chart is complete. She wants to save her work and print the chart so she can review it with Carmen.

Saving and Printing Charts

When you print embedded charts, you can print them individually or you can print the worksheet and chart together as one report. Ann wants to print the chart both ways so Carmen can check to see that the chart does a good job of representing their data and so she can also look at the chart alone and concentrate on its individual elements. Save the worksheet with this newly created chart and then print just the chart first.

To save a worksheet and print only a chart:

> 1. Save the workbook with the newly created chart as S_SMP1.xls in the Tut03 folder.
>
> 2. If the column chart is not activated, double-click it to activate it.
>
> 3. Click the **Print Preview** button on the Standard toolbar to preview the chart, then click the **Print** button to display the Print dialog box with the Selected Chart option already selected. See Figure 3-22.
>
> EXCEL 5.0
>
> *The Version 5.0 Print dialog box is different, but it also includes the Print What options with the Selected Chart option checked.*
>
> **Figure 3-22** Print dialog box
>
> option prints activated chart
>
>
>
> 4. Click the **OK** button to complete the print specifications and print the chart.

Now you are ready to print both the chart and the worksheet as one report.

REVIEWING THE CHART **ADVEX 143**

To print a chart and worksheet as one report:

1. Click anywhere outside the chart area to deactivate the chart.

2. Click the **Print Preview** button 🔍 on the Standard toolbar to display the preview window. Use the scroll bars or the Page Down and Page Up keys to examine the worksheet. Note that the chart is divided between page 1 and page 2.

   Ann prefers to have the entire worksheet report appear on one page, so this situation needs to be corrected.

3. Click the **Setup** button, click the **Page** tab, select the **Fit to Scaling** option button with 1 page wide by 1 page tall, then click the **OK** button to display the automatically scaled report. See Figure 3-23.

Figure 3-23 ◀
Scaled
one-page report
with column
chart

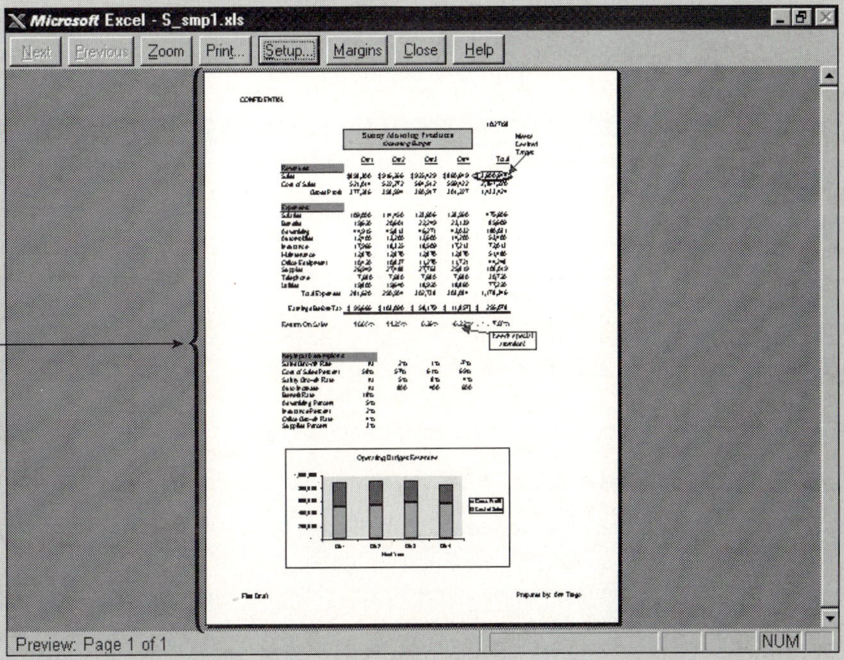

page scaled to
include chart

4. Click the **Print** button to display the Print dialog box with the Selected Sheet(s) option selected, then click the **OK** button to print Ann's one-page report.

With her two printouts in hand, Ann is ready to review the chart with Carmen.

Reviewing the Chart

Carmen thinks Ann's chart does a good job of comparing Sales, Cost of Sales, and Gross Profit for the four quarters. However, she notices a few things that need to be added, as indicated in Figure 3-24. First, she asks Ann to add the subtitle "Sunny Morning Products." Then, Carmen asks her to change the size and attributes of the titles. She recommends that Ann make them larger and display them in italics. Also, Carmen isn't pleased with the number format for the y-axis. Although the comma format with no decimals is satisfactory, she wants this y-axis scale to appear with the currency symbol and with a zero as the starting value. She also asks Ann to change the scale on the y-axis so the value labels are easier to read. Next, Carmen explains that they will need to make copies of the chart for the managers and because of SMP's one-color printer and copier, Ann will need to modify the chart. She will have to create a black-and-white copy of the chart with different patterns for the two planning items rather than the different colors. Finally, Carmen asks Ann to add a note that points to the value for Qtr 4 to indicate that the overall height of the stacked column represents Sales. Ann understands what she needs to do and gets right to work.

Figure 3-24
Carmen's suggested changes to the stacked column chart

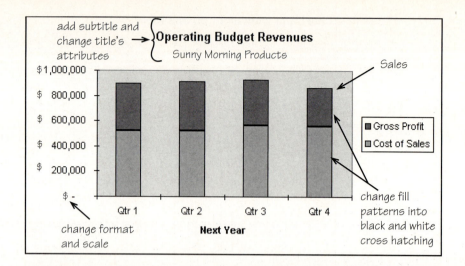

Adding and Changing Titles

First, Ann plans to add the subtitle for the chart. She will also change the point size of the title and subtitle to improve their appearance. Before you can make a change to an object on a chart—edit, move, resize, delete, or copy it—you need to select the object that you want to change. The appearance of handles indicates that an object is selected; text objects are surrounded by a border. You need to click individual chart objects to select them. Add the text "Sunny Morning Products" to the title of the chart.

To add a subtitle line to a chart's title:

1. Double-click anywhere on the chart to activate it.

2. Click the **Operating Budget Revenues** title to select it; confirm the selection by noting the appearance of the handles and border surrounding the text. The mouse pointer changes to an I-beam I for selecting text within the title text box.

3. Click to the right of the last character in the title to place the edit cursor at that location for adding text. The pointer appears as a vertical bar to indicate the insertion point, and the border disappears.

4. Press the **Enter** key to add a second text line. Note that pressing the Enter key does *not* complete the entry, as it often does with other activities in Excel.

5. Type **Sunny Morning Products** as the subtitle.

Changing point sizes and fonts for text in a chart is the same as changing them for cells in the worksheet—you select the text that you want to format and then select the desired formatting option. Ann wants the size of the Operating Budget Revenues title to be 12 points so it stands out, and she wants to italicize the subtitle. Begin by formatting the title by changing its point size.

To change the point size of a text object on a chart:

1. Select the **Operating Budget Revenues** title on the chart by clicking and dragging the I-beam pointer I over it. The selected text is highlighted.

2. Click the **Font Size** list arrow on the Formatting toolbar, then click **12**, the desired point size.

Next, italicize the Sunny Morning Products subtitle.

3. Select the **Sunny Morning Products** subtitle.

4. Click the **Italics** button *I* on the Formatting toolbar to apply that attribute to the selected text.

5. Click anywhere outside the title text box to finish changing the chart title.

You can change the appearance of any text objects on your chart using this procedure. Now that the chart title is complete, Ann needs to revise the number format for the y-axis.

Changing Axis Number Formats

Although you could use the Currency Style button on the Formatting toolbar to add the currency symbol to the value labels on the y-axis, that would not change the appearance of the starting value. You revise the number format for the y-axis using the Number setting sheet.

To change the number format of a y-axis:

1. Click the **y-axis** to select it, as indicated by a handle at each end of the axis.

2. Right-click the **y-axis** to display the shortcut menu for use with that object, click **Format Axis** to display the Format Axis dialog box, then click the **Number** tab to display that setting sheet. See Figure 3-25.

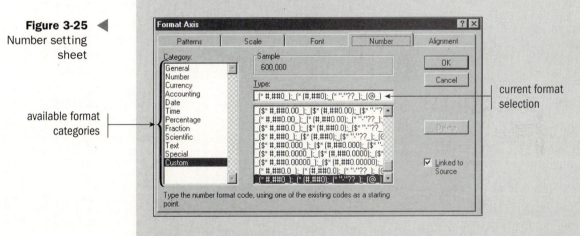

Figure 3-25 Number setting sheet

available format categories

current format selection

3. Click **Currency** in the Category list, click the **Use $** check box to check it, set the Decimal Places to **0**, select negative numbers displayed in red with parentheses, then click the **OK** button to apply this format to the y-axis.

Click Currency in the Category list, then click the OK button because the default Format Code is appropriate.

EXCEL 5.0

Changing the Axis Scale

Ann wants to revise the y-axis scale so that the major units displayed are $250,000 rather than $100,000. She thinks this interval will make the chart easier to read, as Carmen requested.

To change a y-axis scale:

1. Double-click the **y-axis** to display the Format Axis dialog box, then click the **Scale** tab to display that setting sheet.

2. Click and drag the I-beam pointer I over the current Major Unit value to select it.

3. Type **250000** as the new value for Major Unit, then press the **Enter** key to complete the scale specification and return to the chart with the revised axis scale.

Controlling Colors and Fill Patterns

Recall that Carmen wants Ann to change the colors of the chart to black and white so it can be copied more readily. Making this change requires that Ann select two fill patterns to replace the different colors assigned to each data series. A **fill pattern** is a design used to fill an area of a chart to differentiate it from another area of the chart. This will allow the managers to more easily distinguish the two data series. Change the color and fill pattern for the data series included on Ann's stacked column chart.

To change the fill pattern and color for a data series:

1. Select the **Gross Profit** data series by clicking it on the chart. You can click any one of the four bars to select the data series.

2. Double-click the **Gross Profit** data series for any of the four quarters to display the Format Data Series dialog box, then click the **Patterns** tab to display that setting sheet. See Figure 3-26.

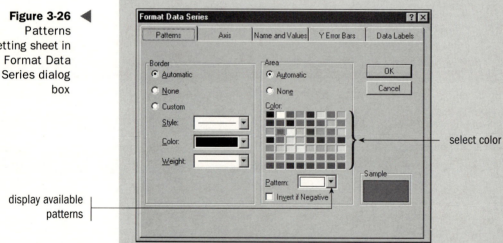

Figure 3-26
Patterns setting sheet in Format Data Series dialog box

3. Click the **Pattern** list arrow to display the palette of patterns, then click the **diagonal** pattern (fourth from the left in the second row from the top) to select it.

4. Click the color **black** (left most color in the top row), then click the **OK** button to apply that pattern and color to the Gross Profit data series on the chart.

Now complete the fill patterns for the stacked column bar chart.

5. Double-click the **Cost of Sales** data series to select it and display the Format Data Series dialog box.

6. Click the **Pattern** list arrow and select the **diagonal** fill pattern (third from the left in the second row) and choose **black** as its color, then click the **OK** button.

Ann's stacked column chart is almost complete. She still needs to add the note that Carmen suggested.

> **CHANGING FILL PATTERNS FOR DATA SERIES**
> - Click the data series to select it.
> - Double-click the same data series to display the Format Data Series dialog box.
>   *or*
>   Right-click the data series to display the shortcut menu, then click Format Data Series to display that dialog box.
> - Click the Pattern list arrow to display the available patterns.
> - Choose the desired pattern from the palette.

Adding Graphic Objects to Charts

Carmen suggests one more enhancement that will help with her presentation—adding graphic objects to the chart. You can add the same graphic objects to a chart that you can place in a worksheet. These graphic objects are also *added on top of the chart*, so they can sometimes cover important information unless they are carefully positioned.

Carmen asks Ann to add a text box to the column chart that points to the top of the stacked column for Qtr 4 to emphasize that the total height of the stacked bars represents Sales. The text in a text box can come from a cell within the worksheet or you can type it manually, as you did for the chart title and subtitle. The advantage of obtaining the text from a worksheet cell is that if the cell content is changed, the text box is automatically updated. Add the text box to Ann's chart.

To add a graphic object to a chart:

1. Click the **Drawing** button on the Standard toolbar to display the Drawing toolbar, then click the **Text Box** button on the Drawing toolbar to change the pointer to a crosshair ✚ for specifying the location and size of the text box.

   TROUBLE? If the Drawing toolbar is covering the location where you want the text box, then click and drag the title bar of the text box to reposition it.

2. Move the pointer to where you want the upper-left corner of the text box to be, click and drag the pointer to the opposite corner, then release the mouse button. Refer to Figure 3-27 for the approximate size and location of the text box. When you release the mouse button, the box outline disappears and you are in Edit mode.

3. Click the **formula bar** and press **=** to begin specifying a cell that contains the text. The insertion point and I-beam pointer appear in the formula bar, while a border indicates the text box location on the chart.

4. Click anywhere in the worksheet to begin specifying the cell reference using pointing and to display the scroll bars. The outline of the text box disappears, although the text box remains selected so that you can specify its content by pointing, as denoted by the Enter mode indicator.

5. Use the vertical scroll bar to scroll the worksheet so cell A7 is visible, click **A7**, which is the cell that contains the desired text, then click the **Enter** button to finish specifying the formula and display the text in the text box. See Figure 3-27.

Figure 3-27
Text from cell A7 appears in text box

selected object

cell reference formula

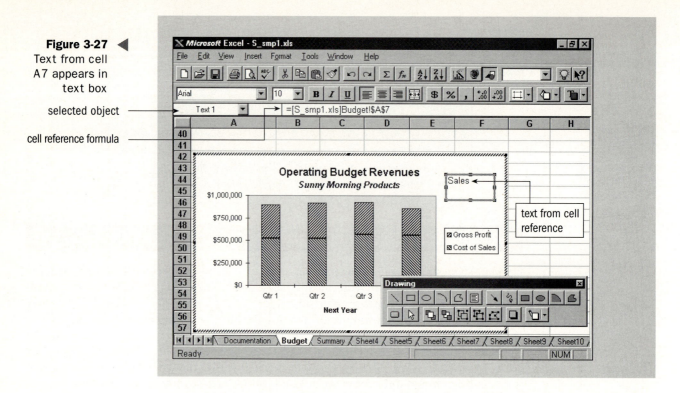

Ann has the text she wants for her chart, but she would like to center it in the text box.

To center text both horizontally and vertically in a text box:

1. Double-click the **text box** to display the Format Object dialog box, then click the **Alignment** tab to display that setting sheet.

2. Select the **Center** option button for both the Horizontal and Vertical Text Alignment, then click the **OK** button to apply these attributes to the text box.

3. Change the font size of the Sales text to 12.

   Ann has completed her text box, and it can now be unselected.

4. Click anywhere outside of the text box to unselect it. The text box displays as desired without a border.

   Next, add an arrow to the chart as the last enhancement.

5. Add an arrow graphic object that points to the top of the Qtr 4 column from the Sales text, then close the Drawing toolbar.

6. Save the workbook as S_SMP1.xls in the Tut03 folder.

If you want to take a break and resume the tutorial at a later time, you can do so now. Close the workbook and exit Excel. If you are on a network, leave Windows running. If you are using your own computer, you may exit Windows and shut down the computer. When you resume the tutorial, place your Student Disk in the disk drive, launch Excel, then continue with the tutorial.

● ● ●

Creating a Pie Chart

According to Ann's sketch in Figure 3-3, she needs to create a pie chart showing the expenses for the year. She will create this chart using steps similar to the ones used in developing her column chart. However, unlike the column chart, which has two data series, the pie chart has only one data series—the values for the expenses in the Total column. In creating her chart, Ann decides to place it in a separate chart sheet so it is easier for Carmen to access as she reviews next year's expenses. Create Ann's chart and place it in a separate chart sheet.

To create a pie chart in a separate chart sheet:

1. Scroll the worksheet as needed and select the nonadjacent ranges **A12:A21** and **F12:F21**, which contain the expense item labels and their annual data values.

2. Click **Insert**, point to **Chart**, then click **As New Sheet** to display the ChartWizard – Step 1 of 5 dialog box. Because the chart is placed in a separate sheet, the pointer for specifying the location and size of the chart does not appear.

3. Verify that the range for the chart data **=$A$12:$A$21**, **$F$12:$F$21** appears in the Range text box, then click the **Next>** button to proceed to the ChartWizard – Step 2 of 5 dialog box.

4. Click **Pie** as the desired chart type, click the **Next>** button to display the ChartWizard – Step 3 of 5 dialog box, click **7** as the desired chart format, then click the **Next>** button to display the ChartWizard – Step 4 of 5 dialog box.

5. Verify that the **Data Series in Columns** option is selected, click the **Next>** button to display the ChartWizard – Step 5 of 5 dialog box, verify that the **Add a Legend? No** option is selected, type **Operating Budget Expenses** as the chart title, then click the **Finish** button to display the pie chart in the Chart1 Chart sheet. See Figure 3-28.

Figure 3-28 ◀
Ann's pie chart in the Chart1 sheet

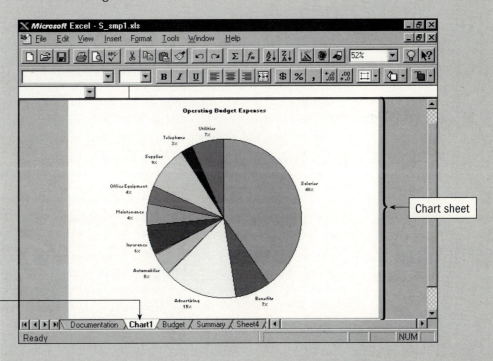

default sheet name

6. Double-click the **Chart1** sheet tab to display the Rename Sheet dialog box, type **Expenses Pie Chart** in the Name text box, then click the **OK** button.

7. Click and drag the **Expenses Pie Chart** tab so that sheet appears after (to the right of) the Summary sheet.

8. Save this as the S_SMP2.xls workbook in the Tut03 folder.

Ann's pie chart satisfies her initial design. However, she now thinks it would be better to move Salaries to the lower-left area of the chart so the other expenses appear on the right side of her chart with more room for the planning item names. To do this, she needs to rotate the pie chart until the Salaries slice appears in the desired location.

To change the rotation of a pie chart:

1. Right-click the chart to display the shortcut menu, click **Format Pie Group** to display that dialog box, then click the **Options** tab to display the degrees of rotation for the first slice, which is the Salaries data. See Figure 3-29.

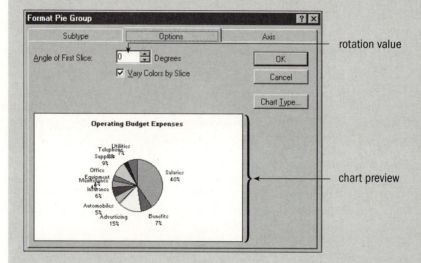

Figure 3-29 ◄
Format Pie Group dialog box with Options settings

2. Click the **Degrees** increase arrow until Angle of First Slice is 160, then click the **OK** button to display the pie chart with that rotation. As you click the increase arrow, you can preview the rotation of the pie chart in the setting sheet.

Now Ann thinks that the Benefits slice would be more distinct if she were to **explode**, or separate, it from the other slices. Exploding is best used to draw attention to the one or two most important data points in a pie chart.

3. Click the **pie chart** itself so that all the slices are selected, as indicated by a handle at the outside edge of each slice.

4. Click the **Benefits** slice to select it, then click and drag it to explode it from the rest of the pie chart. As you drag, a dotted line indicates the new position of the slice. When you release the mouse button, the Benefits slice is exploded.

TROUBLE? If all the slices exploded, it is because they were all selected when you performed the drag. Click the Undo button to unexplode the chart, click anywhere outside of the pie, click anywhere on the pie, then repeat Step 4.

EXPLODING PIE CHART SLICES

- To explode a single pie slice, click the slice once to select the whole chart, then click it again to select that single slice.
  or
  To explode all the slices, click the chart once to select the whole chart.
- Drag the slice away from the center to the position you want.

To explode several individual slices, click and drag each slice one at a time.

Ann thinks her pie chart looks great and that Carmen will be pleased with it. However, she still wants to add two more enhancements to her chart. She wants a subtitle that better describes the chart data and a note that points out the human resource expenses. You change and add text objects on a chart that is in a separate chart sheet the same way as on a chart placed in a worksheet. Add these enhancements to Ann's pie chart.

To make enhancements to a chart in a chart sheet:

1. Select the **chart title** and add the subtitle **Total Expenses Comparison**.

2. Add a text block that contains **Human Resource Expenses** and place it on the chart, as shown in Figure 3-30. Choose the **Shadow** and **Round Corners** options for the border. Include the arrows as shown in the figure.

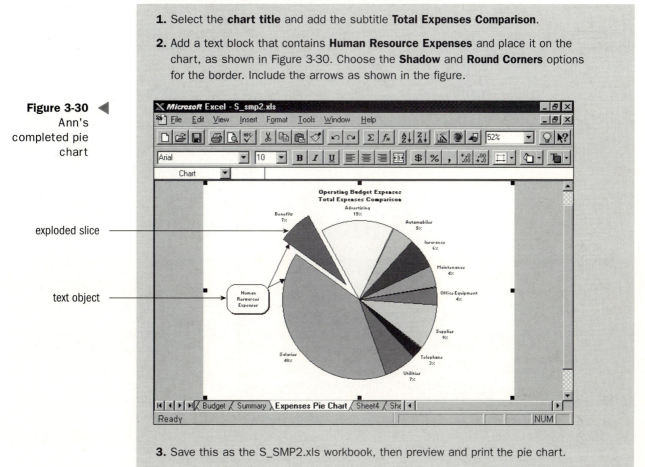

Figure 3-30 ◀ Ann's completed pie chart

exploded slice

text object

3. Save this as the S_SMP2.xls workbook, then preview and print the pie chart.

Performing a What-If Analysis with Charts

Carmen has been analyzing the Total expenses for next year's Operating Budget, as shown in Ann's pie chart. The management committee may ask her to find a way to trim expenses, and she wants to examine how decreasing some expenses will affect the overall budget. In Excel, when you change a data value in the worksheet area that supplies the data values for a chart, the chart is automatically updated. Also, for some chart types, when you change a data value on the chart, the data in the worksheet area is updated. A side-by-side column chart is one of the easiest to use when changing data values. Carmen agrees to meet with Ann to examine several different what-if situations. First, Ann needs to create a side-by-side column chart of selected budget expenses by quarter to be used in the what-if analysis.

To create a side-by-side column chart for a what-if analysis:

1. Click the **Budget** tab to make it the active worksheet, then select the nonadjacent ranges **A5:E5** and **A15:E21**, which contain the data Ann wants to use for the what-if analysis.

2. Create a side-by-side column chart in a separate chart sheet, using column chart format **6**, and give it the title **Selected Budget Expenses**. Include a legend.

   TROUBLE? If the x-axis labels are not all visible, click the x-axis to select it, right-click the x-axis to display the shortcut menu, click Format Axis, click the Alignment tab, click the middle vertical orientation option, then click the OK button.

3. Name this sheet **Expenses** and move it to the right of the Expenses Pie Chart tab. See Figure 3-31.

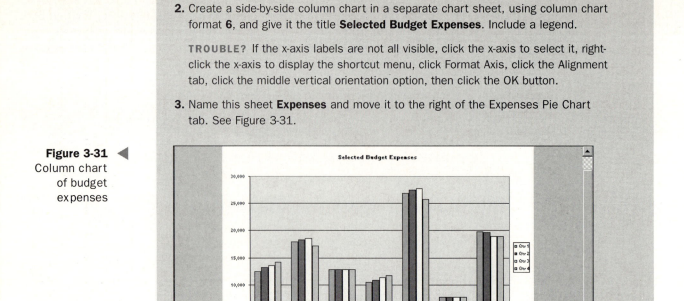

Figure 3-31
Column chart of budget expenses

your x-axis labels may have a vertical orientation

selected expenses

In the Operating Budget, the Utilities data values are numeric constants that are entered for each quarter. A what-if analysis is most readily performed on constants that are input, rather than on calculated formulas. Carmen and Ann agree to limit their analysis to the constants that are input. Use the column chart to perform a what-if analysis on expense items in Qtr 1 and Qtr 2.

To perform a what-if analysis by changing data values on a chart:

1. Click the **Utilities** column data marker for Qtr 2 to select the entire Qtr 2 data series.

2. Click the **Qtr 2 Utilities** column to select that single data marker.

3. Move the pointer to the top of the column until it changes to ↕. You are ready to do the what-if.

4. Click and drag the top of the column downward until **17,000** is displayed in the reference area, then release the mouse button to accept that data value. See Figure 3-32. As you drag the column, the reference area displays the new value, a tick mark on the y-axis indicates the value, and the size of the revised column is outlined. When you release the mouse button, the new data value is placed in the worksheet area for the data series.

Figure 3-32
What-if value entered by changing the column's height

new data value appears while dragging top of column

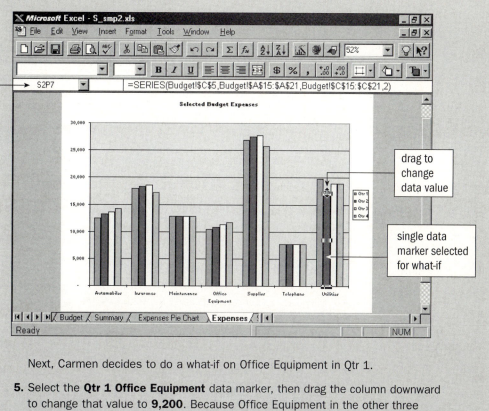

Next, Carmen decides to do a what-if on Office Equipment in Qtr 1.

5. Select the **Qtr 1 Office Equipment** data marker, then drag the column downward to change that value to **9,200**. Because Office Equipment in the other three quarters is calculated using the value in Qtr 1, changing that value changes all four values.

6. Activate the Budget worksheet and verify that the data values for Utilities in Qtr 2 and Office Equipment in Qtr 1 through Qtr 4 were revised by the changes made using the chart.

   TROUBLE? If the Budget worksheet tab is not visible, use the worksheet scroll buttons above the Ready status indicator to scroll the worksheet tabs until the Budget tab is visible.

7. Save this as the S_SMP2.xls workbook in the Tut03 folder. Preview and print the Selected Budget Expenses chart.

Carmen now has a better idea of how a decrease in some expenses over the year will affect the budget.

Creating a 3-D Column Chart

After completing these charts, Ann decides to pursue several of the other possible charts she discussed with Carmen. With their concern about expenses next year, Ann thinks a 3-D column chart of the expenses would be useful for comparing expenses across the four quarters.

A 3-D column chart displays data as three-dimensional columns plotted on either two or three axes. A two-axis 3-D column chart looks similar to a 2-D column chart. The axes are the same in both types of graphs. In the two-axis 3-D column chart shown in Figure 3-4, one axis references expense items and the other axis references dollar amounts. A legend is used to refer to the different quarters.

ADVEX 154 **TUTORIAL 3** CREATING AND PRINTING CHARTS

A three-axis 3-D column chart adds a third axis, which references the information contained within the legend. In the three-axis 3-D column chart shown in Figure 3-4, the third axis references the four quarters. A three-axis chart allows you to compare data series by category without having to refer to a legend. This feature of three-axis 3-D charts makes the data easier to view. Ann decides that a three-axis chart will provide the best comparison for Sunny Morning Products expenses. She wants to modify her 2-D expense comparison column chart for this view of her data.

To create a three-axis column chart from a 2-D chart:

1. Activate the **Expenses** Chart sheet, right-click the chart to display the shortcut menu, then click **Chart Type** to display the Chart Type dialog box.

   TROUBLE? If the shortcut menu did not display Chart Type, click the edge of the chart to make sure the entire chart is selected, then repeat Step 1.

2. Select the **3-D Chart Dimension** option button, then double-click **3-D Column** to select that chart type and display the 3-D chart. You can specify this 3-D chart format either in the Chart Type dialog box or with the ChartWizard when you create the chart.

3. Click the legend to select it, then press the **Delete** key to remove the legend. The legend is not needed with this chart because the third axis in the chart provides the information contained in the legend.

4. Click anywhere on the chart's grayed background to activate it, then increase the width of the chart to include the area previously occupied by the legend.

   TROUBLE? If the Format Chart Area dialog box appeared, click the Cancel button, then click the grayed background of the chart to activate it.

Ann is pleased with the arrangement of this three-axis column chart, but some of the columns are not visible. One disadvantage of three-axis 3-D column charts is that some columns that appear at the back of the chart may be obscured by taller columns in the front. Ann needs to revise the chart by changing its **View**, which consists of its elevation, rotation, and perspective. The **elevation** sets the height from which you appear to look down on or view the chart data. The **rotation** establishes the sideways appearance of the chart, that is, the extent to which you view the data from the side. The **perspective** specifies the ratio of the width of the front-to-back distance, or how far away the rear data appears to be from the front of the chart. When you need to change all three aspects of the chart view, the elevation, rotation, and perspective, use the settings in the Format 3-D View dialog box to preview your changes as you try different settings.

HELP DESK

Index

FORMATTING THE VIEW OF 3-D CHARTS

Double-click the Help button to display the Help Topics Dialog box, then click the Index tab.

Keyword	Topic
3-D charts in Excel	Format the parts of and perspective in 3-D charts

In this situation, Ann only needs to adjust two characteristics of her 3-D chart view, rotation and elevation. She can use the mouse pointer to make these changes. You can adjust the elevation and rotation by dragging a corner of the plot area. The **plot area** is the area of the chart where the data is displayed by the data marker, such as a bar or line. Use the mouse pointer to change the rotation and elevation of Ann's chart so that the columns are more visible.

CREATING A 3-D COLUMN CHART **ADVEX 155**

To change the view of a three-axis 3-D chart using the mouse pointer:

1. Click the bottom right corner of the plot area to select it and display a handle at each corner of the plot. The pointer changes to the cross hair ✛ for altering the view.

2. Hold down the mouse button to display an outline of the current view of the plot. See Figure 3-33.

Figure 3-33 ◀
Outline indicates plot view

chart outline

drag corner to change rotation and elevation

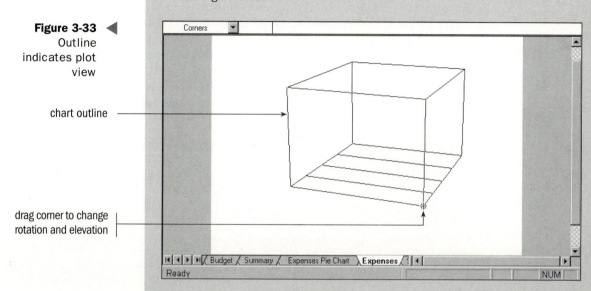

TROUBLE? If the outline did not appear when you held down the mouse button, then move the mouse slightly to display it.

3. Drag the corner of the plot until it appears similar to that shown in Figure 3-34. If you don't succeed on the first attempt, then try again.

Figure 3-34 ◀
Rotation and elevation modified by dragging plot

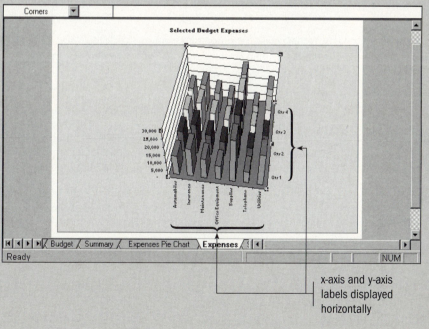

x-axis and y-axis labels displayed horizontally

4. Save this as the S_SMP2.xls workbook, then preview and print the Expenses chart.

Ann believes that this three-axis 3-D version of the Expenses chart will help Carmen as she further examines the expenses for next year's Operating Budget.

Preparing a Combination Chart

A combination chart is a single chart that displays data in more than one way. For example, a combination chart might show several data series as columns and another data series as a line. By combining different chart types, you create an overlay effect. The data series can use the same y-axis, or you can use a second y-axis if the values of the data series vary widely. In Excel, 2-D charts can be combined, but 3-D charts cannot because of the difficulty in showing the third dimension with different displays of the data.

Ann needs to create a chart that displays all the data in her Summary sheet for the four quarters except Earnings Before Tax. Because the Return On Sales values are percent data values that are all less than 1, the difference between them from quarter to quarter cannot be distinguished if Return On Sales is plotted on the same scale as the other data in her Summary sheet. Also, she wants to draw attention to the Return On Sales data. Create a combination chart that displays this data and place it in the Summary sheet.

To create a combination chart:

1. Click the **Summary** sheet tab, then select the nonadjacent ranges **A7:E7**, **A9:E10**, **A12:E12**, and **A16:E16**, which contain the desired data series Cost of Sales, Gross Profit, Total Expenses, and Return on Sales, for Ann's chart.

2. Click the **ChartWizard** button ☒ on the Standard toolbar.

3. Scroll the worksheet window and specify the location of the chart in the range **A19:F35**.

4. Using the ChartWizard dialog boxes, select **Combination** as the chart type, select **2** as the Combination chart format, select the **Row** option for the Data Series, type **Operating Budget Summary** as the Chart Title, type **Next Year** as the Category (X) Axis Title, then click the **Finish** button. Excel automatically assigns both Total Expenses and Return On Sales as line chart types because it equally divides the data series between the column and line types.

   The Total Expenses data series needs to be changed from a line format to a column format in the chart.

5. Double-click the **chart** to activate it, click the **Total Expense line** in the chart to select it, then double-click the **Total Expense line** to display the Format Data Series dialog box.

6. Click the **Axis** tab, select the **Primary Axis** option button to assign this data series to the other axis, then click the **OK** button.

7. Right-click the chart to display the shortcut menu, then click **Format Line Group 2** to display the Format Line Group dialog box. Because the line for the Total Expenses data series is the most recent one that was switched to the primary axis, Excel calls it Format Line Group 2.

8. Click the **Chart Type** button, then double-click **Column** as the chart type to display the desired chart. See Figure 3-35.

Figure 3-35 ◀
Combination chart

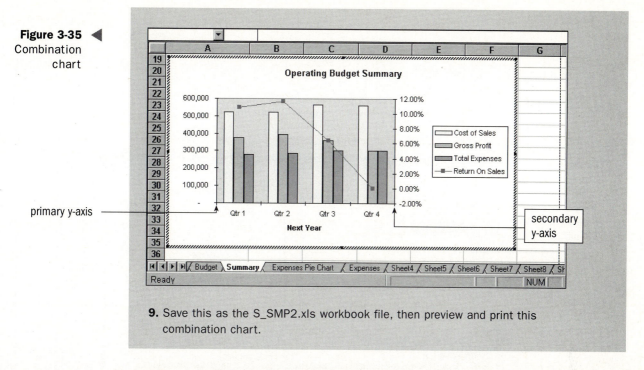

9. Save this as the S_SMP2.xls workbook file, then preview and print this combination chart.

Ann is satisfied that the combination chart provides a good summary of next year's Operating Budget.

Creating a Picture Chart

Carmen plans to send a memo to the Sunny Morning Products management committee informing them of the budget review meeting. She decides to include a version of the budget summary chart you just created with her memo. To enhance the appearance of this chart, she wants Ann to use a graphic or **picture** to liven up the display of the Gross Profit columns on the chart. Although Ann could add pictures to Cost of Sales and Total Expenses, she feels that using them with Gross Profit will provide more impact for this chart. She has some appropriate graphic picture files that she created several weeks ago using the Windows Paint program. Once a chart is created, you can replace its plain data markers with more interesting pictures. This replacement can occur any time and does not need to be done immediately upon creating a chart.

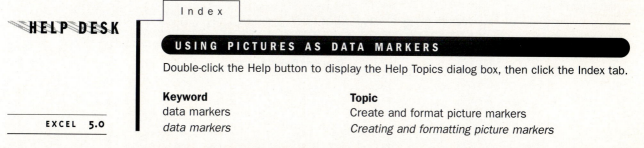

Change the plain column data markers to pictures in the Operating Budget Summary chart.

To use pictures as data markers on a column chart:

1. Make sure the chart is activated, then click the **Gross Profit** data series, which will have the picture marker applied to it.

2. Click **Insert**, then click **Picture** to display the Picture dialog box. If Tut03 is not the current default folder or directory, then select the Tut03 folder to display a list of available graphic files. Click the **c_sunny.bmp** file to display a preview of it. See Figure 3-36.

The Picture dialog box contains Directories and Drives boxes for selecting the Tut03 directory. Click the Preview Picture option button to view the highlighted picture file.

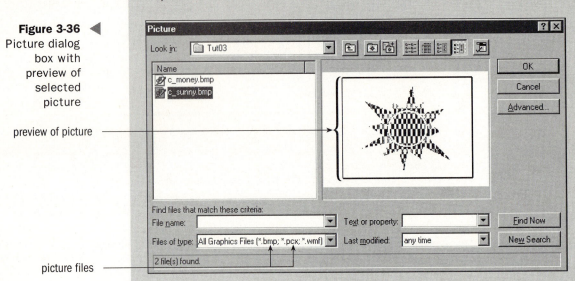

Figure 3-36 ◀
Picture dialog box with preview of selected picture

preview of picture

picture files

3. Click the **OK** button to place this picture in the column. The picture is stretched to fill the entire bar, but you will change that later to make the display more appealing.

Next, stack the pictures in the columns to make a more appealing display.

4. Double-click the **Gross Profit data series** to select it and display the Format Data Series dialog box. Click the **Patterns** tab, select the **Stack** option button for the Picture Format, then click the **OK** button. See Figure 3-37.

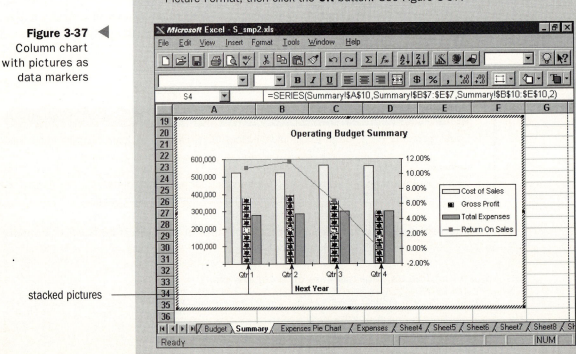

Figure 3-37 ◀
Column chart with pictures as data markers

stacked pictures

INTEGRATING WINDOWS PROGRAMS **ADVEX 159**

5. Double-click the edge of the plot area to select the chart object and display the Format Plot Area dialog box. Select **white** (top row, second from left) as the color, then click the **OK** button to complete this change to the chart. The white chart background makes it easier to duplicate the chart for distribution.

6. Save this as the S_SMP2.xls workbook in the Tut03 folder.

REFERENCE **window**

USING PICTURES AS DATA MARKERS

- Create a column or bar chart.
- Select the data series to be represented by the picture data marker.
- Click Insert, click Picture to display that dialog box, and review the list of available files containing pictures.
- Select the desired picture file and click the **OK** button for the stretched picture.
- If appropriate, double-click the data series, click the Patterns tab, select the Stack option button, and click the OK button for stacked pictures.

Ann has completed the chart, and is ready to integrate it into Carmen's memo to the management committee.

Integrating Windows Programs

Instead of attaching the Summary chart as a separate page of the memo, Carmen wants to integrate it into her memo, which she has created using Microsoft WordPad, the word processor program that comes with Microsoft Windows 95. **Integrating programs** is the transferring and sharing of data among different software tools. A Windows **object** is an Excel range or chart that you can use in another program. The object is copied from the **source**, or **server** program, and the copy is pasted into the **destination**, or **client**, program. For Carmen's integration, Excel is the source, and WordPad (or Write for Windows 3.1) is the destination program. An easy method of sharing information between Windows programs is to **paste** an object from a source program into a destination program with a *copy* of the selected object placed in the destination document. When you paste a copy of an object from a source program into a destination program, you have no connection to the document file from which you transferred the object. Once the paste is completed, any direct relationship to the source document is lost. If you want to change the object, you need to locate the original source document file, make the desired changes using the appropriate program, then replace the old copy of the object in the destination program with the revised copy of the object.

HELP DESK

Index

INTEGRATING PROGRAMS

Double-click the Help button to display the Help Topics dialog box, then click the Index tab.

Keyword	Topic
copying between applications	Drag and drop information between applications
copying, to other applications	*Dragging data between applications*

EXCEL **5.0**

ADVEX 160 **TUTORIAL 3** CREATING AND PRINTING CHARTS

Because Carmen does not anticipate any changes in the Operating Budget before she sends her memo, pasting the Excel chart into the memo is the easiest method for her program integration. All that she needs to do is to copy the chart to the clipboard in Excel, launch the word processing program with her already prepared text of the memo, and paste the Excel chart object into the word processing document.

To copy a chart object to the clipboard:

1. Make sure the chart is activated, then click the **Summary** chart near the thick gray border to make sure the entire chart is selected. Another set of eight handles appears just inside the border to indicate that the entire chart object is selected. That is, the chart is activated and the *entire* chart object is selected.

   TROUBLE? If the thick gray border did not appear at the very perimeter of the entire chart, then the chart is not selected. Double-click the chart, then repeat Step 1.

2. Click the **Copy** button 🗐 on the Standard toolbar to copy the entire chart object to the clipboard.

Next, you need to launch the word processing program and open the partially completed memo.

To launch a word processing program:

EXCEL 5.0

1. Click the **Start** button, point to **Programs**, click **Accessories**, then click **WordPad**. *For Windows 3.1, launch Write from the Accessories program group.* Maximize this program window.

2. Click **File** on the WordPad menu bar, then click **Open**. Double-click **C_SMP1.WRI** in the Tut03 folder. The text of Carmen's memo displays in the document window.

   TROUBLE? If no filenames are listed in the file list box, select the *.WRI file type to display the filename for selection.

3. Position the edit cursor I at the bottom of the document. Press the **Enter** key once to ensure adequate space between the last line of the memo and the chart.

With the document file open in the active window and a copy of the chart object in the clipboard, you are ready to paste the copy into the destination document.

To integrate a chart object into a memo by pasting it:

EXCEL 5.0

1. Click the **Paste** button 🗐 on the WordPad Standard toolbar to paste the chart into the memo.

   Click Edit, then click Paste in Write to paste the chart.

EXCEL 5.0

2. Click the **Print** button 🖨 on the WordPad Standard toolbar to print the memo with the chart.

   Click File, click Print, then click the OK button in Write to print the memo. See Figure 3-38.

INTEGRATING WINDOWS PROGRAMS **ADVEX 161**

Figure 3-38
Integrated program with Excel chart

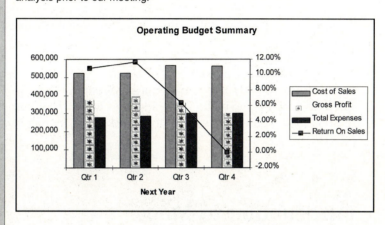

3. Close WordPad (*for Windows 3.1, close Write*) and do *not* save the integrated document. It is best if you do *not* save the document because the picture objects require too much space on your Student Disk. For this reason, you should exercise care in saving Excel charts that include pictures as the data markers.

4. Close the S_SMP2.xls workbook.

> **INTEGRATING PROGRAMS WITH COPY AND PASTE**
>
> - Select the Excel chart or worksheet range.
> - Copy the object to the clipboard.
> - Launch the destination program and open the document in which the object will be placed.
> - Click where you want the object inserted.
> - Click the Paste button to place the copy of the object from Excel into the destination document.
>   *or*
>   Click Edit, then click Paste to place the copy at the specified destination.

Carmen's memo is complete. She's ready to duplicate it and send it to the management committee.

If you want to take a break and resume the tutorial at a later time, you can do so now. Exit Excel. If you are on a network, leave Windows running. If you are using your own computer, you may exit Windows and shut down the computer. When you resume the tutorial, place your Student Disk in the disk drive, launch Excel, then continue with the tutorial.

Introduction to Maps

The Excel **Data Map feature** allows you to link worksheet data to geographic maps. When you view your data as a coded map, you can easily see the trends and relationships in it. For example, you could use mapping to translate US census data into a map in which states with populations between 0 and 20 million appear in red, states with populations between 21 and 100 million appear in blue, and so on. The range of numbers assigned to a particular color is called an interval, or **spread**. Excel automatically divides your data into intervals with equal numbers of items and then assigns colors (or patterns) to each interval. You can optionally specify an equal spread or values for each interval. After you create a map, you can change the colors, as well as the range of numbers assigned to those colors, in order to improve the appearance of the map. *If you are using Excel Version 5.0, you cannot create maps because this feature is available beginning with Version 7.0; you should skip this section of the tutorial and proceed to the end of the tutorial assignments and cases.*

A variety of maps are available for displaying your data; several of these are provided with Version 7.0, while many others can be purchased separately. The following maps are provided with Excel:

- World countries
- United States by state
- Canada by province
- Europe by country
- Mexico by estado
- United Kingdom by standard region
- Australia by state

INTRODUCTION TO MAPS **ADVEX 163**

HELP DESK

EXCEL 5.0

Index

USING THE EXCEL DATA MAP FEATURE

Double-click the Help button to display the Help Topics dialog box, then click the Index tab.

Keyword
mapping data
not available

Topic
Displaying data in a map

Carmen asks Ann to prepare a map of next year's expected sales by state for her presentation. Ann plans to create a map that divides the sales figures into intervals with an equal number of items in each interval. States with the same sales figures in the same interval will appear in the same pattern. Ann completes her planning analysis sheet for creating the map (Figure 3-39).

Figure 3-39 ◀
Planning
analysis sheet
for Ann's map

Planning Analysis Sheet

My goal:

Prepare a map showing expected sales by state for next year's Operating Budget

What results do I want to see?

Map of USA with expected sales displayed by state in one of four intervals with approximately the same number of states in each interval

What information do I need?

Expected sales for next year by state with state geographic codes

---

Ann prepares the data for next year's Operating Budget in a workbook named C_SMP2.xls (Figure 3-40). For her own reference, she places the state names in column A. Then she organizes the data series for the map in columns, with column B containing the predefined two-character geographical abbreviations for each location, column C holding the data identifying the sales regions, and column D containing the sales data for each geographic location. Although Excel only requires two data series (in columns B and D) for a map, Ann may want to use the second data series for Sunny Morning Products' sales regions in another map. You can find out more about map geographical names by examining the MAPSTATS.xls workbook file that is installed with Excel, or by accessing the Excel on-line Help.

Figure 3-40
Data arranged for creating an Excel map

column headings for reference

map abbreviations

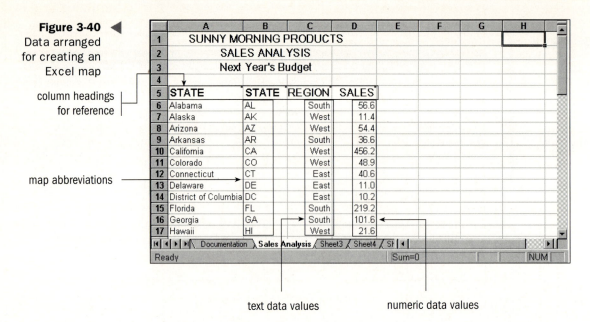

text data values

numeric data values

Ann's finished map will look like Figure 3-41. The expected sales data is grouped into four categories with a fill pattern on the map.

Figure 3-41
Ann's expected sales map

Map menu

Map toolbar

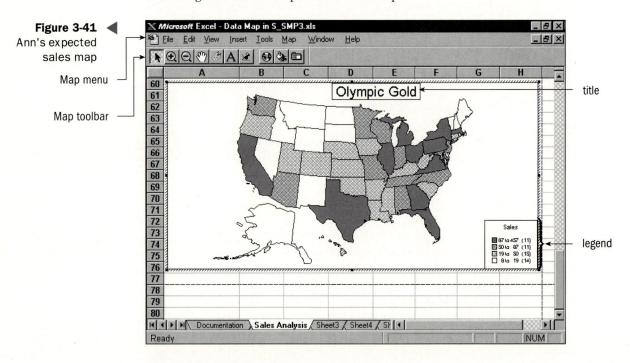

title

legend

Creating a Map

Ann wants to create a map from the data she prepared by state. Open her workbook and review its organization in preparation for creating this map.

To open the workbook and review the data for creating a map:

1. Open the C_SMP2.xls workbook located in the Tut03 folder on your Student Disk. Then save the workbook as S_SMP3.xls in case you want to create this map again. The open workbook appears, as shown previously in Figure 3-40.

CREATING A MAP **ADVEX 165**

2. Review Ann's Sales Analysis worksheet. Observe the arrangement of the two-character geographical map codes, which correspond to the two-letter state abbreviations used by the US Postal Service. For US maps, you can use either the entire state name or its two-letter abbreviation as the geographical identifier.

According to Ann's plan, she wants to create the map for the expected sales data by state.

To create a map:

1. Make sure that the Sales Analysis worksheet is displayed and select the range **B5:D56**, which contains the data series arranged in columns as required for producing an Excel map. Notice that the column headings are included in the selected range.

2. Scroll the worksheet window until cell A60 is positioned in the upper-left corner of the window. Ann's map is to be an embedded object that is placed in the worksheet. This is the location for the upper-left corner of the embedded map. Do not click the mouse at this location, or you will unselect the range you want for the map.

TROUBLE? If you clicked A60 by mistake, repeat Steps 1 and 2.

3. Click the **Map** button 🌑. The pointer changes to a crosshair **+** to indicate that Excel is ready for you to specify the location of your new map.

4. Click and drag the pointer from cell **A60** to cell **H76** to outline the map's location and size. When you release the mouse button, the Multiple Maps Available dialog box opens. You will use this dialog box to select your map.

TROUBLE? If the Unable to Create Map dialog box appeared, you selected the wrong data and the geographic codes were not recognized. Click the Cancel button and repeat Steps 1 through 4.

TROUBLE? If this message is displayed: "Microsoft Data Map is not installed. To Use Data Map you must run Setup and choose to add Microsoft Data Map," seek the assistance of your instructor or technical support person.

5. Click **United States (AK & HI Inset)** to select it as the desired map, then click the **OK** button and wait for the map to be drawn.

6. Click the **Close** button ☒ in the Data Map Control dialog box so the entire map and legend are visible. See Figure 3-42. By default, Excel uses the data in the leftmost column for the geographical names and the data in the rightmost column for the values that are initially plotted. A thick gray border surrounds the entire map to indicate that it is activated.

TROUBLE? If your legend does not match the default legend and intervals shown in Figure 3-42, your default is set for Use Compact Format. This will be corrected when you format the legend later in this tutorial.

Figure 3-42
Ann's initial map

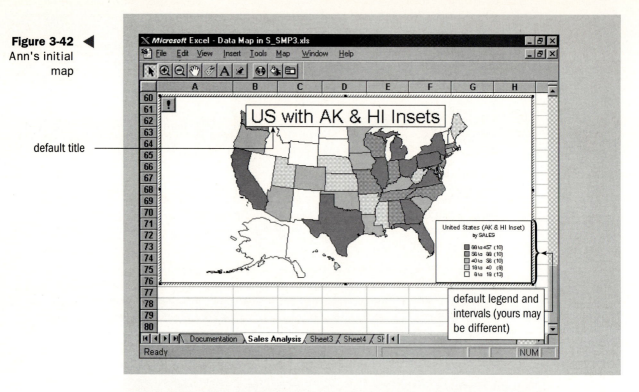

default title

default legend and intervals (yours may be different)

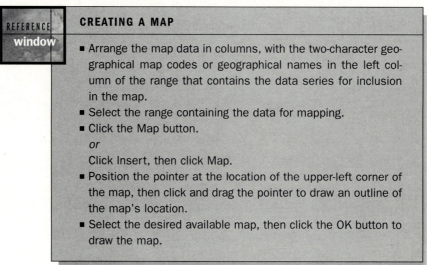

REFERENCE window

CREATING A MAP

- Arrange the map data in columns, with the two-character geographical map codes or geographical names in the left column of the range that contains the data series for inclusion in the map.
- Select the range containing the data for mapping.
- Click the Map button.
  or
  Click Insert, then click Map.
- Position the pointer at the location of the upper-left corner of the map, then click and drag the pointer to draw an outline of the map's location.
- Select the desired available map, then click the OK button to draw the map.

As she reviews her map, Ann notices several characteristics that she wants to change. First, she wants to add her own title to the map. Second, she does not need all the categories Excel has provided for distinguishing data. Finally, the legend title is not appropriate and needs to be changed. Begin modifying the map by changing its title.

To change a map title:

1. Click the **map title** to activate it (as indicated by the box surrounding the title).

2. Click the **map title** again to begin editing it. Use the I-beam pointer I to highlight the current text, and then type **Olympic Gold** as the new map title.

3. Right-click the **map title** to display the shortcut menu, click **Format Font** to display the Font dialog box, select **16** as the font size, then click the **OK** button to finish changing the format of the new map title.

> **TROUBLE?** If the shortcut menu did not display the Format Font menu choice, you right-clicked the map and not its title. Repeat Step 3.
>
> 4. Click anywhere on the map other than on the title to end the edit.
>
>   The desired title displays on the map, but is in the wrong location.
>
> 5. Click the **title** to activate it. Move the pointer on top of the title until it changes to ✥, then click and drag it so it is centered at the top of the map, as shown previously in Figure 3-41.
>
> 6. Click anywhere on the map other than the title to deactivate it.

Now Ann is ready to change the five data categories used for displaying the sales data on the map. She wants only four data intervals for differentiating the data values. Adjust Ann's data intervals to improve the comparison among the states.

To change data categories and legends:

> 1. Click **Map**, click **Value Shading Options** to display that dialog box, click the **Number of value ranges** list arrow and select **4** in the scroll list, then click the **OK** button to finish this change. See Figure 3-43. The map is redrawn with four intervals.

Figure 3-43 ◀
Value Shading Options dialog box

number of intervals

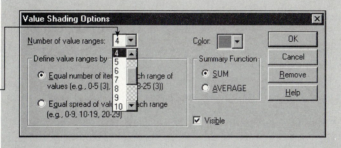

> 2. Double-click the **legend** to display the Edit Legend dialog box, change the Title to **Sales**, delete the **Subtitle**, then click the **OK** button to complete the changes to the legend.
>
>   **TROUBLE?** If the options in the Edit Legend dialog box are grayed out, uncheck the Use Compact Format check box to turn that option off, then repeat Step 2.
>
> 3. Move the pointer on top of the legend so it changes to ✥, then click and drag the legend so it is in the extreme lower-right corner of the map, and release the mouse button.
>
> 4. Save the workbook with the newly completed map as S_SMP3.xls.
>
>   Ann is ready to print her map.
>
> 5. Click **File**, click **Print Preview** to display the Preview window, click the **Print** button, then click the **OK** button to initiate printing.
>
>   **TROUBLE?** If the map did not appear in the Preview window, close the Preview window, click anywhere in the worksheet outside the map, click the map to select it, then repeat Step 5.

Modifying a Map

When Ann initially selected her data for the map, the range included the marketing regions. However, when she used the Excel default map setting, this data was not included in her map. Once a map is created, the Data Map Control dialog box lets you drag the column heading buttons to change the data displayed. Ann now needs to modify her map so both the sales and region data is displayed. She revises her planning analysis sheet (Figure 3-44).

Figure 3-44 Ann's revised plan for the sales map

Planning Analysis Sheet

My goal:

Prepare a map showing expected sales by state and identified by marketing region for next year's Operating Budget

What results do I want to see?

Map of USA with expected sales indicated by dots and grouped by marketing region

What information do I need?

Expected sales for next year by state with state geographic codes and marketing region name

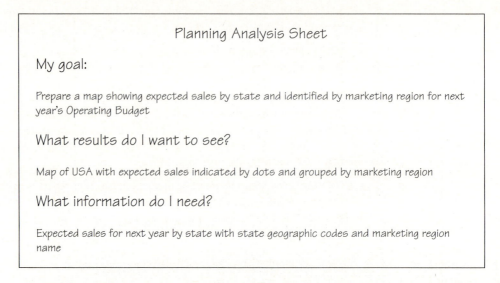

Each marketing region will be a different color, while the sales in each state are indicated using dots with each dot as $10,000 of sales.

To change the data displayed on a map:

1. Make sure the map is activated and click the **Show/Hide Data Map Control** button on the Map toolbar to redisplay the Data Map Control dialog box. See Figure 3-45.

Figure 3-45 Data Map Control dialog box

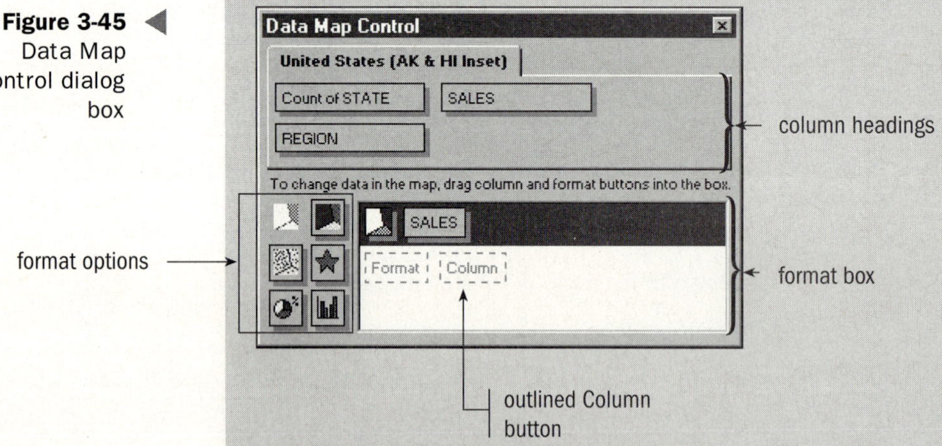

2. Click and drag the **Sales** button out of the format box at the bottom of the dialog box to remove that data from the map. The pointer changes to when it is out of the format box. When you release the mouse button, the map is displayed without any data.

3. Click and drag the **Region** button for that column heading into the format box and place it on top of the outlined Column button. The pointer changes to while you drag the column heading box. When you release the mouse button, the map is redrawn with the four marketing regions appearing in red, blue, green, and yellow.

MODIFYING A MAP **ADVEX 169**

4. Click and drag the **Sales** button for that column heading into the format box and place it on top of the outlined Column button. When you release the mouse button, the Sales data appears on the map as dots to indicate the sales in each state.

5. Close the Data Map Control dialog box and review the revised map.

Ann doesn't like the placement of the legends and she's concerned that the red and blue colors will not print well on her black-and-white printer. She needs to change these features of her map.

To change a map legend:

1. Double-click the **REGION** legend to select it and display the Edit Legend dialog box. Change the Title to **Regions** and delete the **Subtitle**. Then click the **OK** button to complete this modification.

   TROUBLE? If the options in the Edit Legend dialog box are grayed out, uncheck the Use Compact Format check box to turn that option off, then repeat Step 1.

2. Click and drag the **Regions** legend to the extreme lower-right corner of the map.

3. Double-click the **SALES legend** to select it and display the Edit Legend dialog box. Change the Title to **Sales**, and delete the **Subtitle**. Click the **Font** button for the title, select **9** as the Size, then click the **OK** button.

   TROUBLE? If the options in the Edit Legend dialog box are grayed out, uncheck the Use Compact Format check box to turn that option off, then repeat Step 3.

4. Click the **Edit Legend Entries** button to display the Edit Legend Entry dialog box and edit the Type new legend entry text box so it shows **1 Dot = $10,000**.

5. Click the **Font** button to display the Font dialog box, select **8** as the Size, click the **OK** button for the Font to return to the Edit Legend entry dialog box, click the **OK** button for the Edit Legend Entry, then click the **OK** button for the Edit Legend to finish changing this legend.

6. Click and drag the **Sales legend** to the bottom of the map and place it in the location of the Gulf of Mexico.

Now Ann needs to fix the red and blue colors for the Central and West regions.

To change category shading colors:

1. Click **Map** on the menu bar, then click **Category Shading Options** to display that dialog box.

2. Click **Central** and change its color to **white**.

3. Click **West** and change its color to **turquoise** (the color immediately above white in the scroll list of colors).

4. Click the **OK** button to finish changing the shading colors and redraw the map with these colors. See Figure 3-46.

Figure 3-46
Map with sales and regions

modified legends

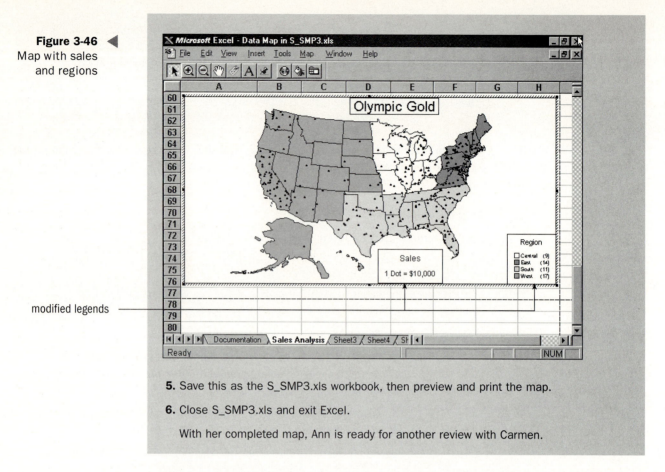

5. Save this as the S_SMP3.xls workbook, then preview and print the map.

6. Close S_SMP3.xls and exit Excel.

With her completed map, Ann is ready for another review with Carmen.

Ann has finished Carmen's charts and map for her meeting next Tuesday with SMP's management committee. They match Ann's design and meet Carmen's requirements. Ann is certain the charts and map will allow Carmen to make an impressive and informative presentation.

Tutorial Exercises

For exercises 1 through 7, launch Excel and open the workbook for Canyon Creek Wood Products (CCW), E_CCW1.xls, in the Tut03 folder or directory, then immediately save it as S_CCW1.xls. This worksheet is used to analyze the components of CCW's cost of goods sold. The costs are entered in millions of dollars. Review this worksheet. Prepare a column chart and a pie chart by performing the following:

1. Create the pie chart of 1998 cost of goods sold, as sketched in Figure 3-47. Select appropriate colors and patterns to differentiate the slices and format the text labels before you print this chart. Place this chart in a separate chart sheet named "Pie Chart."

Figure 3-47

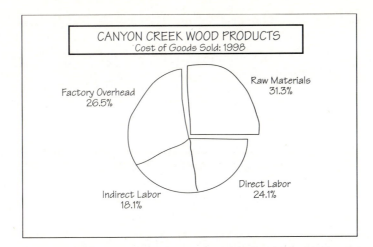

2. Save the S_CCW1.xls workbook in the Tut03 folder. Preview and print the pie chart.
3. Create the 3-D stacked column chart specified by the rough sketch in Figure 3-48 as an embedded chart in the same sheet as the cost of goods sold data. Select appropriate colors and patterns to differentiate the columns when you print this chart.

Figure 3-48

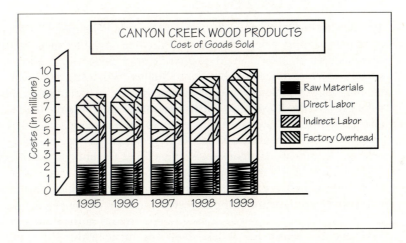

4. Select point sizes, then use boldface and italics with the titles to improve the chart's appearance.
5. Add at least one drawn object of your choice to the chart to highlight some aspect of the chart's content.
6. Save the workbook as S_CCW1.xls in the Tut03 folder. Preview and print the worksheet and chart.
7. Design a chart of your choice using the CCW data. Create and print it. Save it as the S_CCW1.xls workbook. Write a paragraph explaining the message the chart communicates.

For exercises 8 through 12, open the E_CCW2.xls workbook in the Tut03 folder, which contains sales data for 1998 for Canyon Creek Wood Products (CCW). Review the worksheet. Prepare a map by performing the following:

8. Create a map of the sales that displays only sales, with the sales arranged in seven intervals with approximately the same number of states in each interval. Choose US with AK & HI Insets as the appropriate map type.
9. Modify the chart title and legend title so they describe the contents of the map. Position the legend so it does not cover any of the map.

ADVEX 172 TUTORIAL 3 CREATING AND PRINTING CHARTS

10. Click the Map Labels button, click the OK button, then click your state to add a label to it. Click the Select Objects button to turn off the labeling option.
11. Save this as the S_CCW2.xls workbook in the Tut03 folder. Preview and print the map.
12. Create a different map of your choice using the sales data for CCW. Save it as the S_CCW2.xls workbook in the Tut03 folder. Preview and print the map. Write a paragraph explaining the message communicated by your map.

13. Design a chart of your choice; it can be a chart you see in a magazine or newspaper or you can use one of the other workbooks on your Student Disk to design the chart. Include at least one drawn object. Create and print the chart you design. Save the workbook as S_***10.xls in the Tut03 folder. You can use your initials for the three-letter descriptive abbreviation to replace the asterisks. Write a paragraph explaining the message communicated by your chart.
14. Create a map of your choice. Obtain data from a magazine or newspaper for the map or locate the MAPSTATS.xls workbook file. If you use data from the MAPSTATS.xls file, use the Windows clipboard to copy this data to a new workbook and create the map. Use Help to look up any additional information you need to complete the map. Write a paragraph explaining what message the map communicates.

Case Problems

1. Managing Quality for Antel Computer Chips Antel Computer Chips (ACC) manufactures computer memory chips for several IBM clone computer manufacturers. ACC's reputation has been built on its high-quality memory chips sold at a low cost. ACC emphasizes product quality through a Total Quality Management system. As each batch of memory chips is manufactured, a sample of chips is tested to establish the percentage of defectives. Kathy Bowden performs these tests and plots the data on a control chart to determine whether any significant changes have taken place in the quality of the chips produced. If a change is detected, Kathy takes corrective actions in the manufacturing process. A control chart consists of three lines: the upper control limit (UCL), the lower control limit (LCL), and the percentage of defectives in each sample from a batch. The UCL and the LCL are calculated using a common statistical formula for control charts that provides a measure of the expected variation of the percentage of defectives among the batches. Control charts are used to spot trends in the number of defectives. Whenever the percentage of defectives falls outside either the upper or the lower control limits, corrective action is usually required.

Kathy has generally performed these tests and drawn the control charts by hand; however, she believes that using Excel would produce more accurate control charts. Kathy has built the workbook in which the control charts will be created. Create the necessary control charts for Kathy by completing the following:

1. Launch Excel and open the P_ACC1.xls workbook located in the Tut03 folder on your Student Disk. Immediately save the file as S_ACC1.xls. Scroll the worksheet to the right to see all of Kathy's data.
2. Prepare a control chart, as shown in the sketch in Figure 3-49, on a separate chart sheet. Give this sheet an appropriate name. Change the colors and styles so the lines for UCL and LCL are black and contain no data markers, while the line for Defectives is a different style than the UCL and LCL lines and includes data markers. Use the Help menu if necessary to alter the data makers for the UCL and LCL lines. Save the workbook as S_ACC1.xls in the Tut03 folder. Preview and print the control chart.

Figure 3-49

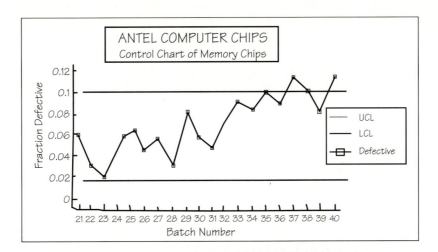

3. Review the control chart. Does there appear to be a problem with the memory chip manufacturing process? Explain your interpretation of this control chart.
4. To indicate that a problem with the memory chip manufacturing process may exist, add the text "Increasing Defectives" with arrows pointing to appropriate data points on the chart. Surround this text with a geometric shape of your choice. Save this as workbook S_ACC1.xls. Preview and print the revised control chart.
5. Review the control chart. Describe how the chart is useful in spotting problems in the memory chip manufacturing process. Write a short paragraph describing other features that could be used to further enhance the chart.
6. Create a side-by-side column chart for the control chart in a separate chart sheet. Give this sheet an appropriate name. Include a descriptive chart title and label both the x- and y-axis. Compare the line chart with this column chart. Which one is easier for you to understand? Write a paragraph describing why you think one chart format is better than the other for displaying this data.
7. Save the workbook as S_ACC1.xls in the Tut03 folder. Preview and print the chart.

2. Work Sampling for Guardian Mutual Insurance Guardian Mutual Insurance (GMI) is a large nation-wide insurance company that sells insurance for both individuals and businesses. GMI employs a staff of 127 computer programmers to build and maintain management information systems to serve their agents.

Steve Michaels was recently hired by Susan Gentry as a junior systems analyst for the Claims Management System at GMI. Susan's staff is classified into three different levels: SA2, SA3, and SA4. The SA2 staff level, Steve's classification, is generally new hires, the SA3 staff level consists of analysts with two to five years of experience, and the SA4 staff level is made up of systems analysts with six or more years of experience. Susan wants to measure the productivity of her staff. She asks Steve to conduct a work sampling study to determine how the different staff levels spend each day. Work sampling is a procedure in which an individual's activities are recorded at random times throughout the day to determine the relative amount of time spent on each activity. Steve collects the data for this study and summarizes the information in an Excel workbook. He meets with Susan to review the worksheet. She is pleased with Steve's results, but she thinks that charts would better communicate the information from the work sampling study. In preparation for creating these charts, Steve develops his planning analysis sheet (Figure 3-50). He is now ready to create the charts for Susan's upcoming staff meeting.

ADVEX 174 **TUTORIAL 3** CREATING AND PRINTING CHARTS

Figure 3-50 ◀

Planning Analysis Sheet

My goal:

Prepare charts showing the time spent on various job activities performed by systems analysts at different job classification levels

What results do I want to see?

A bar chart showing the results of the work sampling study

A pie chart showing the average time spent on various activities throughout the day by all job classification levels

What information do I need?

The results of the work sampling study

1. Launch Excel and open the workbook P_GMI1.xls in the Tut03 folder that contains the summary of Steve's work sampling study. Save it immediately as S_GMI1.xls in case you want to redo this case problem.
2. Review Steve's worksheet. Notice that Steve has formatted the cells as *percentages* and included a row containing the *average* for each job activity.
3. Create a column chart of the three staff levels and their respective percentages for a typical work day. Include the titles "Typical Work Day" and "Work Sampling" on your chart. Select appropriate colors and patterns to differentiate the bars for printing this chart.
4. Include the y-axis title "Percent of Day" and x-axis title "Job Activity." Format the y-axis range as a percentage with zero decimal places.
5. Change the font size of the title to 14 and the subtitle to 12. Add boldface and/or italics to enhance these titles.
6. Save the workbook as S_GMI1.xls. Preview and print both the worksheet and the column chart.
7. Using the same chart, change the chart orientation from column to bar; that is, from a vertical to horizontal arrangement.
8. Change the color of the SA2 bars to black, the SA3 bars to white with black striped cross-hatching, and the SA4 bars to white.
9. Print the chart only, and save the workbook as S_GMI1.xls.
10. Create a pie chart of the average portion of each day spent on the six activities in the Typical Work Day.
11. Place the title "Typical Work Day" on the chart. Select a different font for the chart title and give it a point size of 18.
12. Use a chart format that labels and displays the percentage of the slices of the pie chart using the six daily activities. Explode the slice that shows the average Program Coding percent. Is this less than half of a systems analyst's typical work day activities?
13. Add a graphic object to the chart that includes your answer to the preceding question and include an arrow that points to the Program Coding slice.
14. Save the workbook as S_GMI1.xls in the Tut03 folder. Print the worksheet and the pie chart.
15. Compare the column (vertical) and bar (horizontal) charts. Which chart do you feel is the easiest to understand? Why?
16. Create a comparative stacked column chart with each column as one job classification and each activity as one data range. That is, the job activity data series are arranged by column. Use two rows for the legend text. Place the chart in a separate chart sheet. Give this sheet an appropriate descriptive name.

Add appropriate titles and patterns to the chart. Change point sizes and typefaces, together with using boldface and italics, to improve the appearance of the chart. Save it as S_GMI1.xls and print the chart. Why is the total height of each stacked column the same? What does this represent? Which column format produces the same chart with data values that are not percentages like these?

17. Create a 3-D column chart with three axes of the job classifications and activities. Place the chart in a separate chart sheet. Give this sheet an appropriate descriptive name. Include an appropriate name on the chart. Adjust the chart's rotations and elevation so that all the columns are visible. Save it as S_GMI1.xls and print the chart.

18. Susan visits a number of college campuses each year, speaking to groups such as the student chapters of the Data Processing Management Association. Many of these students believe that systems analysts spend most of their time coding programs. Does the data from Steve's work sampling study support this opinion of the students? Explain your answer.

Comprehensive Applications

The Comprehensive Applications in this tutorial continue from the preceding tutorials.

1. Profit Planning for Valley Gas Alliance At VGA, Amanda Barclay and Dennis Corbin have reviewed the various management reports you have produced. To better understand the relationships underlying their projected income statement, they have requested the preparation of several charts for use as an integral component of their annual review. For ease of reference, they prefer each chart in a separate chart sheet with an appropriate descriptive name.

1. Open the P_VGA1.xls workbook in the Tut03 folder or directory that contains next year's plan with the data to be charted. Save this as the S_VGA1.xls workbook in the Tut03 folder before you begin creating your charts.

2. Create a stacked column chart of the Residential and Industrial Gas sold for the four quarters in the year. The height of each stacked column will also indicate Total Gas Sold. Add a drawn object to the chart that indicates this meaning for the overall column height. Include titles and a legend for this chart. Preview and print it.

3. Create a line chart comparing Total Sales, Total Expenses, Interest Expense, and Net Income for the quarters. Include appropriate titles and a legend. Preview and print this chart.

4. Create a combination chart of the Net Income and Return on Investment for each quarter. Include appropriate titles and a legend. Plot Return on Investment on the second y-axis. Preview and print this chart.

5. Create a pie chart of Cost of Sales, Marketing and Selling, General and Administration, and Depreciation for the year. This pie chart will show Amanda and Dennis the breakdown of each dollar of expenses. Include text and percentage labels on each pie slice. Explode the entire pie. Include an appropriate title. Preview and print this chart.

6. Create a pie chart of Total Expenses, Interest Expense, Income Taxes, and Net Income for the year, with Net Income as the only exploded slice. Include text and percentage labels on each pie slice. Include an appropriate chart title. Save the workbook as S_VGA1.xls in the Tut03 folder. Preview and print this chart.

7. Design a chart of your choice for communicating the VGA data. Create and print the chart you design. Save it as the S_VGA1.xls workbook. Write a paragraph explaining the message communicated by your chart.

2. Production Planning for Oak World Furniture Todd and Robin like to see visual presentations of data. Although you have produced an impressive array of management reports, they have requested that you create several charts. Todd is considering having these charts added to the Briefing Book prepared for each of Oak World's quarterly management meetings. At your last review meeting with Todd, Robin, and Sam, they requested several charts. For ease of reference, they want each chart in a separate chart sheet with an appropriate descriptive name.

1. Open your S_OWF1.xls workbook in the Tut02 folder or directory that contains the quarterly plan with the data to be charted. If you did not create this worksheet in Tutorials 1 and 2, then see your instructor to receive the file you will need to complete this Comprehensive Application. Save this workbook in the Tut03 folder before you start building your charts.

2. Create a stacked column chart of Sales by product for the three months in the quarter. Robin has indicated that the height of each column will also indicate the Total Sales for the quarter. Add a drawn object to the chart that indicates this meaning for the overall column height. Include titles and a legend for this chart. Preview and print it.

3. Create a line chart that compares Total Sales, Cost of Sales, Operating Expenses, and Operating Profit for the three months in the quarter. Include appropriate titles and a legend. Preview and print this chart.

4. Create a 3-D 2-axis column chart of the number of units of Tables, Chairs, and Sofas sold for the three months in the quarter. Include appropriate titles and legends. Include at least one drawn object on the chart to add an explanation of any aspect of the chart that you choose. Preview and print this chart.

5. Create a pie chart of the Cost of Sales, Operating Expenses, and Operating Profit for the Total quarter. This pie chart will show Todd and Robin the breakdown of each dollar of sales. Explode the Operating Profit slice of this chart. Include text and percentage labels for each slice. Preview and print this chart.

6. Create a pie chart of Sales by product for the entire quarter, with Sofa Sales exploded. Include text and percentage labels for each slice. Save the workbook as S_OWF1.xls in the Tut03 folder. Preview and print this chart.

7. Design a chart of your choice for communicating the Oak World data. Create and print the chart you design. Save it as the S_OWF1.xls workbook. Write a paragraph explaining the message communicated by your chart.

TUTORIAL 4

Automating Tasks Using Macros

Making the Operating Budget Workbook Easier to Use

OBJECTIVES

In this tutorial you will learn how to:

- Review an application with a recorded macro

- Plan and record Excel macros

- Run a macro using menu commands

- Run a macro using a button object

- Run a macro using a shortcut key

- Create an Auto_Open macro

- Review a module sheet

- View Visual Basic for Applications code

- Print a module sheet

- Edit macro code

CASE

Sunny Morning Products

Carmen's meeting with the management committee to review the Sunny Morning Operating Budget for next year went well. Several committee members made suggestions for modifying some of the numbers in the budget, and Carmen asks Ann to produce a few alternative versions of the budget using these new values. In an effort to minimize the amount of work this will entail, Ann wants to modify the workbook to make it easier to navigate and use. Since many of the tasks involved in using the workbook tend to be repetitive, Ann wants to create several macros. A **macro** is a program within Excel that automates frequently performed tasks. She feels that the macros will make her more productive as she tests several budget alternatives. In addition, she thinks the macros will make the workbook easier to use for other members of the budget team who are not as familiar with Excel.

Ann decides to add the following macros to the workbook:

View Chart	moves directly to chart section
Print Chart	displays chart in Print Preview window
Assumptions	moves to Key Input Assumptions section
Reset Data	resets initial assumption values
Print Budget	displays Key Input Assumptions and Operating Budget in Print Preview window
Auto_Open	opens Excel workbook in Full Screen view

Ann will use these macros to simplify the tasks she and the budget team have to perform when using this workbook.

Introduction to Macros

A macro automatically performs a series of Excel operations, such as menu selections, dialog box selections, range selections, or keystrokes. Macros simplify the use of workbooks for both experienced and novice users. They can make your work more productive while helping you make fewer errors. For example, you can create macros to automate the following tasks:

- Move through a large worksheet quickly.
- Add a date and time stamp to a cell in the current worksheet.
- Extract data from an Excel list and create a chart.
- Print several reports from a worksheet, each with different print specifications.
- Apply a common set of formats to any sheet in a workbook.

Running a Sample Macro

Ann has already created two macros that make it easier to view and print the Chart section of the budget worksheet. Before you create the other macros Ann has planned for the workbook, take a quick look at what macros are all about by running the macros Ann has already created.

To open the C_SMP1.xls workbook:

1. Launch Excel.

2. Click the **Open** button 🖼 on the Standard toolbar to open Ann's workbook, C_SMP1.xls, located in the Tut04 folder or directory on your Student Disk. Then save the workbook as S_SMP1.xls in the Tut04 folder in case you want to restart the tutorial. As the workbook opens, notice that Ann has added the macros and their descriptions to the Documentation sheet.

   Now, move to the Budget sheet.

3. Click the **Budget sheet tab** to display the Operating Budget worksheet. See Figure 4-1. Notice the two button objects at the top of this sheet—View Chart and Print Chart. As you click each button, Excel executes a macro.

Figure 4-1 ◄
Operating budget with two button objects

button objects —

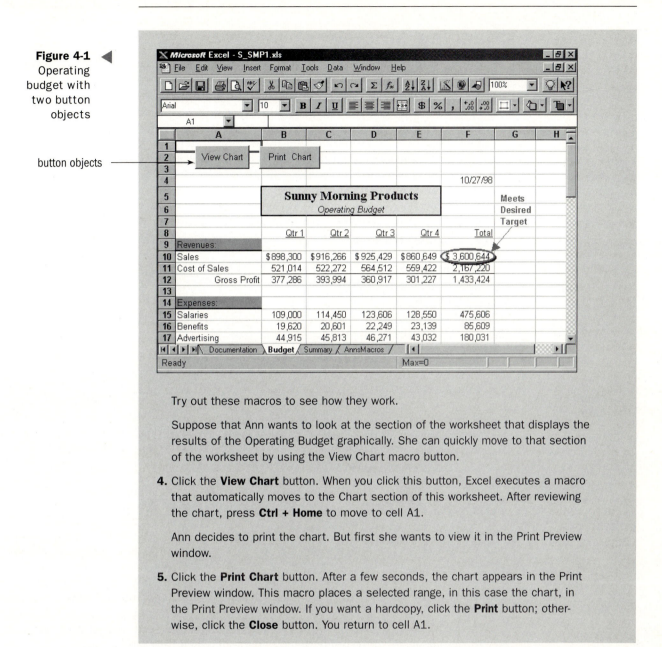

Try out these macros to see how they work.

Suppose that Ann wants to look at the section of the worksheet that displays the results of the Operating Budget graphically. She can quickly move to that section of the worksheet by using the View Chart macro button.

4. Click the **View Chart** button. When you click this button, Excel executes a macro that automatically moves to the Chart section of this worksheet. After reviewing the chart, press **Ctrl + Home** to move to cell A1.

Ann decides to print the chart. But first she wants to view it in the Print Preview window.

5. Click the **Print Chart** button. After a few seconds, the chart appears in the Print Preview window. This macro places a selected range, in this case the chart, in the Print Preview window. If you want a hardcopy, click the **Print** button; otherwise, click the **Close** button. You return to cell A1.

You have seen how Excel macros can help you work more productively. Now, you will create the remaining macros Ann needs to add to the budget worksheet.

Creating Macros

You can create a macro in two ways: you can use the **macro recorder** to record your keystrokes and mouse actions as you perform them (recording the selection of ranges, menu commands, dialog box options, etc.), or you can write your own macros by entering a series of commands in the Visual Basic for Applications (VBA) programming language that tell Excel how to do a particular task.

The easiest way to create a macro in Excel is to use the macro recorder. When you record a macro, Excel translates your keystroke and mouse actions into a macro command that you can play back (run) whenever you want to repeat those particular keystrokes and mouse actions.

In this tutorial, you will create your macros using the macro recorder. In later tutorials you will write your own macros using VBA.

Planning Macros

As with most complex projects, you need to plan your macro. Decide what you want to accomplish and the best way to go about doing it. Once you know the purpose of the macro, you can more easily carry out the keystrokes or mouse actions before you actually record them. Going through each step before recording a macro might seem like extra work, but it reduces the chances of error when you actually create the macro.

Ann realizes that the Operating Budget workbook is large, and that much of the information cannot be displayed on the screen at one time. Previously she has moved to various sections in this worksheet by using the arrow keys, Page Up or Page Down keys, or the Go To command. This approach takes time, and she often becomes frustrated because she doesn't always remember where a particular section is located. She can move to different sections within the workbook more quickly through the use of a macro that goes directly to the desired section. She has already created one macro—View Chart—to help go immediately to the chart.

Ann will need to use the Key Input Assumptions section to create the what-if analyses requested by the management committee. So the next macro Ann will create will go directly to the Key Input Assumptions section of the budget worksheet. She sits down at her computer and goes through the steps she plans to include in the macro before actually recording them. This way she will be familiar with the steps she will include in the macro, and the chances for errors in her macro are fewer. Figure 4-2 lists the steps Ann plans to include in her macro.

Figure 4-2 ◀
Macro planning
sheet

Action	Result
Press F5, double-click KEY_ASSUMPTIONS	Moves to Key Input Assumptions section
Click A32	Positions the cell pointer

Recording the GotoAssumptions Macro

After planning the macro, you are ready to record it. Before you record a macro, make sure your worksheet is set up exactly as you want it to exist at the time you play back the recorded macro. This may involve opening a specific workbook, activating a specific sheet in which you want the macro to run, and moving to the location where you want to start recording. Otherwise the macro may not work as planned, and you may have to record it again.

When you record a macro, you name and describe it. You can also set up a shortcut key to run the macro, and specify the workbook in which to store the macro.

To record a macro to move to a named range:

1. If necessary, click **A1** in the Budget worksheet.

    Now start the macro recorder.

2. Click **Tools**, point to **Record Macro**, then click **Record New Macro** to display the Record New Macro dialog box. See Figure 4-3.

Figure 4-3 ◀
Record New
Macro dialog
box

enter name of
macro here

add to macro
description here

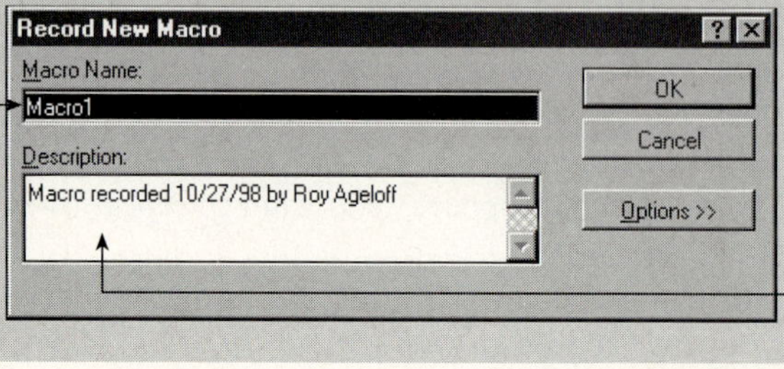

RECORDING THE GOTOASSUMPTIONS MACRO **ADVEX 181**

TROUBLE? If the Macro dialog box opens, you clicked Macro instead of Record New Macro. Click Cancel and repeat Step 2.

Excel proposes Macro1 as the default name for the macro. This macro name consists of the word "Macro" and a number corresponding to the number of macros you have recorded in this work session. You should change the macro name to a name more descriptive of what the macro will do. Name the macro GotoAssumptions.

3. Type **GotoAssumptions** in the Macro Name text box.

   A macro name entered in the Macro Name text box can be up to 46 characters long; it must begin with a letter, and it can contain only letters, numbers, and the underscore character. No spaces or other punctuation marks are permitted.

   Notice that Excel provides a brief description indicating the date the macro is to be recorded and by whom. You can add additional comments to explain the purpose of the macro.

4. Click anywhere within the **Description** text box. If the insertion point is not at the end of the description, move there. Press the **Enter** key to start a new line. Type **Moves to the Key Input Assumptions section**. See Figure 4-4.

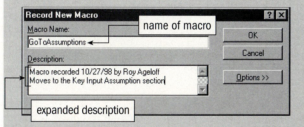

Figure 4-4
Record New Macro Dialog box after changes to Macro name and description

5. Click the **OK** button to start recording the macro. See Figure 4-5. Excel returns to the worksheet and the message "Recording" appears in the status bar. You are now in Record mode and all keystrokes and mouse clicks will be recorded until you stop the macro recorder.

Figure 4-5
Worksheet with macro recorder on

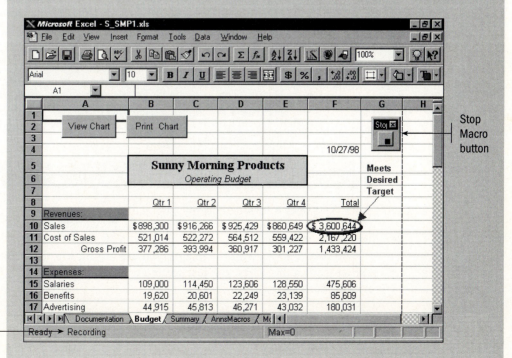

indicates macro recorder is on

Notice that the Stop Recording toolbar is also displayed, either as a floating toolbar, or directly under the Formatting toolbar. This toolbar contains a single button, the Stop Macro button. When you have finished entering all tasks, you can use the Stop Macro button to stop the macro recorder.

TROUBLE? If a warning message appears indicating that the macro name already exists, click Yes and proceed to Step 6. Excel replaces the existing macro with whatever you now record.

Now perform the tasks you want recorded.

6. Press **F5** to display the Go To dialog box. Double-click the range name **KEY_ASSUMPTIONS**. Excel highlights the range A33:E42.

7. Click **A32** to make it the active cell.

   You have completed the actions that you want recorded; next you will stop the macro recorder.

8. Click the **Stop Macro** button ■. Notice that the message "Recording" is no longer displayed on the status bar.

   TROUBLE? If you forget to turn off the macro recorder, it continues to record all of your actions. If this happens to you, you may need to delete the macro and record it again. To delete the macro, click Tools, click Macro, select GotoAssumption in the Macro Name/Reference list, then click the Delete button.

   TROUBLE? If the Stop Macro button is not displayed, click Tools, point to Record Macro, then click Stop Recording to stop the macro recorder.

You have completed recording your first macro. Now test the macro by running it.

RECORDING A MACRO

- Click Tools, point to Record Macro, then click Record New Macro to display the Record New Macro dialog box.
- In the Macro Name text box, type a name for the macro.
- In the Description text box, type a description of the macro.
- Click the OK button. The macro recorder starts recording.
- Perform the tasks you want the macro to automate.
- Click the Stop Macro button, or click Tools, point to Record Macro, then click Stop Recording to stop the recording process. The recorded macro appears in a module sheet.

Running the GotoAssumptions Macro

After recording a macro, you can play it back, or run it, at any time. When you run a macro, you are telling Excel to execute the previously recorded instructions contained within the macro.

The first time you run the macro, you are testing it to determine whether it works as expected. Run the macro you just created to see if it automatically moves to the Key Input Assumptions section.

To run a macro using menu commands:

1. Press **Ctrl + Home** to move to cell A1.

2. Click **Tools**, then click **Macro** to display the Macro dialog box. See Figure 4-6. A list of all macros found in all open workbooks appears in the Macro Name/Reference list box.

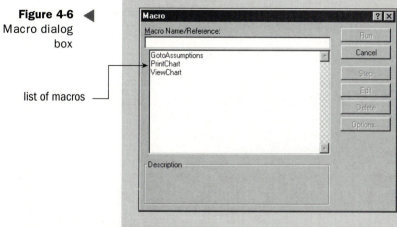

Figure 4-6
Macro dialog box

list of macros

Select the name of the macro you want to run.

3. Click **GotoAssumptions** to display GotoAssumptions in the Macro Name/Reference box, then click the **Run** button. Excel executes the GotoAssumptions macro and moves to cell A32 of the Key Input Assumptions section.

You did it; your first macro ran successfully.

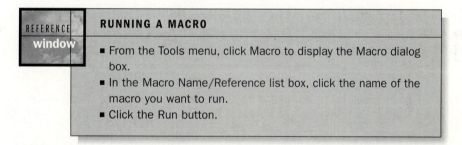

RUNNING A MACRO

- From the Tools menu, click Macro to display the Macro dialog box.
- In the Macro Name/Reference list box, click the name of the macro you want to run.
- Click the Run button.

Assigning the GotoAssumptions Macro to a Button Object

You can use the Macro command on the Tools menu to run macros that you execute infrequently, but this approach is inconvenient if you need to run the macro often. There are several ways to make it easier to run a macro. You can:

- use a shortcut key that enables you to run the macro by using a combination of the Ctrl key and a letter.
- assign the macro to the Tools menu.
- assign the macro to a button on a worksheet.
- assign the macro to a button on a toolbar.
- assign the macro to a graphic object.
- use a custom menu.

For example, to attach the macro to a button object, you place the button object in a worksheet and assign the macro to it. You can then run the macro by clicking the button. This approach makes the macro easier to use. It will speed up your own work, as well as make the macro easier for others to run. Ann knows that other people on the budget team will need to change and update values in the Key Input Assumptions section too. Assign the GotoAssumptions macro to a button object.

To place a button object in the worksheet and assign a macro to the button:

1. Press the **Ctrl + Home** to return to cell A1.

   Display the Drawing toolbar.

2. Click **View**, click **Toolbars**, click the **Drawing** check box to select this toolbar, then click the **OK** button. The Drawing toolbar displays in the worksheet window. See Figure 4-7.

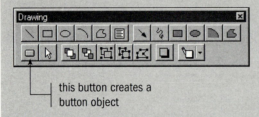

Figure 4-7 ◀
Drawing toolbar

this button creates a button object

Now place a button in the worksheet.

3. Click the **Create Button** button on the Drawing toolbar. Now move the mouse pointer to the position in the worksheet where you want the button to appear.

4. Position the mouse pointer to the right of the Print Chart button. Click and drag the mouse pointer until it is the size and shape you want the button to be. When you release the mouse button, the Assign Macro dialog box opens. See Figure 4-8.

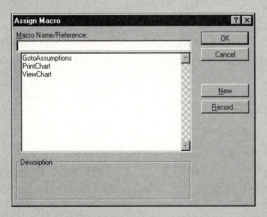

Figure 4-8 ◀
Assign Macro dialog box

5. Click **GotoAssumptions** in the Macro Name/Reference list box, then click the **OK** button. The macro is assigned to the button object. The button object appears on the worksheet.

   TROUBLE? If the button is too small, too large, or in the wrong location, you can resize or move it just as you move or resize any object. If the button is not selected, press the Ctrl key, while moving the mouse pointer on top of the button, then click the mouse. Selection handles appear around the button, indicating that you can move or resize it.

   TROUBLE? If the Drawing toolbar is in the way, click and drag it to move it out of the way, or click the Drawing toolbar Close button to remove it from the screen.

Now change the name of the button to one that indicates the function of the macro assigned to it.

6. Highlight the label on the button and type **Assumptions**. See Figure 4-9.

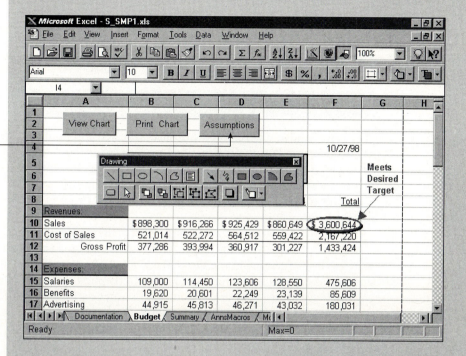

Figure 4-9
Button object with descriptive label

executes GotoAssumptions macro

TROUBLE? If you're in the Key Input Assumptions section, you accidentally executed the macro while typing the title. Press Ctrl + Home to get back to cell A1. Now select the button by pressing the Ctrl key while moving the mouse pointer on top of the button, then click the mouse button. Selection handles appear around the button. Repeat Step 6.

7. Click anywhere in the worksheet to deselect the button.

8. If you haven't already removed the Drawing toolbar, remove it now.

Now Ann wants to test the button to make sure it executes the macro.

9. Click the **Assumptions** button. The Key Input Assumptions section of the Budget worksheet is displayed. Your macro worked.

10. Save the workbook.

REFERENCE window

ASSIGNING A MACRO TO A BUTTON OBJECT ON A WORKSHEET

- Click the Create Button button on the Drawing toolbar.
- Position the mouse pointer where you want the button, then click and drag the mouse pointer until the button is the size and shape you want.
- Release the mouse button. The button appears in the worksheet with a label and the Assign Macro dialog box opens.
- Select the name of the macro that you want to assign to the button from the Macro Name/Reference list box.
- Click the OK button.

ADVEX 186 **TUTORIAL 4** AUTOMATING TASKS USING MACROS

HELP DESK

Index

ASSIGNING MACROS

Double-click the Help button to display the Help Topics dialog box, then click the Index tab.

EXCEL 5.0

Keyword	**Topic**
Assigning macros	Assign a macro
Assigning macros	*All topics are appropriate*

Viewing the GotoAssumptions Macro

As you may have realized, you can successfully record and run a macro without looking at or understanding the instructions underlying it. For simple macros this approach is fine. There will be times, however, when you may welcome the greater flexibility that comes from understanding the concepts underlying the recorded macro. For instance, if you want to confirm that the macro was recorded properly, or you want to edit or delete a macro, you will need to display its text.

Excel stores recorded macros in a special sheet called a **module** sheet and places the sheet at the end of the workbook. As Excel records your actions, it translates them into a series of instructions in the **Visual Basic for Applications** (VBA) programming language, and places the corresponding instructions in the module sheet. When you run the macro, the instructions are read and executed in sequence, thereby duplicating the actions you performed when you recorded the macro.

Move to the module sheet Module1 and view the VBA code for the GotoAssumptions macro you just created.

To view the VBA code for a macro:

1. Click **Tools**, then click **Macro** to display the Macro dialog box.

2. Click **GotoAssumptions** in the Macro Name/Reference list box, then click the **Edit** button to display the module sheet where the recorded macro is located. You will also see the Visual Basic toolbar automatically appear when you display the module sheet. See Figure 4-10. Notice that the module sheet is not oriented to rows and columns; it is oriented to lines of code organized into blocks called **procedures**.

You can also view your macro by moving to the last sheet in the workbook, select the worksheet tab labeled Module1 and scroll to the GotoAssumptions macro.

Figure 4-10
Module1 module sheet

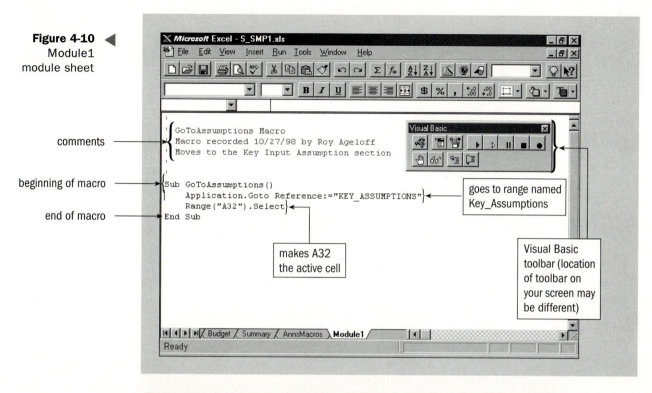

VIEWING THE MACRO CODE

- Click Tools, then click Macro to display the Macro dialog box.
- Click the macro you want to display in the Macro Name/Reference list box.
- Click the Edit button to open the module sheet and display your macro.

Visual Basic Toolbar

The Visual Basic toolbar shown in Figure 4-11 simplifies working with macros. You can use several of the buttons on this toolbar to record, run, and stop recording macros. You use the Record Macro button to begin recording a macro by displaying the Record Macro dialog box; the Stop Macro button to stop recording a macro; and the Run Macro button to run a recorded macro by displaying the Macro dialog box. The other buttons on this toolbar are used for more advanced tasks that will be covered in later tutorials.

Figure 4-11
Visual Basic toolbar

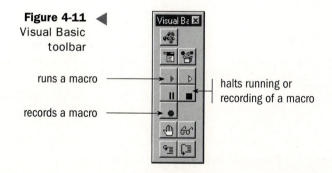

The Visual Basic toolbar typically displays whenever you activate a module sheet, and is automatically removed from the screen when you leave the module sheet.

ADVEX 188 **TUTORIAL 4** AUTOMATING TASKS USING MACROS

HELP DESK

EXCEL 5.0

> Index
>
> **VISUAL BASIC TOOLBAR**
>
> Double-click the Help button to display the Help Topics dialog box, then click the Index tab.
>
> **Keyword**
> Toolbars
> *Visual Basic toolbar*
>
> **Topic**
> module window
> *Visual Basic toolbar*

Visual Basic Code

The VBA code of a typical macro has the following components:

Comments are statements that explain or document what is happening. Any line of the module that is preceded by an apostrophe is a comment and is ignored by Excel when the macro is run. Comments are displayed in green to help you distinguish them from statements that cause Excel to do something. In Figure 4-10, Excel includes as comments the macro name, date recorded, and the description you entered in the Record New Macro dialog box.

Sub/End Sub are keywords, recognized as part of the VBA programming language, that mark the beginning and end of a macro. The keyword Sub in the line

```
Sub GotoAssumptions()
```

signals the start of the macro. It is followed by the macro name GotoAssumptions and then by the left and right parentheses. The keyword End Sub signals the end of the macro. Sub and End Sub, along with other keywords, appear on the screen in blue. All keywords appear in blue to indicate that they are valid Excel keywords.

Macro code is the series of statements between the Sub and End Sub keywords representing the body of the macro. The body contains the VBA translation of the actions you performed while recording the macro. In Figure 4-10, the line

```
Application.Goto Reference:="KEY_ASSUMPTIONS"
```

is the VBA equivalent of pressing F5 and selecting the range named KEY_ASSUMPTIONS.

The next line

```
Range("A32").Select
```

is the VBA equivalent of clicking A32 to make it the active cell.

Now that you have created, run, and viewed your first macro, you're ready to create your next macro, ResetData.

If you want to take a break *and resume the tutorial at a later time, you can do so now.* Close the workbook and exit Excel. If you are on a network, leave Windows running. If you are using your own computer, you may exit Windows and shut down the computer. When you resume the tutorial, place your Student Disk in the disk drive, launch Excel, then continue with the tutorial.

● ● ●

Recording the ResetData Macro

Every time Ann wants to perform a new what-if analysis with the Operating Budget, she needs to change the input values back to their original values before testing another set of assumptions. The next macro you create will automate the resetting of several input assumption values back to their original settings, making it easier for Ann to compare operating budgets with different assumptions.

Figure 4-12 shows the steps Ann plans to incorporate in her ResetData macro.

Figure 4-12
Steps for Ann's ResetData macro

Actions	Results
Click C34, type .02	reset QTR 2 Sales Growth Rate
Click D34, type .01	reset QTR 3 Sales Growth Rate
Click E34, type −.07	reset QTR 4 Sales Growth Rate
Click B35, type .58	reset QTR 1 Cost of Sales Percent
Click C35, type .57	reset QTR 2 Cost of Sales Percent
Click D35, type .61	reset QTR 3 Cost of Sales Percent
Click E35, type .65	reset QTR 4 Cost of Sales Percent
Click C36, type .05	reset QTR 2 Salary Growth Rate
Click D36, type .08	reset QTR 3 Salary Growth Rate
Click E36, type .04	reset QTR 4 Salary Growth Rate

Now record the ResetData macro.

To start the macro recorder:

1. Activate the Budget sheet. If the Key Input Assumptions section does not display, click the **Assumptions** button to move to this section of the worksheet.

2. Click **Tools**, point to **Record Macro**, and then click **Record New Macro** to display the Record New Macro dialog box.

3. Change the name of the macro by typing **ResetData** in the Macro Name text box.

   Next, enter a brief description in the Description text box.

4. Place the cursor at the end of the default description by clicking at the end of the text in the **Description** text box. Press the **Enter** key to move to a new line, and type **Reset input assumption values to their original values** in the Description text box.

   The Record New Macro dialog box has additional settings that are not shown unless you click the Options>> button in the Record Macro dialog box.

5. Click the **Options>>** button. Excel expands the Record Macro dialog box to show several additional settings that you can control. See Figure 4-13.

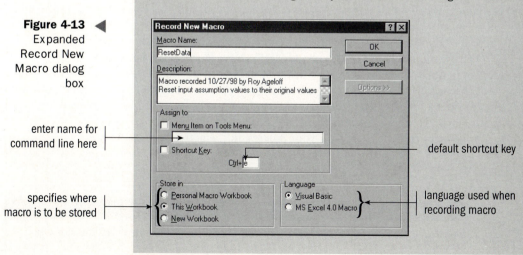

Figure 4-13
Expanded Record New Macro dialog box

enter name for command line here

default shortcut key

specifies where macro is to be stored

language used when recording macro

Before selecting some of these options for the ResetData macro, you need to understand what each option means.

Setting Recording Options

Excel provides several additional options for recording macros that are related to assigning and storing the macro, and specifying the language used to record the macro.

Assigning Macros

In the Assign to section of the Record New Macro dialog box, you can assign the macro to the Tools menu, to a shortcut key combination, or both.

If you want to access a macro no matter where you are in the worksheet, you can assign your macro to a command on the Tools menu. The macro is run when you select the command. To do this, select the Menu Item on Tools Menu check box, and then type the command name as you want it to appear on the Tools menu. The command appears at the bottom of the Tools menu. To run the macro, select the command.

A quick way to run a macro is to assign it to a shortcut key, a key you press along with the Ctrl key to run the macro. The shortcut key can be an uppercase or a lowercase letter. If you use this option, you can run the macro by holding down the Ctrl key and pressing the shortcut key.

HELP DESK

Index

ASSIGNING A MACRO TO THE TOOLS MENU

Double-click the Help button to display the Help Topics dialog box, then click the Index tab.

Keyword	**Topic**
Not Available	
Tools menu	*Adding a macro to the Tools menu*

EXCEL 5.0

Macro Storage Locations

You can also choose where you want to store macros. As you can see from Figure 4-13, the Store in section of the dialog box displays three possible locations.

By default, Excel stores the recorded macro in the active workbook (This Workbook). Macros stored in a workbook are available only when the workbook is open. If a workbook is closed, the macros stored within the workbook can't be run. Use this option to store macros that you plan to use only with this workbook.

If you use some macros on a regular basis, you may want to make them available at all times. When you select the Personal Macro Workbook option, Excel stores the macro in a special workbook file named PERSONAL.xls. When you start Excel, this workbook is opened automatically, making the macros in it available to any open workbook.

You can also store the macro in a separate (New Workbook) workbook file. If you select this option, Excel opens another workbook to record the macro. You use this approach to create a workbook that stores a group of macros that are related to a particular application. For example, a Certified Public Accountant might have a set of macros that are used with all workbooks containing financial statements of the firm's clients.

In this tutorial you will store your macros in the active workbook.

HELP DESK

Index

PERSONAL WORKBOOK

Double-click the Help button to display the Help Topics dialog box, then click the Index tab.

Keyword	**Topic**
Personal Macro Workbook	Recording into the correct module
Not available	

EXCEL 5.0

SETTING RECORDING OPTIONS **ADVEX 191**

Macro Language

Finally, Excel gives you two options for the language used to record your macros. By default, macros are translated into the VBA language. Alternatively, you can elect to record your macros in the older Excel 4 Macro language. Since Microsoft does not plan to make future enhancements to the Excel 4 Macro language, in this text you will record your macros using the Visual Basic option.

Now that you have a better idea of the types of options you have for storing and assigning macros, continue to record the ResetData macro and assign Ctrl + r as the shortcut key for running this macro.

To assign a shortcut key to the macro:

1. Click the **Shortcut Key** check box to select this option.

2. Click the **Ctrl +** text box, remove the default, "e," and type **r**. The "r" represents "reset."

TROUBLE? Shortcut keys are case-sensitive. To assign an uppercase letter as a shortcut key, you must hold the Shift key as you type the letter. Also, note that you cannot use special characters and numbers as shortcut keys.

TROUBLE? When selecting keys to use for shortcuts, take care to avoid conflicts with Excel default shortcut keys. Excel suggests shortcut keys that will not conflict with existing shortcut keys.

3. Click the **OK** button. Excel returns to the worksheet and displays the message "Recording" in the status bar, and the Stop Recording toolbar is displayed.

Now perform the tasks you want recorded.

To record the tasks for the ResetData macro:

1. Click **C34**, then type **.02**. Notice that in order to record the original values, you are reentering the same numbers that are currently stored in these cells.

2. Click **D34**, then type **.01**. Click **E34**, then type **-.07**.

Now set the original values for Cost of Sales Percent.

3. Enter **.58** in cell B35, **.57** in cell C35, **.61** in cell D35, and **.65** in cell E35.

Now set the values for Salary Growth Rate.

4. Enter **.05** in cell C36, **.08** in cell D36, and **.04** in cell E36.

5. Click **A32**.

You have completed the actions that you wanted to include in the macro; now stop the macro recorder.

6. Click the **Stop Macro** button ▣.

TROUBLE? If this button does not appear on your screen, click Tools, point to Record Macro, then click Stop Recording to stop recording the macro.

Assigning the ResetData Macro to a Button Object

To make it easier to use, you will assign the ResetData macro to a button.

To assign a macro to a button:

1. Make sure the Budget worksheet is the active sheet. Press **Ctrl + Home** to return to cell A1. Display the Drawing toolbar.

   Place a button object in the worksheet.

2. Click the **Create Button** button on the Drawing toolbar. Position the mouse pointer to the right of the Assumptions button. Click and drag the mouse pointer until you get the desired size and shape, then release the mouse button. The Assign Macro dialog box is displayed.

3. Click **ResetData** in the Macro Name/Reference list box, then click the **OK** button. You have assigned the macro ResetData to the button object.

   TROUBLE? If you assigned the wrong macro to the button object, you can open the Assign Macro dialog box by right-clicking the button object and selecting Assign Macro. Then select the desired macro.

   Now change the label describing the button to be more descriptive.

4. With the button still selected, highlight the label on the button object, then type **Reset Data**. See Figure 4-14.

Figure 4-14 ◀
Budget sheet after Reset Data button added

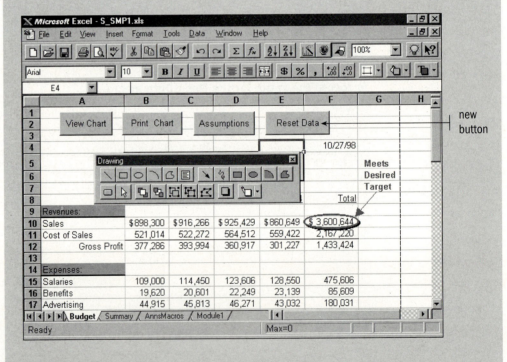

5. Click anywhere in the worksheet to deselect the button.

6. Remove the Drawing toolbar.

7. Save the workbook as S_SMP1.xls.

Running the ResetData Macro

After recording a macro, you should test your macro by running it. To test this macro, you need to first enter a new set of values.

To run the ResetData macro using the Reset Data button:

1. Click the **Assumptions** button to move to the Key Input Assumptions section.

2. Enter **.03** in cell C34, **.02** in cell D34, and **-.06** in E34.

3. Press **Ctrl + Home** to move the active cell to A1. Observe that the Operating Budget reflects sales for the second quarter of $925,249, third-quarter sales of $943,754, and $887,129 in the fourth quarter.

   After reviewing the Operating Budget, Ann decides to try another set of input values. But first, she remembers she must reset the input assumption values.

4. Click the **Reset Data** button to return to the initial input values. Notice that Sales Growth Rate for the second quarter is reset to 2%, the third quarter to 1%, and the fourth quarter to -7%. See Figure 4-15. Your macro worked as planned.

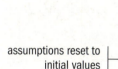

Figure 4-15
Assumptions reset to original values

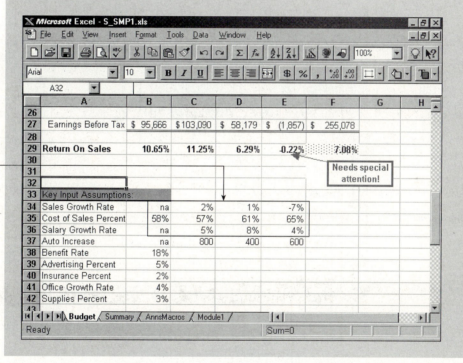

assumptions reset to initial values

Recall that you can also use the shortcut key Ctrl + r to run the ResetData macro. Run the macro again using the shortcut key, but first enter a new set of input values. This time, change the values for both Sales Growth Rate and Cost of Sales Percent.

To run the macro using the shortcut key:

1. Click **C34**, then type **.04** to change Sales Growth Rate in the second quarter to 4%. Click **B35**, then type **.6** to change Cost of Sales Percent for the first quarter.

   Now examine the operating budget with these revisions.

2. Press **Ctrl + Home** to move the active cell to A1. Notice that the Operating Budget reflects Sales Growth Rate for the second quarter of $934,232 and Cost of Sales in the first quarter of $538,980.

   Now reset the expense values using the shortcut key.

ADVEX 194 **TUTORIAL 4** AUTOMATING TASKS USING MACROS

> **3.** Press **Ctrl + r**. Excel resets the initial input values in the Key Input Assumptions section of the worksheet.

Now Ann can run this macro using a shortcut key, the Reset Data button, or the Macro command on the Tools menu. It's her preference.

Viewing the ResetData Macro

Now switch to the module sheet to see what the macro looks like.

To view the ResetData macro:

> **1.** Click **Tools**, then click **Macro** to display the Macro dialog box.
>
> **2.** Click **ResetData** in the Macro Name/Reference list box, then click the **Edit** button to display the module sheet where the recorded macro is located. See Figure 4-16.
>
> A workbook can include many module sheets and each module sheet can contain many macros. In fact, if you scroll the module sheet you will see that there are two macros in this sheet—GotoAssumptions and ResetData.

Figure 4-16 ◄
Visual Basic
code for the
ResetData
macro

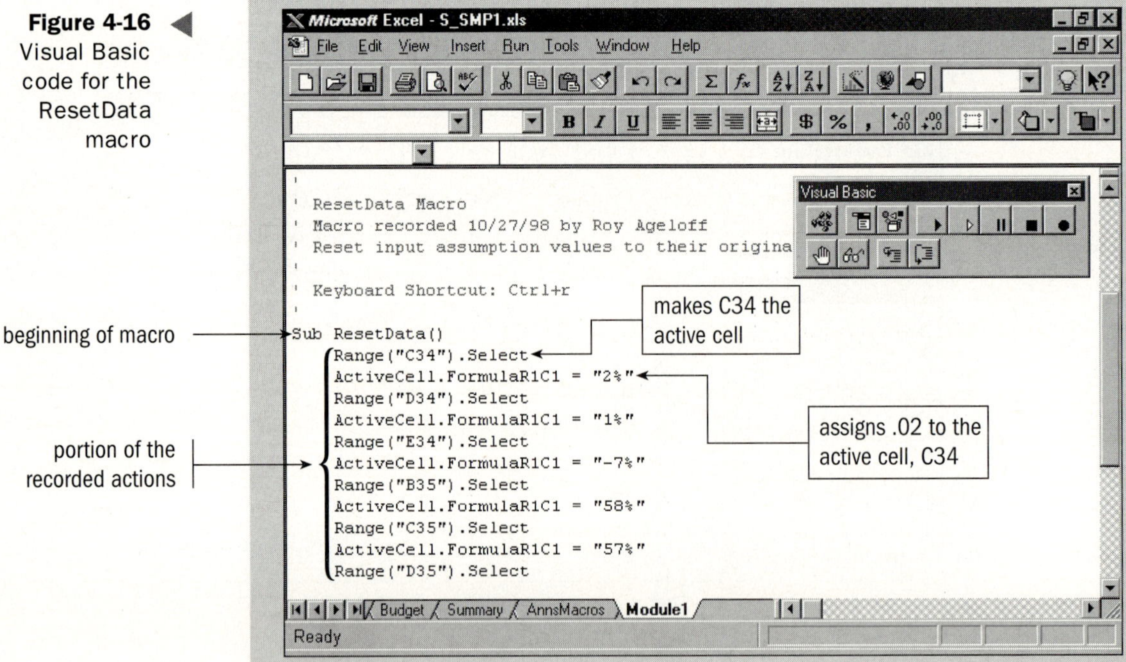

While there are many more lines of code in the ResetData macro than in the GotoAssumptions macro, there are only two basic instructions, which are repeated throughout the macro. The first statement

```
Range("C34").Select
```

tells Excel to make cell C34 the active cell. The second statement

```
ActiveCell.FormulaR1C1 = "2%"
```

is equivalent to typing .02 in the active cell, cell C34. The remaining statements are just variations on the previous two. Essentially, they make other cells the active cell and enter the original assumption values into each active cell.

Recording the PrintBudget Macro

Because your worksheets may be large, containing input sections, data, tables, reports, charts, etc., you will probably want to use a macro to help you simplify the steps for printing different parts of a worksheet. Also, the addition of one or more print macros will make the printing process much easier for other users.

After making changes to certain input values and viewing the revised Operating Budget, Ann wants to print a hardcopy of the budget to share with others. A macro to print the Operating Budget, along with the Key Input Assumptions, will simplify this task. As part of the print specifications, she wants the information to fit on one page. She will be printing only part of a worksheet, so she needs to specify the print area for the portion of the worksheet she is printing. Before printing, she will view the output in the Print Preview window. Figure 4-17 shows the planning for this macro. Record this macro for Ann.

Figure 4-17 ◀
Plans for the PrintBudget macro

Action	Result
Click File, click Page Setup...	Opens Page Setup dialog box
Click Sheet tab, click Print Area text box, enter ReportandInput	Sets print area
Click Page tab, click Fit To option button	Scales output
Click Print Preview	Opens print preview window
Click Close	Closes print preview window
Click A1	Makes A1 the active cell

To start the macro recorder:

1. Make sure the Budget sheet is the active worksheet, and A1 is the active cell.

   Now start the macro recorder.

2. Click **Tools**, point to **Record Macro**, then click **Record New Macro** to display the Record New Macro dialog box.

   Excel proposes Macro3 as the name for the macro. Change the name of the macro to PrintBudget.

3. Type **PrintBudget** in the Macro Name text box.

   Add an additional comment to explain the purpose of the macro.

4. Place the cursor at the end of the default description. Press the **Enter** key and type **Print preview Operating Budget and Key Input Assumptions**.

5. Click the **OK** button to start the macro recorder.

Now perform the tasks you want recorded.

To record a print macro:

1. Click **File**, then click **Page Setup** to display the Page Setup dialog box.

   By default, Excel prints the entire worksheet. To print only a part of the worksheet, you must specify the part you want. Previously, a range name ReportAndInput was defined to refer to the area to be printed. Enter this name in the Print Area text box.

2. Click the **Sheet** tab of the Page Setup dialog box, select the text in the **Print Area** text box, then type **ReportAndInput**.

   Now set up the print settings so the print area fits on one page.

3. Click the **Page tab**, then select the **Fit to option** button. Make sure the settings indicate fit to 1 page(s) wide by 1 tall.

   Review the output on the print preview screen.

4. Click the **Print Preview** button on the right side of the dialog box to preview the output. See Figure 4-18.

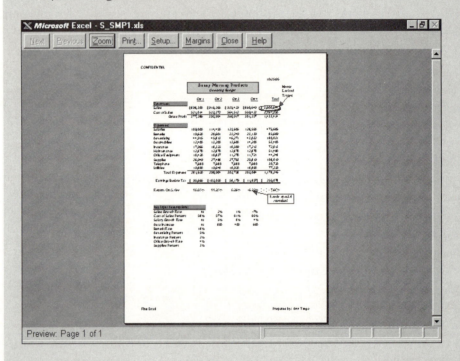

Figure 4-18
Operating budget and key Input Assumptions in print preview

5. Click the **Close** button to close the Print Preview window and return to the Budget sheet. Note that you cannot stop the macro until you leave the Print Preview window.

6. Press **Ctrl + Home** to make A1 the active cell.

   You have completed the tasks to print the Operating Budget and the Key Input Assumptions section; now turn off the macro recorder.

7. Click the **Stop Macro** button ■ to stop recording the macro.

Before running the macro, assign the PrintBudget macro to a button object.

To place a button object in the worksheet and assign a macro to the button:

1. Make sure the Budget worksheet is the active sheet, cell A1 is the active cell, and the Drawing toolbar is displayed.

2. Place a button in the worksheet to the right of the Reset Data button. The Assign Macro dialog box is displayed.

   Assign the PrintBudget macro to this button.

3. Click **PrintBudget** in the macro list box, then click the **OK** button. The macro is assigned to the button object. The button appears in the worksheet.

4. Change the label on the button to **Print Budget**. See Figure 4-19.

Figure 4-19 ◀
Budget sheet after Print Budget button added

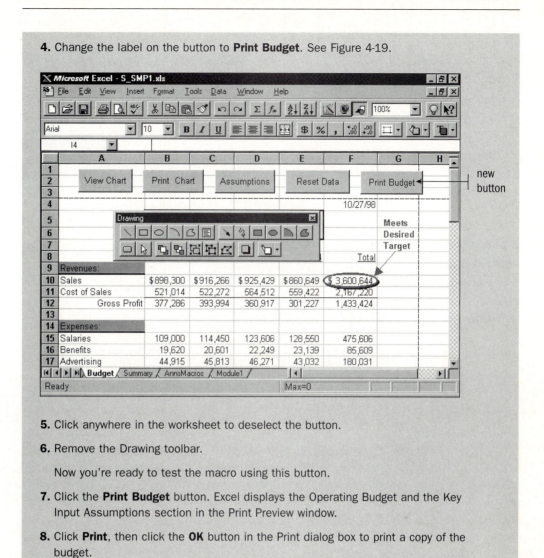

5. Click anywhere in the worksheet to deselect the button.

6. Remove the Drawing toolbar.

   Now you're ready to test the macro using this button.

7. Click the **Print Budget** button. Excel displays the Operating Budget and the Key Input Assumptions section in the Print Preview window.

8. Click **Print**, then click the **OK** button in the Print dialog box to print a copy of the budget.

The Print Budget button properly executed the PrintBudget macro.

Viewing the PrintReport and InputAssumptions Macro

Now view the Visual Basic code for the macro by switching to the module sheet.

To view the PrintBudget macro:

1. Click **Tools**, then click **Macro** to display the Macro dialog box.

2. Click **PrintBudget** in the Macro Name/Reference list box, then click the **Edit** button to display the module sheet where the recorded macro is located. See Figure 4-20. Press the **Page Down** key to view all the code for this macro. Notice that the VBA code for this macro is lengthy. When you record a macro that makes selections from a dialog box, Excel records all possible settings in the dialog box even though you may only change one or two of them.

Figure 4-20
Visual Basic code for the PrintBudget macro

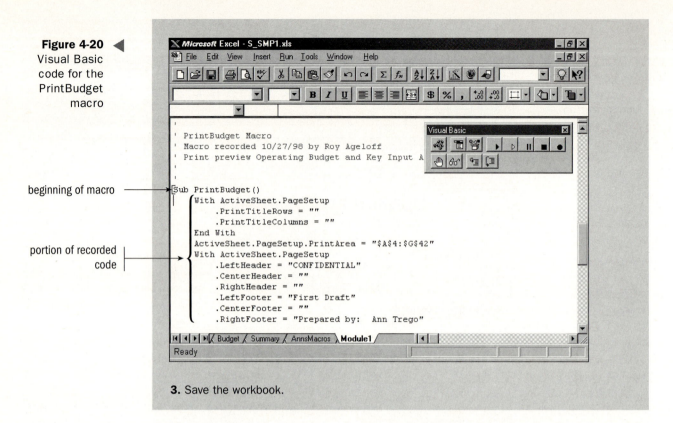

3. Save the workbook.

If you want to take a break and resume the tutorial at a later time, you can do so now. Close the workbook and exit Excel. If you are on a network, leave Windows running. If you are using your own computer, you may exit Windows and shut down the computer. When you resume the tutorial, place your Student Disk in the disk drive, launch Excel, then continue with the tutorial.

● ● ●

Running a Macro Automatically

At some point you may want to change the initial setting of a workbook for an application to work the way you want it to. For example, you may want to add a custom menu or a customized toolbar, or change some program-wide settings, such as the calculation mode, the default file path, or the standard font. You may want these settings available as soon as your macro begins. So, instead of having to change these settings each time, you can have Excel automatically make these adjustments when a workbook is opened. When you assign the **reserved macro name** (a name that has a predefined meaning to Excel) Auto_Open to a macro, Excel will automatically run that macro whenever you open the workbook.

Auto_Close, another reserved macro name, will run automatically whenever the workbook is closed. The Auto_Close macro is often included in a workbook that contains an Auto_Open macro. For example, if you have changed some setting using the Auto_Open macro, when you close the workbook you may need to reset the setting using an Auto_Close macro when you close the worksheet.

RUNNING A MACRO AUTOMATICALLY **ADVEX 199**

HELP DESK

EXCEL **5.0**

Index

AUTO_OPEN MACROS

Double-click the Help button to display the Help Topics dialog box, then click the Index tab.

Keyword
Auto_Open Procedures
Auto open files

Topic

opening a workbook automatically

Recording and Running the Auto_Open Macro

Ann would like the workbook to display in Full Screen view immediately upon opening the workbook file. This view displays more of the information in the worksheet and reduces screen clutter. **Full Screen view** removes the title bar, formula bar, toolbars, and status bar from the screen. Instead of having other users change these settings every time the workbook is opened, you can create macros that automatically do it.

Ann wants to create an Auto_Open macro to open the workbook in Full Screen view. Creating an Auto_Open macro is no different than creating any other macro, except you must assign Auto_Open as the macro name.

Create and test the Auto_Open macro.

To record an Auto_Open macro:

1. Make sure the Budget worksheet is the active sheet, and cell A1 the active cell.

2. Click **Tools**, point to **Record Macro**, and then click **Record New Macro** to display the Record New Macro dialog box.

3. Type **Auto_Open** in the Macro Name text box.

   Next, enter a brief description in the Description text box.

4. Add the text **Automatically opens workbook in Full Screen view** at the end of the default description in the Description text box.

5. Click the **OK** button. Excel returns to the worksheet and displays the message "Recording" on the status bar.

   Now record the actions for this macro.

6. Click **View**, then click **Full Screen**. The title, formula, and status bars and the worksheet window are removed from the window, and the Full Screen toolbar displays in the window.

   You have completed the steps to include in the macro; now stop the macro recorder.

7. Click the **Stop Macro** button ▪.

   TROUBLE? If the Stop Macro button is not on the screen, click Tools on the menu bar, point to Record Macro, then click Stop Recording.

To test this macro, you first need to save and close the workbook.

To save and close the workbook, and run the Auto_Open macro:

1. Make sure cell A1 in the Budget sheet is the active sheet.

2. Click **View**, then click **Full Screen** to return to Normal view.

ADVEX 200 **TUTORIAL 4** AUTOMATING TASKS USING MACROS

3. Save the file as **S_SMP2** in the Tut04 folder or directory on your Student Disk. The macros, which are stored in the module sheet, are part of the workbook. When you save the workbook, the module sheet is saved along with it.

4. Click **File**, then click the **Close** button to close the workbook.

5. Open the file **S_SMP2.xls** in the Tut04 folder or directory on your Student Disk. The workbook opens in Full Screen view. See Figure 4-21.

Figure 4-21 ◀
Workbook opened in Full Screen view

	A	B	C	D	E	F	G	H
1								
2	View Chart	Print Chart	Assumptions	Reset Data		Print Budget		
3								
4						10/27/98		
5		**Sunny Morning Products**					Meets	
6		*Operating Budget*					Desired	
7							Target	
8			Qtr 1	Qtr 2	Qtr 3	Qtr 4	Total	
9	Revenues:							
10	Sales	$898,300	$916,266	$925,429	$860,649	$ 3,600,644		
11	Cost of Sales	521,014	522,272	564,512	559,422	2,167,220		
12	Gross Profit	377,286	393,994	360,917	301,227	1,433,424		
13								
14	Expenses:							
15	Salaries	109,000	114,450	123,606	128,550	475,606		
16	Benefits	19,620	20,601	22,249	23,139	85,609		
17	Advertising	44,915	45,813	46,271	43,032	180,031		
18	Automobiles	12,400	13,200	13,600	14,200	53,400		
19	Insurance	17,966	18,325	18,509	17,213	72,013		
20	Maintenance	12,870	12,870	12,870	12,870	51,480		
21	Office Equipment	10,420	10,837	11,270	11,721	44,248		
22	Supplies	26,949	27,488	27,763	25,819	108,019		
23	Telephone	7,680	7,680	7,680	7,680	30,720		
24	Utilities	19,800	19,640	18,920	18,860	77,220		

Budget / Summary / AnnsMacros / Module1 /

click here to return to Normal View (location of Full Screen button may be different)

Printing Macros

Although you may not fully understand Visual Basic code at this point, you can find that printing the macro will help you better visualize the instructions that have been recorded. You can use the hardcopy as a reference tool from which to work. As you study the hardcopy instruction code, you may notice changes you could make to improve the code, or you may add additional instructions. You should also file the hardcopy as part of the documentation that you assemble for your workbook.

To print the macros, the module sheet must be the active sheet. Print the Visual Basic code.

To print a copy of all macros in a module sheet:

1. Click **Tools**, then click **Macro** to display the Macro dialog box.

2. Click **PrintBudget** in the Macro Name/Reference list box, then click the **Edit** button to display the module sheet where the recorded macros are located.

3. Click **File**, then click **Print**.

4. Click the **OK** button. See Figure 4-22.

PRINTING MACROS **ADVEX 201**

```
                                    Module1


'
' GoToAssumptions Macro
' Macro recorded 10/27/98 by Roy Ageloff
' Moves to the Key Input Assumption section
'
'
Sub GoToAssumptions()
    Application.Goto Reference:="KEY_ASSUMPTIONS"
    Range("A32").Select
End Sub
'
' ResetData Macro
' Macro recorded 10/27/98 by Roy Ageloff
' Reset input assumption values to their original values
'
' Keyboard Shortcut: Ctrl+r
'
Sub ResetData()
    Range("C34").Select
    ActiveCell.FormulaR1C1 = "2%"
    Range("D34").Select
    ActiveCell.FormulaR1C1 = "1%"
    Range("E34").Select
    ActiveCell.FormulaR1C1 = "-7%"
    Range("B35").Select
    ActiveCell.FormulaR1C1 = "58%"
    Range("C35").Select
    ActiveCell.FormulaR1C1 = "57%"
    Range("D35").Select
    ActiveCell.FormulaR1C1 = "61%"
    Range("E35").Select
    ActiveCell.FormulaR1C1 = "65%"
    Range("C36").Select
    ActiveCell.FormulaR1C1 = "5%"
    Range("D36").Select
    ActiveCell.FormulaR1C1 = "8%"
    Range("E36").Select
    ActiveCell.FormulaR1C1 = "4%"

    Range("A32").Select
End Sub
'
' PrintBudget Macro
' Macro recorded 10/27/98 by Roy Ageloff
' Print preview Operating Budget and Key Input Assumptions.
'
'
Sub PrintBudget()
    With ActiveSheet.PageSetup
        .PrintTitleRows = ""
        .PrintTitleColumns = ""
    End With
    ActiveSheet.PageSetup.PrintArea = "$A$4:$G$42"
    With ActiveSheet.PageSetup
        .LeftHeader = "CONFIDENTIAL"
        .CenterHeader = ""
        .RightHeader = ""
        .LeftFooter = "First Draft"
        .CenterFooter = ""
        .RightFooter = "Prepared by:  Ann Trego"
        .LeftMargin = Application.InchesToPoints(0.75)


                                    Page 1
```

Figure 4-22 ◀
Hard copy of
the four macros
(Page 1)

ADVEX 202 **TUTORIAL 4** AUTOMATING TASKS USING MACROS

Module1

```
            .RightMargin = Application.InchesToPoints(0.75)
            .TopMargin = Application.InchesToPoints(1)
            .BottomMargin = Application.InchesToPoints(1)
            .HeaderMargin = Application.InchesToPoints(0.5)
            .FooterMargin = Application.InchesToPoints(0.5)
            .PrintHeadings = False
            .PrintGridlines = False
            .PrintNotes = False
            .PrintQuality = 300
            .CenterHorizontally = True
            .CenterVertically = False
            .Orientation = xlPortrait
            .Draft = False
            .PaperSize = xlPaperLetter
            .FirstPageNumber = xlAutomatic
            .Order = xlDownThenOver
            .BlackAndWhite = False
            .Zoom = False
            .FitToPagesWide = 1
            .FitToPagesTall = 1
        End With
        ActiveSheet.PrintPreview
        Range("A1").Select
End Sub
'
' Auto_Open Macro
' Macro recorded 10/27/98 by Roy Ageloff
' Automatically opens workbook in full screen view
'
'
Sub Auto_Open()
        Application.DisplayFullScreen = True

End Sub
```

Figure 4-22 ◀
Hard copy of
the four macros
(Page 2)

Related Macro Topics

Before concluding this tutorial, you should learn about a few other topics that you may find useful when working with macros.

Editing a Macro by Recording at a Particular Location

What can you do if you discover that you forgot a step in a recorded macro? For example, Ann decides she wants to test some alternative budget scenarios involving the Benefit rate. When you created the ResetData macro, the Benefit Rate was not one of the input assumptions that was reset. Ann would like to reset the benefit rate to 18 percent in the ResetData macro.

You can add new tasks to an existing macro by recording the new task at a location you specify within the macro. To control where a new task appears in the module sheet, move the insertion point to the position where you want to continue recording. Then, from the Tools menu, select Record Macro and Mark Position for Recording. When you're ready to record, switch to the sheet where you want to record the new task, and select Tools, Record Macro, Record at Mark to add the tasks to an existing macro.

Now, modify the ResetData macro by recording one task—setting cell B38 to .18—as the final step in the macro.

To modify the ResetData macro:

1. Click **Tools**, then click **Macro** to display the Macro dialog box.

2. Click **ResetData** in the Macro Name/Reference list box, then click the **Edit** button to display the ResetData macro.

3. To specify where you want to start recording, move the insertion point to the end of the line **ActiveCell.FormulaR1C1="4%"** (two lines above the End Sub statement). Press the **Enter** key. A blank line is inserted. See Figure 4-23.

Figure 4-23
ResetData macro with blank line added

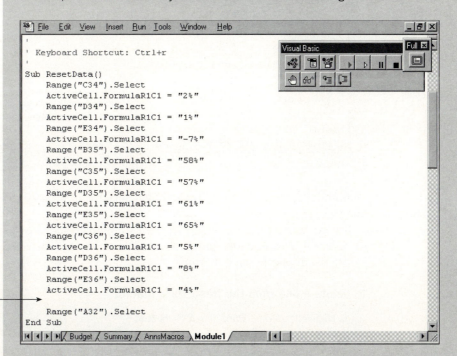

blank line where new code will be added

4. Click **Tools**, point to **Record Macro**, then click **Mark Position for Recording**.

5. Activate the Budget worksheet, then click **A38**.

6. Click **Tools**, point to **Record Macro**, then click **Record at Mark**.

ADVEX 204 TUTORIAL 4 AUTOMATING TASKS USING MACROS

Now perform the additional action.

7. Click **B38**, type **.18**, then click **A32**.

8. Click the **Stop Macro** button ■. The generated code is inserted at the insertion point.

Ann wants to confirm that the new code has been added to the macro. View the ResetData macro.

To view the ResetData macro:

1. Click **Tools**, then click **Macro** to display the Macro dialog box.

2. Click **ResetData** in the Macro Name/Reference list box, then click **Edit** to display the module sheet, where the recorded macro is located. Scroll to the End Sub statement. See Figure 4-24. Notice that two new lines have been added: **ActiveCell.FormulaR1C1 = "0.18"** and **Range("A32").Select**.

Figure 4-24 ◄
Modified
ResetData
macro

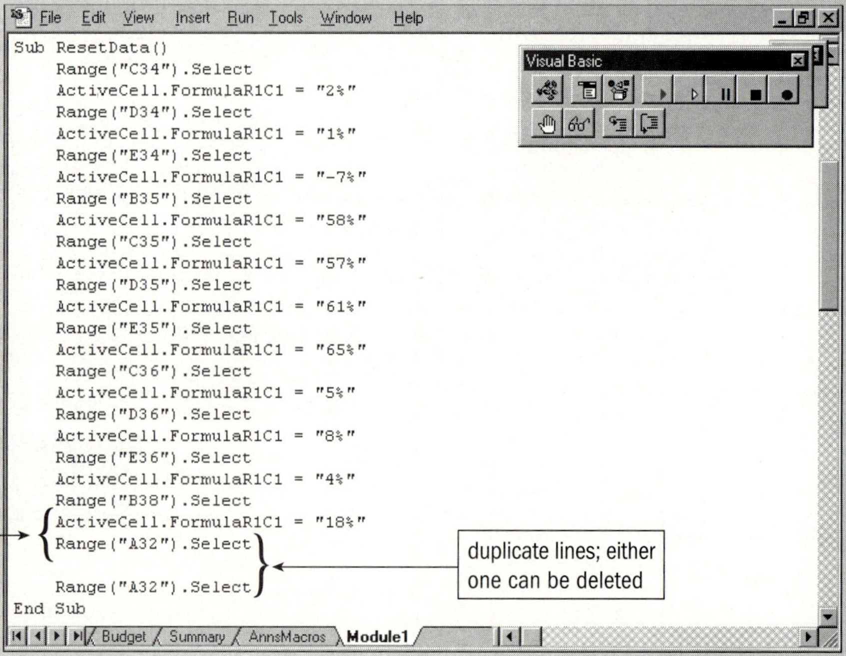

```
Sub ResetData()
    Range("C34").Select
    ActiveCell.FormulaR1C1 = "2%"
    Range("D34").Select
    ActiveCell.FormulaR1C1 = "1%"
    Range("E34").Select
    ActiveCell.FormulaR1C1 = "-7%"
    Range("B35").Select
    ActiveCell.FormulaR1C1 = "58%"
    Range("C35").Select
    ActiveCell.FormulaR1C1 = "57%"
    Range("D35").Select
    ActiveCell.FormulaR1C1 = "61%"
    Range("E35").Select
    ActiveCell.FormulaR1C1 = "65%"
    Range("C36").Select
    ActiveCell.FormulaR1C1 = "5%"
    Range("D36").Select
    ActiveCell.FormulaR1C1 = "8%"
    Range("E36").Select
    ActiveCell.FormulaR1C1 = "4%"
    Range("B38").Select
    ActiveCell.FormulaR1C1 = "18%"
    Range("A32").Select

    Range("A32").Select
End Sub
```

new code →

duplicate lines; either one can be deleted

Budget / Summary / AnnsMacros \ Module1 /

Ann notices that the line **Range("A32").Select** is duplicated. She decides to remove the line from the macro.

If your macro contains code you want to remove, activate the module sheet, highlight the selected lines of code, and press the Delete key to delete the lines from the module. Delete the duplicate line for Ann.

To delete a line from the ResetData macro:

1. Highlight the line **Range("A32").Select**

2. Press the **Delete** key. The line is removed.

Once you understand VBA code, you can make your macros easier to understand and more efficient by eliminating unnecessary lines or editing the code so it works the way you want.

| REFERENCE window | **RECORDING CHANGES TO AN EXISTING MACRO**
■ Activate the module sheet that contains the macro you want to change.
■ Position the insertion point where you want the new code inserted.
■ Click Tools, point to Record Macro, then click Mark Position for Recording to tell Excel where you want new commands inserted.
■ Activate the worksheet you want to use for recording.
■ Click Tools, point to Record Macro, then click Record at Mark to resume the recording of the existing macro.
■ Perform the actions you want added to the macro.
■ Click the Stop Macro button. |

Deleting Macros

Although you won't delete any macros in this tutorial, if you change your mind after recording a macro, or just get confused and want to start over, you can easily delete your macro.

To delete a macro, click Tools, then click Macro to display the Macro dialog box. Then select the macro you want to delete from the macro list and click Delete. You can also delete a macro by activating the module sheet, highlighting the VBA code for the selected macro, and pressing the Delete key.

Stopping a Macro During Execution

Finally, if you want to stop a macro before it has finished executing all its tasks, press the Escape key or Ctrl + Break; a Macro Error dialog box appears. In the Macro Error dialog box, click the End button to shut down the macro or the Continue button to resume running the macro.

You have successfully completed your introduction to macros. You can now exit from Excel and, if you want, turn off your computer. When you want to complete the exercises at the end of this tutorial, you will need to launch Excel again.

To close the workbook and exit Excel:

1. Save the workbook in the Tut04 folder or directory.
2. Close the workbook and exit Excel.

In this tutorial you have made the Sunny Morning Products operating budget easier to use and navigate by creating macros for common tasks. In the next tutorial, you will reap the benefits of these macros when you create several more to help the staff at Sunny Morning Products execute some what-if alternatives in the budget.

Tutorial Exercises

Open the file E_MAC.xls in the Tut04 folder and save the workbook as S_MAC.

1. Record a macro that changes the page setup to landscape orientation. Name the macro Landscape and assign the shortcut key Ctrl + l to it. (*Note:* The shortcut key is lowercase L, not the number 1.)
2. Create a macro that changes the page setup to portrait orientation. Name the macro Portrait and assign the shortcut key Ctrl + p to it.
3. Use the shortcut key to run the Landscape macro.
4. Activate the worksheet Data2 and print the Monthly report.

5. Use the shortcut key to run the Portrait macro.
6. Activate the worksheet Data1 and print the Five-Year Statistics report.
7. Examine the VBA code of the Landscape macro. Identify the line in the macro that sets the orientation to landscape.
8. Activate the Data worksheet and highlight B2:B26. Run the CurSty macro. What is the function of this macro?
9. When the CurSty macro is finished, the range that was selected remains highlighted. Modify the CurSty macro so the last step in the macro makes cell A1 the active cell.
10. Highlight cells C2:C26 and run the modified CurSty macro. Did the modified macro work?
11. Save your workbook.

Case Problems

1. Formatting a Workbook at the Good Tastn Donut Shoppe Good Tastn Donut Shoppe is a family-owned chain of retail donut stores located throughout New England. Currently there are 15 stores. Each week the sales manager prepares a workbook that summarizes the previous week's sales by store. Sales data for each store is entered into a separate sheet within the workbook. The layout of the report titles, column headings, and row labels for each store is identical (Figure 4-25). Prepare a macro that the sales manager can use to copy the report layout into each sheet in the workbook. Perform the following steps to record your macro:

1. Open a new workbook.
2. Start the macro recorder. Name the macro SheetSetup. Enter a description. Assign the shortcut key Ctrl + s to this macro. Enter the text and formatting, as shown in Figure 4-25.

Figure 4-25

3. Stop the macro recorder.
4. Move to Sheet2 in the workbook and run your macro using the Macro command on the Tools menu.
5. Move to Sheet3 and run the macro using the shortcut key.
6. Save the workbook as S_FORMAT in the Tut04 folder or directory on your Student Disk.

2. Creating General-Purpose Macros at TeleMart Jim Felton, hired as a personal computer specialist at TeleMart, finds that his Excel skills are in great demand at his new job. In the short time he has been with TeleMart, Jim has observed that many employees in a number of departments could work much more efficiently if they used macros more effectively. Jim could benefit the company quickly by creating a set of general-purpose macros that could be distributed to the interested departments. Assist Jim in creating these macros.

Open a new workbook and record the following macros:

Date/Time Macro-Create a macro that places today's date and the current time in a worksheet cell. Perform the following actions to record the macro.

COMPREHENSIVE APPLICATIONS — ADVEX 207

1. Make A1 the active cell before starting the macro recorder.
2. Turn the macro recorder on. Name the macro Timestamp and assign the shortcut key Ctrl + t to it. Record the following:
   - Enter the Now() function in cell A1.
   - Format the cell using the AutoFit selection (Format, Column, AutoFit).
   - Copy the cell to the clipboard.
   - Paste the clipboard to cell A1 using the Paste Special—Values option.
   - Press the Escape key.
   - Turn off the macro recorder.
3. Test the macro. Move to any cell in Sheet2 of this workbook. Run the macro using the shortcut key.
4. Why do you think the Paste Special command was used in this macro?

Wrap Text Macro-Create a macro to make it easier to wrap text within a cell.

5. Click B1 in sheet1. Turn the macro recorder on. Name the macro WrapText and assign the shortcut key Ctrl + w to it. Record the following:
   - From the Format menu, click Cells.
   - Click the Alignment tab and click the Wrap Text check box. Close the Format Cells dialog box.
   - Turn the macro recorder off.
6. Move to any blank cell and type the label "Adjusted Salaries." Test the WrapText macro.

GridlinesOff macro-Create a macro that turns off the Gridlines option in the worksheet. Perform the following actions to record the macro.

7. Move to any cell in Sheet1. Turn on the macro recorder and name the macro GridlinesOff. Assign the shortcut key Ctrl + g to it. Record the following:
   - From the Tools menu, click Options.
   - Click the View tab, then click the Gridlines check box. Close the Options dialog box.
   - Turn the macro recorder off.
8. Test the macro. Move to any cell in Sheet2 and run the macro using the shortcut key.
9. Save the workbook as S_GENRL in the Tut04 folder or directory.

Comprehensive Applications

1. Updating Five-Year Financial Summaries at Fradin and Parker Adam Naftalin, an accounting major, is spending his summer working for Fradin and Parker, a CPA firm. The firm maintains a workbook containing a five-year financial summary for each of its 100 clients. Each client's data is shown in a separate sheet. Figure 4-26 shows a typical sheet. One of Adam's assignments is to update each of these 100 worksheets so that each sheet reflects each company's latest five-year financial history. To update each of the 100 worksheets, Adam has to delete the data for the oldest year, move the data for years 2 through 5 to the columns for years 1 through 4, and enter the most recent year in the year 5 column.

Figure 4-26 ◀

	A		B		C		D		E		F		G
1	All-Heart Stores, Inc.												
2			1989		1990		1991		1992		1993		
3	**Operating Results**												
4	Net Sales	$	20,649	$	25,811	$	32,602	$	43,887	$	55,484		
5	Cost of Sales	$	16,057	$	20,070	$	25,500	$	34,786	$	44,175		
6	Sales & General Expense	$	3,268	$	4,070	$	5,152	$	6,684	$	8,321		
7	Interest	$	136	$	138	$	168	$	1,658	$	3,226		
8	Taxes	$	488	$	632	$	752	$	945	$	1,172		
9	Net Income	$	837	$	1,076	$	1,291	$	1,608	$	1,995		
10													
11	**Financial Position**												
12	Current Assets	$	3,631	$	4,713	$	6,415	$	8,575	$	10,198		
13	Property & Equipment	$	2,662	$	3,430	$	4,712	$	6,434	$	9,793		
14	Total Assets	$	6,360	$	8,198	$	11,389	$	15,443	$	20,565		
15	Current Liabilities	$	2,066	$	2,845	$	3,990	$	5,003	$	6,754		
16	Long Term Debt	$	1,193	$	1,273	$	1,899	$	3,278	$	4,845		
17	Shareholder's equity	$	3,008	$	3,966	$	5,366	$	6,990	$	8,759		
18													

ADVEX 208 TUTORIAL 4 AUTOMATING TASKS USING MACROS

Adam realizes that this task will be very repetitious. If he were to do it manually he would have many opportunities for errors. So he has created a macro to automate it. After updating each company's five-year financial history, he has to print each statement. Again, he has developed a macro to simplify his work.

Create the macros that Adam has developed. Do the following:

1. Open the workbook P_SUM1.xls in the Tut04 folder or directory and immediately save it as S_SUM1.
2. Develop a macro that automates the task of
   - deleting the data for year 1.
   - moving the financial data for year 2 to 5 to its new location.
   - formatting the column for year 5 using the Accounting Format code ($*#,##0_).

As you develop this macro, name the macro Updte5Year, and assign the macro to the Tools menu with the name Update 5-Year Summary.

3. After you have stopped the macro recorder, add the data for the fifth year (see Figure 4-27).

Figure 4-27 ◀

	A	G	H
1	All-Heart Stores, Inc.		
2		1994	
3	**Operating Results**		
4	Net Sales	$67,345	
5	Cost of Sales	$53,444	
6	Sales & General Expense	$10,333	
7	Interest	$ 517	
8	Taxes	$ 1,358	
9	Net Income	$ 2,333	
10			
11	**Financial Position**		
12	Current Assets	$12,115	
13	Property & Equipment	$13,175	
14	Total Assets	$26,441	
15	Current Liabilities	$ 7,406	
16	Long Term Debt	$ 7,960	
17	Shareholder's equity	$10,752	
18			

4. Record a second macro to print the five-year summary. The printed output should fit on one page and include a footer that includes the date and filename (remove the page number). The printout should not print gridlines. As you develop the macro, name the macro Print5Year, and assign the macro to the Tools menu with the name Print Summary.
5. Move to the sheet named Green & Porch and test the Updte5Year macro.
6. Add the data for the fifth year (Figure 4-28), then use the Print5Year macro to print the updated five-year summary for Green & Porch.

Figure 4-28 ◀

	A	F	G
1	Green & Porch		
2		1994	
3	**Operating Results**		
4	Net Sales	$393,700	
5	Cost of Sales	$258,661	
6	Sales & General Expenses	$105,905	
7	Interest	$ 34,252	
8	Taxes	$ 4,331	
9	Net Income	$ 9,449	
10			
11	**Financial Position**		
12	Current Assets	$ 4,600	
13	Property & Equipment	$ 845	
14	Total Assets	$ 5,445	
15	Current Liabilities	$ 661	
16	Long Term Debt	$ 1,732	
17	Shareholder's equity	$ 1,169	
18			

COMPREHENSIVE APPLICATIONS **ADVEX 209**

7. Print the macros.
8. Save the workbook.

2. Stock Portfolio for Juan Cortez Your close friend, Juan Cortez, works as an accountant at a local manufacturing company. While in college with a double major in finance and accounting, Juan dabbled in the stock market and expressed an interest in becoming a financial planner and running his own firm. To that end, he has continued his professional studies in the evenings with the aim of becoming a certified financial planner within the year. He has already begun to provide financial planning services to a few clients. Because of his hectic schedule as a full-time accountant, part-time student taking evening classes, and part-time financial planner with client visits on weekends, Juan finds it difficult to keep up with some of the data processing needs he has for his clients. You have offered to assist him until he can complete his studies for the certified financial planner exams.

Juan asked you to set up a worksheet to keep track of a stock portfolio he has set up for one of his clients.

Open a new workbook and do the following:

1. Figure 4-29 shows the data you will enter into the worksheet. For each stock, you enter its name, the number of shares, and the purchase price. Periodically, you will also enter the current price of each stock so that Juan can review the changes with his client.

In addition to entering the data, you need to make the following calculations:
   - Cost = No of shares * Purchase Price
   - Current Value = No of shares * Current Price
   - Gains/Losses = Current Value minus Cost
   - Totals for Cost, Current Value, and Gains/Losses

Below the table, Juan wants a column chart comparing cost (column D) vs. the current value for each stock so that the client can graphically see the changes that have occurred in the portfolio.

Figure 4-29

	A	B	C	D	E	F	G	H	I
1				**Stock Portfolio**					
2									
3	**Stock**	**No of shares**	**Purchase Price**	**Cost**	**Current Price**	**Current Value**	**Gains/ Losses**		
4	PepsiC	100	$ 50.25		$ 52.50				
5	FordM	250	$ 31.00		$ 30.00				
6	AT&T	50	$ 60.00		$ 61.25				
7	IBM	100	$ 90.25		$ 95.75				
8	Xerox	50	$ 138.00		$ 134.00				
9	Totals								
10									
11									

2. After you have completed the requirements specified in Question 1, add the following macros to simplify the use of this worksheet.
   - Prepare a macro that clears the Current Price column. Name the macro ClearPrice. Reenter the Current Price data from Figure 4-29, then test the macro.
   - Prepare a macro that prints the portfolio report without including your chart. Use the following specifications: output on one page; no gridlines; remove page number from the footer; include today's date in the right-hand section of the footer; include the word "Confidential" in the left-hand section of the footer. Do not include information in the header and center the report horizontally on the page. Name the macro PrintTable.
   - Prepare another macro that prints the portfolio report and the chart with the following specifications: output on one page; no gridlines; remove the page number from the footer; include today's date in the right-hand section of the footer; include the word "Confidential" in the left-hand section of the footer. Do not include information in the header and center the report horizontally on the page. Name the macro PrintAll.

ADVEX 210   **TUTORIAL 4** AUTOMATING TASKS USING MACROS

3. Attach each macro to a button object. You decide where to place the buttons, remembering to provide a descriptive label for each button.
4. Test each macro.
5. From the financial section of your newspaper, look up the current price of each stock (all of the stocks in this case are listed on the New York Stock Exchange daily). Use the ClearPrice macro, then enter the current prices. Use your print macros to print the revised stock portfolio.
6. Print the macros.
7. Save your worksheet as S_STOCK in the Tut04 folder or directory on your Student Disk.

TUTORIAL 5

Preparing and Examining What-If Alternatives

Developing the Best Operating Plan

OBJECTIVES

In this tutorial you will learn how to:

- Understand different methods of preparing what-if alternatives
- Explore alternatives with goal seeking
- Use Goal Seek for creating backward solutions
- Use one-input and two-input data tables
- Perform a what-if analysis on a data table
- Use Scenario Manager in evaluating what-if alternatives
- Find optimal solutions using Solver
- Examine optimal solutions
- Automate what-if alternative exploration with macros

Sunny Morning Products

Travis wants SMP to at least make a profit and if possible to hit $4 million in sales next year. He needs to determine if and how this can occur by exploring their business operating plan. He wants an expanded plan that shows how many bottles of Olympic Gold orange juice and Thirst Quencher SMP needs to sell in order to cover its costs of operations *and* make a profit. When Carmen specified the initial sales revenue, she estimated sales for both products to total 276,400 bottles at an average price of $3.25 per bottle. While this was a good overall price estimate, SMP sells its premium orange juice at a higher price than its sports Thirst Quencher. Travis needs to refine their price estimate. He expects that SMP can sell its orange juice for $3.34 per bottle and its Thirst Quencher for $3.06 per bottle. He now needs this refinement included in their Operating Budget. This revision in the plan will allow him to examine the impact of alternative product mixes (that is, the number of each of these two Olympic Gold products he expects to sell) on SMP's total sales and profits.

Travis asks Ann to help him prepare a version of the Operating Budget that allows him to explore alternative product mixes for next year. Travis and Ann discuss the line items and data values they need in the worksheet. These include the expected number of bottles and the selling price per bottle for both orange juice and Thirst Quencher. Ann gathers all the information she needs and prepares a draft of the revised Operating Budget with an initial product mix of bottles of orange juice and Thirst Quencher (Figure 5-1).

Figure 5-1
Ann's draft of SMP's revised Operating Budget

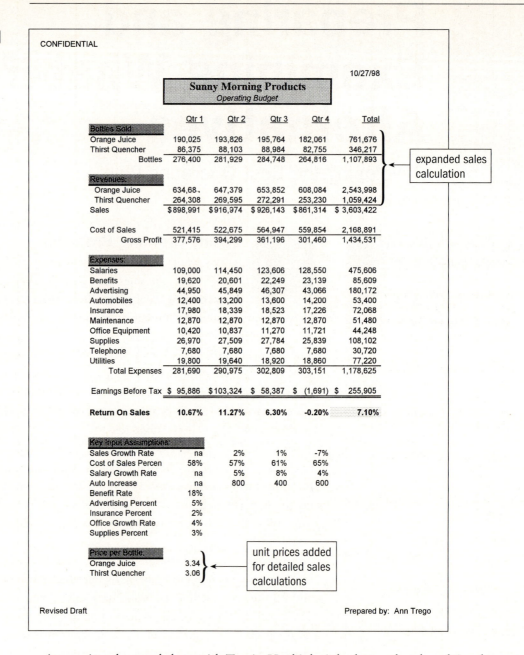

Ann reviews her worksheet with Travis. He thinks it looks good and explains that next they need to do several what-if analyses that will calculate the Earnings Before Tax based on the product mix they might sell. They will explore several different alternatives in order to assess the potential profitability and weigh the possibility of achieving his desired goal of $4 million in total sales. They discuss the range of sales for the bottles of Olympic Gold that might occur next year. What would happen to Earnings Before Tax and Return On Sales as sales change? Which product mixes are most profitable? Ann considers these questions and develops a planning analysis sheet in preparation for evaluating Travis's alternative product mixes (Figure 5-2).

SUNNY MORNING PRODUCTS **ADVEX 213**

Figure 5-2 ◄
Ann's planning
sheet

Planning Analysis Sheet

My goal:

Prepare alternative analyses to determine the best product mix of orange juice and Thirst

Quencher sales that are profitable and may reach $4 million total sales.

What results do I want to see?

Projected Income Statement for each of the following alternatives:

- Product mix for annual ROS of 15%

- Product mix for break even

- Varied product mix options

What information do I need?

Orange juice price per bottle = 3.34

Thirst Quencher price per bottle = 3.06

Orange juice bottles [Qtr 1] = 190025

Thirst Quencher bottles [Qtr 2] = 86375

Range of product mix alternatives for Qtr 1

- Orange juice   150000 to 190000 bottles sold

- Thirst Quencher   30000 to 120000 bottles sold

What other calculations will I perform?

Orange juice sales = Orange juice bottles sold * Orange juice price per bottle

Thirst Quencher sales = Thirst Quencher bottles sold * Thirst Quencher price per bottle

Sales = Orange juice sales + Thirst Quencher sales

In this tutorial you will use Ann's workbook with the revised Operating Budget worksheet to learn how to use Excel in exploring various what-if alternatives. Figure 5-3 summarizes the application of analysis alternatives to different situations.

Figure 5-3 ◄
Selecting an
analysis
method

Analysis Method	Situation
What-If	Enter one or more known input data values and display a single solution
Goal Seeking	Find a single input constant that produces a known target value for a single formula and display a single solution
Data Table	Calculate and display a series of different solution values for one or more formulas from a given series of known what-if constants that are input data values for one or two different cells
Scenario	Calculate several different what-if solutions for an organized series of up to 32 different input constants, all located in separate cells, with one solution displayed at a time
Solver	Find the optimal solution for two or more input decision data values that are restricted by a set of one or more constraint conditions and display that single solution

Retrieving the Worksheet

First you need to retrieve and examine Ann's worksheet in preparation for exploring alternative what-if analyses.

To retrieve the workbook:

1. Launch Excel.

2. Open Ann's C_SMP1.xls workbook in the Tut05 folder or directory on your Student Disk. Then save the workbook as S_SMP1.xls in the Tut05 folder in case you want to restart this tutorial.

In calculating the number of bottles sold in the Operating Budget, Ann uses **constants**, or values that will not change, for the first quarter of the plan. For the remaining quarters she uses a growth rate to determine the number of bottles sold. The price per bottle is expected to remain constant throughout the year, and this value, in conjunction with the number of bottles sold each quarter, is then used to calculate the sales revenue for each product. The revenue for the two products is then summed to determine the Sales amount. Examine Ann's worksheet and inspect the formulas she uses to calculate these planning items.

To examine the formulas used in calculating Sales:

1. Activate the **Budget** worksheet.

2. Click **B7**. This cell contains a constant, 190025, for the number of bottles of orange juice sold.

3. Examine cell **B8**, which contains the number of bottles of Thirst Quencher sold.

4. Click cells **C7**, **D7**, and **E7**. Note the use of the Sales Growth Rate for the bottles sold in each of these quarters and that the ROUND function is used to eliminate partial bottles sold; that is, SMP doesn't sell a 0.573 bottle. Either a full bottle is sold, or no bottle is sold.

5. Click cells **C8**, **D8**, and **E8** to see that the growth rates for the number of bottles of Thirst Quencher sold each quarter are the same as those for orange juice.

6. Click cells **B12**, **C12**, **D12**, and **E12** to examine the formulas for calculating the orange juice Sales amounts for each quarter. Note that these formulas do *not* use the ROUND function.

7. Click cells **B13**, **C13**, **D13**, and **E13** to inspect the formulas for calculating the Thirst Quencher Sales amount for each quarter. Note the use of the same price per bottle in each quarter.

8. Examine the formulas in cells **B14** through **F14**, which calculate the Sales revenue.

9. Scroll to **A48** and review the Price per Bottle key input assumptions. Note that the same price is used in each quarter.

10. Inspect other cells in the worksheet and review the formulas used in their calculations. Confirm that the formulas for Cost of Sales, all the expenses, Earnings Before Tax, and Return On Sales are those you created in Tutorial 2.

Now that you have an understanding of the formulas that Ann will use in calculating the revised Operating Budget, you are ready to explore alternative product mixes.

Examining Alternatives with Goal Seeking

Travis and Ann decide to use goal seeking to evaluate several product mix alternatives. **Goal seeking**, also known as backward solving, is the process of repeatedly changing a constant used in calculating a formula until the formula yields the result you want. The constant is in the **adjust cell**, or the **changing cell**, and the formula that is calculated using that constant is in the **target cell**, or **set cell**. Starting with the answer you want for a formula and finding a constant that gives that result is known as working backwards to get the solution.

Travis wants to see how many more bottles of orange juice need to be sold to make the annual sales equal to his desired target of $4,000,000. Remember that the number of bottles sold for the year is calculated using the number of bottles sold in Qtr 1 (the constant) and the growth rate for each quarter. Ann does not want to change any formulas, only constants, so she decides to adjust the number of bottles of orange juice sold in Qtr 1 until the Sales value in the Total column is $4,000,000.

There are two backward solving methods you can use to obtain a goal-seeking solution: trial-and-error, and the Excel Goal Seek feature.

Using the Trial-and-Error Method to Perform Goal Seeking

The **trial-and-error method** of goal seeking is exactly what it sounds like: you enter values in the adjust cell until the goal value is attained in the target cell. Travis and Ann will adjust the number of bottles of orange juice in Qtr 1 until the Sales value in the Total column equals $4,000,000. Use Ann's worksheet to evaluate Travis's goal-seeking alternative for $4,000,000 in sales for the year.

To use the trial-and-error method of goal seeking:

1. Scroll the worksheet so that row 5 is the first row displayed in the worksheet window.

2. Click **B7**, the adjust cell.

3. Enter **210000**. A larger number of bottles is picked because the Sales value is less than the desired amount and Ann wants it to increase. The Total Sales value in cell F14, the target cell, changes to $3,870,836, which is still less than the desired goal. The number of bottles of orange juice in Qtr 1 needs to be higher.

   Now try 220000.

4. Enter **220000** in cell B7. The Sales value in the Total column is $4,004,713. This is just slightly more than the desired goal value, so the number of bottles of orange juice in Qtr 1 needs to be between 210000 and 220000. See Figure 5-4.

Figure 5-4
Trial-and-error goal-seeking solution

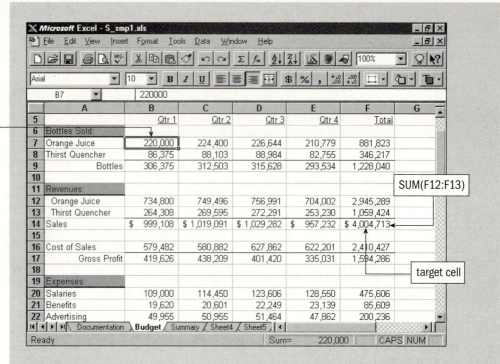

5. Enter **219000** in cell B7. The Sales value in the Total column is $3,991,326, which is now slightly less than the desired goal value.

6. Enter **219648** in cell B7. The Sales value in the Total column is now $3,999,997, which is very close to the desired goal. If you try other values, you will find that this is the closest one to $4,000,000, because partial bottles are not allowed. Of course, you might have tried entering several other values before arriving at this number of bottles sold. A very close, but not exact, result occurs frequently when one or more of the formulas that are used in calculating the cells between the adjust cell and the target cell contains the ROUND function which is the situation for the cells calculating the number of bottles sold. In such a situation, you need to determine how close to the target value your results need to come.

7. Save this as the S_SMP1.xls workbook in the Tut05 folder. Then preview and print the Budget worksheet.

REFERENCE window

PERFORMING TRIAL-AND-ERROR GOAL SEEKING

- If necessary, split the worksheet window so that the target and adjust cells are both visible.
- Click the adjust cell to select it.
- Enter a new trial value and observe the result in the target cell.
- Continue entering new values in the adjust cell until the desired goal result appears in the target cell.

Although trial-and-error is not the most efficient way to do goal seeking, it does produce the desired result without rewriting any formulas. With some practice, goal seeking by trial-and-error provides a reasonable method for exploring what-if alternatives where a goal value is known for a formula.

Using Goal Seek to Find a Solution

Excel includes the **Goal Seek** feature, which is a built-in mathematical procedure that automatically carries out a series of trial-and-error solutions in an efficient way for you. With Goal Seek, all you need to do is specify the target cell, the desired goal value, and the adjust cell. Excel quickly calculates a solution that satisfies the goal you specified. With Goal Seek, *only a single cell* can be adjusted in obtaining the solution for the desired goal value.

Travis wants to explore a second what-if alternative. He wants to find the product mix that provides him with a break-even point for the year. **Break even** occurs when revenues are equal to expenses; that is, the Earnings Before Tax and Return On Sales are zero. This what-if helps Travis establish the minimum number of bottles that must be sold to avoid suffering a loss for the year. Like many other business managers, Travis is keenly interested in the sales volume that is the dividing point between profit and loss. Under these conditions, Travis expects that the relationship between the number of bottles of orange juice and Thirst Quencher sold would be the same as the initial ratio of 190,025 to 86,375; that is, 2.2 bottles of orange juice to each bottle of Thirst Quencher. SMP's marketing staff has established this relationship of the number of bottles of orange juice sold to the number of bottles of Thirst Quencher sold based on several years of prior sales. The break-even solution using this ratio then establishes the minimum acceptable sales level for SMP.

To find a break-even solution:

1. Split the worksheet window horizontally and scroll the worksheet as necessary so that rows 5 through 15 display in the top window, and rows 30 through 35 display in the bottom window. See Figure 5-5.

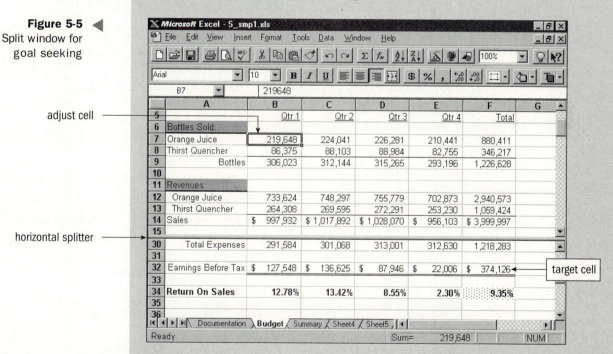

Figure 5-5 Split window for goal seeking

2. Verify that cell **B8** contains its initial value of **86,375**.

3. Click **B7** and enter the formula **2.2*B8**, which represents the ratio between the number of bottles sold of the two products. The ratio between the number of bottles of orange juice and Thirst Quencher remains constant at 1 to 2.2.

4. Click **F32**, the target cell.

5. Click **Tools**, then click **Goal Seek** to display the Goal Seek dialog box with cell F32 already specified as the Set cell. See Figure 5-6.

Figure 5-6
Goal Seek dialog box with target cell specified

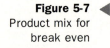

Now enter the goal value.

6. Click the **To value** text box to select it, then type **0** (zero), the target value for break even.

Next, enter the adjust cell.

7. Click the **By changing cell** text box to select it, click and drag the Goal Seek dialog box towards the bottom of the window so that cell B8 is visible, then click **B8** to specify it as the desired adjust cell. Notice that Excel enters this cell reference as an absolute reference.

8. Click the **OK** button to obtain the goal-seeking solution. Wait for Excel to calculate the solution, then click the **OK** button in the Goal Seek Status dialog box to return to Ready mode. See Figure 5-7. Because the ROUND function is used, this is a value that is close to zero, but may not be exactly zero. In this case, it is $3.00, and is close enough to zero for Travis's needs. Note that Total Sales could be as low as $2,744,981 and SMP would just break even for the year.

Figure 5-7
Product mix for break even

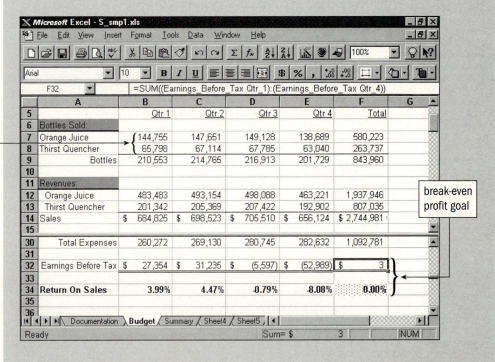

9. Save the S_SMP1.xls workbook.

REFERENCE window

USING GOAL SEEK

- If necessary, split the worksheet window so that the target cell and the adjust cell are both visible in the worksheet window.
- Click Tools and then click Goal Seek to display that dialog box.
- Enter the target cell reference in the Set cell text box.
- Enter the goal value for the target cell in the To value text box.
- Enter the adjust cell reference in the By changing cell text box.
- Click the OK button or press the Enter key.

Exploring Alternatives with Data Tables

Travis and Ann consider the different alternatives that have been explored. In each situation, a single solution was produced and the results printed. Although this gives Travis a good idea of how different product mixes affect the potential profitability of SMP, he needs to look at several different worksheet printouts to compare alternatives. Travis would like to be able to compare the results for several alternatives by having the results for these alternatives displayed as a table in one report.

He decides to use a data table, also known as a what-if table. A **data table** provides a shortcut for calculating and displaying results for a *series* of what-if alternatives all in one operation. The table shows the results of a formula using a series of input data values for a selected cell, all located together in the worksheet. You place the table in a cell range of the worksheet from which you can easily review and conveniently compare the results for the different solutions of the worksheet.

There are two types of data tables—one-input and two-input. A **one-input table** allows you to change one input data value and capture calculated values for one or more different formulas. A **two-input table** enables you to change two input data values and display the calculated results for a single formula. You can use either a row or a column arrangement with a one-input data table. For a column arrangement, the input data values reside in a cell range in a column with the calculated values placed in adjacent columns, and similarly for a row arrangement.

Travis and Ann decide to prepare a data table to evaluate alternative numbers of bottles sold during the year. The questions they want to address are

- What are the Earnings Before Tax in each of the four quarters of the plan and for the year when the number of bottles of Thirst Quencher sold in Qtr 1 ranges from 30,000 to 120,000 in increments of 10,000, while all other assumptions for the plan remain unchanged? The relationship of 2.2 bottles of orange juice to each bottle of Thirst Quencher, as determined from their marketing analysis, remains in effect.

- What are the Earnings Before Tax for the year when the number of bottles of Thirst Quencher sold ranges from 30,000 to 120,000 in increments of 10,000 *and* the number of bottles of orange juice sold varies from 150,000 to 190,000 in increments of 10,000, while all other planning assumptions remain unchanged? The relationship of 2.2 bottles of orange juice to each bottle of Thirst Quencher is *not* applied for this analysis, because the mix of the two products could vary.

- Which product mixes of orange juice and Thirst Quencher are profitable for the year (that is, which combinations exceed break even)?

One-Input Data Table

First, Travis and Ann want to determine the Earnings Before Tax in each of the four quarters and for the year when the number of bottles of Thirst Quencher sold in Qtr 1 varies from 30,000 to 120,000 bottles sold. Because they will change the value in only one cell, they can use a data table with one input variable.

In general, a one-input table with a column arrangement is organized as illustrated in Figure 5-8. The table resides in a range of cells set apart from the main worksheet input area. A series of input values is placed in the first, or leftmost, column of the table. The top row of the table contains one or more formulas that are calculated using each input value. The results for each formula are displayed in the same column as the formula in the rows immediately below it. The upper-left corner of a one-input table can either be blank or contain a label for documentation. The **input cell** is a cell located outside the data-table area, whose value is replaced by the series of input values. When the data table is calculated, the input cell is temporarily given each of the data values from the series of input values in the leftmost column of the data table range. The entire worksheet is recalculated and the results of each of the designated formulas are then stored in the appropriate row of the data table. The values in the table can then be used for exploring different what-if alternatives.

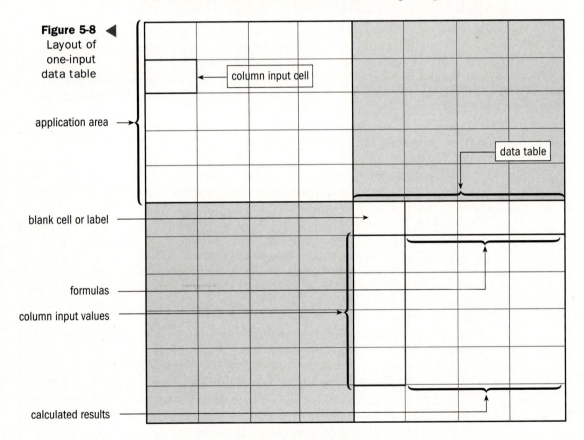

Figure 5-8
Layout of one-input data table

The first thing you need to do to create a data table is to select an area of your worksheet to hold the results. Ann decides to use the area immediately below and to the right of the Operating Budget because this location allows her to insert or delete rows and columns in either the area containing her existing Operating Budget or the area containing the data table, without affecting the other worksheet area. When Ann applies the general design scheme for completing the layout of her data table, the worksheet window is divided into horizontal and vertical panes in preparation for calculating the results (Figure 5-9).

Figure 5-9
Worksheet setup for Ann's one-input data table

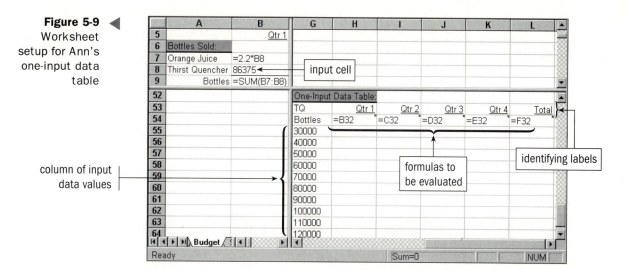

Begin constructing a one-input data table to address Travis's question—what are the Earnings Before Tax each quarter and for the year when the number of bottles of Thirst Quencher sold in Qtr 1 varies from 30,000 to 120,000, in increments of 10,000? In setting up the table, you can place identifying text labels above the table and a descriptive label in its upper-left corner.

To identify a data table and label the left column of the table for documentation:

1. Reduce the width of column A to **14**. This will allow all the columns of the data table to be displayed.

2. Move the horizontal window splitter so that rows 5 through 9 are visible in the top pane, then scroll the bottom pane to view rows 52 through 64. The top of the data table will be placed at row **52**, which is below the worksheet area occupied by the current Operating Budget.

    TROUBLE? If you cannot see rows 52 through 64 in the bottom pane, switch to the full screen view. Click View, then click Full Screen.

3. Split the window vertically so that columns A and B are visible in the left pane, then scroll the right pane so that columns G through L are displayed, as shown previously in Figure 5-9.

4. Enter the **labels** in cells G52, G53, and G54, then enter the **column titles** in H53:L53 as documentation for the data table, as shown previously in Figure 5-9.

Next, enter the input data values in the left column of the table, using drag-and-fill to create an AutoFill series of values.

To enter input data table values using drag-and-fill to fill in the series of numbers:

1. Enter **30000** and **40000** in cells G55 and G56, respectively. You input two values to give Excel the increment for the series.

2. Select the range **G55:G56** to establish the starting value and the increment of 10,000 for the data series.

3. Move the mouse pointer over the fill handle in the lower right corner of the selection until the pointer changes to **+**.

4. Click and drag the pointer to cell **G64** to specify the range you want to fill with the series. An outline appears around the range G55:G64.

> **5.** Release the mouse button to complete the series of values for the number of bottles of Thirst Quencher sold.
>
> **TROUBLE?** If you did not select the correct range to create a data series from 30,000 to 120,000 in increments of 10,000, then click the Undo button and repeat Steps 2 through 5.

Now set up the formulas whose values will be stored in the data table when it is calculated—in this table, the Earnings Before Tax for each of the four quarters and the year. Cell formulas that reference each of the cells B32, C32, D32, E32, and F32, where the Earnings Before Tax values are calculated, provide a convenient method for collecting these values from the application area of the worksheet. When these formulas are entered in the top row of the data table, their data values are displayed. Enter these formulas in cells H54:L54.

To enter formulas for displaying calculated results:

> **1.** Click **H54**, then enter the formula **B32** to display the value for this formula.
>
> **TROUBLE?** If the text B32 appeared in the cell instead of a numeric value, you did not enter B32 as a formula. Repeat Step 1.
>
> **2.** Copy the formula from cell **H54** to cells **I54:L54**. The current values for Earnings Before Tax are displayed. See Figure 5-10.

Figure 5-10
Setup for one-input data table

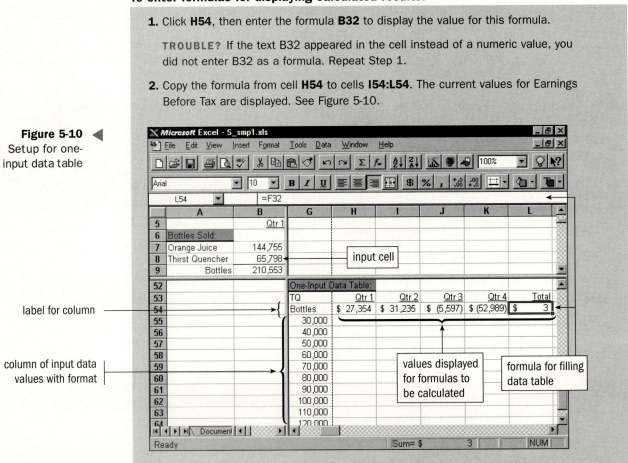

Because the calculated values, and *not* the formulas, are displayed in cells H54:L54, which reference other cells in the worksheet, you may want to include additional documentation with your data table so it is easier to review its content. Excel allows you to add a text note to a cell for this documentation. A **text note** is a descriptive comment that is associated with a cell and is displayed whenever the pointer is positioned on top of the cell. A cell does not need to be selected to display its note. A red dot appears in the top right corner of a cell with a note. Add text notes to the cells that contain the formulas used in the data table.

To attach a text note to a cell:

1. Click **H54** to select it for adding a note.

2. Click **Insert**, then click **Note** to display the Cell Note dialog box. See Figure 5-11.

Figure 5-11
Cell Note dialog box

cell

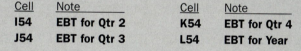

3. Type **EBT for Qtr 1** as the Text Note, then click the **OK** button to finish entering the note.

4. Position the mouse pointer on top of cell **H54** to display the note. You do not need to select the cell to view the note.

Click H54, hold down the Shift key, and press the F2 key to display the note. Click the Close button to close the Cell Note dialog box.

5. Enter the following notes to document the other cells in the top row of the data table:

Cell	Note	Cell	Note
I54	EBT for Qtr 2	K54	EBT for Qtr 4
J54	EBT for Qtr 3	L54	EBT for Year

This completes the setup of the one-input data table, as shown previously in Figure 5-9.

REFERENCE window

ADDING A TEXT NOTE TO A CELL

- Click the cell to which you want to add a text note.
- Click Insert, then click Note to display the Cell Note dialog box.
  or
  Hold down the Shift key and press the F2 key to display the dialog box.
- Type the text you want for the note in the Text Note box.
- Click the OK button.

Once the data table is set up, it is ready to receive the calculated results. Now recalculate the worksheet, using the input data values from the data table.

To calculate and display results in a data table:

1. Select the range **G54:L64**, which contains the data table. This includes the formulas in the top row and the input data values in the leftmost column.

2. Click **Data**, then click **Table** to display the Table dialog box. See Figure 5-12. The Table dialog box allows you to specify either the Row or Column Input Cell. With a one-input data table you use only one of these two input cells; the other one remains blank.

Figure 5-12
Table dialog box

cell reference entered for data in leftmost column

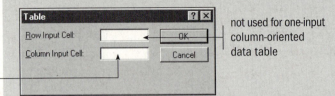

not used for one-input column-oriented data table

3. Click the **Column Input Cell** text box to select it, because this data table is arranged as columns.

4. Click **B8** to specify the input cell that will be given the input data values for calculating the results, then click the **OK** button to carry out the calculations. This may take a few minutes, because the entire worksheet is recalculated for each of the input data values and the results are placed in the corresponding row in the table. See Figure 5-13.

Figure 5-13
Completed one-input data table

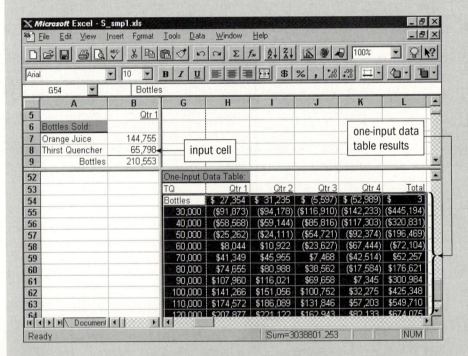

5. Save this as the S_SMP2.xls workbook in the Tut05 folder, then select, preview, and print the data table in range G52:L64. Use the Selection option in the Print What options of the Print dialog box so you print only the selected data table.

> **REFERENCE window**
>
> **USING A ONE-INPUT DATA TABLE WITH A COLUMN ARRANGEMENT**
>
> - Set up the table as a column arrangement in a convenient cell range, with the input data values in the leftmost column and the formulas to be calculated in the top row.
> - Select the range of cells that contains the entire data table, with both the input values and calculated results cell selected.
> - Click Data, then click Table to display that dialog box.
> - Click the Column Input Cell text box to select it.
> - Click the input cell in the worksheet to specify that cell reference.
> - Click the OK button.

HELP DESK

EXCEL 5.0

> Index
>
> **CREATING A ROW-ORIENTED DATA TABLE**
>
> Double-click the Help button to display the Help Topics dialog box, then click the Index tab.
>
> | Keyword | Topic |
> |---|---|
> | data tables | Fill in a one-variable, row-oriented data table |
> | data tables | Filling in a one-input data table |

In reviewing the one-input data table, Travis sees that, with a 2.2 ratio, all combinations of the number of bottles of Thirst Quencher sold are profitable for the year except those from 30,000 bottles to 60,000 bottles. He decides to take a closer look at the profitable product mixes for next year.

Two-Input Data Table

Travis and Ann want to evaluate the profitability of various product mixes of Thirst Quencher and orange juice where the relationship is different than 2.2 bottles of orange juice for each bottle of Thirst Quencher. This what-if evaluation involves two input data values.

In general, a two-input data table is arranged as illustrated in Figure 5-14. The table is in a range of cells with one set of input data values in the leftmost column of the table and the second set of input data values in the table's top row. The upper-left corner of the two-input table holds the single formula, whose results are recorded in the data table for each pair of inputs from the left column and the top row. Note that you can evaluate only one formula as a two-input data table. When the data table is calculated, Excel places each pair of input values into the designated input cells in the application area of the worksheet and calculates the entire worksheet. The results of the single formula are then placed in the calculated results area of the data table. Both the Row and Column Input Cells in the Table dialog box are specified in calculating the two-input data table.

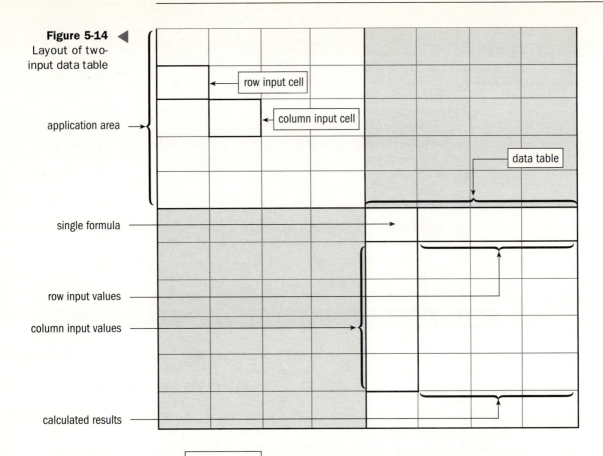

Figure 5-14 Layout of two-input data table

HELP DESK

EXCEL 5.0

Index

SETTING UP A DATA TABLE

Double-click the Help button to display the Help Topics dialog box, then click the Index tab.

Keyword	Topic
data tables	Enter initial values for a data table
data tables	Filling in a two-input data table

Ann can use the same worksheet area as for the one-input data table, since the same number of bottles of Thirst Quencher sold will be one of the inputs. However, the data table setup needs to be modified for the second input. Set up the data table area with the second series of input data values, using drag-and-fill.

To set up the second input data series using drag-and-fill:

1. Select **H53:L64**, which contains the data table results, and press the **Delete** key to remove the contents of these cells.

2. Delete row **54** because it is not needed for the revised data table. Note that the location of the data table below and to the right of the Operating Budget area allows you to remove this row without affecting the layout of the budget.

3. Click **G52** and edit the label to read **Two-Input Data Table**.

4. Enter **150000** and **160000** in cells H53 and I53, respectively, then use the fill handle to complete the series in the range **H53:L53** for the number of bottles of orange juice sold.

5. With the cell range **H53:L53** still selected, click the **Underline** button to remove the underlining from these cells.

6. Format the range **H53:L53** using the Comma format with no decimals.

Next, enter the formula for displaying the calculated results in the upper-left corner of the data table range.

To enter a single formula for displaying the calculated results that appear in a data table:

1. Click **G53**, then enter the cell formula **F32**, which references the cell where Earnings Before Tax for the year is calculated.

2. Format cell **G53** as currency with no decimals, then attach the note **EBT for Year** to the cell for documentation.

This completes the setup of the two-input data table. See Figure 5-15.

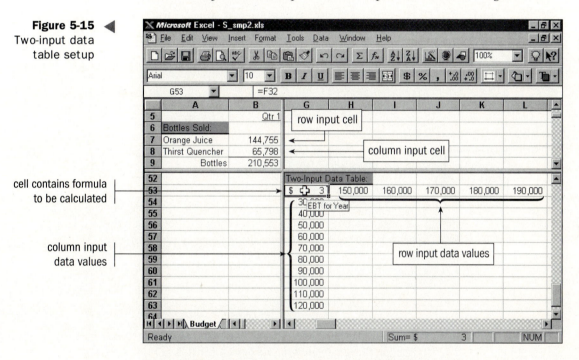

Figure 5-15
Two-input data table setup

The table is ready for calculating the results.

To calculate and store results in a two-input data table:

1. Select the range **G53:L63**, which contains the row and column of input data values, with the formula in the upper-left corner of the range.

2. Click **Data**, then click **Table** to display the Table dialog box with the cursor located in the Row Input Cell text box.

3. Click **B7**, which is the input cell for the row data values. Although this cell contains a formula, the values from the top row of the data table are substituted for this formula as each recalculation is performed.

4. Click the **Column Input Cell** text box, then click **B8**, which is the input cell for the column data values.

Figure 5-16
Completed two-input data table

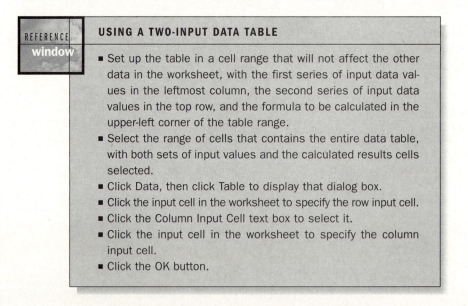

5. Click the **OK** button to calculate and display the results in the data table, then click **G53** to unselect the entire data table. Your screen should look like Figure 5-16.

6. Save this as the S_SMP2.xls workbook.

REFERENCE window

USING A TWO-INPUT DATA TABLE

- Set up the table in a cell range that will not affect the other data in the worksheet, with the first series of input data values in the leftmost column, the second series of input data values in the top row, and the formula to be calculated in the upper-left corner of the table range.
- Select the range of cells that contains the entire data table, with both sets of input values and the calculated results cells selected.
- Click Data, then click Table to display that dialog box.
- Click the input cell in the worksheet to specify the row input cell.
- Click the Column Input Cell text box to select it.
- Click the input cell in the worksheet to specify the column input cell.
- Click the OK button.

Travis reviews the results in the data table and learns the product combinations of orange juice and Thirst Quencher that must be sold in order for SMP to be profitable next year. These are those product mixes with Earnings Before Tax values that are positive numbers in the data table. While these combinations yield a profit that is less than his $4 million sales goal, they clearly establish the minimum acceptable sales combination without incurring a loss—Travis's worst-situation alternatives.

Charting Data Table Results

Travis thinks that a chart of the two-input data table would give him a better understanding of the relationships among his alternatives for the minimum acceptable product mixes. He asks Ann to create a line chart that compares the results for the number of bottles of Thirst Quencher sold with the number of bottles of orange juice sold. Ann decides to place the chart in a separate chart sheet in the workbook.

To create a line chart of data table results:

1. Select the range **G53:L63**, which contains the data table.

2. Click **Insert**, point to **Chart**, then click **As New Sheet** to display the ChartWizard - Step 1 of 5 dialog box.

3. Click the **Next>** button to accept the previously selected range.

4. In the ChartWizard - Step 2 of 5 dialog box, click **Line** to select the chart type, then click the **Next>** button.

5. In the ChartWizard - Step 3 of 5 dialog box, click **1** to select the format type, then click the **Next>** button.

6. In the ChartWizard - Step 4 of 5 dialog box, enter **1** in the Use First Column(s) text box, enter **1** in the Use First Row(s) text box, then click the **Next>** button. This specifies the input row and column from the data table as the legend and the x-axis labels, respectively.

7. In the ChartWizard - Step 5 of 5 dialog box, type **EBT for Orange Juice vs. Thirst Quencher Sales** as the chart title, type **Thirst Quencher** as the x-axis title, type **EBT** as the y-axis title, then click the **Finish** button to display the chart. See Figure 5-17.

Figure 5-17
Line chart compares two-input data table results

8. Rename the Chart1 sheet **Table Chart**, move the tab after the Summary sheet, then print the line chart.

9. Click the **Budget** tab to return to the sheet with the data table, then save this as the S_SMP2.xls workbook.

Ann reviews the chart with Travis. It is easier for him to see those alternatives that are not break even. After reviewing the chart, he's confident that SMP will be able to sell enough bottles of Olympic Gold so that they will make a profit and possibly attain his ambitious goal of $4 million in sales.

Performing a What-If Analysis on a Data Table

Once a data table is set up and calculated, you can use it to perform what-if analyses by changing any of the row and column input data values and having the table immediately recalculated as you make these new entries. Travis wonders what would happen to the EBT for the year if the number of bottles of Thirst Quencher sold was 20,000 rather than 30,000 as the first entry in the data table. Make this what-if change to the data table and observe the outcome.

To perform a what-if on a data table:

1. Click **G54** to make it the active cell where the new value is entered.

2. Enter **20000** as the new number of bottles of Thirst Quencher sold. Excel recalculates this row in the data table. See Figure 5-18. Notice that the other input data values for the number of bottles of Thirst Quencher sold in column H did not change, because the data values were placed in the cells by completing a series. If the other data values in the column had been obtained using a formula that incremented each one by 10,000, then all the data values in the column would be recalculated together with the entire data table.

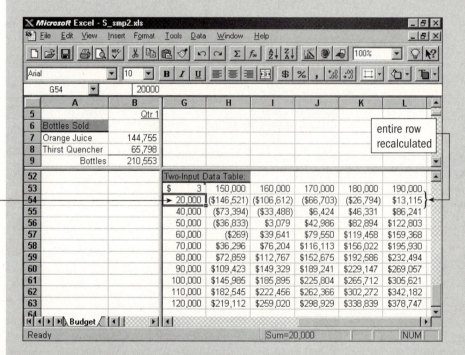

Figure 5-18
What-if peformed on data table

what-if value entered

3. Click **H54** and observe the TABLE(B7,B8) function, which specifies that this cell obtains its value as a data table calculation with inputs in cells B7 and B8. This TABLE function causes the values to be recalculated when new input values are entered.

4. Close the workbook without saving it.

If you want to take a break and resume the tutorial at a later time, you can do so now. Exit Excel. If you are on a network, leave Windows running. If you are using your own computer, you may exit Windows and shut down the computer. When you resume the tutorial, place your Student Disk in the disk drive, launch Excel, then continue with the tutorial.

Understanding Scenarios

After further review, Travis wants Ann to perform various what-if analyses with her worksheet, where more than one or two data values are changed in developing the Operating Budget for next year. You know that a what-if analysis is conducted whenever one or more data values are revised and the effect of this change is observed on other calculated cells. Ann plans to use a feature of Excel called Scenario Manager to organize and track the different what-if alternatives for her.

A **scenario** is a set of values that you use to calculate the outcome of a worksheet model. In Excel, you can name and save different sets of values with the worksheet. Scenarios are useful when you work with uncertain variables. For example, in creating the budget, Travis is uncertain of the Revenues, the Cost of Sales, and the Salaries expenses. Ann can define different values for these planning items, then switch between the scenarios to perform what-if analyses. She discusses the alternatives with Travis and organizes them in her planning analysis sheet (Figure 5-19).

Figure 5-19 ◀

Ann's planning analysis sheet for alternative scenarios

Planning Analysis Sheet

My goal:

Prepare alternative plans for prices per bottle, cost of sales percents, and salary growth rates for next year

What results do I want to see?

Operating Budget for each alternative

What information do I need?

Most likely case —
    Price of orange juice = 3.34
    Price of Thirst Quencher = 3.06
    Cost of Sales Percent = 58%, 57%, 61%, 65%
    Salaries Growth Rate = na, 5%, 8%, 4%

Best case —
    Price of orange juice = 3.39
    Price of Thirst Quencher = 3.17
    Cost of Sales Percent = 56%, 55%, 59%, 62%
    Salaries Growth Rate = na, 4%, 6%, 2%

Worst case —
    Price of orange juice = 3.29
    Price of Thrist Quencher = 2.93
    Cost of Sales Percent = 61%, 59%, 63%, 65%
    Salaries Growth Rate = na, 6%, 8%, 5%

Changing cells, or input cells, contain the values you use in a scenario. These are the cells on which a key formula depends, but the cells themselves usually do not contain formulas. For any one scenario, you can have up to 32 changing cells in Excel.

Before creating a scenario, you first specify the values you want in the changing cells, and then apply a name to this range of changing cells. Then you enter the name of the scenario in the Scenario text box in the WorkGroup toolbar. To switch between scenarios, you click the Scenario text box list arrow in the WorkGroup toolbar, and then select the scenario that you want displayed in your worksheet.

ADVEX 232 TUTORIAL 5 PREPARING AND EXAMINING WHAT-IF ALTERNATIVES

HELP DESK

EXCEL 5.0

Index

USING SCENARIO MANAGER

Double-click the Help button to display the Help Topics dialog box, then click the Index tab.

Keyword	**Topic**
scenarios	Scenario Manager
Scenario Manager	*Overview of Using Scenario Manager*

Naming Changing Cells

Before creating a scenario, you should give range names to the changing cells. These range names will then appear in the Scenario Manager dialog boxes and reports that you will use as you create the different scenarios. These range names are usually easier to work with than cell references because you can easily understand them. When you apply a range name to changing cells, each cell needs to be named individually. This is different from the way you have named ranges previously. For example, the Cost_of_Sales_Percent range refers to all the cells for this planning item. For scenarios, these cells need individual names, such as COS_Pct_Q1, COS_Pct_Q2, and so on. Review the range names currently used in the budget, such as those used for the Cost of Sales Percent and the Salary Growth Rate, and then assign range names to the individual changing cells for the prices per bottle.

To review the current use of range names in the Budget worksheet and include a scenario name for printing:

1. Open the S_SMP1.xls workbook and save it as S_SMP3.xls in the Tut05 folder. By using this version of the workbook, you eliminate the what-if tables, which are not used in creating these scenarios. Although you can use scenarios with what-if tables, they are considered separately in this tutorial so that you can individually explore their features.

2. Unsplit the window and scroll the Budget worksheet so that cell A36 is positioned in the upper-left corner.

3. Click the **Name** box list arrow, scroll the list, then click **Cost_of_Sales_Percent** to select that range and confirm that this range name references all cells used for the Cost of Sales Percent planning item.

4. Click the **Name** box list arrow, scroll the list as required, then click **COS_Pct_Q1** to select that range name, which specifies a single cell and represents the range names for the individual input cells of the scenario.

5. Click cells **C39**, **D39**, **E39**, **C40**, **D40**, and **E40** to confirm that individual range names are already assigned to these cells.

6. Click cells **C37**, **B49**, and **B50** to observe that individual names are not assigned to these cells.

7. Click **C37** and enter the text **Most likely case** to identify the currently active scenario when printing the worksheet. This helps you document which scenario is displayed.

UNDERSTANDING SCENARIOS **ADVEX 233**

Now assign the remaining changing cells' range names for use in the scenario.

To enter individual range names for changing cells used in scenarios:

1. Click **C37**, click the **Name** box, and enter **Scenario_name** as the range name for this cell, which is used to help identify the scenario.

2. Enter the range names for the prices per bottle as follows:

Cell	Range name
B49	**Price_OJ**
B50	**Price_TQ**

Creating Scenarios

With all of the ranges named appropriately, Ann is ready to use Scenario Manager to organize her what-if analyses for the three cases—most likely, best, and worst. Scenario Manager creates a scenario consisting of one set of changing data values and gives that scenario a name. You can think of Scenario Manager as storing the changing data values for an individual scenario on pieces of tape. Once you create a scenario, you can select it, and the changing data values for that scenario will be pasted over the ones that currently display in the worksheet. In this manner, Scenario Manager allows you to store and view a number of different what-if alternatives.

According to Ann's planning analysis sheet, she needs to create three scenarios—one for the most likely alternative, one for the best-case alternative, and one for the worst-case alternative. The most likely scenario is the set of numbers already in the worksheet. All Ann has to do is select the changing cells and name that scenario. Then, she will create the best-case and worst-case scenarios.

Name the most likely scenario for Ann's what-if analysis. The first action is to display the WorkGroup toolbar.

To display the WorkGroup toolbar and create the Most likely case scenario:

1. Click **View**, then click **Toolbars** to display the Toolbars dialog box.

2. Scroll the Toolbars list and click the **WorkGroup** check box to select that toolbar, then click the **OK** button to display it below the Formatting toolbar.

   Now create the Most likely scenario from the data already in the worksheet.

3. Select the nonadjacent ranges **C37**, **B39:E39**, **C40:E40**, and **B49:B50**, which contain all the changing cells for the scenario.

4. Click the **Scenario** text box, type **Most likely case** to create this scenario, then press the **Enter** key. See Figure 5-20.

Figure 5-20
Most likely case data values

WorkGroup toolbar

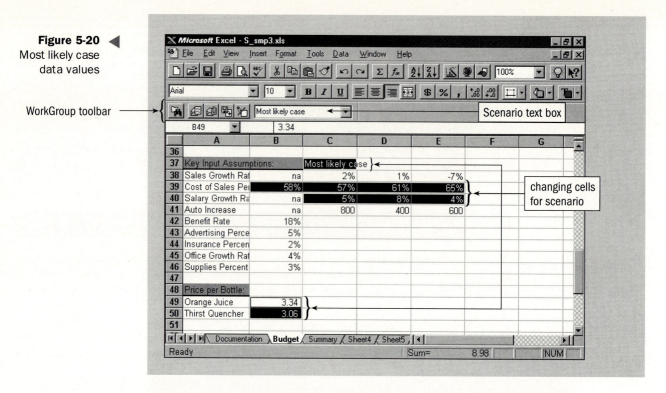

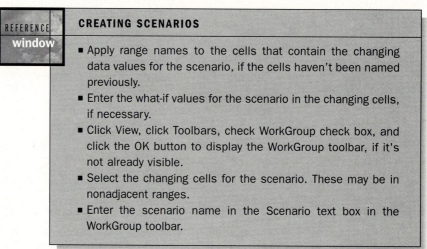

CREATING SCENARIOS

- Apply range names to the cells that contain the changing data values for the scenario, if the cells haven't been named previously.
- Enter the what-if values for the scenario in the changing cells, if necessary.
- Click View, click Toolbars, check WorkGroup check box, and click the OK button to display the WorkGroup toolbar, if it's not already visible.
- Select the changing cells for the scenario. These may be in nonadjacent ranges.
- Enter the scenario name in the Scenario text box in the WorkGroup toolbar.

With Ann's original data named as the most likely case, she is ready to create her best and worst cases. She could do this by entering new data in the worksheet, selecting the changing cell, then typing the scenario name in the Scenario text box in the WorkGroup toolbar. However, this method would require her to remember the changing cells for the scenario. Fortunately, once you have created the first scenario, the Excel Scenario Values dialog box prompts you with the changing cells for additional scenarios so you don't need to remember the changing cells. Use the Scenario Values dialog box to revise the changing values for the best- and worst-case scenarios.

To use the Scenario Values dialog box for changing values to create additional scenarios:

1. Click **Tools**, then click **Scenarios** to display the Scenario Manager dialog box. See Figure 5-21.

Figure 5-21
Scenario Manager dialog box

scenario name

cells used for scenario

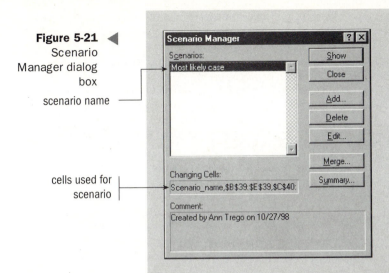

2. Click the **Add** button to display the Add Scenario dialog box, then type **Best case** in the Scenario Name text box. See Figure 5-22.

Figure 5-22
Scenario Name text box

enter new name

verify cells for scenario

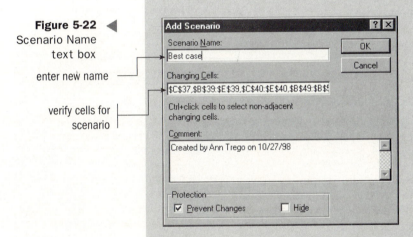

3. Click the **OK** button to display the Scenario Values dialog box. See Figure 5-23. Note the appearance of the range names for each of the input data values, rather than their cell references.

Figure 5-23
Scenario Values dialog box

range names identify cells

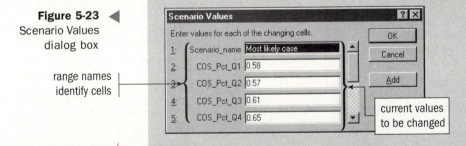

current values to be changed

4. Type **Best case** in the Scenario_name text box.

5. Using Ann's planning analysis sheet in Figure 5-19, type all the other data values for this scenario. Note that this dialog box shows only five data values at a time, and you need to use the scroll bars to display the other data values in this scenario. When you are finished, click the **OK** button to return to the Scenario Manager dialog box.

Once you have added one scenario, you can immediately add other scenarios without closing the Scenario Manager dialog box. Create the worst-case scenario.

To add the worst-case scenario to the Scenario Manager dialog box:

1. Click the **Add** button to display the Add Scenario dialog box, then type **Worst case** as the Scenario_name.

2. Click the **OK** button to display the Scenario Values dialog box and type **Worst case** for the Scenario_name.

3. Using Ann's planning analysis sheet in Figure 5-19, type all the other data values for this scenario, then click the **OK** button to return to the Scenario Manager dialog box.

4. Click **Best case** in the Scenarios list to select it, click the **Show** button so that these values with their solutions are displayed in the worksheet, then click the **Close** button. See Figure 5-24.

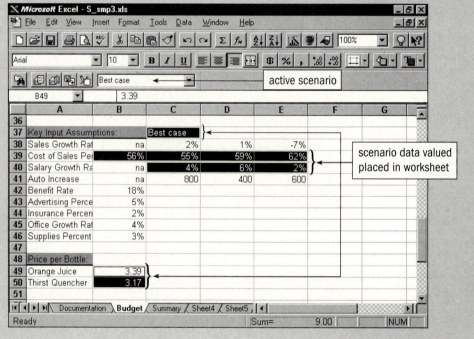

Figure 5-24
Display of Best case scenario solution

Once Ann's scenarios have been created, it is easy to individually display the solutions for each scenario for review and printing.

To display alternative scenarios:

1. Scroll the worksheet so that cell A19 appears in the upper-left corner of the worksheet window.

2. Click **F34** to make it the active cell. This will keep the worksheet area from being scrolled as you select each scenario. When you select a different scenario, Excel always displays an area of the worksheet that contains the active cell.

3. Click the **Scenarios** list arrow on the WorkGroup toolbar to display a list of available scenarios. See Figure 5-25.

Figure 5-25
List of available scenarios

list of available scenarios

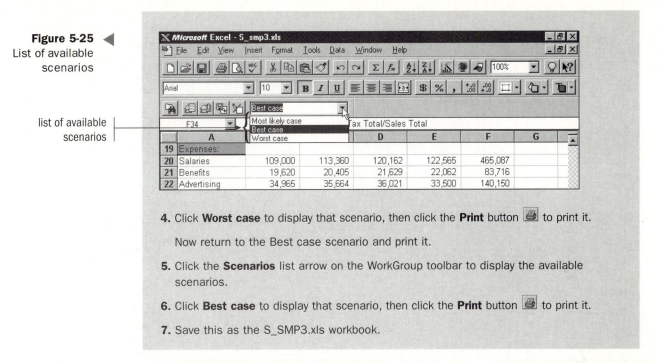

4. Click **Worst case** to display that scenario, then click the **Print** button to print it.

   Now return to the Best case scenario and print it.

5. Click the **Scenarios** list arrow on the WorkGroup toolbar to display the available scenarios.

6. Click **Best case** to display that scenario, then click the **Print** button to print it.

7. Save this as the S_SMP3.xls workbook.

Once you create a scenario, Excel allows you to edit it or delete it at any time, using the Scenario Manager dialog box.

Creating a Scenario Summary

Switching among different scenarios is useful, but Travis also wants to view the results for all the scenarios at one time. This will help him compare the results. A **scenario summary** is a single table that displays the changing cell values and selected results for each scenario. He asks Ann to prepare a scenario summary that will enable him to compare the Earnings Before Tax for each quarter and the year. In order to create a scenario summary report, the changing cells must be in the same worksheet as the result cells, which fortunately is the way Ann has organized her scenarios. A scenario summary table is placed in a new sheet that is inserted in the workbook. Create this summary table.

To create a scenario summary:

1. Click **Tools**, then click **Scenarios** to display the Scenario Manager dialog box.

2. Click the **Summary** button to display the Scenario Summary dialog box, select the **Scenario Summary** option button, then type **Earnings_Before_Tax** in the Result Cells text box to use that range name to specify the results you want to see. See Figure 5-26. You can also specify the result cells by selecting them in the worksheet.

Figure 5-26
Scenario Summary dialog box

Summary option

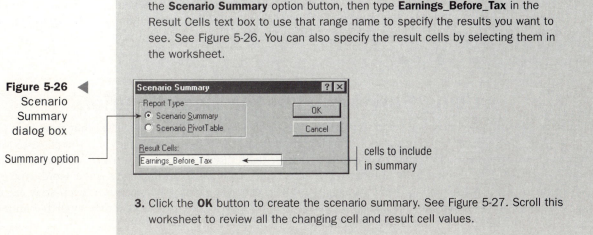

cells to include in summary

3. Click the **OK** button to create the scenario summary. See Figure 5-27. Scroll this worksheet to review all the changing cell and result cell values.

Figure 5-27
Scenario Summary worksheet

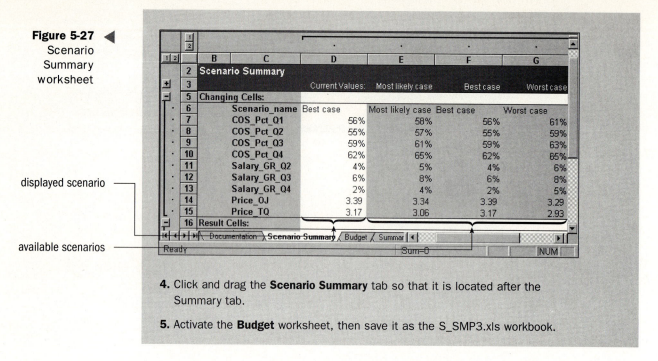

displayed scenario

available scenarios

4. Click and drag the **Scenario Summary** tab so that it is located after the Summary tab.

5. Activate the **Budget** worksheet, then save it as the S_SMP3.xls workbook.

Ann has successfully created the three scenarios to help Travis develop next year's budget. She brings her three printouts and the summary to his office and they both review the what-if scenarios. Travis tells Ann that she did a great job preparing these worksheets and that they will be very useful in determining the best way to meet next year's sales expectations.

Remove the WorkGroup toolbar from the worksheet window because it is no longer needed.

To remove the WorkGroup toolbar:

1. Click **View**, then click **Toolbars** to display the Toolbars dialog box.

2. Click the **WorkGroup** check box to unselect that toolbar, then click the **OK** button. The toolbar is no longer displayed.

3. Close the workbook.

If you want to take a break and resume the tutorial at a later time, you can do so now. Exit Excel. If you are on a network, leave Windows running. If you are using your own computer, you may exit Windows and shut down the computer. When you resume the tutorial, place your Student Disk in the disk drive, launch Excel, then continue with the tutorial.

• • •

Using Solver to Find the Best Solution[1]

Travis reviews the scenario reports with Carmen. Carmen suggests that now that they have determined several product mixes that will ensure that they meet next year's sales goals, they need to determine whether the limited capacity of their production equipment will affect these numbers. SMP uses three machines in producing Olympic Gold—the juicing machine, the blending machine, and the bottling machine. Each machine is cleaned and serviced on a regular basis, therefore limiting the production time available on these

---

[1] Note to instructors: The following section covers advanced concepts. If the level of material is not appropriate for your students, this section may be skipped without loss of continuity in the text.

machines. Also, the two products, Thirst Quencher and Olympic Gold orange juice, each require a different amount of production time.

Given their production limitations, Carmen recommends that Travis and Ann determine the **optimal**, or best, mix of orange juice and Thirst Quencher that SMP can produce to maximize its sales revenues in a quarter. This would assist Travis in making sure that SMP is using its limited resources in the most efficient manner.

Carmen describes a mathematical technique called **linear programming**, which is used to find the optimal, or most efficient, way of using limited resources to achieve a business objective, such as the product mix of Olympic Gold that maximizes sales revenues. Linear programming is often referred to as an **optimization** technique. In Excel, the **Solver** feature finds optimal solutions to linear programming problems. It makes use of a mathematical procedure that calculates different trial solutions until it finds the best one— this is similar to goal seeking, where trial solutions are calculated in closing in on the final solution value.

Formulating the Problem

With linear programming, you explore a business model in which **decision variables** represent the quantities of different products that can be produced. For SMP, these are the number of bottles of orange juice and of Thirst Quencher. It is common practice to refer to the decision variables by the symbols $X_1, X_2, ..., X_n$ when you formulate, or plan, your linear programming model. When you enter these symbols in the worksheet, they become specific cell references. However, it is usually best to begin by formulating the problem in general, rather than immediately writing Excel cell references.

The only requirement for optimization is that you need to have at least one constraint. The **constraints** in an optimization problem specify the restrictions on the available resource alternatives—for SMP, this is the limited amount of machine time. The use of constraints in a business model distinguishes a linear programming solution from a goal-seeking solution. With goal seeking, you indicate a specific target value. In linear programming, you indicate the constraints, which are then used by Solver to determine a best or optimal value. Constraints are usually expressed using these three general relationships:

A less than or equal to constraint:	$f(X_1, X_2, ..., X_n) \leq b$
A greater than or equal to constraint:	$f(X_1, X_2, ..., X_n) \geq b$
An equal to constraint:	$f(X_1, X_2, ..., X_n) = b$

In each situation, the constraint is some function (represented by the $f(\ )$ notation) of the decision variables (represented by X_1 and X_2) that must be less than or equal to, greater than or equal to, or equal to some specific value (represented by the letter b).

For example, at SMP the amount of time used for each machine must be less than the amount of available time for that machine. If Travis wanted to make sure that a minimum number of bottles of orange juice were produced, then a greater than constraint would ensure that this minimum was achieved.

The result that you are looking for in an optimization problem is stated as an objective function in the general form:

MAXIMIZE (or MINIMIZE):	$f(X_1, X_2, ..., X_n)$

The **objective function** identifies a relationship of the decision variables that is to be either maximized or minimized. For example, Travis wants to maximize the sales revenue associated with the product mix of bottles of orange juice and bottles of Thirst Quencher.

Putting these pieces together, the general formulation of an optimization problem is

MAXIMIZE or (MINIMIZE):	$f(X_1, X_2, ..., X_n)$
Subject to the constraints:	$f(X_1, X_2, ..., X_n) \leq b_1$
	$f(X_1, X_2, ..., X_n) \geq b_k$
	$f(X_1, X_2, ..., X_n) = b_m$

where $X_1, X_2, ..., X_n$ are the decision variables.

In this formulation, there may be any number of less than or equal to, greater than or equal to, or equal to constraints. The goal of optimization is to find the values of the decision variables that maximize (or minimize) the objective function without violating any of the constraints. You usually want to maximize profits or revenues, whereas you want to minimize costs or expenses.

For example, Travis wants to determine the maximum sales revenues from orange juice and Thirst Quencher, given the prices per bottle of $3.34 and $3.06 respectively, and 24,300 minutes of available time on the juicing machine, 25,600 minutes of available time on the blending machine, and 26,700 minutes of available time on the bottling machine.

This method of optimization is known as linear programming because the objective function and constraints are **linear**. That is, the decision variables are only multiplied by a constant coefficient and not by any other decision variables. This is the exact situation that exists for SMP's production mix optimization.

Travis asks Bill Hodges, the production manager at SMP, to collect the data on the available machine time and the amount of time required on each machine for a bottle of orange juice or a bottle of Thirst Quencher. Bill studies their production operations and prepares the information for Travis (Figure 5-28).

Figure 5-28
Bill's notes for the production mix

from the desk of
Bill Hodges
Sunny Morning Products, Production Department
One Orangewood Avenue, Garden Grove, CA 92640

The available time on each of the three production machines during a three-month quarterly production period is as follows:

Juicing machine   24,300 minutes
Blending machine   25,600 minutes
Bottling machine   26,700 minutes

These times include appropriate allowances for cleaning and maintaining each machine.

The time in minutes required on each machine to produce one bottle is as follows:

	Orange juice	Thirst Quencher
Juicing machine	0.11	0.04
Blending machine	0.08	0.12
Bottling machine	0.09	0.11

Travis and Ann review the production mix information from Bill. Then Ann develops her planning analysis sheet in preparation for determining the optimum product mix (Figure 5-29). The constants that specify the amount of time required for each bottle of Olympic Gold on each machine represent the basic recipe of production. These constants are known as the **technical coefficients** of the optimization constraints. In preparing her plan, Ann includes a fourth constraint to indicate that the values for the decision variables must be positive numbers. This is a common constraint for most optimization problems and is often handled automatically by Solver.

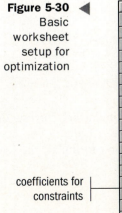

Figure 5-29
Ann's planning sheet for optimization

> *Planning Analysis Sheet*
>
> **My goal:**
> Determine the optimum product mix of orange juice and Thirst Quencher for a quarter that maxmizes the sales revenues
>
> **What results to I want to see?**
> Number of bottles of orange juice and of Thirst Quencher
> Sales revenue for each product and the total
> Juicing machine, blending machine, and bottling machine time used
>
> **What information do I need?**
> Orange juice price per bottle = 3.34
> Thirst Quencher price per bottle = 3.06
> Juicing machine time per bottle for orange juice = 0.11
> Juicing machine time per bottle for Thirst Quencher = 0.04
> Blending machine time per bottle for orange juice = 0.08
> Blending machine time per bottle for Thirst Quencher = 0.12
> Bottling machine time per bottle for orange juice = 0.09
> Bottling machine time per bottle for Thirst Quencher = 0.11
> Juicing machine available time = 24300
> Blending machine available time = 25600
> Bottling machine available time = 26700
>
> **What calculations will I perform?**
> Decision variables: X_1 = bottles of orange juice
> X_2 = bottles of Thirst Quencher
> MAXIMIZE $3.34 * X_1 + 3.06 * X_2$
> Subject to: $0.11 * X_1 + 0.04 * X_2 \leq 24300$
> $0.08 * X_1 + 0.12 * X_2 \leq 25600$
> $0.09 * X_1 + 0.11 * X_2 \leq 26700$
> $X_1, X_2 \geq 0$

Most of the effort in solving an optimization problem involves setting it up in the worksheet in an arrangement that readily supports using Solver to find the best solution. Ann begins creating her Excel worksheet by entering the constants for the prices per bottle, the times used per bottle, and the total available time (Figure 5-30). Ann still needs to add the formulas for the optimization before she uses Solver to find her optimal solution. Although Solver does not require this specific arrangement, it is often the easiest way for you to understand the components of your optimization.

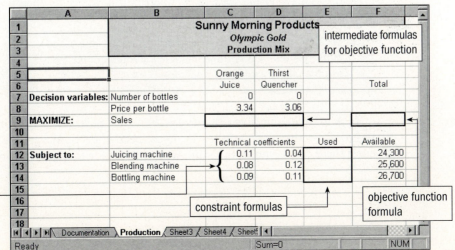

Figure 5-30
Basic worksheet setup for optimization

coefficients for constraints

Setting Up the Optimization Worksheet

Open Ann's worksheet and examine it in preparation for adding the optimization formulas.

To open the workbook with the basic optimization setup:

1. Open Ann's C_SMP2.xls workbook in the Tut05 folder or directory on your Student Disk. Then save the workbook as S_SMP4.xls in the Tut05 folder in case you want to redo this optimization.

2. Click the **Production** tab to view that worksheet, which contains the optimization data.

3. Review the worksheet's contents and verify that the cells contain the constants that are the technical coefficients of the optimization formulas. See Figure 5-31.

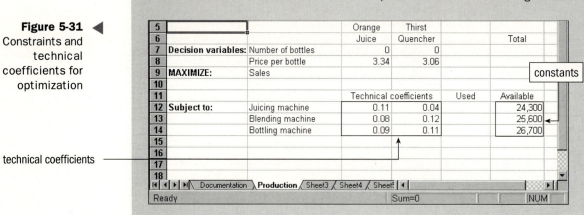

Figure 5-31
Constraints and technical coefficients for optimization

technical coefficients

Ann needs to add the formulas for the sales revenue and each of the constraints to her worksheet. Also, she wants to include a formula for the total bottles produced, although this is not required for the optimization, because Travis wants to know this production volume. In Excel, you can create formulas that summarize and extend the Solver solution to provide additional information that supports management decision-making, such as the total number of bottles sold, which is of interest to Travis. Enter the optimization formula.

To enter the optimization formula:

1. Click **C9** and enter the formula **C8*C7**, which is the price per bottle of orange juice multiplied by the number of bottles.

2. Copy the formula from **C9** into **D9** for calculating the Thirst Quencher sales.

3. Click **F9**, then enter the formula **SUM(C9:D9)**. This is the target cell with the formula that is to be maximized using Solver.

4. Click **F7**, then enter the formula **SUM(C7:D7)**. This calculates the total number of bottles sold and is the additional information that Travis wants, but it is not used in finding the optimal solution.

In Ann's planning sheet (Figure 5-29), each constraint is a formula that consists of a technical coefficient multiplied by its respective decision variable. Although you could enter these cell formulas the same way you did for the optimization formulas, the Excel

SUMPRODUCT function provides a convenient method for specifying these calculations. The syntax for the SUMPRODUCT function for use with optimization is

SUMPRODUCT(*array range 1*, *array range 2*)

In general, one array range specifies the decision variables while the other array range indicates the technical coefficients. Each element in the first array is multiplied by its corresponding element in the second array and these results are summed. When the optimization is solved, these formulas indicate the amount of each machine resource used in obtaining the optimal solution. Enter the constraint formulas using the SUMPRODUCT function.

To enter constraint formulas:

1. Click **E12** to make it the active cell. Each constraint is a formula that resides in a single cell in the worksheet.

2. Click the **Function Wizard** button to display the Function Wizard - Step 1 of 2 dialog box, click the **Math & Trig** Function Category to select it, scroll the Function Name list to display SUMPRODUCT, click **SUMPRODUCT** to select it, then click the **Next >** button to display the SUMPRODUCT Function Wizard - Step 2 of 2 dialog box. See Figure 5-32. Only the array1 and array2 entries are used with the constraint formulas.

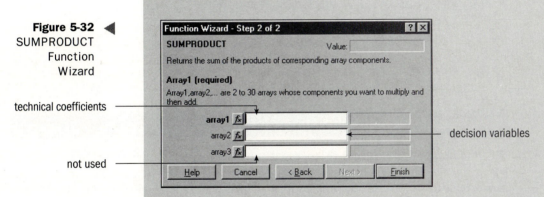

Figure 5-32
SUMPRODUCT Function Wizard

3. Click and drag the Function Wizard dialog box to the top of your screen so that the decision variables and the constraints are both visible.

4. Select the range **C12:D12**, which contains the technical coefficients for the Juicing machine. As you select them, the range displays in the array1 text box.

5. Click the **array2** text box to make it active, then select the range **C7:D7**, which contains the decision variables. Press **F4** to apply absolute referencing to these cells. The absolute references will ensure that the decision variables remain correctly specified when you copy the constraint formula.

6. Click the **Finish** button to finish specifying the SUMPRODUCT function, which performs the calculations for the Juicing machine constraint.

7. Copy the constraint formula from **E12** to **E13:E14**, then click **E14** to unselect the range. The absolute references ensure that the decision variables are still specified. See Figure 5-33.

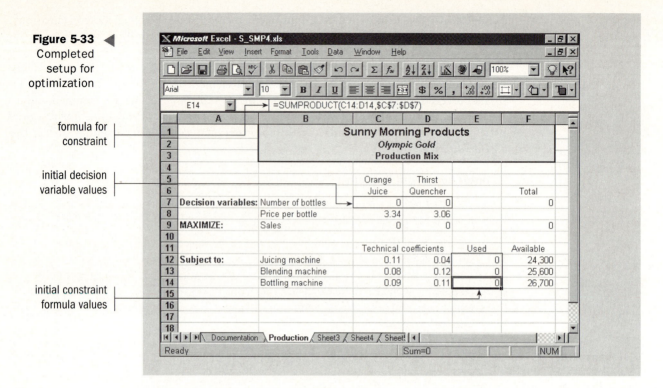

Figure 5-33 Completed setup for optimization

formula for constraint

initial decision variable values

initial constraint formula values

This completes the setup of the optimization problem. Ann is now ready to use Solver to find the optimal solution.

Finding the Optimal Solution

When you use Solver to find the optimal solution, you must identify a target cell, the changing cells, and the constraints that apply to your problem. These elements define the **parameters** for the optimization problem, and you specify them using the Solver Parameters dialog box. The **target cell** is a single cell that you want to maximize or minimize—in Ann's worksheet this is cell F9 for the Total Sales. The **changing cells** are the cells that Excel changes to obtain the desired maximum or minimum for the target cell—these are the decision variables of the number of bottles of each product. The **constraints** are the formulas that are limited by the available values.

HELP DESK

EXCEL 5.0

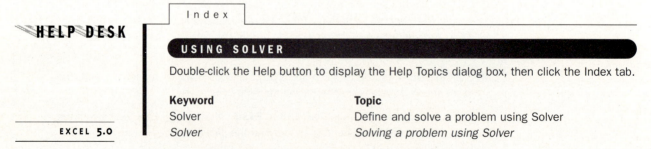

First, display the Solver Parameters dialog box and specify the target cell and the changing cells.

To specify the target cell and changing cells in Solver:

1. Click **Tools**, then click **Solver** to display the Solver Parameters dialog box. Click and drag the dialog box to the top of the screen so that you can see the cells you need to reference to specify the optimization problem.

TROUBLE? If Solver does not appear in the Tools menu, it may not be installed on your computer. See your instructor or lab administrator for assistance.

2. The Set Target Cell text box is active, so click **F9** to select it as the target cell. See Figure 5-34.

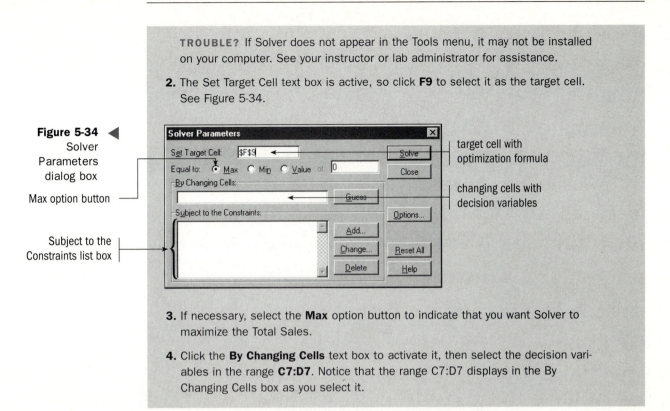

Figure 5-34
Solver Parameters dialog box

Max option button

Subject to the Constraints list box

target cell with optimization formula

changing cells with decision variables

3. If necessary, select the **Max** option button to indicate that you want Solver to maximize the Total Sales.

4. Click the **By Changing Cells** text box to activate it, then select the decision variables in the range **C7:D7**. Notice that the range C7:D7 displays in the By Changing Cells box as you select it.

Ann is now ready to specify the constraint parameters for Solver for each of the three constraints. These constraints represent the maximum amount of time available on each machine.

To enter constraints in Solver:

1. Click the **Subject to the Constraints** list box to make it active, then click the **Add** button to display the Add Constraint dialog box.

2. Click **E12** to place its cell reference in the Cell Reference text box. Recall that this cell contains the constraint formula for the Juicing machine.

3. Click the **Constraint** list arrow to display the list of available comparisons for the constraint, then click the **<=** option to select it.

4. Click the **Constraint** text box to make it active, then click **F12** to specify this constraint limit of the available time for the Juicing machine. The first constraint for the Juicing machine is now complete in the Add Constraint dialog box. See Figure 5-35.

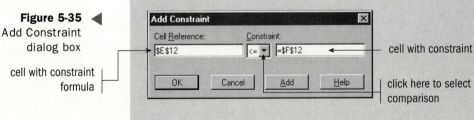

Figure 5-35
Add Constraint dialog box

cell with constraint formula

cell with constraint

click here to select comparison

5. Click the **Add** button to finish entering the first constraint for the Juicing machine and immediately begin adding another constraint.

6. Enter the constraint for the Blending machine.

7. Enter the constraint for the Bottling machine, then click the **OK** button to return to the Solver Parameters dialog box. See Figure 5-36. Note that it is not necessary to include Ann's fourth constraint for the non-negative values of the decision variables, because Solver will automatically include this condition as it searches for the solution.

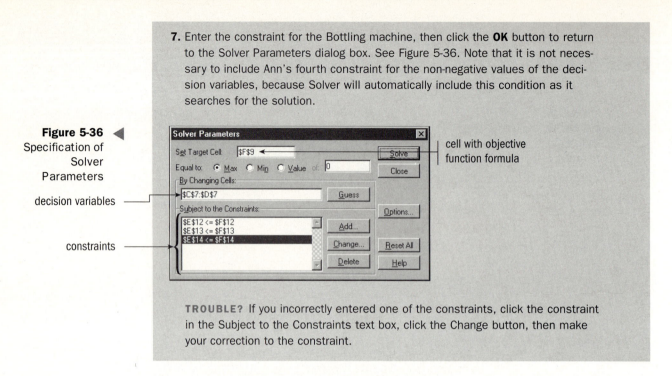

Figure 5-36
Specification of Solver Parameters

decision variables

constraints

cell with objective function formula

TROUBLE? If you incorrectly entered one of the constraints, click the constraint in the Subject to the Constraints text box, click the Change button, then make your correction to the constraint.

Now that Ann has specified the target cell, the changing cells, and the constraints, she is ready to use Solver to obtain an optimal solution to her product mix problem.

To generate the solution using Solver:

1. Click the **Solve** button. After a short time, the Solver Results dialog box opens and displays the message "Solver found a solution. All constraints and optimality conditions are satisfied." See Figure 5-37.

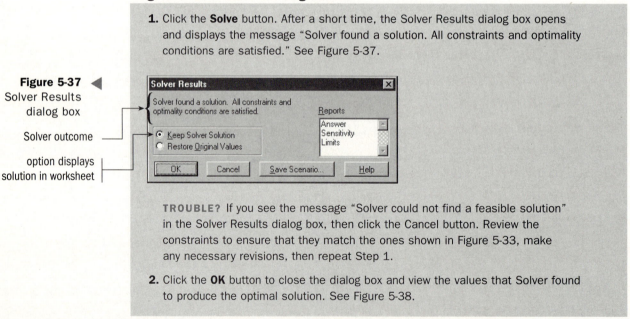

Figure 5-37
Solver Results dialog box

Solver outcome

option displays solution in worksheet

TROUBLE? If you see the message "Solver could not find a feasible solution" in the Solver Results dialog box, then click the Cancel button. Review the constraints to ensure that they match the ones shown in Figure 5-33, make any necessary revisions, then repeat Step 1.

2. Click the **OK** button to close the dialog box and view the values that Solver found to produce the optimal solution. See Figure 5-38.

Figure 5-38
Optimal solution produced by Solver

objective function formula

solution values for decision variables

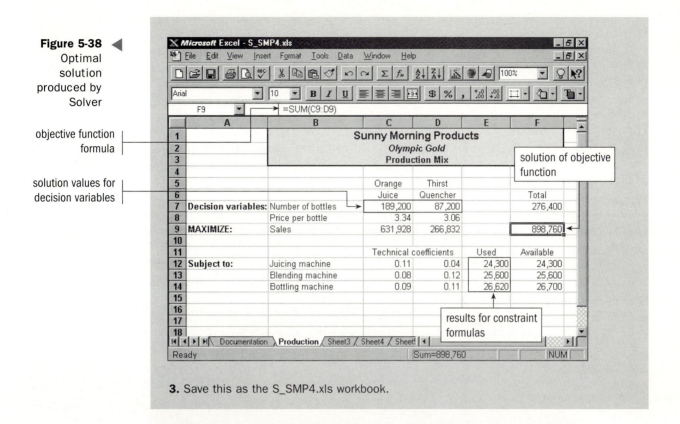

solution of objective function

results for constraint formulas

3. Save this as the S_SMP4.xls workbook.

USING SOLVER

- Create a worksheet that contains the labels, values, and formulas for the optimization problem you want to solve.
- Click Tools, then click Solver to display the Solver Parameters dialog box.
- Enter the cell reference for the cell you want to maximize or minimize in the Set Target Cell text box.
- Enter the cell references for the cells that contain the decision variables that Excel can change to find the solution in the By Changing Cells text box.
- Use the Add button to add constraints that limit the changes that Solver can make to the decision variables, then click the OK button to return to the Solver Parameters dialog box.
- Click the Solve button to generate a solution.
- Click the OK button to return to the Ready mode to view the solution.

Changing Constraints

As Travis reviews this optimal solution, he realizes that they did not include their historical sales of 2.2 bottles of orange juice to each bottle of Thirst Quencher. Considering the sales analysis by the marketing staff, Travis believes that SMP should continue with its emphasis on orange juice sales and wants to extend the analysis so that at least 2.2 bottles of orange juice are sold for each bottle of Thirst Quencher. Although they may sell a higher ratio of orange juice to Thirst Quencher, 2.2 is the minimum acceptable ratio. He writes out his new constraint:

$$X_1 \geq 2.2 * X_2$$

Because this constraint does not have a constant that specifies the available limit, Travis needs to rewrite the formula:

$$X_1 - 2.2 * X_2 \geq 0$$

Because his technical coefficient for the orange juice, X_1, is 1, he didn't include it in his formulation of the constraint, but he will need to use the 1 in his worksheet. Zero becomes his value for the available limit.

When Solver finds a solution, it starts with an initial solution and uses a mathematical procedure that calculates a number of trial solutions as it attempts to find the optimal solution. Depending on the starting values, an optimal solution may not be found. This situation is illustrated in the next section. As a result, it is usually best to have Solver start with decision variable values of zero as it searches for the optimal solution. Reset the decision values to zero, then change the worksheet to include the new constraint.

To revise the worksheet to include the new constraint and reset the decision variables:

1. Click **B15**, then enter **Marketing mix** as the identifying text.

2. Click **C15**, then enter **1** as the technical coefficient for orange juice.

3. Click **D15**, then enter **-2.2** as the technical coefficient for Thirst Quencher.

4. Copy the formula from **E14** to **E15** to specify the constraint formula.

5. Click **F15**, then enter **0** (zero) as the limit for this constraint.

6. Enter **0** (zero) in cells **C7** and **D7** to reset the decision variables. Only the decision variables are being set to their initial starting value; all the Solver parameters remain at their previous settings.

Now Ann is ready to specify the new constraint as a Solver parameter and produce a new optimal solution.

To include a new constraint and produce a revised optimal solution:

1. Click **Tools**, then click **Solver** to display the Solver Parameters dialog box.

2. Click the **Add** button to display the Add Constraint dialog box.

3. Enter the Cell Reference, comparison, and Constraint for the new Marketing mix constraint, then click the **OK** button. See Figure 5-39.

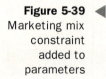

Figure 5-39
Marketing mix constraint added to parameters

Marketing mix constraint

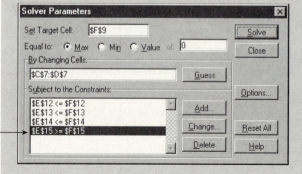

TROUBLE? If you entered the wrong constraint, click Change, correct the constraint, then click the OK button.

4. Click the **Solve** button to produce the revised optimal solution and display the Solver Results dialog box.

5. Click the **OK** button to close the dialog box and return to Ready mode. Notice that the total number of bottles sold and the total sales are only slightly reduced by the additional constraint.

6. Save this as the S_SMP4.xls workbook.

ADDING CONSTRAINTS AFTER OBTAINING A SOLVER SOLUTION

- Enter zeros for the decision variables to reset them.
- Click Tools, then click Solver to display the Solver Parameters dialog box.
- Use the Add button to add the new constraints, then click the OK button to return to the Solver Parameters dialog box.
- Click the Solve button to generate a solution.
- Click the OK button to return to Ready mode to view the solution.

Using Integer Constraints

As Travis reviews the results, he notices that the total number of bottles appears to be off by one—an apparent error due to rounding. Solver found a solution for the decision variables that is *not* an integer or "whole number" of bottles. Although one bottle may not be significant when 275,745 bottles are produced, other situations exist in which this may make a significant difference. For example, if you were producing airplanes, such round-off would not be acceptable. Because the decision variable values are determined by Solver, the Excel ROUND function *cannot* be used in obtaining an integer solution. Rather, you need to specify for Solver that the decision variables must be integers. Solver allows you to specify each decision variable individually, so that some decision variables can be integers, while others are not.

Ann needs to specify that the decision variables in cells C7 and D7 must contain integer values.

To specify integers for decision variables:

1. Enter **0** (zero) in cells **C7** and **D7** to reset the starting point for the solution.

2. Click **Tools**, then click **Solver** to display the Solver Parameters dialog box.

3. Click the **Add** button to display the Add Constraint dialog box.

4. The Cell Reference is active, so click **C7** to specify that decision variable for the bottles of orange juice.

5. Click the **Constraint** list arrow to display the list of available constraint comparisons, then click **int**. "Integer" is displayed in the Constraint text box. Click the **OK** button to finish specifying the constraint. When you specify an integer constraint, you do not specify a cell reference or numeric value in the Constraint text box.

6. Click the **Add** button to redisplay the Add Constraint dialog box and specify the integer constraint for the number of bottles of Thirst Quencher. Then click the **OK** button to return to the Solver Parameters dialog box. See Figure 5-40.

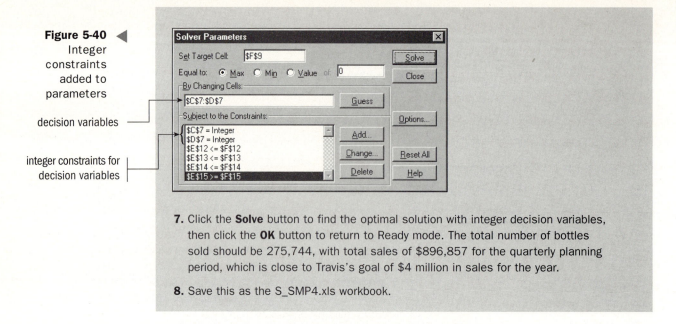

Figure 5-40
Integer constraints added to parameters

decision variables

integer constraints for decision variables

7. Click the **Solve** button to find the optimal solution with integer decision variables, then click the **OK** button to return to Ready mode. The total number of bottles sold should be 275,744, with total sales of $896,857 for the quarterly planning period, which is close to Travis's goal of $4 million in sales for the year.

8. Save this as the S_SMP4.xls workbook.

Ann is curious. She wonders what would happen if she tried to find a solution by providing Solver with different starting values for the decision variables. Try it and see what happens.

To observe the effect of different starting values on a Solver solution:

1. Click **D7**, then enter **0** (zero) as the desired starting value. Do *not* change the value in C7.

2. Click **Tools**, click **Solver** to display the Solver Parameters dialog box, click the **Solve** button to find a new solution, then click the **OK** button to return to Ready mode so you can review the solution. See Figure 5-41.

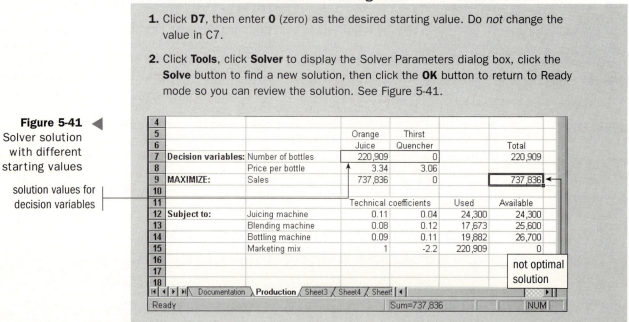

Figure 5-41
Solver solution with different starting values

solution values for decision variables

Solver found a different solution, in which no Thirst Quencher is produced. The total number of bottles and the total sales are less than those found in the previous solution. In optimization, this situation of finding a solution that appears to Solver to be optimal, but is not actually an optimal linear programming solution, is known as a **local maximum** or **local minimum**. This occurs because of the manner in which Solver carries out its trials in searching for an optimal solution. For this reason, it is suggested that you always use zeros as the initial starting values for your decision variables, as was illustrated in the prior Solver solutions. For further discussion of various optimization situations, see *Spreadsheet Modeling and Decision Analysis*, Cliff T. Ragsdale, Course Technology Incorporated, 1995.

> **REFERENCE window**
>
> **ADDING INTEGER CONSTRAINTS AFTER OBTAINING A SOLVER SOLUTION**
>
> - Enter zeros for the decision variables to reset them.
> - Click Tools, then click Solver to display the Solver Parameters dialog box.
> - Click the Add button to display the Add Constraint dialog box.
> - Click the cell reference for the decision variable that you want to be an integer.
> - Select the int option for the constraint.
> - Click the Add button and add any additional integer constraints for your decision variables.
> - Click the OK button to return to the Solver Parameters dialog box.
> - Click the Solve button to generate a solution.
> - Click the OK button to return to Ready mode to view the solution.

Printing Solver Reports

Once you obtain an optimal solution with Solver, there are three reports you can generate to summarize different aspects of the results. The **Answer Report** lists the target cell and the changing cells, with their original and final values. The **Sensitivity Report** provides information about how sensitive the current solution is to small changes in the available resources. The **Limits Report** lists the target cell and the changing cells, with their respective lower and upper limits. The **lower limit** is the smallest value the changing cell can have while holding all other changing values fixed and still satisfying the constraints. The **upper limit** is the greatest value for the changing cell. The Answer Report is the only one available with an integer solution, because the Sensitivity Report and Limits Report are not meaningful with integer constraints.

Travis wants Ann to produce the Answer Report for their review. The Answer Report does not provide any information that could not be determined from the solution shown in their Production sheet. However, the format of this report is a convenient summary of the solution displayed in a standard way for all optimization problems. You can generate the Answer Report in Ready mode.

To produce an Answer Report from Ready mode:

1. Enter **0** (zero) in cells **C7** and **D7** to reset the starting point for the solution.

2. Click **Tools**, then click **Solver** to display the Solver Parameters dialog box. Review the parameters to ensure that you still have all six constraints specified, including the integer constraints.

3. Click the **Solve** button to recalculate the solution and display the Solver Results dialog box.

4. In the Reports list box, click **Answer** to select that report.

5. Click the **OK** button to calculate a new solution, to create the report as a separate worksheet in your workbook, and to return to Ready mode. The sheet is inserted in the workbook before the worksheet that contains your Solver solution.

6. Click the **Answer Report 1** tab and scroll the window to view that report. See Figure 5-42. Notice that Excel automatically creates Names by combining the row planning item names with the column headings. A **binding constraint** is one where all the available resources are used and an equality condition exists for the constraint. For this solution, these are those for the Marketing mix and the integer values of the decision variables. The **slack** is the amount of the unused resource. For the Juicing machine, this appears as zero because there is only 0.06 minute of unused time and the value is rounded off on display. For most practical purposes, any constraint with zero slack is a binding constraint. For this solution, there are 94 minutes of unused time on the Blending machine and 160 minutes of unused time on the Bottling machine.

Figure 5-42
Answer Report for Solver solution

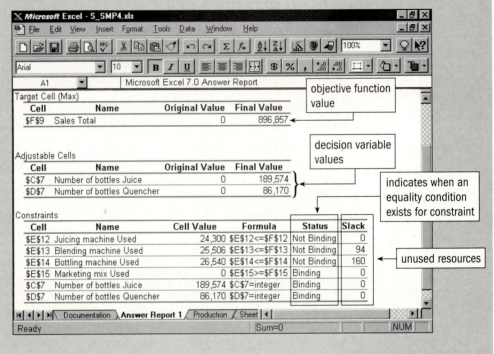

7. Save this as the S_SMP4.xls workbook, then print the Answer Report.

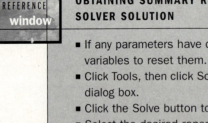

OBTAINING SUMMARY REPORTS AFTER OBTAINING A SOLVER SOLUTION

- If any parameters have changed, enter zeros for the decision variables to reset them.
- Click Tools, then click Solver to display the Solver Parameters dialog box.
- Click the Solve button to generate a solution.
- Select the desired reports in the Reports list box.
- Click the OK button to return to Ready mode to view the solution.
- Click the worksheet tab to view the desired summary report.

Understanding the Results

Travis and Ann review their Answer Report. He explains to her that because the Juicing machine has no slack, they could increase the available time on just this one machine, thereby increasing the total number of bottles produced and sold. Of course, this assumes that all the coefficients and other available resources remain constant. But depending on how much they increased the Juicing machine time, their production might become limited by the available time on the other two machines. Travis wonders how much the total sales might increase if more time is made available on the Juicing machine.

The **shadow price** for a constraint indicates the amount by which the objective function value changes when the amount of the available resource for that constraint is increased by one unit. The shadow price for the Juicing machine would indicate how much the Total Sales would increase if that machine's available time was increased by one minute. Travis wants to know this increase as he considers adding more Juicing machine time. In Solver, the Sensitivity Report identifies the shadow price as the **Lagrange multiplier**—this is a mathematical term that describes the underlying concept of how the shadow prices are calculated by Solver. (For further discussion, see *Spreadsheet Modeling and Decision Analysis,* Cliff T. Ragsdale, Course Technology Incorporated, 1995.) However, in order to obtain shadow prices, you need to relax or remove the integer constraints. Considering their production volumes, Travis is willing to remove these constraints to obtain this information. Delete the current Answer Report and reset the solution in preparation for obtaining a new set of Solver reports.

To delete an Answer Report and reset the solution:

1. Click the **Answer Report 1** tab, if necessary, to make it the active sheet.

2. Click **Edit**, click **Delete Sheet** to display the Microsoft Excel message box, then click the **OK** button to remove this sheet from the workbook.

3. Enter **0** (zero) in cells **C7** and **D7** in the Production worksheet to reset the solution.

Now the new reports can be produced with the desired information.

To produce Solver reports:

1. Click **Tools**, then click **Solver** to display the Solver Parameters dialog box.

2. Click the **$C$7 = Integer** constraint, then click the **Delete** button to remove this constraint.

3. Click the **$D$7 = Integer** constraint, then click the **Delete** button to remove it.

4. Click the **Solve** button to find a new solution and display the Solver Results dialog box.

5. In the Reports list box, click **Answer**, then drag the mouse pointer down the list to select all three reports.

6. Click the **OK** button to calculate a new solution, to create each of the reports as a separate worksheet in your workbook, and to return to Ready mode. The sheets are inserted in the workbook before the worksheet that contains the Solver solution.

7. Click the **Sensitivity Report 1** tab and scroll the window to view that report. See Figure 5-43. This report displays the final values for the changing cells and the constraints. The shadow price of $37 for the Juicing machine indicates that, if the amount of available time on this machine is increased by one minute, then the total sales will increase by $37, rounded to the nearest dollar.

Figure 5-43
Sensitivity Report for Solver solution

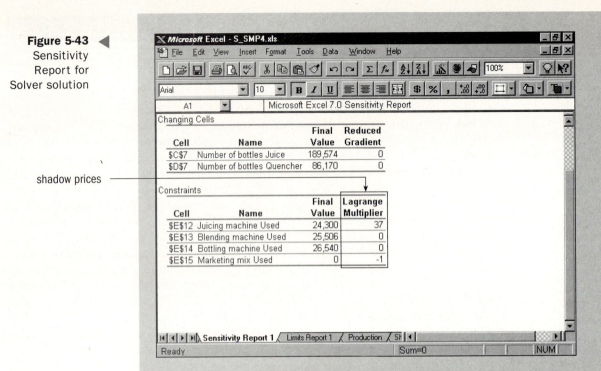

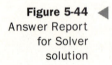
shadow prices

8. Scroll the worksheet tabs as necessary and click the **Answer Report 1** tab and scroll the window to view that report. See Figure 5-44. For this solution, the binding constraints are those for the Juicing machine and the Marketing mix.

Figure 5-44
Answer Report for Solver solution

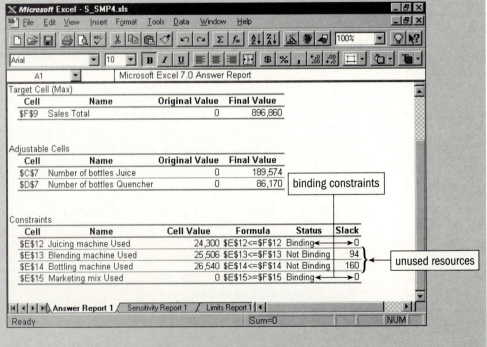

9. Click the **Limits Report 1** tab and scroll the window to view that report. See Figure 5-45. This report displays the final values for the optimization function and the decision variables.

Figure 5-45
Limits Report for Solver solution

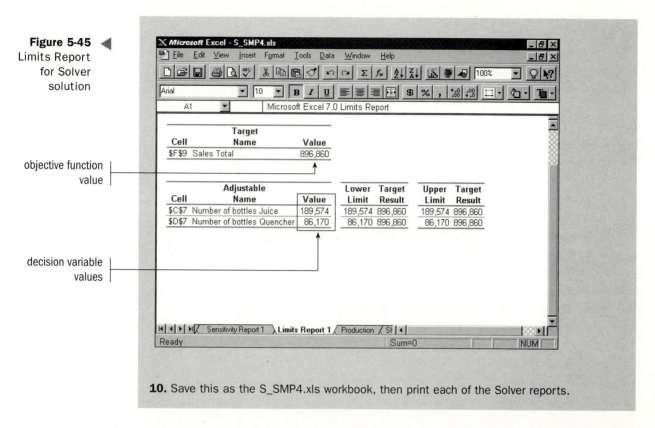

10. Save this as the S_SMP4.xls workbook, then print each of the Solver reports.

Reviewing the reports with Travis has given Ann a much better understanding of linear programming. She has found Solver to be an invaluable decision-making tool, despite the numerous steps and considerations to be made in setting the problem up properly. Travis reminds her that the use of macros could simplify the process for her.

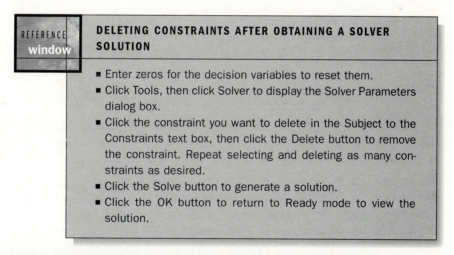

REFERENCE window

DELETING CONSTRAINTS AFTER OBTAINING A SOLVER SOLUTION

- Enter zeros for the decision variables to reset them.
- Click Tools, then click Solver to display the Solver Parameters dialog box.
- Click the constraint you want to delete in the Subject to the Constraints text box, then click the Delete button to remove the constraint. Repeat selecting and deleting as many constraints as desired.
- Click the Solve button to generate a solution.
- Click the OK button to return to Ready mode to view the solution.

Using Macros with What-If Alternatives

Macros are useful in automating repetitive worksheet activities that you carry out in what-if evaluations with data tables, scenarios, and optimizations. You can set up the new conditions for any of these, and then use a macro to carry out the new solution for you. Ann is considering using a macro with the product mix optimization. This would allow her to change any of the technical coefficients or resource availability amounts, set the initial values of the decision variables to zero, and then find a new optimal solution. In this manner, she can readily explore other alternatives as Travis evaluates their Operating Budget. Ann prepares a planning analysis sheet for her macro (Figure 5-46).

Figure 5-46 ◀
Ann's plan for an optimization macro

~~~
                    Planning Analysis Sheet
My goal:
Create a macro for exploring alternative what-if analyses for the product
mix optimization
What results do I want to see?
Product mix optimization solutions with different technical coefficients and
available resources
What information do I need?
Production worksheet set up with product mix optimization for solving and printing
Button to run macro
What macros do I want?
Set initial values of decision variables to zero and solve optimization
~~~

Ann does a walkthrough of the steps for her macro and completes her macro planning sheet (Figure 5-47).

Figure 5-47 ◀
Ann's macro planning sheet for finding another optimal solution

Action	Result
Click C7	Position the cell pointer
Enter 0	Reset decision variable to zero
Click D7	Position the cell pointer
Enter 0	Reset decision variable to zero
Click Tools, click Solver	Display Solver Parameters dialog box
Click Solve button	Accept current setting and find optimal solution
Click OK button	Accept optimal solution and return to Ready mode
Click F9	Position cell pointer on optimal solution value

Macro Planning Sheet

Record Ann's macro for finding an alternative optimal solution.

To record a macro for running Solver:

1. Click the **Production** tab to display that worksheet, which contains the product mix optimization.

   Click C7 to position the cell pointer before you start recording the macro. This helps avoid potential problems with relative references in the macro.

2. Click **Tools**, point to **Record Macro**, then click **Record New Macro** to display the Record New Macro dialog box.

3. In the Macro Name/Reference text box, enter **RunSolver** as the macro name, then click the **OK** button to start recording. The Stop Macro button displays on the screen.

EXCEL 5.0

Now perform the actions listed in Ann's macro planning sheet, and as you do, watch their execution.

4. Click **C7** and enter **0** (zero), then click **D7** and enter **0** (zero). This sets the initial starting values for Solver.

5. Click **Tools**, click **Solver** to display the Solver Parameters dialog box, then click the **Solve** button to calculate the solution and display the Solver Results dialog box.

6. Click the **OK** button to return to Ready mode, then click **F9** to place the cursor on the optimal result.

7. Click the **Stop Macro** button ■ to stop recording the macro.

To make it easier to run her macro, Ann wants to use a macro button located in the same worksheet. Create a macro button and assign the RunSolver macro to it.

To create a macro button and assign a macro to the button:

1. Click the **Drawing** button to display that toolbar, then, if necessary, drag it to the left so that cells E18:F21 are visible.

2. Click the **Create Button** button and draw the macro button. See Figure 5-48. When you release the mouse button, the Assign Macro dialog box opens.

Figure 5-48 ◄
Macro button
for Solver

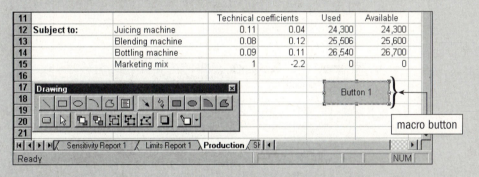

3. Click the **RunSolver** macro to select it, then click the **OK** button to assign that macro to the button.

4. Select the **Button 1** text of the macro button by highlighting it, type **Run Solver** as the button name, then click any cell outside the macro button to finish assigning this name to the button.

5. Click the **Close** button on the Drawing toolbar so that it is removed from your display.

With the macro recorded and assigned to a button, Ann is ready to test it to make sure it works correctly. While she does this, she wants to explore a what-if alternative for the Juicing machine. Bill thinks that they can make an adjustment to the machine that would reduce the time per bottle of orange juice to 0.09 minutes. Test the macro and find this alternative solution.

EXCEL 5.0

To test the macro for a different solution:

1. Click **C12** and enter **0.09** as the new technical coefficient.

   Click C7 to position the cell pointer before running the macro.

2. Click the **Run Solver** button to execute the macro. Although the macro recorded all the steps for its execution, it still pauses when it reaches the Solver Results dialog box. This allows you to keep the new solution or discard it while the macro is executed.

3. Click the **OK** button to accept the solution and continue executing the macro. Cell F9 is selected as the active cell and the macro terminates its execution. See Figure 5-49.

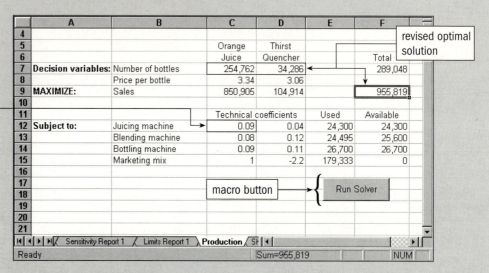

Figure 5-49 ◄
Revised optimal solution using the macro

revised coefficient

TROUBLE? If the macro failed to run Solver, review the macro code shown in Figure 5-50, make any necessary changes to your macro code (located in the Module1 module sheet, the last sheet in the workbook), then repeat Steps 2 and 3.

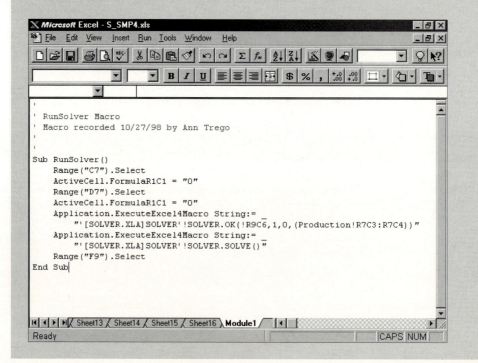

Figure 5-50 ◄
Macro for running Solver

TUTORIAL EXERCISES **ADVEX 259**

4. Save this as the S_SMP4.xls workbook, then print this what-if alternative.

5. Close the file, and exit Excel.

Travis and Ann review their linear programming results with Bill. The Answer Report and Sensitivity Report helped them identify the Juicing machine as a limiting factor in their production process and an area of concern in their planning. They are pleased with the possible increase in sales revenue from the adjustment to the Juicing machine. Overall, Travis feels that the outlook for the future of SMP is bright, and he is confident that they can produce the necessary bottles of Olympic Gold orange juice and Thirst Quencher to meet the requirements that they laid out in their Operating Budget. Bill returns to the plant to schedule the change to the Juicing machine.

Tutorial Exercises

For Exercises 1 through 7, launch Excel and open the E_GZG1.xls workbook for Grandma Zambinos Goodies (GZG), which manufactures and markets snack foods. Save this as the S_GZG1.xls workbook in the Tut05 folder. The snack food industry is very competitive, so GZG likes to keep close track of monthly sales. Prepare an analysis of GZG's monthly sales by doing the following:

1. Review the Analysis worksheet and its formulas. How are monthly sales per employee calculated? How are the sales of chips and cookies calculated? How are the sales of snack bars calculated? Why is this a good method for calculating the snack bar sales?

2. Find the Total Sales value that is needed for GZG to achieve $50,000 in Sales per Employee with all other conditions remaining constant. Print this solution.

3. Find the Total Sales and Sales per Employee that are required for a break-even Operating Profit with all other conditions remaining the same. Save this as the S_GZG2.xls workbook in the Tut05 folder, then print this solution.

4. The chip sales percent could vary from 25% to 35% in increments of 1%, while the cookie sales percent varies from 40% to 50% in increments of 1%. Create a data table of the operating profit for this analysis. Include appropriate labels to identify the contents of the data table. Print the data table, then close the workbook. Why does the same value appear for the operating profit for all combinations in the table?

5. Open the S_GZG2.xls workbook in the Tut05 folder. The manufacturing cost percent could vary from 7% to 15% in increments of 1%, while the selling expense percent varies from 34% to 44% in increments of 1%. Create a data table of the operating profit. Save this as the S_GZG3.xls workbook in the Tut05 folder, then print the data table.

6. Create a chart of the results from Exercise 5 that show the operating profit for the different combinations of manufacturing cost percent and selling expense percent. Place the chart in a separate chart sheet. Place appropriate titles on the chart, the x-axis, and the y-axis. Save this as the S_GZG3.xls workbook, print the chart, then close the workbook.

7. Open the E_GZG1.xls workbook in the Tut05 folder. Save it as the S_GZG4.xls workbook. Using the Analysis sheet, create three different scenarios—most likely, best-case, and worst-case—for the number of salespeople and the four key input assumptions. The most likely case is the one that currently appears in the worksheet. The best-case and worst-case data is as follows:

	Best case	Worst case
Salespeople	127	184
Chips sale percent	32%	24%
Cookie sales percent	48%	43%
Manufacturing cost percent	10%	16%
Selling expense percent	35%	43%

Include a text label in the worksheet that identifies the case when the worksheet is printed. Save this as the S_GZG4.xls workbook in the Tut05 folder. Print each of the three scenarios, print a scenario summary, then close this workbook.

For Exercises 8 through 11, open the E_GZG2.xls workbook for Grandma Zambinos Goodies, and save it as S_GZG5.xls. Prepare an analysis of the product mix by doing the following:

8. Review the Production worksheet and its formulas. A carton is the unit of production for each product, where one carton contains several dozen units of individual products. The available resource is the amount of production time that can be scheduled, and the technical coefficients for each of the three processes—mixing, baking, and packaging—specify the amount of time required for each carton of product.

9. The linear optimization is specified as follows:

Decision variables:
X_1 = cartons of chips
X_2 = cartons of cookies
X_3 = cartons of snack bars

MAXIMIZE $\quad 143 * X_1 + 231 * X_2 + 256 * X_3$

Subject to:
$0.10 * X_1 + 0.30 * X_2 + 0.20 * X_3 \leq 7900$
$0.10 * X_1 + 0.40 * X_2 + 0.50 * X_3 \leq 11600$
$0.30 * X_1 + 0.20 * X_2 + 0.25 * X_3 \leq 8700$
$X_1 \geq 9900$
$X_2 \geq 14700$
$X_3 \geq 7300$

Add the constraint equations in the range F11:F16, using the SUMPRODUCT function.

10. Use Solver to find the optimal solution. What is the amount of the Total Sales? How many cartons of each product should be scheduled? Print the Production sheet, which contains the solution.

11. Generate an Answer Report. Print this report. Save this as the S_GZG6.xls workbook in the Tut05 folder.

Case Problems

1. Financial Performance Reporting for Hot Wheels Manufacturing Hot Wheels Manufacturing (HWM) supplies steel and aluminum wheels to world-wide automakers such as Alfa Romeo, BMW, Ferrari, Honda, Chrysler and Ford. HWM owns manufacturing plants world-wide, and is regarded as an industry leader in both quality and styling. HWM has experienced explosive growth, resulting in a stock price that has more than tripled in the last three years. However, a weakened global economy caused this year's sales to be sluggish and HWM management is concerned about stockholders' reactions.

Dan Sanchez is a financial analyst for HWM. His manager, Michelle Bierer, asked him to take last year's financial performance report worksheet and add a contract that has just been signed to make sales appear higher to the shareholders, so HWM's stock price does not decrease. The stockholders like to see at least a 10% return on sales amount each year. While earning his undergraduate degree from UCLA, Dan took several classes in business ethics and is considering whether what he has been asked to do is ethical.

HWM's customary policy for recording sales is that the sale is recorded when delivery is made. This policy is in accordance with generally accepted accounting principles (GAAP), the guidelines that accountants follow in stating a company's financial position. HWM's books closed on December 31, and the delivery date of the new contract is not until January 27.

Dan doesn't know what to do. He is anxious to prove himself in this new job, but doesn't want to do anything unethical. He decides to edit Michelle's worksheet to include the revised numbers, since Excel makes such revisions very easy. But he plans to prepare two reports: one with the actual performance numbers *and* one with the revised numbers. He'll create two scenarios in order to *document both sets of numbers* in his worksheet. That way, it will be clear that the revised numbers don't merely replace the actual numbers. Dan also plans to talk to Michelle, but he's not sure what to say yet. Dan's first step is to develop a planning analysis sheet (Figure 5-51).

Figure 5-51 ◄

> ## Planning Analysis Sheet
>
> ### My goal:
> Develop alternatives to improve the stock price based on this year's financial performance
>
> ### What results do I want to see?
> Return On Sales should meet the shareholders' expectation for last year, which is 10%
>
> ### What information do I need?
> Last year's worksheet file. This file needs to include range names and scenarios.
>
> ### How will the new contract affect key financial numbers?
> - The wheel prices would increase from 65 Steel and 95 Aluminum to 70 Steel and 105 Aluminum as a result of the substantially higher prices of the new contract
> - The new contract would cause Total Wheels Sold to increase from a minimum of 680,000 units to a maximum of 725,000 units

Make the necessary adjustments to Dan's worksheet to reflect the new contract with the automaker to determine whether it meets the shareholders' objective of a 10% return on sales for Michelle.

1. Open the P_HWM1.xls workbook in the Tut05 folder, which contains last year's financial performance *without* the new contract. Save the worksheet as S_HWM1.xls in the Tut05 folder.
2. Review the worksheet. Notice that the worksheet has a key assumptions section and that all dollar amounts are stated in thousands, except the prices per unit.

ADVEX 262 **TUTORIAL 5** PREPARING AND EXAMINING WHAT-IF ALTERNATIVES

3. Create these named ranges for the planning items:

Planning item name	Range name for data value	Cells
Return On Sales	RETURN_ON_SALES	B39
Total Wheels Sold	WHEELS_SOLD	B11
Steel Wheel Price	PRICE_STEEL	B44
Aluminum Wheel Price	PRICE_ALUMINUM	B45

4. Use the ROUND function to eliminate any potential rounding errors that may exist in the worksheet. (*Hint:* Total Expenses = 43,559.)

5. Save the worksheet as S_HWM2.xls. Preview and print your worksheet.

6. Perform the following what-if alternatives. Preview and print the worksheet after each alternative.
    a) What would the Return On Sales be if the Total Wheels Sold value is 680, which reflects the new contract Michelle informed Dan about? (*Hint:* Return On Sales = 9.5%.)
    b) What if the Total Wheels Sold value was 725? (*Hint:* Net Income = 5,960.)
    c) Save the worksheet as S_HWM3.xls.

7. Use goal seeking to determine the number for the Total Wheels Sold for a 10% Return On Sales. Print this solution. (*Hint:* Use a decimal.)

8. Create the following scenarios with the names "Actual" and "Revised" to identify each scenario:

	Actual	Revised
Wheels sold	632	725
Price steel	65	70
Price aluminum	95	105

   Save the worksheet as S_HWM4.xls in the Tut05 folder. Preview and print each scenario. Print a scenario summary for the Return On Sales. (*Hint:* Return On Sales = 8.4% for the Actual scenario and 11.5% for the Revised scenario.)

9. Add one more named range to the worksheet with the name TITLE for cell A2. Create an Actual scenario that includes the title "Income Statement— Actual" and a Revised scenario that includes the title "Income Statement— Revised." These scenarios use the same data as specified in Question 8. Save the worksheet as S_HWM4.xls. Preview and print each scenario. If these are the reports that Dan gives to Michelle, does this help with his dilemma? Is this better than just having the scenarios in the worksheet file? Why?

10. Numbers are easily changed in an Excel worksheet. Scenarios allow you to save both an original and a revised set of numbers in the same worksheet. Is the addition of the new contract to the income statement ethical? Should Dan say something to Michelle or just make the changes she requested? Why? What would you do if you were in Dan's position? Other than restating financial results, what could Michelle do in her report to the shareholders?

11. To gain an even better understanding of the potential effect of the new contract on the Return On Sales, Michelle asks Dan to prepare a data table that contains the Return on Sales when the Total Wheels Sold value varies from 680 to 730 in increments of 10. Recall that these sales are in thousands of units. Prepare the data table for the actual wheel prices and for the revised wheel prices. Use the scenarios to establish the wheel prices for each scenario. Print the data table created for each scenario.

12. Create a chart of the Return On Sales versus the Total Wheels Sold for the Revised scenario. Place the chart in a separate Chart sheet. Use appropriate titles for the chart, the x-axis, and the y-axis. Print the chart. Save this as the S_HWM5.xls workbook in the Tut05 folder.

13. Open the P_HWM1.xls workbook and save it as S_HWM6.xls in the Tut05 folder. Review the workbook and formulate a goal-seeking question. Why is this goal seeking? Then perform the goal-seeking analysis and print a report of the solution. Save this report in the same file. Write a summary that explains the goal-seeking results.

14. Formulate a two-input variable data table by selecting the input cells and the range of values to be explored for each. Describe why you selected these inputs to explore using a data table. Open the P_HWM1.xls workbook and save it as S_HWM7.xls in the Tut05 folder. Then create this data table. Produce a chart from the data table results and include appropriate titles and legends. Print the data table and the chart. Save them in the same file.

2. Evaluating Training Benefits for Upland Electric Upland Electric Industries (UEI) is a diversified electric utility holding company that provides essential services in energy, financial services, freight transportation, and real estate development to the people of the midwest. Heidi Yun manages the Information Center within the Information Systems Department at the corporate headquarters of UEI. She is considering expanding the services provided by the Information Center to include additional training in the use and application of personal computer software tools, such as presentation graphics and desktop publishing. Heidi's proposed training facility would accommodate up to 12 participants in one class, with a PC available for each participant.

An important aspect of personnel and human resource management for any training program like Heidi's is an evaluation of training effectiveness. Heidi wants to evaluate her program using a cost/benefit analysis that compares the costs of providing training with the expected increases in employee productivity. Training costs include instructors, equipment, materials, facilities, and participants' time. Potential training benefits include the dollar value of productivity increases, turnover rate reductions, and absenteeism rate reductions. In order to obtain approval for her training program, the benefits must be greater than the costs; that is, the cost/benefit ratio must be less than one. Heidi has developed a worksheet containing the cost/benefit analysis for next year's operation of the training program. Although she carefully estimated the costs and benefits, they may vary due to changes in business conditions. Heidi wants to obtain a better understanding of these variations by using data tables to answer the following questions:

a) What are the total costs, total benefits, net benefits, and cost/benefit ratio when the number of trainees varies from 30 to 42 in increments of two trainees?

b) What are the total costs, total benefits, net benefits, and cost/benefit ratio when the training days per trainee vary from 6 to 10 in increments of one day?

c) What are the net benefits when the number of trainees described in Question a) is combined with the training days per trainee in Question b)?

d) What is the cost/benefit ratio when the number of trainees described in Question a) is combined with the training days per trainee in Question b)?

Heidi also wants to know the number of trainees required to break even when the costs are equal to the benefits; that is, when net benefits are zero. Complete the following to answer these questions:

1. Open the workbook P_UEI1.xls in the Tut05 folder, which contains Heidi's cost/benefit analysis. Immediately save the worksheet as S_UEI1.xls in the same folder.

2. Review Heidi's Benefits worksheet and examine the formulas used to calculate the expected costs and benefits. What is the current cost/benefit ratio? Is this ratio acceptable? That is, is it less than one?

3. Use goal seeking to determine the number of trainees needed to break even; that is, when the net benefits are zero and the cost/benefit ratio is one. Preview and print the worksheet for this solution. Then return the number of trainees to its original value of 36.

4. Enter a data table to calculate the answer to Question a). Save this as S_UEI2.xls in the Tut05 folder, then preview and print the data table. Circle the minimum number of trainees required for total benefits to just exceed total costs on your printed report.

5. Create a data table to calculate the answer to Question b). Save it as S_UEI3.xls in the Tut05 folder, then preview and print it. On your printed report, circle the minimum training days per trainee necessary for total benefits to just exceed total costs.

6. Enter a data table to calculate the answer to Question c). Save it as S_UEI4.xls in the Tut05 folder, then preview and print it.

7. Create a chart, in a separate chart sheet, that compares the net benefits for the training days per trainee with the number of trainees, using the results from the data table for Question c). Plot the number of trainees, on the x-axis. Title the chart and both the x-axis and y-axis. Label the legend appropriately. Save this in the same S_UEI4.xls file and print the chart.

8. Develop the data table for Question d). Create a chart like the one in Problem 7 except plot the cost/benefit ratio on the y-axis. Save this as S_EUI5.xls in the Tut05 folder, then preview and print the data table and the chart. Close the worksheet file.

9. Compare the results for Problems 3 and 4 above. How does the break-even value you found in Problem 3 compare with the result you circled in Problem 4? What is the difference between the two results?

10. Create the following scenarios with the names "Most likely," "Best case," and "Worst case" used to identify each scenario:

Planning item	Range name for data	Best case	Worst case
Training per day	COST_PER_DAY	1,250	1,700
Number of trainees	TRAINEES	42	30
Training days per trainee	TRAIN_DAYS	10	6

Open the P_UEI1.xls workbook in the Tut05 folder and immediately save is as S_UEI6.xls in the same folder. Insert two rows below row 4. The most likely scenario is the one with the currently displayed data in the Benefits worksheet. Use the above range names to identify the cells with changing data values.

Also, add one more range name to the worksheet at cell A4 with the name TITLE. Enter "Most Likely Case" as the text label in this cell and center the cell's alignment across columns A through C. Then, when a different scenario is displayed, its name should appear in this cell. Save the workbook in the same S_UEI6.xls file. Preview and print each scenario. Generate and print a scenario summary that displays the net benefits and cost/benefit ratio results. Close the file.

11. Open the P_UEI1.xls workbook and save it as S_UEI7.xls in the Tut05 folder. Review the workbook and formulate a goal-seeking question. Why is this goal seeking? Then perform the goal-seeking analysis and print a report of the solution. Write a summary that explains the goal-seeking results.

12. Formulate another two-input data table by selecting the input cells and the range of values to be explored for each. Describe why you selected these inputs to explore using a what-if table. Open the P_UEI1.xls workbook and save it as S_UEI8.xls in the Tut05 folder. Then create this data table. Produce a chart from the data table results and include appropriate titles and legends. Print the final report, including the data table and the chart. Write a summary that interprets your data table results.

3. Scheduling Employees for Trophy's Sports Grill Jessica Perez is the assistant manager at Trophy's Sports Grill, located in the Hazard Center shopping mall and office complex. Trophy's is open every day from 11:00 AM to 1:00 AM, with half the employees scheduled for the first half of the shift and the others for the second half. Friday and Saturday are the busiest days. Monday and Wednesday are moderately busy, with the other days the slowest.

Jessie is responsible for preparing a schedule with adequate associates available to meet the usual demand, without scheduling more associates than necessary. A **scheduling problem** like this is a common category of linear programming applications. All of Trophy's associates work five consecutive days, then have two days off. However, because of the heavy weekend traffic, no associate is scheduled to have both Friday and Saturday off. This means that Jessie can schedule associates for six different shifts that specify their work days.

Jessie created an Excel workbook with the decision variables and constraints arranged for finding the best schedule with a minimum cost. She included the minimum number of associates that are needed for each day. However, she needs to complete the objective function and constraint equations. Complete the following analysis to produce the information that Jessie wants for scheduling the associates:

1. Open the P_TSG1.xls workbook in the Tut05 folder and maximize the window, if necessary, then save it as the S_TSG1.xls workbook in the Tut05 folder.

2. Click the Schedule tab and review the worksheet. The decision variables are the number of associates scheduled for each of the six shifts. The Wage Rate is the weekly wage paid to each associate. The basic wage is $450 per week. Because most workers prefer to have Saturday or Sunday off, a bonus of $20 per day is paid to associates who work on these days. The objective is to minimize the Total Wages, which is the sum of the Wages for each shift—calculated by multiplying the number of Associates by the Wage Rate for each shift. The Needed column of the constraints specifies the minimum number of associates required to meet the usual demand. The Scheduled column shows the number of associates actually scheduled to work that day.

3. Set up the Solver parameters to find a solution to the scheduling problem that minimizes the Total Wages following these additional conditions:
    a) The number of associates scheduled must be greater than or equal to the number of associates needed each day. That is, more associates may be scheduled than are actually needed to ensure that each associate works a five-day week.
    b) Each associate either works an entire shift or has the day off. Partial shifts are not allowed.
4. Use Solver to generate an optimal solution with a minimum Total Wages and to produce an Answer Report.
5. Save the workbook with its current name, then print the Schedule worksheet and the Answer Report.
6. Review the solution. If associates need to schedule additional personal time off to see their physicians or have their cars repaired, which day would you suggest as the best day of the week for them to schedule the appointment? Why?
7. Create a macro that sets the decision variables to zero and then resolves the optimization, using the same constraints, and generates an Answer Report. Assign this macro to a macro button located in the I20:J21 area in the Schedule sheet. Test this macro. Save the workbook as S_TSG2.xls in the Tut05 folder.
8. Formulate a change in the usual demand. Describe a situation that you think might cause this change in the number of associates needed, such as increased customer traffic on Mondays during the football season. Make these changes to the number of needed associates. Use the macro from Problem 7 to find the new optimal work schedule. Save the workbook with its current name, then print the Schedule worksheet and its Answer Report.
9. Formulate any other change to the scheduling problem. Describe the situation that might bring about this change. Make the necessary adjustments to the worksheet to incorporate these changes. Use Solver to obtain a new optimal schedule and its Answer Report. Save this as the S_TSG3.xls workbook in the Tut05 folder. Print the optimal schedule and its Answer Report. Write a summary that explains this optimal schedule.

Comprehensive Applications

The following Comprehensive Application continues from the preceding tutorials.

1. Production Planning for Oak World Furniture Oak World's quarterly management meeting is about to start. Todd and the other operating managers have gathered for your presentation of the next quarter's anticipated financial performance. These meetings are held in the boardroom, which contains a workstation connected to a large-screen color projector. This permits managers to ask questions and immediately review the possible impacts during the meeting. Once you conclude your presentation, the questions begin:

1. Robin is considering lowering the product prices. What will the Return On Sales be if *only* prices on all products are reduced by 5 percent and no other changes are made? That is, these revisions are to Oak World's original quarterly projection. (*Hint:* Multiply by .95 to obtain a 5 percent decrease in prices.) Open your S_OWF1.xls workbook in the Tut02 folder, which contains the quarterly plan that is the "base case." If you did not create this worksheet in Tutorials 1 and 2, then see your instructor to receive the file you will need to complete this comprehensive application. Save this workbook in the Tut05 folder before you start your analysis. Determine the Return On Sales. Print the worksheet, then close this workbook without saving the changes.

2. Sam would like to know the consequence of a drop in table demand by 7 percent in each month, if there are no other changes in their projection. What is the Return On Sales and Income Before Tax with these table sales? (*Hint:* Only the tables sold in July need to be reduced because this reduction is used in calculating the sales for the other two months.) Find the Return On Sales and Income Before Tax. Open the S_OWF1.xls workbook in the Tut05 folder as the starting point for this analysis. Complete the analysis, save this file as S_OWF2.xls in the Tut05 folder, then print the worksheet.

3. If table demand should drop by 7 percent as determined in Problem 2, what table price is necessary to maintain the "base case" Return on Sales for the quarter of 18.04 percent? Assume that under this condition, the same price is charged for tables in all three months of the quarter. Find the table price. Save this revised workbook in the same file, then print the worksheet. Close this workbook. (*Hint:* Revise the table price calculations for August and September so that they are obtained from the prior month, then find the price for July.)

4. Sam is concerned that a labor strike is imminent unless concessions are made to union demands. He would like to see the financial consequences of increasing the number of planned production employees by five for each month during the quarter and increasing all base wages to $18.90 starting in July, if there are no other changes to the projection. Open the S_OWF1.xls workbook in the Tut05 folder to obtain the "base case." Save this as the S_OWF3.xls workbook in the Tut05 folder. Determine the impact on the Return On Sales and Income Before Tax, then print the worksheet.

5. Robin then asks you how much prices must increase to achieve the same "base case" Return On Sales for the quarter of 18.04 percent if the union demands in Problem 4 are met. (*Hint:* Create a new key input assumption cell for the PRICE ADJUSTMENT and modify each of the table, chair, and sofa prices so that they contain formulas that use this cell in their calculations. Give PRICE ADJUSTMENT an initial value of 1 so that the same results appear after you have modified the prices to be formulas.) Save this in the same S_OWF3.xls file, then print the worksheet.

6. What prices are necessary for Oak World to achieve break even under the conditions of the union demands specified in Problem 4? (*Hint:* Use the PRICE ADJUSTMENT in Problem 5 to assist in finding the break-even prices.) Save this in the same S_OWF3.xls file, then print this worksheet solution. Close the workbook.

Todd, Robin, and Sam study your presentation of Oak World's financial plan at the operating meeting. They would like to obtain information concerning several additional alternatives:

7. Sam is still concerned about the imminent strike and the current union demands. In preparation for the next negotiation meeting, Sam would like a table of alternatives for next quarter's plan that displays the quarterly total for Labor, Operating Profit, and Return On Sales when the hourly rate ranges from $17.75 to $20.00 in increments of $0.25. Then, as a different wage rate is negotiated, the bargaining team will have an idea of the impact on Oak World's financial performance. *No other changes* are made to this projection; all other data values are at their original or "base case" values. Open the S_OWF1.xls workbook in the Tut05 folder to obtain the "base case," and then prepare the table Sam requested. Save this as the S_OWF4.xls workbook in the Tut05 folder. Print the data table, then close this workbook.

8. Robin is on the bargaining team with Sam. She suggests exploring an increase in the number of hours worked each month as an alternative concession. She wants to explore hours worked, ranging from 164 hours to 180 hours in increments of 2 hours. Robin wants this arranged as a table of alternatives for next quarter's plan, which displays the quarterly totals for Labor, Operating Profit, and Return On Sales. Prepare this table using the original hourly rate of $17.70. Robins suggests to Sam that it would be better for Oak World to settle for 180 hours per month at the original hourly rate of $17.70 than it would be to increase the hourly rate to $18.20 with the original hours worked of 170 hours per month. Sam agrees that the additional hours would satisfy the work speed-up concern of the union, and should improve quality. Do you agree with Robin? Why or why not? Open the S_OWF1.xls workbook in the Tut05 folder to obtain the "base case" as your starting point. Create the data table and prepare a what-if analysis for the increased hourly rate. Print the statement of operation and data table. Save this as the S_OWF5.xls workbook in the Tut05 folder, then close the workbook. Review the results and write a summary that answers Robin's question.

9. Sam wants to maintain Oak World's profitability and feels that a PRICE ADJUSTMENT is an appropriate strategy in responding to union demands. Considering the union's demands, Sam feels that $18.20 per hour is likely to result from the current negotiations. At this hourly wage, he would like to explore a series of PRICE ADJUSTMENTS ranging from 2 percent to 12 percent, in increments of 1 percent. You recall that you set up the worksheet to include PRICE ADJUSTMENTS in Problem 5 and that you can begin your analysis using that worksheet. Sam wants a data table that shows quarterly results for Total Sales, Operating Profit, and Return On Sales at each of these PRICE ADJUSTMENTS. Open S_OWF3.xls in the Tut05 folder as the starting point for this analysis. Create the data table. Save this as S_OWF6.xls in the Tut05 folder. Print the data table.

10. Sam and Robin decide that you should explore Oak World's profitability for a variety of combinations of PRICE ADJUSTMENTS and hourly wages. They want you to generate a two-input data table that contains the results for the quarterly Return On Sales when the PRICE ADJUSTMENTS vary as specified in Problem 9 and the hourly wages vary as indicated in Problem 7. Modify the data table from Problem 9 to prepare this analysis. Save this as S_OWF7.xls in the Tut05 folder. Print the data table. Create a chart of the Return On Sales and place it in a separate chart sheet. Print the data table and the chart. Close this workbook.

11. Formulate three scenarios for the quarterly projected operations. The "most likely case" is the current data in the S_OWF1.xls workbook. Devise a "best case" and a "worst case" scenario from the analyses in Problems 2 through 10. Create range names for the variables you select for the scenario. Be sure to include one range that identifies the scenario by displaying an appropriate title in the worksheet. Describe why you selected the data values that you changed in the scenarios. Create each scenario. Print the worksheet for each scenario. Save this in the S_OWF8.xls workbook in the Tut05 folder. Write a summary that explains and compares your three scenarios.

2. Market Planning for Home Real Estate Home Real Estate was founded as a full-service real estate company in 1953 by Ronald Burger. Since its founding, Home Real Estate has experienced significant growth. The current operations include three offices in the metropolitan area, staffed by 40 sales associates. Although Ron still provides general direction to the company by serving as the chairman of the board of directors, the day-to-day operations are under the guidance of Warren Bridges, Home's president and chief operating officer. As the business grew, Ron organized it into three divisions: residential sales, commercial sales, and property management. Residential sales are managed by Marge Mills, while Felix Rodriguez is in charge of commercial sales, and J.P. Morgan coordinates the property management of rental real estate.

Park Place Villas is a proposed development of rental units that will be administered by J.P.'s staff in the Property Management Division. Krista Buffet, the project manager for Park Place Villas, is responsible for planning and developing the apartment complex. They have acquired a parcel of land that is adjacent to Central State University and plan to build up-scale apartments that are designed specifically for graduate students. Three types of apartments will be included in the complex: efficiencies, one-bedroom units, and two-bedroom units. Each efficiency requires 520 square feet, each one-bedroom unit requires 740 square feet, and each two-bedroom unit requires 880 square feet.

Krista and J.P. believe that the complex should include no more than 20 one-bedroom units, and that there should be a 1 to 1.5 ratio of one-bedroom units to two-bedroom units. Local zoning ordinances do not allow Home Real Estate to build more than 50 units at this property location, and restrict the complex to a maximum of 40,000 square feet. Krista has already agreed to lease 4 efficiency units, 5 one-bedroom units and 8 two-bedroom units as a result of her pre-construction promotion of the project. Her market studies indicate that efficiencies can be rented for $450 per month, one-bedrooms for $550 per month, and two-bedrooms for $650 per month. Krista needs to finalize the building plans so that the construction will be completed in time for occupancy by the beginning of the fall semester. She needs to know how many rental units of each type they should include in the complex to maximize the potential monthly rental income.

Krista considers the conditions she needs to satisfy and writes out the formulation of this allocation problem:

Decision variables:
$$X_1 = \text{efficiency units}$$
$$X_2 = \text{one-bedroom units}$$
$$X_3 = \text{two-bedroom units}$$

MAXIMIZE $\quad 450 * X_1 + 550 * X_2 + 650 * X_3$

Subject to:
$$520 * X_1 + 740 * X_2 + 880 * X_3 \leq 40000$$
$$X_1 + X_2 + X_3 \leq 50$$
$$X_2 \leq 20$$
$$X_1 \geq 4$$
$$X_2 \geq 5$$
$$X_3 \geq 8$$
$$1.5 * X_2 - X_3 = 0$$
$$X_1, X_2, X_3 = \text{integers}$$

1. Open a new Excel workbook.
2. Using Sheet 1, create and name a Documentation sheet for this analysis.
3. Using Sheet 2, create an Analysis sheet. Enter the text labels, constants, and formulas for the optimization. Include appropriate titles and headings to clearly identify the worksheet and its contents. Use a page header and footer that also include appropriate identifying information.
4. Solve the optimization and produce an Answer Report. Save this as the S_HRE1.xls workbook in the Tut05 folder. Print the Documentation worksheet, the Analysis worksheet, and the Answer Report.
5. Krista wants to be able to explore several different allocation alternatives and needs to generate additional optimal solutions. To accommodate her analysis, she wants a macro added to the Analysis worksheet that resets the decision variables to zero and then resolves the optimization, including producing another Answer Report. Create this macro and assign it to a macro button that you place in the Analysis sheet. Test the macro. Save this as S_HRE2.xls in the Tut05 folder. Print the module worksheet that contains the macro.
6. Create a scenario named "Base case" for the current optimization. The scenario should include the data values for the rent per unit, the size of each unit, the maximum available complex square feet, the maximum number of units allowed in the complex, the maximum number of one-bedroom units allowed, and the ratio of one-bedroom to two-bedroom units. Give a range name to each of these data values for use with the scenario. Include a title in the Analysis worksheet that identifies the scenario and include this as part of the scenario. Save this as the S_HRE3.xls workbook in the Tut05 folder, then print the worksheet with this scenario. Write a summary of this solution that describes potential options Krista might want to consider in finalizing the building plans. Indicate why you think she should consider these options.
7. Krista has filed a variance request with the local zoning board. This variance would permit a maximum complex size of 45,000 square feet with 60 units in the complex. With this variance, she would increase the limit on one-bedroom apartments to 30 units with a 1 to 1.25 ratio of one-bedroom units to two-bedroom units. Create a scenario named "Variance" that contains these revised data values. Use the macro to find the optimal solution for this scenario. Save this as the same S_HRE3.xls file. Print the Analysis worksheet and the Answer Report.
8. Formulate a third scenario for this optimization. Describe why you think these changes should be considered. Use the macro to find the optimum solution. Save this as the same S_HRE3.xls file. Print the analysis and the Answer Report. Write a summary of this optimal solution that Krista could send to J.P.

TUTORIAL 6

Analyzing Data and Preparing Forecasts

Controlling Costs and Forecasting Sales

OBJECTIVES

In this tutorial you will learn how to:

- Use the AVERAGE, MIN, MAX, MEDIAN, STDEV, PMT, and YIELD functions

- Build in decisions, using the IF and VLOOKUP functions

- Perform complex comparisons, using the AND, OR, and NOT functions

- Develop a forecast, using regression analysis

- Create a growth rate forecast by applying regression analysis

- Create a template workbook

- Use a read-only template workbook

- Develop a macro used with a template workbook

CASE

Sunny Morning Products

The Operating Budget that Travis and his staff have been developing will eventually be the basis for forecasting a five-year plan for Sunny Morning Products. Therefore, Travis wants this budget to be as streamlined and as accurate as possible. As he discusses the various expenses itemized in next year's Operating Budget with his staff, they continually compare one expense item to another to understand where changes might be made. They realize that, as in most other businesses, their single largest operating expense is employee salaries and benefits, and it is also the toughest expense to control. Therefore, their analysis has been focusing on the other expense items, which they can more easily control. Travis holds a meeting with the budget team to ask each person on the team to determine an area where he or she feels costs could be cut, and develop a plan for doing so.

Bill Hodges tells the team about last month's International Juicers and Processors Equipment Faire in London, which he attended in the hope of finding a new juicing machine that would increase their capacity to produce Olympic Gold. He found one that would allow them to increase their production capacity by 25 percent, but it costs $1,500,000. He decides to determine the most economical way for SMP to purchase this machine, and limit its drain on next year's operating expenses. He also agrees to compile a detailed report on production costs, to be used to analyze how sales could affect production costs quarter by quarter.

Carmen and Ann offer to develop an expense analysis summary of all the expense items other than salaries. They feel that this will be helpful in interpreting their budget, and determining the most likely areas for controling costs. Travis thinks this is a good idea, and asks Ann to revise their Operating Budget to include this expense analysis section.

Introduction to Applying Functions

Carmen wants Ann to add an expense analysis section to the Sunny Morning Products Operating Budget that includes the largest expense, the smallest expense, the average expense, the median expense, and the expense standard deviation. Ann considers the request and develops a planning analysis sheet in preparation for making the modifications to their existing Excel workbook (Figure 6-1).

Figure 6-1
Ann's planning analysis sheet

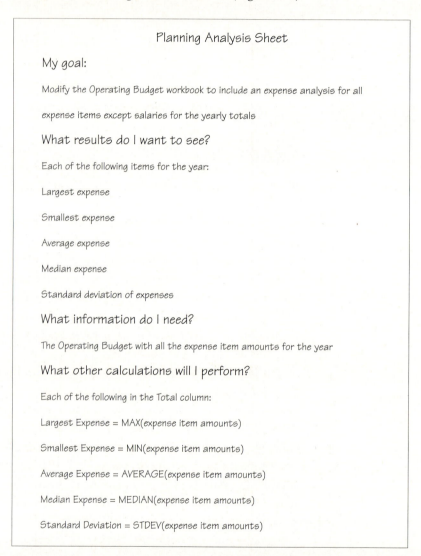

Notice from the planning sheet that Ann intends to obtain these values by using the Excel statistical functions MAX, MIN, AVERAGE, MEDIAN, and STDEV. As you learned in Tutorial 2, an Excel function is a calculation tool that performs a predefined operation. Excel provides many functions that help you enter formulas for calculations and other specialized tasks, such as statistical analysis, even if you don't know the mathematical details of the calculations. You are already familiar with the SUM function, which adds the values in a range of cells you specify. Excel contains more than 100 different functions, classified into ten types, some of which you have already used: Date & Time (for example, TODAY), Database, Engineering, Financial, Information, Logical, Lookup & Reference, Mathematical (for example, SUM and ROUND), Statistical, and Text. These function categories are described in Figure 6-2, and some of the more common Excel functions are listed in Figure 6-3. By using the Function Wizard button and the All Function Category selection, you can display a list of all the Excel functions and obtain a description of each function.

INTRODUCTION TO APPLYING FUNCTIONS **ADVEX 273**

Figure 6-2 ◀
Excel function categories

Function Category	Example Functions in this Category
Financial	Calculate loan payments, depreciation, interest rate, internal rate of return
Date & Time	Display today's date and/or time; calculate the number of days between two dates
Math & Trig	Round off numbers; calculate sums, logs, sines, cosines, and factorials; generate random numbers
Statistical	Calculate averages, standard deviations, and frequencies; find minimums, maximums, and medians; count the numbers in a list
Lookup & Reference	Look for a value in a range of cells; find the row or column location of a reference
Database	Perform crosstabs, averages, counts, and standard deviations for an Excel database
Text	Convert numbers to text or text to numbers; compare two text entries; find the length of a text entry
Logical	Perform comparisons for conditional calculations
Information	Return information about the formatting, location, or contents of cells, including error values
Engineering	Convert binary to hexadecimal and binary to decimal; perform calculations on complex numbers

Figure 6-3 ◀
Selected Excel functions

Function	Description
ABS(formula)	Calculates the absolute value of a formula result
AVERAGE(range)	Calculates the average of values
COS(formula)	Calculates the cosine of an expression
COUNT(range)	Counts the nonblank cells in a range
DAY(date)	Displays the day number of a date
EXP(formula)	Calculates e (2.71828) raised to the power of the formula result
GROWTH(y-range, x-range,new-x-value)	Calculates a value, using an exponential growth curve
INT(formula)	Displays the formula results as an integer
INTERCEPT(y-range, x-range)	Finds the intercept of a linear regression line
ISERROR(formula)	Returns TRUE if the formula result is any error value
ISNUMBER(formula)	Returns TRUE if the formula result is a number
ISTEXT(formula)	Returns TRUE if the formula result is text

ADVEX 274 TUTORIAL 6 ANALYZING DATA AND PREPARING FORECASTS

Figure 6-3
Selected Excel
functions
(continued)

Function	Description
LN(formula)	Finds the natural logarithm of the formula result
LARGE(range-list, position)	Finds the largest value specified by position from the maximum value in a list
LEFT(text,num-chars)	Returns the leftmost characters from a text value
LEN(text)	Finds the number of characters in a text string
LINEST(y-range, x-range,constant,stats)	Returns the parameters of a linear regression line
LOGEST(y-range, x-range,constant,stats)	Returns the parameters of a growth rate or exponential trend line
LOWER(text)	Converts text to lowercase
MAX(range-list)	Finds the maximum value in a list
MEDIAN(range-list)	Finds the median of the values in a list
MIN(range-list)	Finds the minimum value in a list
MONTH(date)	Displays the month number of a date
NPV(interest-rate,range)	Calculates the net present value of cash flows
PMT(principal,rate,term)	Calculates a loan payment
RIGHT(text,num-chars)	Returns the rightmost characters from a text value
ROUND(formula, decimals)	Rounds to specified decimal places
RSQ(y-range,x-range)	Calculates the R-square between the lists of values
SIN(formula)	Calculates the sine of an expression
SLN(cost,salvage,life)	Calculates straight-line depreciation
SMALL(range-list, position)	Finds the smallest value specified by position from the minimum value in a list
SLOPE(y-range,x-range)	Calculates the slope of a linear regression line
SQRT(formula)	Performs a square root of the formula result
STDEV(range-list)	Calculates the standard deviation of sample values
SUM(range-list)	Adds the values in a range
TODAY()	Displays today's date from the computer's clock

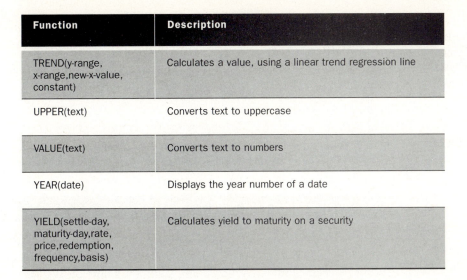

Figure 6-3
Selected Excel functions (continued)

Function	Description
TREND(y-range, x-range,new-x-value, constant)	Calculates a value, using a linear trend regression line
UPPER(text)	Converts text to uppercase
VALUE(text)	Converts text to numbers
YEAR(date)	Displays the year number of a date
YIELD(settle-day, maturity-day,rate, price,redemption, frequency,basis)	Calculates yield to maturity on a security

Describing Data with Functions

Descriptive statistics provide measures of a data series, so that several statistical values can be used to describe a large group of many data values. Using descriptive statistics, you can analyze a few descriptive measures that provide a summary of your data series. Excel contains a number of functions that provide shortcut methods of calculating many different statistics. You can apply several of these statistical functions to calculate the descriptive statistics that summarize Ann's expenses.

Retrieving the Workbook

First you need to retrieve and examine Ann's worksheet in preparation for inserting the expense analysis section and analyzing the results, using the statistical functions.

To retrieve the Operating Budget worksheet:

1. Launch Excel and open Ann's C_SMP1.xls workbook file in the Tut06 folder or directory on your Student Disk. Then save the workbook as S_SMP1.xls in the Tut06 folder in case you want to restart this tutorial.

2. Click the **Budget** tab and review Ann's worksheet. Look at the expense amounts in the Total column that Ann wants to summarize.

Add an expense analysis summary section to Ann's worksheet. First, you need to enter the labels for the expense analysis section in the worksheet and then you can enter the functions.

To create the Expense Analysis section in Ann's worksheet:

1. Scroll the worksheet so that cell A19 is in the upper-left corner of the worksheet area.

2. Split the worksheet horizontally below row 29, then scroll the bottom pane so that cell A52 is in the upper-left corner of the pane.

3. Enter labels in **A52:A57**, as shown in Figure 6-4. Include the border for underlining in cell A52 and select an appropriate background color for that cell.

    TROUBLE? If you cannot see rows A52 through A57 in the bottom pane, click View and then Full Screen to change your view to full screen. The bottom pane should now display rows A52 through A57.

Figure 6-4
Expense Analysis summary section of report

labels for summary

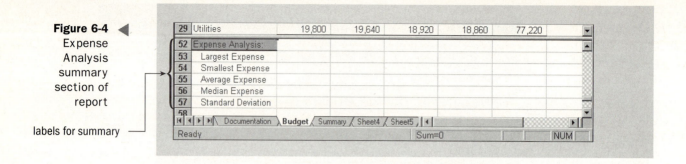

Using the MAX and MIN Functions

With the Expense Analysis section set up in the worksheet, you can now apply the appropriate functions. There are a few different ways to enter a function into a worksheet. Begin by entering the MAX function, using the Function Wizard.

To enter the MAX function using the Function Wizard to find the expense with the largest value:

1. Click **F53** to make it the active cell. The values for the expense analysis summary are placed in the Total column, where the values being summarized are located.

2. Click the **Function Wizard** button f_x to display the Function Wizard - Step 1 of 2 dialog box.

3. In the Function Category list, click **Statistical** because MAX is a statistical function.

4. Click **AVEDEV** or any other name that appears in the **Function Name** box to activate that box.

5. Press **M** to scroll the Function Name list, and click **MAX**, which is the first function listed that begins with the letter M.

6. Click the **Next>** button to display the Function Wizard - Step 2 of 2 dialog box. See Figure 6-5.

Figure 6-5
Function Wizard - Step 2 of 2 dialog box for MAX function

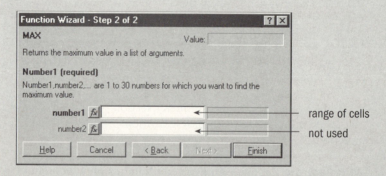

range of cells
not used

7. Select the range **F21:F29**, using pointing, as the number1 parameter for the MAX function. Since you have selected a range that contains a series of values, you do not need to specify the number2 parameter.

   TROUBLE? If the dialog box covers the range, drag it to the left so that the range is visible for doing the selection.

8. Click the **Finish** button to display the result calculated by the MAX function. The largest expense is $180,172.

Now add the function for calculating the smallest expense, using the range named Expenses, which defines cells F21:F29.

To use the MIN function to find the smallest value using a named range:

1. Click **F54** to make it the active cell.

2. Click the **Function Wizard** button to display the Function Wizard - Step 1 of 2 dialog box. The Statistical Function Category is already selected from the last set of steps.

3. Click any name that appears in the **Function Name** box to activate that box.

4. Press **M** to scroll the Function Name list to MAX, which is the first one that begins with the letter M.

5. Scroll down the list until MIN appears, click **MIN**, then click the **Next>** button to display the Function Wizard - Step 2 of 2 dialog box.

6. Click and drag the dialog box to the right as needed to display the Name box, then click the **Name** box list arrow to display the list of defined names.

7. Scroll the list until Expenses appears, then click **Expenses** to place that range name in the number1 parameter text box of the MIN Function Wizard.

8. Click the **Finish** button to display the result calculated by the MIN function. If necessary, scroll the bottom pane so that cell A52 is in the upper-left corner. See Figure 6-6.

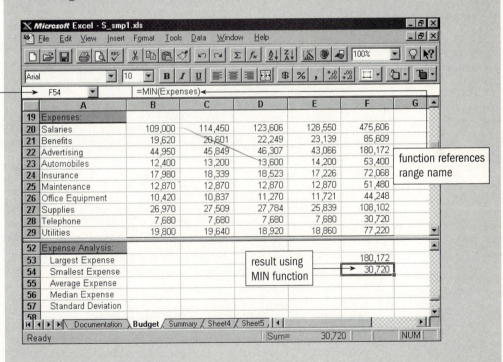

Figure 6-6
Expense summary with values calculated using functions

Now that you have included these statistical functions in the budget, save the workbook.

9. Save the workbook as S_SMP1.xls.

>
> **ENTERING FUNCTIONS USING RANGE NAMES**
> - Click the cell where you want the formula with the function to appear.
> - Click the Function Wizard button to display the function list and select the desired function.
> or
> Type the function name, including the open parenthesis.
> - Click the Name box list arrow and select the named range.
> or
> Use pointing to select the desired cell range.
> - Click the Finish button or press the Enter key to complete the specification.

Using the AVERAGE, MEDIAN, and STDEV Functions

Several descriptive statistics provide an *overall summary* of the data series. **AVERAGE** is a statistical function that represents a "summary" of the data by providing one measure that tells more about the data series than any other value. The average is also known as the arithmetic mean, or just the mean. It is calculated by finding the total value of the data series, and then dividing that total by the number of individual values in the data series. Add the function for the average of the expense items other than salaries to the expense analysis.

To use the AVERAGE function to find the arithmetic mean of the expenses:

1. Click **F55** to make it the active cell.
2. Type **=AVERAGE(** to begin the formula.
3. Select the range **F21:F29** for the number1 parameter. This range contains the expense items for which the average is to be calculated.
4. Press the **Enter** key to finish entering the function. It is not necessary to type the closing parenthesis, since no other arithmetic is included with this function. The average expense amount is $78,113.

Next, you need to calculate the median expense item. The **median** is the number in the middle of a set of numbers; that is, half the numbers have values that are greater than the median and the other half have values that are less. Find the median expense, excluding salaries.

To use the MEDIAN function to find this expense value:

1. Click **F56** to make it the active cell.
2. Type **=MEDIAN(** to begin the formula.
3. Click the **Name** box list arrow to display the list of defined names.
4. Scroll the list until Expenses appears, then click **Expenses** to place that range name in the function.
5. Press the **Enter** key to complete the cell entry. As with the AVERAGE function, it is not necessary to type the closing parenthesis. The median expense is $72,068.

Last, Ann needs to calculate the sample standard deviation, using the Excel STDEV function. This is a measure that summarizes the dispersion of the data values from the average. A small standard deviation indicates that all the data values in a series have values that are near the average or mean, whereas a large standard deviation indicates that the data values are considerably larger or smaller than the average. Find the standard deviation of the expenses, excluding salaries.

To use the STDEV function to find the standard deviation of the expense values:

1. Click **F57** to make it the active cell.

2. Enter the STDEV function to calculate this statistic on the range **F21:F29**. You can use the Function Wizard and the Name box, as desired, in entering this formula. The standard deviation of the expenses is $44,891, indicating that there is considerable deviation from the average, because the standard deviation is more than half of the average. This completes the expense summary calculations. See Figure 6-7.

Figure 6-7 ◀
Completed expense analysis

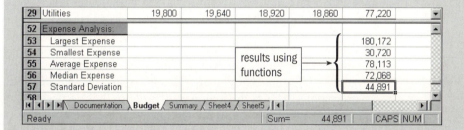

3. Preview and print the **Budget** sheet, using a Page Setup that fits all the output on a single page with a portrait orientation. Save this as the S_SMP1.xls workbook in the Tut06 folder.

4. Close the workbook.

Ann's summary of the total expenses for the year is complete and she can now share it with Travis and Carmen as they further analyze where expenses need to be reduced.

Using Functions for Financial Analysis

Much of financial analysis involves calculations that include interest rates, such as calculating loan payments, annuity payments, and bond yields. Sometimes you know the principal amount, for example the amount of a loan, and want to find the monthly or annual payment; other times you know the payment and want to find the interest rate. Excel financial functions are available that allow you to calculate any value you want to find when the other values for the financial formula are known. The PMT function calculates a periodic loan payment, such as a monthly payment, when the loan amount, interest rate, and loan duration are known. On the other hand, the YIELD function calculates an interest rate when the price, duration, and amount of interest paid are known. Each of these functions will help Carmen and Travis with their decision-making at Sunny Morning Products.

Calculating a Loan Payment with PMT

Bill Hodges believes that the new juicing machine he priced at last month's International Juicers and Processors Equipment convention will greatly increase productivity and sales for SMP. However, the initial cost of the machine could have a significant impact on the Operating Budget. He intends to recommend financing this machine with a bank loan and wants Ann's help in determining what the monthly payments would be. He estimates that they can finance the entire cost of the equipment with a loan at an annual interest rate of nine percent and a repayment period of seven years.

Ann knows that Excel has a financial function that is perfect for this type of calculation—PMT. The syntax of the PMT function is

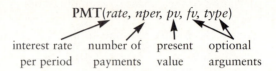

The *rate* argument is the interest rate per period. Usually interest rates are expressed as annual rates. For example, a 10% interest rate means that if you borrow $1,000 for a year, you must pay back the amount of the loan—$1,000—plus an additional $100 in interest at the end of the year. The *nper* argument represents the total number of payments required to pay back the loan. You must be consistent about the units you use for *rate* and *nper*. For example, if the payments for the loan are due monthly, then the interest rate must be a monthly rate. You need to carefully match the period interest rate to the term of the loan in months, quarters, or years.

The *pv* argument is the principal or total amount of the loan. The *fv* argument is the future value, or a cash balance at the end of the loan, and can be omitted if there is no desired ending balance, which is usually the situation for a loan payment. Using the *fv* argument indicates that you are making a loan payment *plus* placing an amount in a savings account, so that the loan is paid and you have a desired savings account balance at the end of the loan's duration. The *type* argument is **1** or **0** to indicate whether the loan payments are made at the beginning or the end of each time period, respectively. If *type* is omitted, a value of zero is assumed for payments at the end of each time period, which is the most usual situation for loan payments.

HELP DESK

Index

PMT FUNCTION

Double-click the Help button to display the Help Topics dialog box, then click the Index tab.

Keyword	Topic
PMT worksheet function	

In many situations, you only want to calculate the amount of a loan payment, without including the calculation of a future cash balance. In this case, the optional arguments are not used and the PMT function makes use of only three arguments. So to calculate the loan payment for the juicing machine, the formula would be

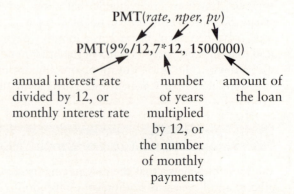

Ann has planned, sketched, and partially completed the worksheet for the loan analysis. Open Ann's partially completed worksheet for the new juicing machine.

USING FUNCTIONS FOR FINANCIAL ANALYSIS ADVEX 281

To review the loan analysis worksheet:

1. Open Ann's partially completed worksheet, C_SMP2.xls, in the Tut06 folder and immediately save it as S_SMP2.xls.

2. Click the **Payment** tab and review the contents of the worksheet with the data values already entered for the interest rate, term, and loan amount.

Notice in Ann's worksheet that the interest rate is given as an annual percentage. Ann will have to convert it to a monthly amount in order to calculate the monthly payment using the PMT function. Add the loan payment calculation to Ann's worksheet.

To calculate a monthly loan payment using the PMT function:

1. Click **B11**. This is where you want the monthly loan payment to be calculated.

2. Click the **Function Wizard** button to display the Function Wizard - Step 1 of 2 dialog box.

3. Click **Financial** in the Function Category list because PMT is a financial function.

4. Scroll through the list of financial Function Names, then double-click **PMT** to display the Function Wizard - Step 2 of 2 dialog box.

5. Use pointing to select the cell references and type the remaining parts of the formulas for each of the *rate*, *nper*, and *pv* arguments. See Figure 6-8. Be sure to include the division by 12 to convert the annual interest rate to a monthly interest rate, and the multiplication by 12 to convert the number of years to the number of months. Leave the *fv* and *type* arguments blank, because you are not using them for this loan payment calculation.

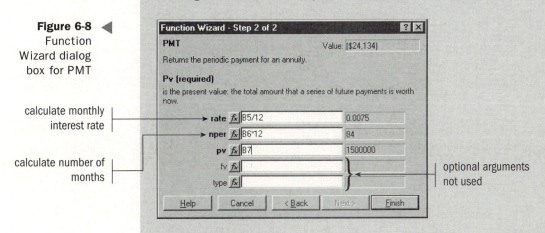

Figure 6-8
Function Wizard dialog box for PMT

calculate monthly interest rate

calculate number of months

optional arguments not used

6. Click the **Finish** button to display the calculated monthly loan payment. See Figure 6-9. Notice that Excel displays the payment as a negative number. This is because it is a business expense that is an amount paid.

Figure 6-9
Monthly loan payment for new Juicing Machine

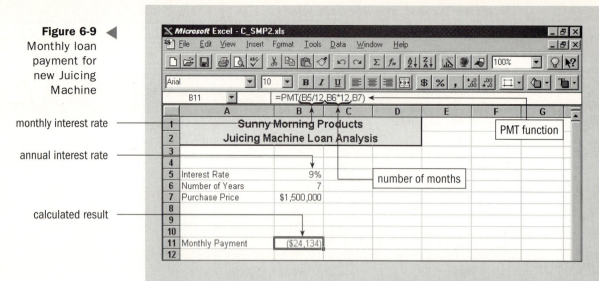

7. Edit cell **B11** and place a minus (–) before the PMT function so that the result is displayed as a positive number. You need to determine whether you want the results to appear as a negative number or not. If not, then you need to use the minus, as you did here.

8. Save the workbook as S_SMP2.xls, then preview and print the loan payment analysis.

USING PMT TO CALCULATE A MONTHLY PAYMENT

- Click the cell where you want to display the monthly payment amount.
- Type =– (that is, equal sign and minus) to start the formula and include the minus so that the payment is displayed as a positive number.
- Click the Function Wizard button, select the Financial category, select the PMT function, and click the Next> button.
- Click the cell containing the annual interest rate, then type /12.
- Click the nper text box, click the cell containing the number of years, then type *12.
- Click the pv text box, then click the cell containing the principal.
- Click the Finish button.

Instead of selecting the function from a list, you can type PMT(and use pointing to specify the cell references for the interest rate, duration, and/or loan amount.

Calculating a Lease Payment with PMT

Bill shows Travis and Carmen the loan payment and they agree that it is high. However, Bill is convinced that the demand for Olympic Gold over the next five years can only be satisfied by installing a larger juicing machine. As they discuss the options, Carmen suggests that perhaps they could lease the machine rather than buy it. Bill's information for leasing indicates that the machine would have a residual value of 44 percent of its original price at the end of the lease. They discuss this option with Ann and ask her to determine their monthly payment under a lease arrangement. A lease payment has two components; a payment amount for the principal reduction, the same as for a loan, and interest on the **residual value**, that is, the balance at the end of the lease. One advantage of leasing is that you do not pay the entire cost of the leased equipment, so there is a residual value at the end of the lease period. You only pay interest on the residual value during the lease period. Since you do not repay the entire principal amount, the monthly payment for leasing is less than the monthly payment for purchasing, and is the reason most people decide to lease rather than purchase equipment.

To calculate a monthly lease payment with a residual value at the end of the lease:

1. Edit the text label in cell A2 so that the title is **Juicing Machine Lease Analysis**.

2. Click **B6** and enter **5** as the Number of Years.

3. Click **A8** and enter the text **Residual Percent**, then click **B8** and enter **44%** for that amount.

4. Click **A9** and enter the text **Residual Value**, then click **B9** and enter the formula **B7*B8**.

5. Edit the formula in cell **B11** so that the payment is calculated on the amount of the principle reduction (that is, the Purchase Price minus the Residual Value) and interest is paid only on the Residual Value (that is, the Residual Value multiplied by the Monthly Interest Rate). The monthly lease payment for the juicing machine is $22,387. See Figure 6-10.

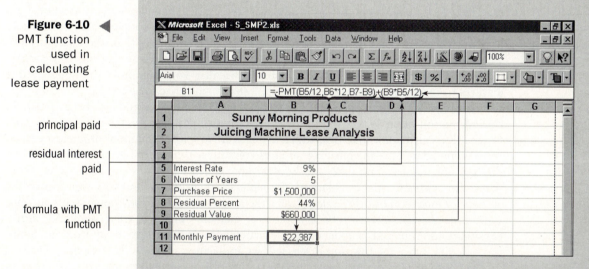

Figure 6-10
PMT function used in calculating lease payment

6. Save the workbook as S_SMP3.xls in the Tut06 folder, then preview and print the lease payment analysis. Close the workbook.

The budget team agrees that the best alternative is for Sunny Morning Products to lease the juicing machine because that involves a lower monthly payment and they expect to replace it in five years.

If you want to take a break and resume the tutorial at a later time, you can do so now. Exit Excel. If you are on a network, leave Windows running. If you are using your own computer, you may exit Windows and shut down the computer. When you resume the tutorial, place your Student Disk in the disk drive, launch Excel, then continue with the tutorial.

Calculating a Bond Interest Rate with YIELD[1]

Carmen's responsibilities at Sunny Morning Products include cash management. When they have excess cash, she invests in corporate bonds to earn a higher rate of interest until the cash is needed for improving their bottling operations. Carmen frequently buys previously issued bonds that are traded on the New York Bond Exchange. This allows her to choose bond maturities that match SMP's long-range plans. The typical bond she buys is scheduled to pay interest every six months, so the amount of interest paid is known. Carmen is considering purchasing several General Motors Acceptance Corporation (GMAC) bonds in order to invest their excess cash for last month. She is considering a series of GMAC bonds with the following terms:

October 15, 1998 settlement date   6.75% coupon
April 15, 2002 maturity date $96.25 price
Interest paid semiannual $100 redemption value
30/360 day count basis

Although bonds like this are most often sold with an actual redemption value, or face value, of $1,000, the custom in trading bonds is to state the bond price relative to $100. For example, the GMAC bond Carmen is considering has an actual redemption value of $1,000, but the current trading price is stated as $96.25. This means that the actual price to buy one bond is $962.50.

The coupon rate on a bond is the interest rate that the bond pays based on its redemption value. Once bonds are initially issued, they often trade at a price that is more or less than their face value. When a bond trades at a lower price than its redemption value, then the true interest rate received on the bond is greater than the coupon rate. This occurs because when the bond matures, the amount received is greater than the amount paid, which increases the amount of interest received. This true interest rate for a previously issued bond is known as the **yield to maturity**, because you must hold the bond until it matures to receive the difference between the settlement price, or purchase price, and the redemption value of the bond. And of course a settlement price could also be greater than the redemption value, in which case the yield to maturity is then less than the coupon rate.

Financial calculations like this, which are concerned with the amount of interest earned between two dates, are the most common use of date arithmetic in business. That is, when the beginning and ending dates are known, how much interest is earned between those dates? For some financial calculations, the interest rate is known and you want to find the amount of interest. For other calculations, the amount of interest is known and you want to find the effective interest rate. A number of financial functions are available for different situations. You need to understand and match your analysis with the appropriate financial function. Once the function is selected, its application is relatively straightforward.

The complexities of all the calculations to determine the yield to maturity, or effective interest rate, for Carmen's GMAC bonds are readily handled in Excel by the YIELD function. Whereas the PMT function finds the amount of a loan payment given an interest rate, the YIELD function determines the effective, or true, interest rate, given the amount paid for the bond. The syntax of the YIELD function is

YIELD(*settlement, maturity, rate, pr, redemption, frequency, basis*)

| date bond purchased | date bond matures | stated interest rate on bond | purchase price paid for bond | amount received at maturity date | number of times per year interest payments received | days per month and year used for interest calculations |

---

[1] The following section covers advanced concepts. If the level of this material is not appropriate for your students, you can skip this section without loss in continuity of the text.

The *settlement* argument is the purchase date of the bond, expressed as a **serial date** number like those obtained from the computer's clock with the TODAY function. The *maturity* argument is the bond's maturity date, and is also expressed as a serial date number. The *rate* argument is the bond's annual coupon, or stated, interest rate. The *pr* argument is the bond's price per $100 of face value. It is important that you remember to enter the price relative to $100 of face value. The *redemption* argument is the bond's value per $100 of face value. This is normally 100. The *frequency* argument is the number of times per year interest is paid on the bond—this is usually 2 for semiannual or 4 for quarterly. The *basis* argument is the manner in which the number of days per month and year are used in determining the bond's interest. For example, is interest calculated based on 360 days in a year or 365? The National Association of Security Dealers uses 30 days in each month and 360 days per year; the Excel YIELD function considers this a 30/360 basis. This is the default value, which is automatically used if you do not include the *basis* argument in the function. Several other bases are available, including one that follows European conventions.

HELP DESK

Index

YIELD FUNCTION

Double-click the Help button to display the Help Topics dialog box, then click the Index tab.

Keyword	Topic
YIELD worksheet function	
YIELD function	

EXCEL 5.0

Ann created an Excel workbook for Carmen to use in doing yield to maturity calculations in analyzing different bonds. Wherever she can, Carmen likes to obtain a yield of at least seven percent. Use serial dates and the YIELD function to determine the effective interest rate on the GMAC bonds that Carmen is considering.

To use the YIELD function to calculate yield to maturity for a previously issued bond:

1. Open the C_SMP3.xls workbook in the Tut06 folder, then immediately save it as the S_SMP4.xls workbook in the Tut06 folder.

2. Click the **Yield** tab and review the data entered in the worksheet. Note that the dates remain to be entered.

3. Click **B5**, then type **Nov 15, 1998** and press the **Enter** key to enter that settlement date. Although Excel displays it as 15-Nov-98, it is stored as a serial date number for use in any date calculations, including those of the YIELD function. A number of other financial functions also include similar serial dates.

4. Click **B6**, then type **May 15, 2002** and press the **Enter** key to enter it as a serial date.

5. Click **B12** to make it the active cell, where the yield to maturity is to be calculated.

6. Click the **Function Wizard** button [fx] to display the Step 1 of 2 dialog box, click **Financial** to select that Function Category, scroll the Function Name list until you locate the YIELD function, then double-click **YIELD** to display the Step 2 of 2 dialog box.

   TROUBLE? If the YIELD function did not appear in the Function Name list, then the Analysis ToolPak Add-In is not available. Click Cancel to exit from the Function Wizard. Click Tools, click Add-Ins to display the Add-Ins dialog box, click the Analysis ToolPak check box, then click the OK button. Repeat Step 6. If the add-in is still not available, see your instructor or technical support person.

7. Click and drag the dialog box to the right so that the data in column B is visible, then click **B5** to select the settlement date. Notice that the serial date 36114 appears in the text box to the right of the settlement text box.

8. Use pointing to enter the cell reference for the *maturity* and note the serial date of 37391, then enter the cell references for the *rate*, *pr*, and *redemption*. See Figure 6-11.

Figure 6-11 ◀
YIELD arguments entered in Step 2 dialog box

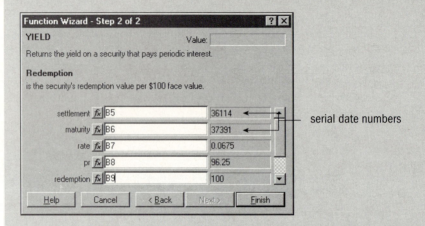

9. Scroll the list of arguments, using the scroll bar, and enter **B10** as the cell reference for *frequency*, then click the **Finish** button to calculate the desired yield. See Figure 6-12. It is not necessary to enter a value for the *basis* argument, since you are using the default.

Figure 6-12 ◀
Yield to maturity for GMAC bond

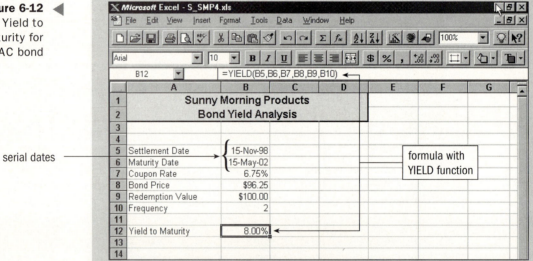

10. Preview and print the worksheet. Save the workbook as the S_SMP4.xls file, then close it.

Because the current yield to maturity is greater than Carmen's desired rate of seven percent, she phones her securities dealer to place an order for 50 bonds at a cost of $962.50 per bond. SMP should have adequate cash for the future production capacity expansion that Travis and Bill are planning.

Building in Decisions

Travis received a report from Bill on their production costs. He meets with Carmen and Ann to review Bill's report to determine the impact of this information on their Operating Budget. The current Cost of Sales Percents vary between 57 percent and 65 percent from quarter to quarter. Bill's report indicates that these costs are likely to change as the sales change from quarter to quarter. He expects that the cost percent will decrease when total sales increase. Based on her discussion with Travis and Carmen, Ann sketches the decision table shown in Figure 6-13. A **decision table** details various conditions that can occur and the appropriate action to take for each condition.

Figure 6-13
Decision table for cost percents

IF CONDITIONS:	THEN ACTIONS:
Sales	Cost Percent
Less than $900,000	63%
$900,000 or more	58%

Excel provides two methods for building the logic of a decision table into formulas, the IF and VLOOKUP functions.

Using the IF Function

In Excel the IF function allows you to make comparisons, like those in Ann's decision table, that test a condition to determine which action Excel should take. The IF function has this general form:

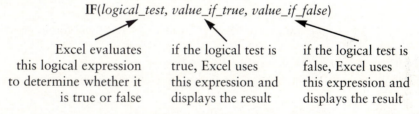

IF(*logical_test, value_if_true, value_if_false*)

- Excel evaluates this logical expression to determine whether it is true or false
- if the logical test is true, Excel uses this expression and displays the result
- if the logical test is false, Excel uses this expression and displays the result

logical_test is any value or expression that can be evaluated to true or false. The most common situation is to use a *logical_test* that compares the values of two different expressions or formulas using a relational operator. The form of the IF function is then

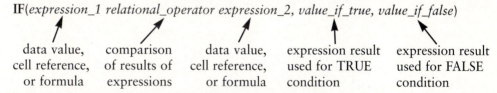

IF(*expression_1 relational_operator expression_2, value_if_true, value_if_false*)

- data value, cell reference, or formula
- comparison of results of expressions
- data value, cell reference, or formula
- expression result used for TRUE condition
- expression result used for FALSE condition

expression is any Excel formula or data value. Formulas can consist of functions, including another IF function. Data values can include text strings, such as "yes" or "no." The relational operators are used to compare the two expressions (Figure 6-14). They indicate the comparison that is to be made, such as Sales <= 900,000.

Figure 6-14
Relational operators

Operator	Symbol
Equal to	=
Not equal to	<>
Less than or equal to	<=
Less than	<
Greater than or equal to	>=
Greater than	>

An IF function is evaluated by Excel in this manner:

- Calculate the values for *expression_1* and *expression_2*.
- Compare the results of *expression_1* and *expression_2* using the *relational_operator* and obtain either a true or a false outcome.
- If the outcome is true, calculate and display the result of the *value_if_true* expression.
- If the outcome is false, calculate and display the result of the *value_if_false* expression.

Examples of several IF functions and their components are illustrated in Figure 6-15.

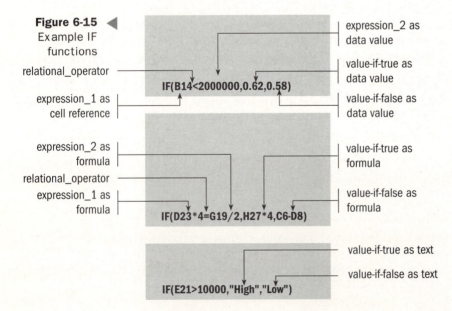

Figure 6-15
Example IF functions

Ann decides to set up a separate assumption section to display the cost percent values, then reference these values in the IF function. Although she could enter the values directly into the IF function, this arrangement makes it easier for Ann and Carmen to review and change these cost percent values. Set up the assumption area for the cost percents as illustrated in Figure 6-16.

Figure 6-16
Assumption area set up with cost percents

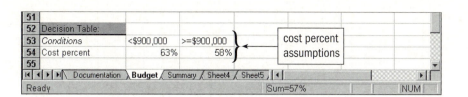

To set up the assumption area for the Cost percents in the decision table:

1. Open the **C_SMP1.xls** workbook in the Tut06 folder and immediately save it as **S_SMP5.xls** in the same folder.

2. Click the **Budget** tab and move the cell pointer to cell **A52**. Then enter the text labels **Decision Table:**, **Conditions**, and **Cost percent**, as shown in Figure 6-16. Apply underlining, borders, and shading as shown. Italicize the Conditions label.

3. In cells **B53** and **C53**, add the labels identifying the conditions under which each cost percent should be used, as shown in Figure 6-16.

4. Select the range **B54:C54**. Change the cell format to Percent with zero decimals.

5. Click **B54**. Enter **.63**, the first cost percent from the decision table.

6. Click **C54**. Enter **.58**, the second cost percent from the decision table.

Now that Ann has set up her decision table values, she is ready to enter the IF function to select the Cost of Sales Percent for each quarter. Enter the IF function that implements Ann's decision table.

To include the conditions in the decision table, using the IF function:

1. Click cell **B39**. Enter the formula **IF(B14<900000,$B$54,$C$54)**. (Remember that you can use the Function Wizard to enter the IF function by selecting the Logical function category, and pointing to the specific cell references. Use the F4 (ABS) key to add absolute referencing. You need to include absolute referencing in the formula because the formula will be copied.) This formula checks the value of Sales in cell B14. If the value is less than $900,000, it selects the true-condition value, the cost percent in B54 (63%). If the value in B14 is equal to or greater than $900,000, it selects the false-condition value, the Cost percent in cell C54 (58%).

2. Click **B39** to make it the active cell and copy its contents into **C39:E39**.

3. Click **E39** to make sure that the formula with the IF function appears. See Figure 6-17. Note that the first cell reference in the formula is a relative reference and changes accordingly, but that the references to the cells containing the Cost percents did not change because they are absolute references.

Figure 6-17
IF function implements decision table

relative references

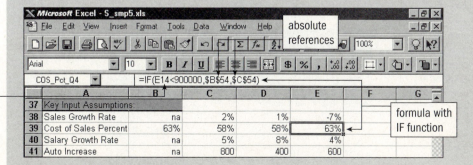

> **TROUBLE?** If cells C39, D39, and E39 contain zeros, you did not include the absolute references for the Cost percents. Edit the formula in cell B39 so that it matches the formula in Step 1, then repeat Steps 2 and 3.
>
> 4. Scroll the worksheet to view the Cost of Sales, which is now $2,178,000 in the Total column, and the Return On Sales, which is 6.85%.

An important reason for including a decision table in a worksheet is that as you do different what-if analyses, you want the appropriate value selected from the decision table for the data values in your particular what-if analysis. Perform a what-if analysis using the built-in decision table.

To do a what-if analysis with a built-in decision table:

> 1. Scroll the worksheet so that row 5 is the top row.
> 2. Click **B7**, the cell whose value you want to change.
> 3. Enter **200100**, an increase in the number of bottles of orange juice sold in Qtr 1.
> 4. Note that the Cost of Sales in the Total column is now $2,212,891, then scroll the worksheet so that row 39 is visible and observe that the Cost of Sales Percent in Qtr 1 is now 58% rather than 63%. The value was automatically selected by the IF function in calculating this what-if alternative.
> 5. Scroll the worksheet and enter the initial value of **190025** in cell B7, then save this modified worksheet as S_SMP5.xls in the Tut06 folder.

REFERENCE window

BUILDING IN DECISIONS USING THE IF FUNCTION

- Click the cell where you want to display the result of the decision.
- Use the Function Wizard to enter the *logical_test*, the *value_if_true* expression, and the *value_if_false* expression.
  or
  Enter the IF function by typing the formula.
- Edit the formula and type any additional arithmetic to be performed with the result of the IF function.
- Click the Enter button or press the Enter key.

After reviewing Ann's worksheet, Carmen and Ann decide that sales, which have been increasing steadily, may surpass $1 million per quarter (that is, $4 million for the year). They formulate a revised decision table to include a reduction in costs when sales exceed $1 million (Figure 6-18).

Figure 6-18 ◀
Decision table for cost percent with additional discount

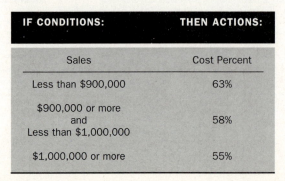

IF CONDITIONS:	THEN ACTIONS:
Sales	Cost Percent
Less than $900,000	63%
$900,000 or more and Less than $1,000,000	58%
$1,000,000 or more	55%

Because this decision table contains three conditions, only two IF functions are necessary for its implementation. The false-condition value is actually another IF function nested inside the first one. First, a new Cost percent value is added to the decision table area, then the Cost of Sales Percent formula is modified so that it considers all three conditions. Make these changes to Ann's worksheet now.

To modify a decision table to include three conditions:

1. Click **C53**, then enter **<$1,000,000** as the new condition label for the Cost percent of 58%.

2. Click **D53**, then enter **>=$1,000,000** as the third condition label.

3. Click **D54**, enter **.55** as the Cost percent, and format this cell as Percent with zero decimals.

4. Click **B39**. Replace the false-condition in the formula ($C$54) with **IF(B14<1000000,$C$54,$D$54)**. The complete formula should now read **IF(B14<900000,$B$54,IF(B14<1000000,$C$54,$D$54))**. The second IF function is evaluated only if the first IF function is evaluated as false. This means that the sales amount in cell B14 has to be greater than $900,000 for the second IF function to be evaluated.

   Now copy the formula with the IF function into the other three quarters of the plan.

5. Select **B39**, then copy that cell's formula into cells **C39**, **D39**, and **E39**.

6. Click **E39** to confirm that the desired formula with the nested IF function appears in that cell. See Figure 6-19.

Figure 6-19
Expanded decision table implemented

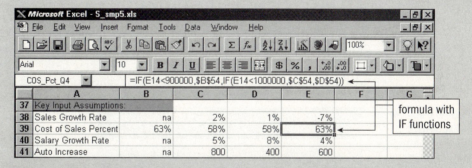

Now the decision table is ready for testing all three sales amounts.

7. Scroll the worksheet window so that cell A5 is in the upper-left corner, split the window horizontally below row 17, and scroll the bottom pane so that cell A37 is in the upper-left corner.

8. Click **D7** in the top pane and enter **219000** as the number of bottles of orange juice sold in the third quarter. Compare the Sales values to the Cost of Sales Percent values to confirm the correct operation of the decision table. See Figure 6-20. The correct Cost of Sales Percent value should be selected for each of the quarterly Sales values, as described by the decision table in Figure 6-18.

Figure 6-20
Cost of Sales Percent values selected for appropriate Sales values

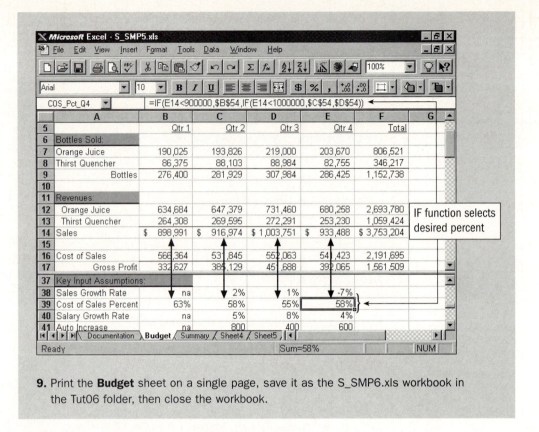

9. Print the **Budget** sheet on a single page, save it as the S_SMP6.xls workbook in the Tut06 folder, then close the workbook.

Using a Table Lookup

At the next operating budget meeting, Ann and Carmen distribute the decision table and the revised budget to Travis and Bill. Bill reminds everyone of the impact the new juicing machine will have on production costs for Olympic Gold. Bill suggests that they expand the decision table to include the additional conditions shown in Figure 6-21.

Figure 6-21
Expanded decision table for cost percent

IF CONDITIONS:	THEN ACTIONS:
Sales	Cost Percent
Less than $900,000	63%
$900,000 or more and Less than $1,000,000	58%
$1,000,000 or more and Less than $1,100,000	55%
$1,100,000 or more and Less than $1,200,000	53%
$1,200,000 or more	51%

This decision table could be implemented using a total of four nested IF functions, with each subsequent IF function acting as the false-value for the previous IF function. This would be a rather complex formula to set up, and Excel limits the nesting of IF functions to a maximum of seven *value_if_true* and *value_if_false* arguments. Excel provides another method for implementing complex decision tables like this. First, you enter a table of values, known as a **lookup table**, in a convenient cell range. Excel then uses an input value, called the **lookup value**, to look up another value in the table; this is called a **table lookup**.

Excel performs table lookups with the VLOOKUP and HLOOKUP functions. VLOOKUP searches vertically down a column until it finds the input value, then it looks across to the right for the lookup value. HLOOKUP searches horizontally across a row until it finds the lookup value, then it looks down for the input value. Only the VLOOKUP function is discussed here.

The syntax of the VLOOKUP function is

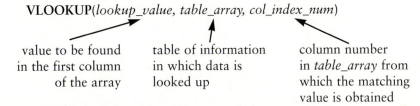

VLOOKUP(*lookup_value*, *table_array*, *col_index_num*)

value to be found in the first column of the array

table of information in which data is looked up

column number in *table_array* from which the matching value is obtained

The *lookup_value* argument is the input value or expression. Excel searches down the leftmost column in the table, column index number 1, until it finds a value that is equal to or less than the input value. The *table_array* argument is the range in the worksheet containing the lookup table. The *col_index_num* argument is the column number of the lookup table that Excel should look in *after* it finds the input value. The first column in the lookup table range is always numbered one, with the other columns in the table numbered from left to right. A lookup table can have as many columns as you choose, but the first column must always contain the input values where Excel searches for the match.

Ann decides that it would be easier to add this lookup table if she used her original worksheet before the IF functions were added to it, so she doesn't need to remove the information she already entered for the IF formulas.

To prepare for implementing the lookup table:

1. Open the C_SMP1.xls workbook in the Tut06 folder and immediately save it as S_SMP7.xls in the same folder.

2. Click the **Budget** tab, press the **F5** (Go To) key to open the Go To dialog box, enter **A52** in the Reference text box, then click the **OK** button. Then scroll the worksheet so that A43 is in the upper-left corner of the worksheet window.

3. Enter **Lookup Table for Cost of Sales Percent:** in cell A52 as the table's title. Enter **Sales** in cell B53 and **Cost percent** in cell C53 as column headings. Use underlining, shading, and alignment as appropriate. See Figure 6-22.

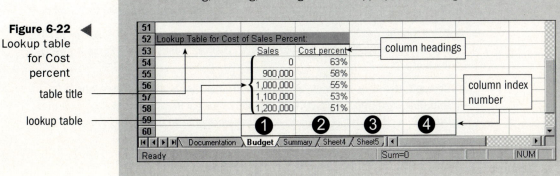

Figure 6-22
Lookup table for Cost percent

ADVEX 294 **TUTORIAL 6** ANALYZING DATA AND PREPARING FORECASTS

4. Enter the data values shown in Figure 6-22 for **Sales** and **Cost percent**. Remember to enter the Cost percent values as decimal numbers. Your screen should look like Figure 6-22. Format cells **B54:B58** (the Sales values) as Numbers with thousands separators and no decimals. Format cells **C54:C58** (the Cost percent values) as Percent with zero decimals.

With the table in place, Ann is ready to add the VLOOKUP functions to the formula for calculating the Cost of Sales Percent. Then she can use test values to make sure that the VLOOKUP function works as she expects. **Test values** are example data values that might occur in preparing different what-if alternatives. Incorporate the expanded decision table into Ann's worksheet.

To include decision table conditions for the Cost percent, using the VLOOKUP function:

1. Scroll the worksheet so that cell A37 is in the upper-left corner of its window, then split the window horizontally below row 46. The worksheet area is now ready for entering the Cost of Sales Percent formula, which is calculated using the Cost percent from the lookup table.

2. Click **B39** in the top pane. Enter the formula **VLOOKUP(B14,$B$54:$C$58,2)**. (Remember to use pointing and the F4 (ABS) key as appropriate.) This selects the desired Cost percent from the lookup table for use in calculating the Cost of Sales.

   Now you need to copy the formula with the VLOOKUP function to the cells that specify the Cost of Sales Percent for the other three quarters of the plan.

3. Copy the formula from cell **B39** into cells **C39:E39**.

4. Click **E39** to confirm that the desired formula with the VLOOKUP function appears in this cell. See Figure 6-23.

Figure 6-23 ◀
LOOKUP
function used to
calculate Cost
of Sales
Percent

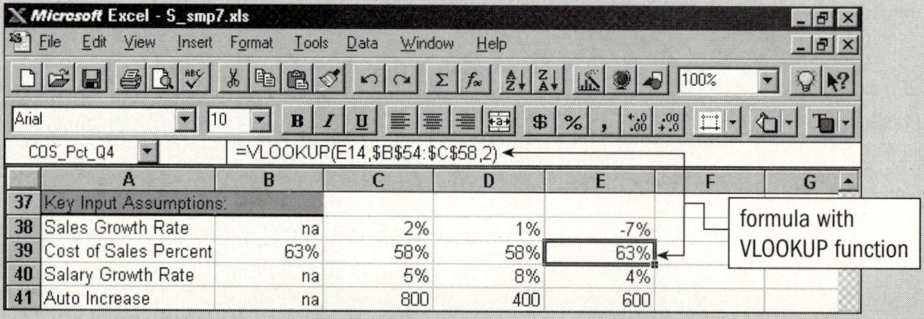

5. Save this modified workbook as S_SMP7.xls.

   Next, test the other entries in the decision table to make sure it works correctly.

6. Scroll the top pane so that the bottles of orange juice (row 7) and Sales (row 14) are visible, then scroll the bottom pane so that the Cost of Sales Percent (row 39) is visible.

7. Click **D7**, then one at a time enter these test values in the cell: **219,000**, **250,000**, **280,000**, and **300,000**. As you enter each value in cell D7, confirm that the correct Cost of Sales Percent is selected from the lookup table.

8. Close the workbook without saving it.

> **REFERENCE window**
>
> **BUILDING IN DECISIONS USING THE VLOOKUP FUNCTION**
>
> - Click the cell where you want to display the result of the lookup function.
> - Use the Function Wizard to choose VLOOKUP, use pointing to specify the *lookup_table* and *table_array*, then type the *col_index_num*.
>   or
>   Type the VLOOKUP function with its arguments.
> - Specify any additional arithmetic performed with the result of the VLOOKUP function.
> - Click the Enter button or press the Enter key.

Carmen is pleased with the results and is confident that this provides a better picture of the cost of producing Olympic Gold. She calls Travis to arrange a meeting with him.

Using Logical Functions

Excel provides three logical functions: AND, OR, and NOT. Two of these functions, AND and OR, evaluate up to 30 conditions that can be either true or false. The AND and OR functions are useful for testing multiple conditions for use in IF functions. The NOT function negates or reverses a condition that you test as true or false. Figure 6-24 describes these logical functions in greater detail.

Figure 6-24
Logical functions

Function	Description
AND(logical1, logical2, ..., logical30)	Each logical condition is evaluated; if they are all true, the function returns a value of TRUE; otherwise, a value of FALSE is returned.
OR(logical1, logical2, ..., logical30)	Each logical condition is evaluated; if one or more is true, the function returns a value of TRUE; otherwise, a value of FALSE is returned.
NOT(logical condition)	The logical condition is evaluated as true or false, then its value is reversed.

Travis discusses the costs of Olympic Gold with Bill. Not only does their cost percent decrease as their sales volume increases, but during the second quarter, they can purchase oranges at lower cost than during the other quarters, because it is the peak harvest time. Ann helps them sketch out a revised decision table that combines these two sets of conditions (Figure 6-25).

Figure 6-25
Compound decision table for cost percent

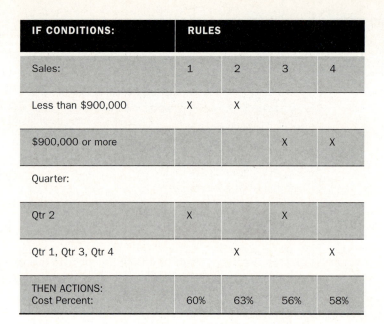

When several different conditions are specified in a decision table, a common practice is to list the different conditions, arranged as shown in Figure 6-25. This layout readily accommodates several different conditions that can occur in some combination. The **rules** indicate the occurrence of a particular combination of conditions. The "X" specifies the occurrence of that condition. For example, in Figure 6-25, Rule 1 is the combination of Sales less than $900,000 *and* the Qtr 2 of the plan where the Cost Percent value is 60%.

Instead of using nested IF functions for a more complex situation like this compound decision table, a better approach is to use an IF function for each rule. The *value_if_false* is set to zero. Then the IF functions for each rule are added together. This allows you to concentrate on each rule individually. The IF functions for Ann's compound decision table are shown in Figure 6-26. An AND function is used for each rule because both conditions must be satisfied. The OR function is used to select the appropriate quarter, while the NOT function provides an alternative to using the OR function with its three arguments.

Figure 6-26
IF functions for compound decision table

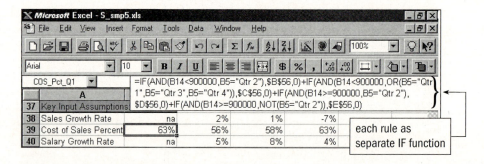

Ann considers the workbooks she has already created and decides that it would be easier to include this compound decision table in the workbook to which she added her first decision table.

To prepare for implementing the compound decision table:

1. Open the S_SMP5.xls workbook in the Tut06 folder.

2. Click the **Budget** tab and move the cell pointer to **A52** to view the current decision table.

3. Enter the conditions and Cost percent, as shown in Figure 6-27. Notice that the conditions and actions match those from the decision table in Figure 6-25. The text labels in B54:E55 are documentation that help you identify the conditions from the decision table.

Figure 6-27 ◀
Compound decision table values

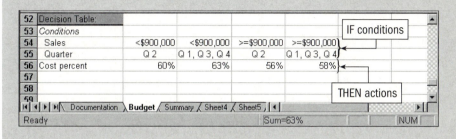

With her decision table set up, Ann is ready to use the logical function in determining the Cost of Sales Percent.

To include the compound decision table for the Cost percent, using logical functions:

1. Scroll the worksheet so that cell **A37** is in the upper-left corner of its window, then split the window horizontally below row 46. Scroll the bottom pane so that the decision table is visible.

2. Click **B39** in the top pane. Enter the formula
   = IF(AND(B14<900000,B5="Qtr 2"),$B$56,0)
   +IF(AND(B14<900000,OR(B5="Qtr 1",B5="Qtr 3",B5="Qtr 4")),$C$56,0)
   +IF(AND(B14>=900000,B5="Qtr 2"),$D$56,0)
   +IF(AND(B14>=900000,NOT(B5="Qtr 2")),$E$56,0)
   Type this as a continuous formula and let Excel continue on the next line automatically. This formula selects the desired Cost of Sales Percent from the Cost percent values in the decision table.

3. Copy the formula from cell **B39** into cells **C39:E39**.

4. Click **E39** to confirm that the desired formula with the compound decision table appears in that cell. See Figure 6-28.

Figure 6-28 ◀
IF and logical functions used to implement compound decision table

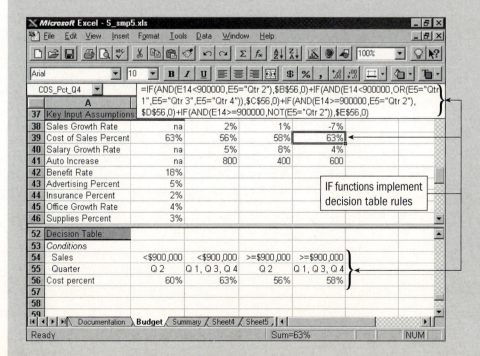

ADVEX 298 TUTORIAL 6 ANALYZING DATA AND PREPARING FORECASTS

5. Save this as the same S_SMP5.xls workbook.

Next, test the other entries in the decision table to make sure it works correctly.

6. Scroll the top pane so that the bottles of orange juice (row 7) and Sales (row 14) are visible, then scroll the bottom pane so that the Cost of Sales Percent (row 39) is visible.

7. Click **B7**, then enter **180,000**. Confirm that the correct Cost of Sales Percent of 60% is selected for Qtr 2 with Sales less than $900,000.

8. Close the workbook without saving it.

In Ann's formula, the NOT(B5="Qtr 2") function could have also been entered as the conditional expression (B5<>"Qtr 2"). Because the NOT function reverses a logical condition, you can often write an equivalent logical condition without the NOT function. This lets you select the method that is easiest for you to understand.

Travis and Bill feel that this alternative is the best representation of the possible change in the costs of producing Olympic Gold. They are ready to meet with Carmen to discuss these costs.

If you want to take a break and resume the tutorial at a later time, you can do so now. Exit Excel. If you are on a network, leave Windows running. If you are using your own computer, you may exit Windows and shut down the computer. When you resume the tutorial, place your Student Disk in the disk drive, launch Excel, then continue with the tutorial.

● ● ●

Forecasting with Regression Analysis[2]

Carmen and Travis want to extend the business plan for Sunny Morning Products to be a five-year plan. They have been discussing how they might determine the number of bottles of Olympic Gold that would be sold in each of the next five years. If they could determine this sales forecast, then they could use it as the base for expanding their business plan. First, they need to analyze past sales to create a representational model of sales in bottles. They are concerned only with forecasting the total number of bottles of Olympic Gold because they are confident that they will continue to sell 2.2 bottles of orange juice for each bottle of Thirst Quencher. Second, they can use the representational model to forecast future sales. The budget team at SMP can use the Excel Data Analysis Tools, an add-in program of custom Excel commands and features useful in doing this type of forecasting.

Regression analysis is a statistical technique that applies, or fits, a straight line to a series of historical or actual data values. With regression, you discover a straight line that best matches your actual or observed data, using a statistical procedure known as **least-squares analysis** that minimizes the distance between your observed, or actual, data and the calculated line, or estimated data. The linear regression produces an equation for a simple straight line that can be used as a representational model to project estimates of possible future results. The general equation of a simple linear regression is

$$Y = mX + b$$

where Y = dependent variable
X = independent variable
m = slope of straight line
b = intercept constant

---

[2] The following section covers advanced concepts. If the level of this material is not appropriate for your students, you can skip this section without loss in continuity of the text.

For their analysis, Carmen and Ann have identified annual sales in bottles as the dependent variable. This is the one they would like to project into the future. They will use time in years as the independent variable. So their general regression line equation is

BOTTLES = *m* * (YEAR) + *b*

where BOTTLES is the dependent variable and YEAR is the independent variable.

With Carmen's guidance, Ann compiles data on the number of bottles of Olympic Gold sold during the past 10 years (Figure 6-29). They will use this data to discover the slope (*m*) and the intercept (*b*) of a regression line, which they can then apply to forecast future sales.

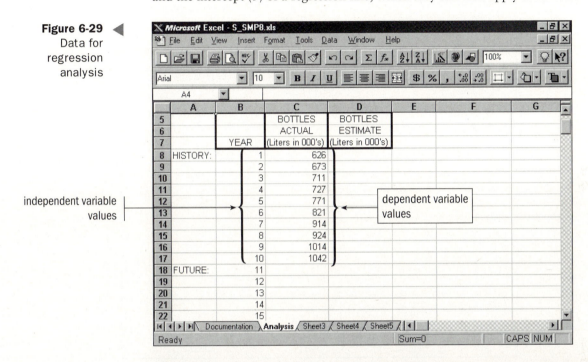

Figure 6-29 Data for regression analysis

Performing Regression Analysis

Carmen and Ann will analyze the actual data for yearly bottles shown in Figure 6-29 as a means of forecasting future bottles sold. In performing their analysis, they will fit a straight line to this data. A key question that they need to answer is how closely the fitted regression line matches their data. The **R-square value** is a statistical measure of how well the calculated straight line matches the observed data values. An R-square value of 1.00 means that all the observed data values are exactly on the straight line, whereas an R-square value of 0 indicates that it is not possible to fit a straight line to the observed data. Although Carmen and Ann understand that the R-square value of a regression analysis provides a measure of the fit of the straight line, they need a picture to show Travis how well the calculated, or estimated, regression line matches the actual data. Ann will produce a chart as part of this analysis so that she can review the quality of the line with Travis. Since Carmen and Travis are interested in a five-year projection, they will include that data in the initial data setup. You can organize your data in either rows or columns. Because several pairs of data values are typically used with regression analysis, the column arrangement often works best, and is the one used in this example.

Ann considers the steps that are necessary to carry out this regression analysis and creates a planning analysis sheet for her linear regression analysis (Figure 6-30).

ADVEX 300 TUTORIAL 6 ANALYZING DATA AND PREPARING FORECASTS

Figure 6-30 ◀

Ann's linear regression planning sheet

> Planning Analysis Sheet
>
> My goal:
>
> Use a linear regression business model to prepare a five-year forecast of the number of bottles of Olympic Gold that are expected to be sold based on the number of bottles sold during the past ten years
>
> What results do I want to see?
>
> Actual number of bottles sold for past ten years
>
> Summary output of linear regression analysis with slope (m), intercept (b), and R-square value
>
> Estimated number of bottles sold for past ten years based on linear regression formula
>
> Chart of actual and estimated data values to visually review the regression results
>
> Five-year forecast of bottles sold, using the linear regression equation
>
> Chart of actual data together with the five-year forecast to view the historical and anticipated future sales
>
> What information do I need?
>
> Actual number of bottles sold in thousands of liters for the past ten years
>
> What calculations will I perform?
>
> Linear regression analysis to find slope (m) and intercept (b)
> Estimate Bottles = m * Year + b [for past ten years
> and next five years]

Ann has already set up the worksheet with the data for the regression analysis. Take a look at this worksheet.

To retrieve the workbook file and review the setup of the data for the regression:

1. Open the C_SMP4.xls workbook and save it as S_SMP8.xls in the Tut06 folder.

2. Click the **Analysis** tab to view the worksheet with the sales data, then inspect the contents of the worksheet, observing that the input data values are all constants. See Figure 6-29, shown previously. The YEAR in column B is the independent variable, while the BOTTLES ACTUAL in column C is the dependent variable. You can arrange your data in either rows or columns, but columns is most effective for this situation.

Now you can execute the regression analysis on the data, using the Excel Data Analysis features that are provided by the Analysis ToolPak. This ToolPak add-in must be available before you calculate the regression.

FORECASTING WITH REGRESSION ANALYSIS **ADVEX 301**

To perform the regression analysis and display a summary of the results:

1. Scroll the worksheet so that cell A5 is in the upper-left corner and all the data is visible.

2. Click **Tools**, then click **Data Analysis** to display the Data Analysis dialog box. See Figure 6-31.

Figure 6-31
Data Analysis dialog box

Scroll list of available data analysis tools

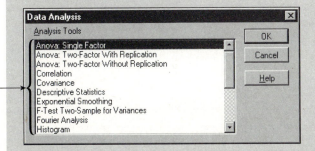

TROUBLE? If Data Analysis does not appear on the Tools menu, then the Analysis ToolPak Add-In is not available. Click Add-Ins to display the Add-Ins dialog box, check Analysis ToolPak, then click the OK button. Repeat Step 2. If the add-in is still not available, see your instructor or technical support person.

3. Scroll the list of Analysis Tools, then double-click **Regression** to display the Regression dialog box. See Figure 6-32. Drag the dialog box to the right so that the data in columns B and C is visible.

Figure 6-32
Regression dialog box

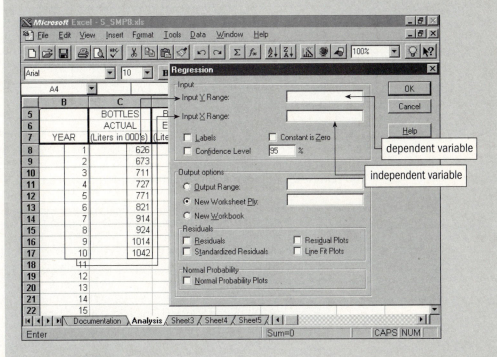

dependent variable

independent variable

4. The Input Y Range text box is active, so select the range **C8:C17** by using pointing. This specifies the dependent variable.

5. Click the **Input X Range** text box to make it active, then select the range **B8:B17** to specify the independent variable.

6. Select the **Output Range** option button to indicate that you want the output summary in the same worksheet as your data. This makes it convenient to refer to the calculated output values.

7. Click the **Output Range** text box to make it active and type **F5** as the cell that designates the upper-left corner of the output area for the summary.

8. Check the **Residual Plots** and **Line Fit Plots** check boxes to specify that you want to automatically produce these charts as part of the output summary.

9. Click the **OK** button to complete the specification of your regression and calculate the results, click **F7** to unselect the Summary Output range, then scroll the worksheet so that cell F7 is in the upper-left corner. See Figure 6-33.

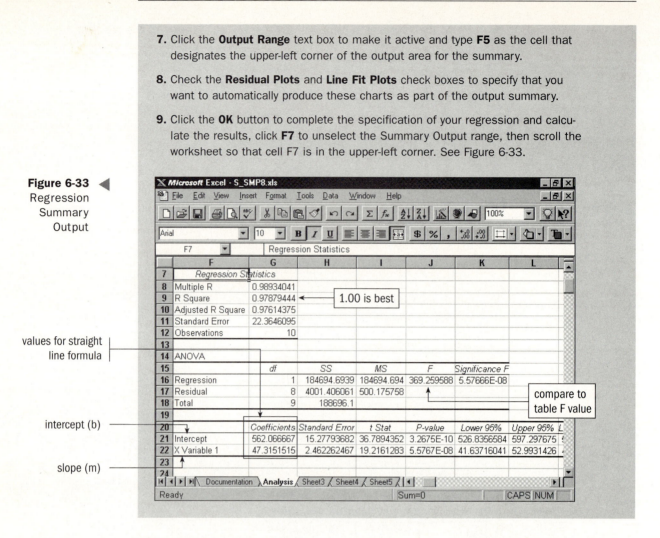

Figure 6-33
Regression Summary Output

The Intercept or constant (*b*) of 562.06 appears in cell G21, while the X Variable 1 or coefficient of 47.315 is the slope (*m*) of the line. The R Square of 0.97879444 indicates a very, very good match between the actual data and the calculated regression line, since 1.00 represents a perfect match and 0 indicates no match at all.

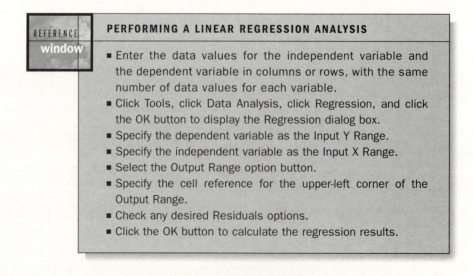

REFERENCE window

PERFORMING A LINEAR REGRESSION ANALYSIS

- Enter the data values for the independent variable and the dependent variable in columns or rows, with the same number of data values for each variable.
- Click Tools, click Data Analysis, click Regression, and click the OK button to display the Regression dialog box.
- Specify the dependent variable as the Input Y Range.
- Specify the independent variable as the Input X Range.
- Select the Output Range option button.
- Specify the cell reference for the upper-left corner of the Output Range.
- Check any desired Residuals options.
- Click the OK button to calculate the regression results.

In Figure 6-33, you can use the F statistic value of 369.259 to determine whether the slope, intercept, and R square may have occurred by chance. (If you conclude that they occurred by chance, then you should *not* use the regression equation to forecast future values.) You can do this by comparing the calculated F statistic to a value from a table of F-critical values that you can find in many statistics textbooks. For many situations, you can read the F-table using an Alpha value of 0.05 for the degrees of freedom (df) for your regression. In a statistical table, the degrees of freedom are often abbreviated as v1 and v2, where v1 is the Regression df and v2 is the Residual df in the Summary Output. The F-critical value for Alpha = .05, v1 = 1, and v2 = 8 is 5.32. If the calculated F value is greater than the table F value, you can conclude that the regression equation did *not* occur by chance. So, while the R-square value is a good quick test for the quality of the regression line and the one used in this tutorial, the F value provides a stronger test of the many assumptions that underlie a regression line and should be checked before using the regression line for important business decisions. However, the statistical foundation of the F test is beyond the scope of this book. For further discussion of regression assumptions and tests, see *Data Analysis with Microsoft Excel 5.0 for Windows*, Kenneth N. Berk and Patrick Carey, Course Technology Incorporated, 1995. Because the regression line successfully passes the F test, it is a good prediction model for Carmen and Travis to use in forecasting the number of bottles sold.

HELP DESK

Index

INTERPRETING LINEAR REGRESSION RESULTS

Double-click the Help button to display the Help Topics dialog box, then click the Index tab.

Keyword	**Topic**
regression, linear	LINEST
Regression tool	

EXCEL 5.0

Ann now needs to calculate the BOTTLES ESTIMATE column, using the Intercept (*b*) and the X Variable 1 slope (*m*) determined from the regression. This will allow her to chart the data for Travis to inspect. Calculate the BOTTLES ESTIMATE by using the regression equation.

To develop the formula for calculating the estimate of bottles sold during the actual years 1 through 10:

1. Scroll the worksheet so that cell B6 is in the upper-left corner and the independent variable values in column B are visible.

2. Click **D8** to select that cell for entering the formula for the estimated value.

3. Enter the formula **ROUND($G$22*B8+$G$21,0)** to calculate the estimated number of bottles. This uses the X Variable 1 slope from G22 and the Intercept from G21. Absolute references are used for the slope and the intercept so that this formula can be copied.

4. Copy the formula from **D8** into **D9:D17** for the other estimates, then click **D17** to unselect the copy range. See Figure 6-34.

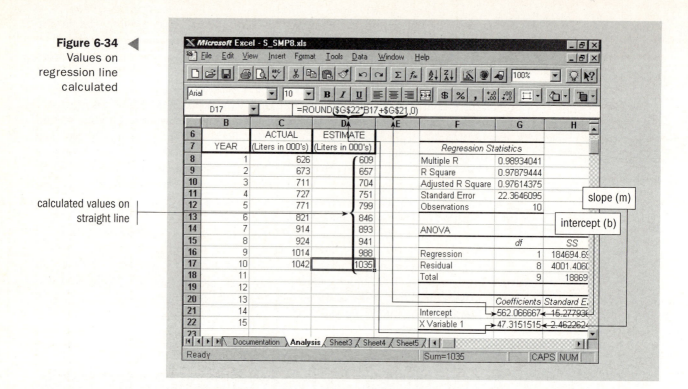

Figure 6-34
Values on regression line calculated

calculated values on straight line

The ROUND function is used here, rather than just changing the format to display integers, so that all values are calculated and displayed as integers. Also, these integer values are more readily used as data labels on a chart.

According to the planning sheet, Ann now needs to examine the chart that compares the BOTTLES ACTUAL to the BOTTLES ESTIMATE as a means of visually reviewing the quality of the regression line to forecast future sales. Look at this chart.

To examine the chart that compares the actual and estimated bottles sold for the past 10 years:

1. Scroll the worksheet window so that cell F25 is in the upper-left corner and the Residual Output is displayed. See Figure 6-35. The Predicted Y values are the same as those calculated for the BOTTLES ESTIMATE. Only constants appear in these cells, but they were calculated using the same formula you entered in column D. The Residuals values are the difference between the actual and predicted value for each observation. You could have created your own formula for these as well. Each residual is a measure of the distance of the calculated regression line estimates from the actual values. Values close to zero are most desirable.

Figure 6-35
Residual Output from regression

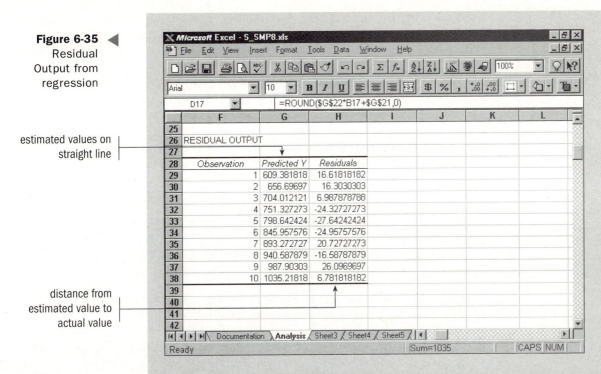

estimated values on straight line

distance from estimated value to actual value

2. Scroll the worksheet so that cell O4 is in the upper-left corner. This displays the two requested plots, the residuals and the line fit. Click the **X Variable 1 Line Fit Plot** chart to select it, then drag the bottom handle down to row 20 to enlarge the chart. See Figure 6-36. You could enhance the chart by changing the default titles to more meaningful names. However, this version of the chart is satisfactory for visually examining the match between the actual and estimate of bottles sold.

Figure 6-36
X Variable 1 Line Fit Plot

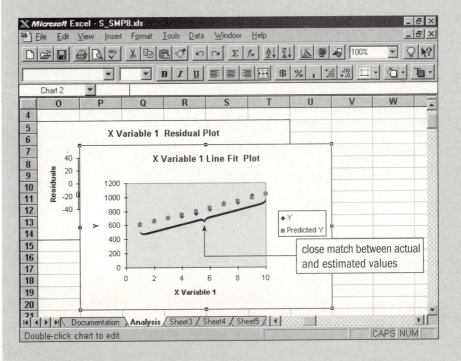

close match between actual and estimated values

TROUBLE? If only one chart is displayed, you did not select both the Residuals Plot and the Line Fit Plot in the Regression dialog box. Repeat the regression analysis, select both plots, and write the new results over the current results.

ADVEX 306 TUTORIAL 6 ANALYZING DATA AND PREPARING FORECASTS

The chart in Figure 6-36 shows the relationship between the BOTTLES ACTUAL and the BOTTLES ESTIMATE. Because the two lines closely match, Ann is convinced that the regression line provides a good representational model for projecting the future sales of Olympic Gold.

Now Ann is ready to calculate the forecast BOTTLES for years 11 through 15. These estimates of the future number of bottles sold are placed in the same column as the BOTTLES ACTUAL for the prior 10 years. This will allow Ann to develop a chart that is a *single line* that combines the 10 years of historical data with the 5-year forecast. Placing the data in the same column creates one contiguous data range for graphing as a single line. Enter the formulas for calculating the forecasted BOTTLES.

To calculate the BOTTLES for the five years of the forecast:

1. Scroll the worksheet window so that B6 is in the upper-left corner, then click **C18**, which is the location of the formula for the first year of the forecast.

2. Enter the formula **ROUND($G$22*B18+$G$21,0)** to calculate the forecasted number of bottles. Again, this uses the slope from G22 and the intercept from G21.

3. Copy the formula from **C18** into **C19:C22** for the other forecast years, then click **C22** to unselect the copy range. See Figure 6-37.

Figure 6-37
Forecasted values use regression line formula

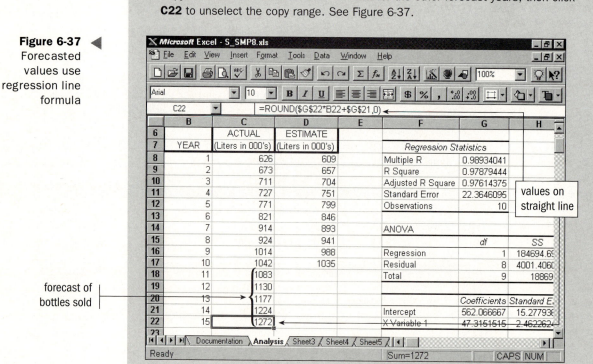

forecast of bottles sold

PREPARING A FORECAST USING A LINEAR REGRESSION FORMULA

- Perform the regression analysis and obtain the Summary Output results.
- Enter the data values for the independent variable for the forecast, using the same column or row arrangement used for the regression analysis.
- Enter the formula for calculating the first forecast dependent variable value; that is: (X Variable 1 coefficient * independent variable value) + Intercept coefficient.
- Apply absolute referencing to the X Variable 1 coefficient and the Intercept coefficient.
- Copy the formula for calculating the dependent variable value to the cells whose values you want to forecast.

You can conduct a more limited form of linear regression analysis with forecast data values using the INTERCEPT, SLOPE, and TREND functions. The INTERCEPT and SLOPE functions calculate these components of the regression line formula, while the TREND function calculates an estimated value from the regression formula. Also, when extending a data series using AutoFill, by using the right mouse button to extend the series, you can select a Linear Trend. However, these methods do *not* provide you with the regression statistics that should be reviewed to ensure that a valid relationship is being used, and that the relationship did not occur by chance.

With Ann's estimates placed in column B with the BOTTLES ACTUAL, the data is arranged for creating a chart with a single line. This permits Ann to develop the chart with the combined historical and forecast data. Prepare this chart and place it in a separate chart sheet.

To produce the chart combining actual and future bottles sold:

1. Select the range **B8:C22**, which contains the desired data for the chart.

2. Click **Insert**, point to **Chart**, then click **As New Sheet** to display the Chart Wizard - Step 1 of 5 dialog box with the desired range specified.

3. Click the **Next>** button to display the Chart Wizard - Step 2 of 5 dialog box, then click **XY (Scatter)** to select that chart type. An XY (Scatter) chart is usually the best to use with regression data because the x-axis data may not always be equal-interval data.

4. Click the **Next>** button to display the Chart Wizard - Step 3 of 5 dialog box, then click **2** to select a format that displays the data using both symbols and lines.

5. Click the **Next>** button to display the Chart Wizard - Step 4 of 5 dialog box. All the settings are appropriate for the desired chart. The Data Series columns should specify **Use First 1 Column(s) for X data**, and **Use First 0 Row(s) for Legend text**.

6. Click the **Next>** button to display the Chart Wizard - Step 5 of 5 dialog box, select the **No Add a Legend** option button, type **Actual and Forecast Sales** as the Chart Title, type **Year** as the Category (X) title, type **Bottles** as the Value (Y) title, then click the **Finish** button to complete the chart. See Figure 6-38.

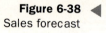
Figure 6-38
Sales forecast

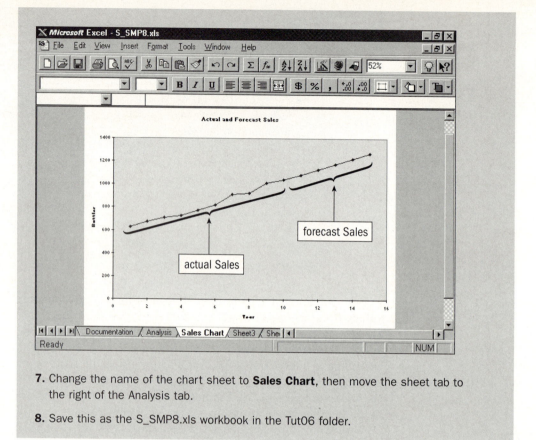

7. Change the name of the chart sheet to **Sales Chart**, then move the sheet tab to the right of the Analysis tab.

8. Save this as the S_SMP8.xls workbook in the Tut06 folder.

Ann's linear regression sales forecast is complete. She is ready to print the results.

To print the forecast analysis and chart:

1. If necessary, click the **Sales Chart** tab to select that chart sheet, then print the chart.

2. Click the **Analysis** tab to select that sheet, select the range **A1:G24**, and print it in the landscape orientation on a single page by using the necessary Page Setup options.

3. Click the **Save** button to re-save the workbook with these print settings, then close the workbook.

Ann and Carmen have completed the analysis they need to establish a linear representational model for preparing a forecast of the number of bottles of Olympic Gold that Sunny Morning Products expects to sell during the next five years.

Preparing a Growth Rate Forecast

Carmen and Ann selected a business model with a constant amount of increase each year (also known as a **linear change**) for their initial analysis. That is, the same increase amount is added to each prior year's estimated value to arrive at the next year's estimated value, as illustrated in Figure 6-39. After further discussion with Travis, they believe that a growth rate model, illustrated in Figure 6-40, may be a better representation. A **growth rate** is a compounded increase from year to year. Many business, economic, and biological situations are described by growth rates. These include salary increases, interest rates, inflation rates, and population increases. A comparison of a growth rate of 10 percent to a linear increase of $10 is illustrated in Figure 6-41. Notice that the linear increase is a straight line, whereas the growth rate is an upward-sloping curve. Least-squares regression analysis is performed on a straight line, not an upward-sloping growth curve that is *not* a straight line. In order to use least-squares regression analysis on data that is other than a straight line, you must change the curved data to a straight line. A number of different transformations can be performed, so the key question is: What is the most appropriate transformation for growth rate data that occurs in so many different business situations?

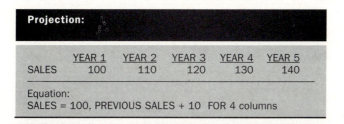

Figure 6-39
Constant amount (linear) change projection technique

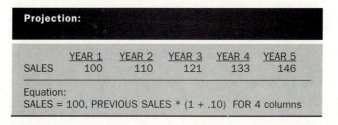

Figure 6-40
Constant growth rate projection technique

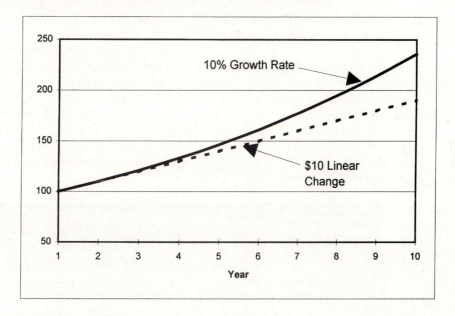

Figure 6-41
Growth Rate versus Linear Change

When a constant growth rate is plotted on a semi-logarithmic chart, that is, one with a linear x-axis scale and a logarithmic y-axis scale, a straight line is produced (Figure 6-42). The slope of this straight line is the growth rate. As a result, you can use regression analysis to find the straight line for the growth rate when the data for the dependent variable is transformed to a logarithmic scale.

Figure 6-42
Semi-logarithmic plot with straight line for constant growth rate

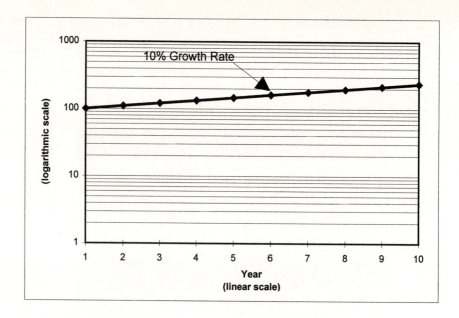

In order to obtain a growth rate representational model, Ann needs to use natural logarithms (base *e*, where the constant *e* is approximately 2.718282), since natural logarithms produce the appropriate compounding growth rate transformation. Changing a data value from its initial scalar value, such as 626, to a logarithm, such as 6.439, is known as doing a **transformation** on the data. The value 6.439 is the exponent of *e* in the formula $626 = e^{6.439}$. A **scalar value** is a number measured on a scale. Once Ann's data is transformed, the regression is performed on the natural logarithms of the bottles data, using the same least-squares procedure used previously to determine the line's slope and intercept for the linear regression. Then estimated values are determined by using the regression equation. Since these estimates are a natural logarithm, they must be converted back to the regular scalar data values of the BOTTLES ESTIMATE. In Excel, the LN and EXP functions provide Ann with an easy and convenient method of converting the initial bottles sold data to natural logarithms and then converting it back to the desired estimated bottles sold values. Ann carried out these operations to produce the worksheet shown in Figure 6-43.

Figure 6-43
Growth rate regression analysis

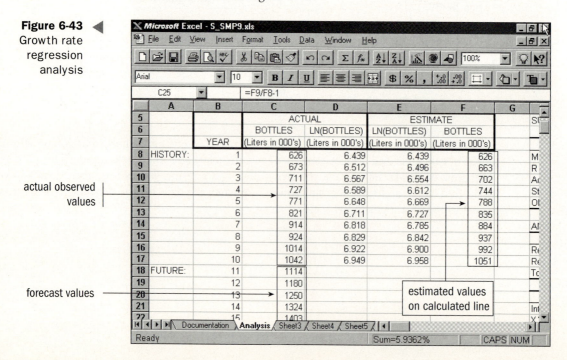

Ann performed the regression using YEAR in column B as the independent variable and LN(BOTTLES) in column D (the natural logarithm of the bottles sold) as the dependent variable. LN(BOTTLES) ESTIMATE in column E is calculated by using the regression equation Intercept constant (*b*) and X Variable 1 coefficient (*m*) in the same manner as for the linear analysis. The EXP function converts these natural logarithms to the ESTIMATED BOTTLES. The key equations are

Cell	Formula	Description
D8	LN(C8)	Log transformation
E8	$I$22*B8+$I$21	Regression line equation
F8	EXP(E8)	Scalar transformation
C25	(F9/F8) - 1	Growth rate equation

The equation in C25 is used to obtain the growth rate as a ratio between the BOTTLES ESTIMATE data values of two adjacent years: you can use any two years in the range. The value 1 is subtracted to obtain the growth rate from the multiplier applied from one time period to the next.

Ann prepared a planning analysis sheet for performing the regression analysis to determine the annual growth rate in the number of bottles sold (Figure 6-44).

Figure 6-44 ◀
Ann's growth rate regression planning analysis sheet

Planning Analysis Sheet

My goal:

Use a growth rate business model to prepare a five-year forecast of the number of bottles of Olympic Gold that are expected to be sold based on the number of bottles sold during the past ten years.

What results do I want to see?

Actual number of bottles sold for past ten years

Summary output of linear regression analysis with slope (m), intercept (b), and R-square value =

Estimated number of bottles sold for past ten years based on growth rate regression formula

Five-year forecast of bottles sold using the growth rate regression equation

What information do I need?

Actual number of bottles sold in thousands of liters for the past ten years

What calculations will I perform?

Transform linear Bottles Actual data to natural logarithms by using the LN function

Do linear regression analysis to find slope (m) and intercept (b)

Estimate LN(Bottles) = m * Year + b

Transform the natural log Bottles Estimate values to linear Bottles Estimate, using the EXP function

Growth rate = (Bottles Estimate [year n] / Bottles Estimate [year n-1]) - 1

{calculated for any two adjacent years}

Ann has already set up the worksheet with the data for the analysis. Retrieve the C_SMP5.xls workbook and examine its setup.

ADVEX 312 **TUTORIAL 6** ANALYZING DATA AND PREPARING FORECASTS

To review the setup of the worksheet data for the growth rate regression analysis:

1. Open the C_SMP5.xls workbook and save it as the S_SMP9.xls file in the Tut06 folder.

2. Click the **Analysis** tab to view the worksheet with the historical data and column titles for the regression analysis. See Figure 6-45.

Figure 6-45 ◀
Worksheet set up for growth rate regression analysis

independent variable values

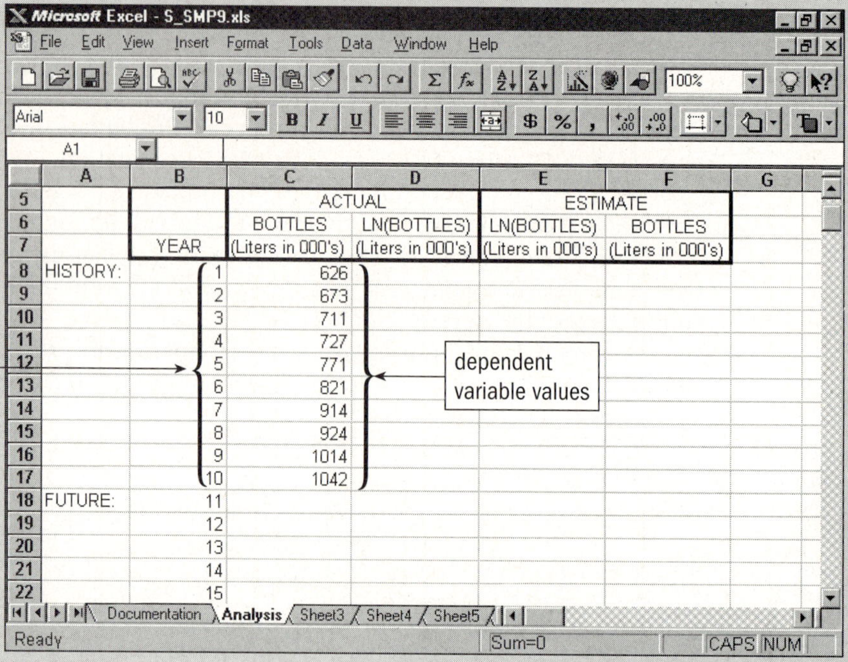

Now Ann can use the LN function on the input scalar data values to perform the natural logarithm transformation. In using least-squares regression analysis, you can use a number of different transformations when the best-fit model is something other than a straight line. The data is transformed to a straight-line representation so that the least-squares method can be used, because least-squares regression analysis can only be used to fit straight lines. A logarithmic transformation is only one of the many alternatives that you may learn about as you learn more about statistics and regression analysis. Add the LN function to the worksheet.

To transform the linear actual bottles sold to natural logarithms:

1. Scroll the worksheet so that cell B5 is in the upper-left corner and all the data is visible.

2. Click **D8**, then enter the formula **LN(C8)**. You can use pointing, and if desired, the Function Wizard.

3. Copy the formula from **D8** into **D9:D17** for the other years.

Next, carry out the least-squares regression on the transformed bottles sold data.

To perform the regression analysis:

1. Click **Tools**, then click **Data Analysis** to display the Data Analysis dialog box.

2. Scroll the list of Analysis Tools, then double-click **Regression** to display the Regression dialog box.

3. Complete the entries in the Regression dialog box as shown in Figure 6-46. In order to point to the Input Y Range, Input X Range, and Output Range cells, you can drag the dialog box to the right or down so that the cells are visible.

Figure 6-46 ◀ Entries for growth rate regression

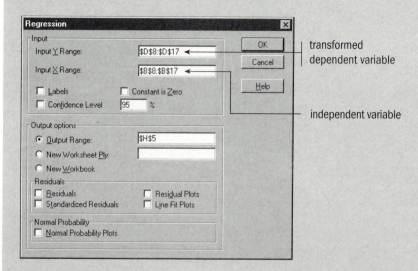

4. Click the **OK** button to complete the specification of the regression analysis and calculate the results, click **H7** to unselect the Summary Output range, then scroll the worksheet so that cell H7 is in the upper-left corner. See Figure 6-47. Note that this growth rate regression has an R-square of 0.9874, which is very close to 1 and indicates a very good match between the estimated and actual data.

Figure 6-47 ◀ Logarithmic transformation regression Summary Output

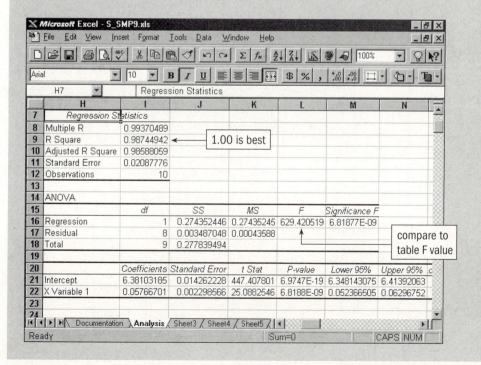

ADVEX 314 TUTORIAL 6 ANALYZING DATA AND PREPARING FORECASTS

PERFORMING A GROWTH RATE REGRESSION ANALYSIS

- Enter the data values for the independent variable and the dependent variable in columns or rows, with the same number of data values for each variable.
- Use the LN function to transform the dependent variable values to natural logarithm values in a separate column or row.
- Click Tools, click Data Analysis, click Regression, and click the OK button to display the Regression dialog box.
- Specify the dependent variable transformed with the LN function as the Input Y Range.
- Specify the independent variable as the Input X Range.
- Select the Output Range option button.
- Specify the cell reference for the upper-left corner of the Output Range.
- Check any desired Residuals options.
- Click the OK button to calculate the regression results.

Ann can now calculate the LN(BOTTLES) ESTIMATE by using the Intercept constant (*b*) and the X Variable 1 slope (*m*) determined from the regression analysis. That is, the straight-line equation is used to calculate the estimated number of bottles as a logarithm.

To calculate the LN(BOTTLES) ESTIMATE using the regression equation:

1. Scroll the worksheet so that cell B5 is in the upper-left corner and the independent variable values in column B are visible.

2. Click **E8** to make it the active cell for entering the formula for the estimated value.

3. Enter the formula **$I$22*B8+$I$21** to calculate the estimated number of bottles. The absolute references are included for copying the formula. Because these are logarithmic values that raise *e* to a power, you should *not* round them. Rounding would cause a significant error because you would be rounding a power of *e*.

4. Copy the formula from **E8** into **E9:E17** for the other estimates, then click **E17** to unselect the range. See Figure 6-48.

Figure 6-48
Estimated number of bottles as a logarithm

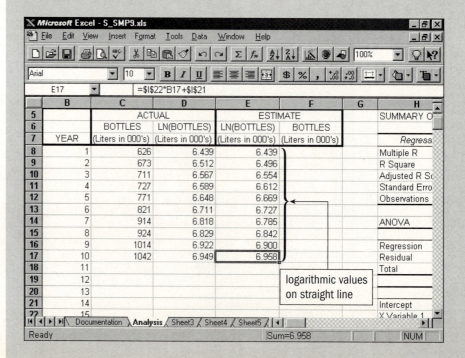

Next, transform the natural log values for the BOTTLES ESTIMATE to linear data values.

To transform the natural log bottles estimate to a linear scale:

1. Click **F8** to make it the active cell.

2. Enter the formula **EXP(E8)**, using pointing and the Function Wizard as desired.

3. Copy the formula from **F8** to **F9:F17** for the other years, then click **F17**. See Figure 6-49.

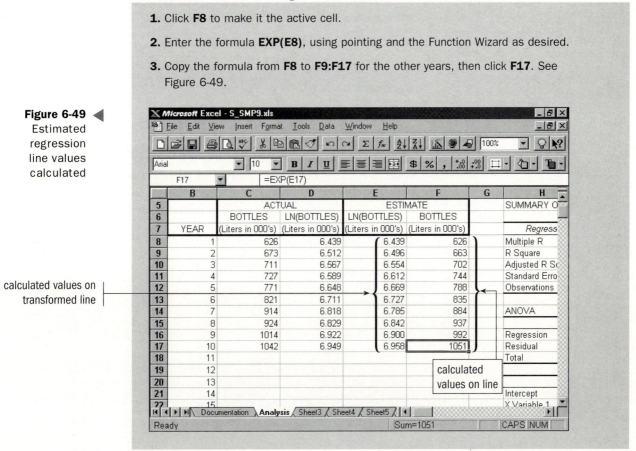

Figure 6-49 ◄ Estimated regression line values calculated

The formulas for carrying out the transformation of the growth rate regression appear as shown in Figure 6-50.

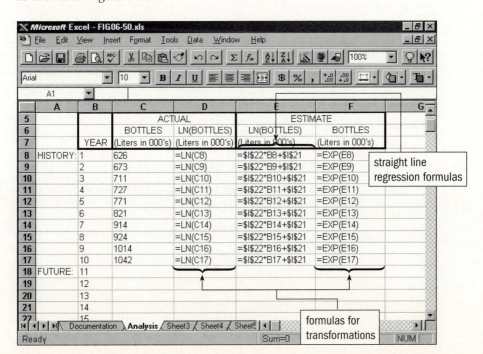

Figure 6-50 ◄ Equations for growth rate regression

Now calculate the growth rate by using the BOTTLES ESTIMATE in any two adjacent years. Enter the formula for this calculation.

To calculate the growth rate:

1. Click **C25** to select it as the active cell at a convenient location for calculating the growth rate.

2. Enter the formula **F9/F8–1** and format the cell as a percentage with four decimal places. The growth rate appears as 5.9362%.

FINDING THE GROWTH RATE

- Perform the regression analysis, using the dependent variable values transformed with the LN function, and obtain the Summary Output results.
- Enter the formula for calculating the logarithmic estimated value for the first dependent variable; that is: (X Variable 1 coefficient * independent variable value) + Intercept coefficient
- Apply absolute referencing to the X Variable 1 coefficient and the Intercept coefficient.
- Copy the formula for calculating the estimated values for the dependent variable to the other cells for the logarithmic estimated values.
- Use the EXP function to transform the logarithmic estimated values to their original linear scale.
- Enter a formula that calculates the growth rate by dividing the second estimated dependent variable value by the first estimated dependent variable value and then subtracting 1.

The growth rate model produces a higher R-square value, 0.9874, which indicates that this is a better "fit," or representation of the number of bottles sold relationship, than the linear increase model. This is frequently the situation with business data that is recorded from year to year. Carmen and Ann are convinced that the growth rate model is the better representation of this forecast of the bottles sold. Travis concurs with this assessment and supports their decision to use this growth rate of 5.9362 percent for their forecast of the number of bottles sold for the next five years.

To complete the growth rate analysis, Ann needs to calculate the forecast BOTTLES for years 11 through 15. As for the linear regression, these estimates are placed in the same column as the BOTTLES ACTUAL for the prior 10 years in the event that Ann decides to produce a chart that combines the 10 years of historical data with the 5-year forecast. Enter the formulas for calculating the forecasted BOTTLES.

To calculate the BOTTLES for the five years of the forecast:

1. Scroll the worksheet window so that B8 is in the upper-left corner, then click **C18**, which is the location of the formula for the first year of the forecast.

2. Enter the formula **F17*(1+C25)** to continue the forecast values from those found with the regression analysis. That is, you want to extend the forecast along the calculated regression line, and the next period's value is calculated from the prior period's value, which occurs in a growth rate formula.

3. Click **C19** and enter the formula **C18*(1+$C$25)**, which continues the forecast along the regression line. The absolute reference prepares the formula for copying it.

4. Copy the formula from **C19** into **C20:C22** for the other years of the forecast. See Figure 6-51.

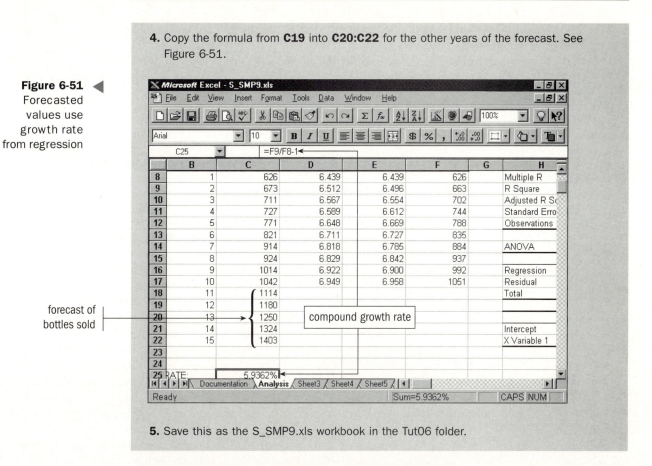

Figure 6-51
Forecasted values use growth rate from regression

5. Save this as the S_SMP9.xls workbook in the Tut06 folder.

Like a linear regression, a more limited form of a growth rate regression analysis to forecast data values can be conducted using the LOGEST and GROWTH functions. The LOGEST function calculates a value that is (1 + growth rate) and is in a form that can be used directly as the multiplication factor. The GROWTH function calculates the estimated values. Although the least-squares calculations still require the use of a logarithmic transformation, Excel does that automatically in calculating these functions. Also, when extending a data series using AutoFill, by using the right mouse button to extend the series, you can select a Growth Trend. As with the linear regression, these methods do not provide you with the regression statistics, such as the R-square, that should be reviewed to ensure that you are using a valid relationship. On the other hand, with functions, if you change an input data value, the regression is automatically recalculated by Excel, whereas you must re-do the Data Analysis commands to obtain a revised regression.

Ann's growth rate regression analysis and forecast is complete. She has the forecast for the next five years and is ready to print the results.

To print the growth rate analysis and forecast:

1. Click the **Analysis** tab to select that sheet, if necessary.

2. Select the range **A1:F25** and print it in the landscape orientation on a single page by using the appropriate Page Setup options.

3. Click the **Save** button to re-save the workbook with these print settings, then close the workbook.

Creating and Using a Template Workbook

A **template** is a pre-formatted workbook that contains the labels and formulas needed for analysis, but does not contain any data values, so you can use it with any set of data. Because the formulas, formatting, and macros are built into a template, you can focus on the data without having to develop the worksheet from scratch. Travis and Carmen want Ann to create a template for forecasting the number of bottles of Olympic Gold. Then when she needs to do another forecast, all she has to do is open the template and enter the necessary data. This also makes it easier for her to share the templates with Carmen and Travis so they can use the workbook to conduct analyses on their own.

A template is created like any other workbook, with the same planning, documentation, and testing. The primary difference is removing any unwanted test data before saving the workbook as a template. In Excel a template is saved with the .xlt extension rather than the .xls extension, to distinguish it as a template. Once a workbook is saved as a template, then you use it like any other workbook and Excel prevents you from inadvertently changing it.

When you create a template, it is a good idea to protect all the cells in the workbook except those that you want the user to be able to change. This helps to ensure that a formula isn't accidentally replaced by a value entered by the user.

Ann's regression analysis workbook can be set up as a template for use by Carmen, Travis, and others at SMP. This worksheet already has been built and tested, so all Ann needs to do is add the features to make it a shareable template.

To modify a previously built and tested workbook for use as a template:

1. Open the **S_SMP9.xls** workbook file in the Tut06 folder.

2. Click the **Documentation** tab, then edit the contents of cells **B5** and **B9**, as shown in Figure 6-52. Insert row **14** and enter the text as shown.

Figure 6-52
Revised Documentation sheet

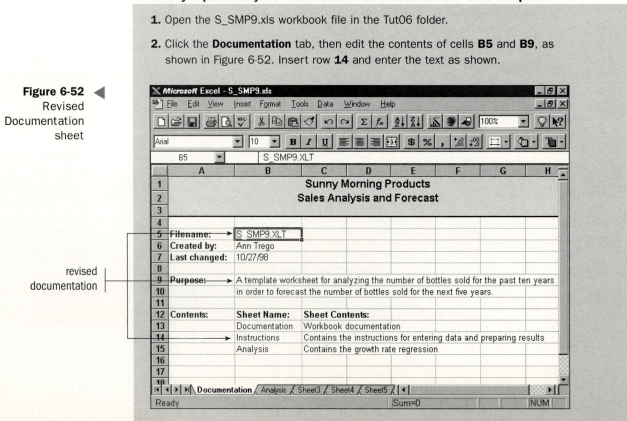

3. Click **B5**, then turn on protection for this sheet.

4. Create an Instructions sheet and place it between the Documentation sheet and the Analysis sheet. See Figure 6-53. So that the instruction step numbers appear with a period, type an apostrophe before each step number, for example **'1.** for Step 1. Spell check your instructions and make any necessary corrections.

Figure 6-53
Instructions sheet

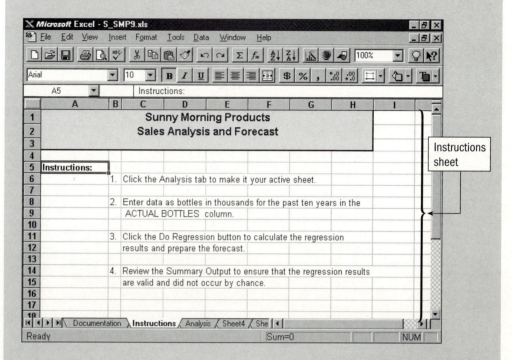

5. Click **A5** in the Instructions sheet, then turn on protection for that sheet.

6. Click the **Analysis** tab to make it the active sheet.

7. Select the nonadjacent ranges **C8:C17** and **H5:P24**, which contain the regression input data and calculated results, then press the **Delete** key to remove them from the worksheet. This removes the unwanted data from the template.

8. Right-click the selected **C8:C17** and **H5:P24** ranges, click **Format Cells**, click the **Protection tab**, unselect the **Locked** option button, then click the **OK** button so that these cells are not locked when protection is turned on. You need to lock both the cells for the input data values and those for the regression results.

9. Turn on protection for this sheet so that only the unlocked cells can be changed when using the template. To prevent changes to the cells of a worksheet, it is necessary to protect each worksheet individually. Protecting the workbook prevents deleting or moving sheets in the workbook, but not the cells of individual worksheets.

Now you are ready to test the protection of the worksheet and save it as a template.

To test the protection of a template:

1. Click **A8**, then type **10**. The Excel message box appears, indicating that you cannot change this locked cell. Click the **OK** button to return to Ready mode.

2. Hold down the **Ctrl** key and press the **Home** key to position the worksheet, click **C8** to position the cell pointer at this location for the user of the template, then click the **Documentation** tab to return to that sheet.

Now you are ready to save this as a template workbook.

To save the workbook as a template:

1. Click **File**, click **Save As** to display that dialog box, click the **Save as type** list arrow, click **Template** to select that file type, then select the **Tut06** folder on your Student Disk.

2. Click the **Options** button to display the Save Options dialog box, then check the **Read-Only Recommended** check box. This will cause a message to be displayed when the workbook is opened so that it cannot inadvertently be saved with unwanted data that would corrupt the template.

3. Click the **OK** button to return to the Save As dialog box, select the Tut06 folder on your Student Disk as the location for the file, click the **Save** button to save this as the S_SMP9.xlt template workbook, then close the workbook.

Click the OK button to save the workbook, then close it.

CREATING A TEMPLATE WORKBOOK

- Prepare and test the workbook that is to be made into a template.
- Select the cells that you want the template user to be able to change and unlock them.
- Remove any unwanted data from the template.
- Turn on protection so that text labels and formulas cannot be accidentally changed by the user.
- Click File, click Save As to display that dialog box, then select Template as the Save as type.
- Click the Options button, check Read-Only Recommended, then click the OK button.
- Select the folder where the template is to be saved, then click the Save button to finish saving the template with the .xlt extension.

When you open an .xlt template workbook, Excel recognizes the special purpose of this workbook and suggests that you open it as read-only so that any changes to its contents are *not* saved in the same file. **Read-only** means you can look at and use the workbook, but you cannot save the file using the *same* filename without responding to several questions that make sure you really want to replace the template. This prevents accidentally replacing the template file with a modified version of it.

Version 5.0 does not provide this option when you open a workbook. Instead, it modifies the workbook's filename. For example, Excel Version 5.0 would open the S_SMP9.xlt workbook as S_SMP91, with the 1 automatically appended to the filename so that the original template is not replaced.

You can use the read-only feature for opening an .xlt template workbook to distinguish the processing of a template workbook from any other Excel workbook. Open the template workbook to test the read-only feature.

To open an .xlt template workbook:

1. Click the **Open** button to display the Open dialog box, then click **S_SMP9.xlt** to select the desired template workbook.

2. Click the **Open** button; the Excel message box opens. See Figure 6-54. This message box allows you to open the file as read-only.

   Click the OK button; the workbook is opened without the message box and a 1 is appended to the filename displayed in the title bar, so it appears as S_SMP91.

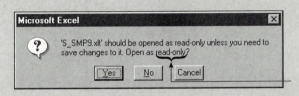

Figure 6-54 ◀ Message box for opening template as read-only

3. Click the **Yes** button, the workbook is opened, and Excel returns to Ready mode.

   The workbook is already available in Ready mode.

Now change the template workbook and attempt to save it.

To attempt to save a read-only template workbook:

1. Click the **Analysis** tab to display that sheet.

2. Enter **624** in cell C8.

3. Click the **Save** button; a warning message box opens, reminding you that the workbook is read-only. See Figure 6-55.

   The Save As dialog box opens with a suggested filename of S_SMP91.xls for saving the file.

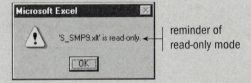

Figure 6-55 ◀ Warning message for read-only template

4. Click the **OK** button; the Save As dialog box opens without a value for the filename. In order to save the template, you must specify a filename. This feature prevents you from inadvertently changing a workbook that you have created as a template.

   Notice that the extension is automatically changed to .xls so that the workbook is not saved as a template unless you specifically change the file extension.

5. Click the **Cancel** button to return to Ready mode, then close the workbook without saving the changes.

Ann's template is nearly ready for distribution to Carmen and Travis. They could use it as an effective template as it is; however, Ann wants to add a macro that carries out the regression so that the template is even easier to use.

Using Macros with Template Workbooks

Ann has now created a template for forecasting the number of bottles of Olympic Gold. However, she realizes that Travis and Carmen are concerned with the quality of any regression they use for forecasting. Therefore they will want to see the Summary Output.

ADVEX 322 **TUTORIAL 6** ANALYZING DATA AND PREPARING FORECASTS

Each time, they will want to recalculate the regression and display a new summary; these activities need to be performed separately. This can be a tedious process. Ann decides that a macro would be the best way to modify the growth rate forecasting model so that Carmen or Travis can enter new data, then click a macro button and have Excel recalculate the regression results and forecast. She has already ensured (by using the Protection feature) that only new data values can be entered and no formulas can be revised.

In order to execute the regression calculations and place the Summary Output in the worksheet, the sheet must be unprotected. However, you want the sheet protected during data entry, prior to running the macro, and after the macro is executed. As a result, you need to turn protection off and on during the macro's execution. Ann does a walkthrough of the steps for her macro and writes out her macro planning sheet (Figure 6-56).

Figure 6-56 ◀
Ann's macro planning sheet for doing another regression analysis

Macro Planning Sheet

Action	Result
Click Tools, click Protection, click Unprotect	Turn off protection
Select H5:P24	Select the current Summary Output range
Press the Delete key	Remove the old summary so it can be replaced by the new summary without an error message
Click Tools, click Data Analysis, double-click Regression	Display the Regression dialog box
Type D8:D17 as the Y Range	Specify the dependent variable values
Type B8:B17 as the X Range	Specify the independent variable values
Select the Output Range option	Request the output in the current sheet
Type H5 as the Output Range	Specify the cell reference for the upper-left corner of the output
Click OK button	Finish regression specifications and calculate regression output
Hold down the Ctrl key and press the Home key	Unselect the Summary Output area and position the cell pointer at A1
Click Tools, click Protection, click Protect Sheet, click OK button	Turn on protection without a password

In preparation for creating the macro, the worksheet data is set up for doing a regression analysis. This avoids errors in fitting a straight line that would occur because the data was removed in creating Ann's template.

To prepare the worksheet for creating the macro:

1. Open the S_SMP9.xlt workbook so that you can add the macro to it.

2. Click the **Analysis** tab to display that worksheet.

3. Enter this data for the ACTUAL BOTTLES:

Year	Bottles	Year	Bottles
1	626	6	821
2	673	7	914
3	711	8	924
4	727	9	1014
5	771	10	1042

You need to have a set of data available when you do the regression in order to record the macro; otherwise, the #NUM! error values would prevent the calculation of the regression results.

With the worksheet set up with test data, record the macro that does the regression analysis.

To record the macro for calculating the regression:

1. Click **Tools**, point to **Record Macro**, click **Record New Macro** to display the Record New Macro dialog box, type **Regression** in the Macro Name text box, then click the **OK** button to begin recording the macro.

2. Click **Tools**, point to **Protection**, then click **Unprotect Sheet** to turn off protection. Protection needs to be turned off in order for the regression to be performed.

3. Select **H5:P24**, which contains the current Summary Output, then press the **Delete** key. You always want to remove the old summary before you place the new results in the same cells. If you don't do this, a message appears when the macro is executed, prompting you to approve writing over the prior results. Removing the old results avoids the message and allows you to calculate several regressions one after the other.

4. Click **Tools**, click **Data Analysis**, then scroll the Analysis Tools list and double-click **Regression** to display its dialog box.

5. Complete the Regression dialog box as shown in Figure 6-57 and click the **OK** button.

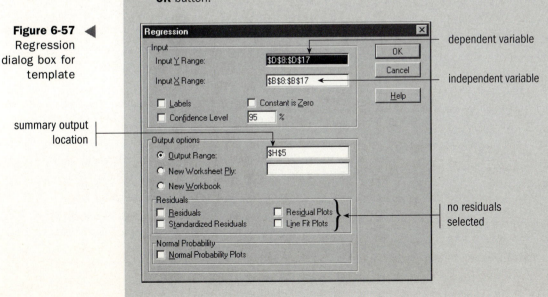

Figure 6-57 Regression dialog box for template

ADVEX 324 **TUTORIAL 6** ANALYZING DATA AND PREPARING FORECASTS

6. Hold down the **Ctrl** key and press the **Home** key to unselect the Summary Output area and position the cell pointer at A1.

7. Click **Tools**, point to **Protection**, click **Protect Sheet**, then click the **OK** button to turn on protection.

8. Click the **Stop Macro** button ■ to terminate recording the macro.

Next, place the macro button in the worksheet to execute the Regression macro once the new data is entered. You cannot place a macro button in a protected worksheet, so the protection needs to be turned off to do this. Because of this, you need to turn protection on and off several times as you build your template workbook. Although this takes some extra effort, remember that when the template is complete it is to be used by several associates, and then all this protection is handled automatically by the template. Add the macro button to the worksheet.

To create a macro button for executing the macro:

1. Turn off the worksheet protection.

2. Scroll the worksheet window so that cell H2 is visible. This is where you want the macro button to be placed.

3. Click the **Drawing** button to display that toolbar.

4. Click the **Create Button** button, draw the macro button on top of cell H2, click **Regression** to assign that macro name to the button, then click the **OK** button.

5. Select the default button name and change it to **Do Regression**. Click **G2** to finish naming the macro button, then close the Drawing toolbar.

6. Click the **Do Regression** button to test the operation of the macro.

The workbook revisions are complete, with the macro included for executing the regression analysis after new data is entered. Ann is finished creating and testing the template workbook for Carmen and Travis. All she needs to do now is save it.

To save the completed template workbook:

1. Unprotect the worksheet, since protection was turned on when you executed the macro and Excel automatically locked the cells for the Regression Summary range.

2. Delete the data values in cells **C8:C17**, then delete the regression **Summary Output** in cells **H5:P24**. Since this is a template, you don't want to save the old data and results in the template workbook.

3. Turn on protection so it will be enabled when the workbook is opened. This is necessary because it was turned off to remove the summary data from the worksheet.

4. Hold down the **Ctrl** key and press the **Home** key to position the worksheet, then click **C8** to position the cell pointer at that location for the user of the template.

   Click the Module1 tab and edit the macro by deleting the specific file reference [S_Smp91], which occurs three times in the REGRESS function. See Figure 6-58. You need to scroll to the right in order to find all three occurrences. This change is required because Excel automatically changes the filename for the template file, and the filename is then recorded in the macro. By removing the reference to the filename in the macro, you can then save the workbook with the desired filename and avoid the conflict with the filename selected by Excel.

EXCEL 5.0

Figure 6-58
Module1 macro sheet with filename reference for deletion

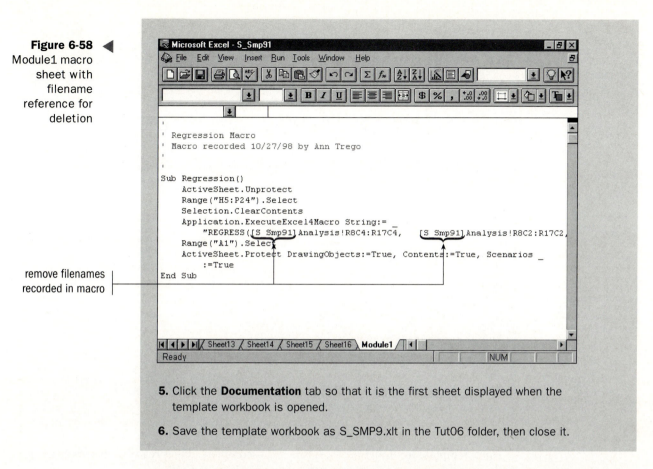

remove filenames recorded in macro

5. Click the **Documentation** tab so that it is the first sheet displayed when the template workbook is opened.

6. Save the template workbook as S_SMP9.xlt in the Tut06 folder, then close it.

Before Ann shares her regression analysis template with Carmen and Travis, she wants to test it to make sure it works correctly.

To test the template:

1. Open the S_SMP9.xlt workbook template in the Tut06 folder as read-only.

2. Click the **Analysis** tab.

3. Enter this data for the ACTUAL BOTTLES:

Year	Bottles	Year	Bottles
1	624	6	819
2	678	7	921
3	717	8	927
4	723	9	1018
5	764	10	1042

4. Click the **Do Regression** button to execute the macro.

5. Review the results. The growth rate should be 5.9522%. See Figure 6-59. Compare the R-square value to 1.0, then compare the calculated F to the table F value of 5.32. You should conclude that this is a good regression equation that can be used for forecasting sales.

Figure 6-59
Regression results with template

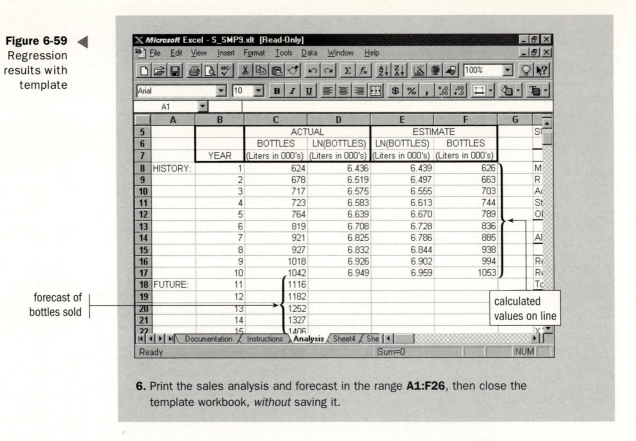

6. Print the sales analysis and forecast in the range **A1:F26**, then close the template workbook, *without* saving it.

Ann's template for doing the sales forecast is complete. She is ready to distribute copies of the template workbook files to her other associates at SMP.

Travis and his budget team have significantly fine-tuned the SMP Operating Budget for next year, and produced a forecast for sales over the next five years. They are ready to make any necessary changes to their Operating Budget to reflect their refined estimate of the number of bottles of Olympic Gold that Sunny Morning Products can expect to sell. Travis will use their forecast in planning production equipment and staffing expansions.

Tutorial Exercises

For Exercises 1 through 4, launch Excel and open the E_RUC1.xls workbook in the Tut06 folder and save it immediately as S_RUC1.xls. This workbook contains the prices of the vehicles in inventory at Ray's Used Cars. Ray Williams wants a summary of the prices for his current stock of automobiles. Prepare this analysis by completing the following tasks:

1. On the Prices sheet, enter appropriate functions in C44:C48 to calculate each of the summary items, as indicated by the labels in A44:A48.
2. Review the available statistical functions, then choose two additional functions for Ray's price summary. Place labels for these in A49 and A50. Enter the formulas with these functions in C49 and C50.
3. Save the workbook as S_RUC1.xls. Preview and print the Prices worksheet, making sure that your output fits on a single page. Close the workbook and save any print settings.
4. Write a paragraph describing why you selected the two additional functions.

For Exercises 5 through 7, launch Excel and open the E_FIG1.xls workbook in the Tut06 folder, and save it immediately as S_FIG1.xls. This workbook contains the annual year-end bonuses for the sales and marketing staff of the Falcon Industries Group (FIG) four marketing regions. Joseph Santoro, FIG's assistant marketing manager, laid out the

TUTORIAL EXERCISES **ADVEX 327**

basic worksheet with a key assumptions area that contains the cost percent and the bonus percent. Note that the cost of sales is equal to the sales multiplied by the cost percent. Finish Joseph's analysis by performing the following tasks:

5. Modify Joseph's Bonus worksheet to include the conditions in the decision table shown in Figure 6-60 for determining the bonus rate that is applied to the sales in each region. Use IF functions to implement this decision table. The bonus is then calculated by multiplying the gross profit by the bonus rate for each region. (*Hint:* Total Bonus = $14.9 million.)

Figure 6-60 ◀

IF CONDITIONS:	THEN ACTIONS:
Sales (in millions)	Bonus Percent
Less than $200	2.0%
$200 or more and Less than $400	4.0%
$400 or more	7.0%

6. Save this workbook as S_FIG1.xls. Preview and print the worksheet.
7. Display the formulas in the worksheet, using the Formula option in the View settings sheet in the Options dialog box. Select Options on the Tools menu to display this dialog box. Print the worksheet to confirm the use of the IF functions for the decision table implementation. Close the workbook without saving it.

For Exercises 8 through 14, launch Excel and open the E_HEP1.xls workbook in the Tut06 folder, then save it immediately as S_HEP1.xls. This workbook calculates the payroll for employees of Home Energy Products (HEP), a company that markets and installs insulation, thermal windows, and storm doors. Renee Salinas is responsible for preparing the weekly payroll report. Revise her worksheet by doing the following tasks:

8. Try to change the pay rate for Mike Phillips to $11.25. What happens when you attempt to make this change? Why can't you change the pay rate?
9. Try changing the regular hours worked for Brigid Rodriquez to 38. What happens when you attempt to make this change?
10. Turn off protection for the Payroll worksheet. The password is HEP. Repeat the change in Exercise 8.
11. Add the withholding tax table in Figure 6-61 to Renee's worksheet. Name the range that contains the table "TAX_TABLE."

ADVEX 328 **TUTORIAL 6** ANALYZING DATA AND PREPARING FORECASTS

Figure 6-61 ◀

Withholding Tax Table

Gross Pay	Federal Tax Rate	State Tax Rate
Less than $200	5%	0%
$200 or more and Less than $400	9%	2%
$400 or more and Less than $700	11%	5%
$700 or more and Less than $1,000	15%	6%
$1,000 or more	18%	8%

12. The Federal and State tax withheld is calculated by multiplying the selected tax rate from the table by the gross pay for each employee. Modify the worksheet to include the formulas that calculate taxes withheld. Use the VLOOKUP function to implement this decision table by referencing the table's range name. Save the worksheet as S_HEP1.xls. (*Hint:* Total Net Pay = $2,875.46.)

13. Preview and print the worksheet, including the decision table for the withholding tax. If your printer allows, print the report in the landscape mode.

14. Display the formulas in the worksheet, using the Formula option in the View settings sheet in the Options dialog box. Select Options on the Tools menu to display this dialog box. Print the worksheet to confirm the use of the VLOOKUP function for the decision table implementation. Close the workbook without saving it.

15. Explore a financial function of your choice, other than PMT and YIELD. Create a workbook that includes a Documentation sheet and a sheet with your financial function. Use individual cells to enter all your data, with appropriate labels identifying the data values. Use the function to calculate the desired result and include a label to identify this result. Write a paragraph explaining the analysis performed with your financial function. Save this as S_FUN1.xls. Preview and print each of your worksheets in the workbook.

16. Convert your workbook from Exercise 15 into a template workbook. Save the template as S_FUN1.xlt. Test the template. Print the worksheet with the financial function.

Case Problems

1. Product Pricing for Rollerblade, Inc.[3] Rollerblade, Inc. (RBI) introduced the first in-line skates just over a decade ago. In-line skates are now one of the fastest-growing segments of the sporting goods industry. In-line skates look something like a ski boot, with four or five wheels lined up in a row, rather than two in front and two in back, like traditional roller skates. RBI is preparing to introduce the all-new Bravoblade line of skates, which incorporates an innovative braking mechanism called Active Brake Technology (ABT). ABT allows a skater to brake simply by moving the braking foot forward with all wheels on the ground.

---

[3] Adapted from "Fast Track," *World Traveler*, November, 1993, pp. 21–26.

CASE PROBLEMS **ADVEX 329**

Noel Shadko, a product analyst in RBI's marketing department, is responsible for analyzing the expected operating results for the new Bravoblade line of skates. She prepared a Projected Statement of Operations to analyze next year's expected profitability of this product line. However, the number of skates sold, the price per pair of skates, and the manufacturing costs may vary. Noel wants to examine these conditions to better understand the risks associated with this new product rollout. Perform the following tasks to produce the information Noel wants:

1. Launch Excel and open the P_RBI1.xls workbook. This is the Projected Statement of Operations that Noel developed. Save the workbook as S_RBI1.xls and review its content.

2. The cost of goods sold table in Figure 6-62 reflects the lower costs experienced as the production volume increases. Add this lookup table to the workbook in a separate sheet named "Lookup Table," so it is isolated from the current report. Name the range that contains the table "Cost_Of_Goods" for reference in the formulas you use to implement this decision table. Include the appropriate formulas that calculate the Raw materials and the Direct labor costs for next year by selecting the correct cost percent from the lookup table for use in place of the constants currently used in these formulas. Save the worksheet as S_RBI2.xls. Then preview and print the worksheet, including the decision table for the cost of goods sold.

Figure 6-62 ◀

Cost of Goods Table		
Sales	Raw Material Percent of Sales	Direct Labor Percent of Sales
Less than $3,000,000	49%	24%
$3,000,000 or more and Less than $4,000,000	46%	21%
$4,000,000 or more and Less than $5,000,000	44%	19%
$5,000,000 or more and Less than $6,000,000	42%	17%
$6,000,000 or more	39%	16%

3. Design a test to validate the application of all the entries in the cost of goods table. Perform the test and write a paragraph describing your test. Close the workbook *without* saving it.

4. Open your S_RBI2.xls workbook as your starting point. Find the number of pairs of Bravoblades that need to be sold to just break even. Save the workbook as S_RBI3.xls, then preview and print the Projected Statement of Operations.

5. Reset the number of Skates sold to the initial value of 75,000 pairs, then find the Price per pair that RBI needs for break even. What is this price?

6. Formulate a goal-seeking question using the worksheet from Problem 2. Why is this goal seeking? Perform the goal-seeking analysis and print a report of the solution. Save this as the S_RBI4.xls file. Write a summary interpreting your goal-seeking results.

7. Develop and sketch another decision table for a different planning item that is used with the Projected Statement of Operations. Your sketch of the decision table should be similar to those illustrated in this tutorial. Describe the business situation represented by your decision table. Implement this decision table. Save it as the S_RBI4.xls file in the Tut06 folder. Preview and print the results.

2. Evaluating Stock Performance for Stagecoach Investments Ricardo Sussman is a rising star portfolio analyst at Stagecoach Investments. Ric uses the beta coefficient as a measure of relative performance of the stocks selected for inclusion in the portfolio he manages. A stock's beta is a number that compares the stock's return to those of a broadbased market index of stocks. When a line is plotted with the market index as the independent variable and an individual stock's return as the dependent variable, the beta is the slope of the line. A stock's return includes both its dividend yield and its price appreciation. A beta of 1.0 indicates that the returns of an individual stock are exactly the same as those for the market index. A beta of 0.5 indicates that the individual stock's return increases (or decreases) one half as fast as the market index. That is, a 10 percent increase in the market index return would result in a five percent increase in the return of an individual stock. On the other hand, for a stock with a beta of 2.0, a 10 percent increase in the market index is expected to produce a 20 percent increase in the return on the individual stock.

Although *The Value Line Investment Surveys* regularly compute and publish individual stock beta estimates, Ric has a special need to determine the beta for Ford Motor. His sense of the stock market in preparing special analyses such as this is a key factor in his success at Stagecoach. Ric collected the percentage rate of return data for both Ford Motor Company and the Standard and Poor's 500 Market Index. He entered this year-end data for each of the last 10 years in his P_SCI1.xls workbook in preparation for computing Ford Motor's beta. Finish his analysis by completing the following:

1. Launch Excel and open the worksheet P_SCI1.xls in the Tut06 folder. Immediately save the workbook as S_SCI1.xls.
2. Review Ric's Beta worksheet with the data for the percentage rate of return for Ford Motor and the S&P 500 Market Index.
3. Using the Market Index as the independent variable and the Ford Motor return as the dependent variable, perform a linear regression analysis.
4. Save this as the S_SCI2.xls workbook in the Tut06 folder. Print the results, containing both Ric's input data and your regression results. What is Ford Motor's beta? Using your pencil, circle it on your printout. (*Hint:* The beta is the slope of the regression line.)
5. Is there a good relationship between Ford Motor's return and the S&P Market Return? Why? Write down the summary results you used to reach this conclusion and explain your answer.
6. Using the Market Index as the independent variable, enter formulas to calculate the estimated, or predicted, percentage rate of return for Ford Motor by using the linear regression equation. That is, each data value of the Market Index is used to calculate a corresponding predicted rate of return for Ford Motor. Locate these predicted rates of return to the right of the Market Index column in your worksheet. On a separate chart sheet, prepare an XY chart of these results with the Market Index as the x-axis. The actual Ford Motor rates of return and the estimated Ford Motor rates of return are plotted on the y-axis. Select format 1 for the XY (Scatter) chart so that the points on the chart are not connected by a line. This will make the chart easier to view and interpret. Label the x-axis "Percentage Rate of Return (Market Index)" and the y-axis "Percentage Rate of Return (Ford Motor)." Place "Characteristic Line for Ford Motor" as the title at the top of the chart. Save this as S_SCI2.xls in the Tut06 folder, then print the chart.

Comprehensive Applications

The Comprehensive Applications in this tutorial continue from the preceding tutorials.

1. Production Planning for Oak World Furniture Sam Sherwood, production manager of Oak World, has analyzed the labor required to meet production requirements and developed the decision table in Figure 6-63.

Figure 6-63

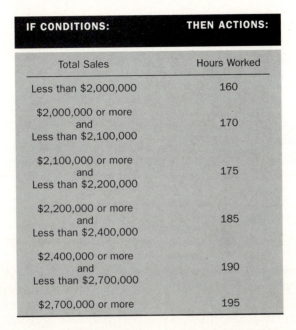

IF CONDITIONS:	THEN ACTIONS:
Total Sales	Hours Worked
Less than $2,000,000	160
$2,000,000 or more and Less than $2,100,000	170
$2,100,000 or more and Less than $2,200,000	175
$2,200,000 or more and Less than $2,400,000	185
$2,400,000 or more and Less than $2,700,000	190
$2,700,000 or more	195

Sam and Todd want you to modify their monthly plan for the next quarter to include this decision table for calculating the labor expense for each month. Do the following analyses to produce the information that Robin and Sam want so that they can gain a better understanding of their business:

1. Open your S_OWF1.xls workbook in the Tut02 folder, which contains the quarterly plan that is the "base case." If you did not create this worksheet in Tutorials 1 and 2, then see your instructor to receive the file you will need to complete this comprehensive application. Save this workbook in the Tut06 folder before you start your analysis.
2. The Hours Worked decision table in Figure 6-63 reflects the additional labor required to increase production. Add this decision table to the worksheet to determine the hours worked in *each* quarter.
3. Modify the formulas for calculating Labor so that they use the appropriate number of Hours Worked in *each* quarter.
4. Save this as the S_OWF2.xls workbook in the Tut06 folder. Print the Projected Statement of Operations, including the decision table area.
5. Test all the entries in the decision table by changing the tables sold in July. Write a paragraph describing your test and the results for each entry in the decision table. Replace the initial value of 1,060 as the number of tables sold in July.
6. Develop and sketch another decision table for use with the Projected Statement of Operations. Your sketch of the decision table should be similar to those illustrated in this tutorial. Describe the business situation represented by your decision table. Implement this decision table. Save the workbook as S_OWF3.xls in the Tut06 folder. Preview and print the results, including the decision table. If necessary, use page breaks to appropriately divide the printout.

ADVEX 332 TUTORIAL 6 ANALYZING DATA AND PREPARING FORECASTS

2. Market Planning for Valley Gas Alliance Martin Simmons, the marketing director at VGA, has collected the following data on the total gas sales during the past 10 years. He wants you to analyze this data and develop the best representational model for gas sales that can be used to forecast future gas sales.

Year	Gas Sales (in BCF)*	Year	Gas Sales (in BCF)*
1989	507	1994	636
1990	548	1995	686
1991	561	1996	701
1992	577	1997	712
1993	591	1998	769

* BCF = billions of cubic feet

Do the following analyses to produce the information that Martin wants for forecasting sales:

1. Launch Excel and create a new workbook.
2. Using Sheet 1, create and name a Documentation sheet for this analysis.
3. Using Sheet 2, create an Analysis sheet. Enter the text labels and Martin's data for this analysis. Use a page header and footer that include appropriate identifying information.
4. Martin wants you to perform a linear regression analysis on this data to consider as a forecast model that can be applied to future gas sales. Save this as the S_VGA1.xls workbook in the Tut06 folder. Print your analysis. Is this a "good" representational model? Why or why not?
5. To assist Amanda, Mark, and Dennis in understanding this linear representational model, Martin wants you to prepare a chart that compares the actual and predicted gas sales for the 10-year period. Label the axis and give the chart an appropriate title. Save this in the same S_VGA1.xls workbook, then print the chart. Does this confirm your answer to Problem 4? Why or why not?
6. Martin wants you to do another regression analysis to determine the growth rate of gas sales for the last 10 years. Recall that a growth rate regression analysis requires a logarithmic scale. Save this as the S_VGA2.xls workbook in the Tut06 folder. Print this analysis. Is this a "better" representational model than the one from Problem 4? Why or why not?
7. Using the best forecast model, prepare a five-year projection of gas sales. Save this as the S_VGA3.xls workbook in the Tut06 folder. Print this forecast with its actual data.
8. Create a chart, in a separate chart sheet, that shows the last 10 years of historical data combined with the five-year forecast. Use appropriate titles for the chart and each axis. Save this in the same S_VGA3.xls workbook, then print the chart.
9. Because Martin continually updates the gas sales forecast, start with the workbook from Problem 8 and create a template that he can use. Design the template so that Martin can input the year number for the first year of actual data and have all the other 14 years automatically calculated. Protect the worksheet so that Martin can only enter the beginning year and the gas sales for the last 10 years. Create a macro that calculates the regression summary for his review. Include macros that print the regression summary, the actual and forecast gas sales, and the chart. Assign each macro to a button so it's easy for him to use. Save this as the S_VGA4.xlt template workbook in the Tut06 folder.
10. Test the operation of the template workbook. Write a paragraph that describes your test procedure.
11. Prepare hardcopy documentation by printing each sheet in the workbook, including the one that contains your macros. Neatly organize these in a Sales Forecasting Manual that Martin can use to help him understand the operation of this template.

TUTORIAL 7

Consolidating Workbook Results

Providing Executive Information

OBJECTIVES

In this tutorial you will learn how to:

- Design multidimensional business models
- Consolidate multiple workbook files
- Link workbook files
- Create 3-D consolidation formulas
- Group workbooks for editing
- Tile workbook windows
- Create array range formulas
- Work with outline groups
- Audit worksheet formulas
- Expand consolidations that use 3-D formulas
- Create macros for consolidation

CASE

Sunny Morning Products

Because of the success of their operations in California, Sunny Morning Products' Board of Directors approved building a second plant in Florida to expand the production of Olympic Gold. Carmen, Travis, and Bill worked for several months finalizing the arrangements for this expansion. With each plant arranged as a separate business unit, the new organizational structure of Sunny Morning Products appears as shown in Figure 7-1.

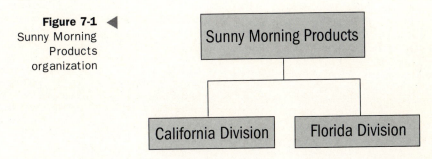

Figure 7-1
Sunny Morning Products organization

Ann is developing an executive information system for the senior management of Sunny Morning Products. An **executive information system**, or EIS, provides top management with the status of key factors critical to running a business, such as budgeted revenues, expenses, and profits. Ann is working with Carmen to determine what information is needed in the EIS. The two met earlier this week to discuss the requirements. Carmen explained that in addition to the EIS containing the correct information, it should summarize the corporate results in a way that she can examine quickly. The EIS should consolidate, or add, the results from the two divisions (California and Florida) to determine the performance of the company as a whole.

Introduction to Workbook Consolidation

Consolidation is the process of combining the results from several different worksheets or workbooks into one worksheet or workbook. A consolidation can provide a summary of data for an entire group of departments or divisions. For example, each individual workbook might contain the data for a separate business entity, such as a department or division. When you combine or consolidate this data into one workbook or worksheet, the summary provides an overall picture of the whole business entity.

Consolidation is one component of **multidimensional** worksheet modeling. Typically, business consolidation employs the three dimensions of (1) variables, planning items, or accounts, (2) time periods, and (3) business units, as illustrated in Figure 7-2. The worksheet is usually organized with the variables and time periods placed in the rows and columns of a worksheet, while the third dimension, business units, is composed of data from multiple worksheets. These worksheets can be arranged as individual Excel workbook files or as multiple worksheets within a single workbook. There are strengths and weaknesses to each design arrangement, with tradeoffs between the ease of doing the consolidation once and the effort required to set up the consolidation for repetitive updating. This tutorial explores the implementation of multidimensional modeling by using multiple worksheets for consolidation.

Figure 7-2
Multi-dimensional worksheet modeling

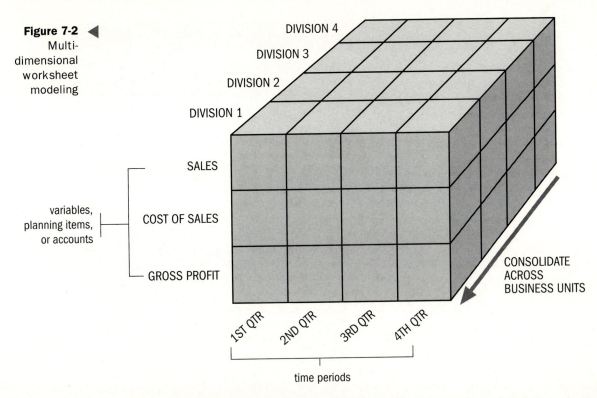

Because consolidation is such a common business activity, Excel provides several different methods of creating these summaries. These methods involve different arrangements of destination and source worksheets or workbooks and the use of unlinked or linked workbooks (Figure 7-3, on the following page). Several different procedures are examined in this tutorial.

Figure 7-3
Selected Excel consolidation methods

Consolidation Method	Description
By Position	A single, unlinked worksheet is used as the destination workbook to consolidate data from worksheets in individual source workbooks that have an identical physical layout.
With 3-D Formulas	SUM functions are used in a destination worksheet to consolidate data from other source worksheets in the same workbook. The detail source data is placed in separate worksheets in the workbook. The data in the source worksheets may be entered directly, copied, or obtained using links to other workbooks. Identical physical layouts facilitate the 3-D SUM function consolidation.
With Groups	Rows and/or columns are automatically inserted into a single destination worksheet and linked to the source workbooks. The consolidation is performed using SUM functions automatically created by Excel. The detail source data is placed in the same worksheet as the summary consolidated data.
By Category	A single, unlinked worksheet is used as the destination workbook to consolidate data from source worksheets in individual workbooks that have identical row and column names, without any duplicate names within each source worksheet.

Ann considers their requirements at SMP and develops her planning analysis sheet in preparation for completing the EIS (Figure 7-4). She brings her plan to Carmen for her approval. Carmen thinks all the critical information is present and gives Ann the go-ahead to create the EIS.

Figure 7-4
Ann's planning analysis sheet

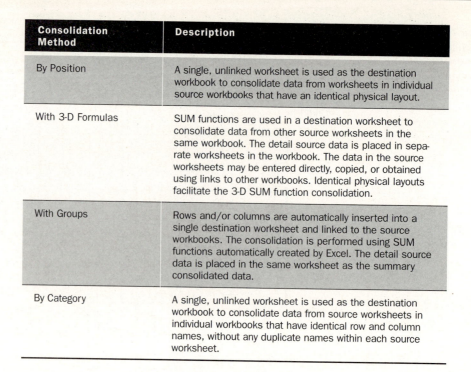

Planning Analysis Sheet

My goal:
Develop an EIS that displays critical information for review by senior management

What results do I want to see?
Current budgeted results for bottles sold, revenues, cost of sales, expenses, earnings, and return on sales by quarter summarized at the corporate level

What information do I need?
Current budgets from each division in a separate workbook file that uses an arrangement of data that is suitable for combining results to produce the corporate summary

What calculations will I perform?
Add the budgeted results for each division to yield the corporate summary

Based on her planning analysis sheet, Ann designs a workbook that presents the critical information thoroughly and clearly. Figure 7-5 shows Ann's corporate worksheet sketch for the EIS. This is the same layout Ann used previously for the Operating Budget, because she is summarizing the information prepared using that layout. You'll examine the formulas used later.

INTRODUCTION TO WORKBOOK CONSOLIDATION **ADVEX 337**

Figure 7-5 ◀
Ann's corporate
worksheet
layout

10/27/98

Sunny Morning Products
Corporate Consolidated Operating Budget

	Qtr 1	Qtr 2	Qtr 3	Qtr 4	Total
Bottles Sold					
Orange Juice	XXX,XXX	XXX,XXX	XXX,XXX	XXX,XXX	XXX,XXX
Thirst Quencher	XXX,XXX	XXX,XXX	XXX,XXX	XXX,XXX	XXX,XXX
Bottles	XXX,XXX	XXX,XXX	XXX,XXX	XXX,XXX	XXX,XXX
Revenues					
Orange Juice	XXX,XXX	XXX,XXX	XXX,XXX	XXX,XXX	XXX,XXX
Thirst Quencher	XXX,XXX	XXX,XXX	XXX,XXX	XXX,XXX	XXX,XXX
Sales	$XXX,XXX	$XXX,XXX	$XXX,XXX	$XXX,XXX	$XXX,XXX
Cost of Sales	XXX,XXX	XXX,XXX	XXX,XXX	XXX,XXX	XXX,XXX
Gross Profit	$XXX,XXX	$XXX,XXX	$XXX,XXX	$XXX,XXX	$XXX,XXX
Expenses					
Salaries	XXX,XXX	XXX,XXX	XXX,XXX	XXX,XXX	XXX,XXX
Benefits	XXX,XXX	XXX,XXX	XXX,XXX	XXX,XXX	XXX,XXX
Advertising	XXX,XXX	XXX,XXX	XXX,XXX	XXX,XXX	XXX,XXX
Automobiles	XXX,XXX	XXX,XXX	XXX,XXX	XXX,XXX	XXX,XXX
Insurance	XXX,XXX	XXX,XXX	XXX,XXX	XXX,XXX	XXX,XXX
Maintenance	XXX,XXX	XXX,XXX	XXX,XXX	XXX,XXX	XXX,XXX
Office Equipment	XXX,XXX	XXX,XXX	XXX,XXX	XXX,XXX	XXX,XXX
Supplies	XXX,XXX	XXX,XXX	XXX,XXX	XXX,XXX	XXX,XXX
Telephone	XXX,XXX	XXX,XXX	XXX,XXX	XXX,XXX	XXX,XXX
Utilities	XXX,XXX	XXX,XXX	XXX,XXX	XXX,XXX	XXX,XXX
Total Expenses	XXX,XXX	XXX,XXX	XXX,XXX	XXX,XXX	XXX,XXX
Earnings Before Tax	$XXX,XXX	$XXX,XXX	$XXX,XXX	$XXX,XXX	$XXX,XXX
Return On Sales	**XX.X%**	**XX.X%**	**XX.X%**	**XX.X%**	**XX.X%**

Knowing that she needs the same information from each plant, Ann decides to create a template workbook. As defined in Tutorial 6, a template is a workbook that already contains the labels and formulas needed for analysis and that can be readily used with other sets of data. It is easier to consolidate worksheets if the worksheets to be consolidated and the final worksheet are *exact images* of each other, as provided by Ann's templates. After Ann creates and saves a master division template workbook, she changes the title and saves it under a new filename for each division. She then sends the template workbook files to the California and Florida offices, where the data for the divisions is entered.

For SMP's organizational structure, consolidation is a two-step process. First Ann prepares the results for each business unit, then she adds together the individual business unit results to get the overall company result. As illustrated in Figure 7-6, a workbook containing a Budget worksheet is prepared for the California (C_SMP1CA.xls) and Florida (C_SMP1FL.xls) divisions. These results represent the source files and are then consolidated in the Corporate worksheet (C_SMP1.xls), or the destination file, to produce this aggregate summary.

Figure 7-6
Consolidation system overview

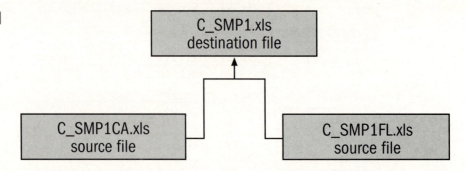

Using her planning analysis sheet, Ann prepares a data flow diagram (DFD) that depicts the overall plan for processing the operating budget consolidation (Figure 7-7). This helps Ann and Carmen understand their consolidation activities and explain them to other associates. The data flow diagram illustrates the flow of data for the interactions among the processes, workbook files, and external documents, such as data input notes and printed reports. The data flow diagram depicts the actions necessary for Ann to carry out the consolidation and produce meaningful, accurate reports of the operating budget for the SMP corporation. Figure 7-7 shows the use of the template workbook files in the preparation of the division and corporate reports, which goes beyond merely identifying the individual workbook files, as shown in Figure 7-6. As depicted in the DFD, budget preparation takes place in these two processes:

P.1–Prepare Division Budget. Data is obtained for each division and entered into the Budget worksheet in that division's workbook to produce the division's budget report. Workbook files (F.1 and F.2) containing the formulas and report layout are accessed in preparing these reports.

P.2–Prepare Corporate Budget. Data is consolidated from the individual divisions to generate the consolidated corporate report. A workbook file (F.3) provides the framework for carrying out the consolidation and producing the report.

Figure 7-7
Data flow diagram (DFD) of consolidation processing

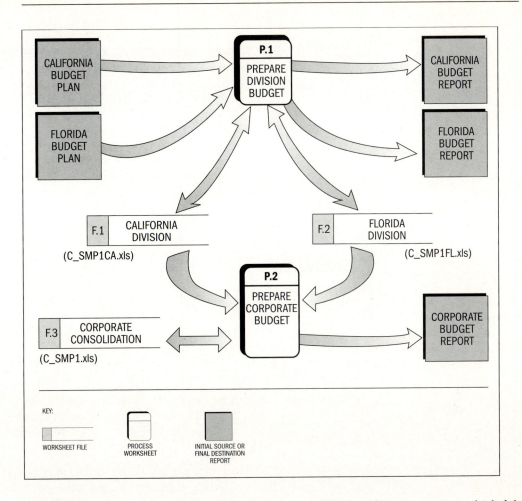

The DFD reflects a common practice in the consolidation of business units, which follows the two-step process of preparing results for individual business units and then consolidating them to obtain a corporate summary. If an organization had three levels rather than just two, this processing could be performed across each level. That is, departments could be consolidated into divisions, and then the divisions could be consolidated to the corporate level.

In this tutorial you will use Ann's template workbook and the workbooks from the California and Florida divisions to learn how to use Excel in consolidating worksheet results.

Retrieving the Workbooks

First you need to retrieve and examine the template workbook Ann prepared for summarizing the results from the files provided by the divisions.

To retrieve and examine the template workbook for the consolidation:

1. Launch Excel, and open Ann's workbook C_SMP1.xls in the Tut07 folder on your Student Disk. Immediately save this corporate template workbook as S_SMP1.xls in the Tut07 folder in case you want to restart the tutorial.

2. Click the **Corporate** tab to view that worksheet. See Figure 7-8.

Figure 7-8
Corporate worksheet template

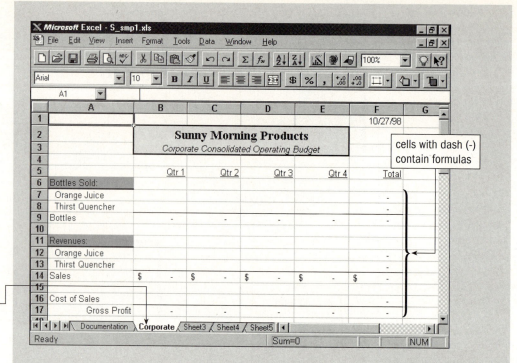

Corporate sheet for consolidation

Ann's template does not yet contain any data; remember, this is a template that will receive data from the division workbook files. Review Ann's template workbook and the formulas used to calculate Bottles, Sales, Gross Profit, Total Expenses, and Return On Sales.

3. Click **B9**. The SUM function in that cell sums the bottles of orange juice and Thirst Quencher sold. These values are zeros now because there is no data to sum.

4. Click **B14**. The SUM function in this cell sums the orange juice and Thirst Quencher revenues.

5. Click **B17**. The Gross Profit is calculated as before by subtracting the Cost of Sales from the Sales.

6. Press the **Page Down** key or scroll the worksheet to display the expenses. Inspect the formulas in cells B30, B32, and B34. The #DIV/0! error value appears in B34:F34 because the data in the worksheet is zeros.

Now examine the workbook that Ann received from the California division.

To examine the California division workbook:

1. Open the C_SMP1CA.xls workbook file located in the Tut07 folder on your Student Disk. Immediately save this as file S_SMP1CA.xls in case you want to restart the tutorial.

2. Click the **Budget** tab to view that sheet. See Figure 7-9. Note that the data values are calculated using the same formulas as those developed in Tutorial 2.

Figure 7-9
Budget for the California division

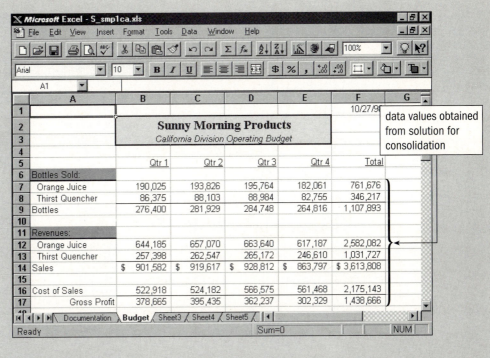

3. Click the **Name** box list arrow to display the list of defined range names, then click **Results**. This range encompasses the worksheet area containing the data to be consolidated from the California division into the corporate results. Ann set up this range when she created the division template.

Next, review the workbook for the Florida division.

To examine the Florida division workbook:

1. Open the C_SMP1FL.xls workbook file located in the Tut07 folder on your Student Disk. Immediately save this as file S_SMP1FL.xls in case you want to restart the tutorial.

2. Click the **Budget** tab to view that sheet. See Figure 7-10. Inspect the cell contents to verify the use of constant values and formulas. The formulas are the same as those for the California division; only the input data values are different.

Figure 7-10
Budget for Florida division

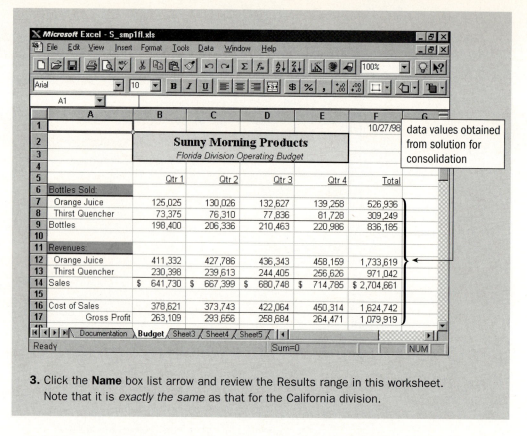

3. Click the **Name** box list arrow and review the Results range in this worksheet. Note that it is *exactly the same* as that for the California division.

Now that each division has submitted completed operating budget workbooks created using her template, Ann is ready to consolidate them into the Corporate worksheet.

Consolidating Multiple Workbook Files

When you consolidate worksheets in Excel, the data values from specified ranges (called **source areas**) are consolidated using a summary function. Most consolidations utilize the SUM function. However, if your business situation requires you to find the average, maximum, or minimum value for data being consolidated between workbooks, you can use the appropriate Excel function in your consolidation. The results of the consolidation are then displayed in a separate specified range, which for Ann is her Corporate worksheet. Because Ann wants the results from the source files for each division to be added to the Corporate worksheet, she will use the SUM function in performing the consolidation.

A consolidation can occur in one of two ways. You can consolidate data **by position**, which is the method to use when the source data in the source areas or files is arranged in the exact same order, and with the exact same labels, and the destination area or range also reflects this order. You perform a consolidation using the **by category** method when the data in the source areas or files does not reflect the same order, but does use the same labels. For example, you could not use "Orange Juice" for "Bottles Sold" and then again for "Revenues." Consolidation by category requires the use of *unique* row and column labels.

Ann will use the consolidation by position method to perform her consolidation of the operating budget data because the source files have been created using the template she provided to the California and Florida divisions, so the order and the labels for the data are the same.

When you perform a consolidation operation, you specify the range in the source files that will be combined and placed in the destination file. The placement of the cell pointer in the destination file designates the upper-left corner of the range where the incoming data will be located. *The consolidated data will replace the corresponding data values in the destination file, but leave the formulas in the destination file intact.*

CONSOLIDATING MULTIPLE WORKBOOK FILES **ADVEX 343**

HELP DESK

EXCEL 5.0

Index

CONSOLIDATING DATA

Double-click the Help button to display the Help Topics dialog box, then click the Index tab.

Keyword	Topic
consolidating data	Consolidate data
consolidating data	*overview of consolidating data*

Ann wants the results from the source files for each division to be added to the Corporate worksheet to produce the consolidated corporate results. Consolidate the data from the California and Florida divisions into the corporate workbook, using the consolidation by position method.

To consolidate data for the California division using the by position method:

1. Click **Window** to display the Window menu, then click **S_SMP1.xls** to make the corporate results worksheet the current worksheet. The other open workbook file-names are displayed on this menu. You do not need to close the workbook files for the California and Florida divisions before carrying out the consolidation.

   TROUBLE? If S_SMP1.xls does not appear on the Windows menu, the file is not open, and you need to open it now.

2. Press **Ctrl + Home** to position the cell pointer at cell A1 and display the upper-left corner of the worksheet. Remember that the division worksheets and the corporate results worksheet are *exact images* of each other, and the Results range in both the California and Florida division worksheets encompasses the range B7:E30.

3. Click **B7** to position the cell pointer at the upper-left corner of the range where the incoming data range from the source file will be located. This is critical because it establishes where the consolidated data is placed in the worksheet.

4. Click **Data**, then click **Consolidate** to display the Consolidate dialog box. Verify that SUM is the function used for the consolidation.

5. Click the **Browse** button to display the Browse dialog box, which is similar to the Open dialog box and allows you to select workbook files.

6. Double-click **S_SMP1CA.xls** in the Tut07 folder to select that file for the consolidation and display its name in the Reference text box of the Consolidate dialog box.

   You want to consolidate a range from the source file, not the entire worksheet.

7. Click to the right of the ! (exclamation mark) in the **Reference** text box, then type **Results** to reference that range. You could have also typed the cell references of the range, in this case B7:E30.

8. Click the **Add** button to specify the consolidation. The reference displays in the All References list box, which indicates all the files that are currently used in the consolidation. See Figure 7-11. Excel remembers these consolidation references and they stay in effect until you change them.

Figure 7-11
Consolidate dialog box

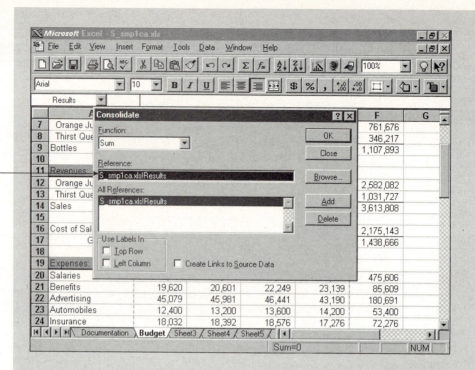

workbook and range specification

9. Click the **OK** button. The numeric values in the source file are added into the current worksheet.

10. Click **B7** to make it the active cell and unselect the range that was consolidated. The current worksheet now displays the results for the California division, as shown previously in Figure 7-9.

CONSOLIDATING DATA USING THE BY POSITION METHOD WITH A DATA RANGE

- Click the cell that is the upper-left corner of the range where you want data from the incoming source file located.
- Click Data, then click Consolidate to display the Consolidate dialog box.
- Click the Browse button to display the Browse dialog box.
- Click to the right of the ! (exclamation mark) in the source filename in the Reference text box, then type the range name or the cell references to specify the workbook and source range for the incoming data.
- Click the Add button to complete the consolidation reference.
- Click the OK button to replace the data values in the current worksheet with incoming consolidated data values.

The results of the California division have been successfully consolidated into the blank template workbook for the corporate results. Now consolidate the results for the Florida division.

To consolidate data for the Florida division:

1. Verify that the cell pointer is still located at **B7**, the upper-left corner of the range where the incoming source range from the Florida division file will be located.

CONSOLIDATING MULTIPLE WORKBOOK FILES   **ADVEX 345**

2. Click **Data**, then click **Consolidate** to display the Consolidate dialog box. Again, verify that SUM is the function used for the consolidation.

3. Click the **Browse** button to display the Browse dialog box for selecting the source workbook file.

4. Double-click **S_SMP1FL.xls** to select that file for the consolidation and display its name in the Reference text box.

5. Click to the right of the ! (exclamation mark) in the **Reference** text box, then type **Results** to specify that range.

6. Click the **Add** button to specify the consolidation. The reference appears in the All References list box, which indicates all the files that are currently used in the consolidation. See Figure 7-12.

Figure 7-12
Consolidate dialog box with all incoming data specified

both consolidation source workbooks specified

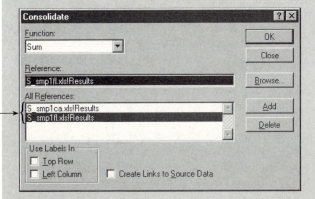

7. Click the **OK** button to add the numeric values in this source file into the current worksheet, then click **B7** to make it the active cell and unselect the range that was consolidated. The current worksheet now displays the corporate totals. See Figure 7-13.

Figure 7-13
Consolidated corporate results

consolidated data values as constants

results from consolidation

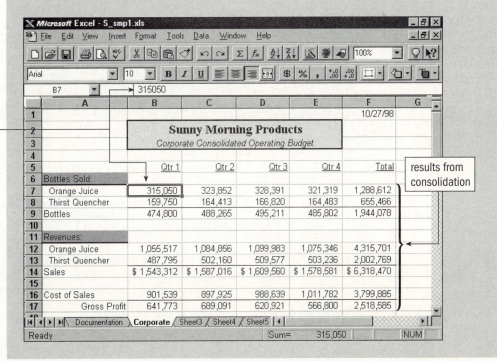

ADVEX 346 **TUTORIAL 7** CONSOLIDATING WORKBOOK RESULTS

Now that the division workbooks have been consolidated, take a look at the results.

To review the consolidated results:

1. Scroll down the worksheet window to examine the entire budget. Look at the contents of cells B7, B8, B9, B12, B13, and B14 to see how Excel brought in the consolidated constant data values, but did *not* replace the formulas with constant data values. Inspect several other cells to observe that only the data values were consolidated and that the formulas were *not* replaced by constant data values.

2. Press **Ctrl + Home** to return the cell pointer to cell A1 when you've finished examining the budget.

3. Save the worksheet as the S_SMP1.xls workbook in the Tut07 folder, then preview and print the Corporate worksheet. Your report should look similar to the one in Figure 7-5.

Ann has the EIS consolidated report that Carmen wants and she sets up a meeting to review it with her. During their meeting, Carmen reminds Ann that some of the data from the California division may be changing, and to contact Bill Hodges to confirm that the data in the consolidation report is accurate.

Updating Consolidated Results

Bill phones Ann to advise her that the California workbook he sent her needs to be revised to reflect the possibility of a last-minute expected increase in the number of bottles of orange juice sold to a total of 200,025 in the first quarter. Bill wants the new value entered in California's Budget sheet, while Ann needs the revision included in the corporate consolidation. Revise the California budget and then update the consolidation.

To revise source data values and update a consolidation:

1. Click **Window**, then click **S_SMP1CA.xls** to activate that workbook.

2. Scroll the window as necessary, then click **B7** to make it the active cell.

3. Enter **200,025** as the new number of bottles of orange juice sold in the first quarter, then observe the revised calculation of the worksheet's results.

4. Click **Window**, then click **S_SMP1.xls** to switch to that workbook and make it the active window. Note that the value in B7 of 315,050 was *not* changed when the value was revised in the California workbook.

The consolidation needs to be repeated in order to update the Corporate results.

5. Click **B7** to make it the active cell for the incoming consolidation.

6. Click **Data**, then click **Consolidate** to display the Consolidate dialog box. Note that the incoming ranges specified in the All References text box are the ones you previously specified.

7. Click the **OK** button to repeat the consolidation and replace the old data values with the new results. Click **B7** to make it the active cell and unselect the consolidation range.

8. Save the worksheet as the S_SMP1.xls workbook in the Tut07 folder, then preview and print the Corporate worksheet. Close all the workbooks without saving them again. Bill's last-minute change is not saved because Carmen wants him to verify this change before it is included in the copy of the report for the management committee.

Using this method of consolidation, Ann retains *control* over *when* the results from Bill are included in the corporate summary. If Ann is in the middle of an analysis for Carmen, she may *not* want the results to be immediately and automatically included in the corporate summary. On the other hand, using this method means that Ann needs to remember to manually repeat the consolidation when a revised workbook is received from one of the divisions. You should consider this control capability when deciding on the most appropriate way to perform a consolidation.

With the update completed, Ann is now ready to review the revised consolidation with Carmen.

If you want to take a break and resume the tutorial at a later time, you can do so now. Exit Excel. If you are on a network, leave Windows running. If you are using your own computer, you may exit Windows and shut down the computer. When you resume the tutorial, place your Student Disk in the disk drive, launch Excel, then continue with the tutorial.

● ● ●

Linking Workbook Files

Ann sits down with Carmen to review the revised consolidation processing. Carmen is pleased with the worksheet and her ability to review the results directly on the computer or from a printed report. Although she likes the control this method provides, she would like Ann to consider a way to streamline the inclusion of the changes Bill phoned in for the California division. She asks Ann if there is some way to set up the EIS worksheet so that when she receives updated workbooks from the divisions, the results would automatically appear in the corporate results workbook. Then, whenever Carmen is using the EIS, she knows that it will contain the most current information.

Ann reviews her design. She still wants to implement the same design; it is just that when updated division workbook files are stored on Carmen's computer, the corporate results need to be immediately and automatically available for her. Ann decides to link the division workbook files to the corporate workbook file. A **link** is a dynamic connection between a *source* and a *destination* workbook. If you edit the source workbook, your changes automatically appear in the destination workbook, because Dynamic Data Exchange (DDE) shares the information between the workbook files. You establish links by using **linking formulas** in the *destination* workbook file that refer to cells in the *source* workbook file. Linking formulas include a file reference as part of the formula. The file reference can refer to an open workbook file or to a file on disk. A formula with a file reference can automatically obtain the value from the linked workbook when you open the file.

Consolidating with 3-D Formulas

Ann created a multiple-sheet file that she set up for linking the data from the divisions. This file has three sheets that she named Corporate, California, and Florida. This allows Carmen to have all the results in one file, so she can more easily examine and compare the corporate results with those for the divisions. With this arrangement, the consolidation is performed by using SUM functions in the Corporate sheet. These functions add the results from the California and Florida sheets in the third dimension across the sheets of these business units, as illustrated previously in Figure 7-2. A **3-D formula** is used, because the SUM function adds *across* the sheets. The syntax of a SUM function with a 3-D formula is

=SUM(sheet-name-1**:**sheet-name-2**!**cell-reference)

Sheet-name specifies the beginning and end of the third dimension of the range of cells for the front-to-back, across-sheet orientation of the range. *Sheet-name-1* indicates the first sheet for the range, and *sheet-name-2* specifies the last sheet for the range. *Cell-reference*

specifies the cell to be summed in each of the sheets in the sheet dimension of the cell range. This is usually a single cell, but could be a range. For a consolidation, the common practice is to add a single cell from each of the sheets in the sheet dimension of the range.

The data in these division sheets is obtained from their respective, individual workbook files using linking formulas. Determine how the file-linking feature can be used with the EIS by reviewing the SUM functions in the Corporate sheet of the new multisheet workbook Ann has created.

To review a consolidation sheet with SUM functions:

1. Open the C_SMP2.xls workbook in the Tut07 folder and immediately save it as S_SMP2.xls in case you want to restart the tutorial. This workbook contains the four sheets Documentation, Corporate, California, and Florida.

2. Review this multiple-sheet file. Notice that Ann has already set up the division sheets with the desired labels and that the consolidation in the Corporate sheet is performed using the SUM function. The SUM functions have been entered for all the planning items except for the expenses.

   Next, Ann enters the remaining SUM functions for the expense planning items.

3. Click the **Corporate** tab to activate that sheet, if necessary.

4. Scroll the worksheet so that A19 is in the upper-left corner of the window.

5. Click **B20** to make it the active cell for entering the SUM function.

6. Press **=** to start the formula, then type **SUM(** to begin the function.

7. Click the **California** tab, scroll the worksheet, then click **B20** to specify that cell.

8. Shift-click the **Florida** tab; that is, hold down the Shift key while you click the worksheet tab. This specifies the range California:Florida!B20, which goes across the worksheets in the third dimension.

9. Press the **Enter** key to complete the specification of the SUM function for the consolidation and return to the Corporate sheet, then click **B20** to make it the active cell. Note the 3-D SUM function formula. See Figure 7-14.

Figure 7-14
3-D SUM function adds across worksheet

3-D SUM function

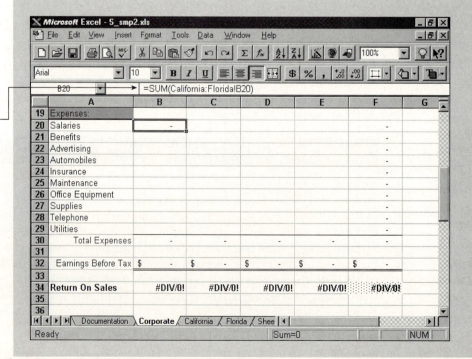

LINKING WORKBOOK FILES · **ADVEX 349**

HELP DESK

EXCEL 5.0

Index

ENTERING A REFERENCE TO ANOTHER WORKSHEET

Double-click the Help button to display the Help Topics dialog box, then click the Index tab.

Keyword	**Topic**
range of cells, references to	Enter a reference to another worksheet
range, sheet	*Enter a reference to a range of worksheets in a workbook*

Although you could enter each of the other SUM function formulas in the Corporate sheet in the same manner, you can also copy this formula, with its relative reference to the other cells in the Corporate sheet.

To copy a 3-D SUM function formula for an across-the-sheets 3-D consolidation:

1. Copy the formula from **B20** into **C20:E20** for the Salaries expense, using the fill handle. The relative references for the cell are revised, while the sheet references remain unchanged.

2. Copy the formulas from **B20:E20** into **B21:E29**. When the formula is copied into B29:E29, the underline border is removed from the cells in row 29 and needs to be replaced.

3. Click **F29** to make it the active cell with the desired cell format, then click the **Format Painter** button to select the format.

4. Select **B29:E29** to place the selected format in those cells. The SUM function formulas are complete for consolidating the data from the California and Florida sheets in this workbook.

5. Press **Ctrl + Home** to make A1 the active cell.

6. Save this as the S_SMP2.xls workbook in the Tut07 folder.

Using the Group Edit Mode

As Ann built the consolidation formulas and referenced the California and Florida sheets, she noticed that the column widths were not set like those in the Corporate sheet and that the formulas for the Earnings Before Tax in columns C, D, and E were missing. She needs to fix the column widths and these formulas in both sheets. By using the Group edit mode, Ann can make these changes in both of her worksheets at the same time. The **Group edit mode** allows you to enter formulas, set column widths, and make other worksheet revisions that *affect all the worksheets in a group at one time*. You turn on the Group edit mode by clicking the first sheet to select it and then shift-clicking the last sheet to select all the sheets between them for doing the group edit. Revise the California and Florida sheets using the Group edit mode.

To use the Group edit mode in creating and revising worksheets:

1. Click the **California** tab to select that worksheet.

2. Shift-click the **Florida** tab to select that worksheet and turn on the Group edit mode, so that "[Group]" is displayed on the title bar. See Figure 7-15. The California sheet remains displayed because it was selected first. If there were any sheets between the California and Florida sheet, these would also be selected.

Figure 7-15
Group edit mode turned on

Group edit mode indicator

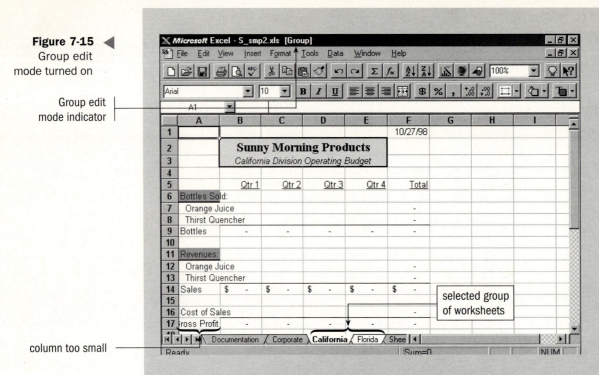

selected group of worksheets

column too small

3. Set the width of column **A** to **18** and of columns **B:F** to **11**.

4. Copy the formula from **B32** into **C32:E32**.

5. Right-click the **California** tab to display the shortcut menu, then click **Ungroup Sheets** to turn off the Group edit mode.

6. Click the **Florida** tab to view that worksheet and note that the changes made in the California sheet were also made to that sheet. See Figure 7-16.

Figure 7-16
Changes made to both sheets simultaneously

Group edit mode turned off

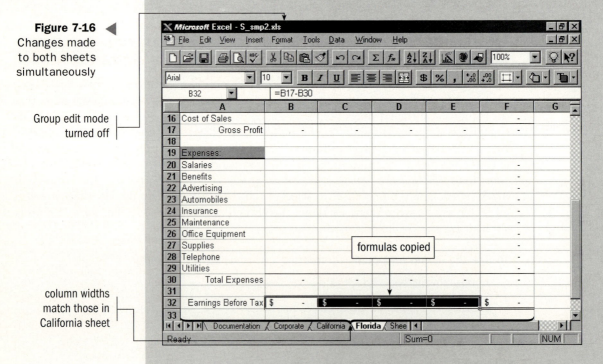

formulas copied

column widths match those in California sheet

7. Click the **Corporate** tab, then save this as the S_SMP2.xls workbook in the Tut07 folder.

| REFERENCE window | USING GROUP EDITING ACROSS WORKSHEETS
■ Click the sheet tab of the first worksheet in the group.
■ Shift-click the sheet tab of the last worksheet in the group.
■ Enter text, data, or formulas, or make changes to any sheet in the group; all the sheets are revised simultaneously.
■ Right-click the sheet tab of any sheet in the group to display the shortcut menu, then click Ungroup Sheets to turn off the Group edit mode. |

Ann has the individual division sheets set up as she wants them and is ready to obtain the data for these sheets. The Group edit mode allowed her to readily change these sheets, knowing that the changes would be identical in both.

Using Formulas to Link Workbooks

Ann's Corporate sheet is complete and ready for consolidating the division data. The next activity is to link the division worksheets in this workbook with the Budget worksheets in the individual division workbooks. With a linking formula, a cell in one workbook is linked to a cell in another workbook. As a result, you can link any source cell to any destination cell and the source and destination worksheets do *not* need to be exact images, as is required when you use the Data Consolidate command. You can create the linking formulas by typing them or by using pointing. Because pointing greatly reduces the chance of incorrectly specifying the linking workbook file, it is usually the preferred method and the one applied in this tutorial. When you create formulas with a file reference that links worksheets in two different workbook files, a convenient means of building these formulas is to open both workbook files and **tile** the windows so that they are arranged side-by-side. This allows you to create the linking formulas using pointing and ensures that the correct workbook file reference is used. Tile the two workbook files in preparation for creating the linked file references.

To tile workbook windows for easy reference:

1. Open the S_SMP1CA.xls workbook in the Tut07 folder that you created previously and that contains the data for the California division.

2. Click the **Budget** tab to activate that sheet, if necessary.

3. Click **Window**, then click **S_SMP2.xls** to display that worksheet in the active window.

4. Click **Window**, click **Arrange** to display the Arrange Windows dialog box, select the **Tiled** option button, then click the **OK** button to tile the windows with the corporate results worksheet and the California division worksheet in adjacent windows. See Figure 7-17. Notice that the active window displays on the left.

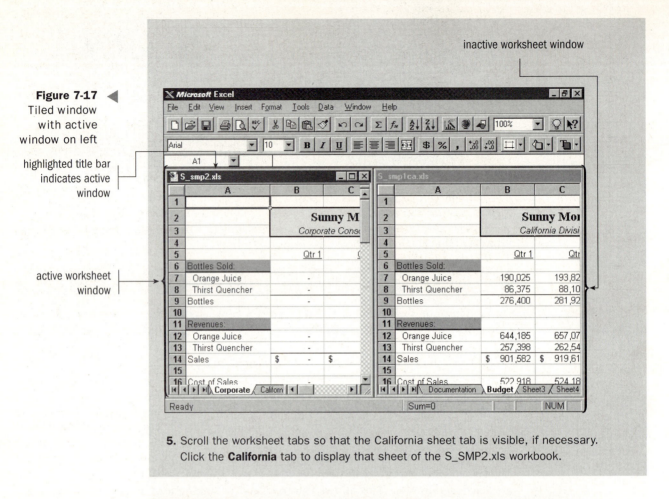

Figure 7-17
Tiled window with active window on left

highlighted title bar indicates active window

active worksheet window

inactive worksheet window

5. Scroll the worksheet tabs so that the California sheet tab is visible, if necessary. Click the **California** tab to display that sheet of the S_SMP2.xls workbook.

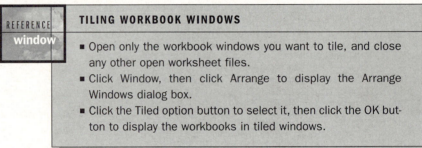

REFERENCE window	**TILING WORKBOOK WINDOWS**
	▪ Open only the workbook windows you want to tile, and close any other open worksheet files.
	▪ Click Window, then click Arrange to display the Arrange Windows dialog box.
	▪ Click the Tiled option button to select it, then click the OK button to display the workbooks in tiled windows.

You need to link the Budget worksheets for the California and Florida divisions to their respective sheets in the corporate results workbook. To do this, you need to place a linking formula in the corporate results workbook. The linking formula identifies the workbook and the range from which the data will be retrieved. The syntax for a linking formula is

= [filename.xls]sheet-name!range

Filename.xls is the name and extension of the workbook file. It may include the file's disk drive identifier and path. *Range* is the cell reference or range name of the data you want to retrieve from the specified file. Pointing is the easiest and safest method of specifying a linking formula. Use pointing to create linking formulas in the corporate results workbook that reference data in the California division's Budget worksheet.

To create a formula with a linked workbook file reference:

1. Scroll the S_SMP2.xls window so that cell A6 is in the upper-left corner, then click **B7** to make it the active cell where the linking formula will be created.

2. Press **=** to begin entering an Excel formula.

3. Click anywhere in the **Budget** sheet of the S_SMP1CA.xls workbook to make it the active window.

4. Click **B7** to select that cell reference for the formula.

5. Press the **F4** key three times to remove the absolute reference for the B7 cell reference.

6. Press the **Enter** key to finish specifying the linking formula and display the value from the Budget sheet in the California sheet, then click **B7** to make it the active cell. See Figure 7-18.

Figure 7-18
Formula with linked workbook file reference

linking formula with workbook reference

cell contains linking formula

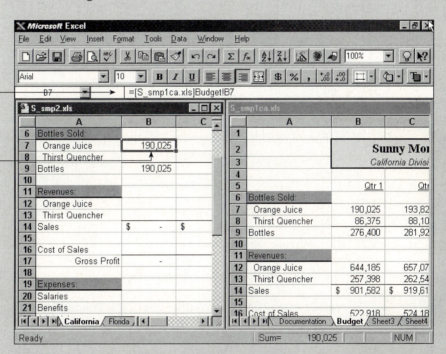

7. Copy the formula from **B7** into **C7:E7**, using the fill handle to finish copying the linking formula that specifies the number of orange juice bottles sold.

USING FORMULAS TO LINK EXCEL WORKBOOKS

- Tile the worksheets to be linked.
- Click the destination workbook sheet to activate it.
- Click the cell in the sheet of the destination workbook where you want the linked formula.
- Begin entering the formula until you need to specify a linked reference.
- Click the source workbook sheet to make it active.
- Click the cell reference in the source sheet.
- Continue entering the formula.

Instead of using pointing to create the linked file reference formula, you can type the entire formula. When typing the formula, be careful to include the correct path.

ADVEX 354 **TUTORIAL 7** CONSOLIDATING WORKBOOK RESULTS

Once Ann has created the linking formula using a relative reference, she can copy it into all the other cells in the California sheet that obtain their data values from the Budget sheet in the S_SMP1CA.xls workbook. Although Ann could create each of the linking formulas individually, copying a linking formula is usually the easiest method. Complete the linked file references in the California sheet of the S_SMP2.xls workbook by copying the linking formula.

To complete the linked formula references for the California division:

1. Click the **Maximize** button 🗗 for the workbook window so that the California sheet of the S_SMP2.xls workbook fills the entire worksheet window. This makes it easier to copy the linking formulas.

2. Scroll the window so that cell A6 is in the upper-left corner, then click **B7** to make it the active cell so its contents can be copied to other cells in this worksheet.

3. Click the **Copy** button 🗐 to copy the contents of cell B7 to the clipboard.

4. Select **B8:E8**, then click the **Paste** button 📋 to copy the linking formula to these cells. The underline border is removed by this copy. You can replace it after all the formulas have been copied.

5. Select **B12:E13**, then click the **Paste** button 📋 to copy the formula to these cells.

6. Select **B16:E16**, then click the **Paste** button 📋; again the formula is copied. These multiple copies are performed so that the linking formulas do not appear in blank cells or destroy the other formulas in the sheet.

7. Select **B20:E29**, then click the **Paste** button 📋 to copy the formula for all the expenses. This finishes creating the formulas with the linked reference to the California division workbook.

The underline borders were removed from the cells B8:E8, B13:E13, B16:E16, and B29:E29 as the formulas with the linked workbook file references were copied. Now replace these borders using the Format Painter.

To replace formatting removed by copying a linking formula:

1. Scroll the worksheet as necessary, then click **F8** to make it the active cell.

2. Click the **Format Painter** button 🖌 to select the format.

3. Select **B8:E8** to place the desired format in those cells.

4. Place the format from cell **F13** in cells **B13:E13**.

5. Place the format from cell **F16** in cells **B16:E16**.

6. Place the format from cell **F29** in cells **B29:E29** to complete the linking formulas for the California sheet. See Figure 7-19.

LINKING WORKBOOK FILES **ADVEX 355**

Figure 7-19 ◄
Completed
California sheet
with linking

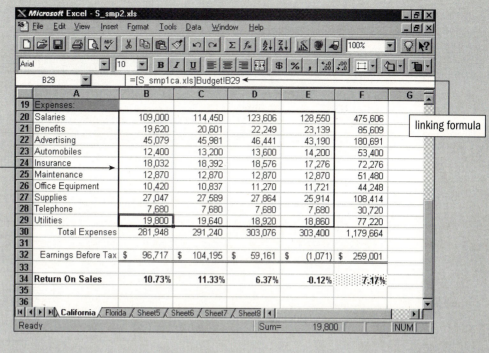

values obtained with
linking formulas

7. Save this as the S_SMP2.xls workbook.

8. Select the S_SMP1CA.xls workbook and close it without saving it, then maximize the S_SMP2.xls workbook, if necessary.

Now create the linked workbook file references for the Florida division.

To create the linked workbook references for the Florida division:

1. Open the S_SMP1FL.xls workbook. This window replaces the maximized S_SMP2.xls workbook window and is the active window.

2. Click the **Budget** tab to make it the active sheet.

3. Click **Window**, then click **S_SMP2.xls** to display the open worksheet in the active window.

4. Click **Window**, click **Arrange** to display the Arrange Windows dialog box, select the **Tiled** option button, then click the **OK** button to tile the windows with the corporate results workbook and the Florida division workbook in adjacent windows.

5. Build the linked workbook file reference formulas in the Florida sheet of the S_SMP2.xls workbook. These formulas are created in the same manner as those for the California sheet.

Now set the column widths to their defaults for the California and Florida sheets.

6. Set the width of column **A** to **18** and **B:F** to **11**, using the Group edit mode.

7. Save the S_SMP2.xls workbook. Then preview and print the Corporate worksheet with the consolidated results. See Figure 7-20.

Figure 7-20
Consolidated results from linked workbooks

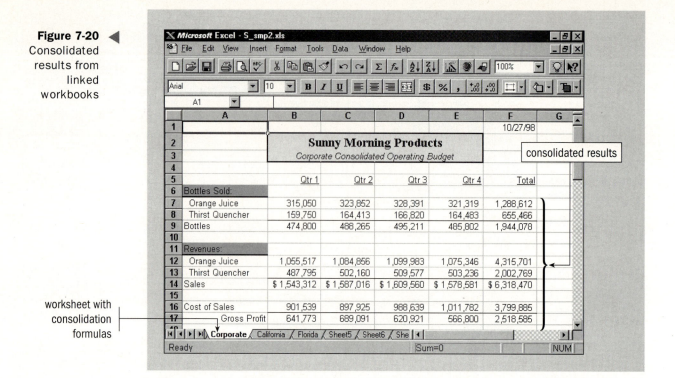

Ann shows Carmen the new multiple-sheet workbook. She explains that linking formulas with the workbook file references preserves the data integrity among the linked files so that the workbooks all display exactly the same data values. Ann demonstrates this by making a change in one of the source workbooks.

To demonstrate the data integrity of calculations between linked workbooks:

1. Tile the **S_SMP2.xls** and **S_SMP1FL.xls** workbook file windows, if necessary, then make sure that the **Budget** sheet of the S_SMP1FL.xls workbook is active.

2. Click **B7** in the Budget sheet of the S_SMP1FL.xls workbook for the Florida division.

3. Type **145,025** and press the **Enter** key, then click **B7**. Observe that the value in cell B7 in the Florida sheet of the S_SMP2.xls workbook is immediately updated. See Figure 7-21. If both workbooks were not open at the same time, the values in the S_SMP2.xls workbook would be updated when you opened that file or used the Edit Links Update Now command.

Figure 7-21
Revised value automatically updates linked file formula

value automatically updated

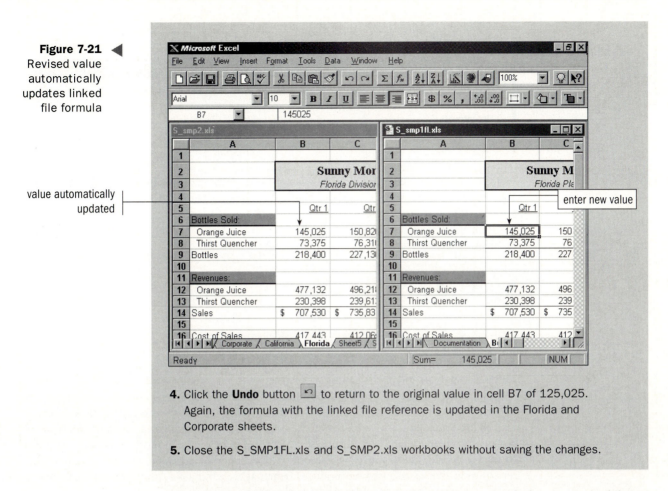

4. Click the **Undo** button to return to the original value in cell B7 of 125,025. Again, the formula with the linked file reference is updated in the Florida and Corporate sheets.

5. Close the S_SMP1FL.xls and S_SMP2.xls workbooks without saving the changes.

Ann knows that setting up the linking formulas takes more work than just consolidating data. However, the workbook with the linking formulas will provide Carmen with the automatic updates she wants, which were not available with the Data Consolidate command.

Ann can use the criteria shown in Figure 7-22 to help her decide whether to use the Data Consolidate command or the linking formula method. When few changes are expected for the formulas of an EIS, linked file references provide the automatic updates and are Carmen's preferred arrangement. If Ann or Carmen needed to do a consolidation "on the fly," then Data Consolidate is easier because it usually requires less effort to set up.

Figure 7-22
Strategy for consolidating or linking workbooks

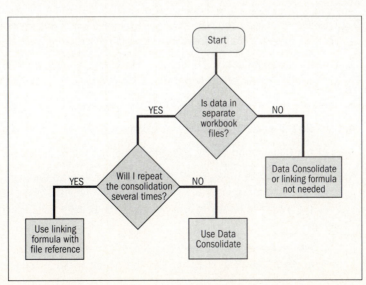

ADVEX 358　TUTORIAL 7 CONSOLIDATING WORKBOOK RESULTS

HELP DESK

EXCEL 5.0

Index

WHEN TO LINK WORKBOOKS

Double-click the Help button to display the Help Topics dialog box, then click the Index tab.

Keyword	**Topic**
linking cells in worksheets and workbook	When to link workbooks
links, workbook, creating	*Creating links between workbooks*

If you want to take a break and resume the tutorial at a later time, you can do so now. Exit Excel. If you are on a network, leave Windows running. If you are using your own computer, you may exit Windows and shut down the computer. When you resume the tutorial, place your Student Disk in the disk drive, launch Excel, then continue with the tutorial.

● ● ●

Using Arrays to Link Workbooks

Array ranges are rectangular ranges of cells that Excel treats as a single group. An array range allows you to specify a *single* formula that is applied to all the cells in the range. That is, rather than entering or copying a repetitive formula in each cell of a range, you apply an array formula to all the cells in the array. When Ann created the linking formulas for her consolidation workbook, she created the linking formula with its relative reference and then copied it to all the other cells in the destination worksheet that are linked to the worksheet in the source workbook. She thinks that array ranges may give her a better solution that is easier to maintain. Carmen agrees and asks Ann to test this alternative using a consolidation workbook with the three sheets for Corporate, California, and Florida. Ann can begin her development using the same C_SMP2.xls workbook she used previously with the linking formulas. As before, the consolidation is performed with the SUM functions in the Corporate worksheet. In preparation for creating this alternative implementation, open the C_SMP2.xls workbook and enter the SUM functions for doing the consolidation in the Corporate sheet.

To copy the SUM function formulas for the across-sheet 3-D consolidation:

1. Open the C_SMP2.xls workbook in the Tut07 folder and immediately save it as S_SMP3.xls in case you want to restart this section of the tutorial. This workbook contains the four sheets Documentation, Corporate, California, and Florida.

2. Click the **Maximize** button 🗗 of the S_SMP3.xls workbook to fill the workbook window with the workbook, then click the **Corporate** tab to make it the active sheet.

3. Scroll the worksheet so that A12 is in the upper-left corner of the window.

4. Click **B12** to make it the active cell whose formula you want to copy.

5. Click the **Copy** button 📋 to copy the formula to the clipboard.

6. Select **B20:E29** as the destination range, then click the **Paste** button 📋 to place the SUM function in those cells, for performing the across-sheet consolidation. The underline border is removed from the cells in row 29 and needs to be replaced.

7. Click **F29** to make it the active cell, click the **Format Painter** button 🖌, then select cells **B29:E29** to place the desired format in these cells.

8. Save this as the S_SMP3.xls workbook in the Tut07 folder.

Now you are ready to use array ranges in linking the data values from the Budget worksheets in the individual workbooks for the California and Florida divisions to their respective worksheets in the corporate results workbook. The first activity is to tile the workbooks so it is easy to use pointing in creating the linking array range formula.

To tile workbook windows for creating linking array formulas:

1. Open the S_SMP1CA.xls workbook in the Tut07 folder.

2. Click the **Budget** tab to make it the active sheet.

3. Click **Window**, then click **S_SMP3.xls** to display that open workbook in the active window.

4. Click **Window**, click **Arrange** to display the Arrange Windows dialog box, select the **Tiled** option button, then click the **OK** button to finish tiling these two workbook windows.

5. Click the **California** tab to display that sheet of the S_SMP3.xls workbook.

The Budget worksheet for the California division is ready to be linked to the California sheet of the corporate results workbook, using array range formulas. You will place the array formula in the corporate results workbook. The array range formula identifies the source workbook and range of the data. The syntax of the array range formula is

={[filename.xls]sheet-name!range-reference}

Filename.xls is the name and extension of the workbook file. *Range-reference* is the range of cells in the source worksheet. The array formula is enclosed in braces, ({}), that distinguish an array formula from other Excel formulas. Create the linking array formulas in the corporate results workbook.

To create an array range formula with a linked workbook file reference:

1. Click anywhere in the **Budget** sheet of the S_SMP1CA.xls workbook to make it the active window.

2. Click the **Name** box list arrow to display the list of defined names, then click **Bottles_Sold** to select that range of cells. Ann named this range when she created her template workbook as a convenient method for referencing these cells. The same cells could be referenced by selecting the range B7:E8.

3. Click the **Copy** button 🖺 to copy the range to the clipboard.

4. Click anywhere in the **California** sheet of the S_SMP3.xls workbook to make it the active window.

5. Click **B7**, the upper-left corner of the destination for the array range.

6. Click **Edit**, then click **Paste Special** to display that dialog box. See Figure 7-23. Then click the **Paste Link** button to enter the array range formula in cells B7:E8 of the California sheet. When you link array ranges, Excel requires only that the ranges be the same size and shape. They do not need to be the same cell references in both sheets.

Figure 7-23
Paste Special dialog box

option used with Paste Link

creates array range linking formula

7. Click anywhere in the S_SMP3.xls workbook window to activate it.

8. Click **E8** and review the formula in that cell. See Figure 7-24. The formula in cells B7:E8 of the California sheet are all the *same* because of the array range formula with the linking reference. Using this array range for the linking formula means that the underline border remains displayed as the format for the cells in row 8.

Figure 7-24
Same array formula appears in all cells of the array

same formula in all cells of destination range

array range formula

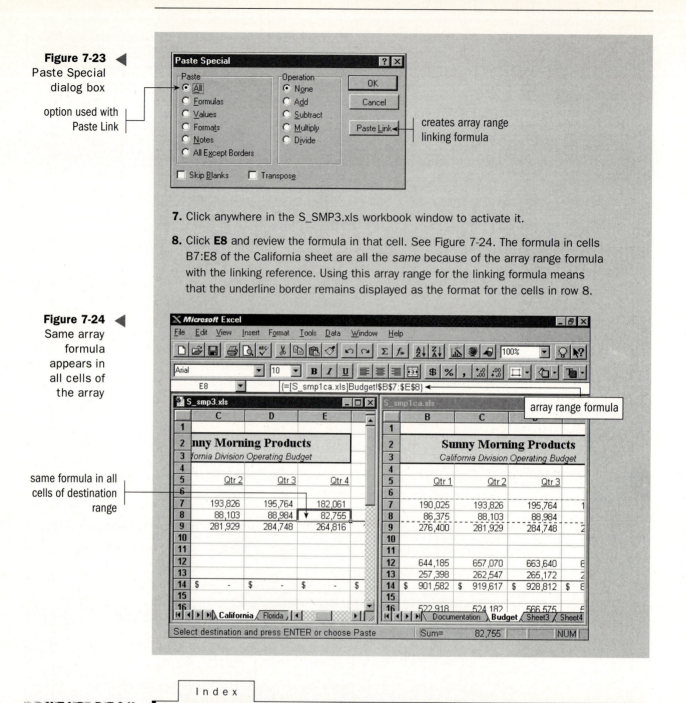

HELP DESK

Index

USING ARRAY RANGES

Double-click the Help button to display the Help Topics dialog box, then click the Index tab.

Keyword
range of cells, array ranges
ranges, array

Topic
Select an array range
Selecting an array range

EXCEL 5.0

Next, you must add the array formulas with the linking references to the California worksheet for the Revenues, Cost of Sales, and Expenses, using the same procedure. Complete these linked file references in the California sheet of the S_SMP3.xls workbook.

To complete the array range linked formula references for the California division:

1. Copy the **Revenues** range from the Budget sheet of the S_SMP1CA.xls workbook to the clipboard and use the **Paste Link** command to place that array range at cell **B12** in the California sheet of the S_SMP3.xls workbook.

2. Copy the **Cost_of_Sales** range from the Budget sheet of the S_SMP1CA.xls workbook to the clipboard and use the **Paste Link** command to place that array range at cell **B16** in the California sheet of the S_SMP3.xls workbook.

3. Copy the **Expenses** range from the Budget sheet of the S_SMP1CA.xls workbook to the clipboard and use the **Paste Link** command to place that array range at cell **B20** in the California sheet of the S_SMP3.xls workbook.

4. Review the formulas for Revenues, Cost of Sales, and Expenses in the California sheet of the corporate results workbook to verify that they are all array range formulas. See Figure 7-25.

Figure 7-25
Array range formula for insurance expense

array range formula for all expense items

same formula as other expense items

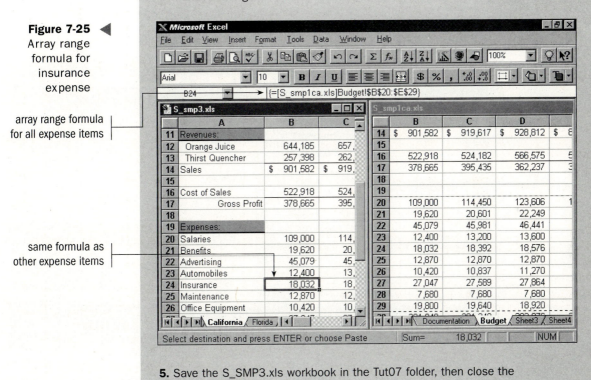

5. Save the S_SMP3.xls workbook in the Tut07 folder, then close the S_SMP1CA.xls workbook without saving it.

Next, you need to create the array range formulas with the linked references for the Florida division's worksheet in the corporate results workbook.

To create the array range formulas with the linked references for the Florida division:

1. Open the S_SMP1FL.xls workbook, then click the **Budget** tab to activate that sheet.

2. Make the S_SMP3.xls workbook the active window, then click the **Florida** tab to activate that sheet.

3. Tile the workbook windows so that it is easier to create the array range formulas.

4. Click anywhere in the **Budget** sheet of the S_SMP1FL.xls workbook to make it the active window, click the **Name** box list arrow to display the list of defined names, then click **Results** to select all these cells.

5. Click the **Copy** button to copy the range to the clipboard.

6. Click anywhere in the **Florida** sheet of the S_SMP3.xls workbook to make it the active window, then click **B7**, which is the upper-left corner of the destination for the array range.

7. Click **Edit**, click **Paste Special** to display that dialog box, then click the **Paste Link** button to enter the array range formula in cells **B7:E30** of the Florida sheet.

8. Click **B10** to make it the active cell. Note that zeros appear in the blank cells of the Florida sheet that contain the array range formula. See Figure 7-26. The original formulas for calculating the Bottles sold, Sales, and Gross Profit are also replaced by the array range formula. However, the correct values are still displayed for these cells.

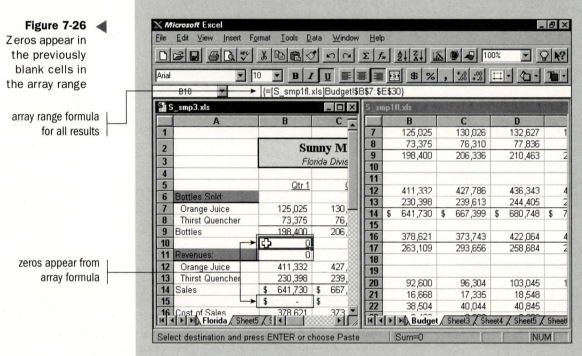

Figure 7-26
Zeros appear in the previously blank cells in the array range

array range formula for all results

zeros appear from array formula

Although the Results array range is convenient for linking all these data values at one time, the zeros need to be removed from the worksheet display. Remove the unwanted zeros from the array range.

To remove unwanted zeros from an array range formula with linking references:

1. Select **B10:E11**, which contains unwanted zeros.

2. Press the **Delete** key to attempt to remove the contents of these cells. An Excel message box appears, indicating that you cannot change part of an array. See Figure 7-27.

Figure 7-27
Message box for attempt to change array

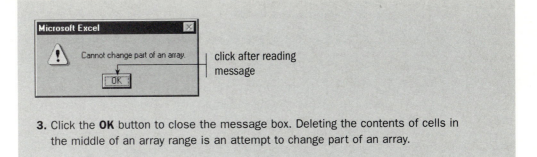

click after reading message

3. Click the **OK** button to close the message box. Deleting the contents of cells in the middle of an array range is an attempt to change part of an array.

A better method is to change the format of the cells with the unwanted zeros so that a zero appears as a blank. Although you cannot change the cell contents, and you cannot insert or delete rows or columns from the array range, you can change the format of cells in an array range. Change the cell format.

To format cells so that zeros appear as blanks for use with an array range linked reference formula:

1. Select **B10:E11**, **B15:E15**, and **B18:E19** as a nonadjacent range, using the Ctrl key to select the additional elements of the nonadjacent range.

2. Right-click any cell in the selected range to display the shortcut menu, click **Format Cells** to display that dialog box, then click the **Number** tab to view that settings sheet.

3. Click **Custom** in the Category list box, scroll the Type list until # ?/? appears, then click **# ?/?**, which is a starting point for a custom number format.

   In the Code text box, type ###, then click the OK button. Click B10 to unselect the range. Continue to Step 5.

4. In the Type text box, edit the # ?/? format so it is **###**, click the **OK** button to apply that format to the selected cells, then click **B10** to unselect the other cells in the nonadjacent range. The ### format displays a zero as a blank. See Figure 7-28.

EXCEL 5.0

Figure 7-28
Zeros formatted to appear as blanks in array range

zeros formatted as blanks

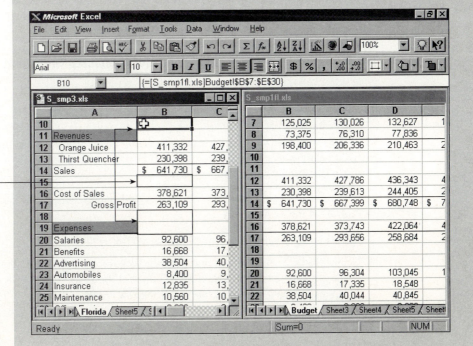

ADVEX 364 **TUTORIAL 7** CONSOLIDATING WORKBOOK RESULTS

5. Save this as the S_SMP3.xls workbook, then preview and print the Corporate sheet.

6. Close the S_SMP3.xls and S_SMP1FL.xls workbooks without saving them.

Ann is pleased with the use of the array ranges to create her linking reference formulas. She decides that this arrangement is best for the Sunny Morning Products corporate consolidation because it contains the corporate consolidation together with the sheets for each division.

Working with Outline Groups

As Carmen reviews the consolidation with Ann, she wonders whether there is some way that Ann can arrange the Corporate sheet of the consolidated results so that she can view either a summary arrangement of this sheet or all the details. She thinks this would help her in explaining their Operating Budget to Travis and the other members of the management committee.

An Excel **outline** enables you to expand or contract the rows and columns of a worksheet so that you see more or less detail. The rows and columns of data that can be expanded or contracted are arranged as **groups**. In the Operating Budget, Carmen is interested in a summarized view that displays only the total Bottles sold, the Gross Profit, the Total Expense, the Earnings Before Tax, and the Return On Sales for the year in the Total column. Here, total Bottles sold and Total Expense are examples of Excel groups. These groups will allow Carmen to quickly present an overview of the proposed Operating Budget to the management committee. However, if any of the committee members has a question concerning these summarized budget items, she will be able to quickly display the details for review and discussion.

Excel can create the groups of a worksheet outline either automatically or manually. To manually outline a worksheet, you select each range that you want to treat as a group individually, whereas to automatically outline a worksheet, you select a range or the entire sheet that you want Excel to organize as groups based on your use of formulas in the worksheet. Automatic outlining works well in most situations if you have not previously created an outline and your formulas in the outline range have a consistent layout. For example, all summary formulas in rows should add cells above and all summary formulas in columns should add cells to the left. This matches the layout of Ann's Operating Budget. Automatically outline the detail of the Corporate worksheet to create Carmen's summary.

To automatically create outline groups for a selected worksheet range:

1. Open the S_SMP3.xls workbook in the Tut07 folder.

2. Click the **Yes** button if the Excel message box displays asking if you want to re-establish the links for this workbook. Excel asks you if you want to update the links whenever you open a workbook that contains any linking formulas. You can change this by clicking Tools, then Options, and then unchecking the Ask to Update Automatic Links check box.

3. Maximize the workbook window, then click the **Corporate** tab, if necessary, to make it the active sheet.

4. Select **A5:F30**, which is the range you want to outline.

5. Click **Data**, point to **Group and Outline**, click **Auto Outline** to automatically create the outline groups, then click **A5** to unselect the range. See Figure 7-29. Group outline symbols appear to the left of the row numbers and above the column letters. The outlining symbols are described in Figure 7-30. Notice that Excel created the outline using the formula references to the rows and columns in this sheet, and not those of the 3-D SUM functions for the consolidation.

WORKING WITH OUTLINE GROUPS **ADVEX 365**

Figure 7-29
Group outline elements

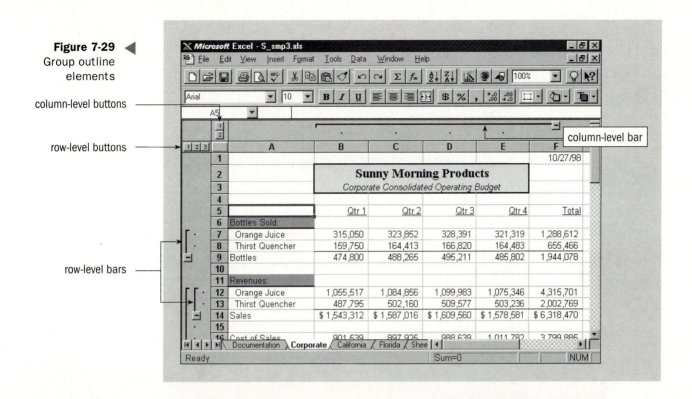

Figure 7-30
Outline symbols and actions

Symbol	Meaning
Show Detail ➕	Click this button to show the detail one level under this button
Hide Detail ➖	Click this button to hide all levels under this button
Row or column Level button ①	Click this button to specify the number of the row or column level to display throughout the outline
Level bars	Designates all rows or columns at a specific level

HELP DESK

EXCEL 5.0

Index

OUTLINING WORKSHEET DATA

Double-click the Help button to display the Help Topics dialog box, then click the Index tab.

Keyword
outlines in Excel
outlines, creating

Topic
Summarize data by outlining a worksheet
Overview of Creating and Removing an Outline

Once Ann has created the outline with these groups, Carmen can click the outline symbols to expand or contract the data displayed. Explore the use of the outline symbols for displaying grouped data.

To use outline symbols for grouped data:

1. Click the **Row level 1** button [1] to collapse the row outline to that level. See Figure 7-31.

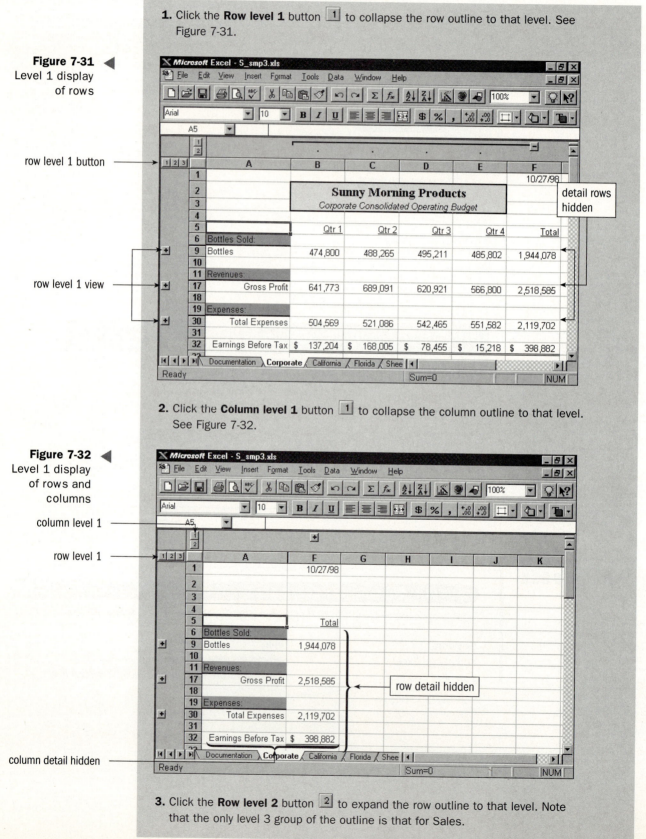

Figure 7-31
Level 1 display of rows

Figure 7-32
Level 1 display of rows and columns

2. Click the **Column level 1** button [1] to collapse the column outline to that level. See Figure 7-32.

3. Click the **Row level 2** button [2] to expand the row outline to that level. Note that the only level 3 group of the outline is that for Sales.

WORKING WITH OUTLINE GROUPS **ADVEX 367**

4. Click the **Show Detail** button ⊞ for Sales to expand that level.

5. Try several other different group-level displays, then click the **Row level 1** button 1 and click the **Column level 2** button 2 .

6. Save this as the S_SMP3.xls workbook, then close the workbook.

Carmen is pleased with this outline arrangement of her worksheet. The outline groups give her the ability to use the outline buttons to **drill down** to, or isolate, the related information in their EIS at lower levels of detail.

HELP DESK

EXCEL 5.0

Index

CLEARING AN OUTLINE

Double-click the Help button to display the Help Topics dialog box, then click the Index tab.

Keyword	**Topic**
outlines in Excel	Remove an outline
outlines, removing	*Removing an outline*

Using Groups to Consolidate Data

Another way to use groups is with the Data Consolidate command, when the references in the destination workbook are linked to the source data workbooks. Ann used the Data Consolidate command in producing the consolidated corporate results shown previously in Figure 7-13. Recall that when she created this consolidated report, she did not link it to the division source files. Rather, when she needed to make a change to one of the source files, she controlled the update by re-doing the consolidation to the corporate workbook. She could have selected an option to create links between the source files and the destination file. This way, any changes she made to the source workbooks would have automatically been reflected in the corporate workbook, the destination workbook. Such a link would automatically create the outline groups and insert rows in the destination worksheet. With this linking, any changes to the source workbooks can be controlled when the revised workbooks are placed in the same folder as the destination workbook. Although Ann is pleased with her linking formulas using array ranges, she wants to evaluate this alternative for Carmen. Implement Data Consolidate with the source data links and automatically create the outline groups.

To create links to the source data for consolidation by position using the Data Consolidate command:

1. Open the S_SMP1.xls workbook in the Tut07 folder, and immediately save it as the S_SMP4.xls workbook.

2. Click the **Corporate** tab to activate that worksheet, if necessary. Then scroll the window so that A1 is displayed in the upper-left corner.

3. Click **B7** to position the cell pointer at the upper-left corner of the range where the incoming data range for the source file will be located.

4. Click **Data**, then click **Consolidate** to display the Consolidate dialog box. Note that the SUM function is still used for the consolidation and references to the source workbooks are the same.

5. Check the **Create Links to Source Data** check box to automatically create the links between the source and destination workbooks.

6. Click the **OK** button to repeat the consolidation and establish the links, then click **B9** to deselect any selected ranges. See Figure 7-33. Note the appearance of the row levels for the outline. Also, the orange juice Bottles Sold value is now located at row 9 rather than row 7, because the linking inserted two rows for each consolidated line item.

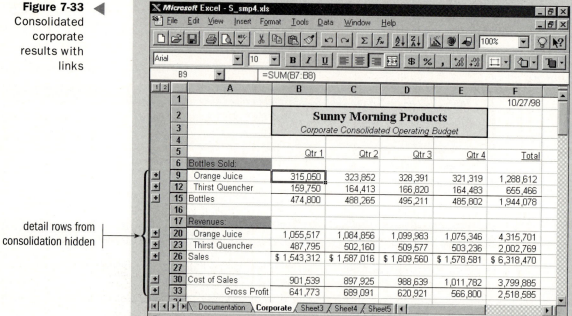

Figure 7-33 Consolidated corporate results with links

detail rows from consolidation hidden

When you use the Create Links to Source Data option, Excel automatically inserts one row for each of the references above the row where the data is consolidated in the destination workbook. Then SUM functions are automatically created to add the detailed data for the summary row. Review the S_SMP4.xls workbook to observe these changes.

To review the linked source data for the Data Consolidate command:

1. Click **B12**. Note that the formula is a SUM function that adds the detail rows 10 and 11.

2. Click the **Show Detail** button ⊞ for the Thirst Quencher bottles sold in row 12 to expand that level. See Figure 7-34. The detail rows appear with the data values from their respective workbooks. However, the planning item names do not appear in column A because they are not part of the Results ranges in the source workbooks.

WORKING WITH OUTLINE GROUPS **ADVEX 369**

Figure 7-34
Detail displayed for Thirst Quencher bottles sold

data not identified

detail rows displayed

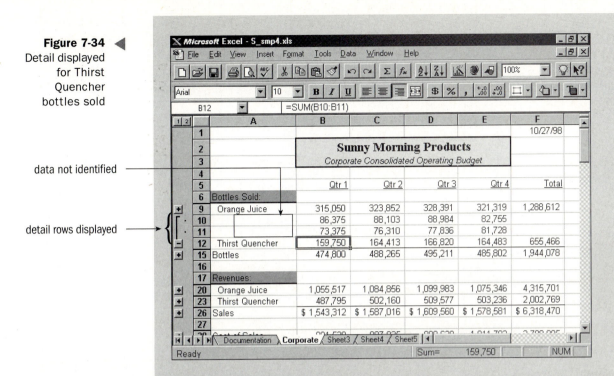

3. Click **B10**. Note the appearance of the linking formula to the Budget sheet in the S_SMP1CA.xls workbook. See Figure 7-35.

   TROUBLE? If your linking formula appears with your disk drive letter and folder name, don't worry. This is not a problem.

Figure 7-35
Link formula for detail level

linking formula

detail displayed

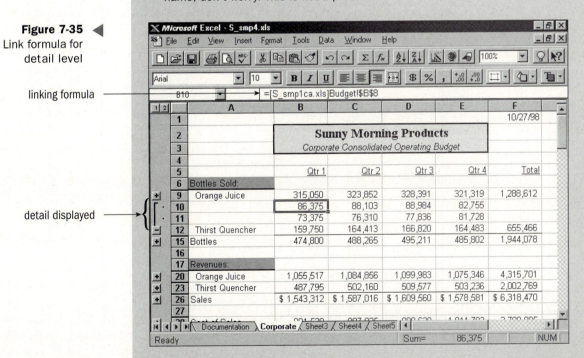

4. Open the S_SMP1CA.xls workbook, then click **B8** in the Budget sheet to make it the active cell.

5. Tile the workbook windows.

6. Enter **88,375** in **B8** as a revised data value, then click **B8** so that it is the active cell. See Figure 7-36. Note that the S_SMP4.xls workbook was automatically updated in the same manner as the other linking formulas in this tutorial.

Figure 7-36
Update consolidation results

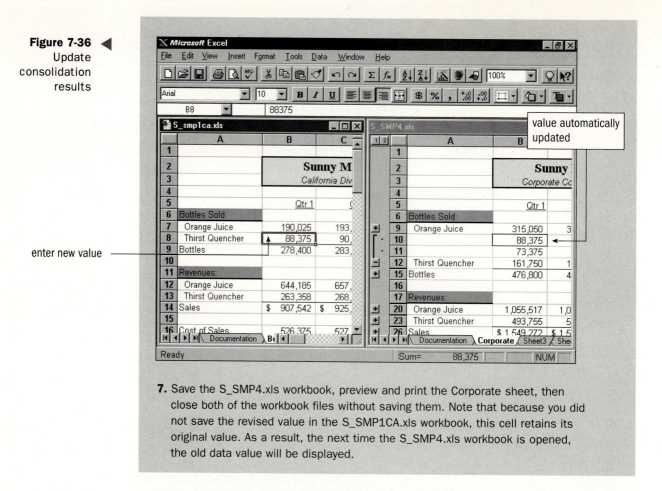

7. Save the S_SMP4.xls workbook, preview and print the Corporate sheet, then close both of the workbook files without saving them. Note that because you did not save the revised value in the S_SMP1CA.xls workbook, this cell retains its original value. As a result, the next time the S_SMP4.xls workbook is opened, the old data value will be displayed.

Although Ann is impressed with this linking and grouping of source data for the consolidation, she thinks that the inclusion of the detail worksheets in the same workbook as the corporate results worksheet provides Carmen with the best arrangement for their consolidation.

If you want to take a break and resume the tutorial at a later time, you can do so now. Exit Excel. If you are on a network, leave Windows running. If you are using your own computer, you may exit Windows and shut down the computer. When you resume the tutorial, place your Student Disk in the disk drive, launch Excel, then continue with the tutorial.

● ● ●

Auditing the Workbook

To keep up with the growing demand for Olympic Gold, Sunny Morning Products has expanded its production capacity by adding a third plant in Arizona. Kurt Suarez, the Arizona division plant manager, prepared their operating budget using the template he received from Ann. After entering the data for the Arizona division, he sent the file to her for inclusion in the corporate results workbook. Ann just received the workbook file and is preparing to integrate it into her summary workbook. Open the file and review it.

To review Kurt's workbook:

1. Open the C_SMP1AZ.xls workbook in the Tut07 folder. The Excel message box displays as the workbook opens, indicating that a circular reference was detected. See Figure 7-37.

AUDITING THE WORKBOOK **ADVEX 371**

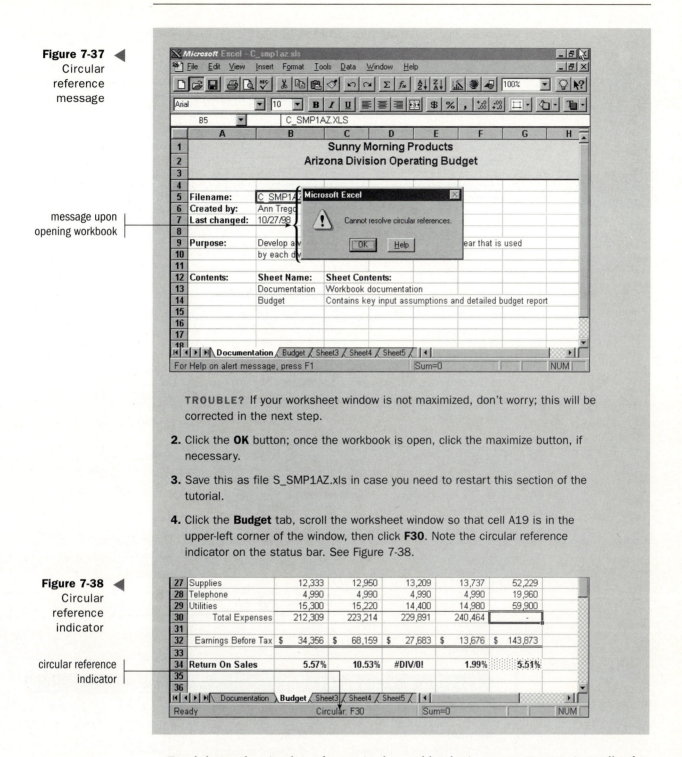

Figure 7-37 ◄ Circular reference message

message upon opening workbook

Figure 7-38 ◄ Circular reference indicator

circular reference indicator

TROUBLE? If your worksheet window is not maximized, don't worry; this will be corrected in the next step.

2. Click the **OK** button; once the workbook is open, click the maximize button, if necessary.

3. Save this as file S_SMP1AZ.xls in case you need to restart this section of the tutorial.

4. Click the **Budget** tab, scroll the worksheet window so that cell A19 is in the upper-left corner of the window, then click **F30**. Note the circular reference indicator on the status bar. See Figure 7-38.

Excel detected a circular reference in the workbook. A **circular reference** is a cell reference in a formula in which the calculated value of the formula in the cell depends on the value in that same cell. Because the cell does not initially contain a value, zero is displayed for the calculated result. There are some specialized applications in which circular references are desirable, such as with the automatic debt borrowing and interest expense calculations that occur in some business planning analyses. However, most circular references are the result of an incorrect cell reference in a formula, and they need to be detected and corrected.

The Excel Circular reference audit feature helps you locate the cell containing the error and displays its cell reference on the status bar. Other audit features help you inspect the overall logic of a worksheet by locating and analyzing formulas and links to other workbooks (Figure 7-39). If you are using a workbook that someone else created, the trace features can quickly identify cells used in formulas. When your own worksheets start to get large and complex, the audit features can help you review their organization. The trace audit features can also make what-if analysis easier by identifying cells that will change when you enter a new what-if value. They can also let you know whether a specific cell or range of cells is referenced by any formulas elsewhere in the worksheet.

Figure 7-39 ◀
Audit analyses

Audit Activity	Description
Trace Precedents	Identifies cells whose results are used directly in calculating a selected cell by displaying tracer arrows
Remove Precedent Arrows	Removes the tracer arrows for precedents of a selected cell
Trace Dependents	Identifies cells that are calculated using the result from the selected cell by displaying blue tracer arrows
Remove Dependent Arrows	Removes the tracer arrows for dependents of a selected cell
Remove All Arrows	Removes all tracer arrows for both precedent and dependent cells
Trace Error	Identifies cells that contain values used to calculate a selected cell's value which is incorrect
Attach Note	Opens the Cell Note dialog box for attaching an explanatory note to the selected cell
Show Info Window	Opens a separate window that displays a selected cell's reference, the formula contained in the cell, and the note attached to the cell
Circular reference	Identifies a cell involved in a circular reference in which the calculated value for a cell depends on the value in the same cell
Edit, Links	Displays the Links dialog box with a list of workbook files linked to the active workbook

HELP DESK

Index

SOLVING CIRCULAR REFERENCES

Double-click the Help button to display the Help Topics dialog box, then click the Index tab.

Keyword	Topic
circular reference formulas	Solving circular reference formulas
circular references	*Overview of solving circular references*

EXCEL 5.0

Correct the cell containing the circular reference identified by Excel.

To find and correct the circular reference:

1. Make sure that **F30** is the active cell and the one that Excel identified with a circular reference.

2. Click **Tools**, point to **Auditing**, then click **Show Auditing Toolbar** to display that toolbar.

3. Click the **Show Info Window** button [icon] to display the information window. See Figure 7-40. Note that the formula is =SUM(B30:F30). The cell is referencing itself.

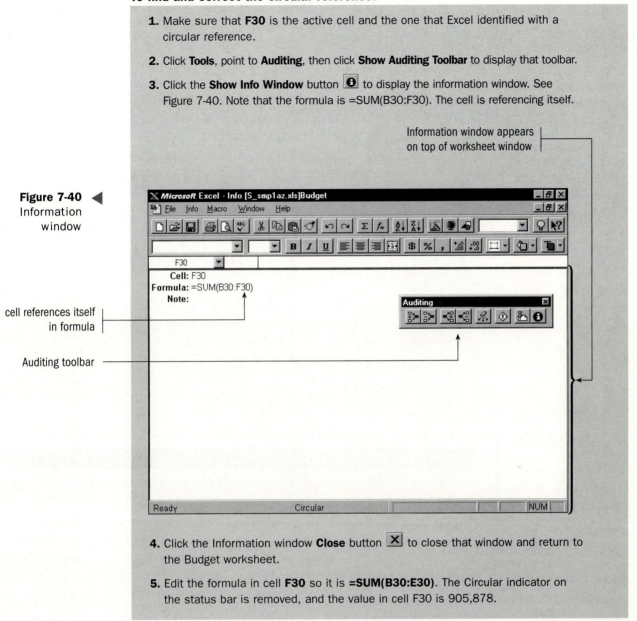

Figure 7-40 Information window

4. Click the Information window **Close** button [X] to close that window and return to the Budget worksheet.

5. Edit the formula in cell **F30** so it is **=SUM(B30:E30)**. The Circular indicator on the status bar is removed, and the value in cell F30 is 905,878.

The #DIV/0! error value appears in cell D34 of the Budget worksheet. Ann is not sure how Kurt managed to cause this situation, but she knows that she must correct it. If she had locked the cells that contain formulas, this situation might have been avoided. Nonetheless, she now needs to correct this condition. The Excel trace error audit feature enables Ann to look at cells that contain error values in order to correct these conditions. Trace the cells used in calculating D34.

To trace an error value displayed in a worksheet:

1. Click **D34**, which displays the #DIV/0! error value.

2. Click the **Trace Error** button on the Audit toolbar to display the trace arrows that show the cells used in the calculation of D34. See Figure 7-41.

Figure 7-41 ◄
Trace arrows for cells used in calculation

trace arrows indicate cells used in formula

Ann sees that the wrong cell was used as the divisor and edits the formula to correct it.

3. Edit the formula in cell **D34** so it is **=D32/D14**. The correct value, 4.19%, replaces the error value.

4. Click the Audit toolbar **Close** button to close it.

5. Save this as the S_SMP1AZ.xls workbook in the Tut07 folder.

Ann is confident that the worksheet is correct and is ready to include it in the Corporate results summary.

HELP DESK

Index

AUDITING WORKSHEETS

Double-click the Help button to display the Help Topics dialog box, then click the Index tab.

Keyword	Topic
auditing formulas	Auditing worksheet visually
auditing	Auditing Buttons Category

EXCEL 5.0

Expanding the Consolidation

Now that all the formulas in the operating budget from the Arizona division are correct, Ann needs to include the results in the Corporate results workbook. This expands her third dimension of the consolidation from two to three detailed division worksheets. Add an Arizona sheet to the Corporate results workbook.

EXPANDING THE CONSOLIDATION **ADVEX 375**

To add a worksheet for consolidation to an existing workbook:

1. Open the S_SMP3.xls workbook in preparation for including the Arizona division in it. Click the **Yes** button to re-establish the links, if necessary.

2. Click the **Sheet5** tab to make it the active worksheet, then change the sheet's name to **Arizona**.

3. Set the width of column **A** to **18** and of columns **B** through **F** to **11**.

4. Make S_SMP1AZ.xls the active workbook, and click the **Budget** tab to make it the active sheet, if necessary.

5. Click the **Name** box list arrow, then click **Budget** to select that range which Ann created when she set up the template.

6. Click the **Copy** button ▣ to copy the range to the clipboard.

7. Activate the workbook S_SMP3.xls, then click the **Arizona** tab to make it the active worksheet.

8. Click **A1** to make this the active cell and position the cell pointer for pasting the contents of the clipboard.

9. Click the **Paste** button ▣ to finish copying all labels and formats from the Budget worksheet, click **A1** to unselect the range, then review the contents of the sheet. Many of the values are zeros because the key assumptions data values were not copied to this sheet.

Now that the Arizona sheet contains all the desired labels and cell formats, you can link the data values from the Budget sheet in the S_SMP1AZ.xls workbook you can link to this Arizona sheet. You can use the same linking arrangement used with the California and Florida sheets. Complete this linking using an array range.

To link the detail and summary workbooks using an array range:

1. Make S_SMP1AZ.xls the active workbook. Confirm that the Budget sheet is still active.

2. Click the **Name** box list arrow, then click **Results** to select that range as the desired array.

3. Click the **Copy** button ▣ to copy the range to the clipboard.

4. Activate the **Arizona** sheet in the S_SMP3.xls workbook.

5. Click **B7** to position the cell pointer at the upper-left corner of the destination for the array range.

6. Click **Edit**, click **Paste Special** to display that dialog box, then click the **Paste Link** button to place the array range formula in **B7:E29**.

7. Change the format of the cells **B10:E11**, **B15:E15**, and **B18:E19** so that these zeros in the array range appear as blanks. See Figure 7-42.

Figure 7-42
Arizona results for corporate consolidation

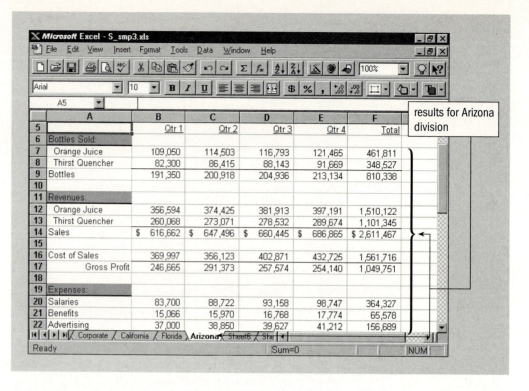

Ann has the data from the Budget sheet of the S_SMP1AZ.xls file linked to its respective Arizona sheet in the S_SMP3.xls workbook with the corporate results. Now she needs to include the Arizona data in the corporate summary. She could modify the SUM function in the Corporate sheet to include the Arizona sheet. However, since the California and Florida sheets already specify the beginning and ending of the 3-D range, it is easier to merely place the Arizona sheet between the other two.

To include a sheet in an already defined 3-D range:

1. Click and drag the **Arizona** tab so that it is between the California and Florida tabs.

2. Click the **Corporate** tab and verify that the results for Arizona are included in these totals. See Figure 7-43.

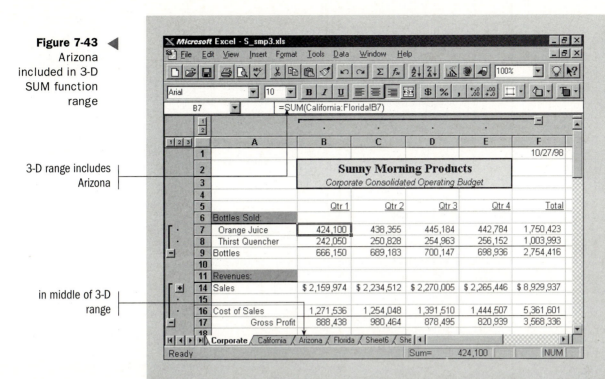

Figure 7-43
Arizona included in 3-D SUM function range

3-D range includes Arizona

in middle of 3-D range

TROUBLE? If the groups are collapsed to level 1, expand them to level 2 so you can view the detailed changes in the consolidated results.

3. Save this as the S_SMP3.xls workbook, preview and print the Corporate sheet, then close this workbook.

Using Macros to Automate Consolidations

When the source and destination workbooks for a consolidation are linked, there is no need to use macros to repeat any commands for a consolidation. As you have seen from the linked workbook examples for Sunny Morning Products, when a data value is changed in a source workbook, it is automatically updated in the destination workbook by the Excel DDE link. The primary use of macros in consolidation is when data is consolidated *without* the use of links between the source and destination workbooks.

When Ann created the S_SMP1.xls workbook consolidation, she needed to repeat the consolidation commands to update the workbook with the data values from the source workbooks. This arrangement allowed her to have additional *control* over when the consolidation was performed, rather than doing it automatically when the source workbook file was updated. When this control is desired, then macros are very useful in repeating the consolidation. The macro can position the cell pointer in the desired location for the consolidation by position, and then repeat the consolidation. For those situations in which Ann needs to manually control the consolidation, she wants to create a macro to simplify the process. First, Ann needs to include the Arizona division in the consolidation, then she can plan and create her macro.

To include the Arizona division in the consolidation:

1. Open the S_SMP1.xls workbook and maximize the workbook window, if necessary.

2. Activate the **Corporate** worksheet, then click **B7** to position the cell pointer at the desired location for the incoming source data from the divisions.

3. Click **Data**, then click **Consolidate** to display the Consolidate dialog box, with the SUM function still used for the consolidation.

ADVEX 378 TUTORIAL 7 CONSOLIDATING WORKBOOK RESULTS

> **4.** Click the **Browse** button to display the Browse dialog box, then double-click **S_SMP1AZ.xls** to select that file for inclusion with the other two divisions.
>
> **5.** Click to the right of the ! (exclamation mark) in the **Reference** text box, type **Results** to specify that range name, click the **Add** button to complete the specification, then click the **OK** button to include this division in the consolidated results.

Next, Ann does a walkthrough of the steps for her consolidation macro and writes out her macro planning sheet (Figure 7-44). Because the source workbooks were previously defined and Excel remembers them, she does not need to include the specification of each workbook in her macro plan. The desired workbook filenames will be included in her recorded macro. However, if she had not previously carried out the consolidation, she would need to include these additional steps in planning her macro. This underscores why it is useful to use a walkthrough to determine the Excel commands you want to include in your macro.

Figure 7-44 ◀
Ann's macro
planning sheet
for repeating the
consolidation

Macro Planning Sheet	
Action	Result
Click B7	Position cell pointer for incoming source data
Click Data, click Consolidate	Display the Consolidate dialog box with the previously specified references
Click OK button	Repeat the previously specified consolidation
Click B7	Unselect the selected range

Now, create a macro for Ann's S_SMP1.xls workbook file that uses manual control for any consolidation updates.

To create a macro for performing a manual consolidation by position:

> **1.** Click **Tools**, point to **Record Macro**, then click **Record New Macro** to display the Record New Macro dialog box.
>
> **2.** Type **Consol** as the macro name, then click the **OK** button to start recording the macro.
>
> **3.** Click **B7** to position the cell pointer at the upper-left corner for the incoming source data. This is one of the most important actions in the macro.
>
> **4.** Click **Data**, click **Consolidate** to display that dialog box with all the references already set up for the consolidation, then click the **OK** button to repeat the con-solidation.
>
> **5.** Click **B7** to deselect the selected range.
>
> **6.** Click the **Stop Macro** button ■ to turn off the macro recorder.
>
> Next, assign the macro to a macro button.
>
> **7.** Create a macro button named **Consolidate** at cells **F2:G2** and assign the Consol macro to it. See Figure 7-45.

Figure 7-45
Macro button for controlled consolidation

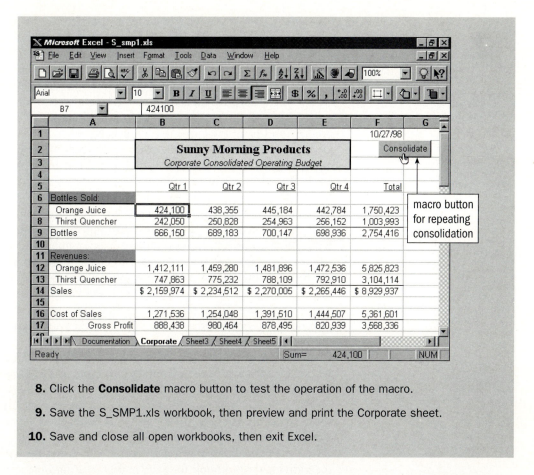

8. Click the **Consolidate** macro button to test the operation of the macro.
9. Save the S_SMP1.xls workbook, then preview and print the Corporate sheet.
10. Save and close all open workbooks, then exit Excel.

Ann has her macro that allows her to control the update of the consolidation. With this macro, Carmen can place updated division files on her computer and review them before she revises her consolidated results.

Carmen and Ann have the consolidation processing they want. Their Operating Budget was readily expanded to include its multidimensional organization for Sunny Morning Products expansion. Carmen is ready to present their consolidated Operating Budget to the Board of Directors. They know that their consolidation will accommodate any last-minute revisions from the California, Florida, or Arizona divisions of SMP.

Tutorial Exercises

Launch Excel and open the E_APT1CO.xls workbook in the Tut07 folder for Aqua Pure Technologies (APT). Cesar Gonzalez, APT's assistant operations manager, uses Excel to plan and coordinate production of the Aqua Clarifier purification system. He receives an Excel workbook file that contains the aggregate production plan from the planners at each of APT's manufacturing operations in North America (NA), South America (SA), and the Pacific Rim (PR). Cesar needs to consolidate the plans from each of these manufacturing operations to produce the Corporate Aggregate Production Plan. Because the data in these workbooks is the number of units of production, the number of production hours, and the number of employees, Cesar does not need to be concerned with any currency conversions. The data is reported in units that make business sense to directly add together. He received the workbooks with the individual plans and laid out his summary worksheet for consolidating the production plans. Consolidate these plans by performing the following:

1. Review Cesar's workbook for the corporate summary. In preparation for doing the consolidation, notice that the range for the quarterly data is blank and that formulas are used in the total column to calculate these values after the consolidation is performed. Examine the range named Plan. Does this range include the cells for all the quarterly data?

2. Open the E_APT1PR.xls workbook from the planner for the Pacific Rim manufacturing operation, and immediately save it as S_APT1PR.xls. This workbook contains at least one error. What is it? Use the Trace Precedents audit tool to examine the error. Print the worksheet that includes the trace arrow.

3. Correct the errors in the S_APT1PR.xls workbook. You have corrected all the errors when there are no zero data values and the total production requirement is 40,250. Save this as the S_APT1PR.xls workbook in the Tut07 folder, then preview and print the corrected worksheet.

4. Open the workbooks from the planners at each of the other two manufacturing operations. These files, identified by the last two characters of the filename, are E_APT1NA and E_APT1SA. Immediately save them as S_APT1NA and S_APT1SA. Examine each workbook, including the ranges named Plan, which contain the data for consolidation. If you want, you can preview and print each of these worksheets. Are the Plan ranges in all three individual operation worksheets and the corporate summary exact images?

5. Use the Data Consolidate command to consolidate the production plans for the three manufacturing operations in the corporate summary workbook. Save this as the S_APT1CO.xls workbook. Preview and print the corporate aggregate production plan. Circle the total production requirement and the total number of production hours required for APT's world-wide manufacturing operations on the printed worksheet.

6. Cesar created the E_APT2CO.xls template workbook, which contains a separate worksheet for each of the manufacturing operations. Open this template, immediately save it as S_APT2CO, then use the Data Consolidate command to place the production plan for *each* manufacturing operation in its respective sheet. Save this as the S_APT2CO.xls workbook, then preview and print the Corporate aggregate production plan worksheet.

7. Revise the consolidation from Question 6 by using the array range Plan to link the individual workbook for each manufacturing operation to its respective sheet in the S_APT2CO.xls workbook. Remember to remove unwanted zeros.

8. Change the beginning inventory for the first quarter in the S_APT1NA.xls workbook to 9,000. Is this change automatically shown in the S_APT2CO.xls workbook? Save the S_APT2CO.xls workbook, then preview and print the Corporate aggregate production plan worksheet. Close the S_APT1NA.xls workbook without saving it.

9. Make S_APT1PR.xls the active workbook. Select the range B9:F13 in the Production Plan worksheet. Create an outline for this range, using the Auto Outline command. How many row and column levels are there? Collapse both the rows and columns to level 1, then preview and print this worksheet. Close this workbook without saving it.

10. Open the S_APT1CO.xls workbook. Create a macro that repeats the consolidation to update the results from the source files. Assign this macro to a button that you place in a convenient location in the Corporate worksheet. Save this workbook. Use the S_APT1PR.xls workbook to create test data with revised values for this consolidation. Which data values did you change? Run the macro in the S_APT1CO.xls workbook. Preview and print the Corporate worksheet. Verify that this consolidation was updated with your revised values. Write a paragraph describing your validation of this consolidation process.

11. Save and close the workbooks.

Case Problems

1. Tracking Bonuses for John Connolly & Sons John Connolly & Sons has been a publisher of textbooks since 1945. John Connolly was the founder of the publishing company and was later joined by his sons, Mark and Brian, when they graduated from college. Over the past 50 years, John Connolly & Sons has established itself as a leading publisher of mathematics and statistics textbooks, which are distributed through their University and Junior College divisions.

John has since retired and turned the control of the family-owned-and-operated company over to Mark, the oldest son. Mark concentrates on the financial area of the company. Brian maintains responsibility for the sales and marketing functions. He is particularly focused on the management of key personnel. Brian recognizes that in order to have sales growth in the publishing industry, outstanding sales associates are needed.

Brian meets regularly with his University and Junior College division managers, Mary Monzo and Brad Anderson. Mary and Brad each manage the sales associates for their respective divisions. Mary's sales associates are responsible for sales to four-year universities. Brad's staff serves the same group of clients, except at junior colleges and technical schools. At the start of each year, Mary and Brad meet with each of their sales associates and set a quota. A five percent bonus is paid to each associate who exceeds the quota. The payment of a bonus as an incentive has improved the productivity of the sales associates.

During his last meeting with Brian and Mary, Brad discussed a system that would track bonuses for each division and sales associate. Your task is to create this system for Brian and his division managers by completing the following:

1. Launch Excel and open Brad's P_JCS1JC.xls workbook in the Tut07 folder, then immediately save it as S_JCS1JC.xls. This workbook contains at least one error. What is it? Use the Trace Precedents audit tool to examine the error. Print the worksheet that includes the trace arrow.

2. Correct the errors in Brad's S_JSC1JC.xls workbook. You have corrected all the errors when there are no zero data values. Save this as the S_JCS1JC.xls workbook in the Tut07 folder. Preview and print the Bonus Detail worksheet.

3. Open the P_JCS1UN.xls workbook in the Tut07 folder and save it as S_JCS1UN.xls. Review the workbook, then preview and print it for your reference.

4. Open the P_JCS1CO.xls workbook in the Tut07 folder, which summarizes the bonuses paid to each division. Use formula references to link the totals from the TOTAL row in each of the division worksheets to the Bonus Summary worksheet. Save this as the S_JCS1CO.xls workbook, then preview and print the summary. Why is linked formula referencing a good method for including the data in this summary workbook?

5. Create a test of the formula linking, using the S_JCS1UN.xls workbook. Do this test, then write a paragraph describing your test and its results.

6. Mary needs to revise her quarterly sales numbers for several associates. She made a quick revision that she saved in the P_JCS2UN.xls workbook, which contains these changes from Accounting. Although the Accounting staff members followed a similar arrangement for the new data, their workbook does not contain the bonus amount or the totals. The quota and quarterly sales data needs to be replaced for each associate in Mary's S_JCS1UN.xls workbook. Open the P_JSC2UN.xls workbook, then review it, including the named range. Use the Data Consolidate command to replace the quota and sales data in the S_JSC1UN.xls workbook with that from the P_JSC2UN.xls workbook. Save your changes.

7. Preview and print the summary in the S_JCS1CO.xls workbook. Was it updated?

8. What is another method that Mary could have used to update her S_JCS1UN.xls workbook with the data from the P_JSC2UN.xls workbook? Repeat the update using this method, then write a paragraph describing your method.

9. Save and close any open workbooks.

2. Reporting Operating Profits for SeaWest Industries SeaWest Industries (SWI) manufactures, constructs, and manages wind farms. A wind farm consists of several hundred wind turbine generators that churn silently in a breeze, producing electricity. SWI recently completed construction of a wind farm in Tehachapi, California that, at the time of completion, was the largest single wind project of its kind. SWI manufacturing operations are organized in two divisions—Micon Wind Turbines in Copenhagen, Denmark and Mitsubishi Wind Turbines in Yokohama, Japan—that make up the Wind Turbine Manufacturing business unit.

Niels Rydder, vice president and chief financial officer of SWI, asked Lisbeth Hether, a financial analyst, to develop a workbook for preparing the quarterly statement of consolidated operating profit for Wind Turbine Manufacturing. The statement of operating profit is a variance report that includes the budget, actual, variance, and percent variance for each line item. Each quarter the two manufacturing divisions use electronic mail to transmit an Excel workbook file containing their operating profit data to the corporate office in San Diego. These workbooks contain data obtained directly from each division's general ledger system and are in local currency—Danish krone (DKK) or Japanese yen—with the appropriate currency exchange rate included in the workbook. The workbook that Lisbeth created includes the operating profit data for each division in local currency and in U.S. dollars (USD). The consolidated statement of operating profit uses USD, because the different local currencies do not produce meaningful results when consolidated. Lisbeth has set up the consolidation workbook and just received the two workbooks from the manufacturing divisions. Niels needs the consolidated statement of operating profit for a meeting tomorrow. Perform the following tasks to produce the information Niels wants:

1. Launch Excel and open the P_SWI1.xls workbook in the Tut07 folder that Lisbeth created with multiple sheets for the Quarterly Statement of Operating Profit. Save the workbook as S_SWI1.xls.

2. Review Lisbeth's workbook by examining each of the three sheets. Notice that the local currency operating statements are in the same worksheet and are immediately to the right of the USD statements, so you can click the horizontal scroll bar to move quickly between the two statements. What formula is used in the Wind Turbines sheet to do the consolidation for the budget and actual amounts? In general, what is the formula for performing the currency conversion to USD for each division? Why is the "#DIV/0!" error value displayed in the cells that calculate the percent variance? Notice that the budget and actual columns in the local currency statements are blank in preparation for receiving the data from the division workbooks. Try using the Name list to access the local currency statements.

3. Examine cells H8 and I8 in the Copenhagen and Yokohama worksheets. Note that these cells contain formulas with text values for the column titles. Because they are formulas, you can place data on top of them with the Data Consolidate command; the values will not be erased, which they would if they were only text labels and not formulas.

4. Open the P_SWI1DK.xls and P_SWI1JP.xls workbooks in the Tut07 folder for the manufacturing operations in Copenhagen and Yokohama, respectively, and immediately save them as S_SWI1DK.xls and S_SWI1JP.xls. Examine their contents, and the named ranges. If you want, print copies of the worksheets in these two workbooks. Compare these worksheets to the line items in the local currency statements. Do the rows and columns of data in the division workbooks match the corresponding data in the operating profit statements?

5. Use the Data Consolidate command to place the local currency data in its respective statement. Where does the cell pointer need to be located while the data consolidation is being done? Save this as the S_SWI1.xls workbook, then preview and print all three USD reports and the two local currency reports. (*Hint*: Wind Turbine Operating Profit Variance = $2,151.)

6. Create a macro that lets Lisbeth do the data consolidation of the division workbooks and print all five of the operating profit statements. Have the macro print all the USD reports first, and then the local currency reports. Place a macro button in a separate sheet named Macros for executing the macro. Save this as the S_SWI2.xls workbook. Execute the macro. Print the macro commands. Is there an advantage to using a macro to do the data consolidations? Why or why not?
7. SWI is considering establishing a third manufacturing division that would be located in Southern California. What changes would need to be made to Lisbeth's workbook to include the reporting for this third division? If the sheet for this new division is a *duplicate* of those for the other two divisions, what is an easy way to handle the currency exchange rate?
8. Create a separate Excel workbook for the proposed Southern California division. This should include the same line items as those used with the other two divisions. Make up the budget and actual data for this division. Save this as the S_SWI1SC.xls workbook, then print the budget. Open the S_SWI1.xls workbook and save it as the S_SWI3.xls workbook. Revise the S_SWI3.xls workbook to include the changes you described in Problem 7 for adding the Southern California division. Use the Data Consolidate command to include the California data in the revised workbook. Save this workbook, then preview and print the Wind Turbine and Southern California operating profit reports.

Comprehensive Applications

The following Comprehensive Application in this tutorial continues from the preceding tutorials.

1. Production Planning for Oak World Furniture At Oak World Furniture, Todd, Robin, and Sam just returned from Ashville, West Virginia, where they completed the negotiations for the purchase of Oak Express Creations, a furniture business specializing in manufacturing affordable oak furniture. With this acquisition, Todd has organized Oak World Furniture Corporation as shown in Figure 7-46. The Oak Country Division is Oak World's main business unit before the acquisition.

Figure 7-46 ◀

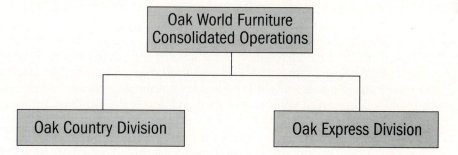

Todd is concerned about controlling the entire business operation. He wants you to create a Projected Statement of Operations for the Oak Express Division, just like that of the Oak Country Division. These results from the Oak Express Division can be consolidated with the old Oak Country Division to produce the corporate plan for the quarter.

Robin and Sam have assembled the following data for the Oak Express Division:

	July	August	September
Management Salaries	29000	29000	29000
General and Administrative	13500	14500	15500
Tables Sold	870		
Sofas Sold	312		
Table Price	450	450	470
Chair Price	100	110	110
Sofa Price	375	375	375
Employees	70	82	90
Hourly Rate	16.50		
Hours Worked	176		
Tables Sold Growth Rate	4%		
Sofas Sold Growth Rate	3%		
Raw Material Percent	28%		
Factory Overhead Percent	16%		
Advertising Percent	8%		
Insurance Percent	3%		

Because of the quality of oak used in the furniture at the Oak Express Division, the raw material percent is more than that for Oak Country. However, the newly acquired operation has less factory overhead.

Todd, Sam, and Robin analyzed their requirements for a corporate consolidation. They determined that the planning items or variables to be consolidated should include the following:

Tables Sold	Overhead
Chairs Sold	Cost of Sales
Sofas Sold	Gross Profit
Tables Sales	Advertising
Chairs Sales	Insurance
Sofa Sales	Management Salaries
Total Sales	General and Administrative
Raw Materials	Operating Expenses
Labor	Operating Profit

Once these items have been consolidated for each of the three months in the quarter, then the total for the quarter is to be calculated. For the Return on Sales, this ratio is calculated for each month in the quarter and for the quarter total.

After you visit with Robin and Todd, you are ready to develop the Oak World Furniture consolidated Projected Statement of Operations by doing the following:

1. Open your S_OWF1.xls workbook in the Tut02 folder, which contains the quarterly plan. If you did not create this workbook in Tutorials 1 and 2, see your instructor to obtain a copy of the file you will need to complete this comprehensive application. Change the title of the report from "Oak World Furniture" to "Oak Country Division." Save this as the S_OCD1.xls workbook in the Tut07 folder.

2. Create a BUDGET named range that includes only the data values for the planning items to be consolidated for the three months. Save this as the same S_OCD1.xls workbook, then preview and print this worksheet.

3. Clone the S_OCD1.xls workbook into the S_OED1.xls workbook by making the changes for the Oak Express Division. Change the report title to "Oak Express Division." Verify the inclusion of the BUDGET range name. Save this as the S_OED1.xls workbook, then preview and print this worksheet. (*Hint*: Operating Profit [Total] = $660,755 and Return on Sales [Total] = 19.90%.)

4. Set up a S_OWF1.xls workbook for performing the consolidation. Title the consolidated report "Oak World Furniture Consolidated Operations." Include a Documentation sheet. Save the workbook, then preview and print the Documentation sheet and the consolidated results sheet.

5. Write a paragraph describing the method of consolidation that you used and why you selected that method.

6. Outline the worksheet with the consolidated results, then collapse the rows and columns to level 1. Save this as the S_OWF1.xls workbook in the Tut07 folder, then preview and print the consolidated results. (*Hint:* Recall that the SUM functions control the levels of your outline.)

7. Using the consolidated data, create a bar chart of the sales revenue by product for the three months in a separate chart sheet. Add the appropriate titles and headings. Save this as the S_OWF1.xls workbook, then preview and print the bar chart. Write a paragraph interpreting the results shown by this chart.

8. Prepare user documentation that describes the operation of the system. These instructions should include the preparation of both the individual business unit reports and the consolidated corporate report.

9. Prepare a data flow diagram (DFD) of Oak World's planning system for inclusion in the system's documentation.

10. Describe the changes to this system that would be necessary if Oak World acquired another division, such as Lazy Days Rockers.

11. Implement the changes that you described in Problem 10. This system should include the same line items as those used with the other two divisions. Make up the data for the Projected Statement of Operations for this division. Use data values that seem reasonable to you based on those used for the other two divisions. Save the workbook with the data for this new division as the S_OWFNEW.xls file in the Tut07 folder, then preview and print the worksheets in this workbook. Save the workbook with the consolidated results for the three divisions in the S_OWF2.xls file in the Tut07 folder, then preview and print the consolidated results.

2. Analyzing Work Centers for Merritt Laboratories, Inc. In 1956, Dr. Joseph P. Merritt founded Merritt Laboratories, Inc (MLI). Dr. Merritt worked as a research chemist for a leading pharmaceutical company prior to founding MLI. He is recognized as one of the premier researchers in the areas of cardiovascular, neural, and respiratory systems. Since he founded MLI, it has grown to become one of the world-wide leaders in the manufacturing of prescription drugs. MLI patents most of its pharmaceutical products, which provides product differentiation in the competitive pharmaceutical industry. Currently, MLI sells over 100 different prescription and non-prescription pharmaceutical products.

The pharmaceutical industry is regulated by the U.S. Food and Drug Administration (FDA). The FDA approves new products only after extensive testing. The FDA also maintains a close watch on the production and effectiveness of existing drugs. MLI produces all of its products at its production facility in Providence, Rhode Island. A work center approach is taken in the production of all of MLI's pharmaceuticals. A work center is made up of a set of machines and machine operators. Each work center works on one batch of product at a time until that batch is complete. MLI production is separated into two groups, Caplet and Tablet. Each group maintains the same work centers in different parts of the factory.

Gabriela Dietz is MLI's production manager. At the end of each month, Gabriela prepares a work center analysis that calculates the amount of machine time available and the efficiency of labor. Machine time available is the amount of time that a machine is not used. Gabriela has set a goal of 7% to 15% machine time available and 90% efficiency of labor. Gabriela presents the results of this analysis at the monthly production review meeting. This month Gabriela is going to be out of town for the meeting and wants you to prepare her analysis by performing the following:

1. Open the P_MLI1CA.xls and P_MLI1TA.xls workbooks for MLI's work groups in the Tut07 folder on your Student Disk, then immediately save them as S_MLI1CA.xls and S_MLITA.xls. How are Machine Time Available and Efficiency of Labor calculated?

2. Construct a third workbook with a sheet that can be used as the consolidated worksheet. Give this sheet an appropriate name. This worksheet should be similar in structure to the worksheets for the Caplet and Tablet groups. Why

do you need formulas in this worksheet to calculate the Machine Time Available and Efficiency of Labor? Use a page header and footer that also include appropriate identifying information.

3. Create a Documentation sheet for this workbook with the consolidation. Make it the first sheet in the workbook, name the sheet, then save it as the S_MLI1WC.xls workbook in the Tut07 folder.

4. Consolidate the Caplet and Tablet groups into the summary worksheet. Did you consolidate the entire worksheet or a cell range? Explain. What could be done to make this Excel process more efficient? Save this as the S_MLI1WC.xls workbook. Preview and print the consolidated report for the work centers. What is the total Machine Capacity?

5. Using the consolidated data, create a bar chart of Efficiency of Labor in a separate chart sheet. Add the appropriate titles and headings. Save this as the S_MLI1WC.xls workbook, then preview and print the bar chart. Based on the efficiency of labor, which work center should Gabriela investigate more closely? Why?

6. To automate the consolidation process, create a macro and macro button that will consolidate the Caplet and Tablet work groups. Save this as the S_MLI1WC.xls workbook. Execute the macro, then print the macro sheet for documentation.

7. Prepare hardcopy documentation of this consolidation by printing each sheet of each workbook, including the one that contains your macro. Neatly organize these into a user manual that Gabriela can reference in preparing her summary each month.

8. Gabriela is considering an alternative solution for MLI's consolidation. Starting with the S_MLI1WC.xls workbook, she wants you to create a workbook that includes three worksheets—one for the Summary worksheet and one for each of the individual manufacturing groups. The consolidation performed with the Summary worksheet is to be implemented using 3-D SUM functions that you create. The data values in the two individual manufacturing group worksheets are to be obtained from the P_MLI1CA.xls and P_MLI1TA.xls workbooks, using linking. Which method of linking did you use? Using the example provided in this tutorial as a guide, draw a DFD for this system of workbooks. Create the multiple-worksheet consolidation workbook. Update the Documentation worksheet to reflect the changes to this workbook. Save this as the S_MLI2WC.xls workbook in the Tut07 folder. Preview and print the Summary worksheet and the Documentation worksheet, then print the formulas used in each of the three calculation sheets. Assemble these printouts and your DFD as the documentation for this application.

9. Create a workbook for a third manufacturing group of your design. The planning items and planning horizon are the same for this workbook as those for the Caplet and Tablet groups. Give this manufacturing group a realistic name of your choice. Use data values that seem reasonable to you based on those used with the other two manufacturing groups. Be sure to include a Documentation sheet in this workbook. Save this as the S_MLI1**.xls workbook. Use a two-letter descriptive abbreviation to replace the asterisks, like that used with the other groups. Preview and print the Documentation sheet and the work center analysis sheet.

10. Include the work center analysis for the manufacturing group from Problem 9 in the S_MLI2WC.xls workbook. The results from this additional manufacturing group should be included in the summary for the work centers. Write a paragraph describing the method you used to include the additional manufacturing group in the summary. Save this as the S_MLI2WC.xls workbook. Preview and print the Summary worksheet and the chart of efficiency of labor.

TUTORIAL 8

Working with Excel Lists

Managing Human Resources Data

OBJECTIVES

In this tutorial you will:

- Identify the elements of an Excel list

- Sort data in a list

- Use a data form to enter, edit, and delete records

- Filter data in a list using AutoFilter

- Insert subtotals into a list

- Summarize a list using pivot tables

Sunny Morning Products

CASE

Sunny Morning Products is a relatively young company, but it is growing rapidly. Currently the company has 75 employees, and Allison Olson, the human resources manager, has been searching for software that will help her to maintain accurate records on the employees at SMP. She has discovered that there are numerous human resource software packages available, but she just doesn't feel she can justify the expense. Human resource software keeps track of employee personal data, employment and salary history data, benefits, employee skills, education, and more. Even the simple packages with limited functionality can cost a thousand dollars or more. Her assistant, Janice Black, suggests using the software already available within Sunny Morning Products. She thinks that Excel provides list features flexible enough to create meaningful reports. Janice can enter the data for SMP's employee's into Excel; then add records when new employees are hired, make changes to records when an employee's status changes, and develop queries and reports in response to requests for information.

Using Excel to maintain the human resource records at SMP will enable Allison to answer requests for personnel-related information from other managers within the company as well as from external organizations.

Introduction to Lists

One of the more common uses of a worksheet is to manage lists of data, such as client lists, phone lists, and transaction lists. Excel provides you with the tools to manage such tasks. Using Excel, you can store and update data, sort data, search for and retrieve data, summarize and compare data, and create reports.

In Excel a **list** is a collection of similar data stored in a structured manner, in rows and columns. Figure 8-1 shows a portion of the Sunny Morning Products employee list that Janice created. Within an Excel list, each column represents a **field** that describes some attribute or characteristic of an object, person, place, or thing. In this situation, an employee's last name, the department in which the employee works, and the employee's annual salary are examples of fields. When related fields are grouped together in a row, they form a **record**, a collection of fields that describes an object, person, place, or thing. For example, the data for each employee—employee number, first name, last name, sex, hire date, department, salary, and classification as salaried or hourly—represents a record at Sunny Morning Products. A collection of related records makes up an Excel list.

Figure 8-1
Portion of Sunny Morning Products Employee List

If you have worked with spreadsheets before, you may associate the term "database" with what Excel now calls a list. Since the introduction of Excel Version 5, Microsoft refers to database tables in Excel worksheets as lists. The term **database** refers to files created using database management software, such as dBASE, Access, and Paradox. In this tutorial we focus on Excel lists. In the next tutorial we will discuss how you can use Microsoft Query to bring data from external databases into Excel workbooks.

Planning and Creating a List

Before you create a list you will want to do some planning. As you spend time thinking about how you will use the list, consider the types of reports, queries, and searches you may need. This process should help you determine the kind of information to include for each record and the contents of each field. As with most projects, the planning you do in advance will help you avoid redesigning the list later.

First, Janice determined her information requirements. As a way of documenting the information requirements of the employee list, she developed a data definition table that describes the fields she plans to maintain for each employee at Sunny Morning Products. Figure 8-2 shows the data definition table Janice developed to define her data requirements. She used this as a guide in creating the employee list.

Figure 8-2 ◀
Data definition
table for
Employee list

Field Name	Description
EMPNO	Employee ID
FIRSTNAME	Employee's first name
LASTNAME	Employee's last name
SEX	Female (F) or male (M)
HIREDATE	Date employee hired
DEPARTMENT	Name of department
SALARY	Annual salary
SALHOUR	Hourly (H) or Salaried (S), indicating whether employee is paid on hourly basis or gets a bi-weekly salary

Once you determine the design of your list, you can create the list in a worksheet. You can use an empty worksheet, or one that already contains data.

When creating a list in Excel, use the following guidelines:

- The top row of the list should contain a **field name**, a unique label describing the contents of the data in the rows below it. This row of field names is sometimes referred to as the **field header row**.

- Field names can contain up to 255 characters. Usually a short name is easier to understand and remember. Short field names also enable you to display more fields on the screen at one time.

- You should boldface the field names, change the font, or use a different color to make it easier for Excel to distinguish between the data in the list and the field names.

- Each column should contain the same kind of information for each row in the list.

- The list should be separated from any other information in the same worksheet by at least one blank row and one blank column so that Excel can automatically determine the range of the list.

- You should avoid blank rows and columns within the list, because Excel determines the range of a list by identifying blank rows and columns.

Now open the workbook that Janice created to help Allison maintain the data on employees at Sunny Morning Products.

To open the C_EMP1.xls workbook:

1. Launch Excel. Then open the workbook C_EMP1.xls in the Tut08 folder or directory; and immediately save it as S_EMP1. xls.

2. Switch to the EmployeeData sheet to display the employee list.

Janice's worksheet contains the list of employees at Sunny Morning Products. Currently there are 75 employees. Each employee record is stored as a separate row (rows 2 through 76). There are eight fields for each employee record (columns A through H). Notice that the field names have been boldfaced to make it easier for Excel to distinguish the field names from the data in the list.

Sorting Data

As human resources manager, Allison needs to distribute copies of a new employee's handbook to every employee in the company. Even though there are only 75 employees, it is easy to miss someone when distributing the copies. She asks Janice to prepare a list of all employees, alphabetized by last name. The list will be initialed by each employee as he or she receives a copy of the handbook. Janice begins to think about the tasks she will need to do to prepare the employee list.

When you initially enter records in a list, each new record is placed at the bottom of the list. To rearrange records in a list, you sort based on the data in one or more of the fields (columns). The fields you use to order your data are called **sort fields** or **sort keys**. For example, to sort the employee list alphabetically by last name, you order the data using the values in the LASTNAME field. LASTNAME becomes the sort field. Because LASTNAME is the first sort field, and in this case the only sort field, it would be the **primary** sort field.

Before you complete Allison's sort, you will need to decide whether you want to put the list in ascending or descending order. **Ascending order** arranges labels alphabetically from A to Z, and numbers from smallest to largest. **Descending order** arranges numbers from largest to smallest, and labels in reverse alphabetical order from Z to A. In both ascending and descending order, blanks are placed at the bottom of the list. For the handbook distribution list she is creating, Janice wants to sort the employee list by last name in ascending order.

Sorting a List Using One Sort Field

To sort data in an Excel worksheet using one sort field, you can use the Sort Ascending and Sort Descending buttons on the Standard toolbar, or you can use the Sort command on the Data menu. The easiest way to sort data if the sort key involves one field is to use the Sort Ascending or Sort Descending buttons on the Standard toolbar. If you are sorting using more than one sort key, you must use the Sort command on the Data menu to specify the columns on which you want to sort.

Produce Janice's alphabetized list by sorting the employee list using LASTNAME as the sort field.

To sort a list using a single sort field:

1. Click any cell in the LASTNAME column.

2. Click the **Sort Ascending** button ![Sort Ascending] on the Standard toolbar. The data is sorted in ascending order by last name. See Figure 8-3. Excel automatically recognizes the adjacent rows and columns as part of the list and sorts the entire list.

Figure 8-3
Employee list sorted by last name

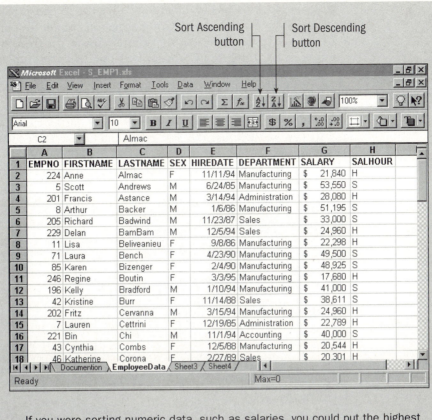

If you were sorting numeric data, such as salaries, you could put the highest salaries first by selecting any cell in the SALARY column and clicking the Sort Descending button.

TROUBLE? If you selected the wrong column before sorting the list, and your data is sorted in the wrong order, you can undo it. To undo a sort, click Edit, then click Undo. Remember that undoing a sort will only work if you act immediately after you have sorted your data.

SORTING USING A SINGLE SORT FIELD

- Click any cell in the column you want to sort by.
- Click the Sort Ascending or Sort Descending button on the Standard toolbar to sort the data.

Sorting a List Using More than One Sort Field

Sometimes sorting by one sort field results in ties. A tie occurs when more than one record has the same value for a field. For example, if you sort the employee list on the DEPARTMENT field, all employees with the same department name would be grouped together. To break a tie you can sort the list on multiple fields. For example, you can sort the employee list by department, and then by last name within each department. In this case, you specify the department field as the *primary* sort field and the last name field as the *secondary* sort field.

As Allison looks over the rather long alphabetized list Janice has created, she realizes that it would be better to have each manager distribute the employee handbooks within each department. To make the list more useful to department managers, the employee records must be arranged alphabetically within each department. So now she asks Janice to sort by department and then alphabetically within each department. To prepare this second list, Janice will need to sort the data using two columns: DEPARTMENT as the primary sort field and LASTNAME as the secondary sort field. Remember, you can use the sort buttons on the toolbar only if you have one sort key. When you have more than one sort key, you will use the Sort command on the Data menu to specify the columns you want to sort.

Now sort the employee list by department, and within department by last name.

To sort the records by department and within department by last name:

1. Click any cell in the list.

2. Click **Data**, then click **Sort** to display the Sort dialog box. See Figure 8-4.

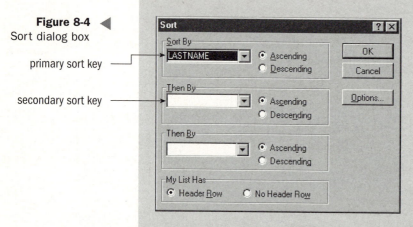

Figure 8-4
Sort dialog box

primary sort key

secondary sort key

3. Click the **Sort By** list arrow to display the list of column headings, then click **DEPARTMENT**.

4. If necessary, click the **Ascending** option button to specify that you want to sort in ascending order.

   Now specify the secondary sort field.

5. Click the first **Then By** list arrow to display the list of column headings, then click **LASTNAME**.

6. Make sure the Ascending option button is selected.

7. Click the **OK** button to sort the records by department and within department by last name. See Figure 8-5.

SORTING DATA **ADVEX 393**

Figure 8-5
Employee list sorted by department and within department by last name

sorted by last name within Accounting Department

sorted by last name within Administration Department

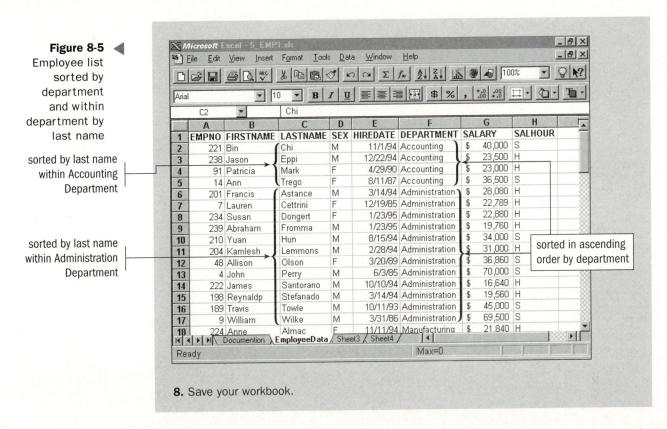

sorted in ascending order by department

8. Save your workbook.

Now Janice has a list of employees sorted by department and within department by last name. This will make the distribution of the company handbook easier.

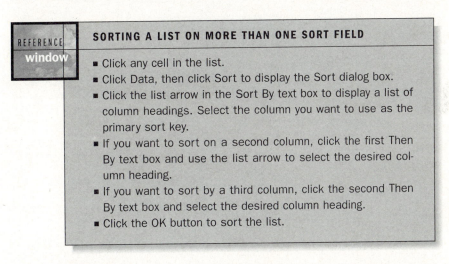

REFERENCE window

SORTING A LIST ON MORE THAN ONE SORT FIELD

- Click any cell in the list.
- Click Data, then click Sort to display the Sort dialog box.
- Click the list arrow in the Sort By text box to display a list of column headings. Select the column you want to use as the primary sort key.
- If you want to sort on a second column, click the first Then By text box and use the list arrow to select the desired column heading.
- If you want to sort by a third column, click the second Then By text box and select the desired column heading.
- Click the OK button to sort the list.

HELP DESK

Index

CUSTOM SORT ORDER

Double-click the Help button to display the Help Topics dialog box, then click the Index tab.

Keyword
Sorting data
Sort order, custom

Topic
Create a custom sort order
Creating a custom sort order

EXCEL 5.0

Maintaining a List Using the Data Form

Allison has received a memo from the sales manager informing her of several employee-related changes in the Sales Department. First, the sales manager has hired an office temp, Mark Hutch, as a regular full-time employee. His record now needs to be added to the employee list. Second, the sales manager held an annual performance review with Kevin Mack, who received an increase in salary for good performance. Kevin's record must be updated to reflect his new salary of $35,000. Finally, Wendy Garabizien has resigned; yesterday was her last day at Sunny Morning Products, so her record needs to be deleted from the employee list. Allison asks Janice to update the employee list to reflect these changes.

One of the easiest ways to maintain a list in Excel is to use a data form. A **data form** is a dialog box in which you can add, find, edit, and delete list records. A data form displays one record at a time, as opposed to the table of rows and columns you see in the worksheet.

Although you can use the worksheet to make changes directly to the list, using the data form can help prevent mistakes that can occur if you accidentally enter data in the wrong column or in a row above or below the correct one. Begin updating the employee list by adding Mark Hutch's data, using the data form.

To add a new record using the data form:

1. Click **A1**.

2. Click **Data**, then click **Form** to display the EmployeeData dialog box. The first record in the list appears. See Figure 8-6. Notice that Excel uses the worksheet name as the title of the data form.

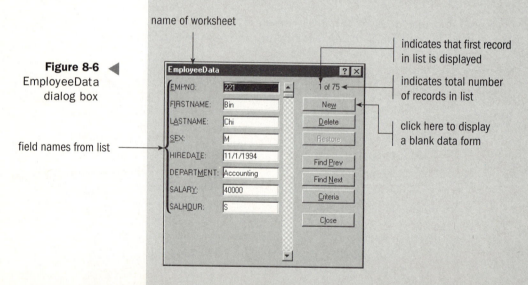

Figure 8-6
EmployeeData dialog box

The names that appear on the left side of the dialog box are taken from the header row of the employee list.

In the upper-right corner of the form, there is information on how many records are in the list and which row is currently selected. The heading row is not included in this count.

Now add the new record.

3. Click the **New** button to display a blank data form. Notice that the label "New Record" appears in the upper-right corner of the data form. Enter the values for the record in the text boxes next to each field name.

4. Type **247** in the EMPNO text box, then press the **Tab** key to move to the FIRSTNAME text box.

TROUBLE? If you pressed the Enter key instead of the Tab key, a blank data form appears. Click the Find Prev button to return to the previous record, the record you were entering, and continue entering the data.

5. Type **Mark** in the FIRSTNAME text box, then press the **Tab** key to move to the LASTNAME text box.

6. Type **Hutch** in the LASTNAME text box, then press the **Tab** key to move to the next text box. Continue entering the remaining data. Remember to press the Tab key after you complete each entry.

SEX	M
HIREDATE	7/15/95
DEPARTMENT	Sales
SALARY	25000
SALHOUR	H

7. Press the **Enter** key to add the record to the bottom of the list.

   If you use the data form dialog box to add a record(s) to a list and you have assigned the range name Database to the Excel list, Excel will automatically extend the range definition to include the new row(s) that you added to the list.

   The data form is blank again, ready for you to add a new record. But since you don't have any new records to add now, return to the worksheet.

8. Click the **Close** button to close the data form dialog box and return to the worksheet.

Confirm that the new record has been added to the employee list. It should appear at the bottom of the list.

To go to the bottom of the list:

1. Click **A2** to make it the active cell.

2. Press **End +** ↓ to move to the last record in the list. Verify that the last record contains the data for Mark Hutch.

   TROUBLE? If you can't tell what the data in some fields represents because the field names are not on the screen, use the Freeze Panes command on the Window menu to lock the top row so the field names are visible as you scroll the list.

3. Press **Ctrl + Home** to return to cell A1.

ADDING A RECORD USING A DATA FORM

- Click any cell in the list.
- Click Data, then click Form to display a data form.
- Click the New button to display a blank data form.
- Type the values for the new record, pressing the Tab key to move from field to field.
- Press the Enter key to add the record.
- When finished adding records, click the Close button.

Now Janice is ready to make other updates to the employee list. She still needs to complete two tasks: change Kevin Mack's annual salary to 35,000, and delete Wendy Garabizien's record. Although you can manually scroll through the list to find a specific record, with larger lists of data this method is slow and prone to error. The quicker and more accurate way to find a record is to use the data form's search capabilities. Janice will use this method to make Kevin Mack's salary change and delete Wendy Garabizien's record.

Using the Data Form to Search for Records

You can use the data form to search for a specific record or group of records. When you initiate a search, you specify the search criteria or instructions for the search. Excel starts from the current record and moves through the list, searching for any records that match the search criteria. If Excel finds more than one record that matches the search criteria, it displays the first record that matches the criteria. You can use the Find Next button in the data form to display the next record that matches the search criteria.

Janice needs to find Kevin Mack's record to change his salary. Use the Excel search capability to find this record.

To search for a record in a list:

1. Make sure the active cell is inside the employee list.

2. Click **Data**, then click **Form** to display the EmployeeData dialog box.

3. Click the **Criteria** button to display a blank data form. The label "Criteria" in the upper-right corner of the data form indicates that the form is ready to accept search criteria.

   Enter the search criteria in the appropriate field.

4. Click the **LASTNAME** text box, then type **Mack**.

   If necessary, you can enter multiple criteria. If you enter multiple criteria, all criteria must be met for Excel to find a match.

5. Click the **Find Next** button to display the next record in the list that meets the specified criteria—LASTNAME equal to Mack. See Figure 8-7.

Figure 8-7
Data form after Kevin Mack's record found

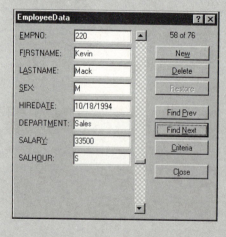

Kevin Mack is the record you're looking for. If this was not the record you were interested in, you could click the Find Next button again and the next record meeting the search criteria would be displayed.

If no records meet the search criteria, no message is displayed. Instead, the data form simply displays the current record.

MAINTAINING A LIST USING THE DATA FORM **ADVEX 397**

6. Double-click the **SALARY** text box, then type **35000**.

7. Press the **Enter** key. The salary for Kevin Mack has been updated.

Now Janice needs to complete her final update, deleting Wendy Garabizien's record.

Using the Data Form to Delete a Record

To delete Wendy Garabizien's record, you will again use the search criteria to find the record. If you enter the full name as the search criteria, the spelling must be absolutely correct; otherwise there will be no match and Wendy Garabizien's record won't be found. As an alternative, the data form allows you to use wildcard characters when you enter search criteria. A **wildcard character** is a symbol that stands for one or more characters. Excel recognizes two wildcards: the question mark and the asterisk.

You use the asterisk (*) wildcard to represent any group of characters. For example, if you use "Gar*" as the search criteria for LASTNAME, Excel will find all the records with a last name that begins with Gar, no matter what letters follow. You use the question mark (?) to substitute for a single character. For example, enter "Richm?n" as the search criteria and you might find Richman, Richmen, or Richmon.

Since there is a chance of entering Wendy Garabizien's name incorrectly, use the asterisk wildcard character to help find her record.

To search for a record using a wildcard search:

1. Click the **Criteria** button to begin entering the search criteria.

2. Click the **Clear** button to clear the previous search criteria.

   Specify the new search criteria.

3. Click the **LASTNAME** text box, then type **Gar***. See Figure 8-8.

Figure 8-8 ◀
Searching for employee using wildcard character

wildcard character

EmployeeData	? X
EMPNO:	Criteria
FIRSTNAME:	New
LASTNAME: Gar*	Clear
SEX:	Restore
HIREDATE:	Find Prev
DEPARTMENT:	Find Next
SALARY:	Form
SALHOUR:	Close

4. Click the **Find Next** button to display the first record in the list that contains the letters Gar as the first three letters of the last name. Karen Garafano is not the record you want to delete.

   TROUBLE? If you did not retrieve Karen Garafano's record, click the Close button, click Data, then click Form before repeating Steps 1 through 4.

5. Click the **Find Next** button to display the next record that contains the letters Gar at the beginning of the name. Wendy Garabizien is the record you're looking for.

6. Click the **Delete** button. A message box appears, warning you that the record will be permanently deleted from the list.

7. Click the **OK** button to return to confirm the record deletion. Wendy Garabizien's record has been deleted from the list, and the next record in the list is displayed in the dialog box.

8. Click the **Close** button to close the data form and return to the worksheet.

9. Save your workbook.

REFERENCE window	**DELETING A RECORD USING A DATA FORM** ■ Click any cell in the list. ■ Click Data, then click Form to display a data form. ■ Locate and display the record you want to delete. ■ Click the Delete button, then click the OK button to confirm the deletion.

HELP DESK

EXCEL 5.0

Index

WILDCARD CHARACTERS

Double-click the Help button to display the Help Topics dialog box, then click the Index tab.

Keyword
Wildcard characters
*

Topic
Using wildcard characters in string comparisons
Using special characters in a search

If you want to take a break and resume the tutorial at a later time, you can do so now. Close the workbook and exit Excel. If you are on a network, leave Windows running. If you are using your own computer, you may exit Windows and shut down the computer. When you resume the tutorial, place your Student Disk in the disk drive, launch Excel, then continue with the tutorial.

● ● ●

Filtering a List Using AutoFilters

The last several weeks have been very busy at Sunny Morning Products. Many of the employees have worked long hours, well beyond the forty-hour week, for which they receive no overtime pay. The payroll clerk has asked Allison for a list of employees who are paid on a per-hour basis. These are the only employees eligible for overtime pay for any hours worked over the normal 40 hours within a week.

To get an idea of how many employees are paid on an hourly basis and who they are, you could scan the entire employee list. However, with large lists locating the data you need can be difficult. Sorting can help because you group the data; however, you're still working with the entire list. You could use a data form, but if you use a data form to find records that meet specified criteria, you will only display one record at a time. A better solution is to have Excel find the specific records you want, displaying only these records in the worksheet. This process of "hiding" certain records and viewing the ones you want is called **filtering** your data. All records that do not meet your criteria are temporarily hidden from view.

FILTERING A LIST USING AUTOFILTERS ADVEX 399

HELP DESK

EXCEL 5.0

Index

FILTERING LISTS

Double-click the Help button to display the Help Topics dialog box, then click the Index tab.

Keyword
AutoFilter, Overview
Filtering lists

Topic
Filter a list
Filtering a list using AutoFilter

Excel's **AutoFilter** feature allows you to filter your data so you only view the records you want. Janice will use this feature to create the list of the hourly employees at Sunny Morning Products.

To display a list using the AutoFilter command:

1. Make sure the active cell is within the employee list.

2. Click **Data**, point to **Filter**, then click **AutoFilter**. See Figure 8-9. List arrows appear next to each column label in the list. To see a list of filtering criteria for a specific column, click the list arrow next to the column heading.

Figure 8-9
Employee list after AutoFilter feature activated

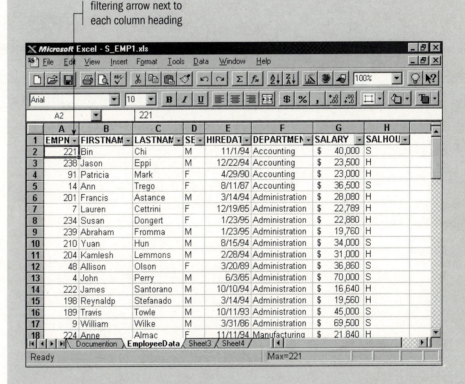

3. Click the **list arrow** in the SALHOUR column, cell H1, to display a list of criteria you can use to filter the data. Besides the unique values H and S in the SALHOUR column, five other choices appear that apply to every column. Figure 8-10 describes each of the other options found in this list.

Figure 8-10
Custom filtering options

EXCEL 5.0

Option	Description
All	Displays all items in the column and removes filtering for the column
Top *n*	Displays the top or bottom *n* items in the list *Top n not available*
Custom...	Specifies more complex criteria
Blanks	Displays rows where the field is blank
NonBlanks	Displays rows where the field is not blank

Now select your criteria for filtering the data.

4. Click **H** to display only records with H in the SALHOUR column. See Figure 8-11. On the status bar Excel displays the number of records found out of the total records in the list. Scroll the list to verify that only records with a value equal to H in the SALHOUR column are visible. Excel hides all rows (records) that do not have the value H in this column. You have filtered the list.

Figure 8-11
Employee list displaying only hourly employees

missing row numbers indicate records hidden

indicates number of records found out of all records in the list

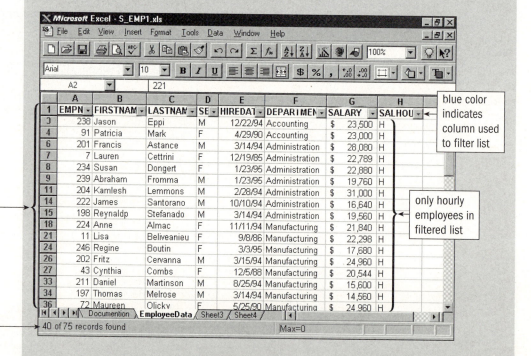

Notice the gaps in the row numbers in the worksheet, and the blue color of row numbers of the filtered records. In addition, the color of the list arrow next to the SALHOUR column changes to blue to let you know that this column has been used to filter the list.

5. Print the filtered list.

You can further restrict the records that appear in the filtered list by selecting entries from another drop-down list. For instance, to view the hourly employees in the Manufacturing Department, simply click the DEPARTMENT column and then click Manufacturing.

To filter out all but the hourly employees in the Manufacturing Department:

1. Click the **list arrow** in the DEPARTMENT column, cell F1, then click **Manufacturing** to display the hourly employees in the Manufacturing department. See Figure 8-12.

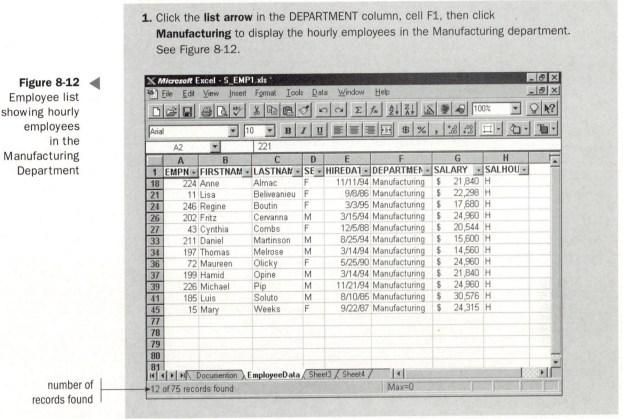

Figure 8-12 ◀
Employee list showing hourly employees in the Manufacturing Department

number of records found

Although you will not do this in this tutorial, you can copy the AutoFiltered data to another worksheet by using the Copy and Paste commands.

Now that Janice has provided the payroll clerk with the various filtered lists, she wants to view all the records in the employee list again.

To restore all the data from the list:

1. Click **Data**, point to **Filter**, then click **Show All**. All the records appear in the worksheet, but all the list arrows remain next to the column headings.

Now that the list again shows all the employee records, Allison has a more complex task for Janice, which requires her to provide specific information based on customized criteria.

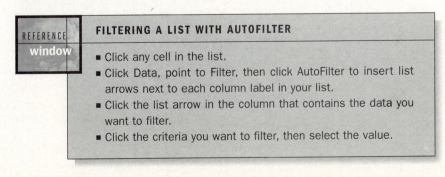

REFERENCE window

FILTERING A LIST WITH AUTOFILTER

- Click any cell in the list.
- Click Data, point to Filter, then click AutoFilter to insert list arrows next to each column label in your list.
- Click the list arrow in the column that contains the data you want to filter.
- Click the criteria you want to filter, then select the value.

Using Custom AutoFilters to Specify More Complex Criteria

Although you can often find the information you need by selecting a single item from a filter list, there are times when you need to specify a custom set of criteria to find certain records. **Custom AutoFilters** allow you to specify relationships other than "equal to" to filter records. For instance, Allison received a memo today from the accounting manager outlining some new tax guidelines affecting employees earning over $50,000 a year. The accounting manager asks Allison to produce a report listing all employees in the Manufacturing and Sales Departments earning more than $50,000 a year. You can develop a custom set of criteria using the Custom option in the AutoFilter list. Janice will use the custom AutoFilter feature to retrieve these records for Allison.

To use a custom AutoFilter to filter a list:

1. Click the **DEPARTMENT** list arrow, then click **Custom** to display the Custom AutoFilter dialog box. See Figure 8-13.

Figure 8-13 ◀
Custom AutoFilter dialog box

operator boxes

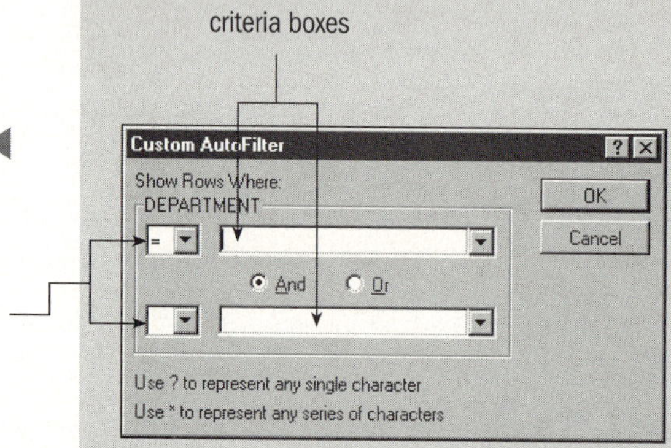

The **operator box**, the narrow list box on the left side of the dialog box, lets you specify the comparison operators (=><>=<=<>), by typing a value or selecting an item from a list.

The **criteria box**, the wider list box, lets you specify the field value by typing a value or selecting an item from a list.

The **And** and **Or** options are used if you want to apply two comparisons for the field. You select **And** to select rows that meet both criteria. You select **Or** to display rows that meet either criterion.

2. Make sure that = is selected in the first operator box.
3. Click the **criteria box** list arrow, then click **Sales** in the list.
4. Click the **Or** option button.
5. Click the **second operator** list arrow, then click = in the list.
6. Click the **second criteria box** list arrow, then click **Manufacturing**. See Figure 8-14.

Figure 8-14 ◀
Custom AutoFilter dialog box showing custom criteria

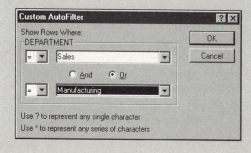

7. Click the **OK** button to display the filtered list consisting of all employees in the Sales and Manufacturing Departments.

   You are only partway there, because you also want to know all the employees in either Sales or Manufacturing who earn more than $50,000. So, further restrict the filtered list to those employees earning more than $50,000.

8. Click the **SALARY** list arrow, then click **Custom** to display the Custom AutoFilter dialog box.

9. Click the **first operator box** list arrow, click **>** in the list of operators, click the **criteria** list box, then type **50000**.

10. Click the **OK** button to view the filtered list—employees in either the Manufacturing or Sales Departments earning more than $50,000. See Figure 8-15.

Figure 8-15
Filtered list showing employees in Manufacturing and Sales earning more than $50,000

Janice shows the list to Allison. Allison approves it, and sends a copy to the accounting manager. Janice can now remove all the filters to return to the original employee list.

To show all records and remove the filter arrows:

1. Click **Data**, point to **Filter**, then click **AutoFilter** to remove all the filters. All the records are displayed and the list arrows no longer appear in the column headings.

HELP DESK

Index

CREATING A CUSTOM AUTOFILTER

Double-click the Help button to display the Help Topics dialog box, then click the Index tab.

Keyword	Topic
AutoFilter, creating custom	
AutoFilter	*Custom AutoFilter dialog box*

EXCEL 5.0

Allison had one other request for information from the Accounting Department, and she meets with Janice to discuss how the employee list can be used in this task.

Inserting Subtotals in a List

Bin Chi, the Sunny Morning Products accountant, is getting ready to start the next budget cycle. He asks Human Resources to provide him with a list of employees sorted by department that includes departmental subtotals for the salary field.

After sorting a list, and filtering out any records you don't want to use, you can summarize the data by inserting subtotals. The Subtotals command offers many kinds of summary information, including counts, sums, averages, minimums, and maximums. The Subtotal command automatically inserts a subtotal line into the list for each group of data in the list. A grand total line is also added at the bottom of the list. Before you can use the Subtotal command, however, you need to sort the list on the field on which you are grouping subtotals.

To supply Bin Chi with the information he requested, Janice will develop a list of employees sorted by department with subtotals inserted after each departmental grouping.

To insert subtotals by department:

1. If the list is not sorted by department, click any cell in the DEPARTMENT column, then click the **Sort Ascending** button 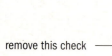 on the Standard toolbar. The list is sorted by department.

    Now insert the subtotals into the list.

2. Click **Data**, then click **Subtotals** to display the Subtotal dialog box. See Figure 8-16.

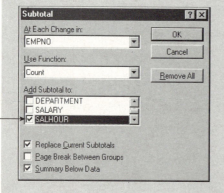

Figure 8-16 ◀
Subtotal dialog box

remove this check ⎯⎯⎯⎯

3. Click the **At Each Change in** list arrow, then click **DEPARTMENT** to select the column containing the group you want subtotals for.

4. Click the **Use Function** list arrow, then click **Sum** to select the function you want to use to summarize the data.

    You want departmental subtotals for salaries.

5. In the Add Subtotal to box, scroll the list and remove any check marks in the category check boxes, then click the **SALARY** check box, the column containing the values you do want to summarize.

6. Make sure the Replace Current Subtotals and the Summary Below Data check boxes are checked.

7. Click the **OK** button to insert subtotals into the list. Subtotals are added to the SALARY column, showing the total salaries for each department. See Figure 8-17.

INSERTING SUBTOTALS IN A LIST **ADVEX 405**

Figure 8-17
Employee list with subtotals

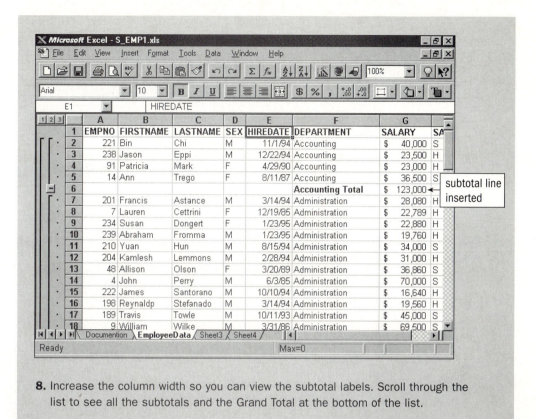

8. Increase the column width so you can view the subtotal labels. Scroll through the list to see all the subtotals and the Grand Total at the bottom of the list.

REFERENCE window

INSERTING SUBTOTALS INTO A LIST

- Sort the list by the column for which you want a subtotal.
- Click a cell in the list.
- Click Data, then click Subtotals to display the Subtotal dialog box.
- In the At Each Change in text box, select the column containing the group you want to subtotal.
- In the Use Function text box, select the function you want to use to summarize the data.
- In the Add Subtotal to text box, select the column containing the values you want to summarize.
- Click the OK button.

HELP DESK

Index

SUBTOTALS

Double-click the Help button to display the Help Topics dialog box, then click the Index tab.

Keyword
automatic subtotals
automatic subtotals

Topic
Automatic subtotals
displaying automatic subtotals in a list

EXCEL 5.0

ADVEX 406 TUTORIAL 8 WORKING WITH EXCEL LISTS

Janice now has the list for Bin Chi. After reviewing and printing the list with subtotals, she can remove the subtotals from the list.

To remove the subtotals from the list:

1. Click **Data**, then click **Subtotals** to display the Subtotal dialog box.

2. Click the **Remove All** button to remove the subtotals from the list.

Using Macros to Automate the Departmental Salary Report

Allison has been providing the Accounting Department on a monthly basis a printed report of employees sorted by department that includes subtotals for the SALARY field. She knows this task involves many steps and asks Janice if there is any way to expedite this process. After some thinking about Allison's request, Janice realizes that a macro can be created to automate this task. She records the macro and assigns the shortcut key Ctrl + p to execute the macro.

To start the macro recorder:

1. Make sure that the EmployeeData sheet is the active worksheet, and A2 is the active cell.

   Now start the macro recorder.

2. Click **Tools**, point to **Record Macro**, then click **Record New Macro** to display the Record New Macro dialog box.

   TROUBLE? If the Use Relative References command is checked (the command under Record New Macro), click Cancel to leave the Record New Macro dialog box. Click Tools, point to Record Macro, then click Use Relative References to uncheck this command. Now repeat Step 2.

   Change the name of the macro to DeptSubtotal.

3. Type **DeptSubtotal** in the Macro Name text box, then click the **Options>>** button. Excel expands the Record Macro dialog box to show several additional settings that you can control.

   Assign the shortcut key Ctrl + p to the macro:

4. Click the **Shortcut Key** check box, then click the **Ctrl+** text box, remove the default, "e," and type **p**. A lowercase "p" represents "print." Click the **OK** button to start the macro recorder.

Now perform the tasks you want recorded.

To record the DeptSubtotal print macro:

1. Click **F2**, then click the **Sort Ascending** button.

2. Click **Data**, then click **Subtotals** to display the Subtotal dialog box.

USING MACROS TO AUTOMATE THE DEPARTMENTAL SALARY REPORT **ADVEX 407**

3. Click the **At Each Change in** list arrow, then click **DEPARTMENT** to select the column containing the group you want subtotals for. Click the **Use Function** list arrow, then click **Sum** in the list to select the function you want to use to summarize the data. In the Add Subtotal to text box, remove any check marks in the category boxes by scrolling the Add Subtotal to list, then click the **SALARY** check box, the column containing the values you want to summarize. Make sure the Replace Current Subtotals and the Summary Below Data check boxes are checked.

4. Click the **OK** button to insert subtotals into the list. Subtotals are added to the SALARY column, showing the total salaries for each department.

   Now display the subtotaled list in the Print Preview window.

5. Click **File**, then click **Print Preview** to preview the output. Click the **Close** button to close the Print Preview window and return to the EmployeeData sheet.

6. Click **Data**, then click **Subtotals** to display the Subtotal dialog box. Click the **Remove All** button to remove the subtotals from the list.

7. Press **Ctrl + Home** to make cell A1 the active cell.

   You have completed the tasks to print the employee list with subtotals; now turn off the macro recorder.

8. Click the **Stop Macro** button ■ on the Stop Recording toolbar to stop recording the macro.

   Now test the macro using the shortcut key.

9. Press **Ctrl + p**. Excel displays the Employee list with subtotals on the print preview screen. If you want a hardcopy, click the **Print** button. If you do not want a copy, click the **Close** button. You return to cell A1.

   TROUBLE? If you get the run-time error "Offset method of range class failed," you need to recreate the macro. First you must remove the check mark next to the Use Relative References command. Click End to remove the error message box, then click Tools, point to Record Macro, and click Use Relative References to deselect this command. Now, repeat Step 2.

10. Save your workbook.

The macro executes as planned; the report with departmental subtotals appears in Print Preview. After you print the report, the subtotal rows are automatically removed from the employee list.

If you want to take a break and resume the tutorial at a later time, you can do so now. Close the workbook and exit Excel. If you are on a network, leave Windows running. If you are using your own computer, you may exit Windows and shut down the computer. When you resume the tutorial, place your Student Disk in the disk drive, launch Excel, then continue with the tutorial.

● ● ●

Allison now wants some tabulated information for an affirmative action report. She first reviewed the data within the worksheet to try to get a feel for whether men and women in comparable positions are making comparable salaries. She became overwhelmed and asks Janice to set up some sort of table.

Creating and Using Pivot Tables to Summarize a List

An Excel list contains a wealth of information, but because of the large amounts of detailed data, it is often difficult to form a clear overall view of the information, as it was for Allison. Janice can use a pivot table to help organize the information for Allison. A **pivot table** is a special type of table that enables you to group and summarize an Excel list into a concise tabular format for easier reporting and analysis. A pivot table summarizes data in different categories using functions such as COUNT, SUM, AVERAGE, MAX, and MIN. Janice has never used a pivot table before. She knows that the Sales Department uses them to organize its sales data for regions and for individual sales representatives. She asks Lee Jeng, the sales assistant, to show her an example of a pivot table so she can become familiar with them before she tries to create one for Allison. Lee shows Janice a pivot table summarizing sales by region and sales representative. See Figure 8-18.

Figure 8-18 ◄
Pivot table summarizing sales by Region by Sales Rep

Sum of Sales	Sales Rep			
Region	1	2	3	Grand Total
East	$84,471	$213,717	$21,231	$319,419
North	$142,740	$328,382	$1,846	$472,968
South	$120,209	$160,128	$41,255	$321,592
Grand Total	$347,420	$702,227	$64,332	$1,113,979

One advantage of pivot tables is that you can easily rearrange, hide, and display different categories in the pivot table to provide alternative views of the data. Figure 8-19 shows the example pivot table rearranged to summarize total sales in each region with the sales reps shown as subcategories within each region. This ability to "pivot" your table, for example, change column headings to row positions and vice versa, gives the pivot table its name and makes it a powerful analytical tool.

Figure 8-19 ◄
Pivot table after being "pivoted"

Sum of Sales		
Region	Sales Rep	Total
East	1	$84,471
	2	$213,717
	3	$21,231
East Total		$319,419
North	1	$142,740
	2	$328,382
	3	$1,846
North Total		$472,968
South	1	$120,209
	2	$160,128
	3	$41,255
South Total		$321,592
Grand Total		$1,113,979

Often you need to show numerical data in graphical formats so that various audiences can get a better feel for the impact of the data. While pivot tables provide valuable reports, you can enhance their effectiveness further by creating charts from them, as illustrated in Figure 8-20. Janice really likes this idea, and decides to keep this option in mind when she creates her pivot table for Allison. First, she needs to review the components of a pivot table.

Figure 8-20
Chart created from pivot table

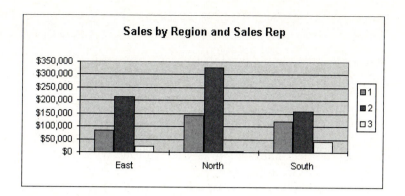

All pivot tables have similar elements. These include **column fields**, **row fields**, and **page fields**. Typically, the values in descriptive fields, such as departments, regions, and sex, appear in pivot tables as rows, columns, or pages. In creating a pivot table, you also specify which fields you want to summarize. Salaries, sales, and costs are examples of fields that you usually summarize. In pivot table terminology these are known as the **data fields**. Now that Janice has a better understanding of what a pivot table consists of, and how it can be used, she is ready to create a pivot table to help Allison compare the average salaries of men and women by department.

Creating a Pivot Table

To create the pivot tables for Allison, Janice can use the PivotTable Wizard to guide her through a four-step process. Although the PivotTable Wizard will prompt Janice for the information necessary to create the table, it will be useful for her to do some preliminary planning about what she wants to summarize. For example, the PivotTable Wizard will require Janice to specify the desired layout for the pivot table.

HELP DESK

EXCEL 5.0

> Index
>
> **OVERVIEW OF PIVOT TABLES**
> Double-click the Help button to display the Help Topics dialog box, then click the Index tab.
>
> **Keyword**   **Topic**
> PivotTables, creating   Analyzing data with a pivot table
> *PivotTable Wizard*   *Overview of creating a pivot table*

Figure 8-21 shows a sketch that Allison gave Janice of the summary information needed for the comparative salary analysis report. Allison wants to compare average salaries for males and females by department.

Figure 8-21
Sketch of table to compare average salaries

Average Salaries by Department for Females and Males			
Department	Females	Males	Totals
Accounting	xx	xx	xx
Administration	xx	xx	xx
Manufacturing	xx	xx	xx
Sales	xx	xx	xx
Totals	xx	xx	xx

Janice can use this sketch to determine the layout she wants for the pivot table.

Defining the Layout of the Pivot Table

In the third step of the PivotTable Wizard you specify which fields contain the data you want to summarize, and specify how the data will be summarized by selecting from functions such as COUNT, SUM, AVERAGE, MAX, and MIN. In addition to identifying the data to be summarized, you also specify how the data is to be arranged; that is, what fields will appear as column, row, and page headings in the pivot table.

In this step the fields are represented by a set of field buttons. You create the layout by dragging the field buttons into any of the four areas of the sample pivot table: ROW, COLUMN, PAGE, and DATA.

In the pivot table Janice is creating, she will categorize average salaries by departments and sex. The values in the DEPARTMENT field will appear as row labels, the values in the SEX field will appear as column headings, and the SALARY field will be the data that is summarized.

Now that Janice has done some planning, she is ready to create the pivot table for Allison.

Most often when creating a pivot table, you begin either with a list stored in a worksheet, or a database stored in an external file. In this case, Janice will use the Employee list in the EmployeeData worksheet to create the pivot table.

To create a pivot table:

1. Click any cell in the list, click **Data**, then click **PivotTable** to display the PivotTable Wizard - Step 1 of 4 dialog box. See Figure 8-22. In this dialog box, you specify the source of the data that is to be used to create the pivot table. You can select from an Excel List; an External Data Source, such as a dBASE file; a Multiple Consolidation Range; or another Pivot Table. To develop the average salaries pivot table you use the Excel list in the EmployeeData worksheet.

Figure 8-22
PivotTable Wizard - Step 1 of 4

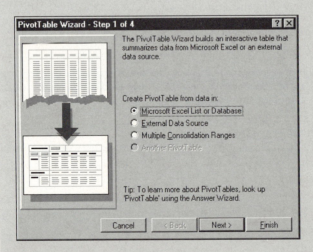

2. Make sure the Microsoft Excel List or Database option is selected, then click the **Next >** button to display the PivotTable Wizard - Step 2 of 4 dialog box. See Figure 8-23.

Figure 8-23
PivotTable Wizard - Step 2 of 4

Excel automatically selects range of list

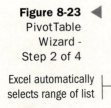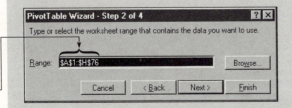

At this point, you need to identify the location of the data you are going to use to summarize in the pivot table.

Since the active cell is located within the range of the Excel list (step 1), the Wizard automatically selects the range of the Employee list, $A$1:$H$76, as the source of data for the pivot table.

3. Click the **Next >** button to display the PivotTable Wizard - Step 3 of 4 dialog box. See Figure 8-24. In this dialog box you specify the layout of the pivot table. Notice the field buttons on the right side of the dialog box and the sample pivot table in the center of the dialog box. They are used to specify the layout of the pivot table.

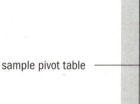

Figure 8-24
PivotTable Wizard - Step 3 of 4

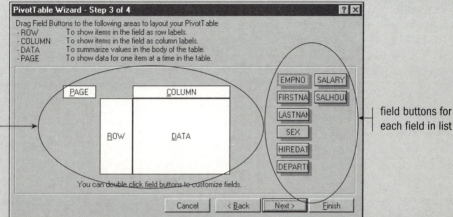

4. Click the **DEPARTMENT** field button and drag it to the ROW area of the sample pivot table. When you release the mouse button, "DEPARTMENT" appears in the ROW section of the sample pivot table. See Figure 8-25. When the Wizard is finished, the pivot table will contain a row label for each unique value in the DEPARTMENT field.

Figure 8-25
Sample pivot table area with DEPARTMENT field button as ROW label

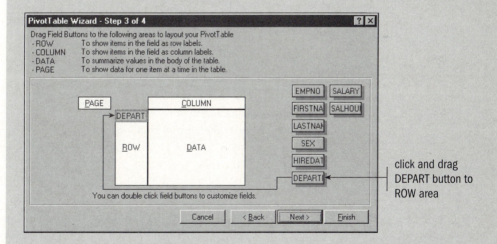

TROUBLE? If you moved the wrong field into the sample pivot table area, you can remove it by dragging it anywhere outside the sample pivot table area.

5. Click and drag the **SEX** field button to the COLUMN area of the sample pivot table. When you release the mouse button, "SEX" appears in the column section of the sample pivot table. When the Wizard is finished, the pivot table will contain a column label for each unique value in the SEX field.

6. Click and drag the **SALARY** field button to the DATA area of the sample pivot table. When you release the mouse button, a Sum of SALARY button appears in the DATA area. See Figure 8-26. When the Wizard is finished, the pivot table will contain the sum of the SALARY field entries for each combination of the SEX and DEPARTMENT field entries.

Figure 8-26
Sample pivot table area with entries in ROW, COLUMN, and DATA areas

SEX field is column label

DEPARTMENT field is row label

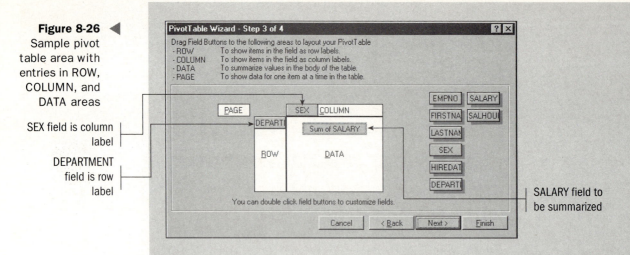

SALARY field to be summarized

By default, the PivotTable Wizard uses the SUM function for calculations involving numeric values in the DATA area, and the COUNT function for nonnumeric values. If you want to use a different summary function, such as AVERAGE, MAX, or MIN, you can double-click the field button in the DATA area and select the summary function from a list of available functions in the PivotTable Field dialog box.

Now compute average salaries.

7. Double-click the **Sum of SALARY** button in the DATA area to display the PivotTable Field dialog box. See Figure 8-27.

Figure 8-27
PivotTable Field dialog box

select this summary function

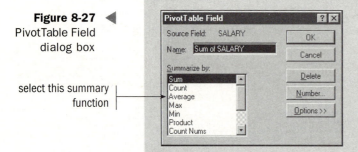

8. Click **Average** in the Summarize by list box, then click the **OK** button to return to the PivotTable Wizard - Step 3 of 4 screen. Notice that the summary button in the DATA area indicates Average of SALARY. The third step is complete.

9. Click the **Next >** button to display the PivotTable Wizard - Step 4 of 4 dialog box. See Figure 8-28.

Figure 8-28
PivotTable Wizard - Step 4 of 4

how you want your pivot table to appear

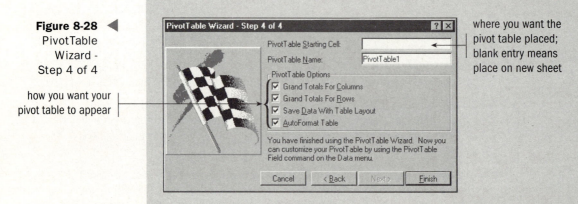

where you want the pivot table placed; blank entry means place on new sheet

In this final dialog box the PivotTable Wizard provides you with a number of options.

For Janice, the default options in this dialog box are appropriate. The pivot table will be placed in a separate worksheet with grand totals for columns and rows.

10. Click the **Finish** button to create the pivot table. A new worksheet containing the pivot table appears. See Figure 8-29. Notice that the field buttons DEPARTMENT and SEX appear as part of the pivot table. Additionally, the Query and Pivot Table toolbar is displayed. Figure 8-30 describes the tools available on this toolbar.

Figure 8-29 ◀ Pivot table showing average salaries for males and females by department

Query and Pivot Table toolbar (your location of this toolbar may be different)

DEPARTMENT field button

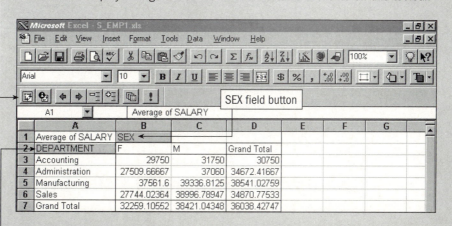

Figure 8-30 ◀ Query and Pivot Table toolbar

Button	Name	Function
	PivotTable Wizard	Accesses the PivotTable Wizard so you can create or modify a pivot table
	PivotTable Field	Displays the PivotTable Field dialog box so you can modify the options for the selected field
	Ungroup	Ungroups the values in a selected field
	Group	Groups selected items; lets you group numeric items, dates, or times into ranges
	Hide Detail	Hides detail lines for a selected field in the pivot table
	Show Detail	Shows detail lines for a selected field in a pivot table
	Show Pages	Copies each page of a page field to a separate pivot table in a new worksheet
	Refresh Data	Updates the contents of the pivot table based on changes made to the source data

11. Rename the worksheet **AvgSalary**.
12. Save your workbook.

ADVEX 414 TUTORIAL 8 WORKING WITH EXCEL LISTS

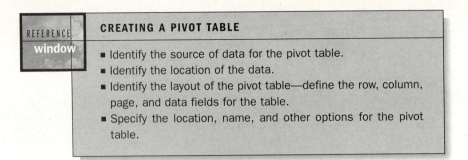

> **REFERENCE window**
>
> **CREATING A PIVOT TABLE**
>
> - Identify the source of data for the pivot table.
> - Identify the location of the data.
> - Identify the layout of the pivot table—define the row, column, page, and data fields for the table.
> - Specify the location, name, and other options for the pivot table.

The pivot table in Figure 8-29 shows the average salaries paid to employees in each department by males and females. Although the data in a pivot table may look like data in any other worksheet, you cannot directly enter or change data in the DATA area of the pivot table, because the pivot table is linked to the source data. Any changes that affect the pivot table must first be made to the Excel list. Later in the tutorial you will update an employee's salary and learn how to reflect that change in the pivot table.

Changing the Layout of the Pivot Table

Although you cannot edit the cells inside the pivot table, there are many ways you can change the layout, formatting, and computational options of a pivot table. For example, once the pivot table is created, you have numerous ways of rearranging, adding, and removing fields.

Repositioning a Field on the Pivot Table

A pivot table summarizes large amounts of data into a readable format. Once you have created the table, you can view the same data from different angles. At the top of the pivot table's ROW and COLUMN areas are field buttons that enable you to change, or pivot, the view of the data by dragging these buttons to different locations in the pivot table.

Allison reviews the tabular format of the pivot table Janice has created, and decides it might be more useful if it displayed males and females as row classifications under departments. Reposition the column headings for the SEX field (females and males) as row labels.

To move a column field to a row field in the pivot table:

1. Click and drag the **SEX** field button below the DEPARTMENT field button. See Figure 8-31. Notice that when you click and drag in the COLUMN area, your mouse pointer changes to . After you drag into the ROW area, the mouse pointer changes to .

Figure 8-31 ◀
Repositioning SEX field button in the pivot table

indicates pivot table is being rearranged

2. Release the mouse button. See Figure 8-32. The pivot table is reordered so that the SEX field is treated as a row field instead of a column field.

TROUBLE? If the SEX field appears to the left of the DEPARTMENT field, undo the last step and repeat Step 1. When you drag the SEX field button, just drag the button under the last "t" in DEPARTMENT. If you drag the button much further to the left, you change the order of the fields.

Figure 8-32
Rearranged pivot table

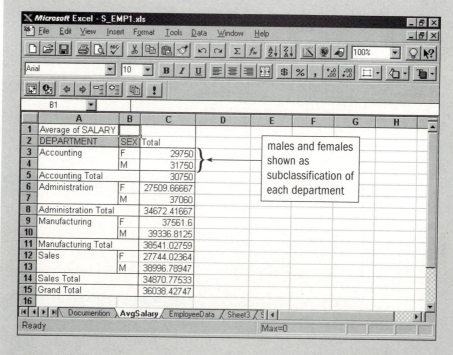

After viewing the pivot table in the new arrangement, Allison decides she prefers the original setup.

3. Click the **SEX** field button and drag it above the DEPARTMENT field button. The pivot table again looks like Figure 8-29.

Allison is pleased with the format of the pivot table. After reviewing it, she recognizes that the Sales Department has the largest discrepancy between salaries for men and women in similar capacities. She schedules a meeting to discuss the issue with the sales manager.

Rearranging Items Within the Pivot Table

Before the meeting with the sales manager, Allison asks Janice to place the Sales Department first in the table. To complete this task, you can change the field order within an area by dragging a field label to a new location within the area. Rearrange the pivot table so that the Sales Department row is the first row in the pivot table.

To move a pivot table item:

1. Click **A6** to place the cell pointer in the cell that contains the label you want to move.

2. Place the mouse pointer on the cell border of cell A6 so the shape of the pointer changes to ⇖.

3. Click and drag the **Sales heading** to cell A3 and release the mouse button. See Figure 8-33. The Sales Department is now the first department in the pivot table.

Figure 8-33
Pivot table with Sales Department as first row

Sales Department now first department

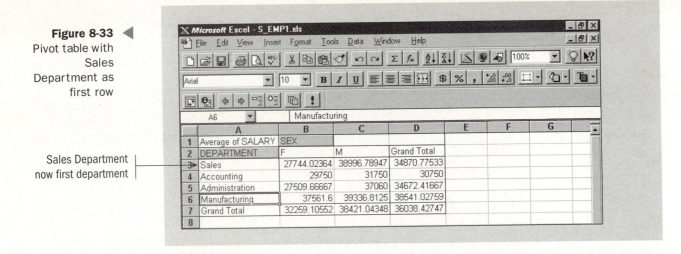

HELP DESK

EXCEL 5.0

Index

PIVOT TABLE PAGES

Double-click the Help button to display the Help Topics dialog box, then click the Index tab.

Keyword
PivotTables
Pivot table pages

Topic
Use page fields in a pivot table
Overview of working with pivot table pages

Formatting Numbers in the Pivot Table

As Allison runs off to a meeting, she mentions to Janice that the numbers in the pivot table are difficult to read and asks her to improve its appearance. You can apply number formats to the cells in the pivot table just as you would format any cell in a worksheet. Unfortunately, if you use this approach and later change the layout of the pivot table, you lose the formatting; it returns to the original format. A better approach, which makes your formatting permanent, is to format the data using the Number option in the PivotTable Field dialog box. Janice will format the average salary using the currency format code at zero decimal places.

To specify the number format for summary data:

1. Click **B3**.

2. Click the **PivotTable Field** button on the Query and Pivot Table toolbar, or click **Data**, then **PivotTable Field** to display the Pivot Table Field dialog box.

3. Click the **Number** button to display the Format Cells dialog box, then click **Currency** in the Category list. Click the **Decimal Places** spinner button twice to reduce the number of decimal places to zero.

   Click the Number button to display the Format Cells dialog box, then click Currency in the Category list. Choose the Format code ($#,###_);($#,##0_) from the list of Currency Format codes.

EXCEL 5.0

4. Click the **OK** button to close the Format Cells dialog box, then click the **OK** button to close the PivotTable Field dialog box. The pivot table is displayed with the format applied to the cells in the DATA area of the table. See Figure 8-34.

Figure 8-34
Pivot table after formatting

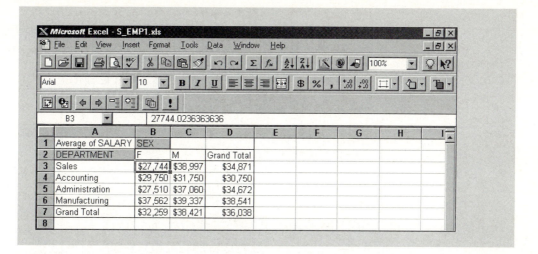

Now the data in the pivot table is much easier to interpret. Janice is pleased with the appearance of the modified pivot table.

Adding a Field to the Pivot Table

You can expand a pivot table by adding columns, rows, page fields, and data fields; this creates a more informative table. For example, Janice believes that a more accurate comparison of average salaries would include the SALHOUR field. Adding this field to the pivot table ensures that average salaries will be based on an additional breakdown that categorizes employees in each department into salaried and hourly classifications as well as by sex. She thinks the additional information will be useful for Allison in her discussion with the sales manager, and she decides to add it to the table before giving it to Allison to review.

To add a field to the pivot table:

1. Click any cell in the pivot table.

2. Click the **PivotTable Wizard** button on the Query and Pivot Table toolbar to display the PivotTable Wizard - Step 3 of 4 dialog box.

3. Click and drag the **SALHOUR** field button into the ROW area, immediately below the DEPARTMENT field button, and release the mouse button. See Figure 8-35.

Figure 8-35
PivotTable Wizard after rearranging field buttons

SALHOUR field added

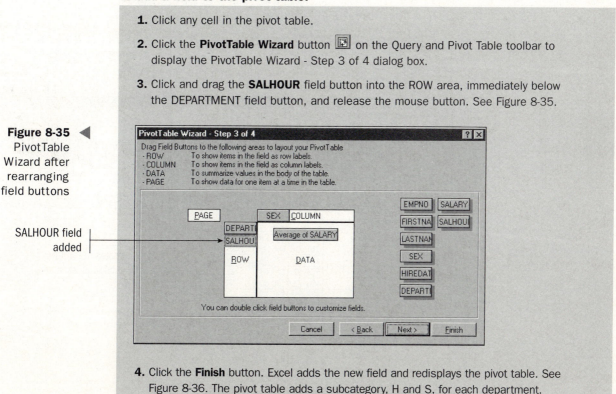

4. Click the **Finish** button. Excel adds the new field and redisplays the pivot table. See Figure 8-36. The pivot table adds a subcategory, H and S, for each department.

Figure 8-36 ◀
Pivot table after SALHOUR field added

field added to pivot table

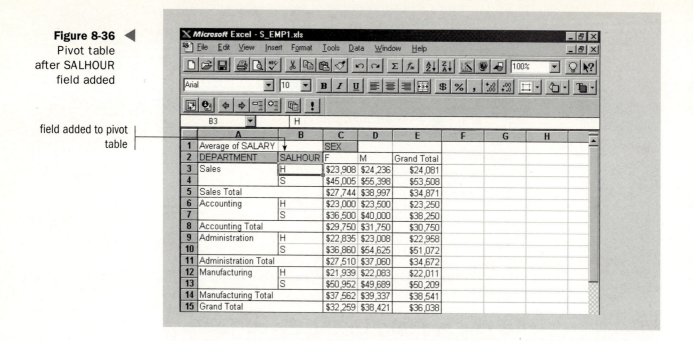

Removing a Field from the Pivot Table

Allison reviews the pivot table showing the data arranged by hourly and salary and by male and female. While she thinks this is important information, she feels the additional breakdown is not needed to show the difference in average salaries between men and women. So she asks Janice to remove the SALHOUR field from the pivot table.

If you decide you want to remove a field from the pivot table, just drag the field button outside the pivot table. Remove the SALHOUR field from the pivot table as Allison requested.

To remove a field from the pivot table:

1. Click and drag the **SALHOUR** field button outside the pivot table range. When the field button is outside the pivot table, a ✗ appears through the button. See Figure 8-37.

Figure 8-37 ◀
SALHOUR field button outside pivot table range

remove this field button

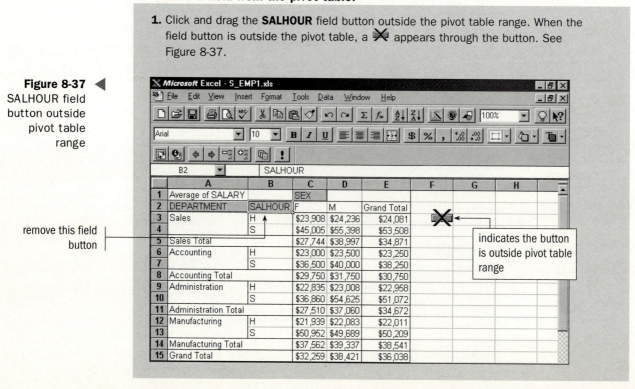

indicates the button is outside pivot table range

2. Release the mouse button. The SALHOUR field is removed from the pivot table. See Figure 8-38. Removing a field from the pivot table has no effect on the underlying list; SALHOUR is still in the employee list.

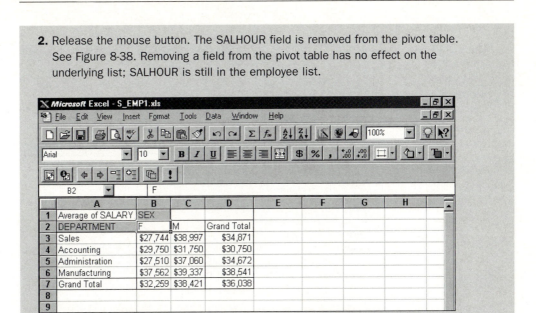

Figure 8-38
Pivot table after SALHOUR field removed

Hiding and Showing Items in the Pivot Table

Allison has decided to focus on the two departments with the greatest differences between men's and women's salaries. Thus, she wants to display only the Sales and Administration Departments in the pivot table. You can keep data in the pivot table without it being visible. In other words, Janice can hide certain data. For example, in this situation, you will hide the Manufacturing and Accounting Department rows of the pivot table, so only the Sales and Administration Departments are visible.

To hide a field item:

1. Click the **DEPARTMENT** field button, then click the **PivotTable** field button on the Query and Pivot Table toolbar to display the PivotTable Field dialog box. See Figure 8-39.

Figure 8-39
PivotTable Field dialog box

select these items to hide

2. Click **Accounting** in the Hide Items list. The Accounting item is highlighted.

3. Click **Manufacturing** in the Hide Items list. The Manufacturing item is highlighted.

4. Click the **OK** button. See Figure 8-40. The list of departments shows only Sales and Administration.

Figure 8-40
Pivot table with two departments hidden

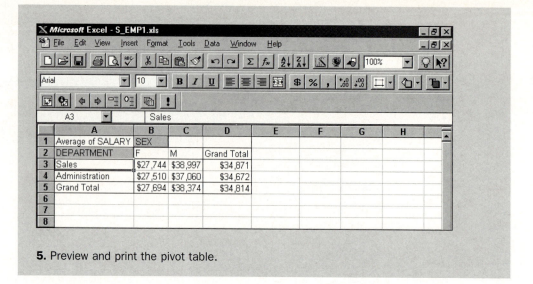

5. Preview and print the pivot table.

After Janice prints the pivot table, Allison asks her to return the two fields so they are no longer hidden.

To show a hidden field item:

1. Click the **DEPARTMENT** field button, then click the **PivotTable Field** button on the Query and Pivot Table toolbar to display the Pivot Table Field dialog box.

2. Click **Accounting** in the Hide Items list to show the item again.

3. Click **Manufacturing** in the Hide Items list to show the item again, then click the **OK** button. The pivot table appears with all four departments visible.

Refreshing the Pivot Table

Recall that in order to change the data in the pivot table, you must make the changes to the original list first; then you need to update the pivot table. To update a pivot table so it reflects the current state of the employee list, you need to update, or "refresh," the pivot table using the Refresh command.

Allison receives a memo from the sales manager stating that Mary Givens, an employee in the Sales Department, received a $1,500 salary increase. Her new salary is $26,000. Update her record in the Employee list and see how this affects the pivot table. (Make note at this point that the average salary for females in the Sales Department is $27,744.) Observe whether there is any change in the pivot table when you update Mary Givens' salary.

To update Mary Givens' salary:

1. Switch to the EmployeeData worksheet, then click any cell in the list.

2. Click **Data**, then click **Form** to display the EmployeeData dialog box.

3. Click the **Criteria** button to display a blank data form.

   Enter the search criteria in the appropriate field.

4. Click the **LASTNAME** text box, then type **Givens**.

5. Click the **Find Next** button to display the next record in the list that meets the specified criteria—LASTNAME equal to Givens.

6. Change Mary Givens' salary to **26000**.

7. Click the **Close** button. The salary for Mary Givens has been updated.

   Now return to the pivot table to observe whether there is any change in the average salary for females in the Sales Department staff.

8. Switch to the AvgSalary worksheet. Notice that the average salary for females in the Sales Department remains at $27,744.

Because the pivot table is not automatically updated when data in the source list is updated, the pivot table must be "refreshed."

To refresh a pivot table:

1. Select any cell inside the pivot table.

2. Click the **Refresh Data** button on the Query and Pivot Table toolbar to update the pivot table. See Figure 8-41. The new average salary for females in the Sales Department is $27,880.

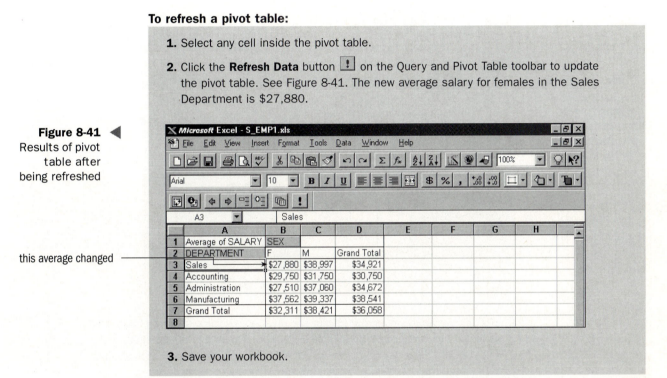

Figure 8-41
Results of pivot table after being refreshed

this average changed

3. Save your workbook.

The table shows that the average salary paid to females is lower in every department than average salaries paid to males. Allison is pleased with the appearance of the pivot table and asks Janice to print it.

If you want to take a break and resume the tutorial at a later time, you can do so now. Close the workbook and exit Excel. If you are on a network, leave Windows running. If you are using your own computer, you may exit Windows and shut down the computer. When you resume the tutorial, place your Student Disk in the disk drive, launch Excel, then continue with the tutorial.

● ● ●

Grouping Data in the Pivot Table

Sometimes the data in an underlying list is structured so that the pivot table does not initially summarize the data the way you want to view it. Dates are a good example of this kind of problem. The pivot table has a feature that lets you group items together to form larger categories.

Allison has asked Janice to create a second pivot table to see how many employees were hired in each year at Sunny Morning Products. This information is to be used in the company's annual report. This new pivot table will be located in its own worksheet.

To create a pivot table:

1. Activate the EmployeeData worksheet, then select any cell in the list.

2. Click **Data**, then click **PivotTable** to display the PivotTable Wizard - Step 1 of 4 dialog box. Make sure the Microsoft Excel List or Database option is selected, then click the **Next >** button to display the PivotTable Wizard - Step 2 of 4 dialog box. Since the active cell is located within the range of the Excel list, the Wizard automatically selects the range $A$1:$H$76 as the source of data for the pivot table.

3. Click the **Next >** button to display the PivotTable Wizard - Step 3 of 4 dialog box.

4. Click and drag the **HIREDATE** field button to the ROW area of the sample pivot table.

5. Click and drag the **LASTNAME** field button to the DATA area of the sample pivot table. The default summary function for nonnumeric data, Count of LASTNAME, is placed in the DATA area of the sample pivot table. See Figure 8-42.

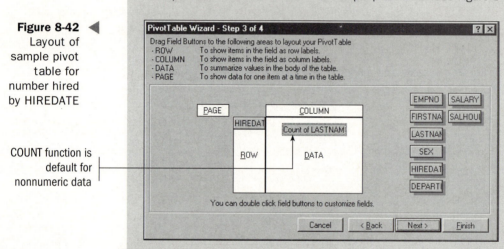

Figure 8-42
Layout of sample pivot table for number hired by HIREDATE

COUNT function is default for nonnumeric data

6. Click the **Next >** button to display the PivotTable Wizard - Step 4 of 4 dialog box, and accept the default options by clicking the **Finish** button to create the pivot table. The pivot table is added to a new sheet and this sheet becomes the active sheet. See Figure 8-43.

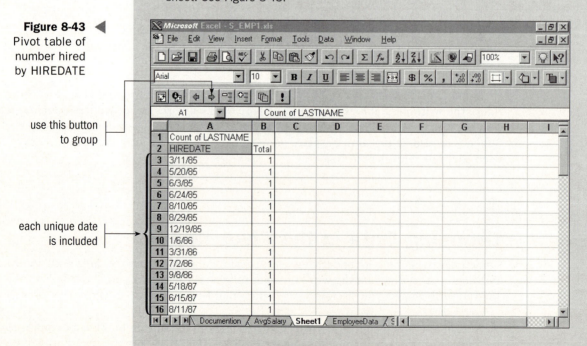

Figure 8-43
Pivot table of number hired by HIREDATE

use this button to group

each unique date is included

7. Rename the worksheet **Hired**.

Notice that the pivot table produces a row for each date on which an employee was hired. The information in the pivot table is not very useful. The pivot table would be more informative if Janice grouped the dates into blocks by year. Group the hire dates by year. First, select one of the cells in the Pivot table containing a value you want to group on.

To group date items in a pivot table:

1. Click **A3** as this is the cell containing the value you want to group on. This cell contains a year value, and Janice wants to group the data by years.

2. Click the **Group** button  on the Query and Pivot Table toolbar to display the Grouping dialog box. See Figure 8-44.

Figure 8-44 ◀
Grouping dialog box

3. Click the default **Months** time interval to deselect it, click **Years** in the By list, then click the **OK** button. See Figure 8-45. The pivot table now summarizes the number of employees hired in each year.

Figure 8-45 ◀
Pivot table after HIREDATE grouped by years

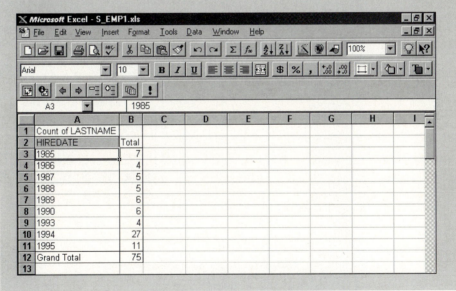

Allison comes by your work area and reviews the number hired by year pivot table. She asks you to present the data graphically.

HELP DESK

Index

GROUPING DATA IN A PIVOT TABLE

Double-click the Help button to display the Help Topics dialog box, then click the Index tab.

Keyword
Pivot tables
Grouping

Topic
grouping data
Overview of grouping

EXCEL 5.0

ADVEX 424 **TUTORIAL 8** WORKING WITH EXCEL LISTS

Creating Charts from a Pivot Table

You can create charts using the data in a pivot table. The process is the same as creating a chart with any other worksheet data. Janice decides to create a two-dimensional column chart to represent the yearly hiring experience at Sunny Morning Products.

To create a chart from a pivot table:

1. Select cells **A2:B11** in the pivot table. When graphing a pivot table, be sure to avoid selecting any columns or rows containing totals.

   TROUBLE? If you are having trouble selecting this range, try placing your mouse pointer in B11 when starting to select the range.

2. Click the **ChartWizard** button and highlight cells **D2:H12**.

3. Click the **Next >** button in the ChartWizard - Step 1 of 5 through ChartWizard - Step 4 of 5 dialog boxes, accepting the defaults for each of the first four ChartWizard dialog boxes.

4. In the ChartWizard - Step 5 of 5 dialog box, click the **No** option button to remove the legend, then type **Employees Hired by Year** in the Chart Title text box.

5. Click the **Finish** button to display the Column chart.

6. Click outside the chart area to deselect it. See Figure 8-46.

Figure 8-46 ◀
Column chart
showing
number of hires
by year

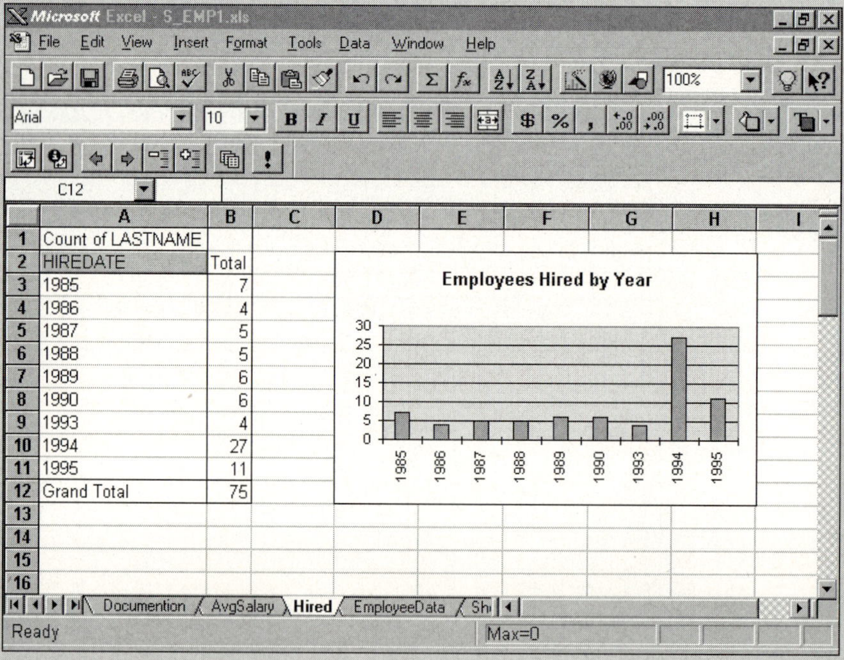

7. Print the pivot table and chart.

Allison is impressed with the chart developed using the data from the pivot table. It graphically shows the recent growth in hiring at Sunny Morning Products, and she thinks it will look impressive in the annual report.

Before you leave the tutorial, save the workbook and exit Excel.

CASE PROBLEMS **ADVEX 425**

To save the workbook:

1. Activate to the Documentation sheet.

2. Click the **Save** button 🖫 to save the workbook with the two pivot tables.

3. Close the workbook and exit Excel.

Tutorial Exercises

Jim Elvers has been using Excel for several months to track his household expenses. Open the workbook E_CHKBK.xls in the Tut08 folder on your Student Disk and save it as S_CHKBK.xls.

1. Identify the fields in this list.
2. How many records in the checkbook?
3. Arrange the checks by check number. Print the list of checks.
4. Arrange the checks by category and within category by date (earliest date first). Print the sorted list.
5. Print all checks written during July 1998 that were for groceries.
6. In which category did Jim spend the most? How much? Print the output that you used to determine the answer.
7. In which category did Jim write the most checks? Print the output that you used to determine the answer.
8. Prepare a report summarizing the total amount spent each month. Print the results.
9. Based on the answer to Question 8, prepare a column chart to graphically show how much is spent each month. Print the table and the chart.
10. Save the worksheet.

Case Problems

1. Inventory of State-Owned Property Emily Morris works in the Planning Division of the State of Rhode Island. This agency is responsible for tracking the land and buildings owned by the state. She has just been assigned the responsibility for overseeing and maintaining these records. Emily visited each site and inspected it; in most cases she found that the data matched the physical inventory she took. So she began her computer tasks by creating an Excel list of important facts about these various properties. Figure 8-47 shows the fields she used in creating the Excel list.

Figure 8-47 ◀

Field Name	Description
Division	Organizational unit that owns property
Land ID	ID that uniquely identifies property
Land Use	Category to classify type of property
Acquired	Year property was acquired
Acreage	Area in acres
Value	Value of property
Description	Brief description of property

Do the following:

1. Open the file P_PROP.xls and immediately save it as S_PROP.xls.
2. Sort the property list by division, and within division display the most recently acquired assets first. Print the sorted list.
3. Prepare a list of all assets under $50,000. Sort the list by land use. Print it.
4. Modify the results of Question 3 by inserting subtotals that show the average value of property under $50,000 *by division*. Which division has the lowest average value? Print this list.
5. Prepare a pivot table, in a separate worksheet, showing the total value of properties by division. Format the numbers in the pivot table (your choice of formatting). Rename the sheet Division. Print the pivot table.
6. Use the results of Question 5 to prepare a pie chart to graphically display the value of properties by division. Place the chart next to the pivot table. Print your pivot table and chart on one page.
7. Prepare a pivot table that provides a count of the number of properties by division by year acquired. In which year did the state acquire the most property? Print the pivot table.
8. Sort the property list by land ID, then save the workbook as S_PROP.xls.

2. Budget Reports at the State Legislature As a student intern working in the budget office at the state legislature, you will be assisting the staff of the budget office as they prepare several reports. The information in these reports must be accurate so that the legislature can make informed decisions based on this data. These reports will be distributed to members of the legislature and media, so the data needs to be clearly and professionally presented.

The director of the budget office has created an Excel list consisting of current and proposed expenditures for each agency within the state. Figure 8-48 shows the fields used in the Excel list.

Figure 8-48 ◀

Field	Description
Division	Major organizational unit
Agency	Organizational unit within a division
Current budget	Current year's budget expenditures for each agency
Proposed budget	Next year's proposed budget expenditures for each agency
PercntChg	Calculated field showing percent change between the proposed budget and current budget for each agency

Do the following:

1. Open the workbook P_GOVT.xls and immediately save it as S_GOVT.xls.
2. The fifth field, PercntChg, has not been included in the worksheet. Add this field to the list. Use the following formula to compute percent change:

$$\frac{\text{proposed budget - current budget}}{\text{current budget}}$$

3. Improve the appearance of the data by formatting the three numeric fields: Current budget, Proposed budget, and PercntChg. You select the appropriate formatting.
4. Sort the list in descending order by the Current budget field. Print the sorted list.
5. Prepare a report that includes subtotals by division for both the Current and Proposed fields. Which division has the highest proposed expenditures? Print the report. After printing the report, remove the subtotals.
6. Prepare a filtered list including records where the percent change is negative. Sort the filtered list by division. Print the list.
7. Prepare a pivot table, in a separate sheet, that summarizes average proposed expenditure by division. Format the pivot table (you select the formatting). Rename the sheet AvgExpenses. Print the pivot table.
8. Prepare a chart based on the pivot table in Question 7. You decide on an appropriate chart type. Remember to include a title for the chart. Print the pivot table and chart on one page.
9. Save the workbook.

Comprehensive Applications

1. Sales Analysis at Medical Technology, Inc. Medical Technology, Inc. distributes supplies to hospitals, medical laboratories, and pharmacies. Records of all customer and accounts receivable data are available to department managers on the company's mainframe computer. Tom Benson, the manager of credit and collections, was reviewing this data and noticed that the outstanding balances of several customers in Rhode Island and Massachusetts appeared to be higher than the average customer balances. He believes the average customer balance to be approximately $4,000. He wants to study these accounts in more detail with the goal of creating a plan to bring these accounts closer to the average balance.

Tom was able to download the necessary data from the company's mainframe, and he set up an Excel list. Figure 8-49 shows the fields included in the list.

ADVEX 428 **TUTORIAL 8** WORKING WITH EXCEL LISTS

Figure 8-49 ◀

Field Name	Description
CustNo	Customer number
Customer	Name of customer
Type	Type of customer: H for hospital, P for Pharmacy, and L for Laboratory
St	State where customer resides
Rep	ID of sales rep
Balance owed	Amount of money owed by customer
YTD sales	Amount of sales with customer since beginning of year

Do the following:

1. Open the workbook P_MEDI.xls, then save it as S_MEDI.xls in the Tut08 folder on your Student Disk.

2. Sort the list by Sales Rep (ascending) and within Sales Rep by year-to-date (YTD) sales (descending). Print the sorted list.

3. Insert subtotals (SUM) on YTD sales by type of customer. Print the list with subtotals. After printing, remove the subtotals.

4. Display all customers with a balance owed above $25000. Sort the list in descending order by balance owed. How many customers in the list? Which customer owes the most? Print the list.

5. Print a list of customers that have the word "lab" anywhere in the customer name. Explain how you got your results.

6. Prepare a pivot table summarizing total YTD sales by Sales Rep. Format the pivot table, then print it.

7. Using the pivot table you prepared in Question 6, hide the sales rep with the lowest total sales. Print the modified pivot table.

8. There appears to be a problem in the collection of money (balance) owed in one state and one type of customer. Identify the state and customer type that has the highest average outstanding balance. Print a report that supports your observation.

9. Create a macro to sort the Customer list by State, within State by Type of Customer, and within Type of Customer by YTD Sales (descending order for year-to-date sales). Name the macro SortByState. Assign the macro to a button. Change the button label to be more descriptive. Place the button to the right of the Customer list. Test your macro. Print the macro code. (*Hint*: As you begin the steps to open the Record New Macro dialog box, if the command Use Relative References is checked, uncheck it before recording the macro.)

10. Save the workbook.

COMPREHENSIVE APPLICATIONS **ADVEX 429**

2. Customer Orders at Baxter Inc. Mel Finder is the owner of Baxter Incorporated. The company specializes in selling plants and gardening equipment to greenhouses and garden shops around the country. The cost of shipping perishable plants and heavy equipment is expensive, and Mel wants to determine which shipping company would be most cost effective for him to use. He decides it would be helpful to analyze the orders to determine the volume of orders from certain regions, shipping patterns, and payment patterns of customers. He has created an order list to help him perform the analysis.

Figure 8-50 describes the layout of the order list.

Figure 8-50 ◀

Field	Description
Order No	Order number
Cust No	Customer number
Order Date	Date ordered
Ship VIA	How order was shipped—FedEx, UPS, or US mail
Order$	Amount of order in dollars
AmtPaid	Amount paid on order
Owed	Amount owed
Paid By	How payment was made—Check, Cash, MC, Visa, or left blank if no payment received
Region	Region where order was made

Do the following:

1. Open the workbook P_ORDRS.xls, then save it as S_ORDRS.xls.
2. Change the Region value from South to North for customer 2163's order on 1/16/98.
3. Sort the Order list by the Region field and within region by the Order$ field (descending order). Print the sorted list so all fields for a record fit on one page.
4. Which orders were shipped via US mail? Sort the orders by region. Print this list.
5. Prepare a report of orders for which no payment has been received (Paid By field is blank). Arrange the report with earliest orders first. Print the report.
6. Find all orders in either the North or East regions above $5,000 and with a balance owed greater than 0. Print the list.
7. Prepare a pivot table of the average Order$ value by the Paid By field. Format the pivot table. Name the pivot table worksheet PaidBy. Print the pivot table.
8. Based on the pivot table in Question 7, prepare a column chart to graphically present this information. Remember to include titles and labels in the chart. Print the pivot table and chart on one page.
9. In which region and in which month did the company have the highest number of orders? What were the total Order$ values in that month? Prepare a report to support your conclusion. Print this report.

ADVEX 430 **TUTORIAL 8** WORKING WITH EXCEL LISTS

10. Prepare a macro to sort the order list by customer number and within customer number by order date (ascending order). Name the macro CustSort. Assign the macro to a button object and place the button in rows 1–3 above the Cust No field name in the Order list. Change the label on the button to read "Cust Sort." Test the macro. Print the sorted list. (*Hint*: As you begin the steps to open the Record New Macro dialog box, if the command Use Relative References is checked, uncheck it before recording the macro.)

11. Prepare a macro that prints all orders that have an amount owed greater than zero. This report will be ordered so that the largest amount owed appears first. Name the macro AmtOwed. Assign the macro to a button object and place the button in rows 1–3 above the Owed field name in the order list. Change the label on the button to read "Who Owes." In this macro your tasks will include filtering records, sorting the filtered records, printing (or print previewing) the filtered list, and removing all filtering arrows from column headings. Use the macro to print the filtered list.

12. Print the code for all macros.

13. Save the worksheet.

TUTORIAL 9

Integrating Excel with Other Windows Programs

Retrieving and Sharing Data with Other Programs

OBJECTIVES

In this tutorial you will learn how to:

- Retrieve data from an external database using MS Query

- Updating linked and embedded Excel objects.

- Create multi-table queries

- Transfer data among programs, using object linking and embedding

- Import ASCII files

Sunny Morning Products

CASE
The management staff at Sunny Morning Products use a variety of Windows programs in carrying out their everyday responsibilities. In addition to using Excel as their spreadsheet software for maintaining budgets and employee data lists, the personnel at SMP use word processing programs to create memos, letters, and reports, and database management system (DBMS) software to maintain detailed records on purchasing, sales, and other accounting transactions. Sometimes the task at hand calls for creating documents using information found in several of these programs; sometimes the information needed is contained in a program that the user doesn't know, but can access using Excel.

For example, Casandra Montoya, vice president of sales at Sunny Morning Products, will attend a sales and merchandising conference in England next month. In preparation for her trip, she checked with her salespeople to see whether there was anything she could do to assist with any accounts located in London. Casandra often makes sales calls on key accounts to help the sales staff maintain good relations with the accounts and to resolve any issues that may exist regarding pricing, quality, and delivery.

For this particular trip, the sales staff has requested Casandra's help with some of the key customers. Casandra has asked her sales coordinator, John Bergeron, for an updated list of the company names, key contacts, and phone numbers for customers located in London.

SMP uses an Access database to keep track of data on customers and their orders. John realizes that it would be simple to find the information in Access, but he is not familiar with Access and isn't scheduled for Access training until after Casandra's trip. So he decides to use Excel and MS Query to retrieve the information Casandra has requested from Access into an Excel worksheet.

External Databases and Queries

In the previous tutorial you learned how to manage and manipulate data in an Excel list. This skill is a good one to have, but you will need to know more, because most businesses use a variety of DBMS software packages in addition to Excel. They use these DBMS to store, maintain, and process their routine business transactions—such as payroll, order entry, invoicing, and accounts receivable—using software packages like Access, dBASE, Paradox, Oracle, or DB2. In the past, when non-computer professionals needed to access data in these external databases, they found the task to be very difficult, and often had to manually re-enter data into a worksheet. Now Excel makes the task of accessing and retrieving data from an external database much easier by including a separate program called Microsoft (MS) Query.

In many situations, you may not be interested in all the records or fields in a database. Instead, you may want to transfer a subset of data that meets certain criteria. In other words, you want to query the database.

A **query** is a question you ask about the data in a database. For example, Casandra wants John to ask the question, "What customers are located in London?" The answer to this question will be the customers she hopes to visit on her trip there.

To query a relational database, you need to understand how a relational database like Access works. Recall from the previous tutorial that in an Excel list, a record is the set of data for a single person, place, or thing stored in a worksheet row. The data relating to each characteristic of the person, place, or thing is stored in columns called fields. Each column is labeled with a field name. The actual data value in a field is called the field value.

Relational databases have the same structure—based on fields and records. A list in an Excel worksheet is referred to as a table in a relational database. Each table in a relational database has a table name.

A relational database often contains more than one table. For example, the Sunny Morning Products Order Entry database consists of two tables. The CUSTOMER table stores data about each customer, and each customer record consists of a Customer ID, Company Name, Contact Name, Contact Title, Address, City, Region, Postal Code, Country, Phone, and Fax. A portion of the CUSTOMER table is shown in Figure 9-1. The second table, ORDERS, stores data about each customer order. Each record in this table consists of an Order ID, Customer ID, Order Date, Required Date, Shipped Date, Order Amount, and Freight. A portion of the ORDERS table is shown in Figure 9-2.

Figure 9-1 ◄
Portion of
CUSTOMER
table

Customer ID	Company Name	Contact Name	Contact Title	Address	City	Region	Postal Code
ALWAO	Always Open Quick	Melissa Adams	Sales Represent	77 Overpass Ave	Provo	UT	84604
ANDRC	Andre's Continental	Heeneth Ghandi	Sales Represent	P.O. Box 209	Bellinghe	WA	98226
ANTHB	Anthony's Beer and	Mary Throneberry	Assistant Sales A	33 Neptune Circl	Clifton Fc	WA	24422
AROUT	Around the Horn	Thomas Hardy	Sales Represent	Brook Farm	Colchest	Essex	CO7 6JX
BABUJ	Babu Ji's Exports	G.K.Chattergee	Owner	Box 29938	London		WX1 5LT
BERGS	Bergstad's Scandin	Tammy Wong	Order Administra	41 S. Marlon St.	Seattle	WA	98104
BLUEL	Blue Lake Deli & Gr	Hanna Moore	Owner	210 Main St.	Port Tow	WA	98368
BLUMG	Blum's Goods	Pat Parkes	Marketing Mana	The Blum Buildin	London		NW1 2BP
BOBCM	Bobcat Mesa West	Gladys Lindsay	Marketing Mana	213 E. Roy St.	Seattle	WA	98124
BOTTM	Bottom-Dollar Mark	Elizabeth Lincoln	Accounting Man	23 Tsawassen B	Tsawass	BC	T2F 8M4
BSBEV	B's Beverages	Victoria Ashworth	Sales Represent	Fauntleroy Circus	London		EC2 5NT
CACTP	Cactus Pete's Fami	Murray Soderholr	Sales Agent	87 Yuca Dr.	Albuquer	NM	87123
CAESM	Caesar's Mediterrar	Olivia LaMont	Marketing Mana	9308 Dartridge A	San Frar	CA	94965

Figure 9-2 ◄
Portion of
ORDERS table

Order ID	Customer ID	Order Date	Required Date	Shipped Date	Order Amount	Freight
10000	FRUGF	1/6/96	2/3/96	1/11/96	135	4.45
10001	MERRG	1/9/96	2/6/96	1/19/96	1316.97	79.45
10002	FOODI	1/10/96	2/7/96	1/13/96	731.8	36.18
10003	SILVS	1/11/96	2/8/96	1/20/96	498.18	18.59
10004	VALUF	1/12/96	2/9/96	1/16/96	3196.2	20.12
10005	WALNG	1/16/96	2/13/96	1/20/96	173.4	4.13
10006	FREDE	1/17/96	2/14/96	1/20/96	87.2	3.62
10007	MORNS	1/18/96	2/15/96	2/7/96	1405	36.19
10008	FUJIA	1/19/96	2/16/96	1/25/96	1171	74.22
10009	SEVES	1/20/96	2/17/96	1/27/96	1530	49.21
10010	SILVS	1/24/96	2/21/96	1/26/96	470	3.01
10011	WELLT	1/25/96	2/22/96	1/30/96	589.05	31.54
10012	LIVEO	1/26/96	2/23/96	1/30/96	1057.6	102.59
10013	RITEB	1/27/96	2/24/96	2/3/96	560.4	50.87
10014	GRUED	1/30/96	2/27/96	2/8/96	192.1	17.67
10015	PICAF	2/1/96	3/1/96	2/16/96	1423.5	22.1

The tables in a relational database are linked by values in **common fields**, which are fields that are common to two or more tables. These links between tables allow you to find the information you need in a database as it is pulled from each linked table. For example, each order in the ORDERS table is linked to a customer in the CUSTOMER table by the Customer ID field, which is common to both tables. In Figure 9-3 the ORDERS table shows that Order ID 10062 was placed by Customer ID ALWAO. Looking in the common field Customer ID in the CUSTOMER table, you find that the customer with Customer ID ALWAO is the Always Open Quick Mart located in Provo, Utah.

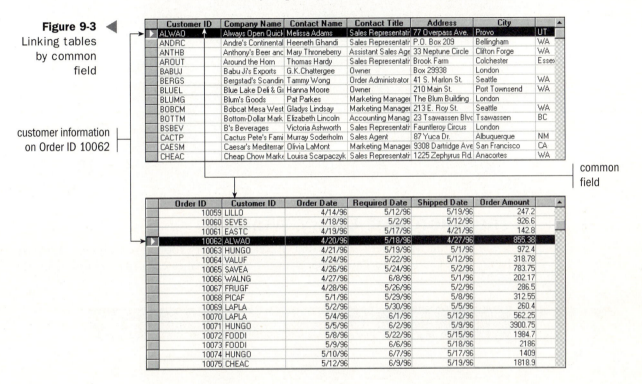

Figure 9-3 Linking tables by common field

customer information on Order ID 10062

common field

Now that you understand the structure of the Order Entry database, you can help John query the database, using MS Query, to obtain the information for Casandra.

Using Microsoft Query

MS Query, a separate program that comes with Excel, allows you to retrieve all or part of a set of data from an external database program and place it in your workbook as an Excel list.

Remember that a query is a question you want to ask about your data. For example, which orders are from customers in Canada? Who is the top salesperson this quarter? Who is our largest customer?

In this case, John needs to query the ORDENTRY database to get an updated list of customers located in London. To retrieve this information, he will need to create a query to retrieve a list of Company Name, Contact Name, and Phone from the CUSTOMER table in the ORDENTRY database and place the data in a worksheet. Begin by opening a new workbook; then run MS Query.

To run MS Query:

1. Launch Excel and open a new workbook.

2. Click **Data**, then click **Get External Data**. The Microsoft Query window displays and then the Select Data Source dialog box opens. See Figure 9-4.

TROUBLE? If you don't see the Get External Data command on the Data menu, click Tools, click Add-In, click the MS Query Add-In check box, then click the OK button and repeat Step 2. If you don't see the MS Query Add-In checkbox, see your instructor or technical support person for assistance.

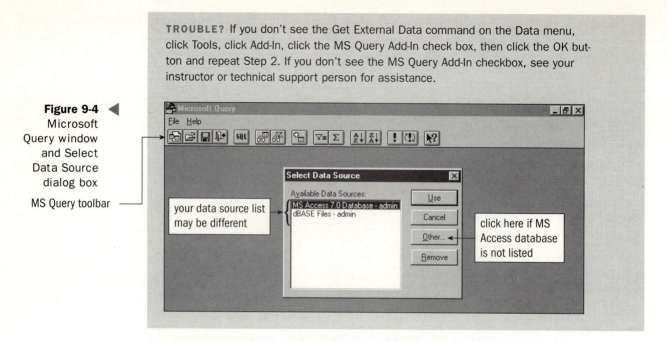

Figure 9-4
Microsoft Query window and Select Data Source dialog box

MS Query toolbar

The Microsoft Query Window

When you run MS Query from within Excel, the Query toolbar displays, as shown in Figure 9-4. The table in Figure 9-5 identifies and describes each of the buttons on the toolbar.

Figure 9-5
Description of MS Query toolbar

Button	Name	Description
	New Query	Displays an empty Query window in which you create a query
	Open Query	Displays the Open Query dialog box, from which you open an existing query for viewing or editing
	Save File	Saves a query's design, replacing any previous version with the current version
	Return Data to Excel	Returns data from MS Query to the original application
SQL	View SQL	Displays the corresponding SQL SELECT statement for the active query in the Query window so you can view or edit the statement
	Show/Hide Tables	Displays or hides the Table pane
	Show/Hide Criteria	Displays or hides the Criteria pane
	Add Table(s)	Displays the Add Tables dialog box, which you can use to add one or more tables to the Table pane in your query
	Criteria Equals	Displays the Add Criteria dialog box, in which you define the criteria that records must meet to be included in the result set
Σ	Cycle Thru Total	Performs a Total calculation on values in the selected field

Figure 9-5
Description of MS Query toolbar (continued)

Button	Name	Description
A↓Z	Sort Ascending	Sorts the records in a query by the values in ascending order (A-Z, 0-9) by the column you select
Z↓A	Sort Descending	Sorts the records in a query by the values in descending order (Z-A, 9-0) by the column you select
!	Query Now	Runs the query and displays the most current result set in the Data pane
(!)	Auto Query	Controls whether the query is run every time you change it
?	Help	Accesses on-line Help

Before John can create the query, he must first select the data source.

Selecting a Data Source

When you create a new query, you have to select a data source for it, telling MS Query the type of database you want to work with and where the data is located.

Because Sunny Morning Products' order entry database is stored as an Access database, John needs to choose Access as the data source. Then he will select the order entry database, which is named ORDENTRY.MDB.

To select the Access database ORDENTRY.MDB:

1. Click MS Access 7.0 Database - admin in the Available Data Sources list in the Select Data Source dialog box, then click the Use button. The Select Database dialog box opens. See Figure 9-6.

   Click MS Access 2.0 Database - Admin from the Available Data Sources list, then click the Use button.

   TROUBLE? If the MS Access Database isn't displayed in the Available Data Sources list, click the Other button to display the ODBC Data Sources dialog box. Click MS Access Database in the Enter Data Source list. Click the OK button to return to the Select Database dialog box. Select the database. Click ordentry.mdb, then click the OK button to select the Select Data Source dialog box. Click MS Access Database, click the Use Button, then go to Step 4.

EXCEL 5.0

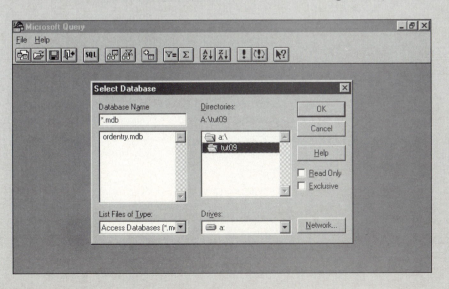

Figure 9-6
Select Database dialog box

Now select the database.

2. If necessary, click the **Drives** list arrow and select the drive in which your Student Disk is located. Click the **Directories** list box and select the **Tut09** folder or directory.

3. Click **ordentry.mdb** in the Database Name list, then click the **OK** button. The Microsoft Query window opens and then the Add Tables dialog box opens. See Figure 9-7. Within the dialog box is a list of all the tables in your data source.

Figure 9-7
Add Tables dialog box

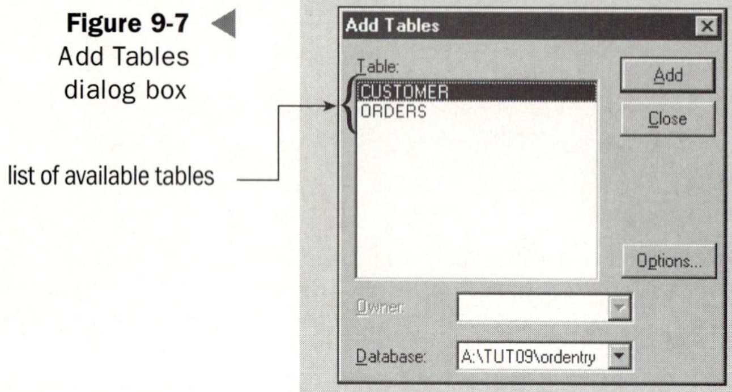

list of available tables

4. Click **CUSTOMER**, then click the **Add** button. See Figure 9-8. The CUSTOMER table appears as a field list at the top of the Query window within the Table pane. You can add as many tables as you need to the Table pane.

Figure 9-8
Customer field list displayed in Table pane

Table pane

field list

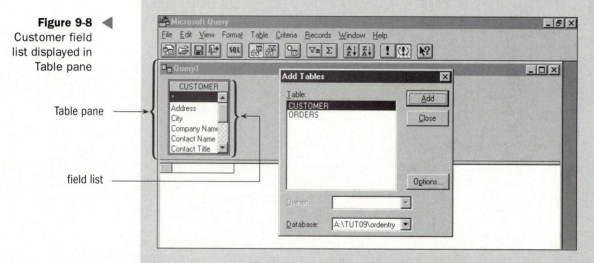

You only need data from the CUSTOMER table.

5. Click the **Close** button to close the Add Tables dialog box.

6. Click the **Show/Hide Criteria** button to display the Criteria pane in the Query window. You use the Query window to design, edit, and run the query. See Figure 9-9.

Figure 9-9
Query window divided into three panes

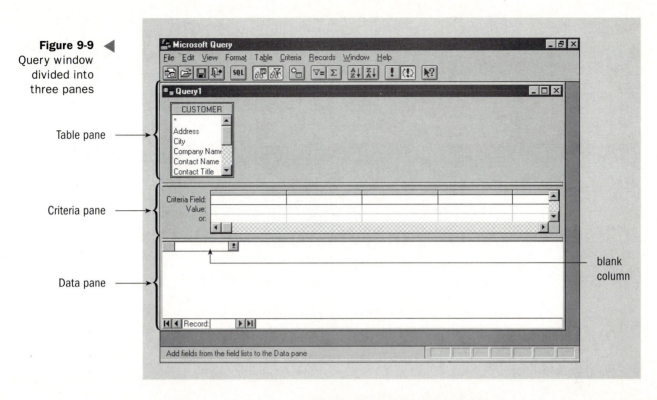

Table pane

Criteria pane

Data pane

blank column

The Query window is divided into three panes: the Table pane, the Criteria pane, and the Data pane.

The tables you use in your query are displayed in the **Table pane**. In the Table pane, you see one or more **field lists** labeled with the name of the table you are working with and an alphabetical list of the fields that each table contains. You enter your search criteria in the **Criteria pane**. The **criteria** are the values you want MS Query to search for. For example, to ask the question "Which customers are located in Canada?" you would enter "Canada" as your criterion and then ask MS Query to search for all records that match this criterion.

The answer to your question—in this case, all the records for customers in Canada—is the **result set**. The result set displays in the Data pane. The **Data pane** displays the fields you select from the field list. The Data pane always displays one empty field box to show you where to add the next field from the field list.

You are now ready to create the query that lists the Company Name, Contact Name, and Phone of all SMP customers located in London.

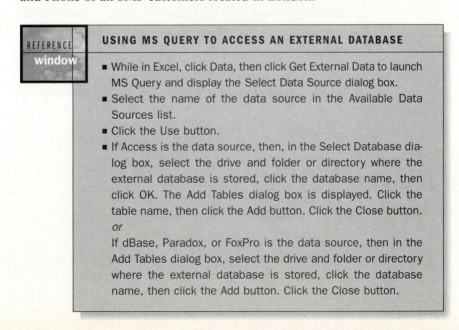

REFERENCE window

USING MS QUERY TO ACCESS AN EXTERNAL DATABASE

- While in Excel, click Data, then click Get External Data to launch MS Query and display the Select Data Source dialog box.
- Select the name of the data source in the Available Data Sources list.
- Click the Use button.
- If Access is the data source, then, in the Select Database dialog box, select the drive and folder or directory where the external database is stored, click the database name, then click OK. The Add Tables dialog box is displayed. Click the table name, then click the Add button. Click the Close button.
  or
  If dBase, Paradox, or FoxPro is the data source, then in the Add Tables dialog box, select the drive and folder or directory where the external database is stored, click the database name, then click the Add button. Click the Close button.

ADDING A DATA SOURCE TO THE DATA SOURCE LIST

- If the Select Data Source dialog box is not already on the screen, click the New Query button to display it.
- If the data source you want to use is not listed in the Available Data Sources list, click the Other button to display the ODBC Data Sources dialog box.
- Click the data source you want to use in the Enter Data Source list, then click the OK button. The data source now appears in the Available Data Sources list of the Select Data Source dialog box.

Querying Only One Table

After you access your data source and specify the table or tables you want to work with, you specify the fields you want in the result set. By default, MS Query updates the result set every time you add a new field to the Data pane. This is called the Auto Query feature. By turning the automatic query feature off, you will speed up the query design process, so before adding fields to the data field, it is a good idea to turn off the Auto Query option.

In this query, John will focus on single-table operations.

To add fields to the Data pane:

1. Click the **Auto Query** button on the toolbar to turn Automatic Query off. The button no longer appears depressed.

2. Click **Company Name** in the Customer field list in the Table pane.

3. Click and drag the **Company Name** field name from the field list to the blank column in the Data pane (lower part of the window). The Company Name field is added to the Data pane. A new blank column appears in the Data pane. See Figure 9-10.

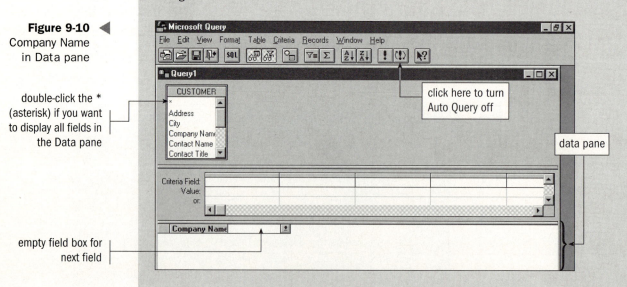

Figure 9-10
Company Name in Data pane

If you decide you no longer need a field, you can remove it from the Data pane by selecting the field in the Data pane and pressing the Delete key.

4. Repeat Steps 2 and 3 to place **Contact Name** and **Phone** in the Data pane. See Figure 9-11.

Figure 9-11
Completed
Data pane

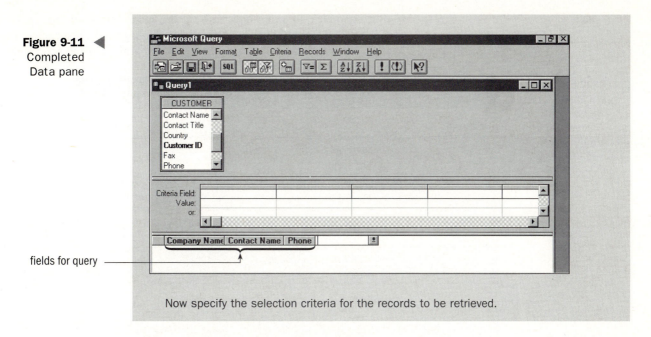

fields for query

Now specify the selection criteria for the records to be retrieved.

Using the Criteria Pane

You use the Criteria pane to control which records are displayed in the Data pane. Criteria are values you enter in the Criteria pane to indicate the records that MS Query needs to look for. The simplest kind of criterion is one where you specify that a field exactly equals some value. This is called an **exact-match** criterion. For example, John wants to retrieve information on customers located in London. The CUSTOMER database contains the field City, which stores the values that identify the customers to retrieve. So he simply needs to specify the field that contains the desired information, and the value in that field that he wants retrieved. These records will display in the Data pane.

To specify criteria to select only customers located in London:

1. Click and drag the field name **City** from the Customer field list to the first Criteria Field cell in the Criteria pane. When you release the mouse button, the field name City appears in the cell, along with a list arrow. See Figure 9-12.

Figure 9-12
City appears in
Criteria pane

field you want to specify criteria for

Criteria pane

2. Click the first **Value** cell, which is located directly below the field name City. Type **London**, then press the **Enter** key. MS Query automatically adds apostrophes around the text, and highlights it.

You can specify more complex selection criteria by using relational operators, logical operators, and other special operators as part of a criteria. Figure 9-13 illustrates many of the operators you can use to select records from an external database using MS Query.

Figure 9-13 ◀
Relational, logical, and special operators used in MS Query

Operator	Description	Sample Entry in Criteria Pane
Relational		
<	Less than	<5
<=	Less than or equal to	<=5
>	Greater than	>5
>=	Greater than or equal to	>=5
=	Equal	=5
<>	Not equal to	<>5
Logical		
AND	All conditions must be true for record to be retrieved	>5 AND <25
OR	At least one condition must be true for record to be retrieved	<2.0 OR >=3.5
NOT	Condition must not be true for record to be retrieved	NOT ("ACC")
Special		
Between	Determines whether a value falls within a lower and upper limit	Between 10 AND 15
In	Determines whether a value is equal to any value in the list of constant values enclosed in parentheses	In ('ACC','HIS','BIO')
Like	Determines whether a character expression matches a search pattern using wildcard characters	LIKE 'SM%'

HELP DESK

Index

OPERATORS

Click Help from the menu bar, then click Search to display the Help Topics dialog box, then click the Index tab.

Keyword
Operators

Topic
Operators

Now run the query. When you run the query, MS Query places the data that answers your question, the result set, in the Data pane.

To run a query:

1. Click the **Query Now** button. The customer records that match the criteria display in the Data pane. See Figure 9-14.

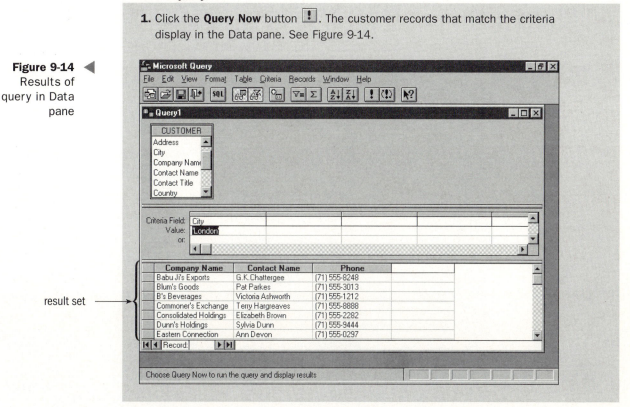

Figure 9-14 ◀ Results of query in Data pane

result set

Now John needs to return, or transfer, the results of the query to Excel.

To return the results of a query to Excel:

1. Click the **Return Data** button to copy the data to Excel. The Excel window opens with the Get External Data dialog box displayed. Notice that the Keep Query Definition and Include Field Names check boxes are checked. The Keep Query Definition option tells Excel to store a copy of the query with the Excel workbook, allowing you to easily update the query results at a later time. The Include Field Names option allows you to list the field names from the query results in the Excel worksheet. In the Destination edit box, Excel proposes to store the results at the current worksheet location. You can accept that location or specify a different one.

2. Change the destination of the returning data to A2 by changing the text in the Destination edit box to **Sheet1!$A$2**, then click the **OK** button.

3. The customers located in London are inserted into the worksheet as an Excel list. Press **Ctrl + Home** to deselect the list and return to cell A1. See Figure 9-15.

Figure 9-15
List of London customers returned to Excel

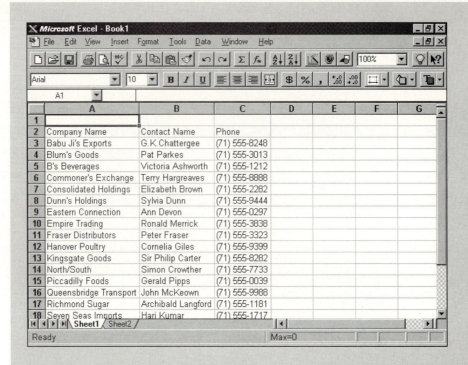

4. Boldface the field names in the field header row, then sort the list on Company Name in ascending order.

5. Print the list.

6. Press **Ctrl + Home**, then save the workbook as S_MSQRY.xls.

7. Click the **Microsoft Query** program button on the taskbar to switch to MS Query. Click **File** on the MS Query menu, then click **Exit** to close MS Query. If Excel is not the active program, click the Microsoft Excel program button on the Taskbar.

Use the Task List to switch to MS Query. Click File on the MS Query menu, then click Exit to close MS Query. If Excel is not the active program, use the Task List to switch to Excel.

WIN 3.1

John now has a report on the customer data Casandra needs.

REFERENCE window

CREATING A QUERY

- Access an external database.
- Select the fields you want to include in the query results by clicking and dragging the field names from the table field list in the Table pane to the blank column field name box in the Data pane.
- If the Criteria pane is not displayed, click the Show/Hide criteria button. To specify criteria, click and drag each field name from the table field list in the Table pane to a blank criteria field name box in the Criteria pane, then enter the value or condition in the text boxes below the field name.
- If the Automatic Query option is on, the results of the query (the result set) immediately display in the Data pane. If the Automatic Query option is not on, click the Query Now button to display the results in the Data pane.
- To return the query results to Excel, click the Return Data button.

QUERYING MORE THAN ONE TABLE   **ADVEX 443**

Querying More Than One Table

Casandra is pleased to get the list of London customers so promptly. As she quickly reviews the list, she realizes that, although Sunny Morning Products has a small base in London, she may not have time to visit all of the accounts on this trip. To help her focus on the key accounts, she asks John to also provide her with the London customers that had the largest sales volume during 1998. She will use this ranking to decide the order of her visits to customers.

In order to determine the largest customer, John will create a pivot table to summarize orders by customer. The Excel pivot table feature can access data from an external database using MS Query. As a first step in creating the pivot table, John will use MS Query to retrieve the records from the ORDENTRY database that meet the criteria—orders during 1998 for customers located in London. These are the records he needs to summarize.

In order to retrieve orders made in 1998 for customers located in London, John needs to retrieve data from more than one table—the CUSTOMER table and the ORDERS table. MS Query will use the common field Customer ID to link, or **join**, the CUSTOMER and ORDERS tables. Once these tables are joined, MS Query can connect each order with the customer that made the order.

Start the PivotTable Wizard and then use Ms Query to retrieve all the sales orders in 1998 made by companies located in London.

To create a pivot table using data from an external database:

1. Click **E1** to make it the active cell. This is the location where you will place the pivot table.

2. Click **Data**, then click **PivotTable** to display the PivotTable Wizard - Step 1 of 4 dialog box.

3. Select the **External Data Source** option button, then click the **Next >** button to display the PivotTable Wizard - Step 2 of 4 dialog box. See Figure 9-16.

Figure 9-16
Step 2 of
PivotTable
Wizard

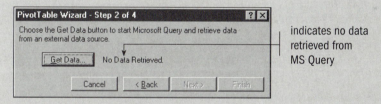

indicates no data retrieved from MS Query

4. Click the **Get Data** button. The Microsoft Query window opens and the Select Data Source dialog box displays.

5. Click **MS Access 7.0 Database - admin** from the Available Data Sources list, then click the **Use** button. The Select Database dialog box opens.

   Click MS Access 2.0 Database - admin from the Available Data Sources list, then click the Use button.

EXCEL 5.0

6. If necessary, click the **Drives** list button and select the drive in which your Student Disk is located, then select the **Tut09** folder, where the database is located. Click **ordentry.mdb** in the Database Name list, then click the **OK** button. The Add Tables dialog box opens.

7. Click **CUSTOMER**, click the **Add** button, click **ORDERS**, click the **Add** button, then click the **Close** button. The CUSTOMER and ORDERS tables display in the Table pane. Scroll the Customer field list until you see the Customer ID. Notice that MS Query displays a line between the two tables to confirm that the tables are joined (linked). See Figure 9-17.

Figure 9-17
CUSTOMERS and ORDERS tables are linked

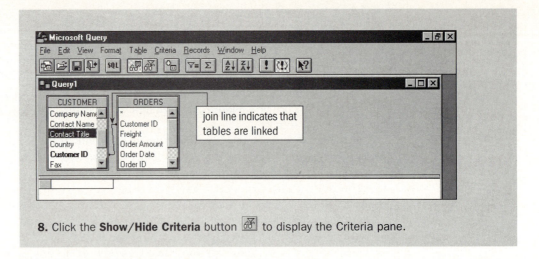

8. Click the **Show/Hide Criteria** button to display the Criteria pane.

Once the tables are joined, you can create the query.

HELP DESK

Index

JOIN

Click Help from the menu bar, then click Search to display the Help Topics dialog box, then click the Index tab.

Keyword	Topic
Join Command	
Joins command	*Join Command (Table Menu)*

EXCEL 5.0

To build a query:

1. Click the **Auto Query** button to turn off automatic query.

2. From the CUSTOMER table, click and drag the **Company Name** field name to the blank text box in the Data pane.

3. From the ORDERS table, click and drag the **Order Amount** field name to the Data pane. The Order Amount field is added to the Data pane.

   Now specify the criteria.

4. Click and drag the field name **City** from the CUSTOMER field list to the first Criteria Field cell in the Criteria pane.

5. Click the **Value** cell directly below the field name City. Type **London**.

6. Click and drag the field name **Order Date** from the ORDERS field list to the second Criteria Field cell in the Criteria pane.

7. Click the **Value** cell directly below the field name Order Date. Type **Between 1/1/98 And 12/31/98**, then press the **Enter** key. Notice that # symbols are automatically placed around the date values.

   You have formed the query by selecting the fields you want to retrieve and the selection criteria. Now run the query.

8. Click the **Query Now** button. See Figure 9-18. The result set contains the order amount for orders during 1998 of customers located in London.

QUERYING MORE THAN ONE TABLE **ADVEX 445**

Figure 9-18 ◀
Query and portion of result set

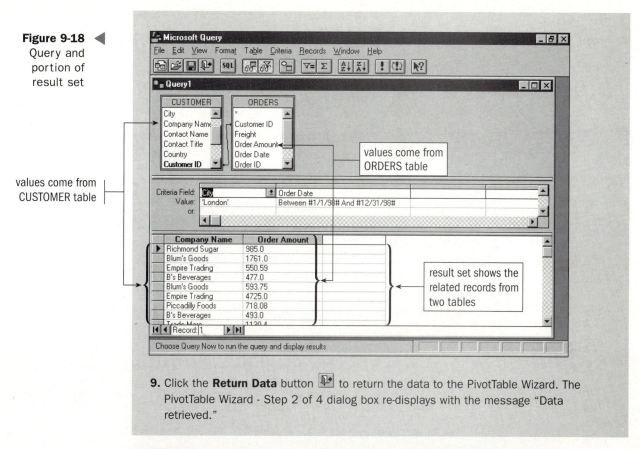

9. Click the **Return Data** button to return the data to the PivotTable Wizard. The PivotTable Wizard - Step 2 of 4 dialog box re-displays with the message "Data retrieved."

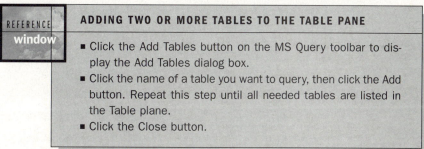

ADDING TWO OR MORE TABLES TO THE TABLE PANE

- Click the Add Tables button on the MS Query toolbar to display the Add Tables dialog box.
- Click the name of a table you want to query, then click the Add button. Repeat this step until all needed tables are listed in the Table plane.
- Click the Close button.

Now that you have retrieved the data, you can finish creating the pivot table. You want the pivot table to show the amount ordered by each customer, so you will use the Company Name as the rows of the pivot table and the Order Amount as the data to be summarized.

To complete the pivot table:

1. Click the **Next >** button. After a pause, the PivotTable Wizard - Step 3 of 4 dialog box opens.

2. Click the **Company** button and drag it to the ROW section of the sample pivot table.

3. Click the **Order Amount** button and drag it to the DATA section of the sample pivot table.

4. Double-click the **Sum of Order Amount** button in the DATA section to display the Pivot Table Field dialog box, click the **Number** button, click **Currency** in the Category list of the Format Cells dialog box, change the Decimal places to **0**. Click the **OK** button to close the Format Cells dialog box, then click the **OK** button to return to the PivotTable Wizard - Step 3 of 4 dialog box. See Figure 9-19.

After selecting Currency in the Category list, use the Format Code $#,###_);$#,##0).

EXCEL 5.0

Figure 9-19
Step 3 of
PivotTable
Wizard

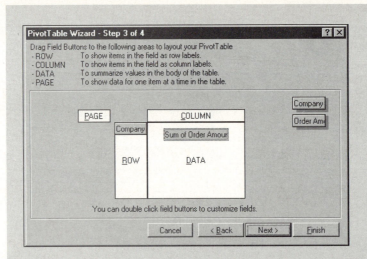

5. Click the **Next >** button. The PivotTable Wizard - Step 4 of 4 dialog box opens. Click the **Finish** button to accept the default options. The completed pivot table appears in the Sheet1 worksheet. You do not need to close MS Query. When you create a pivot table, MS Query automatically closes after the result set is returned to Excel.

6. Decrease the column width of column **D** so that the Total column of the pivot table is in full view.

Next, sort the pivot table by orders in descending order.

7. Click **F3**, then click the **Sort Descending** button 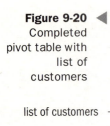 on the toolbar. See Figure 9-20.

Figure 9-20
Completed
pivot table with
list of
customers

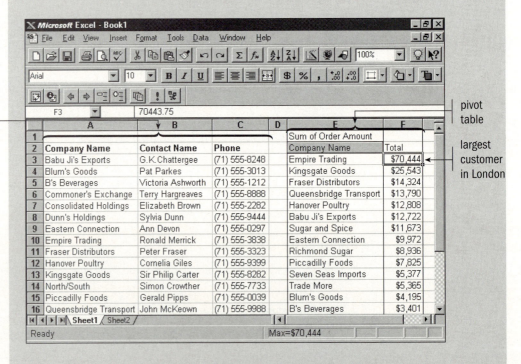

John has now collected the data Casandra needs for her trip to London.

8. Rename the worksheet tab **London Customers** and print the worksheet.

9. Create a Documentation sheet for the workbook, then save and close the workbook.

If you want to take a break and resume the tutorial at a late time, you can do so now. Exit Excel. If you are on a network, leave Windows running. If you are using your own computer, you may exit Windows and shut down the computer. When you resume the tutorial, place your Student Disk in the disk drive, launch Excel, then continue with the tutorial.

● ● ●

Transferring and Sharing Data Among Windows Programs

Every Tuesday morning, the Sunny Morning Products Operations Management Team (OMT) holds a planning and status meeting that includes the heads of each department. At this OMT meeting, each department or functional area presents segments of its annual business plan, along with a year-to-date progress report. The president begins the meeting by apprising the group of the latest developments in the industry and the economy in general. Marketing updates everyone on new marketing research, activities of the competition, etc.; Sales provides a report of sales for the month, quarter, and year. Similarly, Accounting gives a financial picture of how the company is doing, and Human Resources (HR) reports on headcount and hiring status.

As part of her weekly presentation to the OMT, Allison Olson, the director of HR, wants to give a memo to each team member so that everyone will have a hard copy for his or her files showing the employee population data. Currently, Allison's headcount information is in an Excel worksheet and her memo is in WordPad, the word processing program included with Windows 95. Allison would like to link the information from the Excel worksheet with her weekly memo. She also wants this process to be automated so that she doesn't have to repeat a number of steps each week to generate the information she needs for the staff meeting. To do this, Allison needs to transfer data between two programs—Excel and WordPad.

Like Allison, you may occasionally need to exchange data between two or more programs to produce the type of document you require. This type of document is referred to as a **compound document**—a document made up of parts created in more than one program. For example, you may want to incorporate data from a worksheet, as Allison does, or a graphic design, into a word-processed report.

To transfer or share data among programs, you can use pasting, linking, and embedding. Regardless of the method used, a copy of the data appears in the compound document. Figure 9-21 provides a description of each of these methods, and examples of when each method would be appropriate.

Figure 9-21 ◄
Comparison
of methods
for sharing
information

Method of Sharing	Description	Use when
Pasting	Places a snapshot of information into a document	It does not matter if data changes; it is one-time exchange of data
Linking	Inserts an object into a document—only the location of the source document is stored in the destination document	You always want the latest information in the document; or you use the same data in several documents and need to ensure that the data will be identical in each document
Embedding	Inserts an object into a document—the object's data is stored in the destination document	You want the source data to become a permanent part of the destination document; or the source data will no longer be available to the destination document

Pasting Data

You can paste an object, such as a range of cells or a chart, from one program to another using copy-and-paste operations. For example, you can paste a range of cells from an Excel worksheet into a WordPad document, and use it as part of your document.

Once you paste an object from one program into another, that data is now part of the new document, and can only be altered in that document's program. The pasted data becomes a table of text and numbers, just as if you had entered it directly from the keyboard. The pasted data has no link to the source document. For example, if you paste a range of cells from Excel into a WordPad document, you can only edit or change that data using the WordPad commands and features. There is no connection to the Excel worksheet. Once you have pasted the range of cells, any changes in the Excel worksheet are not reflected in the WordPad document. In order for the changes in the worksheet to appear in the WordPad document, you need to repeat the copy-and-paste operations. Pasting is used when you need to perform a one-time exchange of information between programs.

Embedding Data

Another method of sharing data between programs is to embed an object in a document. You embed an object using **Object Linking and Embedding** (OLE). An object is a package of data or information—a range of cells in Excel, or a document in WordPad, for example. OLE (pronounced oh-LAY) allows you to copy an object from one program into another. For example, you can copy a pivot table from Excel and embed it in a WordPad document. The program used to create the original object is the **source** or **server** program (Excel in this case), and the document in which the data was created is the **source document**. The program in which you place the copy (WordPad in this case) is the **destination** or **client** program, and the **destination** or **compound document** is the document that receives the data from another program. The copied object is said to be embedded because it exists as a separate object within the destination document; however, the source program's tools are available for use in editing this object. The embedded copy is not linked to the original source document, which means that changes to the embedded object do not alter the original object, and vice versa. For example, if you embed an Excel worksheet in a WordPad document, the WordPad document doesn't keep a record of the original worksheet location, only the program (Excel) to which it is associated. If you want to update the embedded object, double-click it; the WordPad menu and toolbar change to those used by Excel. You can now use any of the Excel commands to edit or update the Excel worksheet *in place*. If you change a number in a cell within an embedded document, it will appear in the WordPad document when you return to WordPad; however, these changes do not change the original source worksheet. The embedded object is independent from the original source. Figure 9-22 illustrates an embedded object.

Figure 9-22
Illustration of an object after it has been embedded in the destination document

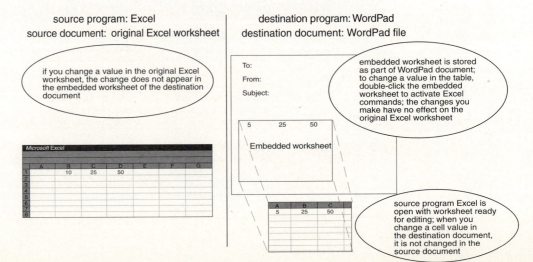

The ability to use the tools and commands of the source program differentiates embedding from pasting. When you embed one object within another, you directly access the source program by double-clicking the embedded object, allowing you to edit the embedded object quickly and easily within your document.

Linking Data

Using OLE, you can also share data between programs by creating a **link** between data copied from one program to another. When an object is linked, the document in the destination program displays an image of the linked object, but the data is stored in the source document. The destination document stores a reference (location and name of source file) to the object in the source program. In other words, it knows where to find the object. Thus, only one copy of the original, or source, object exists. If you make changes to the original object, changes also appear in the destination document. For example, if you link a range of cells from Excel into a WordPad document, the Wordpad document stores a reference to the data source in Excel; the WordPad document does not store the data itself, but instead is sent a copy of the source data through the link that has been established. If you need to change the Excel data, you change it in Excel. The document containing the link is updated either automatically or on demand when the destination document is opened. With only one version of the object, every document containing a link to the source object uses the same copy of the object. Figure 9-23 illustrates a linked object.

Figure 9-23
Illustration of an object after it has been linked to a destination document

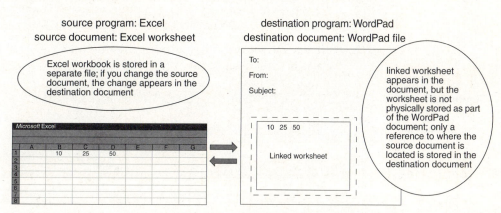

Now Allison needs to transfer and share data between Excel and a word processor program, in this case WordPad, as she writes her memo to the OMT.

Linking an Excel Worksheet to a Word Processor Document

At first, you may think that Allison's employee count memo can be completed by pasting data between programs — in other words, using the Excel Copy command and the word processor's Paste command to copy a section of a worksheet into a document created with a word processor. However, remember that Allison wants the report automated, and does not want to cut and paste her memo every week. The copy-and-paste method of transfer is static in that it shows only a snapshot of your data. The pasted data has no link to the original source. When the numbers change in the original source document, you must repeat the copy-and-paste operation over and over to keep the word processing document current.

Because the employment picture at Sunny Morning Products changes regularly with the rapid growth of the company, a more appropriate method would be to link the two documents. That way, Allison can keep the memo up to date while continuing to use the worksheet for other purposes.

When you use object linking, the linked object appears in the destination document and the data for the object remains stored in the file where it was originally created (the source document). When you make changes in the source document, the information in the linked destination document is automatically updated.

Object linking is a powerful tool and is useful in many situations. In general, you should link rather than embed data when

- the data is likely to change over time, and you need to maintain the data in the source program

- you want to use the same data in several documents and you need to ensure that the data will be identical in each.

By linking the Excel data to the WordPad document, Allison can update the employee list in the Excel worksheet when it changes and be sure that the data in her memo will automatically be updated whenever she accesses it.

Link the pivot table in the Excel worksheet to Allison's memo by first copying the cell range that contains the headcount report to the clipboard; then use the Paste Special command in the word processor to create the link.

To copy an Excel object to the clipboard:

1. Open the workbook C_EMP.xls and immediately save it as S_EMP.xls. This workbook consists of two sheets—the HeadCount sheet, which contains a pivot table of the number of employees in each department broken down by males and females, and the EmployeeData sheet, which represents SMP's employee list.

2. Activate the **HeadCount** sheet. See Figure 9-24. Select the range **A1:D6**, which contains the pivot table data.

Figure 9-24
HeadCount sheet

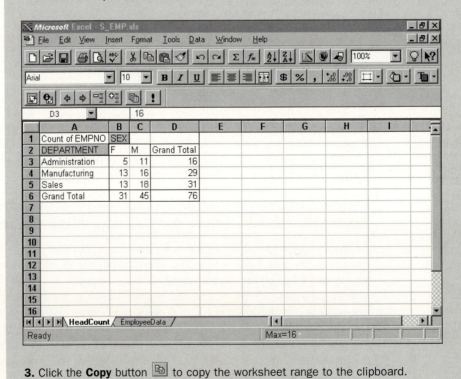

3. Click the **Copy** button to copy the worksheet range to the clipboard.

Allison now needs to launch her word processor so that she can integrate the data into her memo.

Opening Multiple Programs

You can open another program in Windows without exiting the program in which you are currently working. When you open another program, Windows places the new program on the desktop. Recall that in Windows 95 any open program is represented by a program button. To switch between open programs you will click the appropriate button on the taskbar.

To open the Windows word processor program:

1. Click the **Start** button, point to **Programs**, point to **Accessories**, then click **WordPad**. The WordPad document window opens. If necessary, maximize the document window.

   WIN 3.1

   Use the task list for Windows 3.1. to open the word processing program. Press Ctrl + Esc to open the Task List, double-click Program Manager, double-click the Accessories group icon, then double-click Write to open the Write program. Maximize the program window.

   Now Allison is ready to open her memo. Open the file C_Mgtltr, which contains the text of Allison's memo.

2. Click **File**, then click **Open** to display the Open dialog box. Click the **Look in** list arrow, click **3 1/2 Floppy (A:)**, then double-click the **Tut09** folder to display a list of WordPad files on your Student Disk. Double-click **C_mgtltr** in the Look in list box to open the file. See Figure 9-25.

   WIN 3.1

   Click File, then click Open to display the Open dialog box. Click the Drives list arrow and select the drive in which your Student Disk is located. Click the Directories list box and select the Tut09 directory. Double-click the file C_mgtltr to open it.

   TROUBLE? If you don't recognize the file extension for your document, Write uses .wri, and WordPad and Word use .doc.

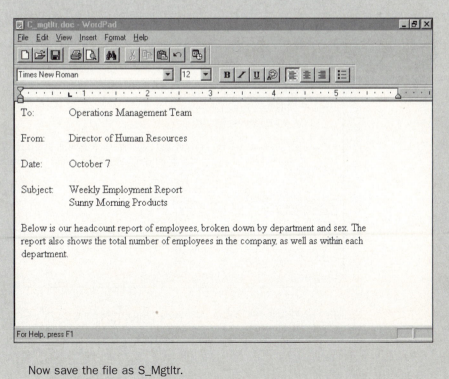

Figure 9-25 Allison's memo

Now save the file as S_Mgtltr.

ADVEX 452　TUTORIAL 9　INTEGRATING EXCEL WITH OTHER WINDOWS PROGRAMS

WIN 3.1

3. Click **File**, then click **Save As** to display the Save As dialog box. Type **S_Mgtltr** in the File Name text box, then click the **Save** button.

Click File, then click Save As to display the Save As dialog box. Type S_Mgtltr in the FileName text box, then click the OK button.

Now Allison will link the headcount report to the employee count memo. To create the link, she can use the Paste Special command. Once the link is established, any changes she makes to the original worksheet data, the employee list, will also appear in the word processor document. Remember, this object is still held temporarily in the clipboard. Now link the headcount report to Allison's memo.

To create a link between an Excel worksheet and a word processor document:

1. Move the insertion point to the blank line directly below the last sentence in Allison's memo. Press the **Enter** key to add a blank line.

2. Click **Edit**, click **Paste Special** to open the Paste Special dialog box, click the **Paste Link** button, then click the **OK** button to copy the contents of the clipboard to the WordPad document.

WIN 3.1

Click Edit, click Paste Special to open the Paste Special dialog box, click Microsoft Excel 5.0 Worksheet in the Data Type list box, then click the Paste Link button to copy the contents of the clipboard to the memo.

3. If necessary, click outside the linked object to remove the selection handles. See Figure 9-26.

Figure 9-26
Linked object in word processor document

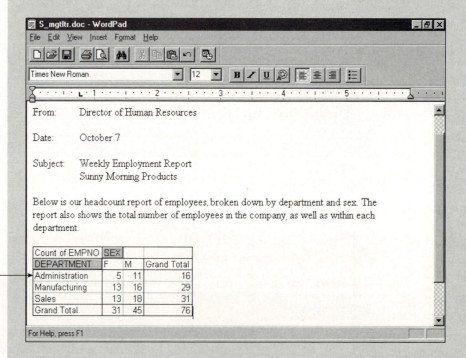

linked object

After reviewing her memo, Allison is ready to print it.

4. Click **File**, then click **Print** to display the Print dialog box. Accept the default print settings and click the **OK** button to print the memo. See Figure 9-27.

Figure 9-27
Allison's printed memo

To: Operations Management Team

From: Director of Human Resources

Date: October 14

Subject: Weekly Employment Report
Sunny Morning Products

Below is our headcount report of employees, broken down by department and sex. The report also shows the total number of employees in the company, as well as within each department.

Count of EMPNO	SEX		
DEPARTMENT	F	M	Grand Total
Administration	5	11	16
Manufacturing	13	16	29
Sales	13	18	31
Grand Total	31	45	76

You have successfully integrated the data from Allison's Excel worksheet into her word processor document. Save the file and exit the word processor.

5. Click **File**, click **Save**, click **File**, then click **Exit** to close the Windows word processor. The Excel windows re-opens, with the pivot table still displayed. Press the **Esc** key to deselect the pivot table.

TROUBLE? *If Excel is not the active window, use the task list to return to Excel. Press the Esc key to deselect the pivot table.*

WIN 3.1

REFERENCE window

LINKING AN EXCEL OBJECT TO A WORD PROCESSING DOCUMENT

- Select the Excel worksheet range or other object.
- Copy the object to the clipboard.
- Open the Windows word processor program and open the document in which the linked object will be placed.
- Position the insertion point where you want to place the linked object. Click Edit, click Paste Special, click the Paste Link button, then click the OK button to place a copy of the linked object from Excel into the word processor document.

ADVEX 454 TUTORIAL 9 INTEGRATING EXCEL WITH OTHER WINDOWS PROGRAMS

Updating the Linked Object

Several days later, Allison receives a memo from the Manufacturing Department indicating that they are ready to hire two candidates that Human Resources recently brought in for interviews. Figure 9-28 shows the data for the employees. She asks her assistant, Janice, to update the employee list.

Figure 9-28 ◀
Data for new employees

Field	Employee 1	Employee 2
EMPNO	250	251
FIRSTNAME	Ellen	Hank
LASTNAME	Merchant	Keller
SEX	F	M
HIREDATE	10/20/98	10/21/98
DEPARTMENT	Manufacturing	Manufacturing
SALARY	24000	24000
SALHOUR	H	H

When you use object linking to copy a table from Excel to a word processor document, the data remains in the Excel worksheet, while a copy of the data also appears as an object in the word processor document. Remember that linked objects are updated in the source program.

Update the employee list with the new information from Manufacturing.

To add the new employees to the Employee list:

1. Activate the **EmployeeData** sheet. Select any cell in the first record of the Employee list.

2. Click **Data**, then click **Form** to display the EmployeeData dialog box. The first record in the list displays.

   Now add the new record.

3. Click the **New** button to display a blank data form.

4. Add the data for the first employee in Figure 9-28 to the data form. Remember to press the **Tab** key after you make each entry.

5. Click the **New** button to add the record to the first blank row at the bottom of the list and display a blank data form.

6. Add the data for the second employee from Figure 9-28. After adding both employees to the list, click the **Close** button to close the EmployeeData dialog box.

TRANSFERRING AND SHARING DATA AMONG WINDOWS PROGRAMS **ADVEX 455**

Because the headcount report is based on a pivot table, Janice needs to refresh the pivot table in order to update it.

To update the pivot table:

1. Activate the **HeadCount** sheet. Make sure that the cell pointer is inside the pivot table.

2. Click the **Refresh Data** button on the Query and PivotTable toolbar to update the pivot table. See Figure 9-29.

   TROUBLE? If your Query and PivotTable toolbar is not displayed, click Data, then click Refresh Data.

Figure 9-29 ◄
Updated pivot table

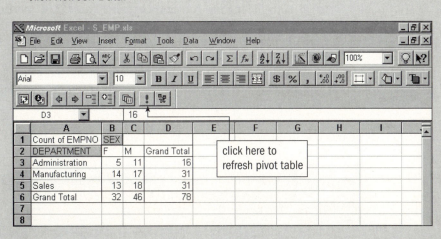

It's Tuesday morning, and Allison is hurrying to get to the OMT meeting. At the last minute, she remembers that she needs to bring the headcount memo to the meeting. Because the memo is linked to her Employee worksheet, she can open the memo and it will include the updated headcount table.

To open and retrieve the memo with the updated headcount table:

1. Launch WordPad, then open the file S_Mgtltr. See Figure 9-30. The memo reflects the latest headcount, 78 employees.

Figure 9-30 ◄
Updated memo

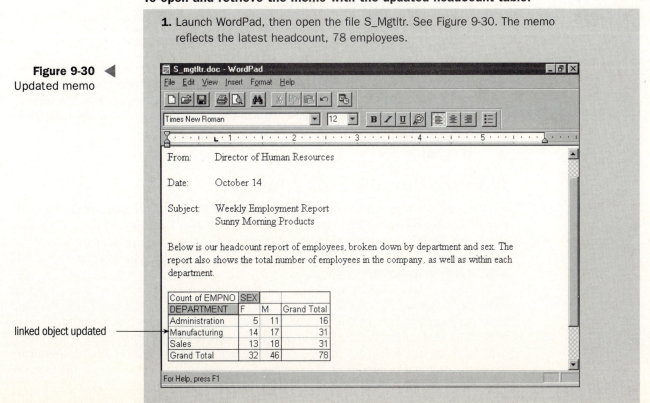

linked object updated

ADVEX 456 TUTORIAL 9 INTEGRATING EXCEL WITH OTHER WINDOWS PROGRAMS

WIN 3.1

> *Launch Write, then open the file S_Mgtltr. Click the Yes button in response to the message "This document contains links to other documents. Do you wish to update links now?" Maximize the window.*
>
> Allison quickly reviews the memo before printing it.
>
> 2. Change the date to **October 14**, then print the document.
>
> 3. Save the document, exit the word processor, return to Excel, then save and close the open workbook.

Satisfied with the memo, Allison brings it to the OMT meeting.

As Janice is working with Allison on her various projects, she is wondering whether there is an alternative method of updating files that are linked. As a matter of fact, there are times when she will be working in the destination program (perhaps WordPad) and need to change some aspect of the linked object. In that case, she can activate the linked object (Excel worksheet) directly from the destination program by double-clicking the object in the destination program. Windows will open Excel and load the linked document (an Excel worksheet, in this case). You can then change the Excel worksheet and the changes will automatically update the WordPad document.

REFERENCE window	**UPDATING A LINKED OBJECT FROM THE DESTINATION PROGRAM**

- Double-click the linked object to launch Excel and open the worksheet file that contains the selected object.
  or
  Launch Excel, then open the worksheet file that contains the object.
- Make the desired changes to the object in Excel.
- Save the revised worksheet.
- Click File, then click Exit to switch back to the destination program.

If you want to take a break and resume the tutorial at a later time, you can do so now. Exit Excel. If you are on a network, leave Windows running. If you are using your own computer, you may exit Windows and shut down the computer. When you resume the tutorial, place your Student Disk in the disk drive, launch Excel, then continue with the tutorial.

Linking Versus Embedding

As you conclude your work on linking, recall that OLE has two components: linking and embedding. If you embed Excel data in another document, a copy of the data is incorporated into that destination document. When embedding an object, remember that the embedded information is not updated if the original source data changes. So why would anyone embed an object?

Embedding data allows you to take a file with you when traveling and using a laptop computer. While away, you can work on your documents and have access to the data and various programs. That portability can be a real advantage. However, the disadvantage with embedded data is that it takes up more disk space. On the other hand, while linked data takes up less disk space, it requires the source document remain available in order to use the destination document. As you can see, you have choices and tradeoffs to make as you consider whether to embed or link an object.

Embedding an Excel Object in a Word Processor Document

In WordPad, you can use the Paste Special command to embed your workbook file in a WordPad document file. Remember that once you embed the file, any changes you make to the embedded file will not be updated in the original workbook data.

Casandra is waiting for one figure so that she can complete her Sales Report—Summarized by State for next week's OMT meeting. As she is working on the report, she receives an urgent call from one of her sales representatives indicating that he needs Casandra in Denver immediately to deal with a customer problem that requires management attention. Casandra realizes that she will not be able to make the next OMT meeting, so she plans to complete her report on the road. She will get the last figure she needs, finish the report, and then fax it to John, who will represent her at the meeting. Before she leaves the office, Casandra decides to embed her data in a memo.

You will embed Casandra's Excel worksheet data in her memo by first copying the cell range that contains the sales report to the clipboard, then using the Paste Special command to complete the embedding.

To embed an Excel object in a word processor document:

1. Make sure that Excel is the active program.

2. Open the workbook C_stsal.xls in the Tut09 folder or directory, and immediately save it as S_stsal.xls.

3. Select the range **A1:D57**, which contains the sales data. Notice that the sales figure for Idaho is missing and that the total sales are currently $3,582.7.

4. Click the **Copy** button to copy the worksheet range to the clipboard.

   Casandra now needs to start her word processor so that she can embed the data into her memo.

5. Launch WordPad *(or Write)* and open the file C_salmem, then immediately save it as S_salmem. See Figure 9-31.

Figure 9-31
Sales memo

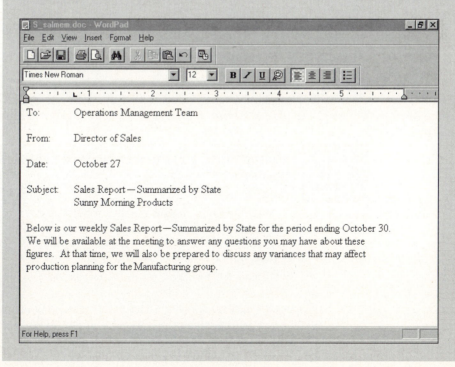

Casandra can now embed her sales report in her memo to the OMT. Remember that this object is still held temporarily on the clipboard.

6. Add a blank line to the bottom of Casandra's memo.

7. Click **Edit**, click **Paste Special** to display the Paste Special dialog box, click the **Paste** button, click **Microsoft Excel Worksheet** in the As list box, then click the **OK** button to copy the contents of the clipboard to the memo. See Figure 9-32.

Click Edit, click Paste Special to open the Paste Special dialog box, click Microsoft Excel 5.0 Workbook, then click the Paste button to copy the contents of the clipboard to the memo.

WIN 3.1

Figure 9-32
Sales table from Excel embedded in word processor document

embedded object

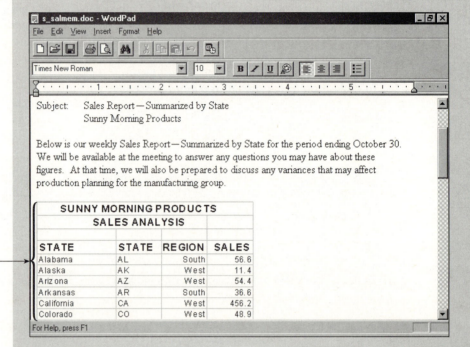

8. If necessary, click anywhere outside the table to deselect it.

9. Save the sales memo, then exit the word processing program and return to Excel. Press the **Esc** key to deselect the table, then close the workbook.

REFERENCE window

EMBEDDING AN EXCEL OBJECT IN A WORD PROCESSING DOCUMENT

- Select the Excel worksheet range or other object.
- Copy the object to the clipboard.
- Open the word processor program and open the document in which the linked object will be placed.
- Position the insertion point where you want to place the linked object.
- Click Edit, click Paste Special, click the Paste button, then click the OK button to embed the object from Excel in the word processor document.

Casandra has successfully embedded the Excel worksheet data in her memo.

Updating the Embedded Object

After arriving in Denver, Casandra gets a call with the missing sales figure—sales in Idaho this quarter were $17.9. She can now enter this number into the worksheet and complete the memo. Open Casandra's word processor document.

To open the word processor program:

1. Start WordPad (*or Write*) and open S_salmem. If necessary, maximize the window.

   Add the new number to the sales list.

2. Double-click the **table** in the memo. See Figure 9-33. Notice that the Excel menu bar and toolbar appear in the word processor window.

   Double-click the table in the memo. Excel is launched.

WIN 3.1

Figure 9-33
Editing the worksheet in place

menus and toolbar change to those used by Excel

embedded object displays with Excel rows and column borders

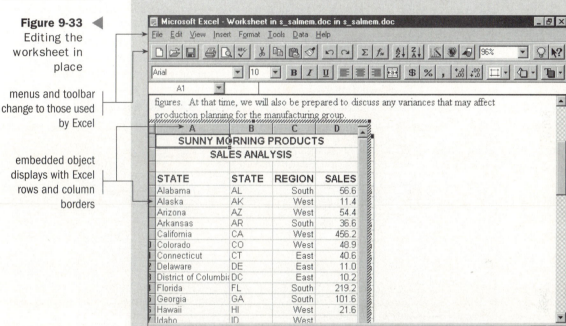

3. Move to the cell containing the data for Idaho, type **17.9**, and press the **Enter** key. Click outside the sales worksheet to return to WordPad. Notice that the Idaho sales figures and the total sales for all states have been updated in the word processing document. Total sales are now $3,600.6. Save the memo and exit WordPad.

   Move to the cell containing the data for Idaho, type 17.9, and press the Enter key. Click File, then click Exit to return to Write. Scroll to the bottom of the table. Click anywhere below the table to deselect it. Notice that the Idaho sales figures and the total sales for all states have been updated in the word processor document. Total sales are now $3,600.6. Save the memo, then exit Write.

WIN 3.1

Satisfied with the updated memo, Casandra faxes it to her assistant.

If you want to take a break and resume the tutorial at a later time, you can do so now. Exit Excel. If you are on a network, leave Windows running. If you are using your own computer, you may exit Windows and shut down the computer. When you resume the tutorial, place your Student Disk in the disk drive, launch Excel, then continue with the tutorial.

● ● ●

Working with Text Files

Casandra assigned John a task to complete while she was away in Denver. She has been conducting a study of the Consumer Price Index (CPI) and its potential relationship to the company's pricing activities over the last several years. She is considering recommending changes to SMP's pricing policies and needs this analysis before she determines the new policy recommendations. The CPI is a measure of the price level facing consumers. The federal government publishes these figures monthly, and Casandra would like to use the government's data in her analysis. In this particular project, Casandra intends to compare the annual increase in the food component of the CPI with the average price increases the company has instituted over several years. She asked John to find the CPI data and to prepare a line chart showing the food segment data from 1960 to the most recent year available.

John remembers that the federal government's Census Bureau stores extensive data on the economy on the Internet. John uses a **Web browser**, software that enables you to use the World Wide Web to find and load documents, and discovers a significant amount of data on the CPI. He notes that the information covers a broad spectrum of consumer prices for food, shelter, upkeep, transportation, etc. Figure 9-34 shows a portion of the file. While John only needs the food segment, he must download the entire file, containing all the consumer price segments. Since the file he downloaded is a text file, he will need to convert it into an Excel file before he can manipulate the data in Excel.

Figure 9-34
View of CPI index from a Web browser

address of document on World Wide Web

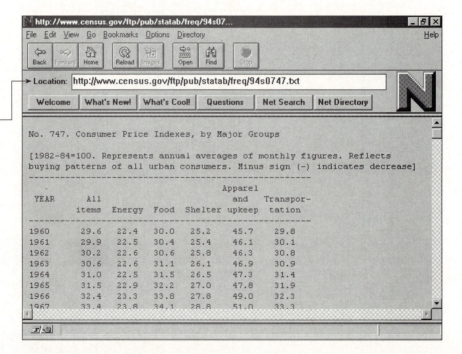

Importing Text Files

Text files, known as **ASCII files**, contain only plain text without any formatting such as special fonts or boldface. Since most programs, both windows and non-windows, can read and write to this type of file, this format is often used to transfer raw data (without formatting information) between various software programs. Using the ASCII files, each line in a text file gets inserted into a single cell in the worksheet. In most cases, this will not be exactly what you need. To get what you really need, you must tell the computer what data goes into each cell, rather than accept a full line of text going into one cell. How can you do this? Fortunately, Excel includes a Text Import Wizard that can simplify the job of importing text files. The Wizard helps break the lines of text into columns. Open the file that John has downloaded from the Internet, and use the Text Import Wizard to import the text file into Excel.

IMPORTING TEXT FILES **ADVEX 461**

To import a text file using the Text Import Wizard:

1. Click **File**, then click **Open** to display the Open dialog box.

   Now indicate that you want to open a text file.

2. Click the **Files of Type** list arrow, then click **Text Files**.

   Click the List Files of Type list arrow, then click Text Files.

3. If necessary, click the **Look in** list arrow, click **3 1/2 Floppy (A:)**, then double-click the **Tut09** folder to display a list of files on your Student Disk.

   If necessary, click the Drives list arrow and select the drive in which your Student Disk is located. Click the Directories list box and select the Tut09 directory.

4. Double-click **PRICEIND.TXT** in the Name list. Excel displays the Text Import Wizard - Step 1 of 3 dialog box. See Figure 9-35.

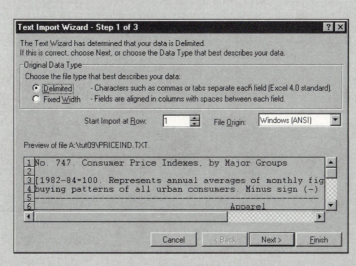

Figure 9-35 ◀
Step 1 of Text Import Wizard

What happens next depends on how the text file was originally formatted. There are two types of text formatting: **delimited text** files and **fixed-width** files. Files with delimiters use special characters, such as commas, spaces, or tabs, to separate fields, allowing Excel to place each field in a new column. Files that do not use delimiters to separate fields often use a fixed width to break each line into separate columns. This type of file is typically more challenging to import. Excel tries to determine whether the file is delimited or fixed width. If necessary, you can change the Excel selection by clicking the appropriate option button.

5. If Fixed Width is not selected, select the **Fixed Width** option button.

   Next, select the starting row to begin importing the data.

6. Click the **Start Import At Row** up arrow until the row number is **7**. This allows you to ignore information such as headings or other identifying information at the beginning of the file that you don't want to import.

7. If you wish, you can scroll the Preview area to examine the text file.

8. Click the **Next>** button to move to the Text Import Wizard - Step 2 of 3 dialog box. See Figure 9-36.

Figure 9-36
Step 2 of Text Import Wizard

click on ruler to add column breaks

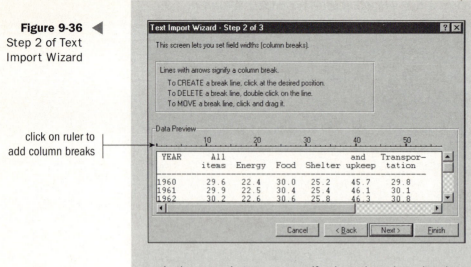

In the second step, you specify where the column breaks are located. The Wizard tries to determine the column breaks for you by displaying vertical lines to represent where the lines will be separated. If the column breaks are not where you want them, you can adjust them.

9. Click at positions **5**, **15**, **22**, **28**, **38**, **44**, and **54** on the ruler to add column break lines. See Figure 9-37.

   TROUBLE? If you added a column break at the wrong position, you can remove it by double-clicking the column break line.

Figure 9-37
Text Import Wizard - Step 2 after column breaks inserted

column break line

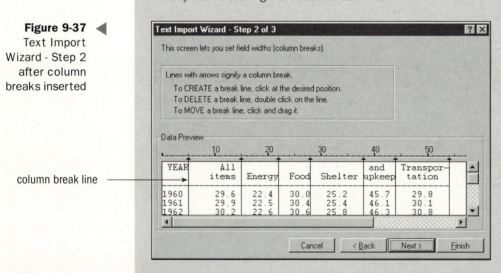

10. Click the **Next>** button to move to the Text Import Wizard - Step 3 of 3 dialog box. See Figure 9-38.

Figure 9-38
Step 3 of Text
Import Wizard

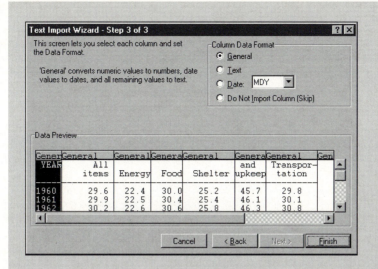

At this point, you specify the formatting to apply to each column. You can also exclude a column from being imported. The current settings in this dialog box are appropriate.

11. Click the **Finish** button. The text file is imported into the active worksheet. See Figure 9-39.

Figure 9-39
Text file imported into Excel

unwanted underline

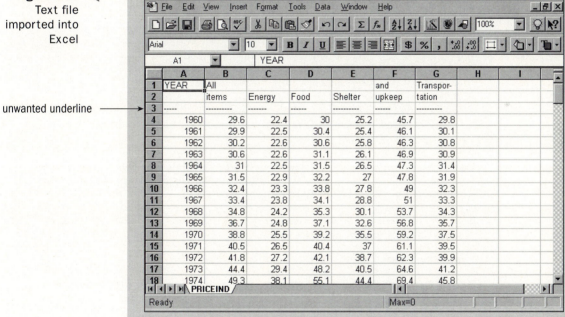

> **REFERENCE window**
>
> **IMPORTING AN ASCII FILE**
>
> - Click File, click Open, select text file format, select a directory, select a filename, then click the OK button to display the Text Import Wizard - Step 1 of 3 dialog box.
> - Select the Fixed Width option button if the fields are arranged in fixed columns.
> - Click the Start Import at Row spinner button to identify the first row to begin importing data.
> - Click the Next> button to display the Text Import Wizard - Step 2 of 3 dialog box.
> - Click positions on the ruler to select column breaks, then click the Next> button to display the Text Import Wizard - Step 3 of 3 dialog box.
> - Select Column and Format option buttons.
> - Click the Finish button to display the converted text in the Excel worksheet.

John thinks that a line chart illustrating the data will help Casandra in creating her report. Now prepare the line chart.

To create a chart:

1. Delete row **3** to remove the unwanted underline.
2. Select cells **A2:A36**. Use the scroll arrow to return to row 2, then press the **Ctrl** key and select cells **D2:D36**.
3. Click the **ChartWizard** button and highlight cells **I4:O15**. The ChartWizard - Step 1 of 5 dialog box opens.
4. Click the **Next >** button in the ChartWizard - Step 1 of 5 dialog box to display the Step 2 of 5 dialog box, click **Line**, then click the **Next>** button to display the Chart Wizard - Step 3 of 5 dialog box.
5. Click format **2**, then click the **Next >** button to display to the Chart Wizard - Step 4 of 5 dialog box. Accept the default settings by clicking the **Next>** button to display to the ChartWizard - Step 5 of 5 dialog box.
6. Select the **No** option button to remove the Legend, then type **Consumer Price Index—Food** in the Chart Title text box.
7. Click the **Finish** button to display the Column chart.
8. Click outside the chart area to deselect it. Use the scroll arrow to view the entire chart. See Figure 9-40.

Figure 9-40
Line chart of CPI index

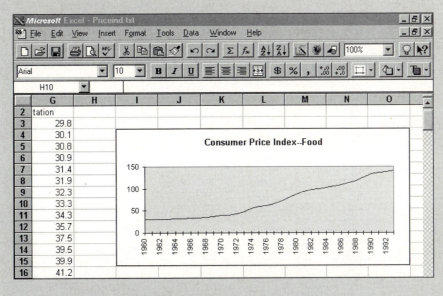

EXCEL 5.0

Now that you have finished importing the text file and charting the CPI, you can save the file and exit Excel.

9. Click **File**, click **Save As**, click the **Save as Type** list arrow, then click **Microsoft Excel Workbook**. Name the file S_CPI.xls, then click the **Save** button.

Click File, click Save As, click the Save Type as list arrow, then click Microsoft Excel Workbook. Name the file S_CPI.xls, then click the OK button.

10. Close the workbook, then exit Excel.

In this tutorial, you have learned how Excel can be used in conjunction with other Windows programs. John now has the CPI data in a chart that Casandra can use in her report on SMP's pricing activities.

Tutorial Exercises

The following exercises will give you an opportunity to compare the features of pasting, linking, and embedding. You will update regional sales data using each approach. Note the differences as you proceed.

1. Launch Excel, open the workbook E_REGION.xls in the Tut09 folder or directory, and save it as S_REGION.xls.
2. Launch WordPad (Write for Windows 3.1 users), open the document E_DEMO1, and save it as S_DEMO1.
3. Divide your screen so that it looks similar to Figure 9-41.

Figure 9-41

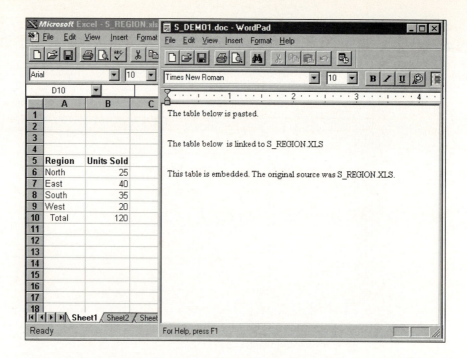

4. Immediately below the line "The table below is pasted," paste the Excel range A5:B10 into the word processor document.
5. Immediately below the line "The table below is linked to S_REGION.XLS," link the Excel table (A5:B10) to the word processor document.
6. Immediately below the line "This table is embedded...," embed the Excel table (A5:B10) in the word processor document.
7. Switch to Excel and increase the number in the North region to 75. Switch to the word processing program and print the document. Comment on the results.

As you answer Exercises 8 through 12, observe what is happening on the screen. What happens when you double-click the linked or embedded object?

8. Switch to the word processor and double-click the embedded table. Change the value in the West region to 60 and click outside the embedded document. Print the document. Why didn't the value in the pasted or linked table change? Describe what occurred on the screen.
9. Double-click the pasted table. What happened? Change the value of the East region to 50. What happened to the total?
10. Switch to Excel and save the workbook as S_REGION.xls, and close the workbook.
11. Return to the word processing program and double-click the linked table. What did you observe? Change the value in the South to 45. What happened in the Excel window? The word processing window? Print the word processing document. Why didn't the value in the embedded table change? What happened on the screen when you double-clicked the word processor document?
12. Save the word processing document. Save, then close the Excel workbook.

In Exercises 13 through 19 you will both link and embed the same Excel document in two separate documents. In particular, focus your attention on the size of the files created by your word processor when you use the two different methods. The next section will help you determine the differences in file size between embedded and linked documents.

13. Open the workbook E_REGION.xls in the Tut09 folder, then save it as S_REGN.xls.

CASE PROBLEMS **ADVEX 467**

14. Switch to the word processor, open E_DEMO2, and save it as S_DEMO2.
15. Immediately below the line "This data is linked to...," link the Excel table to the word processing document. Save the word processing document.
16. While in the word processor, open E_DEMO3 and save it as S_DEMO3.
17. Immediately below the line "This data is embedded...," embed the Excel table in the word processing document. Save the document.
18. Use the Windows Explorer to determine the size in bytes of the two word processing documents—S_DEMO2 and S_DEMO3. Which one is larger? Why?
    Use the Windows File Manager to determine the size in bytes of the two word processor documents—S_DEMO2 and S_DEMO3. Which one is larger? Why?

WIN 3.1

19. Close all files.

Case Problems

1. Reporting Sales for Toy World Store manager Fred Galt must report to the regional manager each week. He faxes a memo each week to the regional sales office indicating his recommendations regarding any special sales or promotions he feels will be needed, based on the summary sales information he includes in the report. Fred maintains a worksheet that summarizes sales in units and dollars for each day of the week. This sales summary is included in his weekly report.

Do the following:

1. Open P_STORE.xls in the Tut09 folder. This is Fred's partially completed worksheet. Save it as S_STORE.xls.
2. Complete the worksheet by computing total sales in dollars for each day by multiplying the number of units sold of each product by the price per unit (the price table is in the upper-right corner). Also, compute total sales for each product and the total sales for the store. (*Hint*: Total Store Sales = $86,993.90.)
3. Save the worksheet.
4. Open the word processing document P_LTR and save it as S_LTR.
5. Link the worksheet range A1:F15 to the memo.
6. Saturday evening, Fred faxes the memo to the regional manager, indicating that sales are on target for the week, and no special promotions are necessary at this time. Update store sales for Saturday using the following data: 22,6,18,14.
7. Print the memo.
8. Save the memo and exit the word processor.
9. Save and close the workbook.

2. Planning 401(k) Investments at CableScan CableScan plans to install a 401(k) plan this year, and Mary Kincaid, benefits administrator, is traveling to the three company sites to introduce the plan and its features. A 401(k) plan is a retirement savings program that allows employees to deduct funds from their weekly pay, before taxes, provided that they invest them directly into various options within the 401(k) plan.

To introduce the 401(k) plan, Mary will hold formal meetings at each location of the company. At the meetings, employees will be provided with an audio-visual presentation that gives an overview of the plan, the administrative procedures, and investment options. Because there are currently no other retirement plans available to the employees, other than personal savings, the company wants to be sure that there is high participation in the 401(k) plan. The goal established by management is that at least 80% of all eligible employees will participate in the plan. To help ensure a high rate of participation, the company will match, dollar for dollar, whatever the employee contributes, up to four percent of the employee's salary. Additionally, employees can contribute up to 20 percent of their salaries. Mary has asked you to work with individual employees after each of the formal presentations.

One of your assignments is to develop a simple investment model that will allow each employee to see the effect (dollar accumulation) of investing a percent of his or her current salary each year at an annual return on investment over a 30-year period.

Figure 9-42 shows the planning analysis sheet that Mary has sketched to assist you in completing the assignment.

As a final output, Mary wants each employee to receive a letter encouraging him or her to participate in the 401(k) plan. You will include in the letter the investment model results for each employee based on his or her individual contribution and the company match.

Figure 9-42 ◀

Planning Analysis Sheet

What information do I need?

Name of employee
Current salary
Percent of salary invested—enter a percent of salary. NOTE: The maximum salary employee can contribute is 20 percent.
Annual rate of return—enter as a percent.

What calculations do I need to perform?

Employee annual contribution = Current salary * percent of salary invested.
Monthly employee contribution = Annual contribution divided by 12. NOTE: Remember maximum employee contribution allowed.
Monthly employer contribution = Employee's annual contribution divided by 12. NOTE: Remember that for every dollar employee contributes, company invests a dollar, up to 4% of employee's salary; company invests nothing above 4% of employee's salary.
Total monthly contribution = monthly employee contribution + monthly employer contribution.
Value of investment at 5, 10, 15, 20, 25, and 30 years. NOTE: use FV (monthly rate of return, number of periods, total monthly contribution).

What output do I want to see?
Letter report similar to Figure 9-43

Do the following:

1. Use the planning sheet (Figure 9-42) to create the investment model worksheet. Use the information in Figure 9-43 to test the model. Include a documentation sheet in the workbook. Save the workbook as S_INVEST.xls in the Tut09 folder.
2. Use your word processor, create a document with the following introductory paragraph:
   Unless you are independently wealthy, win the lottery, or write a best seller, you'll probably need to plan and set aside more funds for retirement than Social Security will provide. The table below shows what you can accumulate over a 30-year period with a monthly payment.

Figure 9-43

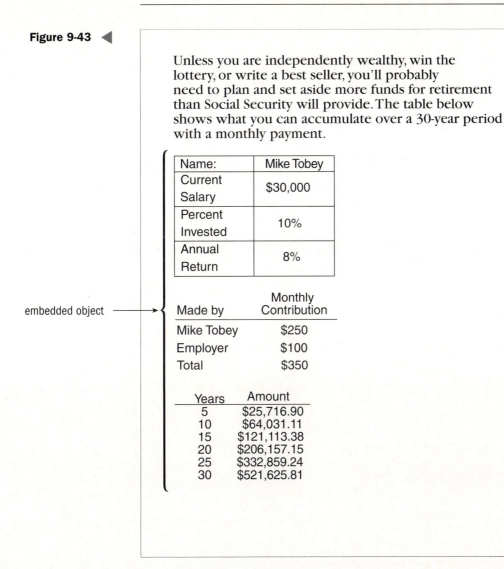

embedded object

3. Embed the investment model worksheet (S_INVEST.xls) after the introductory paragraph in Problem 2. Save the revised letter with the embedded document as S_INVLTR.
4. In Houston, one of the company locations, Fred Alvarez, an engineer at CableScan-Houston, asks you about the 401(k) plan. He supplies you with the following data (Annual Salary $45,000; Invest 5% of salary; Annual rate of return-10%). Use this information in your embedded document to enter this new data.
5. Print the letter for Fred Alvarez.
6. Save and exit the word processor.

Comprehensive Applications

1. Recording Grades in BAC207 at Central State University You have been asked by one of your professors to be a grader for all BAC207 sections of Introduction To Business. Your professor wants you to set up a grade book as an Excel workbook with the following specifications:

- Put each section into a separate worksheet. Figure 9-44 shows the layout of each worksheet.
- Name each sheet with the name of each section. That is, Section 1, Section 2, etc.
- Include a documentation sheet for the workbook.

Figure 9-44

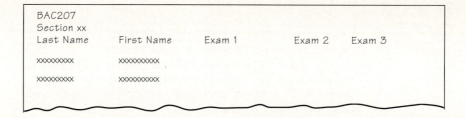

Your professor received a file from the university's Student Record System (SRS) with course rosters for all business courses. The SRS is maintained on the university's mainframe computer. The name of the file is COURSES.TXT. You discover some complications with the file. First, the file is not an Excel file; it is a text file. Second, the file contains more information than you need; you only need the first and last name of the students. Figure 9-45 shows the layout of the text file. Third, the file contains all business courses, not just the BAC207 sections for which you are the grader.

Figure 9-45

Position	Field
3-7	Term code
8-13	Course ID
23	Section
24-31	Last name
32-39	First name
40	Middle initial
54-55	Year of graduation
56-60	Major
61-63	College
64-65	Unit

Do the following:
1. Use the file COURSES.TXT to import the course roster file into Excel.
2. After importing the text file, create the workbook as your professor specified. Remember that each BAC207 section is in a separate worksheet. On each sheet, the names of the students should be sorted by last name (Figure 9-45).
3. Improve the appearance of each sheet.
4. Develop a macro to print all the information for a section. Name the macro PrintGrades. Place a button in each section's grade sheet labeled Print. When this button is clicked, the contents of the entire sheet are printed. Print BAC207 section 2, using your macro.
5. Include a documentation sheet, then print this worksheet.
6. Save the workbook as an Excel file. Name the file S_BAC207.xls.

COMPREHENSIVE APPLICATIONS **ADVEX 471**

2. Record Player Data for Community Youth Soccer League Al Delbet is using a dBASE file to keep track of the players in a youth soccer league for kids eight to eighteen. Originally the database was set up by a friend of Al's but that friend has moved away. The database has functioned well in several areas, such as keeping track of data about players, printing team rosters, and printing mailing labels. However, it does not work well when Al needs answers to questions put to him by the director of the soccer league. For example, one of the questions the director has asked is: which players will move to the next division because they are no longer eligible to play in the division they are in?

Al decided to contact the local college for some assistance. You have been hired to work a few hours a week to help him. Your first task is to examine the dBASE file (SOCCER.DBF) and together with Al, you develop a list of fields and their descriptions (Figure 9-46). While you are discussing the database with Al, he informs you that the data in the file contains active as well as inactive players (Registered = 1 if active, 0 if inactive), but answers to any questions must be based only on active players.

Figure 9-46 ◄

dBASE Field Name	Description
ID_NUMBER	ID assigned player
DIVISION	Division player plays in
LAST	Last name
FIRST	First name
INITIAL	Middle initial
GENDER	Code for Gender (M or F)
BIRTH	Birth date
ADDRESS1	Street number
TOWN	Town
ZIP	Zip code
PHONE1	Phone number
REGISTERED	1 = active, 0 = inactive

Do the following:

Open an Excel workbook and then use MS Query to access the SOCCER.DBF database file located in the Tut09 folder on your Student Disk, then answer the following questions:

1. The league must prepare a summary report of the number of active players, broken down by division and within division by gender. Improve the appearance of the table, then print it.
2. The division director of the Under 8 Coed wants to try to organize the teams by town rather than the draft system that is used by other division directors. Retrieve all the *active* players in the Under 8 Coed division (U08C), then retrieve their first and last names, and towns. Once in Excel, sort by town and within town by last name. Print the list.

ADVEX 472 TUTORIAL 9 INTEGRATING EXCEL WITH OTHER WINDOWS PROGRAMS

3. Each town or village donates money to the league based on the number of *active* players from that town playing in the league. Prepare a pivot table of active players by town. Print the pivot table.

4. Al received a call from the coach of the statewide Olympic Development team. She would like a list of *active female* players in either the Under 14 Girls (U14G) or Under 14 Coed (U14C) divisions, because these players are eligible to try out for the state Olympic Development team. Al asks you to retrieve the first and last names and phone numbers of all eligible players. He wants the data arranged by last name. Print the list.

5. Include a documentation sheet, then print this worksheet.

6. Save the workbook as S_SOCCER.xls.

TUTORIAL 10

Introduction to Visual Basic for Applications

Building Complex Macros Using VBA

OBJECTIVES

In this tutorial you will learn how to:

- Work with VBA objects, properties, and methods
- Write simple procedures
- Create interactive macros
- Control the flow of code
- Repeat actions in code
- Use VBA control structures in creating macros

Sunny Morning Products

CASE

Ann Trego, assistant budget manager for Sunny Morning Products, has been using macros to help prepare SMP's Operating Budget. The macros she has developed have made her work and that of the budget team much more productive. Ann realizes that her work is never static. Not only is the budget team always asking for new or revised reports, she is also constantly searching for better ways to complete her work.

As she used her budget application, she thought of a way to improve the PrintBudget macro used for printing the Operating Budget. She wants to incorporate into that macro some simple, easy-to-use options for printing the summary report and chart that are also part of the workbook. She wants to modify the PrintBudget macro so that once the user clicks the PrintBudget macro button to print the Operating Budget, the macro will prompt the user, asking whether to print the Summary report. If the user responds positively, the macro prints the summary report. In either case, she wants the macro to then ask the user whether to print the budget chart. Again, if the user responds positively, the chart is printed. As Ann thought about what she wants the macro to do she sketched a flowchart of the logic (Figure 10-1). But she wasn't sure how to create a macro to do these tasks, so she went to the company's PC specialist, Mike Balleos, for help. After reviewing Ann's current macro and the flowchart showing her new requirements, Mike realized he could not record these new steps. He would need to manually enter some VBA code to enable the macro to interact with the user and perform some decision-making tasks.

Figure 10-1
Flowchart of modified PrintBudget macro

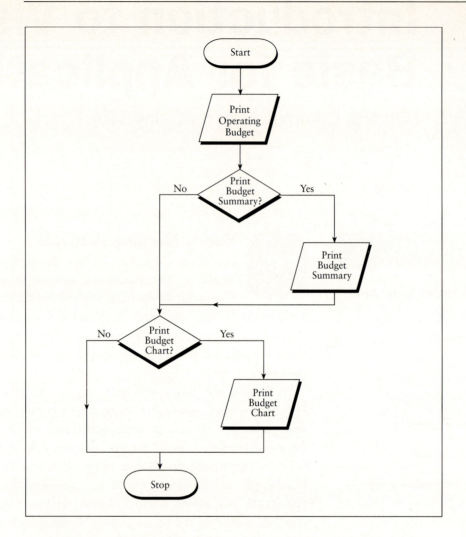

Mike modified the PrintBudget macro by entering eight lines of VBA code. Open the C_SMP1.xls workbook to see how this modified macro works.

To run the modified PrintBudget macro:

1. Open the workbook C_SMP1.xls in the Tut10 folder or directory on your Student Disk. Activate the **Budget** sheet.

2. Click the **Print Budget** button. The Print Preview window displays the SMP Operating Budget. Click the **Print** button, then click the **OK** button in the Print dialog box to print the budget. A message box containing the prompt "Print the Budget Summary" displays. See Figure 10-2.

Figure 10-2
User asked whether to print Budget Summary

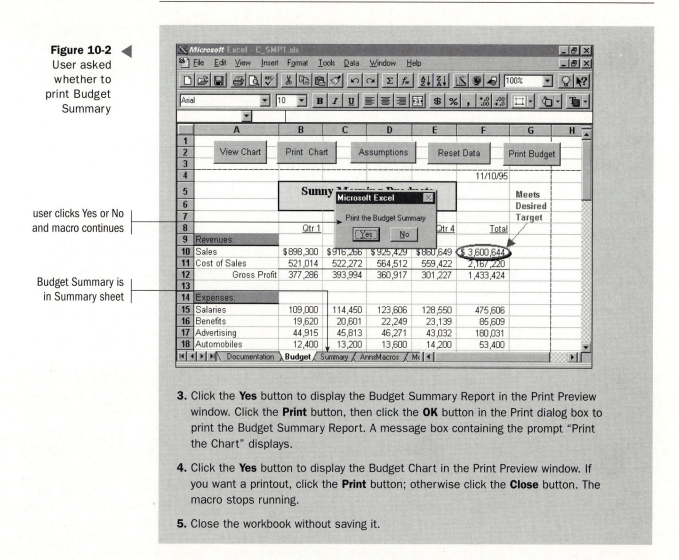

user clicks Yes or No and macro continues

Budget Summary is in Summary sheet

3. Click the **Yes** button to display the Budget Summary Report in the Print Preview window. Click the **Print** button, then click the **OK** button in the Print dialog box to print the Budget Summary Report. A message box containing the prompt "Print the Chart" displays.

4. Click the **Yes** button to display the Budget Chart in the Print Preview window. If you want a printout, click the **Print** button; otherwise click the **Close** button. The macro stops running.

5. Close the workbook without saving it.

Mike's macro is an example of an **interactive macro**. The macro pauses during execution and waits for a user response to a prompt before continuing. You cannot record this type of macro. Mike had to add VBA code manually to the macro in order to satisfy the new requirements. There are many problems that you cannot solve using only the macro recorder. Some understanding of VBA is necessary to develop these types of macros. In this tutorial you will be introduced to the concepts and terminology of VBA, and you will have the opportunity to write some VBA macros.

Overview of VBA

As you recall, in Excel you can automate tasks by using macros. A macro is a sequence of instructions that tells Excel what to do. These instructions are written in a computer programming language called **Visual Basic for Applications** or **VBA**. VBA is an implementation of the Microsoft Visual Basic (VB) language, an **object-oriented** programming language used to develop applications within Windows. VBA is a programming language embedded within Excel that automates tasks and creates macros that use a spreadsheet.

You have already learned to record and run macros, and discovered how useful they can be. When you recorded macros in earlier chapters, you didn't need to understand the VBA code to put the macros to work for you. However, as you need to modify your macros or develop more complex applications, you will find a knowledge of VBA necessary. For example, there are situations where you will want to add decision-making and repetition to your recorded macros. The only way you can do this is to manually add VBA code to your recorded macro. In addition to enhancing recorded macros, you can use VBA to develop powerful applications that include custom commands, menus, dialog boxes, and messages.

Why VBA?

Before the release of Excel Version 5.0, users of Excel used a macro language called XLM. This macro language was a very specialized tool. It could be used to automate tasks for Excel spreadsheets, but it could not be used in any other programs. With the release of Excel Version 5.0, VBA became the primary macro programming language for customizing, simplifying, and automating routine tasks across all major Microsoft programs. The switch to VBA as a common macro language makes it much easier for you to develop solutions to problems that span several programs. Eventually VBA will be used with all of the Microsoft major programs—Excel, its spreadsheet program; Word, its word processing program; PowerPoint, its presentation program; Access, its database program; and Project, its project planning program. Presently VBA is only included in Excel, Project, and Access. Nevertheless, once you have learned VBA using Excel, you will be familiar with many of the statements and techniques needed to develop macros for use with other programs.

Macros Versus Procedures

Programmers use the term **procedure** to describe an automated task, while computer users with a spreadsheet orientation use the term "macro". So what you have been calling a macro is also called a procedure or, technically, a sub procedure, in VBA jargon. In this tutorial, we will use the term "macro," because that is the term you are most familar with.

Within Excel there are two types of procedures: sub procedures and function procedures. A **sub procedure macro**, also known as a **subroutine**, is the most common type of procedure. A sub procedure macro usually contains statements that automate tasks such as formatting a range, performing calculations, printing a worksheet, or copying data. Sub procedure macros are the types of macros Ann has been using to automate tasks in the Operating Budget.

Both sub procedure and function procedure macros have a certain structure, or organization, that you must follow so that Excel knows where the procedure begins and ends. A sub procedure macro always begins with the keyword Sub, followed by the procedure (macro) name, and a pair of parentheses. The procedure ends with the keywords End Sub. The lines in between represent the VBA code. The VBA code follows a certain **syntax**, that is, a set of rules specifying which forms of the language are grammatically correct. Sub procedure macros have the following structure:

```
Sub ProcedureName()
    <VBA statements>
End Sub
```

Figure 10-3 shows a simple procedure that displays the message "Overview of Visual Basic for Applications."

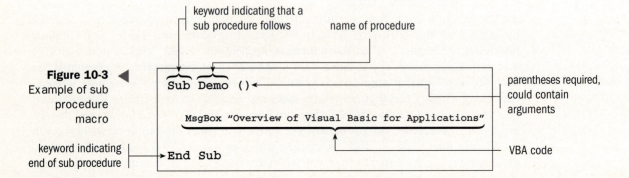

Figure 10-3
Example of sub procedure macro

A function procedure, also called a **user-defined function**, is a function that you create using VBA. User-defined functions work like the Excel built-in functions that you've used in previous tutorials. The SUM function, for example, totals the values in a specified range. A function procedure also takes values from the spreadsheet and uses them to calculate the result, using a formula that you specify in the function procedure. User-defined functions begin with a statement containing the keyword Function, followed by the function name and a set of parentheses enclosing the arguments. User-defined functions end with the End Function keywords. They have the following structure:

```
Function FunctionName (arguments)
    <VBA statements>
    FunctionName=expression
End Function
```

Figure 10-4 is a sample function procedure that calculates the commission in a stock transaction.

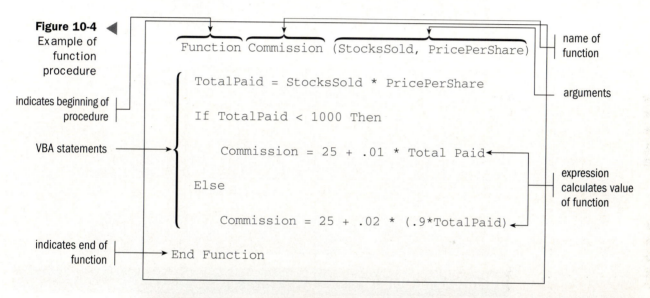

Figure 10-4
Example of function procedure

Storing VBA Code

Whether you create a macro by recording a series of steps or by entering your own instructions manually, Excel stores the VBA code, the instructions that make up a macro, just as it stores worksheets and charts—within a workbook. Recall that the sheets that hold the VBA code are called **module sheets**, or just modules. A workbook can have any number of module sheets. A single module sheet can hold any number of sub or function procedures (up to 4000 lines of code). When the workbook is saved, all module sheets are saved as part of the workbook.

VBA Objects, Properties, and Methods

To develop a VBA application in Excel you need to understand the concepts of objects, properties, and methods, because these are the three main components of VBA code. First you will spend some time on the concept of objects, because the key to understanding VBA is to think in terms of objects.

An **object** is any element in Excel that you can control or manipulate through a VBA program. For example, in Excel, a workbook, a worksheet, a range, a chart, and a button are objects. Excel has over 100 objects that you can control and manipulate. We won't try to address all of them here; you will start by learning a few of the more common ones. Figure 10-5 lists several objects used in Excel. You can find out more about these and other VBA objects by searching for them in the on-line Help facility.

Figure 10-5 ◀
Some Excel objects

Object	Refers To
Application	The Excel program as a whole
Workbook	One Excel file
Sheets	A group of sheets in a workbook (worksheets, chart, modules, dialog sheets)
Worksheet	One worksheet in a workbook
Module	One VBA module in a workbook
Range	A cell or group of cells in a worksheet
Chart	One chart in a workbook

Hierarchy of Objects

It may help to think of objects within Excel in terms of a hierarchy. Think of each object as a container that can hold other objects, and these objects in turn can contain smaller objects, and so on. At the top of the hierarchy is the Application object, in this case Excel. The Application object contains other objects, such as workbooks, menu bars, toolbars, and windows. Each of these objects also contains objects. For example, the Workbook object contains objects such as worksheets, charts, modules, and dialog sheets. Again, each of these objects contains objects. For instance, the Worksheet object contains objects such as ranges, pivot tables, drawing objects, and pageSetup. Figure 10-6 provides you with a graphical view of a portion of this hierarchy.

Figure 10-6
Partial view of the Excel object hierarchy

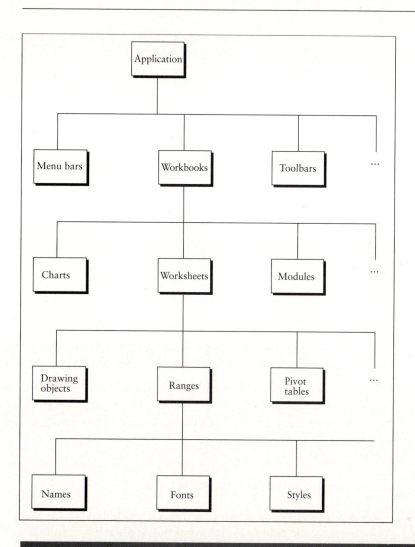

Collections

Some Excel objects consist of a set of objects called a **collection**—a group of related objects. A member in a collection is called an **element** or **item** of the collection. For example, the Workbooks collection consists of all the currently open workbooks. You can refer to the Workbooks collection as a group or you can refer to each workbook as an individual element. Worksheets also come in collections. The set of all worksheets in an open workbook is known as the Worksheets collection. Some examples of collections you may frequently use are shown in Figure 10-7.

Figure 10-7
Some Excel collections

Collection	Description
Workbooks	All currently open workbooks
Worksheets	All worksheets in an open workbook
Sheets	All sheets of any type in a workbook
Charts	All Chart sheets in a workbook

Using VBA to Refer to Objects in Collections

When using VBA to refer to an object in a collection, you will often specify the object's position in the collection or use its name. For example, if you had two workbooks open, C_SMP1.xls and C_SMP2.xls, then you could refer to the first opened workbook by its position in the Workbooks collection with the following VBA expression:

```
Workbooks(1)
```

Workbooks is a VBA keyword that refers to the collection of open workbooks. The index number 1 refers to the first workbook opened in the Workbooks collection. You could also use the name of the object to refer to a specific open workbook. For instance, you could use the expression

```
Workbooks("C_SMP1.XLS")
```

to refer to the workbook C_SMP1.xls in the Workbooks collection. When you use the name of the object, you must always enclose it in quotation marks.

Using VBA to Reference Objects in the Object Hierarchy

When you write VBA code, you often need to refer to all the objects that lie in the hierarchical path to an object. You can do this by listing the objects from left to right—from the outermost "container" inward—with each object (container name) separated from the next by a period. For example, to refer to a workbook named C_SMP1.xls, you can use the expression

```
Application.Workbooks("C_SMP1.XLS")
```

This expression refers to the C_SMP1.xls workbook in the Workbooks collection. The Workbooks collection is contained in the Application object (Excel). If you need to refer to the Budget worksheet in the C_SMP1.xls workbook, you can write the expression

```
Application.Workbooks("C_SMP1.XLS").Worksheets("Budget")
```

To refer to a specific cell, such as B10, in the Budget worksheet, you can write the expression

```
Application.Workbooks("C_SMP1.XLS").Worksheets("Budget").Range("B10")
```

where the expression **Range ("B10")** returns an Excel range object, which in this case is a single worksheet cell, cell B10.

As you can see, expressions can get quite long and referencing an object can be cumbersome if you always have to use the complete hierarchical path. Frequently, you can simplify the expression used to refer to an object by thinking about where you are within the hierarchy. For instance, you can omit the Application reference if the code is executed in Excel; VBA assumes that you mean the Excel application. Thus, you can refer to cell B10 in the Budget worksheet of the C_SMP1.xls workbook using the expression

```
Workbooks("C_SMP1.XLS").Worksheets("Budget").Range("B10")
```

VBA OBJECTS, PROPERTIES, AND METHODS **ADVEX 481**

Further, if you know that the workbook C_SMP1.XLS is the active workbook, you can eliminate the workbook reference and refer to cell B10 in the Budget worksheet as

```
Worksheets("Budget").Range("B10")
```

Continuing, if you know that the Budget worksheet is the active worksheet, you can refer to cell B10 as

```
Rang3e("B10")
```

So at what level in this hierarchical path should your reference to the object begin? If you know the context in which the code will execute, then you can select the appropriate path by knowing where Excel will be when executing the code. For example, if you know that only one workbook will be open and that the workbook has a sheet named Budget, then you can refer to cell B10 of the Budget sheet with the reference

```
Worksheets("Budget").Range("B10")
```

If you're not sure, you can always start at the Application object, in which case your code will execute without error, but it may mean typing long lines of code.

Properties of Excel Objects

Each object has **properties**, a set of characteristics that control its appearance and behavior. A property represents a value or setting that describes an object. For example, a range object refers to one or more cells in a worksheet. The range object has Formula, Font, Row, Column, Value, and other associated properties. A worksheet has Name, Visible (hides or unhides the worksheet), and ProtectContents properties, as well as many others. Excel contains over 100 objects, and each object has its own set of properties. Some examples of Excel objects and their properties are shown in Figure 10-8.

Figure 10-8 ◀
Some properties of Excel objects

Object	Associated Properties	Refers To
Application	ActiveCell	The cell that is active
	ActiveSheet	The sheet that is active
	ActiveWorkbook	The workbook that is active
	ScreenUpdating	Screen updating either on or off
Workbook	ActiveSheet	The sheet in the workbook that is active
	Name	The name of the workbook
Worksheet	Name	The name of the worksheet
	Visible	Hiding or unhiding the worksheet
Range	Formula	The range formula
	Value	The contents of the range
	ActiveCell	The active cell
	Name	The name of the range

When working with properties, you can use VBA to examine an object's current property setting and either take some action based on the current setting or change it. Whether you are examining or changing an object's property, you refer to it by specifying the name of the object followed by a period and the property name.

For example, you can refer to the value in cell B10 (*Value* is a property of a range object) in the Budget sheet as

```
Worksheets("Budget").Range("B10").Value
```

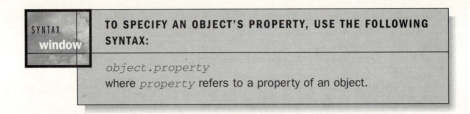

Methods of Excel Objects

In addition to properties, objects have methods associated with them. **Methods are actions you want the object to perform.** For example, you can print the worksheet using the PrintOut method. Sometimes a method will change an object's properties. For example, you can clear the contents of a range object using the Clear method. Figure 10-9 lists some examples of objects and their associated methods.

Figure 10-9
Some methods of Excel objects

Object	Associated Methods	Action
Workbook	Close	Closes a workbook
	Save	Saves a workbook
	Activate	Activates a workbook
Worksheet	Calculate	Recalculates a worksheet
	Select	Selects a worksheet
	PrintOut	Prints a worksheet
Range	Clear	Clears the contents of a range of cells
	Select	Selects a range of cells
	Copy	Copies a range to the clipboard
	Offset	Returns a range offset from the specified range

You refer to an object's method by specifying the name of the object followed by a period and the method name. For example, the statement `ActiveWorkbook.Save` uses the Save method to save the active workbook, and the statement `Worksheets.Add` uses the Add method to insert a new worksheet into the currently open workbook.

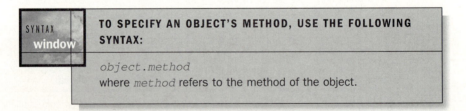

Some methods require additional information to carry out their actions. This additional information is specified as arguments to the method. For example, the statement

`Range("A1:C3").Cut Destination:=Range("C4")`

uses the Cut method to move a range of cells (A1:C3) to the clipboard and pastes the range to a Destination range whose upper left cell is C4. The argument for the Cut method is Destination. You separate the argument value `Range("C4")` from the argument name `Destination` with a colon and an equal sign. You separate the argument from the name of the method `Cut` with a space.

SYNTAX window

TO SPECIFY AN OBJECT'S METHOD, USE THE FOLLOWING SYNTAX:

object.method argument1, argument2,...
where *argument* is a constant, variable, or expression that provides the method with needed information to carry out the specified action. Each argument consists of a name for the argument plus values, which are assigned using the := operator (not the = operator).

Changing Properties of Objects

To change the behavior or appearance of an object, you must change the value of a property associated with the object. For example, to increase the width of a column in a worksheet, you change the column's Width property. So one of the more common tasks when you use objects is to set the values of their properties. For example, to set the Value property of cell B10—a range object—in the Budget worksheet to 5000, you could use the following VBA statement:

```
Worksheets("Budgets").Range("B10").Value = 5000
```

SYNTAX window

TO SET A PROPERTY OF AN OBJECT TO A NEW VALUE, USE THE FOLLOWING SYNTAX:

object.property = expression
where *object* is a reference to an object, *property* is the name of the specific property you want to change, and *expression* is the value to which you want to set the property.

Entering a Simple VBA Macro

To become more comfortable with entering and understanding VBA code, you will plan, create, and run through several simple VBA macros. The first macro illustrates how you can change the properties of range objects using VBA code. While you may consider these examples rather simplistic, it's important for you to focus on the underlying principles. Later in the tutorial you will use the skills you are learning to develop more realistic macros.

You will enter a VBA macro to place the label "Age" in cell A10 and change the cell's font style to boldface. Your procedure will also place the value 25 in cell B10 and increase that cell's font size to 12. Figure 10-10 shows a flowchart of the macro's logic.

Figure 10-10
Flowchart for a simple macro

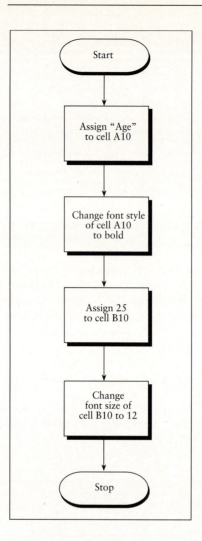

First, to create a VBA macro you need to add the VBA code to a module sheet in the workbook. As you may recall from a previous tutorial, when you record a macro, the VBA code is automatically stored in a module sheet. If there is no module sheet in the workbook, Excel automatically inserts a module sheet for you. If you are not recording the macro and no module sheet exists in the workbook, you need to manually insert a module sheet into the active workbook. Open a workbook, add a module sheet, and then enter the VBA code to perform the tasks for the first VBA macro.

To insert a module sheet:

1. Open the workbook C_DEMO.xls in the Tut10 folder or directory on your Student Disk and immediately save it as S_DEMO.xls.

2. Click **Insert**, point to **Macro**, then click **Module** to insert a module sheet. See Figure 10-11. Excel inserts a blank module sheet in front of the active sheet and makes the new module sheet the active sheet. In addition, Excel automatically displays the Visual Basic toolbar whenever you activate a module sheet.

   When a module sheet is active, the menus on the menu bar change to include commands appropriate for modules.

   TROUBLE? If Excel did not display the Visual Basic toolbar when you activated the module sheet, click View, click Toolbars to display the Toolbars dialog box, select the Visual Basic check box, then click the OK button. The Visual Basic toolbar will display whenever you activate a module sheet.

Figure 10-11
Blank module sheet

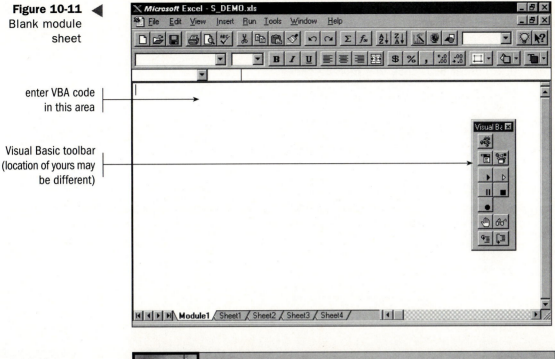

enter VBA code in this area

Visual Basic toolbar (location of yours may be different)

REFERENCE window

INSERTING A MODULE SHEET

- Open a workbook
- Click Insert, click Macro, then click Module
  or
  Click the Insert Module button on the Visual Basic toolbar

Entering a Macro in a Module Sheet

Once the module sheet is inserted in the workbook you can enter the VBA code into the module sheet. You enter code directly by typing the code using the keyboard. Figure 10-12 lists some guidelines to help make your VBA code more readable.

Figure 10-12
Guidelines for more readable code

Key	Comment
Tab key	Indents line
Enter key	Inserts blank line
At end of line, insert space followed by underscore (_)	Splits long lines into multiple line commands

As you enter your lines of code they are automatically formatted for you; the VBA editor capitalizes keywords, bolds others. The VBA editor uses different colors to enhance readability of the code. For example, comments are displayed in green, and VBA keywords are displayed in blue. Your code is checked by VBA for correct syntax as you enter it. If you have a syntax error your line appears in red after you press the Enter key, and a message box appears indicating the syntax error.

You can use the clipboard to cut, copy, and paste your VBA code.

Now enter the macro. As you type the VBA code, you may have many questions about the purpose of each statement. Don't worry if you don't understand a specific statement; each instruction will be explained.

To enter VBA code in a module sheet:

1. Make sure the module sheet is the active sheet.

2. Type the VBA code shown in Figure 10-13.

Figure 10-13 ◀
VBA code for SetValue macro

TROUBLE? If an error message displayed as you pressed the Enter key to move to the next line, you made an error in typing the line of code. Click the OK button to remove the message box, then review the line where the error occurred. Correct the line by retyping, then continue entering the remaining VBA code.

Before running the SetValue macro, review the function of each VBA statement in the macro you just typed.

The statement `Sub SetValue()` indicates the beginning of the macro and the macro name, SetValue.

The statement `Worksheets("Sheet1").Activate` makes Sheet1 the active sheet in the active workbook.

The statement `Range("A10").Value = "Age"` uses the Value property to place the string "Age" in cell A10.

The statement `Range("A10").Font.FontStyle = "Bold"` changes the FontStyle property of cell A10 to bold.

The statement `Range("B10").Value = 25` uses the Value property to assign the value 25 to cell B10.

The statement `Range("B10").Font.Size = 12` changes the FontSize property of cell B10 to 12.

The statement `End Sub` indicates the end of the macro.

The lines that begin with an apostrophe are comment lines that describe the macro. They have no effect on how the macro runs, but they are useful for the user in interpreting the code.

Now run the macro.

To run the macro:

1. Click the **Run Macro** button on the Visual Basic toolbar to display the Macro dialog box.

   TROUBLE? If the Visual Basic toolbar is not displayed, click Tools, then click Macro to display the Macro dialog box and continue to Step 2.

2. If necessary, click **SetValue** in the Macro Name/Reference list box, then click the **Run** button. See Figure 10-14. "Age" appears in cell A10, formatted in boldface. Cell B10 displays the value 25 in 12-point font size.

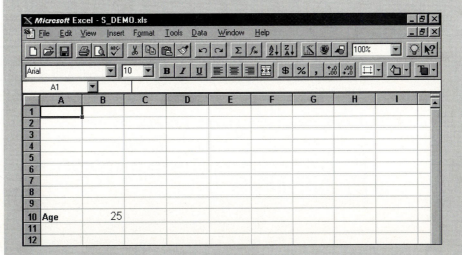

Figure 10-14
Results of SetValue macro

TROUBLE? If a run-time error message displayed on your screen, click the Goto button to return to the SetValue macro and check the line that is highlighted. Correct any discrepancies and repeat Steps 1 and 2.

Now that you have seen how you can use VBA to change the properties of objects, create a VBA macro to determine the settings of an object's property.

Examining Property Settings of Objects

Sometimes you need to know the current setting of a property before your macro performs an additional action. For example, you can examine the Value property of a cell to determine whether to change the cell's Color property. One way to do this is to write a VBA statement that assigns the current setting of a property to a variable.

For example, to store the contents of cell B10—a range object—to a variable named `Cost`, you write the statement `Cost = Range("B10").Value`.

Note that this statement stores the contents of cell B10 temporarily in a memory location named `Cost`. This memory location is called a **variable**. Variables are *not* cells in your worksheet. You'll learn more about variables later in the tutorial.

> **SYNTAX window**
>
> **TO ASSIGN THE CURRENT VALUE OF A PROPERTY TO A VARIABLE, USE THE FOLLOWING SYNTAX:**
>
> *variable = object.property*
> where *variable* is the variable name that holds the returned property value (property setting), and *object.property* is the expression that returns the property of the object you want to assign to the variable.

Look at a VBA macro that examines the current setting of a property. This macro will use the **MsgBox** function to display information about the value of the property in a special type of dialog box called a **message box** while your VBA code is executing. For example, to display the message "The value stored in cell A10 is," you could use the following statement:

```
MsgBox "The value stored in cell A10 is"
```

> **SYNTAX window**
>
> **TO SPECIFY THE MSGBOX FUNCTION, USE THE FOLLOWING SYNTAX:**
>
> **MsgBox** *(prompt, buttons, title)*
> where *prompt* is the message you want to display in the message box. *Buttons* is an optional entry that consists of a number or a constant that specifies the command buttons that appear in the message box. If you omit it, an OK button appears in the message box. *Title* is an optional entry that contains the text that appears in the title bar of the message box. If you omit it, VBA uses the label "Microsoft Excel" as the title.

Now you are going to examine some properties of objects by writing a VBA macro. Figure 10-15 shows a flowchart of the macro's logic.

EXAMINING PROPERTY SETTINGS OF OBJECTS **ADVEX 489**

Figure 10-15
Flowchart of macro to examine object's properties

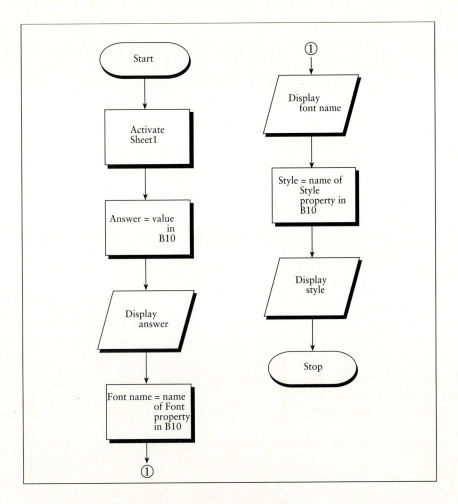

To examine the value of an object's property:

1. Activate the **Module1** module sheet. Place the insertion point at the bottom of the module.

2. Press the **Enter** key several times to insert blank lines.

3. Type the VBA code shown in Figure 10-16.

Figure 10-16
VBA code for GetProperty macro

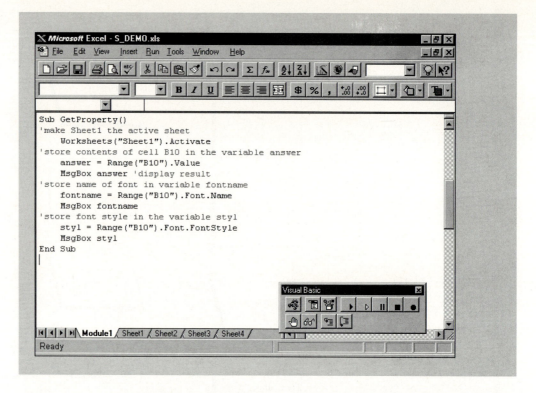

Stop here for a moment and review the function of each statement in the GetProperty macro.

The statement `Sub GetProperty` indicates the beginning of the procedure GetProperty.

The statement `Worksheets("Sheet1").Activate` makes Sheet1 the active sheet in the active workbook.

The statement `answer = Range("B10").Value` gets the value stored in cell B10 and stores it in a variable named *answer*.

The statement `MsgBox answer` displays the contents of the variable *answer*.

The statement `fontname = Range("B10").Font.Name` gets the name of the font that is used in cell B10 and stores that name in the variable *fontname*.

The statement `MsgBox fontname` displays the contents of the variable *fontname*.

The statement `styl = Range("B10").Font.FontStyle` gets the name of the font style that is used in cell B10 and stores that style name in the variable *style*.

The statement `MsgBox styl` displays the contents of the variable *styl*.

Now run the GetProperty macro.

To run the GetProperty macro:

1. Make sure the insertion point is on any line in the **GetProperty** macro.

2. Click the **Run Macro** button on the Visual Basic toolbar to execute the **GetProperty** macro. See Figure 10-17. The value 25 is displayed in a message box.

   TROUBLE? If an error message displays on your screen, click the OK button or the End button, depending on the error. Return to the GetProperty procedure in the module sheet and check each line. Correct any discrepancies and repeat Steps 1 and 2.

Figure 10-17
Message box displays Value property of cell B10

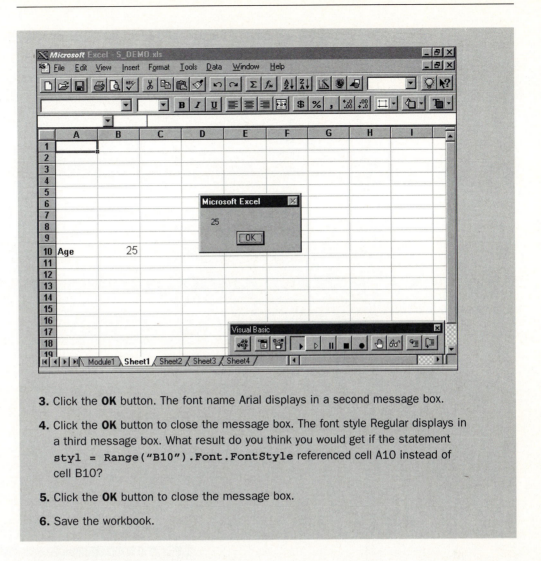

3. Click the **OK** button. The font name Arial displays in a second message box.

4. Click the **OK** button to close the message box. The font style Regular displays in a third message box. What result do you think you would get if the statement `styl = Range("B10").Font.FontStyle` referenced cell A10 instead of cell B10?

5. Click the **OK** button to close the message box.

6. Save the workbook.

If you want to take a break and resume the tutorial at a later time, you can do so now. Close the workbook and exit Excel. If you are on a network, leave Windows running. If you are using your own computer, you may exit Windows and shut down the computer. When you resume the tutorial, place your Student Disk in the disk drive, launch Excel, then continue with the tutorial.

● ● ●

Using VBA to Access an Object's Method

Methods perform actions upon or with data stored by the object. For example, there are many useful range object methods, such as Cut, Copy, and Paste, that transfer the contents of the range object either to or from the clipboard. The Select method makes a specific range object the active object. Another method, Clear, clears everything from a cell or range. The PrintOut method sends a range object to the printer. Take a look at a VBA macro that illustrates the use of these methods.

To use the Select, Copy, PrintOut, and Clear methods of a range object:

1. Activate the **Sheet2** worksheet.

2. Type the following values in Sheet2:

in cell	type the value
A2	5
A5	10
A6	20
B5	30
B6	40

3. Activate the **Module1** module sheet and move the insertion point to the bottom of the module sheet. Enter several blank lines.

4. Type the VBA code shown in Figure 10-18.

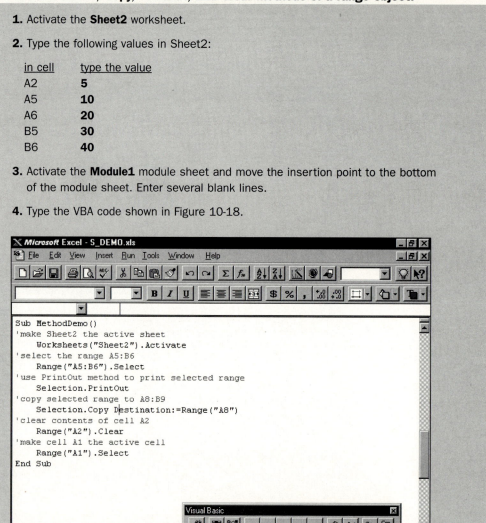

Figure 10-18
VBA code for MethodDemo macro

Before running the MethodDemo macro, review the function of each VBA statement in the procedure.

The statement `Worksheets("Sheet2").Activate` makes Sheet2 the active sheet in the active workbook.

The statement `Range("A5:B6").Select` uses the Select method to select the range A5:B6.

The statement `Selection.PrintOut` prints the currently selected range. Selection returns the currently selected object (A5:B6), which is used by the PrintOut method to print the selected object.

The statement `Selection.Copy Destination:=Range("A8")` returns the currently selected range, A5:B6, to the Copy method, which copies the range to the destination range. Since the destination range is a single cell (A8), Excel uses that cell as the upper-left corner of the copied range. Thus, the contents of cells A5:B6 will be copied to A8:B9.

The statement `Range("A2").Clear` uses the Clear method to clear the contents of cell A2.

The statement `Range("A1").Select` makes cell A1 the active cell.

Now run your macro.

To run the MethodDemo macro:

1. Make sure the insertion point is on any line in the **MethodDemo** macro.

2. Click the **Run Macro** button on the Visual Basic toolbar to execute the **MethodDemo** macro. See Figure 10-19. The range A5:B6 is selected and then printed. The selected range, A5:B6, is copied to A8:B9, the content of cell A2 is erased, and cell A1 is the active cell.

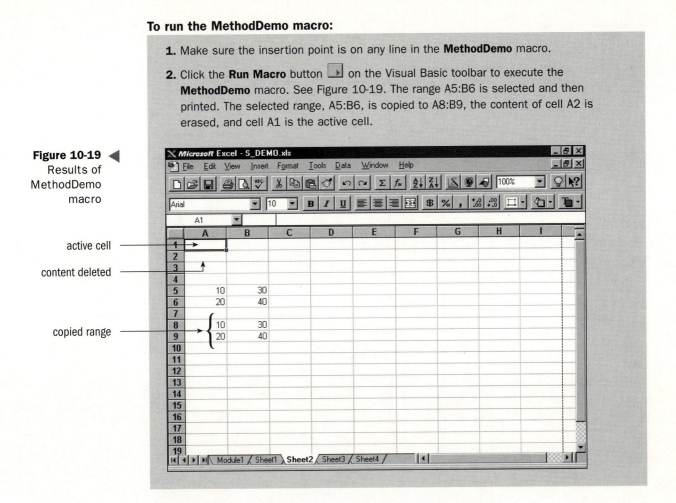

Figure 10-19
Results of MethodDemo macro

Working with Worksheet Objects

Although much of your work with Excel involves range objects, you will find it useful to manipulate other objects as well. For example, you may need to add a worksheet or chart sheet to a workbook. Next you will enter a VBA macro to control worksheet objects by manipulating their properties and methods.

The worksheet object contains a number of methods and properties you may find useful when writing VBA procedures. For example, you can activate a worksheet, add a new worksheet, rename a worksheet, count the number of worksheets in a workbook, or delete a worksheet. Write a VBA macro that illustrates how you can manipulate worksheet objects. Figure 10-20 shows a flowchart of the macro's logic.

Figure 10-20
Flowchart of macro to manipulate worksheet objects

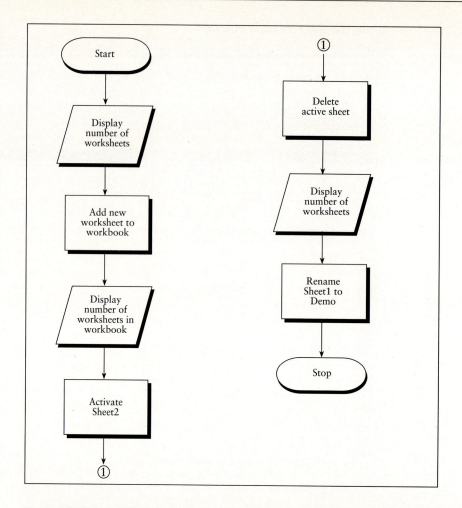

To manipulate worksheet objects using their properties and methods:

1. Activate the **Module1** module sheet and move the insertion point to the bottom of the module sheet. Add several blank lines.

2. Type the VBA code shown in Figure 10-21.

Figure 10-21
VBA code for Worksheet Objects macro

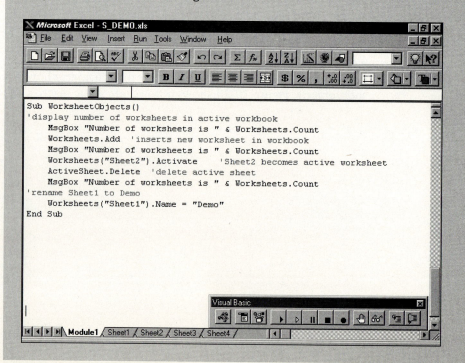

```
Sub WorksheetObjects()
'display number of worksheets in active workbook
    MsgBox "Number of worksheets is " & Worksheets.Count
    Worksheets.Add   'inserts new worksheet in workbook
    MsgBox "Number of worksheets is " & Worksheets.Count
    Worksheets("Sheet2").Activate    'Sheet2 becomes active worksheet
    ActiveSheet.Delete  'delete active sheet
    MsgBox "Number of worksheets is " & Worksheets.Count
'rename Sheet1 to Demo
    Worksheets("Sheet1").Name = "Demo"
End Sub
```

WORKING WITH WORKSHEET OBJECTS **ADVEX 495**

TROUBLE? If an error message displayed when you pressed the Enter key to move to the next line, you did not type the code correctly. Click the OK button to remove the message box, then review the line where the error occurred. Correct the line by retyping, then continue entering the remaining VBA code.

3. Make sure the insertion point is on any line in the **WorksheetObjects** macro. Click the **Run Macro** button ⬜ on the Visual Basic toolbar to execute the **WorksheetObjects** macro. The message box indicates that there are four worksheets in the workbook.

The statement

`MsgBox "Number of worksheets is " & Worksheets.Count` displays this number of worksheets in a message box. The ampersand (&) operator is used to join several text items into one text item. Within the MsgBox statement, the expression `Worksheets.Count` uses the Count property of the Worksheets collection to get the number of worksheets in the active workbook.

TROUBLE? If a run-time error message displayed, click the Goto button and compare the highlighted statement with the corresponding statement in Figure 10-21. Correct your error and continue.

4. Click the **OK** button. See Figure 10-22. Sheet5 is added to the workbook. The message box confirms that there are now five worksheets in the active workbook.

Figure 10-22 ◀
Message box indicates that there are 5 worksheets in the workbook

message box ————

Sheet5 just added ————

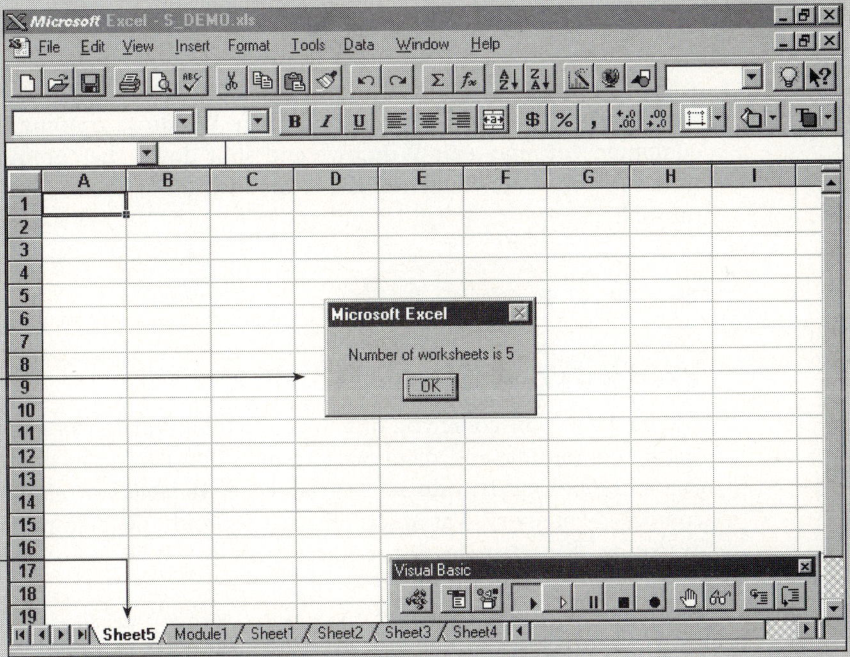

The statement `Worksheets.Add` uses the Add method to add a new member to the Worksheets collection. Notice that a new worksheet, Sheet5, has been inserted into the active workbook. Note also that Sheet5 is now the active worksheet. The statement

`MsgBox "Number of worksheets is " & Worksheets.Count` displays the number of worksheets currently in the workbook in a message box.

5. Click the **OK** button to display the message "Selected sheets will be permanently deleted. Continue?"

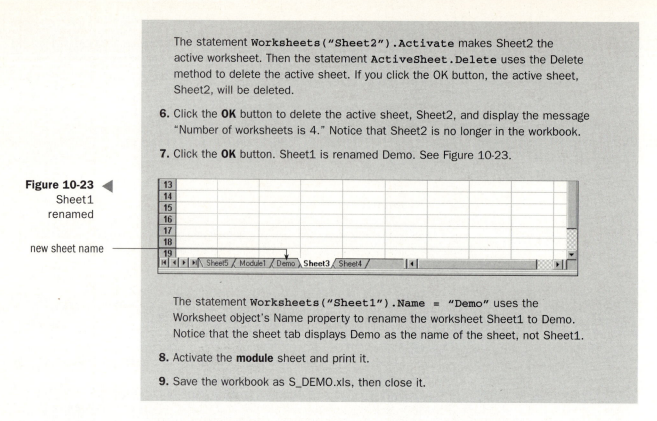

The statement `Worksheets("Sheet2").Activate` makes Sheet2 the active worksheet. Then the statement `ActiveSheet.Delete` uses the Delete method to delete the active sheet. If you click the OK button, the active sheet, Sheet2, will be deleted.

6. Click the **OK** button to delete the active sheet, Sheet2, and display the message "Number of worksheets is 4." Notice that Sheet2 is no longer in the workbook.

7. Click the **OK** button. Sheet1 is renamed Demo. See Figure 10-23.

Figure 10-23
Sheet1 renamed

new sheet name

The statement `Worksheets("Sheet1").Name = "Demo"` uses the Worksheet object's Name property to rename the worksheet Sheet1 to Demo. Notice that the sheet tab displays Demo as the name of the sheet, not Sheet1.

8. Activate the **module** sheet and print it.

9. Save the workbook as S_DEMO.xls, then close it.

If you want to take a break and resume the tutorial at a later time, you can do so now. Exit Excel. If you are on a network, leave Windows running. If you are using your own computer, you may exit Windows and shut down the computer. When you resume the tutorial, place your Student Disk in the disk drive, launch Excel, then continue with the tutorial.

● ● ●

Working with Variables

As you write VBA code, you often need to temporarily store values for use in calculations, testing conditions, and displaying results. In VBA, as in other programming languages, you store temporary values in variables. A **variable** is a named storage location in your computer's memory. Variables are used to hold and manipulate values when a macro is executing. For example, in the statement

`GrowthRate = Worksheets("Budget").Range("B10").Value`

the value in cell B10 in the worksheet Budget is assigned to the variable *GrowthRate*. In this case, once a value is assigned to the variable, you can use it in other parts of your program. For instance, you can take *GrowthRate* and multiply it by *Sales*.

Declaring a Variable

It is often a good idea to "dimension" or declare a variable, although it isn't absolutely necessary. By declaring the variable, you set aside space in memory to hold the variable during execution. To declare a variable, you include a **Dim** statement at the top of your VBA code. Declaring a variable tells VBA the name of the variable you're going to use and the type of data the variable will store. For example, the statement `Dim age as Integer` declares a variable named *age* that will store only integer values.

> **SYNTAX window**
>
> **TO SPECIFY A DIM STATEMENT, USE THE FOLLOWING SYNTAX:**
>
> `Dim` *VariableName* `As` *DataType*
> where *VariableName* is the name of the variable. The name must begin with a letter; it must be 255 characters or fewer, and it can contain spaces or ,!#$%&@ characters; the *DataType*, the type of data you store in a variable, is Integer, String, Currency, or Date, among others.

HELP DESK

EXCEL 5.0

Index

DECLARING VARIABLES

Double-click the Help button to display the Help Topics dialog box, then click the Index tab.

Keyword	Topic
Variables, declaring	Declaring variables
not available	

Getting Information from the User

Until now you have used recorded macros or entered VBA procedures that perform a task without interruption. Occasionally, you may want to temporarily pause the execution of your macro to obtain information from the user. This type of macro, an **interactive macro**, exchanges data with a user by prompting the user for input and then temporarily storing the newly entered data in a variable. For instance, you can have a macro ask users whether or not they want a printed report, or you could have a macro request the name of a file. To get input from the user, you use the **InputBox** function. The InputBox function displays a message in a dialog box that asks the user to enter data, and provides an input area (edit box) where the user enters the data. The dialog box also displays an OK button and a Cancel button. The user must click one of these buttons to continue the execution of the application. For example, to ask the user's name you could use the following VBA code:

```
userName = InputBox( _
        Prompt:="Enter your name", _
        Title:="Student data")
```

Figure 10-24 displays a dialog box generated using the InputBox function.

Figure 10-24
Dialog box generated using InputBox function

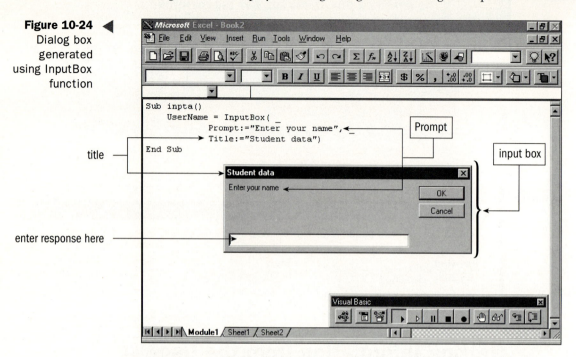

SYNTAX window

TO SPECIFY THE INPUTBOX FUNCTION, USE THE FOLLOWING SYNTAX:

InputBox(*prompt, title*)
where *prompt* is the message you want to display in the dialog box. *Prompt* must be enclosed in quotes. *Title* is an optional argument whose text is displayed in the title bar of the dialog box. The text is enclosed in quotes. If the *Title* argument is not used, the dialog box has no title.
The dialog box also displays the OK and Cancel buttons. If the user clicks the OK button, the InputBox function returns the value he or she entered in response to the prompt as a string value. If the user clicks the Cancel button, an empty character string is returned.

Now combine the concepts of objects, methods, variables, and the InputBox function to create an interactive macro.

Create a macro that asks the user the name of a workbook to open. Figure 10-25 shows a flowchart of the macro's logic.

Figure 10-25
Flowchart of interactive macro

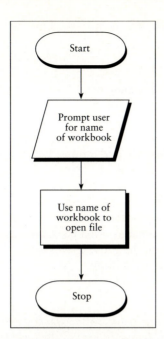

To create a macro that uses the InputBox function:

1. Open a new workbook and immediately save it as S_OPENBK.xls.

   Add a module sheet.

2. Click **Insert**, point to **Macro**, then click **Module** to insert a new module sheet. The module sheet is the active sheet.

3. Type the VBA code shown in Figure 10-26.

Figure 10-26
VBA code for OpenWorkBook macro

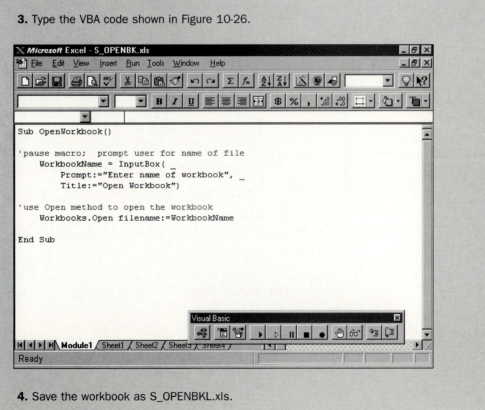

4. Save the workbook as S_OPENBKL.xls.

Stop and review the function of each statement in the OpenWorkBook macro. The statement

```
WorkbookName = InputBox( _
    Prompt:="Enter name of workbook", _
    Title:="Open Workbook")
```

stores the user response in the variable *WorkbookName*. Notice that the statement is continued over several lines by using a space and an underscore (_). These characters are called **line continuation** characters; they make the code more readable. Although this statement takes three lines, it executes as a single statement. The named argument *Prompt* passes, or provides, the message "Enter name of workbook" to the InputBox function. The named argument *Title* passes the caption for the dialog box to the InputBox function.

The statement `Workbooks.Open filename:=WorkbookName` uses the Open method to open a workbook whose name is stored in the variable *WorkbookName*.

Now run the interactive macro OpenWorkBook.

To run the OpenWorkBook macro:

1. Click the **Run Macro** button on the Visual Basic toolbar, if necessary click **OpenWorkBook** in the Macro Name/Reference list box, then click the **Run** button. The input dialog box titled Open Workbook displays. See Figure 10-27.

Figure 10-27
Prompt user for name of file

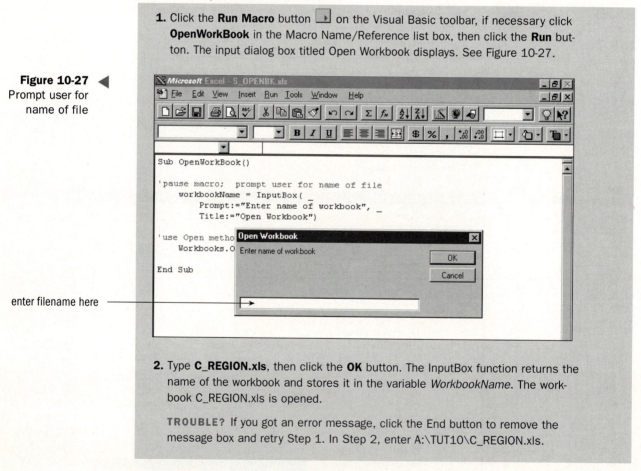

enter filename here

2. Type **C_REGION.xls**, then click the **OK** button. The InputBox function returns the name of the workbook and stores it in the variable *WorkbookName*. The workbook C_REGION.xls is opened.

TROUBLE? If you got an error message, click the End button to remove the message box and retry Step 1. In Step 2, enter A:\TUT10\C_REGION.xls.

This section illustrated how to create an interactive macro to obtain information from a user while a macro is running. Now you will look at several VBA statements that will add power and flexibility to your problem-solving capabilities.

Visual Basic Control Structures

Until now, the macros you have recorded or entered were executed in a linear fashion, one instruction after the other, in the order in which they appeared in the module sheet. This linear approach worked well for the problems you have solved up to now. In many situations, however, you will work on problems that require more flexibility and power in executing macros. You will want to be able to test conditions and run certain statements based on the results of those tests. At other times, you will want to run a group of statements several times. VBA contains statements called **control structures**, which control decision-making and looping. These control structures are functionally equivalent to those found in other programming languages. Figure 10-28 lists the most common control structures found in VBA.

Figure 10-28 ◀
Common
VBA control
structures

Control Structure	Description
If-Then-Else	Tests a condition and alters execution flow based on result of test
Select Case	Branches to one of several code segments based on the value of a variable
For. . .Next	Carries out a repetitive action a specified number of times
Do loop	Carries out a repetitive action while a specific condition is true or until a specific condition becomes true

Now explore these control structures more fully, and learn how you can incorporate these statements into your macros.

Using the If-Then-Else Statement

VBA's If-Then-Else statement is a decision control statement that allows you to make a comparison—the condition—and based on the results of the comparison, execute one or another branch of the macro's code. To help you understand this comparison, Figure 10-29 shows a flowchart depicting the logic of the If-Then-Else statement. In the flowchart, the diamond symbol specifies the condition or decision you are testing. The evaluation of the condition is set up so the results are either true (yes) or false (no). For example, either the employee worked more than 40 hours this week (true) or the employee didn't work more than 40 hours (false). If the condition is true, the macro performs a certain set of tasks. On the other hand, if the condition is false, the macro performs a different set of tasks.

Figure 10-29
Flowchart of If-Then-Else statement

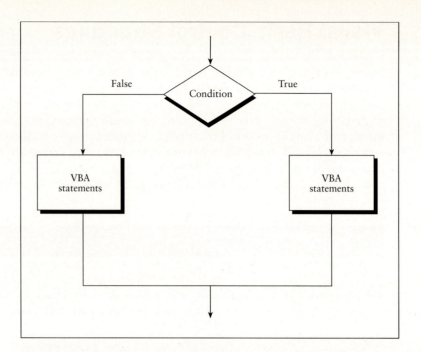

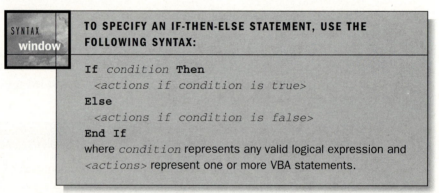

TO SPECIFY AN IF-THEN-ELSE STATEMENT, USE THE FOLLOWING SYNTAX:

```
If condition Then
    <actions if condition is true>
Else
    <actions if condition is false>
End If
```
where *condition* represents any valid logical expression and *<actions>* represent one or more VBA statements.

Now incorporate several VBA commands to develop a macro that illustrates decision-making. In the C_REGION.xls workbook, the workbook you just opened, there is a table that displays regional sales data for Sunny Morning Products in dollars and units. Bill Smith, the sales manager, wants to insert a column chart next to the tabular data that displays one data series, either regional sales in dollars or regional sales in units. Bill wants to be able to switch the data series depending on the type of data he is interested in viewing at any moment. To solve this problem, you will create an interactive macro. While the macro is running, Bill will be asked to enter the data series he wishes to display—sales in units or sales in dollars—on the column chart. Once Bill enters the choice of data series, the macro chooses the appropriate VBA code to display the column chart he requested. Figure 10-30 shows a flowchart of the logic needed to create this macro.

Figure 10-30
Flowchart to determine data series to display

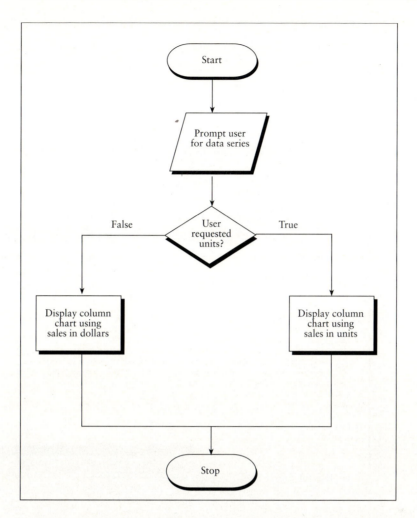

One essential task in this macro is to create a chart using VBA. If you were working with the Excel ChartWizard, creating this column chart would be quite simple. The challenge, however, is to produce the chart using VBA. Which objects, properties, or methods do you use? Within VBA, charts and chart objects have hundreds of properties and methods, too many to try to memorize the commands needed to create a chart. A much easier starting point is to first use the macro recorder to record the process of creating a chart. Once you record the chart macro, you can view and modify the VBA code and use it as you build the macro described in Figure 10-30.

Prepare a column chart to display regional sales in units. While you prepare this chart, record the steps. Then review the objects, properties, and methods found in the recorded macro.

To record a macro to create a chart:

1. Make sure the workbook C_REGION.xls is open. Save it as S_REGION.xls. Make sure Sheet1 is active.

2. Select the range **A2:A6**. Press the **Ctrl** key and select the range **C2:C6**.

3. Click **Tools**, point to **Record Macro**, then click **Record New Macro**. Name the macro **CreateChart**, then click the **OK** button.

4. Click the **ChartWizard** button on the Standard toolbar. Select the range **E2:I11** as the area where the chart should be placed.

5. Accept all default settings in the ChartWizard dialog boxes 1–4, then in the Chart Wizard = Step 5 of 5 dialog box, select the **No** option button to remove the legend from the chart, then click the **Finish** button.

ADVEX 504 · TUTORIAL 10 · INTRODUCTION TO VISUAL BASIC FOR APPLICATIONS

6. Click anywhere outside the chart object to deselect the chart.

7. Click the **Stop Macro** button ▣.

Now examine the VBA code.

To view the VBA code:

1. Activate the **Module1** sheet and review the recorded macro. See Figure 10-31.

Figure 10-31 ◀
VBA code for
CreateChart
macro

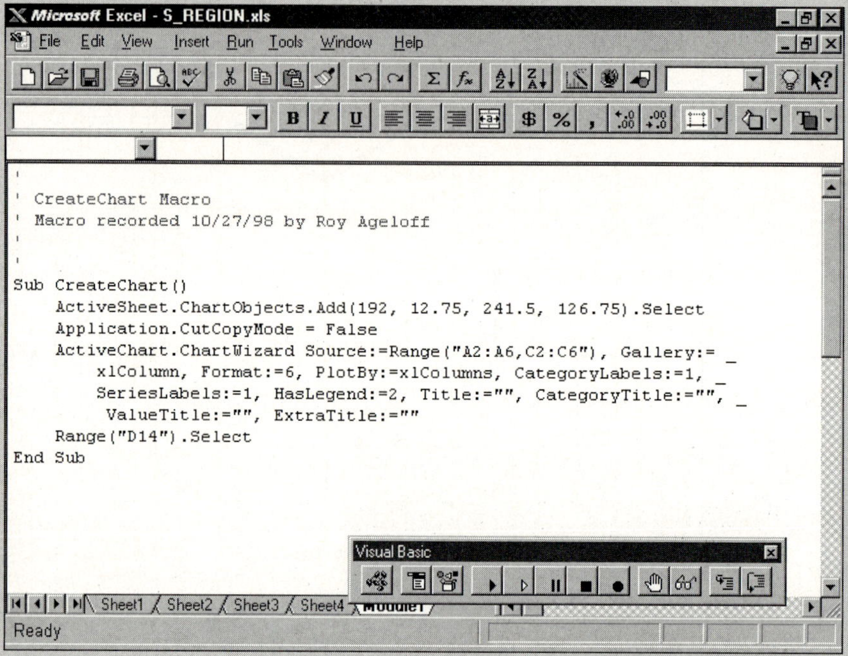

```
'
' CreateChart Macro
' Macro recorded 10/27/98 by Roy Ageloff
'
Sub CreateChart()
    ActiveSheet.ChartObjects.Add(192, 12.75, 241.5, 126.75).Select
    Application.CutCopyMode = False
    ActiveChart.ChartWizard Source:=Range("A2:A6,C2:C6"), Gallery:= _
        xlColumn, Format:=6, PlotBy:=xlColumns, CategoryLabels:=1, _
        SeriesLabels:=1, HasLegend:=2, Title:="", CategoryTitle:="", _
        ValueTitle:="", ExtraTitle:=""
    Range("D14").Select
End Sub
```

Take a minute to review the function of each statement in the macro.
The statement
`ActiveSheet.ChartObjects.Add(192,12.75,241.5,126.75).Select` inserts the container for the chart (your numbers will differ slightly). The first two values (192 and 12.75) are the vertical and horizontal locations of the upper-left corner of the container for the chart. The third and fourth numbers (241.5 and 126.75) are the height and width of the chart's container.

The statement `Application.CutCopyMode = False` cancels the Copy command.

The statement `ActiveChart.ChartWizard` defines the chart that goes inside the container. Note that several arguments are passed to the ChartWizard method to specify values for various properties of the chart.

The argument `Source:=Range("A2:A6,C2:C6")` specifies cells A2:A6 and C2:C6 as the source of data for the chart. The argument `Gallery:=xlColumn` specifies the chart as a column chart. The argument `Format:=6` specifies the sixth chart in the Column gallery. The argument `PlotBy:=xlColumns` tells Excel that the data series is in columns. The argument `CategoryLabels:=1` tells Excel to use the entries in the first column as the category axis labels. The argument `SeriesLabels:=1` tells Excel to use the entries from the first row as the text for the legends; the argument `HasLegend:=2` tells Excel not to display the legend. The four remaining arguments tell Excel that there are no titles for these parts of the chart.

Now that you have recorded the CreateChart macro, use the VBA code to prepare the macro that will allow Bill to select the data series to use when displaying the column chart.

VISUAL BASIC CONTROL STRUCTURES **ADVEX 505**

To create the ChartDataChoice macro:

1. Move to the bottom of the module sheet. Add several blank lines.

2. Type the following VBA code:

```
Sub ChartDataChoice()
   Dim dta As String
   dta = InputBox( _
         Prompt:="Enter Dollars or Units", _
         Title:="Source of Data")
   If dta = "Units" Then
```

Recall from the flowchart in Figure 10-30 that you need a decision structure to complete your macro. You will use the If-Then-Else statement. But rather than type the VBA code to create a chart into the ChartDataChoice macro, you will copy the code from the CreateChart macro to the ChartDataChoice macro.

To copy code from one macro to another:

1. Move the insertion point to the **CreateChart** macro and select all the code following the **Sub CreateChart()** statement, up to but not including the **End Sub** statement.

2. Click the **Copy** button on the toolbar to copy the VBA code to the clipboard.

3. Move the insertion point to the line following the **If-Then** statement in the **ChartDataChoice** macro.

4. Click the **Paste** button to insert the VBA code into the macro.

5. Press the **Enter** key to move to the next line and type **Else**, then press the **Enter** key again.

6. Click the **Paste** button on the toolbar to insert the VBA code again.

7. In the VBA code following the Else clause, change the argument
`Source:=Range("A2:A6,C2:C6")` to `Source:=Range("A2:A6,B2:B6")`
so the Else block in the If-Then-Else statement will supply source data for sales in dollars.

8. Place the insertion point at the bottom of the module sheet and type the following:
```
End If
End Sub
```

Figure 10-32 shows the finished procedure. Compare it to the code you entered. Make any changes. Recall that alignment and indentation are not required for your macro to run, but will make the code easier to read.

Figure 10-32
VBA code for the ChartData Choice macro

entry is case-sensitive: dta must store "Units" for a match to occur: "UNITS" will not result in a match

change range to sales in dollars

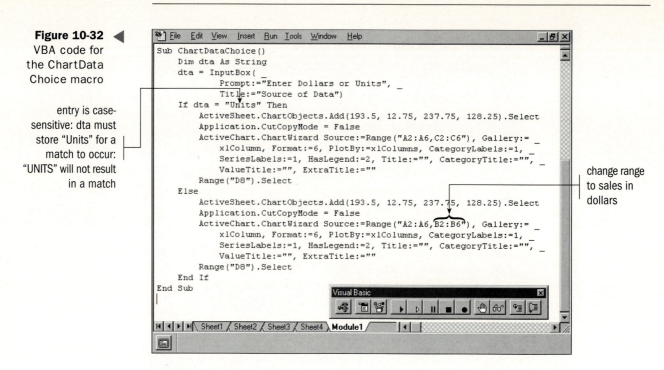

Now test the macro.

To test the macro:

1. Activate **Sheet1**.

2. Click **Tools**, click **Macro** to open the Macro dialog box, click the **ChartDataChoice** macro name, then click the **Run** button. You are prompted to enter Dollars or Units. See Figure 10-33.

Figure 10-33
Input box with prompt for units or dollars

enter "Dollars" exactly as shown

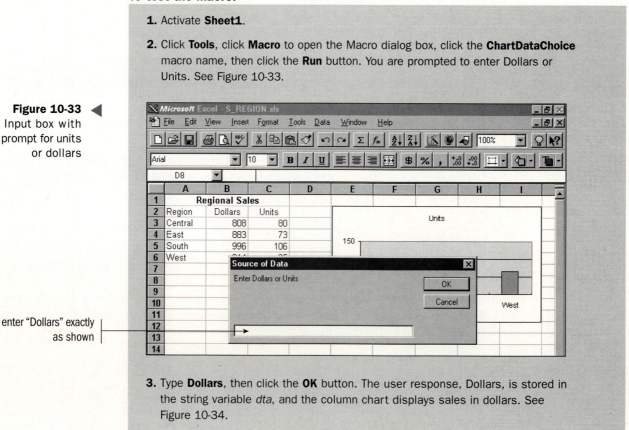

3. Type **Dollars**, then click the **OK** button. The user response, Dollars, is stored in the string variable *dta*, and the column chart displays sales in dollars. See Figure 10-34.

Figure 10-34
Column chart for sales in dollars

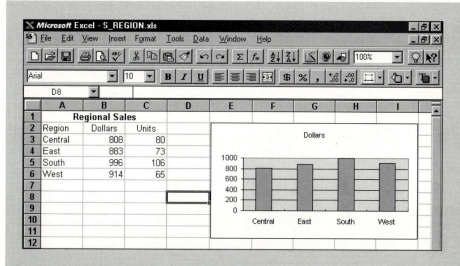

The value stored in *dta* is evaluated in the If-Then-Else statement. If the user enters "Dollars," then the condition is false and the ChartWizard method uses the source data for sales in dollars (B2:B6) to display the chart. However, if the user enters "Units," then the condition is true and the ChartWizard method uses the source data for sales in units (C2:C6) to display the chart.

4. Return to Step 2 and run the macro again. Type **Units** when asked to enter a choice.

   TROUBLE? If the data series for dollars is still displayed, you did not match the case when typing "Units". The entry for Dollars or Units is case-sensitive. Return to Step 2. In Step 3, make sure you type "Units" exactly as shown in the step. One way to avoid a case-sensitive entry of character data is to use the VBA string function Ucase. The function Ucase converts all lower case characters to uppercase characters. By using the Ucase function in the If statement you can compare the user's entry to UNITS without concern for how the entry was typed.

   In the ChartDataChoice macro, change the If statement from
   `If dta = "Units" then`
   to
   `If Ucase(dta) = "Units" Then`

5. Save the workbook as S_REGION.xls, then close it.
6. The workbook S_OPENBK.xls is still open. Save it, then close the workbook.

Now that you have seen how you can use the If-Then-Else statement to make choices, you will take a look at some of the other control structures available in VBA.

If you want to take a break and resume the tutorial at a later time, you can do so now. Exit Excel. If you are on a network, leave Windows running. If you are using your own computer, you may exit Windows and shut down the computer. When you resume the tutorial, place your Student Disk in the disk drive, launch Excel, then continue with the tutorial.

● ● ●

Using the Select Case Statement to Make Multiple Decisions

The decision structure considered in the preceding section involved selecting from one of two alternative paths. Of course, all decisions are not merely between two alternatives. In cases where you want to make a decision in which the user chooses from three or more alternative paths, VBA provides the Select Case statement as an option.

TO SPECIFY THE SELECT CASE STATEMENT, USE THE FOLLOWING SYNTAX:

```
Select Case testexpression
   Case Expressionlist1
       <statements for first case>
   Case Expressionlist2
       <statements for second case>
   ...

   Case ExpressionlistNth
       <statements for Nth case>
   Case Else
       <statements when testexpression does not
       match any of the expressionlists>
End Select
```

The Select Case statement begins with the keywords `Select Case` and ends with the keywords `End Select`. Between these two statements are individual Case clauses that represent different paths the macro can follow. You can have as many Case clauses as needed in a Select Case statement, as indicated by the ellipses (...).

Notice that the `Select Case` clause must include a *testexpression* that is evaluated when the statement is first entered.

When processing the Select Case statement, VBA compares the results of the *testexpression* with the values for each case's *expressionlist*. If a match is found, VBA processes the block statements associated with that case. If the *testexpression* does not match any of the values in the *expressionlists*, VBA then processes the statements listed in the `Case Else` clause or, if no `Case Else` clause is included, VBA processes the instructions following the `End Select` statement.

Figure 10-35 shows abbreviated VBA code of the Select Case structure where one of four regional column charts is displayed depending on the option the user requests.

Figure 10-35
Example of Select Case statement

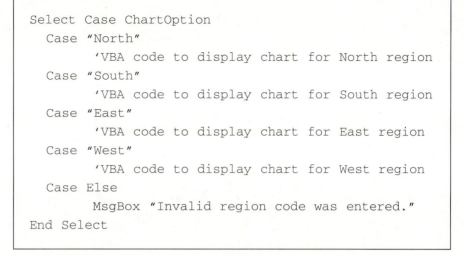

```
Select Case ChartOption
   Case "North"
         'VBA code to display chart for North region
   Case "South"
         'VBA code to display chart for South region
   Case "East"
         'VBA code to display chart for East region
   Case "West"
         'VBA code to display chart for West region
   Case Else
         MsgBox "Invalid region code was entered."
End Select
```

The Select Case structure is a good example of decision-making when there are multiple paths from which to choose.

Using the For...Next Loop Control Structure

One of the limitations of recorded macros is their inability to execute one or more statements repeatedly. This is not a limitation when you are working with VBA code, because it has several commands designed for repeating a series of statements in a loop. A **loop** is a control structure that results in one or more statements being executed repeatedly until a certain condition is met, such as repeating a series of steps a specified number of times.

You use the For...Next loop control structure when you know the number of times you want a series of statements to be performed. For...Next loops automatically increment or decrement a counter to keep track of the number of times a loop has been performed.

Figure 10-36 illustrates the logic of the For...Next loop.

Figure 10-36
Flowchart of For...Next loop control structure

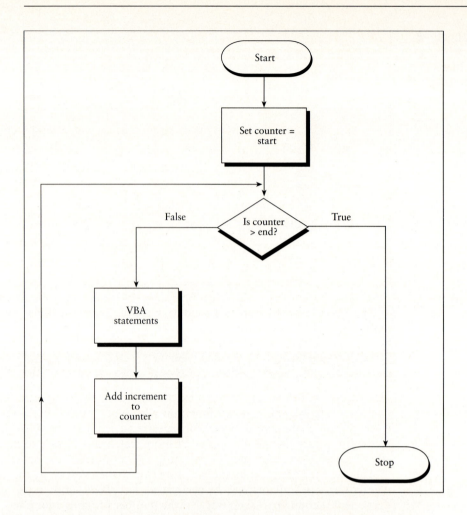

TO SPECIFY A FOR...NEXT LOOP, USE THE FOLLOWING SYNTAX:

For *counter* = *start* **To** *end* **Step** *increment*
 <VBA statements>
Next *counter*

where *counter* is a variable used to count the number of times the program has gone through the loop. *Start* is the initial value of the counter, usually 1. *End* is the final value of the counter. *Increment* is an optional value that defines the increment value for the loop counter. If you leave the increment out, the step value is 1. You can use a negative step value if you want to decrement the counter.

Now that you have reviewed the syntax of the Select Case and For...Next loop statements, examine a macro that incorporates both statements.

Using Select Case and For...Next Statements in a Macro

Bill prepared a worksheet that summarizes sales by state. He wants to use different colors to help quickly identify the states where sales are very high or very low. Sales above 200 units will be displayed in blue, sales below 10 units will be displayed in red, and sales greater than or equal to 10 and less than or equal to 200 will be displayed in black. Bill developed a macro to automatically change the color of each sales value. Figure 10-37 shows a flowchart of the logic of this macro.

Figure 10-37
Flowchart for SetColor macro

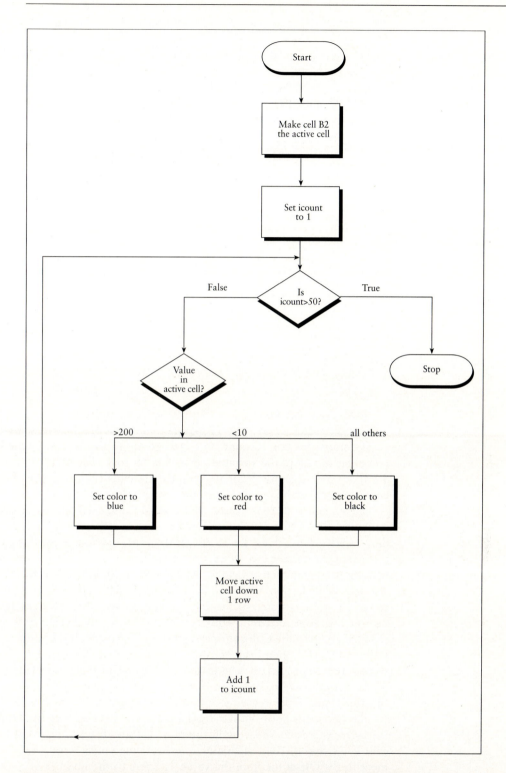

To run a macro using Select Case and For...Next loop statements:

1. Open the C_LOOPS.xls workbook in the Tut10 folder or directory and immediately save it as S_LOOPS.xls. The workbook consists of two sheets: the Sales by State worksheet and the modLoops module sheet. The Sales by State sheet contains a summary of the sales for each of the 50 states within the US.

    Run the macro to set the colors.

2. Click the **SetColor** button to run the SetColor macro. Note that the colors in the Sales column are adjusted—blue if sales are above 200, red if sales are below 10, and all others display in black.

ADVEX 512 TUTORIAL 10 INTRODUCTION TO VISUAL BASIC FOR APPLICATIONS

Now examine the SetColor macro to determine how the code performed its task.

3. Activate the **modLoops** module sheet and review the SetColor macro. See Figure 10-38.

Figure 10-38 ◄
VBA code for
SetColor macro

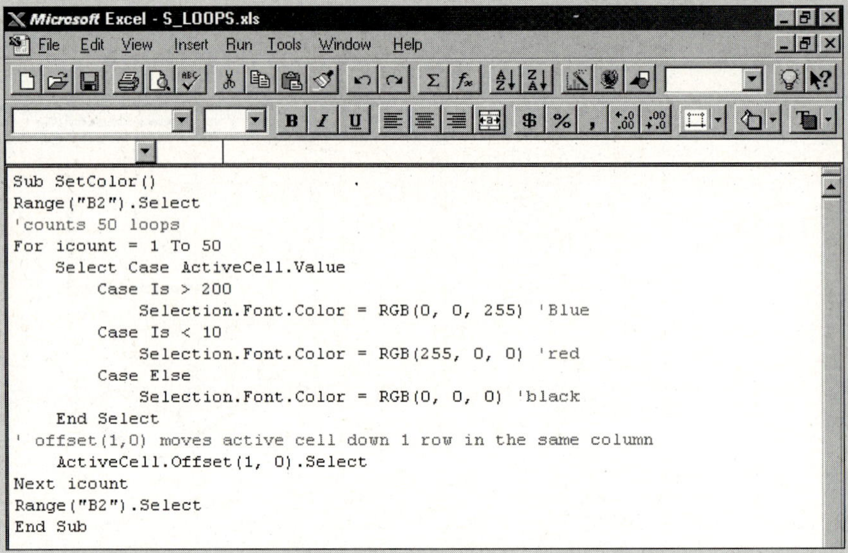

```
Sub SetColor()
Range("B2").Select
'counts 50 loops
For icount = 1 To 50
    Select Case ActiveCell.Value
        Case Is > 200
            Selection.Font.Color = RGB(0, 0, 255) 'Blue
        Case Is < 10
            Selection.Font.Color = RGB(255, 0, 0) 'red
        Case Else
            Selection.Font.Color = RGB(0, 0, 0) 'black
    End Select
' offset(1,0) moves active cell down 1 row in the same column
    ActiveCell.Offset(1, 0).Select
Next icount
Range("B2").Select
End Sub
```

Now review each line of code in the SetColor procedure.

The statement `Range("B2").Select` makes cell B2, the first sales value, the active cell.

The statement `For icount = 1 to 50` indicates the start of the loop. Initially, when you enter the loop, the variable *icount* is set to 1. The value of *icount* is compared to 50. If *icount* is greater than 50, then the statement following the Next statement is executed; otherwise the program executes the statements following the For statement.

The statement `Select Case ActiveCell.Value` indicates the beginning of the case structure. VBA evaluates the expression *ActiveCell.Value* and compares it to the condition in the clause `Case Is > 200`. If the value of the active cell is greater than 200, then the statement `Selection.Font.Color = RGB(0, 0, 255)` is executed. This statement uses the RGB function to assign the color blue (0, 0, 255) to the Color property of the selected cell (Selection). If the value in the active cell is not greater than 200, then the clause `Case Is < 10` is tested. If the value of the active cell is less than 10, then the statement `Selection.Font.Color = RGB(255, 0, 0)` is executed. That statement assigns the color red (255, 0, 0) to the Color property of the selected cell. If the value of the active cell is not less than 10, then the `Case Else` clause is reached and the statement `Selection.Font.Color = RGB(0, 0, 0)` assigns the color black (0, 0, 0) to the Color property of the selected cell. (To learn more about the RGB function, you can highlight the function name while in the module sheet and press the F1 key.)

The statement `ActiveCell.Offset(1, 0).Select` uses the Offset method to move the active cell down one row in the same column from the current location of the active cell. The Offset method calculates a new starting position for *ActiveCell*. The first argument in the Offset method, the value 1, refers to the number of rows up (negative number) or down (positive number) you shift the current selection. The second argument, the value 0, refers to the number of columns left (negative number) or right (positive number) you shift the current selection.

The statement `Next icount` indicates the end of the loop. The value of *icount* is increased by 1 (when *step* is omitted, *value* is assumed to be 1) and program control returns to the For statement, where the value of *icount* is again tested to see if the value is greater than 50. When the value of *icount* is greater than 50, program control moves to the first statement following the **Next icount** statement. The statement `Range("B2").Select` is executed and cell B2 becomes the active cell.

USING THE SELECT CASE STATEMENT TO MAKE MULTIPLE DECISIONS **ADVEX 513**

4. Close the S_LOOPS.xls workbook without saving it.

HELP DESK

Index

OFFSET METHOD

Double-click the Help button to display the Help Topics dialog box, then click the Index tab.

Keyword	**Topic**
Offset method	Offset method

Using the Do...Loop Control Structure

What happens when you want to build a loop, but you don't know in advance how many times to repeat it? Such a situation could occur if you want the statements you are running to be executed repeatedly until the active cell is blank.

A solution to this situation is a control structure called the Do loop. A **Do loop** allows you to repeat a series of statements an indefinite number of times (based on whether a condition is true or false). Many variations of the Do loop structure exist. However, in this tutorial we will focus on the commonly used Do While...loop statement, and leave the other statements for you to investigate using on-line Help.

HELP DESK

Index

DO LOOPS

Double-click the Help button to display the Help Topics dialog box, then click the Index tab.

Keyword	**Topic**
Do statement	Do...Loop statement
not available	

EXCEL 5.0

The Do While...loop statement continues to repeat a series of statements as long as the condition is true. Figure 10-39 illustrates the logic of the Do While...loop statement.

Figure 10-39
Flowchart of Do While...loop control structure

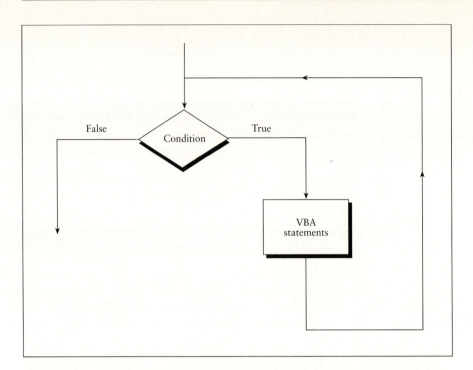

SYNTAX window

TO SPECIFY THE DO WHILE...LOOP, USE THE FOLLOWING SYNTAX:

`Do While` *conditionIsTrue*
  <one or more VBA statements>
`Loop`

where the keywords `Do While` indicate the beginning of the loop. This statement includes a condition that is evaluated before entering the loop. If the condition is true, the statement or statements inside the loop are executed. The keyword `Loop` indicates the end of the loop, and the point at which VBA returns to the `Do While...` statement and tests the condition again. This looping process continues while the condition in the `Do While...` statement is true. Once the condition is false, the program continues execution at the statement following the `Loop` statement.

Recall in an earlier tutorial that Ann developed a worksheet at SMP to calculate a monthly loan payment for a new juicing machine using the PMT function. Now examine a modification of this application in which an interactive macro has been developed to prompt the user for the interest rate of the loan, the number of years of the loan, and the total amount of the loan. Then the macro calculates the monthly loan payment using the information the user has provided. After the macro displays the results of the loan calculation, the user is asked if he or she wants to enter another set of data. If the user indicates Yes, the process of entering data and determining a monthly loan payment is repeated. If the user indicates No, the macro stops processing. Figure 10-40 shows a flowchart of the logic of this macro.

Figure 10-40
Flowchart at
LoanCalc
macro

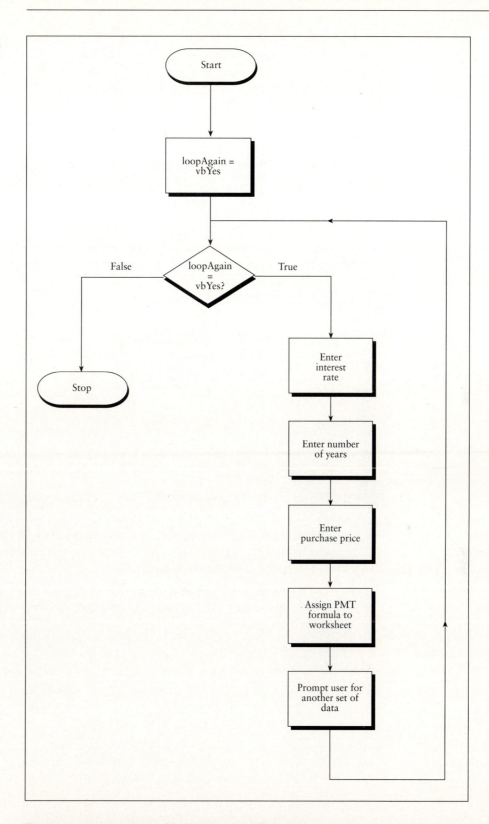

To run a macro using a Do loop control structure:

1. Open the C_LOAN.xls workbook and immediately save it as S_LOAN.xls. The workbook consists of three sheets: the Documentation and Payment worksheets and the modPayment module sheet.

2. Activate the **Payment** worksheet.

   Run the macro to calculate the monthly payment for the loan.

3. Click the **Loan Calculation** button to run the **LoanCalc** macro. An input box with the message "Enter interest rate" displays. Type **.08**, then click the **OK** button. Enter **7** when prompted for number of years, and **1500000** when prompted for the equipment's purchase price.

4. The monthly payment is calculated and displayed as $23,379. In addition, a message box displays asking if you want to enter another set of data. See Figure 10-41. Click the **Yes** button. The macro continues execution.

Figure 10-41
Interactive message box

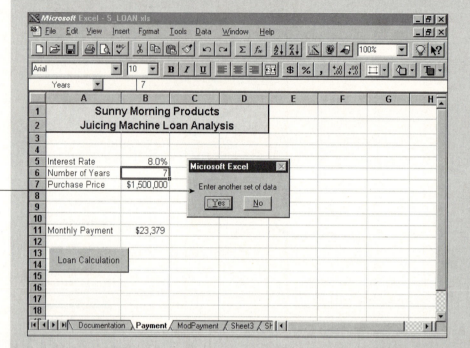

macro halts, waiting for your response; click Yes or No

5. Type **.075** when prompted with the message "Enter interest rate." Then click the **OK** button. Enter **7** when prompted for Number of years, and **1500000** when prompted for the equipment's Purchase Price.

6. The monthly payment is calculated and displayed as $23,007. The message box asking if you want to enter another set of data displays. Click the **No** button. The macro stops execution.

Examine the LoanCalc macro.

7. Activate the **modPayment** module sheet and review the LoanCalc macro. See Figure 10-42.

Figure 10-42
VBA code for LoanCalc macro

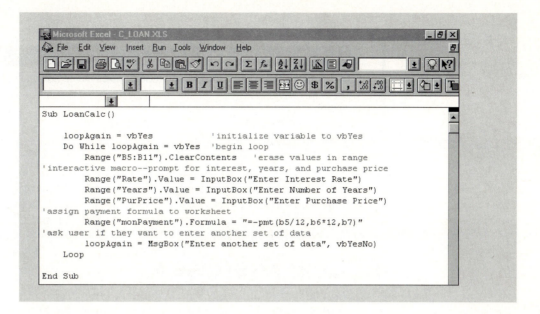

Now review each line of code in the LoanCalc macro.

The statement `loopAgain = vbYes` initializes the variable *loopAgain* with a special VBA constant, vbYes.

The statement `Do While loopAgain = vbYes` begins the Do While...loop. The condition `loopAgain = vbYes` tests true because the previous statement assigned the constant vbYes to the variable *loopAgain*. The statements inside the loop are executed.

The statement `Range("B5:B11").ClearContents` erases the entries in the range B5:B11 before getting a new set of data.

The statements

```
Range("Rate").Value = InputBox("Enter Interest Rate")
Range("Years").Value = InputBox("Enter Number of Years")
Range("PurPrice").Value = InputBox("Enter Purchase Price")
```

prompt the user for input and place the response in the worksheet cells named Rate, Years, and PurPrice, respectively.

The statement

`Range("monPayment").Formula = "=-pmt(b5/12,b6*12,b7)"` assigns the PMT function to the worksheet cell named monPayment. The monthly loan payment is computed and displayed.

The statement

`loopAgain = MsgBox("Enter another set of data", vbYesNo)` is executed. The variable *loopAgain* is assigned the VBA constant vbYes or vbNo, based on the user response to the command buttons in the message box (Figure 10-41). If the user clicks Yes, the constant vbYes is assigned to the variable *loopAgain*; if the user clicks No, the constant vbNo is assigned to *loopAgain*. The VBA constant VbYesNo results in two buttons, Yes and No appearing in the message box.

The statement `Loop` indicates the end of the loop. Program control returns to the Do While... statement, where the condition `loopAgain = vbYes` is tested again. When the result of the test is false, program control moves to the first statement following the Loop statement. The End Sub statement is executed and execution stops.

To close the workbook and exit Excel:

1. Close the workbook without saving the changes and exit Excel.

ADVEX 518 · TUTORIAL 10 · INTRODUCTION TO VISUAL BASIC FOR APPLICATIONS

HELP DESK

EXCEL 5.0

Index

VISUAL BASIC CONSTANTS

Double-click the Help button to display the Help Topics dialog box, then click the Index tab.

Keyword	**Topic**
Visual Basic Constants	MsgBox constants
not available	

You now have a solid introduction to VBA. You've covered a lot of ground, but you've just begun to learn about the power of Visual Basic for Applications. In the next tutorial you will continue your introduction to VBA and develop a complete application. In the process you will learn about creating custom dialog boxes and adding your own menus to the menu bar of the worksheet.

Tutorial Exercises

Before beginning the end of tutorial exercises and cases, you may want to refer to the Tutorial 10 Appendix located after the Comprehensive Applications for this tutorial to learn more about VBA on-line Help and detecting and fixing errors in your macros.

Open E_FOLLOW.xls in the Tut10 folder or directory. Immediately save it as S_FOLLOW.xls, then do the following.

1. Write a macro that sets to bold all cells in the range that makes up the Sales by Division report and sets to italic all cells in the range that makes up the Sales by Location report. Name the macro Prop1. Test it. Print the worksheet.

2. Record a macro that prints only the Sales by Division report. As part of the printout, center the report horizontally on the page, remove all information from the header, and include only the date in the footer. Name the macro PrintDivision. After you record, edit the macro so all extraneous lines are removed. Name the macro PrintDiv. Test it.

3. In Question 2, your macro was placed in a second module sheet. Use the clipboard to move the PrintDiv macro to the same module sheet as the Prop1 macro. After making sure the PrintDiv macro was pasted correctly, delete the empty module sheet.

4. Write a macro that checks each cell in the Sales by Location range and changes the color to blue RGB(0, 0, 255) if the amount is above 1000. Name the macro ChangeColor. Test the macro.

5. Write a macro to display the contents of cell A1 in a message box. Name the macro DisplayCell. Test the macro.

6. Write an interactive macro that prompts the user for a department and stores the department name in cell F1. Name the macro GetDept. Test the macro.

7. Print the VBA code for all the macros.

8. Save the workbook as S_FOLLOW.xls, then close it.

Case Problems

1. Invoicing for INFO-NOW Corporation INFO-NOW Corporation is offering a management seminar on strategic planning. To attract a larger audience, INFO-NOW is offering a discount to multiple attendees from the same company who attend the seminar. Figure 10-43 lists the pricing structure for the seminar.

Figure 10-43

Number of registrants	Charge per attendee
1-3	$125
4-6	$100
7 and over	$75

Each company that plans to send employees to the seminar returns a post card indicating the company name and number of employees planning to attend. INFO-NOW's marketing director, Helen MacClean, wants to use Excel to prepare a new invoice to send to companies who have registered to attend the seminar.

Develop an interactive macro that prompts for the name of a company and the number of employees from that company who plan to attend the seminar. The macro should also compute the total amount due (compute amount due as number of attendees multiplied by the charge per attendee). (*Hint:* Use an If or Select Case statement within the macro to determine the charge per attendee.) Place the input values and the total due into the area of the worksheet you're using for the invoice (Figure 10-44).

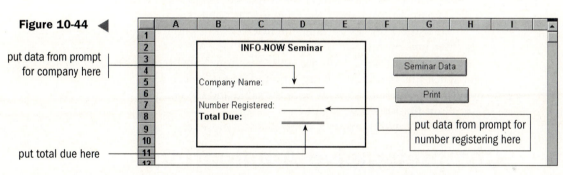

Figure 10-44

To create the interactive macro, do the following:
1. Open a new workbook, and save it as S_SEMNR.xls in the Tut10 folder or directory on your Student Disk. Enter the labels for the invoice (Figure 10-44) in a worksheet. Name the worksheet Invoice.
2. Prepare a flowchart showing the logic of your macro.
3. Write the VBA code. Name the macro Seminar. (*Hint:* If you choose to declare variables in your VBA code, declare them as variant type.)
4. Test the macro.
5. Attach the Seminar macro to a button. Label the button Seminar Data. When this button is clicked, the Seminar macro is executed.
6. Create a second macro to print the invoice. Name the macro PrintInvoice. Attach the PrintInvoice macro to a button labeled Print.
7. Test your application using the following data: Sawyer Foundation, 5 attendees. Enter the data, then print the invoice.
8. Print the VBA code.
9. Save the workbook as S_SEMNR.xls.

2. Sales Analysis for Phar-Maid, Incorporated Phar-Maid, Incorporated, a large pharmaceutical company, sells a wide variety of over-the-counter pain relief products. The Marketing Research Department wants to analyze the sales for each of its pain relief products. Specifically, the company wants to know what percent of sales for each product is advertising.

Figure 10-45 shows the data you have collected on their leading brands of over-the-counter pain relief drugs. You will want to present this data to the Marketing Research Department. Enter this data, compute the percent advertising is of sales, and then improve the table's appearance.

ADVEX 520 **TUTORIAL 10** INTRODUCTION TO VISUAL BASIC FOR APPLICATIONS

Figure 10-45 ◄

Brand	Sales	Advertising	Percent Adv to Sales
Tylenol	855	143	
Advil	360	92	
Vicks	350	27	
Robitussin	205	38	
Bayer	170	44	
Alka-Selzer	160	52	

On the same sheet, create a chart that you believe will best represent the data. Then label the chart.

Next, prepare a macro that prints just the table. After the table is printed, ask the user if he or she wants to print the chart. If the user indicates Yes, the macro automatically prints the chart; if the user indicates No, the macro stops.

To complete the print macro, do the following:

1. Open a new workbook and save it as S_PRINT.xls in the Tut10 folder or directory. Enter the data from Figure 10-45 into a worksheet. Compute the percent Advertising is to Sales for each product. Create a chart that best represents the data. Improve the appearance of the worksheet. Name the sheet Drugs.
2. Prepare a flowchart of the logic for the print macro.
3. Enter the VBA code. Name the macro PrintOption. (*Hint*: You can record portions of this macro and then modify the VBA code.)
4. Attach the PrintOption macro to a button. Label the button Print. When you click this button, the PrintOption macro is executed.
5. Use your macro to print both the table and the chart.
6. Print the VBA code.
7. Save the workbook as S_PRINT.xls, then close it.

Comprehensive Applications

1. Administrative Audit at Alliance Manufacturing You have been given a file of employee data that someone else in Alliance Manufacturing had maintained. However, that individual has left the company to return to college and now you are assigned the task of auditing and cleaning up the administrative records. The company's management wants to use the employee data for planning purposes, but you are uncomfortable using the data for planning until you conduct an audit. You are concerned about the accuracy of the data, especially the accuracy of two fields: Age and Department. For instance, as you scanned the employee list you discovered an employee with an age of 445, an obvious error. You also discover an employee assigned to the Administration Department, a department that was consolidated into the Accounting and Manufacturing Departments a month ago.

You know that no one in the company is over 75 years old, and you also know that the Department field should consist of only three departments: Accounting, Manufacturing, and Sales. In scanning the department codes you observed that there are some spelling errors of otherwise correct department codes.

To perform the audit on the employee data, do the following:
1. Open the workbook P_EMP.xls in the Tut10 folder or directory, and save it as S_EMP.xls.
2. Develop a macro to check each cell in the Age and Department fields. If you find an age greater than 75 or department other than Accounting, Manufacturing, or Sales, change the color of the errant cell to red and the font style to bold. The use of bold and color will quickly help you spot any errors. Prepare a flowchart of the logic of the macro.
3. Enter the VBA code. Name the macro CheckData.
4. Test your macro.
5. Print the employee list with the errors flagged (red and bold). Don't correct the errors.
6. Print the VBA code.
7. Save the workbook.

2. Maintaining Customer Information for M & B Carpets M&B Carpets has been using Microsoft Word to maintain a list of prospective new customers. After attending an Excel workshop, Philip Stallen, the owner, realizes that if the list were maintained in Excel, he could manipulate the data in many different ways. First, he converts the Word file into an ASCII file, P_PROSP.txt. In this ASCII file, every prospective customer's information takes up three lines for name, address, and city/state/zip, followed by a blank line (Figure 10-46). Phil asks you to convert this text file to an Excel file. When you're finished, the prospects data should be structured as an Excel list (Figure 10-47). Develop a macro to perform this conversion by completing the following tasks.

Figure 10-46 ◀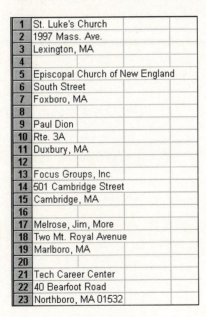

Figure 10-47

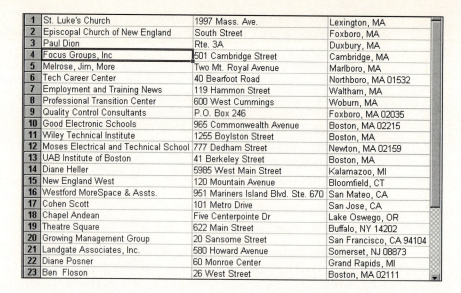

1. Open the file P_PROSP.txt in the Tut10 folder or directory, then import the file into Excel.
2. Prepare a flowchart showing the logic to convert the prospect data (Figure 10-46) to an Excel list (Figure 10-47). The Excel list that you create should be in a different worksheet from the prospect data that you import.
3. Write the VBA code to convert the data. (*Hint:* Use the Offset method to move around within the worksheet.) Name the macro Transfer.
4. Test the macro.
5. Print the Excel list.
6. Print the VBA code.
7. Save the workbook as S_PROSP.xls.

TUTORIAL 10 APPENDIX

On-line Help, Types of Errors, and Debugging Tools

In this tutorial you learned about Excel objects and how to access and change properties of range objects using VBA. You also used several methods to perform tasks with objects. Even after you become comfortable with the concepts involved in manipulating objects, properties, and methods, you will often search to find the ones you need. Because Excel has over 100 objects and more than 500 methods and properties, trying to memorize a list of them is not realistic. As you become more familiar with VBA, you will find that there are tools to guide you through the numerous features, so try not to let the volume overwhelm you.

Using On-line Help

Excel offers an extensive Help system for VBA, the objects that Excel supports, and the properties and methods of those objects.

You can access Help in the following ways:

- In a module sheet, place the insertion point anywhere in an object property, method, function, or other keyword and then press F1 to get context-sensitive Help.

- On the Help menu, click Microsoft Excel Help Topics, then click Getting Started with Visual Basic on the Contents tab.

- On the Help menu, click Excel Help Topics, then look up a specific topic or VBA term on the Index tab.

- For information about an object, method, property, or function, you can use the Object Browser.

Getting Help Using the Object Browser

One of the tools you can use to learn about objects, properties, and methods is the Object Browser. The **Object Browser** provides information on all the available objects in Excel, VBA, and any open modules.

The Object Browser contains separate libraries (computer files) of reference information about the Excel objects available for use in your code, and the VBA statements, functions, and keywords available for your macro. You choose the appropriate library and then the Object Browser retrieves a list with the names of all objects in the selected library. For example, if you choose Excel, you will see a list of all objects used in Excel. On the right side of the Object Browser is the Methods/Properties list, which contains the names of all methods and properties associated with the currently selected object.

The Object Browser is only available when a module sheet is active. Activate a module sheet and try the Object Browser.

To display the Object Browser:

1. If necessary, launch Excel and open a new workbook.

2. Insert a new module sheet.

3. Click **View**, then click **Object Browser** to display the Object Browser dialog box. See Figure 10-48.

Figure 10-48 ◀
Object Browser dialog box

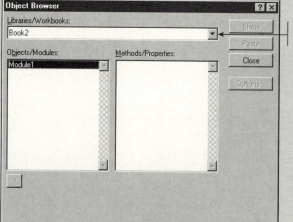

Notice that at the top of the dialog box is a drop-down list of all available libraries and workbooks.

4. If Excel does not appear in the Libraries/Workbooks text box, click the **Libraries/Workbooks** list arrow to display the list of libraries and modules. Click **Excel**. See Figure 10-49. Notice that the list of objects in the Objects/Modules list box changes to show the names of all objects in the Excel library, with the first in the list, AddIn, highlighted. On the right side of the dialog box, all the methods and properties associated with the selected object AddIn are listed in the Methods/Properties list box.

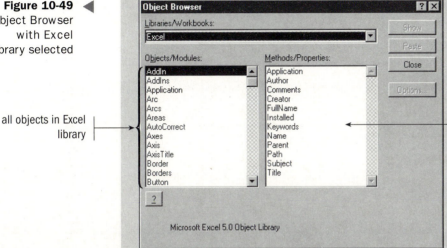

Figure 10-49
Object Browser with Excel library selected

all objects in Excel library

all methods and properties associated with the selected Excel Object AddIn

5. In the Objects/Modules list, scroll to locate **Range**, and click it. The names in the Methods/Properties list change to reflect the methods and properties available for the selected object—Range.

6. Locate and select **Offset** in the Methods/Properties list. The syntax of the Offset method displays at the bottom of the dialog box. See Figure 10-50.

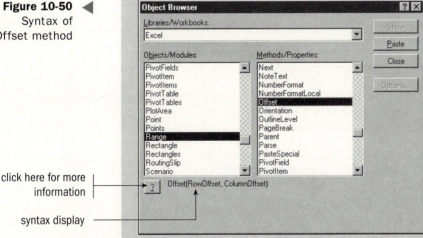

Figure 10-50
Syntax of Offset method

click here for more information

syntax display

In general, the bottom section of the dialog box displays code templates that you can paste into your module. The **code template** lists the method, property, or function name followed by its named arguments, if there are any. You can use the Paste button to copy the Offset template into your procedure and then edit it.

To get more information on the selected method, click the ? button.

ADVEX 526 **TUTORIAL 10** INTRODUCTION TO VISUAL BASIC FOR APPLICATIONS

7. Click the **?** button to display on-line Help about the Offset method. See Figure 10-51. From this Help file you can see other references by selecting See Also, or you can see an example by choosing Example.

Figure 10-51
Visual Basic reference on Offset method

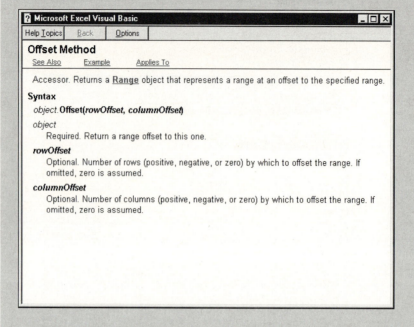

8. Click **Example** to display the Visual Basic Example dialog box. See Figure 10-52.

Figure 10-52
Example of VBA code using Offset method

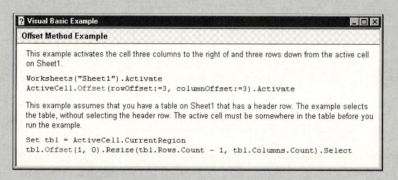

9. Study the example of the Offset method, close all the open Help windows, then close the Object Browser.

ACTIVATING THE OBJECT BROWSER

- Activate a module sheet.
- Click the Object Browser button on the VBA toolbar.
  or
  Click View, then click Object Browser.

Getting Help Using the Macro Recorder

Another way to learn about VBA is to use the macro recorder. The macro recorder is especially useful if you want to insert values or apply formatting to cells. Turn on the macro recorder and record some action you make in Excel, then examine the VBA code. You then can edit the code to remove any unneeded steps or change the procedure.

Encountering Errors in VBA Procedures

As you develop your macros, you are likely to encounter problems; your code may not work perfectly the first time you use it.

Generally, three types of errors can occur: syntax errors, run-time errors, and logical errors. Understanding each type of error will help you find the best solution.

Syntax Errors

Syntax errors, errors in Visual Basic grammar, occur when you mistype a keyword, incorrectly use parentheses, omit quotation marks, etc. Very often you'll discover this type of error as you look over the line you just typed. In addition to your own visual check, the VBA editor checks the statement for syntax errors. If VBA discovers an error, it immediately displays a dialog box containing an error message. If a syntax error occurs, you simply type the correction and continue entering the code.

Sometimes you will not detect syntax errors until you run the macro. When you execute the macro, VBA tries to translate, or **compile**, the procedure into language the computer understands. During this process, if the VBA compiler detects an error, an error message displays. This type of syntax error is called a **compile-time error**. For example, if you forget to conclude the If-Then-Else statement with the keywords End If, VBA will not detect the error until it tries to compile your code.

Intentionally create some syntax errors in a procedure and observe what happens.

To create syntax and compile-time errors:

1. Make sure the **Module1** sheet is the active sheet.

2. In the module sheet, type the following:

```
Sub Syntax1()
     Range("A5).Select
```

Press the **Enter** key. An error message displays. See Figure 10-53. These messages aren't always helpful; you may not be able to figure out the problem or type of error from the information provided. In that case, you can click Help to get a more descriptive explanation. After looking at the line you realize the close double quotes (") were omitted after the 5.

Figure 10-53
Error message displayed in a message box

missing "

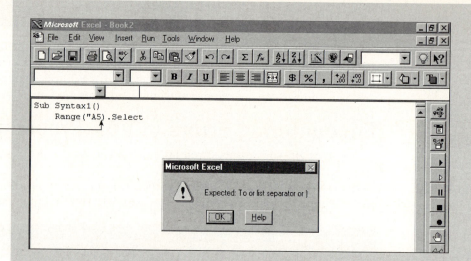

3. Click the **OK** button. The line appears in red, indicating that a syntax error exists in this statement. Edit the line so it appears as `Range("A5").Select`. Move the insertion point to the end of the line, and press the **Enter** key to move to the next line. Now no error message appears. You have corrected the syntax error.

Now enter another syntax error.

4. On a new line, type

    `If Range("A5").Value > 25 Thn`

   Press the **Enter** key. The line of code you just typed appears in red, and an error message displays. Click the **OK** button to remove the message box. Correct the error by replacing `"Thn"` with **Then**. The correct line is

    `If Range("A5").Value > 25 Then`

   Now enter a syntax error that's not detected until the macro is run for the first time.

5. Move to the next line and type each entry on a separate line:

    ```
        MsgBox "Value above 25"
    Else
        MsgBox "Value is 25 or less"
    End Sub
    ```

   You have entered all the VBA code but no error is indicated.

   Now run the macro.

6. Activate the **Sheet1** worksheet. Click **Tools**, click **Macro**, click **Syntax1**, then click the **Run** button. You are returned to the Module1 sheet, the line where VBA encountered a problem is highlighted, and an error message displays. See Figure 10-54. This error is an example of a syntax error that is not caught until you run the macro. As VBA was compiling the macro, it detected the error.

Figure 10-54
Error message appears when macro is run

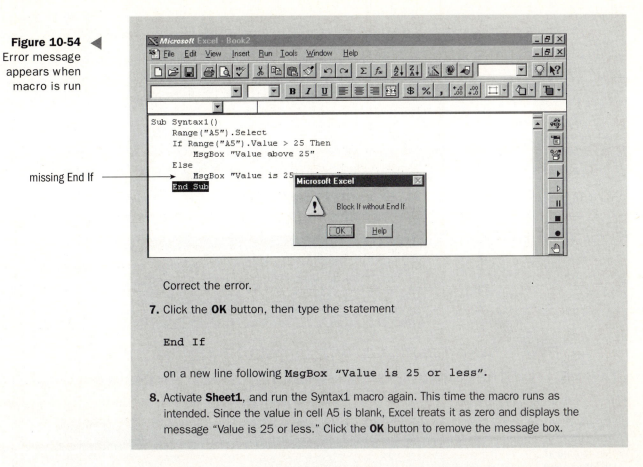

Correct the error.

7. Click the **OK** button, then type the statement

   End If

   on a new line following MsgBox "Value is 25 or less".

8. Activate **Sheet1**, and run the Syntax1 macro again. This time the macro runs as intended. Since the value in cell A5 is blank, Excel treats it as zero and displays the message "Value is 25 or less." Click the **OK** button to remove the message box.

As you write your macros, be aware of some of the more common causes of syntax errors:

- omitting quotation marks before or after a string
- omitting a comma within a list of arguments
- using parentheses with a method when you shouldn't
- misspelling a keyword
- omitting the End statement from a control structure, for example the End If keyword after a multiple-line If-Then-Else statement

Run-time Errors

Even though your application has no syntax errors, it still may not run properly. A second type of error, a run-time error, doesn't occur until after all syntax and compile-time errors are corrected. **Run-time errors** occur when macros are running and can be caused by missing arguments, arguments of the wrong data type, using a property or method with the wrong object, and a number of other things. One common run-time error occurs when you forget to activate the worksheet before running a macro. Now create a run-time error so you can see how this type of error occurs.

To create a run-time error:

1. Activate the **Module1** sheet. The VBA macro that you just correctly ran appears.

   Run the macro with the module sheet active.

2. Click the **Run Macro** button on the Visual Basic toolbar, click the **Syntax1** macro, then click the **Run** button. The error dialog box indicates that run-time error "1004" occurred. See Figure 10-55. The macro failed because the statement `Range("A5").Select` only applies to a worksheet object. It doesn't apply to the module sheet, but you tried to run the macro while the module sheet was the active sheet. Thus, a run-time error occurred.

Figure 10-55 ◀
Run-time error message displayed in error dialog box

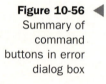

The error dialog box for run-time errors contains several command buttons. Figure 10-56 summarizes each button.

Figure 10-56 ◀
Summary of command buttons in error dialog box

Button	Description
End	Ends the macro
Continue	Continues to run the macro (for most run-time errors this option is not available)
Debug	Goes to the VBA debugger to help track down the run-time error
Goto	Goes to the line in the source code that produced the run-time error
Help	Accesses VBA on-line Help and displays information on the run-time error that has occurred

3. Click the **Goto** button. The statement that caused the run-time error is highlighted. Because the problem in this situation was the result of running the macro with the wrong sheet activated, no changes to the macro are needed. You merely need to activate the correct sheet and run the macro again. In other cases, if you find an error, you will need to make corrections to the VBA code.

4. Activate the **Sheet1** worksheet, then run the macro again. The macro works correctly. Click the **OK** button to remove the message box.

A final suggestion: when trying to correct run-time errors, check for misspelled methods or properties first. A very common mistake is to forget the "s" at the end of a method such as Workbooks or Worksheets. Because Workbook and Worksheet are valid keywords, VBA will not recognize them as syntax errors; however, they will cause an error when you try to run your macro.

Logic Errors

Some errors are never detected by the computer. These **logic errors** are in the logic of your program rather than the syntax of the code. With logic errors your program runs, but the results you get are incorrect. Logic errors are usually the hardest to find because the computer doesn't detect the error and the code seemed perfectly logical to you when you wrote it. Modify the Syntax1 macro to intentionally create a logic error.

To create a logic error:

1. Make sure **Sheet1** is active and enter **20** in cell A5.

2. Activate the **Module1** sheet.

3. Change the If statement from `If Range("A5").Value > 25 Then` to `If Range("A5").Value > 15 Then`

4. Activate **Sheet1**.

5. Run the **Syntax1** macro. The macro ran, but with 20 in cell A5, the message "Value above 25" is not correct. This is an example of a logic error. See Figure 10-57. The logic error occurred because the condition *is value in cell A5 greater than 15* is inconsistent with the message *"Value above 25."*

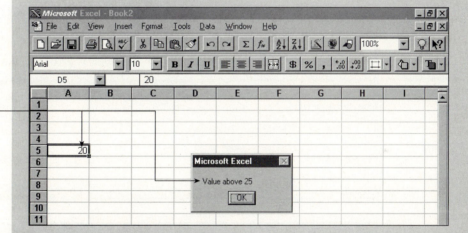

Figure 10-57
Example of logic error

value is not above 25

6. Click the **OK** button to remove the message box, then close the workbook without saving it.

Although logic errors are the toughest to find and correct, with more knowledge and experience you will become successful in discovering what went wrong with your macro and how to correct the problems.

To find logic errors you can use the MsgBox function to display values from your macro as it is running. When a message box displays, the macro is temporarily halted and you can check for errors. When you click a button in the message box, the macro continues. While writing and testing your macro, you can use the message box to display the value of a variable or expression at any point in the code. For example, you can insert a message box into a looping statement to check a value each time the loop repeats its statement block.

Additionally, VBA offers some debugging tools through the Debug window that will help you in the process.

Debugging Macros

As you have already discovered, macros don't always work properly the first time. To find and remove errors that prevent your program from running properly, you will need to learn some debugging skills.

To debug your macro, or correct it, you often need to enter **Break mode**, which is a pause in the execution of a macro. There are several ways to enter Break mode. You enter Break mode automatically when a running macro encounters a run-time error, when a running macro encounters a breakpoint, or when you press the Ctrl + Enter keys to stop the execution of the macro.

When you enter Break mode, you will see a Debug window where you will find the main debugging tools for Excel macros. The Debug window is divided into two parts (Figure 10-58).

The lower section, the **Code pane**, displays the VBA code of the currently running macro.

The upper section consists of either of the Watch or Immediate pane. The **Watch pane** enables you to monitor the values of selected variables, or the property setting of selected objects. The **Immediate pane** enables you to enter VBA code just as you enter code in modules, but in the Immediate pane the statement is executed immediately when you press the Enter key. This method enables you to evaluate expressions, assign new values to variables, and test procedures.

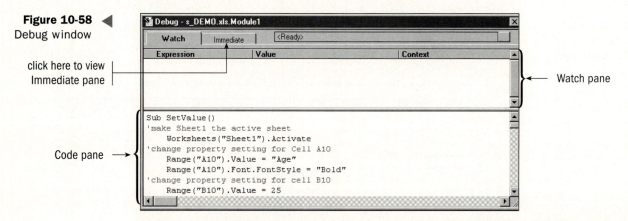

Figure 10-58
Debug window

click here to view Immediate pane

Code pane

Watch pane

Establishing Breakpoints

When debugging a macro, you typically designate one or more lines of your macros as breakpoints. A **breakpoint** is a marker indicating where VBA will suspend the execution of your macro. When you execute a macro that has a breakpoint, execution pauses when the breakpoint is reached; Excel enters Break mode and the Debug window displays. At this point you can view the macro code in the Code pane. You can examine values of variables and properties of objects by defining watch expressions and stepping through the code line by line.

Using the Debug Window to Debug a Macro

Earlier in the tutorial, you ran the SetColor macro, which displayed sales above 200 in blue, sales below 10 in red, and any values in between in black. A modified version of this macro has been created, containing a logic error so that the macro no longer works as planned. Can you find the logic error? First, run the modified macro and observe how the values are colored; then use some of the debugging tools to help locate and correct the error.

DEBUGGING MACROS **ADVEX 533**

To run the SetColor macro:

1. Open the C_DEBUG.xls workbook in the Tut10 folder or directory, and immediately save it as S_DEBUG.xls. Two macro buttons appear in the worksheet. The Reset Color button executes a macro that sets all the values in the Sales column to black. The Set Color button assigns the colors red, blue, or black to the values in the Sales column depending on the value of sales.

2. Click the **Set Color** button. Note that the macro doesn't work as expected. For example, the sales value for Alaska should be red, but it's black; the sales values for Arizona, Arkansas, and others should be black, not red.

Use the debugging tools to help debug the program. First set a breakpoint.

To set a breakpoint:

1. Activate the **ModLoops** module sheet.

   Set the breakpoint.

2. Move the insertion point to the statement `Select Case ActiveCell.Value` in the SetColor macro, then click the **Toggle Breakpoint** button on the Visual Basic toolbar. The background of the statement is colored red to indicate that it contains a breakpoint.

REFERENCE window | **SETTING A BREAKPOINT**

- Move the cursor to the line in your procedure where you want to set the breakpoint.
- Click the Toggle Breakpoint button on the Visual Basic toolbar.
  When macro execution reaches a breakpoint, it switches to Break mode and automatically opens the Debug window.

Establishing Watch Expressions

Sometimes you want to monitor the values of variables and expressions in the macro during the debugging process. To monitor the value of variables and the property settings of selected objects, you can add **watch expressions** that will display in the Watch pane of the Debug window.

Add a watch expression to view the current sales value in the Watch pane.

To add a watch expression:

1. Highlight the expression `ActiveCell.Value` within the statement `Select Case ActiveCell.Value`, then click **Instant Watch** on the Visual Basic toolbar to display the Instant Watch dialog box. Click the **Add** button to add the expression to the Watch pane.

2. Activate the **SalesByState** sheet. Click the **Reset Color** button to execute a macro that returns all the sales values to black.

   Now execute the macro containing the breakpoint.

3. Click the **Set Color** button. The macro executes until the breakpoint is reached, at which point the macro halts execution, enters Break mode, and opens the Debug window. If the Watch pane is not active, click the **Watch** tab. See Figure 10-59. Notice in the Watch pane that the watch expression, `ActiveCell.Value`, is 250 and in the Code pane the statement `Select Case ActiveCell.Value` is placed in a border, indicates that it is the next statement to be executed.

Figure 10-59
SetColor macro in Debug window

watch expression

current value of watch expression

line in border indicates next line to be executed

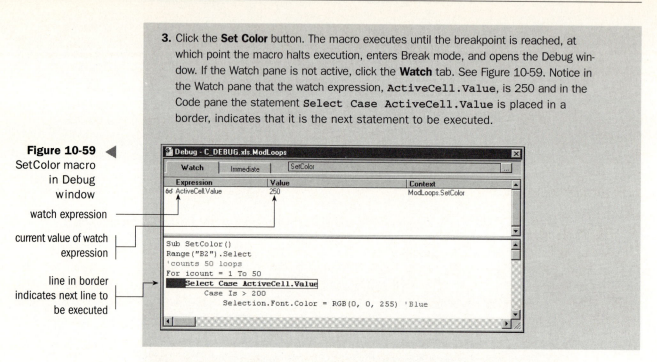

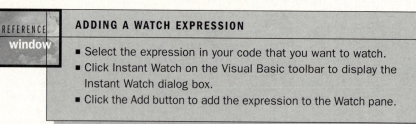

ADDING A WATCH EXPRESSION

- Select the expression in your code that you want to watch.
- Click Instant Watch on the Visual Basic toolbar to display the Instant Watch dialog box.
- Click the Add button to add the expression to the Watch pane.

While execution is halted in Break mode, you can execute the macro one line at a time.

Stepping Through a Macro

One of the most common debugging techniques is to step through the macro code one line at a time. This allows you to examine such things as the current values of variables and properties, as well as trace the flow of the program's logic. You do this by clicking the Step Into button.

To step through the macro a line at a time:

1. Click the **Step Into** button to execute one line at a time. The program executes one line and returns to Break mode. The Code pane indicates that the expression `Case is > 200` is next to be executed. Continue to step through the code line by line.

2. Click the **Step Into** button again. The Code pane now indicates that `Selection.Font.Color = RGB(0,0,255)` is the next line to be executed. This means that the value in the current cell will be displayed in blue. Click the **Step Into** button again. Now the statement `End Select` is the next to be executed, bypassing the other Case clauses. Click the **Step Into** button; the statement `ActiveCell.Offset(1,0).Select` is next to be executed. Click the **Step Into** button. The statement `Next icount` is next to be executed. See Figure 10-60. Notice that the value in the Watch pane changes to 9.4 as the statement `ActiveCell.Offset(1,0).Select` is executed, moving the active cell down one row. You expect this value, 9.4, to be assigned the color red.

Figure 10-60
Stepping through the macro

current value of watch expression

next line to be executed

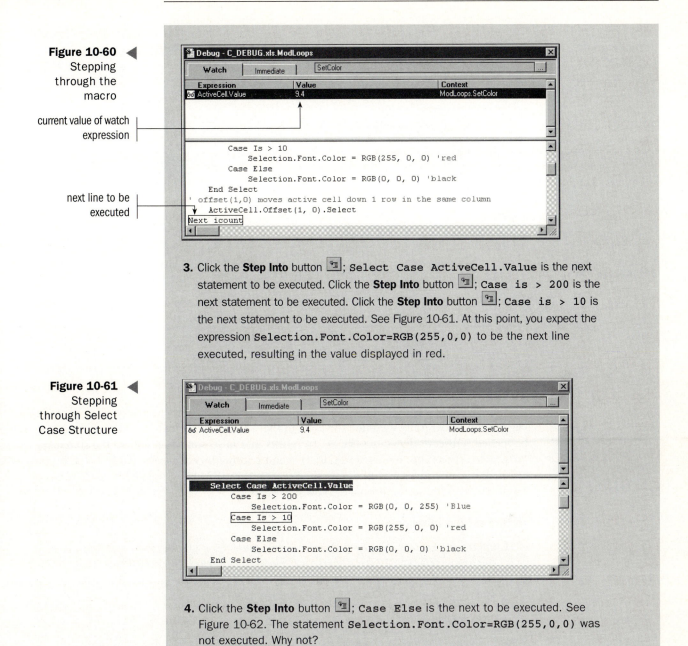

3. Click the **Step Into** button ; `Select Case ActiveCell.Value` is the next statement to be executed. Click the **Step Into** button ; `Case is > 200` is the next statement to be executed. Click the **Step Into** button ; `Case is > 10` is the next statement to be executed. See Figure 10-61. At this point, you expect the expression `Selection.Font.Color=RGB(255,0,0)` to be the next line executed, resulting in the value displayed in red.

Figure 10-61
Stepping through Select Case Structure

4. Click the **Step Into** button ; `Case Else` is the next to be executed. See Figure 10-62. The statement `Selection.Font.Color=RGB(255,0,0)` was not executed. Why not?

Figure 10-62
Case Else is next line

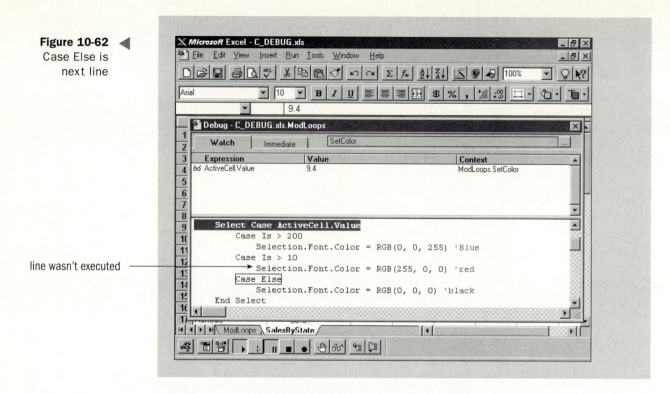

line wasn't executed

When you are stepping through your code and something unexpected occurs, it should trigger you to carefully examine the code in that section of the macro to determine what happened. Observe that `Case is > 10` results in a false condition and so the statement `Selection.Font.Color=RGB(255,0,0)` is not executed, because the value in the active cell is 9.4. You realize that a logic error exists in the VBA code; the line should be `Case is < 10`. You found the problem. Now correct it.

To turn off the breakpoint:

1. Move the insertion point to the line where the breakpoint was assigned, `Select Case ActiveCell.Value`, then click **Toggle Breakpoint** on the Visual Basic toolbar to turn off the breakpoint. Notice that the red background is removed from the line, indicating that the breakpoint is turned off.

   Stop the execution of the macro.

2. Click the **Stop Macro** button on the Visual Basic toolbar. The **SalesByState** sheet is activated.

3. Click the **Reset Color** button to set all the sales values to black.

4. Activate the **ModLoops** module sheet. Change the line `Case is > 10` to `Case is < 10` and activate the SalesByState worksheet.

5. Click the **SetColor** button. The colors assigned to the sales values are now displayed as you expected: blue for Sales > 200; red for Sales < 10; and black for Sales >=10 and <=200.

Debugging your macros is an art; there is no fixed set of steps for you to take when you run up against a bug. Finding and removing a bug requires your knowledge of VBA, experience, and intuition.

TUTORIAL 11

Creating a Custom Application Using VBA

Tracking Rotary Club Sponsorship

OBJECTIVES

In this tutorial you will learn how to:

- Build a complete Excel application

- Insert a dialog sheet into a workbook

- Create a custom dialog box

- Place controls in a dialog box

- Write VBA code to display a custom dialog box

- Write VBA code to transfer data from a custom dialog box to a worksheet

- Modify recorded macros

- Create a custom menu using the Menu Editor

Sunny Morning Products

CASE The Sunny Morning Products corporate headquarters are located in Garden Grove, California. The Garden Grove Rotary Club is beginning preparation for its biggest fund-raising event of the year—the Garden Grove Fair—a three-day festival that attracts some five to ten thousand visitors.

This is a busy time for Ann, the newly elected treasurer of the Rotary Club and assistant budget manager at SMP, the largest corporate sponsor of the festival. The money raised from this festival is used to fund several local charities and community projects.

The Rotary Club raises money on this festival in a number of ways, including charging a small fee for participants to enter the festival, and charging a nominal fee for booth space. Another method of raising funds is through the development of a program booklet. The booklet, distributed to all visitors entering the festival, contains a schedule of events, the layout of the festival grounds, and various promotions from local merchants. Merchants donate $50 to $250 to place an ad containing a greeting or promotion and the name and address of their business.

The Rotary Club president, James Whitmore, has told Ann that last year the record-keeping for money collected for this program booklet was a nightmare. The club was not sure that the merchant participation in the ad booklet was at the level it should be; nor was it sure that merchants who pledged to support the effort paid for their pledges. Some merchants indicated that they had paid for ad space in the booklet, but never saw their promotion appear. This year, James is relying on Ann, with her accounting experience, to devise and implement a tracking system for sponsorship of the festival.

After spending some time learning about the ad booklet fund-raising effort, Ann decided to develop an Excel application to keep a more accurate record of sponsors and how much each sponsor pledged and paid.

Additionally, Ann and James decided to try to increase the level of participation and thus funds raised through the booklet project. They urged the members of the club to solicit even more donations from the local merchants. To encourage members to solicit more participation, they decided to award prizes to members bringing in the most fund-raising dollars through this approach.

Ann also decided to establish a method of tracking merchants who had placed an ad and the pledge and payment amounts. She also wanted to provide a way to report sponsors who had not paid their pledge. Ann decided to set up an Excel list to track each sponsor, the pledge, and the amount paid.

Realizing that she would not be the primary user of this record-keeping system, Ann took into consideration the level of expertise that others would have. Because the Excel application will be used by people who know very little about Excel, she decided to make the application as simple and easy to use as possible.

For simplicity, she developed a data entry form using a custom dialog box. The custom dialog box will be easy to use, but more importantly, it will make the entry of sponsor data less error-prone.

Ann knows that several reports will be requested by club members, so she developed reports to provide summary as well as detail information about the fund-raising. She also added a menu system to guide the user through the various options in the application. She thought this would make it easier for the users to find the tasks they needed.

Ann's sponsorship tracking application utilizes the power and flexibility of VBA to create custom applications in Excel.

Running a Completed Application

Before you develop the application on your own, it will be useful for you to view and use a completed VBA application. This will give you an idea of how you can use the different features of Excel and VBA together. Open the workbook that Ann developed and run the sponsorship tracking application she created.

To open the C_FUND1.xls workbook:

1. Launch Excel and open the workbook C_FUND1.xls in the Tut11 folder or directory on your Student Disk. See Figure 11-1. The workbook consists of four worksheets, four module sheets, and one dialog sheet. Notice the FundRaising menu on the menu bar. Ann added this menu to the worksheet menu bar to help users navigate the fund-raising application.

Figure 11-1
Fund-raising application

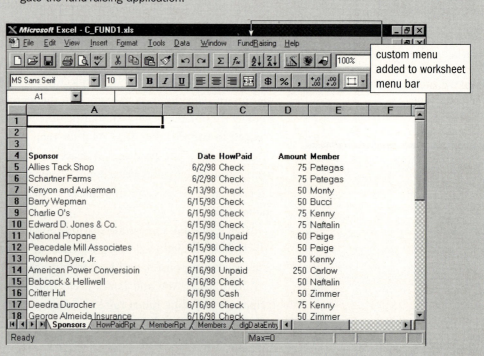

2. Click **FundRaising** to view the menu items available for this application.

3. Point to **Sponsor List** to display the submenu items available on the Sponsor List menu. See Figure 11-2.

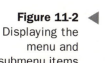

Figure 11-2 ◀
Displaying the menu and submenu items on the FundRaising menu

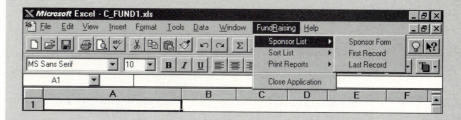

4. Click **Sponsor Form** to display a data entry form. Ann created this custom dialog box to make it easier to enter data for a new sponsor. See Figure 11-3.

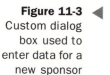

Figure 11-3 ◀
Custom dialog box used to enter data for a new sponsor

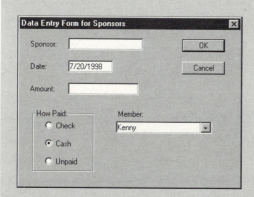

5. Enter the following data in the data entry form. Press the **Tab** key or use the mouse to move between fields in the custom dialog box. Do not press the Enter key.

Sponsor:	**Camelot Kennels**	press the **Tab** key
Date:	**7/20/98**	press the **Tab** key
Amount:	**50**	press the **Tab** key
How Paid:	**Cash**	
Member:	**Carlow**	

6. Click the **OK** button or press the **Enter** key to transfer the data in the data entry form to the Sponsor list. A message box opens asking if you want to enter data for another sponsor. See Figure 11-4. Click the **No** button.

Figure 11-4 ◀
Getting user input with a message box

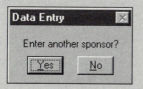

Next confirm that the record has been added to the Sponsor list.

7. Click **FundRaising**, point to **Sponsor List**, then click **Last Record** to see that the record for the sponsor Camelot Kennels was added to the bottom of the Sponsor list.

Now return to the first record in the Sponsor list.

8. Click **FundRaising**, point to **Sponsor List**, then click **First Record** to return to the beginning of the Sponsor list.

Ann wanted to be able to display or print the Sponsor list in three different orders—by Sponsor, by Date, and by Member. She developed three sort macros to perform the sorts, and made them available on the FundRaising menu. Review the various Sort List menu options and how the user accesses each one.

To view the sort options:

1. Press **Alt + R** to display the menu items available on the FundRaising menu, then point to **Sort List** to display the submenu items available on the Sort List menu. See Figure 11-5.

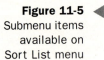
Figure 11-5
Submenu items available on Sort List menu

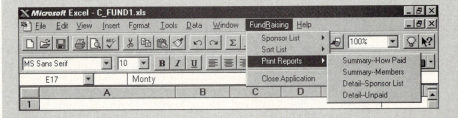

2. Click **By Sponsor** to display the Sponsor list sorted by Sponsor.

   Now sort the Sponsor list by Rotary Club Member.

3. Click **FundRaising**, point to **Sort List**, then click **By Member** to display the Sponsor list sorted by Member.

Now that you have tried two of the options available to sort the Sponsor list, look at the reports Ann developed for the application.

To view the reporting options of the fund-raising application:

1. Click **FundRaising**, then point to **Print Reports** to display the submenu items available on the Print Reports menu. See Figure 11-6.

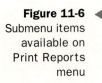
Figure 11-6
Submenu items available on Print Reports menu

   Now review the Summary--How Paid report.

2. Click **Summary--How Paid** to view the pivot table in the print preview window. You may need to click the **Zoom** button to enlarge the print preview display. If you want a printout, click the **Print** button; otherwise, click the **Close** button to return to the Sponsors worksheet.

   Next review the Detail--Unpaid report.

3. Click **FundRaising**, point to **Print Reports**, then click **Detail--Unpaid** to view the sponsors who haven't paid yet. If you want a printout, click the **Print** button; otherwise, click the **Close** button to return to the Sponsors worksheet.

   You have completed your exploration of the reporting options available for the application, and are ready to close the workbook.

4. Click **FundRaising**, then click **Close Application** to close the workbook.

Now that you have viewed the application Ann created, you will develop this application on your own. By reconstructing Ann's application, you can learn the necessary steps in the process and observe the different ways you can use VBA macros in a custom application.

Ann began building the sponsorship tracking application by planning. This step involves determining what the application will do and how it will be laid out in the worksheet.

The second step is to build the working parts of the workbook, such as entering the field names of the Sponsor list. Thirdly, you need to plan and create the custom dialog box that will be used for data entry; then in the fourth step, you determine and create the reports to be generated from the application.

The fifth step in the process is to record or write the VBA code used to automate the various tasks in the application. You then need to test this code and correct any errors.

Finally, you will need to build the menuing system that will allow the user to easily carry out each of the tasks in the application.

You are ready to begin creating the sponsorship tracking application for the Garden Grove Rotary Club. Normally you would develop the application starting with a new workbook. In this case, you'll start with Ann's partially completed workbook. In this way, you can focus your efforts on aspects of VBA that you were introduced to in the previous tutorial, and learn a few new skills as well.

Planning the Application

During the first step, planning, Ann outlined what was needed in the application and how the workbook would be organized. Figure 11-7 shows her planning sheet, which outlines the steps necessary to build the application.

Figure 11-7 ◀
Planning the
application

Planning Analysis Sheet

My goal:
Create an application to track sponsors for the Rotary Club Program booklet

What results do I want to see?
Summary report--How Paid
Summary report--Members
Detail report--Sponsor list
Detail report--Unpaid list

What information do I need?
Sponsor list consisting of five fields: Sponsor name, Date entered, Amount collected or pledged, How paid (Cash, Check, or Unpaid), Member responsible

Steps:
- Build the Sponsor list
- Build the custom dialog box to enter the sponsor data
- Build summary report on amount collected
- Build summary report on how much was raised by each member
- Build macros to transfer information in the custom dialog box to the Sponsor list in the worksheet
- Build macros to sort the Sponsor list in three ways: (1) by Date, (2) by Sponsor, (3) by Member
- Build macros to print reports:
  - Summary Report--member summary
  - Summary Report--total dollars raised
  - Detail Report--entire sponsor list
  - Detail Report--sponsors who still have not paid
- Develop a menuing system to guide the user through the application

Ann also had some sponsor information entered in an Excel list. One of her Excel files has been made available to you to use in re-creating her application. Open the workbook and see what is already available to you.

To open the C_FUND2.xls workbook:

1. Open the workbook C_FUND2.xls in the Tut11 folder or directory and immediately save it as S_FUND2.xls.

In this file, you have a workbook with six sheets, including the worksheets named Sponsors and Members and the module sheets named modDataEntry, modReport, modSortList, and modMisc.

Within the Sponsors worksheet, 36 sponsors represent the current Sponsor list. Figure 11-8 shows the fields in the Sponsor List.

Figure 11-8 ◀
Fields in
sponsor list

Column Label	Description
Sponsor	Name of sponsor
Date	Date record entered
HowPaid	Check, cash, or unpaid
Amount	Amount of donation
Member	Last name of Rotary member who solicited the donation

Within the Sponsors worksheet, you will note that several range names have been defined. These range names will be useful as you construct some of the VBA code. Figure 11-9 shows a list of the range names and their cell locations.

Figure 11-9 ◀
Range names in
the Sponsors
worksheet

Range Name	Address
First	A4
Dtabse	A4:E40
Sponsor	K1
DateEntered	L1
HowPaid	M1
Amount	N1
Member	O1
RecordToAdd	K1:O1

In addition to the Sponsors worksheet, a second worksheet, Members, includes the last names of all members of the Rotary Club. A range name, MemberList, has been assigned to the range A2:A21. In the tutorial you will add an element to the custom data entry form that will make it easier to enter the correct spelling of the last name of a Rotary Club member. At that time, you will use the data in the Members worksheet.

The workbook also contains four module sheets, which contain some of the macros you will need for the application.

Now that you have examined the current status of the S_FUND2.xls workbook, it's time for you to get involved and complete the application. Since the field names for the Sponsor list are already entered and the range names created, there is really no right or wrong place to start. You will begin by developing a form to capture the data for new sponsors.

Creating a Custom Dialog Box

An important aspect of creating a custom application in Excel is managing the way the user interacts with the application. For example, in earlier tutorials you placed buttons in worksheets and assigned them to macros to make it easier for the user to execute the macros. Now we will look at how you can create a form that the user can use to enter data on new sponsors. To do this, you can use VBA's **custom dialog box**. Then you can create macros to display the custom dialog box, update the Sponsor list, update the Dtabse range name, and then tie these three macros together.

An Overview of Dialog Box Controls

A custom dialog box lets you develop a professional-looking interface to get input from users. An **interface** is the means by which the user communicates with the application. The user interacts with the application through objects in the custom dialog box called **controls**. Controls are special drawing objects that you place in a custom dialog box, such as labels, edit boxes, option buttons, check boxes, list boxes, drop-down list boxes, combination drop-down edit boxes, combination list-edit boxes, scroll bars, and spinners. Figure 11-10 illustrates a custom dialog box with the different control objects you can place in it.

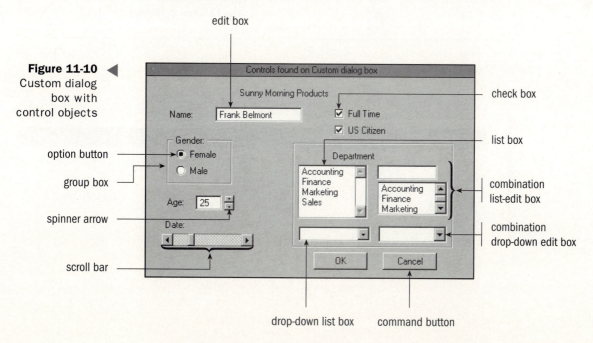

Figure 11-10 ◄
Custom dialog box with control objects

VBA provides 12 controls that you can place in your custom dialog boxes; Figure 11-11 provides you with a quick reference to each type of control.

ADVEX 544 **TUTORIAL 11** CREATING A CUSTOM APPLICATION USING VBA

Figure 11-11 ◀
Controls
available
for custom
dialog box

Type of control	Control Icon	Description
Label		Adds a caption to provide a description for another control.
Edit Box		Enables user to enter text, numbers, cell references, and formulas.
Command Button		Enables user to carry out an action, such as executing a macro or closing a dialog box.
Check Box		Represents a yes/no, true/false, or on/off condition. An empty check box indicates that the check box is off. A box with a check indicates that the option is on. Each check box is independent, so you can select any combination of check boxes.
Option Button		Represents an on/off condition. Usually appears in groups of two or more, and only one of the options in the group can be on at a time.
Group Box		Draws a line around a group of related controls.
List Box		Presents user with a list of options from which to choose.
Drop-down List Box		Lets user choose one item from a list of options. Saves space compared to a list box, because only one item initially appears. To view options, user clicks list arrow.
Combination List-Edit Box		Combines an edit box with a list box. User selects from a list of items or enters an item in the edit box.
Combination Drop-down Edit Box		Offers a list of items when arrow is clicked, but also allows user to type in additional items if item does not appear in the list.
Spinner		Used to enter a value between a minimum and maximum value. User clicks spinner arrow to increase or decrease the value.
Scroll Bar		Used to enter values between a predefined minimum and maximum.

You create the dialog boxes graphically and then display them using VBA code.

HELP DESK

Index

DIALOG BOX CONTROLS

Double-click the Help button to display the Help Topics dialog box, then click the Index tab.

Keyword	**Topic**
Controls (dialog box)	Summary of controls
controls	*Forms Toolbar*

EXCEL 5.0

Building the Sponsor Data Entry Custom Dialog Box

Now that you have an idea of the dialog box controls available in VBA, you can design the data entry form for the sponsorship application. You need to determine the input that is required as well as the layout of the controls in the dialog box. Figure 11-12 shows Ann's sketch of the data entry form. Use this sketch as a guide as you create the custom dialog box.

Figure 11-12 ◀
Sketch of custom dialog box

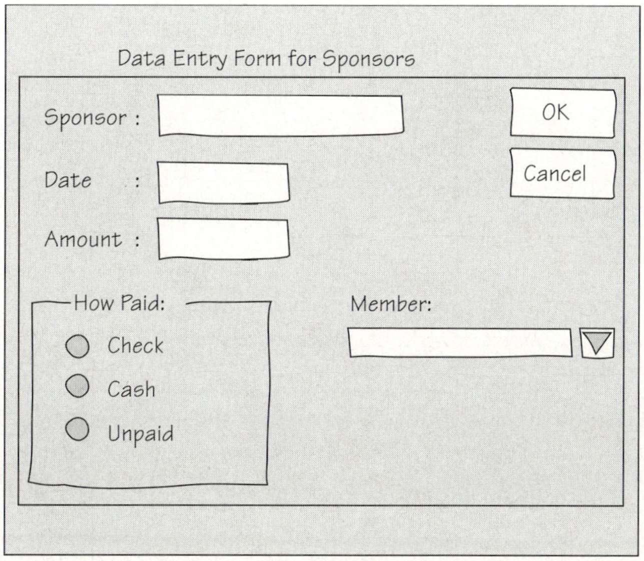

To create a custom dialog box you first insert a new type of sheet, called a dialog sheet, into your workbook. The **dialog sheet** initially contains an empty dialog box frame with two buttons—an OK button and a Cancel button. In this dialog box frame, you draw the controls you need, such as text boxes, check boxes, and drop-down list boxes, to produce your completed custom dialog box.

Insert a dialog sheet into the workbook so you can begin to create the custom dialog box.

To insert a dialog sheet:

1. Activate the **Sponsors** worksheet so that the dialog sheet will be inserted next to it. This step, although not necessary, will make it easier for you to move back and forth between the dialog sheet and the Sponsors worksheet.

2. Click **Insert**, point to **Macro**, then click **Dialog** to insert a new dialog sheet before the current sheet in your workbook. See Figure 11-13. Within the dialog sheet is the default dialog box frame, which includes the OK and Cancel buttons. Each dialog sheet holds one custom dialog box. In addition to the dialog box frame, the Forms toolbar automatically displays when you activate the dialog sheet. You use the buttons on the Forms toolbar to add controls to the dialog box.

Figure 11-13
Dialog sheet immediately after being added to workbook

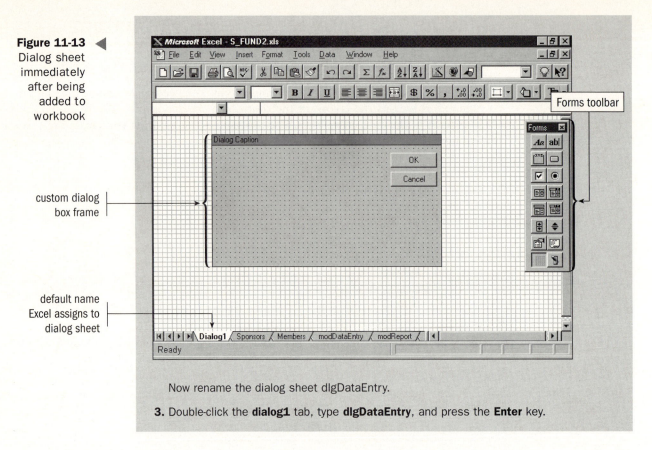

custom dialog box frame

default name Excel assigns to dialog sheet

Forms toolbar

Now rename the dialog sheet dlgDataEntry.

3. Double-click the **dialog1** tab, type **dlgDataEntry**, and press the **Enter** key.

Because the dialog box frame is a separate object, you can move it, resize it, and change its title. As you can see from Ann's sketch, there is quite a bit of information to fit into this dialog box. You need to change the size of the dialog box frame by increasing its height.

To resize the dialog box frame:

1. If the dialog box frame is not selected, click the outside border of the dialog box frame or the title bar to select the dialog box frame. Selection handles appear around the frame.

2. Click and drag the sizing handle in the middle of the bottom border down to increase the height of the dialog box frame.

The caption in the title bar of the dialog box frame is automatically assigned the name Dialog Caption. Change it to a more descriptive name for use by Rotary Club members: Data Entry Form for Sponsors.

To change the title of a dialog box:

1. Click anywhere in the title bar or click the outer border of the dialog box frame to select the frame. Selection handles appear around the frame.

2. Click and drag the pointer over the text in the title bar of the dialog box, type **Data Entry Form for Sponsors**, then click outside the dialog box frame to deselect it. See Figure 11-14.

Figure 11-14
Dialog sheet after being resized and renamed

new title

frame size increased

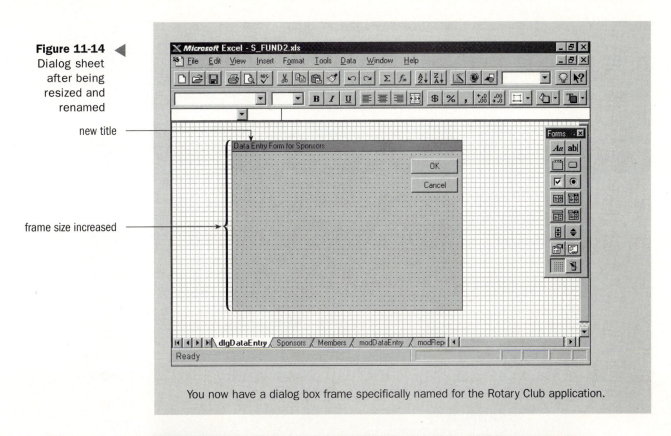

You now have a dialog box frame specifically named for the Rotary Club application.

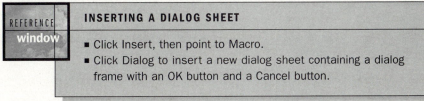

REFERENCE window

INSERTING A DIALOG SHEET

- Click Insert, then point to Macro.
- Click Dialog to insert a new dialog sheet containing a dialog frame with an OK button and a Cancel button.

Placing Controls in the Dialog Box

Now that you have inserted the dialog sheet, you can use the Forms toolbar to add controls to the dialog box. You will use the buttons on the Forms toolbar to add three labels, three text boxes, a group box containing three option buttons, and a combination drop-down edit box to the dialog box.

Placing Descriptive Labels in the Dialog Box

The first controls you will add to the dialog box frame are label controls. These controls put the captions Sponsor, Date, and Amount to the left of the three edit boxes that you will add to the dialog box frame. Review Figure 11-12 to see their placement in the dialog box before adding the Sponsor label control.

To place a label in a dialog box:

1. Click the **Label** button [Aa] on the Forms toolbar and move the + to where you want the first letter of the label to be. Click and drag the mouse pointer in the dialog box to add a label control, then release the mouse button. A default caption appears inside the label control. See Figure 11-15.

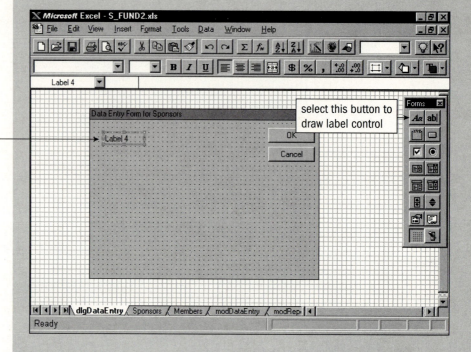

Figure 11-15
Label control with default caption

label control

Now change the text in the label control to a more descriptive caption.

2. Click and drag the mouse pointer over the caption to highlight the text, type **Sponsor:**, then click outside the label control to deselect it.

   TROUBLE? If you pressed the Enter key after typing "Sponsor," then the text for the label disappeared. Pressing the Enter key allows you to enter a second line of text in the label control, but a second line is not needed for this label. Press the Backspace key to return to the first line of text.

3. Using Ann's sketch in Figure 11-12, repeat Steps 1 and 2 to add the label **Date:**.

4. Using Ann's sketch in Figure 11-12, repeat Steps 1 and 2 to add the label **Amount:**. Figure 11-16 shows the dialog box after the three label controls have been added.

Figure 11-16
Dialog box after three label controls added

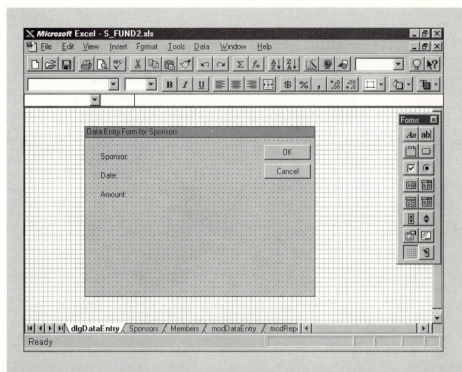

After placing an object in a dialog box, you can move, copy, resize, or delete it. To move an object, select it, then click and drag its edge. To resize an object, select and drag the selection handles. To copy it, use the clipboard, and to delete it use the Delete key.

5. If the label controls are not aligned vertically, select a control and click and drag its edge until they are.

ADDING A CONTROL TO A DIALOG BOX

- Click the button on the Forms toolbar for the control you want to add.
- Position the mouse pointer where you want the top-left corner of the control to display.
- Click and drag the mouse pointer until the control is the size and shape you want.
- Release the mouse pointer. The control is created and VBA gives it a default name.

Creating the Edit Boxes

According to Ann's sketch in Figure 11-12, the custom data entry form needs to have three edit boxes for the sponsor's name, the date the donation is entered, and the amount of the donation. First add the edit box for the sponsor's name.

To add an edit box to a dialog frame:

1. Click the **Edit Box** button on the Forms toolbar, position the + where you want to begin the control, then click and drag the mouse pointer in the dialog box to create an edit box. See Figure 11-17. Notice that in the name box (the area to the left of the formula bar) Edit Box 7, a default name, is assigned to the control.

ADVEX 550   TUTORIAL 11   CREATING A CUSTOM APPLICATION USING VBA

> **TROUBLE?** If your edit box has a different number assigned to its default name, this may be because you had to delete and re-create one of the controls in a previous set of steps. Don't be concerned if your numbers are different. These numbers are assigned by Excel to represent the sequential order in which controls were added to the form.

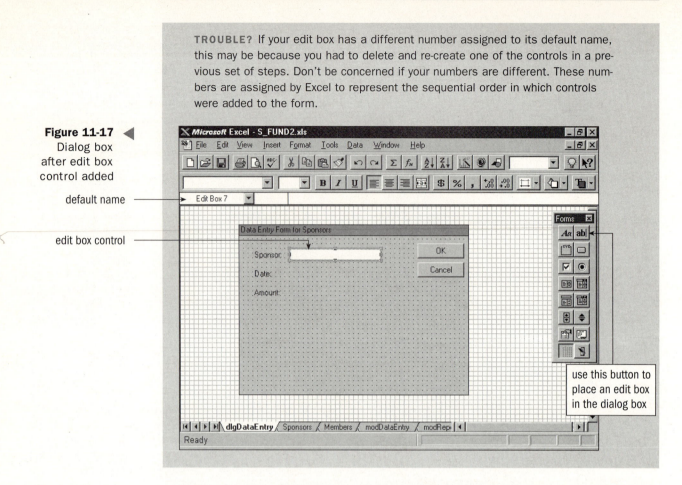

Figure 11-17
Dialog box after edit box control added

default name
edit box control
use this button to place an edit box in the dialog box

When you draw objects in the dialog box frame, Excel automatically names them, using the name of the object type and a sequential number. The name appears in the Name box on the far left side of the formula bar. For instance, when Excel inserted the dialog sheet it contained three objects: Dialog Frame 1, Button 2 (the OK button), and Button 3 (the Cancel button). You now have seven objects in the dialog box, including the dialog frame, the OK button, the Cancel button, three labels (Label 4, Label 5, Label 6), and the edit box (Edit Box 7). Later in the tutorial you will need to access some of the objects (controls) in the dialog box. You will want to use a more descriptive name when you write VBA code to access a control because it will be easier to reference. Rename the edit box you just added.

To rename the edit box:

1. If the edit box is not selected, click the **edit box** so it is selected.

2. Click the **Name** box (the area to the left of the formula bar) to highlight the default name, type **edtSponsor**, then press the **Enter** key. The name edtSponsor displays in the Name box.

Now add the edit box controls for the Date and Amount. Review the sketch of the custom dialog box in Figure 11-12 and place the edit box controls to the right of the corresponding labels in the dialog box.

To add edit boxes for the Date and Amount fields:

1. Click the **Edit Box** button [abl] and add the Date edit box control to the data entry form.

2. Click the Name box to highlight the default name, type **edtDate**, then press the **Enter** key. The name edtDate displays in the Name box.

3. Add the **Amount** edit box control.

4. Rename the Amount edit box **edtAmount**, then click outside the data form to deselect the Amount edit box. Figure 11-18 shows the dialog box after the three edit boxes are placed in the form.

Figure 11-18 ◀
Dialog box after three edit boxes added

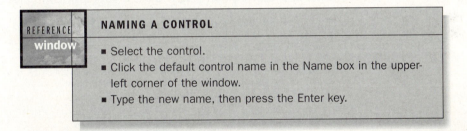

5. If necessary, select a control and move or resize it to improve the alignment and appearance of the dialog box.

REFERENCE window

NAMING A CONTROL

- Select the control.
- Click the default control name in the Name box in the upper-left corner of the window.
- Type the new name, then press the Enter key.

Viewing the Custom Dialog Box

It is a good idea to check your progress periodically when constructing custom dialog boxes, so you can fine-tune your design along the way. You can view a dialog box to see how it will appear to the user by clicking the Run Dialog button on the Forms toolbar to display a fully functioning representation of the dialog box. Once the dialog box is active, you can enter data in the edit boxes. If you click the OK or Cancel button, Excel will close the dialog box.

Later in the tutorial you will create a macro (using a VBA procedure) to run the custom dialog box from the Sponsors worksheet. For now you will use the Run Dialog button on the Forms toolbar to check on your progress as you create your custom dialog box. Run the dialog box to see what it actually looks like at this stage of its development.

ADVEX 552   **TUTORIAL 11**   CREATING A CUSTOM APPLICATION USING VBA

To run a dialog box:

1. Click the **Run Dialog** button on the Forms toolbar to display the dialog box as it will actually appear when the application is run. See Figure 11-19.

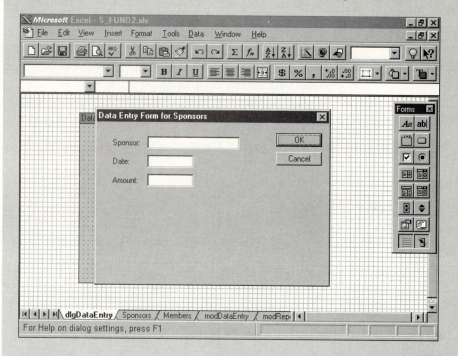

Figure 11-19 ◀
How custom dialog box will look when run

You can interact with the dialog box as the user would, entering data and testing option buttons, drop-down lists, and other controls. When you're finished experimenting, close the dialog box by clicking the OK or Cancel button.

2. Type **Bayleys Auto Shop** in the Sponsor edit box.

3. Press the **Tab** key, then type **7/20/98** in the Date edit box.

4. Press the **Tab** key, then type **100** in the Amount edit box.

5. Click the **OK** button to close the dialog box.

6. If necessary, select a control and move or resize it to improve the alignment and appearance of the dialog box.

7. Save the workbook as S_FUND2.xls in the Tut11 folder or directory.

Creating a Group Box and Option Buttons

Now you want to set up the portion of the custom dialog box where the user enters how the sponsor paid the donation. There are three options: Check, Cash, or Unpaid. To capture this information, you will set up three option buttons within a group box. With an option button group box, only one of the option buttons in the box can be selected. Selecting one option button immediately clears all other option buttons in the group. Although a group box is optional when you only have one set of option buttons, it is required when more than one set of option buttons is used on the same form. First, create the group box, as shown in Ann's sketch in Figure 11-12.

To create a group box:

1. Click the **Group Box** button on the Forms toolbar, position + where you want to begin the control in the dialog box, and click and drag the mouse in the dialog box to create a group box.

2. Change the caption of the group box to **How Paid**. See Figure 11-20.

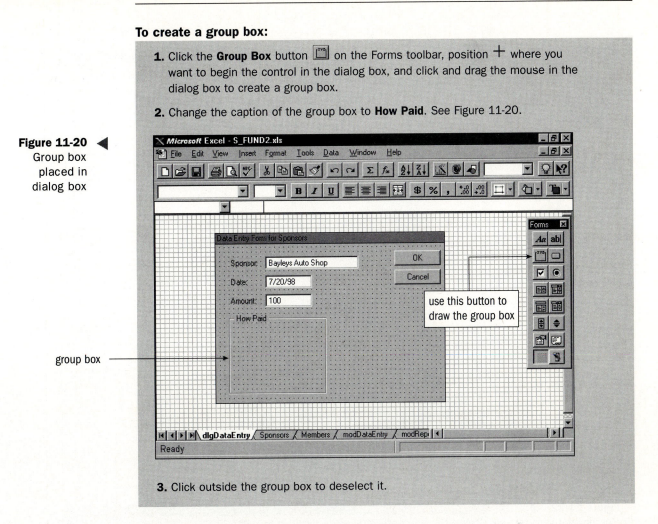

Figure 11-20 ◀ Group box placed in dialog box

3. Click outside the group box to deselect it.

Now place the three option buttons inside the group box. An option button consists of a button and a label.

To create an option button:

1. Click the **Option Button** button on the Forms toolbar; position + where you want to begin the control, then click and drag to create an option button. Keep the frame of the option button inside the border of the group box.

2. Change the label on the option button to **Check**, then click outside the option button control.

3. Click the border of the option button control to select it. Rename the control **optCheck**. Remember to use the Name box to change the name of the object. See Figure 11-21.

Figure 11-21
Dialog box with option button added

name of control ◀──

option button ◀──

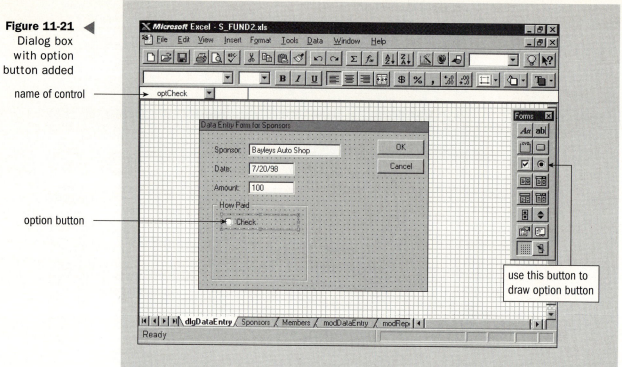

4. Click outside the selected control to deselect it.

5. Repeat Steps 1 through 4 to add the **Cash** option button. Label the option button **Cash** and rename the option button object **optCash**.

6. Repeat Steps 1 through 4 to add the **Unpaid** option button. Label the option button **Unpaid** and rename the object **optUnpaid**. See Figure 11-22.

Figure 11-22 ◀
Dialog box with three option buttons

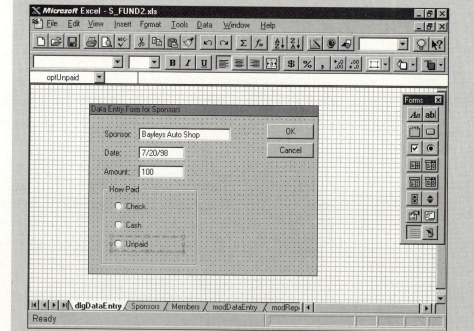

7. If your screen doesn't look like Figure 11-22, use your mouse to resize or move the controls in the dialog box. To move a group of objects together, press and hold the Shift key while clicking the objects you want selected.

Now check your progress.

PLACING CONTROLS IN THE DIALOG BOX **ADVEX 555**

8. Click the **Run Dialog** button [⊡] to display the dialog box, then select the **Cash** option button.

9. Click the **OK** button to close the dialog box.

Now the option buttons shown in Ann's sketch are in place. The last control to be added to the custom dialog box is the combination drop-down edit box.

Creating a Combination Drop-Down Edit Box

In the past, entering Rotary Club member last names caused some problems. Names were occasionally misspelled during data entry. Because the same name was entered differently than the previous entry, the same person would show up on several lines of the Summary Report by Member, as each spelling would be treated as a different person. To eliminate this problem, Ann used a combination drop-down edit box. She used this control to provide a list of members' last names. Then the user need only click the drop-down list arrow to display the list of last names from which to choose. This control also allows the user to enter a last name directly into the edit box if the last name he or she needs is not in the drop-down list. Review the layout of the dialog box (Figure 11-12) to see where this control is to be placed.

To create a combination drop-down edit box control and place a label above it:

1. Click the **Combination Drop-Down edit** button [▦] on the Forms toolbar, position +
where you want to begin the control, then click and drag to create a combination drop-down edit box. See Figure 11-23.

Figure 11-23 ◀
Dialog box after combination drop-down edit box added

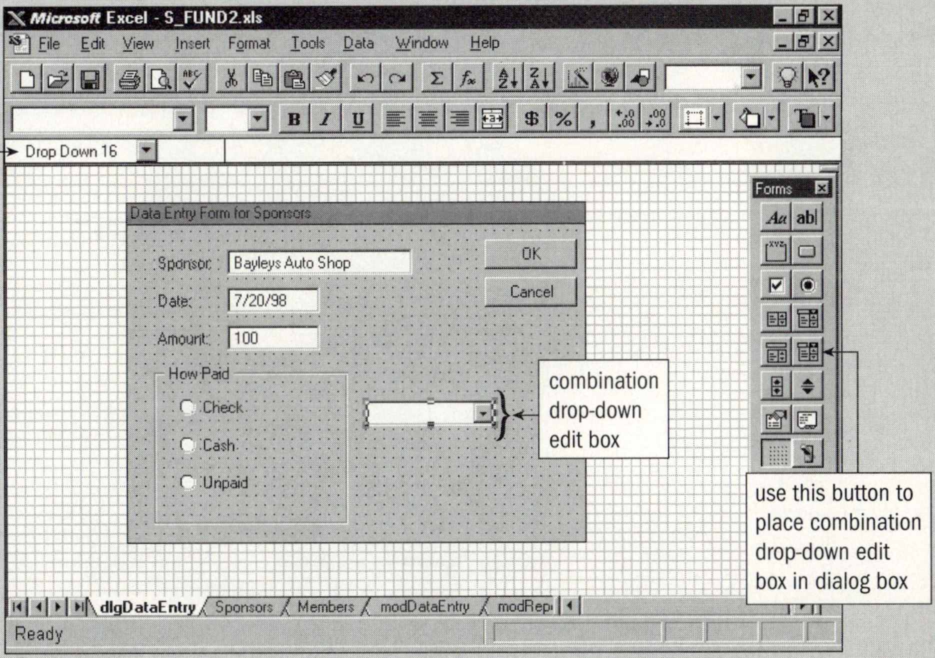

default name

2. Rename the combination drop-down edit box **edtMember**.

3. Use the Label control [Aa] to place the label **Member:** above the combination drop-down edit box. See Figure 11-24.

Figure 11-24
Label control placed above combination drop-down edit box

label control for drop-down edit box

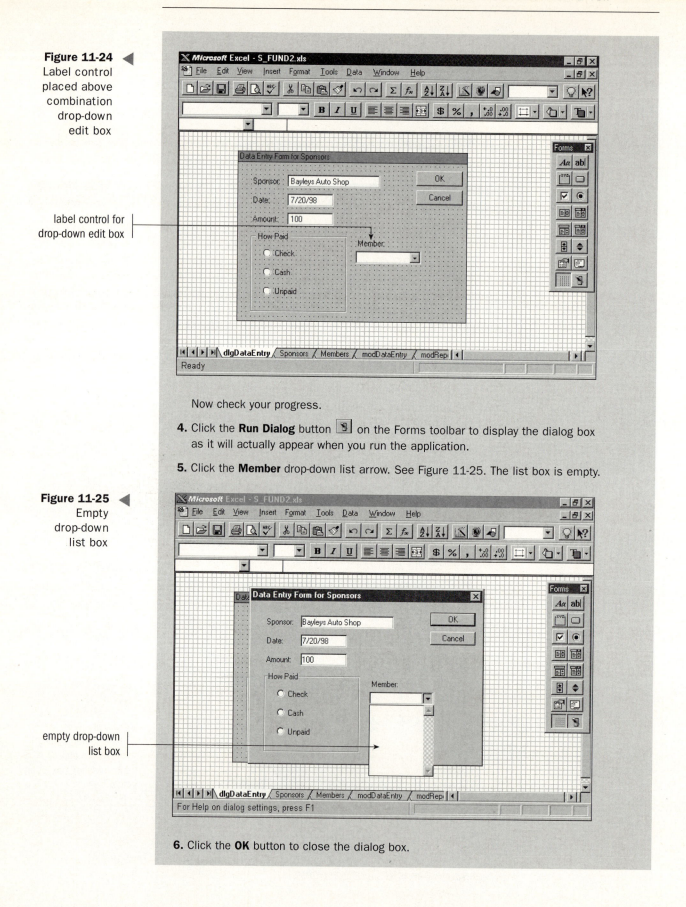

Now check your progress.

4. Click the **Run Dialog** button on the Forms toolbar to display the dialog box as it will actually appear when you run the application.

5. Click the **Member** drop-down list arrow. See Figure 11-25. The list box is empty.

Figure 11-25
Empty drop-down list box

empty drop-down list box

6. Click the **OK** button to close the dialog box.

PLACING CONTROLS IN THE DIALOG BOX **ADVEX 557**

As you observed when running the custom dialog box, the drop-down list box is initially empty. You want the member names to be displayed when the user clicks the drop-down list arrow of this control. To save time, the names of the Rotary Club members have already been entered in the workbook for you in the Members worksheet, cells A2:A21. Now you need to link the combination drop-down edit box to the cells storing the member names to make the combination drop-down edit box functional.

To link a combination drop-down edit box to cells in a worksheet:

1. Double-click the **combination drop-down edit box** to display the Format Object dialog box, and if necessary, click the **Control** tab. See Figure 11-26.

Figure 11-26 ◄
Format Object
dialog box

enter range of
member's list here

number of items
appearing in
drop-down list at
one time

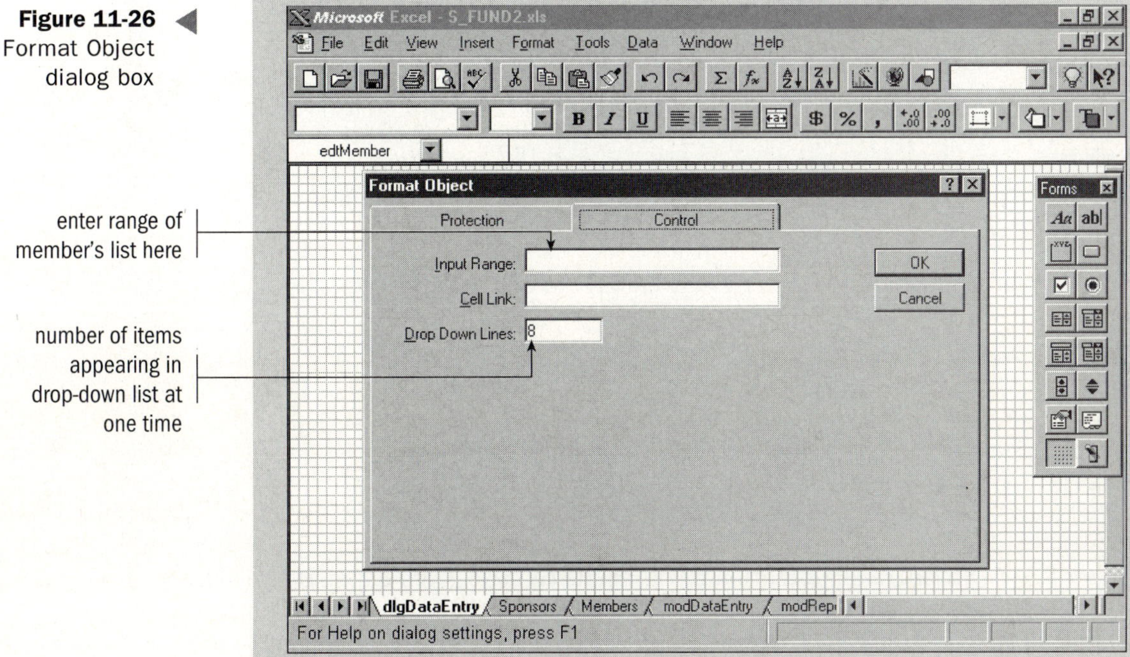

Specify the range of cells that contains the items you want to appear in your drop-down list. The range name MemberList was assigned to cells A2:A21 in the Members worksheet.

2. Type **MemberList** in the Input Range text box, then click the **OK** button. This step links the named range A2:A21 to the combination drop-down edit control.

Now check your progress.

3. Click the **Run Dialog** button ▣ to display the dialog box, then click the **Member** drop-down list arrow to see a list of the first eight members. See Figure 11-27. You can see additional names by clicking the scroll arrow.

Figure 11-27
Drop-down list linked to member names in Members worksheet

drop-down edit list displaying eight member names

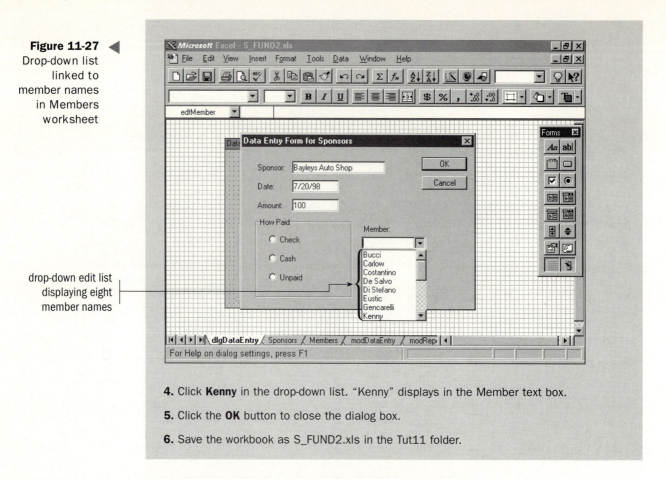

4. Click **Kenny** in the drop-down list. "Kenny" displays in the Member text box.

5. Click the **OK** button to close the dialog box.

6. Save the workbook as S_FUND2.xls in the Tut11 folder.

Congratulations. You have completed the custom dialog box for the sponsor tracking application for the Garden Grove Rotary Club.

If you want to take a break and resume the tutorial at a later time, you can do so now. Close the workbook and exit Excel. If you are on a network, leave Windows running. If you are using your own computer, you may exit Windows and shut down the computer. When you resume the tutorial, place your Student Disk in the disk drive, launch Excel, then continue with the tutorial.

• • •

Testing the Completed Custom Dialog Box

According to Ann's plan, data for a new sponsor is entered in the custom dialog box and then transferred to the Sponsor list. Now that you have created the custom dialog box, enter the data for a new sponsor and confirm that the data is transferred to the bottom of the Sponsor list.

To test a data entry form by entering data:

1. Click the **Run Dialog** button on the Forms toolbar.

2. Enter the following data in the data entry form by typing over the current entry:
   Sponsor: **Michael's Cafe**
   Date: **7/20/98**
   Amount: **150**
   How Paid: **Cash**
   Member: **Olsen**

3. Click the **OK** button to close the dialog box. Now check to see whether the data you just entered has been transferred to the Sponsor list in the Sponsors worksheet.

4. Activate the **Sponsors** worksheet.

5. Scroll to the last record in the Sponsor list, row 40. Notice that the data you just entered in Step 2 has not been transferred to the bottom of the Sponsor list. See Figure 11-28.

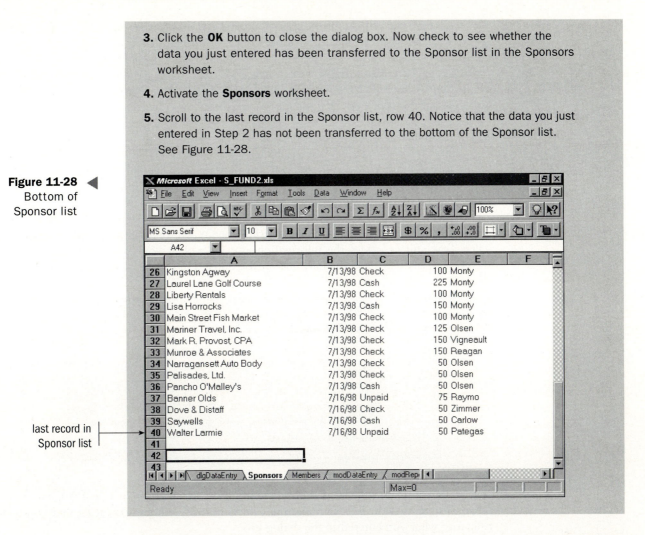

Figure 11-28
Bottom of Sponsor list

last record in Sponsor list

Two problems are illustrated by this set of steps. First, to display the custom dialog box, you had to use the Run Dialog button on the Forms toolbar. While this approach works, a novice user wouldn't know how to use it. You want a simple way for a Rotary Club member to display the data entry form for sponsors. A better approach would allow the user to access the custom dialog box directly from a menu.

A second problem, as you observed, occurs when entering data in a custom dialog box. It does not automatically transfer from the dialog box to the Sponsors worksheet. You need to write a *program* to access the values in the dialog box controls so they can be copied from the dialog box to the worksheet. You do this by writing macros for the application.

Creating Macros to Update the Sponsor List

Creating the dialog box is only the first step in using a custom dialog box. You must also develop VBA code to

- automatically display the customized dialog box
- process the data entered in the dialog box

Displaying the Custom Dialog Box

Up to this point, you tested the data entry form by clicking the Run Dialog button on the Forms toolbar. In the final application, you want the user to be able to display the custom dialog box automatically without having to click the Run Dialog button on the Forms toolbar. You can do this by typing VBA code directly into a module.

Recall that custom dialog boxes are created in dialog sheets. In VBA, each dialog sheet is a DialogSheet object and represents an object in the workbook's DialogSheets collection.

To display a custom dialog box using VBA code, you use the **Show** method of the DialogSheet object. For example, to display the dialog box named dlgDataEntry in the collection of dialog sheets, you would use the following VBA statement:

`DialogSheets("dlgDataEntry").Show`

While the dialog box is displayed, you can interact with its controls. For example, you can enter text in the edit boxes, select an option button, select an item from a drop-down list, and so on. You close the dialog box by clicking either the OK or the Cancel button.

As you close a custom dialog box, the Show method returns a True or False value, depending on which button you clicked. If you clicked the OK button, the Show method returns the value True and processes the information you entered; if you clicked Cancel, the Show method returns False, and the information you entered in the dialog box is not processed.

TO DISPLAY THE CUSTOM DIALOG BOX, USE THE FOLLOWING SYNTAX:

dialogSheets(dialogSheetName).**Show**

where *dialogSheets* represents the collection of DialogSheet objects, *dialogSheetName* is the name of the specific dialog sheet that you want to reference, and **Show** is a method that displays a custom dialog box.

Usually you want to process the changes made in the dialog box only if you choose the OK button to close it. If you choose the Cancel button, you are indicating that you want to ignore what you entered in the dialog box.

Since the Show method returns a True or False value, depending on whether the user clicks the OK or Cancel button, you can write VBA code to determine which button was clicked. You can then use an If-Then-Else statement to test whether or not to process the entries. For example, you could use the following code:

```
If DialogSheets("dlgDataEntry").Show = True Then
        <code to process the data in dialog box>
Else
        <exit without processing data in dialog box>
End If
```

This segment of VBA code displays the custom dialog box until the user clicks the OK or Cancel button. If the user clicks the OK button, the Show method returns a True value. As a result, the If-Then-Else statement will be true; Excel closes the dialog box and processes the data. On the other hand, if the user clicks Cancel, the Show method returns a False value; Excel closes the dialog box and does not process the data.

Returning Data from a Control to the Worksheet

When the user enters data in the custom dialog box, the values are entered in controls, such as edit boxes, check boxes, and option buttons. Most of the time you need to write VBA code to access the current value stored in the control. You use the Value or Text property of the control to get its current value. For example, the following line of code uses the Text property of the EditBox control to assign the data in the edit box named edtSponsor to the worksheet cell named Sponsor:

```
Range("Sponsor") = DialogSheets("dlgDataEntry").EditBoxes("edtSponsor").Text
```

In the above statement, the text stored in the edit box—edtSponsor—of the dialog sheet named dlgDataEntry is assigned to the worksheet cell named Sponsor. You will use similar lines of code to move your data from your custom dialog box into worksheet cells. Figure 11-29 lists sample VBA code for accessing selected controls in a custom dialog box.

Figure 11-29 ◀
Sample VBA
code for
controls

Control name	Sample VBA code to reference control
CheckBoxes	DialogSheets("dlgDataEntry").CheckBoxes("status").Value
DropDowns	DialogSheets("dlgDataEntry").DropDowns("majors").Value
EditBoxes	DialogSheets("dlgDataEntry").EditBoxes("sponsor").Text
Labels	DialogSheets("dlgDataEntry").Labels(1).Caption
ListBoxes	DialogSheets("dlgDataEntry").ListBoxes("category").Value
OptionButtons	DialogSheets("dlgDataEntry").OptionButtons("optCash").Value
Spinners	DialogSheets("dlgDataEntry").Spinners("interest").Value
ScrollBars	DialogSheets("dlgDataEntry").ScrollBars("temp").Value

In the sponsorship tracking application, you will be transferring data from the data entry form to the Sponsors worksheet. Figure 11-30 shows a diagram of the transfer of data between the data entry form and the temporary holding area in the Sponsors worksheet. Figure 11-31 shows the flowchart Ann used to plan this macro.

Figure 11-30
Transfer of data from custom dialog box to temporary holding area

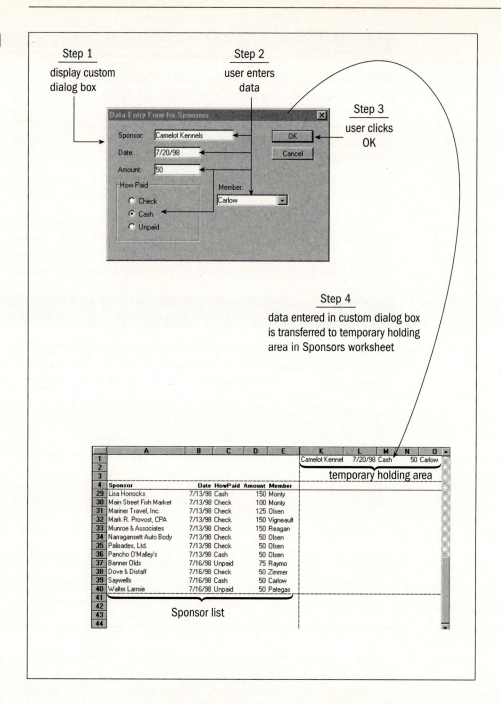

Figure 11-31
Logic to transfer data between custom dialog box and temporary holding area

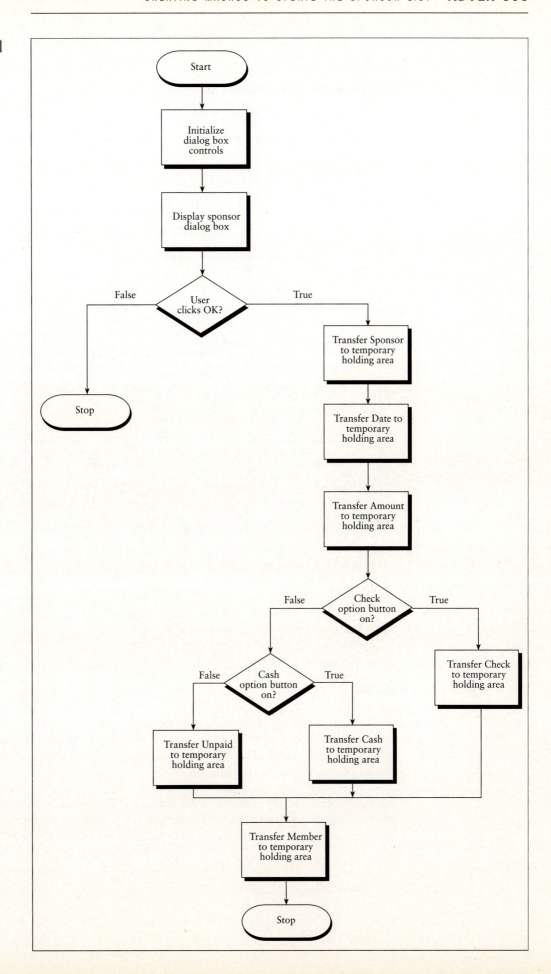

The DisplayForm() macro that Ann wrote is already entered in the module sheet modDataEntry for you. Now examine the macro code.

To examine the DisplayForm() macro:

1. Switch to the **modDataEntry** module sheet.

2. Scroll to the **DisplayForm()** procedure and review the VBA code used to transfer the data from the dialog box into the temporary holding area of the Sponsors worksheet. See Figure 11-32.

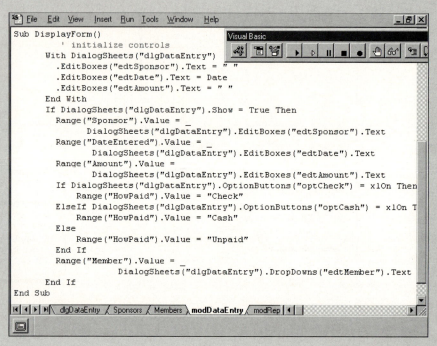

Figure 11-32
Listing of Display Form macro

Now review each line of code in the DisplayForm() macro.

The statements

```
With DialogSheets("dlgDataEntry")
   .EditBoxes("edtSponsor").Text = " "
   .EditBoxes("edtDate").Text = Date
   .EditBoxes("edtAmount").Text = " "
End With
```

allow you to abbreviate the references to the object—DialogSheets(dlgDataEntry)—in each statement between the With and End With keywords. You can also write this code without using the With...End With statements, in which case you would enter three lines instead of five. However, the three lines would be entered as

```
DialogSheets("dlgDataEntry").EditBoxes("edtSponsor").Text = " "
DialogSheets("dlgDataEntry").EditBoxes("edtDate").Text = Date
DialogSheets("dlgDataEntry").EditBoxes("edtAmount").Text = " "
```

The statements in this group set the dialog box controls for Sponsor, Date, and Amount to a desired initial value before the dialog box is displayed. In this case, any text in the edtSponsor and edtAmount edit boxes is cleared out (the control is set to an empty string); the edtDate edit box is set to the current date.

The Show method in the line `If DialogSheets("dlgDataEntry").Show = True Then` displays the dialog box until the user clicks the OK or Cancel button. When the user clicks either button, the dialog box is closed. If the user clicks the OK button, True is returned to the If-Then-Else statement and the data entered in the controls of the dialog box is transferred to the Sponsors worksheet. If the user clicks the Cancel button, False is returned and no action occurs. Most VBA programmers will write the If-Then-Else statement to display the custom dialog box as `If DialogSheets("dlgDataEntry").Show Then` instead of `If DialogSheets("dlgDataEntry").Show = True Then`. Both statements will work.

The statement
```
Range("Sponsor").Value = _
DialogSheets("dlgDataEntry").EditBoxes("edtSponsor").Text
```
assigns the data in the edtSponsor edit box to the Sponsor cell in the active worksheet.

The statement
```
Range("DateEntered").Value = _
DialogSheets("dlgDataEntry").EditBoxes("edtDate").Text
```
assigns the data in the edtDate edit box to the DateEntered cell in the active worksheet.

The statement
```
Range("Amount").Value = _
DialogSheets("dlgDataEntry").EditBoxes("edtAmount").Text
```
assigns the data in the edtAmount edit box to the Amount cell in the active worksheet.

The statement
```
If DialogSheets("dlgDataEntry").OptionButtons("optCheck")=xlOn Then
```
examines the state of each option button to determine which one was selected. If the optCheck option button is *on*, this control stores the Excel constant `xlOn` (l is the letter, not the number). If this is true, Check is assigned to the cell named HowPaid in the active worksheet. If the optCash option button is *on*, then this control stores the Excel constant `xlOn`. If this is true, Cash is assigned to the cell named HowPaid in the active worksheet; otherwise Unpaid is assigned to the cell named HowPaid in the active worksheet. `xlOn` is a special **built-in constant** in Excel that indicates an option button is selected. `xlOff` is the alternative Excel constant that indicates the option is not selected. A number of built-in constants are available for use with various Excel controls.

The statement
```
Range("Member").Value = _
DialogSheets("dlgDataEntry").DropDowns("edtMember").Text
```
transfers the data in the drop-down list named edtMember to the cell named Member in the active worksheet.

Now see whether the data entry form you created and the DisplayForm() macro work as intended. That is, can you display the data entry form, enter the data for a sponsor in the custom dialog box, and then transfer the data from the dialog box to the temporary holding area in the Sponsors worksheet?

To test the DisplayForm() macro:

1. Activate the **Sponsors** worksheet.

2. Click **Tools**, click **Macro** to display the Macro dialog box, click **DisplayForm** in the Name/Reference list box, then click the **Run** button. The data entry form for a new sponsor opens. See Figure 11-33.

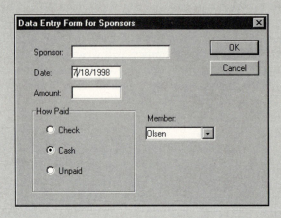

Figure 11-33
Data Entry Form for New Sponsor

TROUBLE? If you received a run-time error, click the Goto button and examine the highlighted line. Then switch to the dialog sheet and check the name box of each control except the label and group box controls. You should have assigned the following names: edtSponsor, edtDate, edtAmount, optCheck, optCash, optUnpaid, and edtMember. If you find a name that must be changed, select the appropriate control, click the Name box, type the correct name, and press the Enter key. When done, repeat Step 2.

3. Enter the following data in the data entry form:
   Sponsor: **Michael's Cafe**
   Date: **7/20/98**
   Amount: **150**
   How Paid: **Cash**
   Member: **Olsen**

RECORDING A MACRO TO ADD THE SPONSOR TO THE SPONSOR LIST **ADVEX 567**

4. Click the **OK** button to close the dialog box. Did it work? Was the data you just entered transferred to the temporary holding area (N1:O1) in the Sponsors worksheet?

   TROUBLE? If you received a run-time error, see Trouble? paragraph in Step 2.

5. Press **F5** to display the Go To dialog box, type **O1** in the Reference text box, then press the **Enter** key to move the active cell to cell O1. See Figure 11-34. The new sponsor record has been transferred to the temporary holding area.

Figure 11-34 ◀
Temporary holding area with transferred record

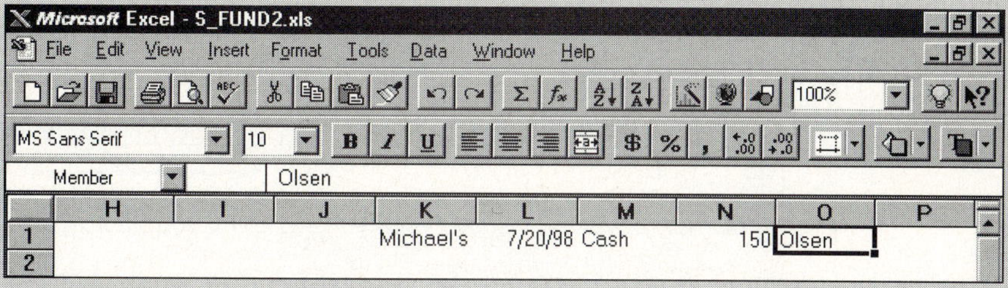

Has the data been transferred to the bottom of the Sponsor list?

6. Move to the last record in the Sponsor list (row 40). Notice that the data for the sponsor, Michael's Cafe, has not been transferred to the bottom of the Sponsor list.

Now create a macro to move the data from the temporary holding area to the bottom of the Sponsor list in the Sponsors worksheet.

Recording a Macro to Add the Sponsor to the Sponsor List

The macro DisplayForm() displays the data entry form and transfers the data entered to a temporary holding area (K1:O1) in the Sponsors worksheet. A temporary holding area is used because this simplifies the VBA code needed to transfer the data from the custom dialog box to the bottom of the Sponsor list. This macro does not place the new sponsor record at the bottom of the Sponsor list.

Now you will record a macro that will copy the data from the temporary holding area to the bottom of the Sponsor list. When Ann was creating the sponsorship tracking application, she decided to record the macro as opposed to writing the VBA code because she wasn't sure of the exact VBA code to use and she knew the macro could just as easily be recorded. Because Ann intended to record the macro, her planning process included the steps she would need to follow while the macro recorder was on. Review Ann's sketch illustrating the steps for this macro as shown in Figure 11-35.

Figure 11-35
Steps to transfer data from temporary holding area to Sponsor list

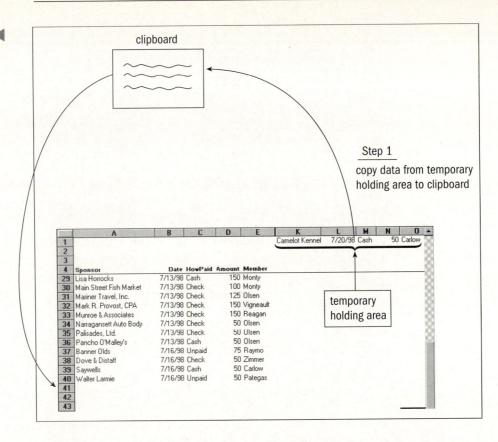

Step 2
determine row immediately following last row in Sponsor list

Step 3
paste contents of clipboard to bottom of Sponsor list

Before you record the macro, move to the bottom of the modDataEntry module sheet and mark the position for recording the macro so the recorded macro will be included with the other data entry macros. If you don't mark the position, the recorded macro will be placed in a new module sheet.

To record a macro in an existing module sheet:

1. Switch to the **modDataEntry** module sheet.

2. Position the insertion point at the last line in the module sheet. Press the **Enter** key to add a few blank lines.

3. Click **Tools**, point to **Record Macro**, then click **Mark Position for Recording**. Now you have told Excel where you want to place the code for the recorded actions.

To record a macro that copies the sponsor record from the temporary holding area to the bottom of the Sponsor list:

1. Activate the **Sponsors** worksheet and click **K1** to make it the active cell.

    Before recording the macro, you need to confirm the Use Relative References command is not selected.

2. Click **Tools**, point to **Record Macro**. If the Use Relative References command is checked, click it to remove the check. If it is not checked, click anywhere in the worksheet to close the Tools menu.

3. Click **Tools**, point to **Record Macro**, then click **Record New Macro** to display the Record New Macro dialog box. Type **AddToList** in the Macro Name text box, then click the **OK** button. The macro recorder is on.

4. Select the range **K1:O1**.

5. Click the **Copy** button on the Standard toolbar.

RECORDING A MACRO TO ADD THE SPONSOR TO THE SPONSOR LIST **ADVEX 569**

6. Press **F5** to display the Go To dialog box, type **First** in the Reference text box, then click the **OK** button to move the active cell to cell A4.

7. Press **End + ↓** to move to the last record in the Sponsor list.

8. Press **↓** to move down one row to the first empty row in the Sponsor list.

9. Click the **Paste** button 📋 on the Standard toolbar to copy the record to the bottom of the list.

10. Press **Ctrl + Home** to return to A1.

11. Click the **Stop Macro** button ■ to stop recording the macro.

Now examine the VBA code for the macro you just recorded.

To view the AddToList macro:

1. Click **Tools**, click **Macro** to display the Macro dialog box, click **AddToList** in the Macro Name/Reference list, then click the **Edit** button. You are now in the modDataEntry module sheet. See Figure 11-36.

Figure 11-36 ◀
VBA code
for AddToList
macro

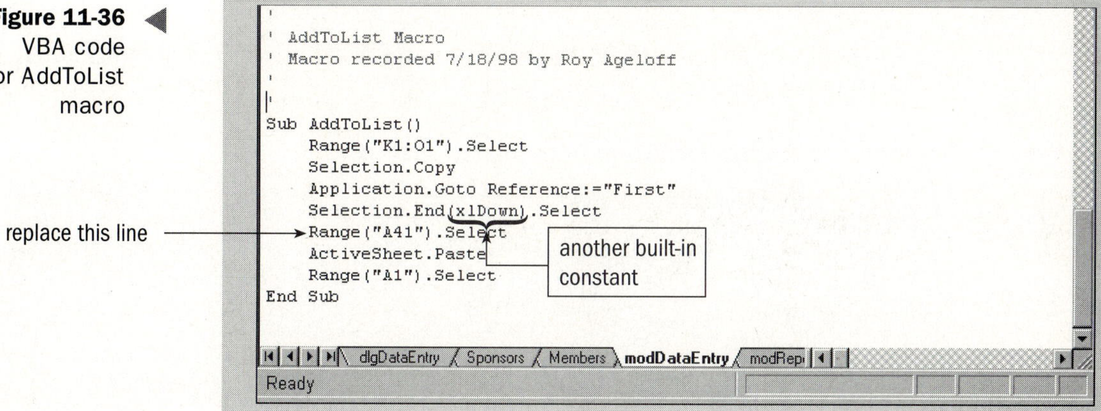

replace this line ⟶

```
'
'  AddToList Macro
'  Macro recorded 7/18/98 by Roy Ageloff
'
'
Sub AddToList()
    Range("K1:O1").Select
    Selection.Copy
    Application.Goto Reference:="First"
    Selection.End(xlDown).Select
    Range("A41").Select
    ActiveSheet.Paste
    Range("A1").Select
End Sub
```

another built-in constant

dlgDataEntry / Sponsors / Members \ **modDataEntry** / modRep‹ ‹ ›
Ready

Recording your actions is often the fastest way to generate VBA code, especially if you're not sure of the correct objects, properties, and methods to use. However, recording doesn't always produce code that does exactly what you want. That situation occurred in this macro. Do you see any problems? There is one. The problem lies with the recorded macro statement `Range("A41").Select`.

This statement must be changed. Have you figured out why? If you use the statement as is, you will always add a new record to the same row, row 41, overwriting what's already in that row in the Sponsor list. Since you are adding records to the Sponsor list, the last record in the range must change for each new record. You need a method that allows you to determine the next empty row in the Sponsor list in which to insert data. You can use the **Offset** method to solve this problem. For example, to move one row down and one column to the left of the current cell, you can use the code `ActiveCell.Offset(1,-1)`. If the active cell is in D10, then `ActiveCell.Offset(1,-1)` returns the range object C11.

>
>
> **TO USE THE OFFSET METHOD, USE THE FOLLOWING SYNTAX:**
>
> `object.Offset(RowOffset,ColumnOffset)`
>
> where *object* is the starting range, `Offset` is a method that returns a range based on its position relative to the starting range, *RowOffset* is the number of rows to shift down (positive number) or up (negative number) from the starting row, and *ColumnOffset* is the number of columns to shift to the right (positive number) or left (negative number) from the starting column.

To modify the AddToList macro:

1. Move the insertion point to the statement `Range("A41").Select`.

2. Replace the statement `Range("A41").Select` with `ActiveCell.Offset(1,0).Select`.

   This new statement uses the Offset method to move down one row from the active cell.

Now test the two procedures, DisplayForm and AddToList, again to ensure that they will execute properly.

To retest the DisplayForm() and AddToList() macros:

1. Activate the **Sponsors** worksheet.

2. Click **Tools**, click **Macro** to display the Macro dialog box, click **DisplayForm** in the Macro Name/Reference box, then click the **Run** button. The data entry form for new sponsors opens.

3. Enter the following data in the data entry form:
   Sponsor: **Almacs Super Store**
   Date: **7/25/98**
   Amount: **100**
   How Paid: **Unpaid**
   Member: **Naftalin**

4. Click the **OK** button to close the dialog box. Has the data you just entered been transferred to the temporary area (K1:O1) in the Sponsors worksheet?

5. Press **F5** to display the Go To dialog box, type **O1** in the Reference text box, then click the **OK** button to move the active cell to cell O1. The data for the new sponsor is in the holding area.

   Now transfer the data from the temporary holding area to the bottom of the Sponsor list.

6. Click **Tools**, click **Macro** to display the Macro dialog box, click **AddToList** in the Macro Name/Reference list box, then click the **Run** button.

7. Scroll to the last record in the Sponsor list, row 42. Notice that the data has been transferred. See Figure 11-37.

Figure 11-37
Last record in Sponsor list

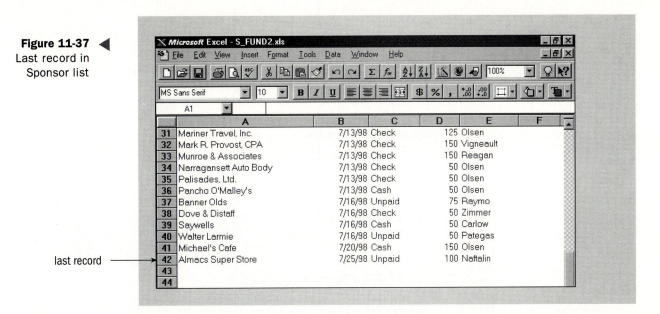

last record

Entering a Macro to Update a Range Name

Ann wanted the sponsorship tracking application to generate four reports for the Rotary Club. These four reports rely on the Sponsor list as the source of data. The range name Dtabse defines the cells currently included in the Sponsor list. As you add records to the Sponsor list, the range of cells representing the Sponsor list changes. Thus, the range name, Dtabse, must change to reflect the new range of the Sponsor list. Unfortunately, as you use the data entry form to capture data on a new sponsor, and the AddToList macro to transfer the data to the Sponsor list, the range name Dtabse is not automatically updated to reflect the new range of the Sponsor list.

If the range name Dtabse does not reflect the current range of the Sponsor list, the Rotary Club reports will not be accurate. The next macro you create will update the range name Dtabse to reflect the current range of the Sponsor list but is not a macro you can record. Type this macro into the modDataEntry module sheet.

To enter a macro to update the range name Dtabse:

1. Activate the **modDataEntry** module sheet, and move the insertion point to the bottom of the module sheet. Press the **Enter** key to insert a few blank lines.

2. Type the VBA code shown in Figure 11-38.

Figure 11-38
VBA code for SetNameRange macro

```
Sub SetRangeName()
    Range("First").Select
    Selection.CurrentRegion.Select
    Names.Add Name:="Dtabse", RefersToR1C1:=Selection
    Range("A1").Select
End Sub
```

Now review each line of code in the SetRangeName macro.
The statement `Range("First").Select` makes the range name First the active cell.

The statement `Selection.CurrentRegion.Select` selects the entire region, the block of cells bounded by blank rows and columns, in which the selected cell resides. In this case, the entire range of the Sponsor list is selected.

The statement `Names.Add Name:="Dtabse", RefersToR1C1:=Selection` updates the range name Dtabse based on the selected range of cells.

You need to test this macro to determine whether it updates the range name.

To test the SetRangeName macro:

1. Activate the **Sponsors** worksheet. Scroll the Sponsor list to determine the current range. The current range is A4:E42.

2. Click **Insert**, point to **Name**, click **Define** to display the Define Name dialog box, then click **dtabse** in the Names in Workbook list. Notice that the Refers to text box indicates that the range is Sponsors!$A$4:$E$40. See Figure 11-39. The current range of the Sponsor list, as you observed in the previous step, is A4:E42.

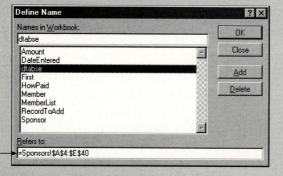

Figure 11-39
Define Name dialog box

current range of dtabse

3. Click the **OK** button to close the Define Name dialog box.

   Now run the SetRangeName macro to update the range name Dtabse.

4. Click **Tools**, click **Macro** to display the Macro dialog box, click **SetRangeName** in the Macro Name/Reference list box, then click the **Run** button. If the macro worked, the range name Dtabse will refer to A4:E42.

5. Click **Insert**, point to **Name**, click **Define**, then click **Dtabse** in the Names in Workbook list. The Refers to text box indicates that the range is $A$4:$E$42. Click the **OK** button.

The macro SetRangeName updated the range name. Now you will tie all the steps together.

Tying the Data Entry Steps Together

Each time you have added a record to the Sponsor list thus far, you have

- run the DisplayForm macro to display the data entry form and transfer the data to the temporary holding area in the Sponsors worksheet
- run the AddToList macro to copy the data from the temporary holding area to the bottom of the Sponsor list
- run the SetRangeName macro to update the range name Dtabse

The last step in the data entry process is to build one macro that will execute all the data entry macros—DisplayForm, AddToList, and SetRangeName—one after the other. In addition, you can add a loop so that the custom dialog box reappears until the user indicates that there is no more data to add.

Figure 11-40 shows the logic of this macro. Now enter the macro.

Figure 11-40
Flowchart showing logic of data entry procedure

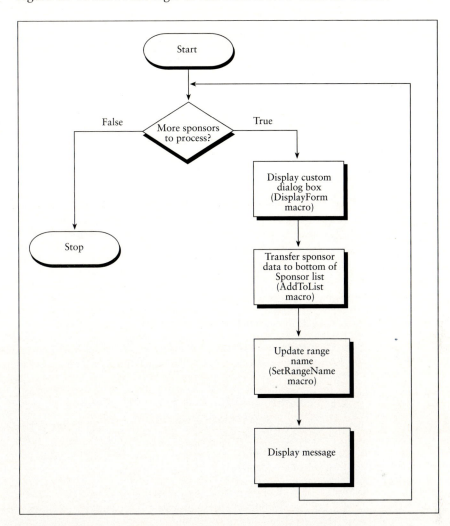

To create a macro to enter and move data to update the Sponsor list:

1. Activate the **modDataEntry** module sheet, and insert a few blank lines at the bottom of the module sheet.
2. Type the VBA code shown in Figure 11-41.

Figure 11-41
VBA code for DataEntry macro

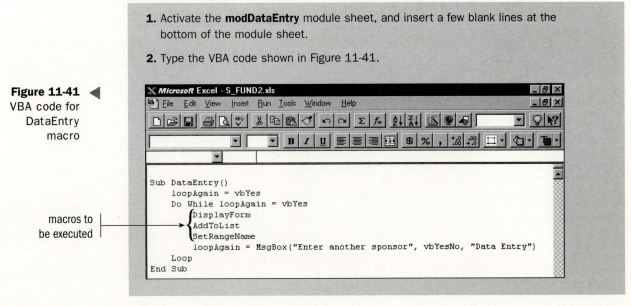

macros to be executed

Now review each line of code in the DataEntry() macro.

The statement `loopAgain = vbYes` assigns the built-in VBA constant vbYes to the variable *loopAgain*.

The statement `Do While loopAgain = vbYes` executes the statements following the Do While. . . statement to the Loop statement as long as the variable *loopAgain* stores the constant vbYes.

The statement `DisplayForm` executes the DisplayForm() macro.

The statement `AddToList` executes the AddToList() macro.

The statement `SetRangeName` executes the SetRangeName() macro.

The statement `loopAgain = MsgBox("Enter another sponsor", vbYesNo, "Data Entry")` displays the message box with the prompt "Enter another sponsor." If the user clicks Yes, the variable *loopAgain* is assigned the constant vbYes. If the user clicks No, *loopAgain* is assigned the constant vbNo.

The statement `Loop` signals the end of the loop. Program control returns to the statement `Do While loopAgain = vbYes`, where the variable *loopAgain* is tested. If the value in *loopAgain* is not VbYes, the statement following `Loop` is executed and the program stops running.

Now test the macro.

To test the DataEntry macro:

1. Activate the **Sponsors** worksheet.

2. Click **Tools**, click **Macro** to display the Macro dialog box, click **DataEntry** in the Macro Name/Reference list, then click the **Run** button. The data entry form opens.

3. Enter the following data:
   Sponsor: **International Pockets**
   Date: **7/28/98**
   Amount: **100**
   How Paid: **Cash**
   Member: **Olsen**

4. Click the **OK** button. The message "Enter another sponsor" displays. See Figure 11-42.

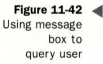

Figure 11-42
Using message box to query user

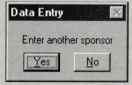

5. Click the **Yes** button. The data entry form displays again.

6. Enter the following data:
   Sponsor: **Purple Cow Gift Shop**
   Date: **7/28/98**
   Amount: **50**
   How Paid: **Unpaid**
   Member: **Olsen**

7. Click the **OK** button. The message "Enter another sponsor" displays.

8. Click the **No** button. The macro stops execution.

Two records have been added to the Sponsor list. Confirm that the records were added to the bottom of the Sponsor list and that the range name Dtabse has been updated. You will use the macro ViewLastRecord already included in the modDataEntry module sheet to view the bottom of the Sponsor list.

To confirm that the records were added to the Sponsor list:

1. Click **Tools**, point to **Macro** to display the Macro dialog box, click **ViewLastRecord** in the Macro Name/Reference list box, then click the **Run** button. See Figure 11-43. The last two records, the records you just entered, are displayed at the bottom of the Sponsor list.

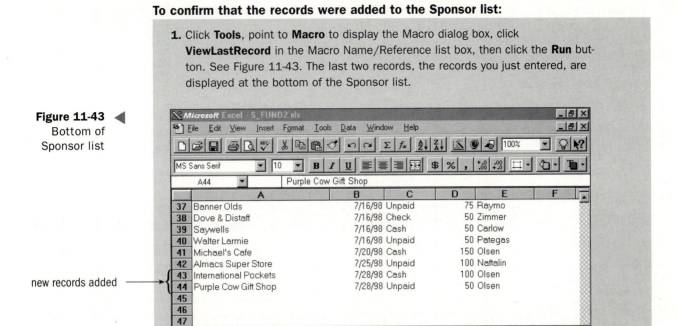

Figure 11-43
Bottom of Sponsor list

new records added

Now see if the range name Dtabse refers to the current range of the Sponsor list—A4:E44.

To check the definition of the range name Dtabse:

1. Click **Insert**, point to **Name**, click **Define** to display the Define Name dialog box, then click **Dtabse** in the Names in Workbook list. The Refers to text box indicates that the range is $A$4:$E$44. Click the **OK** button.

2. Save the workbook as S_Fund2.xls.

The macro SetRangeName updated the range name Dtabse.

If you want to take a break and resume the tutorial at a later time, you can do so now. Close the workbook and exit Excel. If you are on a network, leave Windows running. If you are using your own computer, you may exit Windows and shut down the computer. When you resume the tutorial, place your Student Disk in the disk drive, launch Excel, and continue with the tutorial.

● ● ●

Preparing the Other Macros

In addition to working with data-entry related tasks, you want to automate the sorting, printing, and closing functions of this application. You can do this by recording macros and then modifying them if necessary. Some of Ann's macros for these tasks are already available in the workbook. Figure 11-44 shows the module sheet, macro name, and function of each of the macros that are already included in the workbook.

Figure 11-44 ◀
Macros included
in S_FUND2.xls
workbook

Module Sheet	Macro Name	Macro Function
modSort	SortByDate SortByMember	Sorts Sponsor list by Date Sorts Sponsor list by Member
modReport	PrintHowPaid PrintMember	Refreshes and prints the How Paid pivot table Refreshes and prints the Member pivot table
modMisc	CloseFund	Saves and closes the active workbook

Now you can complete the remaining macros.

Recording a Macro to Sort the Sponsor List by Sponsor

The Rotary Club Fund-Raising committee wants to be able to view the Sponsor list in three different arrangements—by Date, by Member, and by Sponsor. To automate these tasks you will use three macros. Two of these macros have already been recorded, as you can see from Figure 11-44. They are the SortByDate and the SortByMember macros. It is up to you to record the third macro, the SortBySponsor macro. Figure 11-45 shows the planning for this macro.

Figure 11-45 ◀
Planning for
SortBySponsor
macro

Action	Result
Click A4	Cell A4 is the active cell
Click Sort Ascending button on the Standard toolbar	Sponsor list sorted by Sponsor

Before you record the macro, move to the bottom of the modSortList module sheet and mark the position for recording the macro so that the recorded macro will be included in the module sheet with the other sort macros.

To record a macro in an existing module sheet:

1. Activate the **modSortList** module sheet.

2. Position the insertion point in the last blank line in the module sheet.

3. Confirm the Use Relative Reference command on the Record Macro submenu is not checked. If it is checked, deselect it.

4. Click **Tools**, point to **Record Macro**, then click **Mark Position for Recording**. Now you have told Excel where you want to place the SortBySponsor macro.

5. Activate the **Sponsors** worksheet, and select any cell inside the Sponsor list.

6. Name the macro **SortBySponsor**, then start the macro recorder.

7. Click **A4**, then click the **Sort Ascending** button 🔼 on the Standard toolbar. The Sponsor list is sorted in alphabetical order by Sponsor.

8. Click the **Stop Macro** button ⬛.

Now test the macro to verify that it sorts the Sponsor list by Sponsor in ascending order. To test this macro, you first need to arrange the Sponsor list in a different order.

CREATING THE SUMMARY—HOW PAID REPORT **ADVEX 577**

To test the SortBySponsor macro:

1. Click any cell in the **Date** column, then click the **SortAscending** button 🔼 on the toolbar. The Sponsor list is sorted by Date.

2. Click **Tools**, click **Macro** to display the Macro dialog box, click **SortBySponsor** in the Macro Name/Reference list, then click the **Run** button.

The Sponsor list is sorted by Sponsor. Now you need to review which reports the Rotary Club needs, create the reports, and finally record the macros to print preview them.

Creating the Summary—How Paid Report

When Ann created her sponsorship tracking application, she determined that she needed four reports, two of which were summary reports, and two of which were detail reports. The summary reports included one that summarized how the donations were paid, and another to determine the members who solicited the largest donations.

In recreating her application, you need to create the two summary reports, Summary—How Paid and Summary—Members. Both reports are based on the Excel pivot table feature, which you learned how to use in a previous tutorial.

First, create the Summary—How Paid report.

To create the Summary—How Paid pivot table:

1. If necessary, activate the **Sponsors** worksheet, then select any cell in the **Sponsor** list.

2. Click **Data**, then click **PivotTable** to display the PivotTable Wizard - Step 1 of 4 dialog box. Make sure that the **Microsoft Excel List or Database** option is selected, then click the **Next >** button to display the PivotTable Wizard - Step 2 of 4 dialog box.

   Since the active cell is located within the range of the Excel list, the Wizard automatically selects the range $A$4:$E$44 as the source of data for the pivot table. Since you will be inserting new rows in the Sponsor list, specify the range name, not the range address, as the source of data for the pivot table. If you don't identify the source by name, the PivotTable Wizard will not include all your data when you refresh the pivot table.

3. Type **Dtabse**, then click the **Next >** button to display the PivotTable Wizard - Step 3 of 4 dialog box.

4. Click and drag the **HowPaid** field button to the ROW area of the sample pivot table.

5. Click and drag the **Amount** field button to the DATA area of the sample pivot table. The default summary function Sum of Amount is placed in the DATA area of the sample pivot table.

6. Double-click the **Sum of Amount** button in the DATA area to display the PivotTable Field dialog box. Click the **Number** button to display the Format Cells dialog box. Click **Currency** in the Category list, then click the **Decimal Places** spinner to set it to zero. Click the **OK** button to close the Format Cells dialog box, then click the **OK** button to return to the PivotTable Wizard - Step 3 of 4 dialog box.

   Click the Format code $#,##0_);($#,##0) instead of setting the Decimal Places spinner to zero.

7. Click the **Next >** button to go to the PivotTable Wizard - Step 4 of 4 dialog box, and accept the default options by clicking the **Finish** button to create the pivot table. The pivot table is added to a new sheet and this sheet becomes the active sheet. See Figure 11-46.

EXCEL **5.0**

Figure 11-46
Pivot table of amount raised

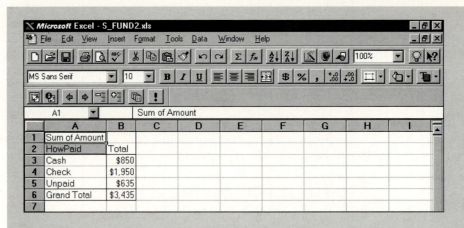

8. Rename the worksheet with the pivot table **HowPaidRpt**.

Creating the Summary—Members Report

A second pivot table is needed to determine which Rotary Club members win the prizes for bringing in the most donations.

To create the Summary—Member pivot table:

1. Activate the **Sponsors** worksheet, then select any cell in the list.

2. Click **Data**, then click **PivotTable** to display the PivotTable Wizard - Step 1 of 4 dialog box. Make sure that the **Microsoft Excel List or Database** option is selected, then click the **Next >** button to display the PivotTable Wizard - Step 2 of 4 dialog box.

   Recall that you need to specify the range name, not the range address, in order for all new data to be included in the pivot table.

3. Type **Dtabse** in the Range text box, then click the **Next >** button to display the PivotTable Wizard - Step 3 of 4 dialog box.

4. Click and drag the **Member** field button to the ROW area of the sample pivot table.

5. Click and drag the **Amount** field button to the DATA area of the sample pivot table. The default summary function Sum of Amount is placed in the DATA area of the sample pivot table.

6. Double-click the **Sum of Amount** button in the DATA area to display the PivotTable Field dialog box. Click the **Number** button to display the Format Cells dialog box. Click **Currency** in the Category list, then click the **Decimal Places** spinner to set it to zero. Click the **OK** button to close the Format Cells dialog box, then click the **OK** button to return to the PivotTable Wizard - Step 3 of 4 dialog box.

   Click the Format code $#,##0_);($#,##0) instead of setting the Decimal Places spinner to zero.

7. Click the **Next >** button to go to the PivotTable Wizard - Step 4 of 4 dialog box, and click the **Finish** button to create the pivot table. The pivot table is added to a new sheet and this sheet becomes the active sheet. See Figure 11-47.

EXCEL 5.0

Figure 11-47
Pivot table of total funds raised by each member

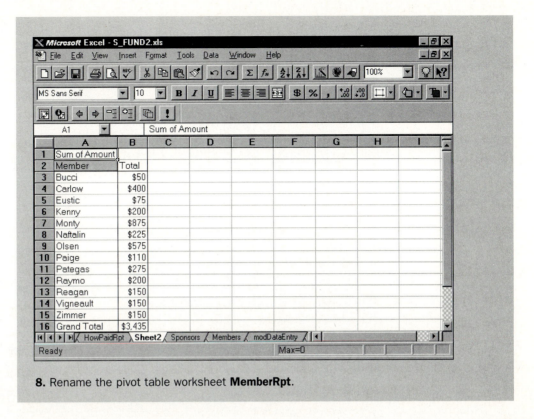

8. Rename the pivot table worksheet **MemberRpt**.

You have now completed the two summary reports used in the application. Next, record the macros to print preview the detail reports.

Recording the Report Macros

Now that you have created the summary reports, four reports are available in the fund-raising sponsorship tracking application. They are Summary—How Paid, Summary—Members, Detail—Sponsor List, and Detail—Unpaid Sponsors.

Ann's macros to print preview the two summary reports are included in your modReport module sheet. Ann used the macro recorder to create these macros. You too will use the macro recorder to create the other two print report macros, which automate producing the detail reports. First, record the macro to print preview the Detail—Sponsor List.

To record the print preview macro:

1. Move to the bottom of the **modReport** module sheet and mark the position for recording the macro so that the recorded macro will be included with the other print report macros, then activate the Sponsors worksheet.

2. Confirm the Use Relative Reference command on the Record Macro submenu is not checked. If it is checked, deselect it.

3. Record the macro. Name the macro **PrintDetail**, then start the macro recorder.

4. Click any cell inside the Sponsor list.

5. Click **File**, then click **Page Setup** to display the Page Setup dialog box.

   By default, Excel prints the entire worksheet. To print only a part of the worksheet, you must specify the part you want. Previously, the range name Dtabse was defined to refer to the Sponsor list. Enter this name in the Print Area text box.

6. Click the **Sheet** tab, click the **Print Area** text box, then type **dtabse**.

   Deactivate the gridlines check box so that gridlines won't appear on the printed output.

7. If necessary, click the **Gridlines** check box to remove the check.

   Review the output on the print preview window.

8. Click the **Print Preview** button at the right of the dialog box to preview the output.

9. Click the **Close** button to return to the Sponsors worksheet.

   You have completed the tasks to print preview the Sponsor list; now turn off the macro recorder.

10. Click the **Stop Macro** button.

Now examine the VBA code.

To view the PrintDetail macro:

1. Click **Tools**, point to **Macro** to display the Macro dialog box, click **PrintDetail** in the Macro list, then click the **Edit** button. You are now in the modReport module sheet. See Figure 11-48.

Figure 11-48
VBA code for PrintDetail macro

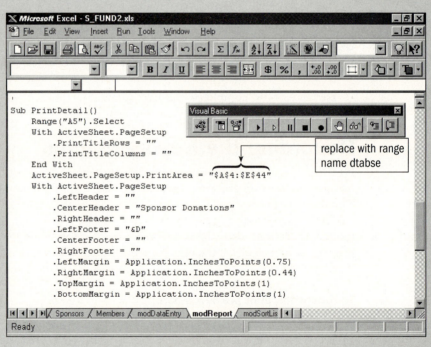

As in an earlier macro that you recorded, there is a problem with this recorded macro. Even though you specified the range name Dtabse as the print area, Excel converts the reference in the recorded macro to an absolute range reference. Thus, the statement `ActiveSheet.PageSetup.PrintArea = "$A$4:$E$44"` must be changed. The range of the print area must reference the range name Dtabse; otherwise, as the Sponsor list grows this macro will still display just the range A4:E44. Modify the PrintDetail macro.

RECORDING THE REPORT MACROS **ADVEX 581**

To modify the PrintDetail macro:

1. Move the insertion point to the statement
   `ActiveSheet.PageSetup.PrintArea = "$A$4:$E$44"`

2. Replace the statement `ActiveSheet.PageSetup.PrintArea = "$A$4:$E$44"`
   with `ActiveSheet.PageSetup.PrintArea = "dtabse"`

   This new statement uses the name dtabse to refer to the print area.

   Now test the macro.

3. Activate the **Sponsors** worksheet and run the **PrintDetail** macro.

Recording a Macro to Print the Unpaid Sponsors Report

It's important for the Fund-Raising committee to get a list of sponsors that haven't paid. The Detail—Unpaid Sponsors report uses the Filter command on the Data menu to display a list of unpaid sponsors. Figure 11-49 shows the steps Ann used to record her macro to display the unpaid sponsors. Record this macro.

Figure 11-49 ◀
Planning for
UnpaidRept
macro

Action	Result
Click Data, click Filter, then click AutoFilter	Sets filter arrows
Select Unpaid from HowPaid column	Displays list of unpaid sponsors
Click File, click Print Preview	Displays unpaid sponsors in print preview window
Click Close	Closes print preview window
Click Data, click Filter, then click AutoFilter	Removes all filter arrows and displays all records

To record the UnpaidRept macro:

1. Mark the positioning for the recording at the bottom of the **modReport** module sheet, then activate the **Sponsors** worksheet, and click any cell inside the **Sponsor** list.

2. Confirm the Use Relative Reference command on the Record Macro submenu is not checked. If it is checked, deselect it.

3. Name the macro **UnpaidRept** and start the macro recorder.

   Now perform the tasks you want recorded.

4. Click **Data**, point to **Filter**, then click **AutoFilter**. List arrows appear next to each column label in the list. To see a list of filtering criteria for a specific column, click the list arrow next to the column heading.

5. Click the **list arrow** in the HowPaid column to display a list of criteria you can use to filter the data. Click **Unpaid** to display a list of sponsors that have not yet paid.

6. Click **File**, then click **Print Preview** to preview the output.

7. Click the **Close** button to return to the Sponsors worksheet.

   Show all records and remove the filter arrows.

ADVEX 582   TUTORIAL 11   CREATING A CUSTOM APPLICATION USING VBA

8. Click **Data**, point to **Filter**, then click **AutoFilter** to remove all the filters. All the records are displayed and the list arrows are removed from the column headings.

You have completed the tasks to print the Unpaid Sponsors report; now turn off the macro recorder.

9. Click the **Stop Macro** button ■.

Now test the macro.

10. Run the **UnpaidRept** macro, then save the workbook.

All the macros for the application are now complete. Your final task will be to create a custom menu to lead the user to the different automated tasks.

If you want to take a break and resume the tutorial at a later time, you can do so now. Close the workbook and exit Excel. If you are on a network, leave Windows running. If you are using your own computer, you may exit Windows and shut down the computer. When you resume the tutorial, place your Student Disk in the disk drive, launch Excel, and continue with the tutorial.

● ● ●

Creating a Custom Menu

Now that you have recorded and modified several macros, you need to develop a simple way to perform the tasks you have automated in the sponsorship tracking application. You could continue to use the method you learned in earlier tutorials, in which you place command buttons in a worksheet and attach each macro to a button. Alternatively, you could tie all the tasks in this application together by customizing the Excel menuing system to suit your needs. Your choice of one method over another will be a matter of personal preference. Since you already know how to implement the first method, try the method Ann chose when she created the sponsorship tracking application: create a custom menu for the user.

You can create a custom menu for your application that will make it easier for a user to complete a specific task. In essence, you are customizing the Excel menu bar to fit your needs. Using the Excel Menu Editor, a tool that enables you to modify menu bars, you can

- Add commands to an existing menu.

- Create a custom menu.

- Delete menus from any menu bar.

- Create custom menu bars.

You can modify the Excel standard menu bars either by using the Menu Editor or by programming in VBA. In this tutorial you will learn how to use the Menu Editor. To learn more about creating menus using VBA, check on-line Help within Excel.

HELP DESK

Index

MENUS IN VISUAL BASIC

Double-click the Help button to display the Help Topics dialog box, then click the Index tab.

Keyword	Topic
Menus in Visual Basic, Menu Bars	Creating new menu bars
not available	

EXCEL 5.0

Understanding Menu Terms

The Excel menuing system consists of several components:

Menu Bar—The set of menus that are available for a window. There are different menu bars available depending on the type of window that is open. For instance, while a worksheet is active, the worksheet menu bar is displayed. This enables you to select appropriate commands while working with a worksheet. When editing a chart, the chart menu bar, the set of menus that applies to the charting environment, is displayed, and when you switch to a module sheet, the module menu bar is displayed.

Menu—A single top-level element of a menu bar. A menu organizes related tasks. For example, on the menu bar you find the Help menu, which provides options related to on-line Help.

Menu Item—An individual item on a menu. When you select a menu from a menu bar, you see a list of all the items available from that menu selection. For example, the Data menu has a Sort menu item. Each menu item performs a specific action when selected. The action may be a task, such as printing, or a step toward a task, such as displaying a dialog box.

Submenu—A second-level menu that is displayed under certain menus. For example, the Insert menu has a submenu called Macro.

Submenu Items—Menu items that appear on a submenu. For example, the Insert, Macro submenu contains the submenu items Module, Dialog, and MS Excel 4.0 Macro.

Figure 11-50 shows the worksheet menu bar, menu items available on the Insert menu, and the submenu items that display when the Macro item is selected.

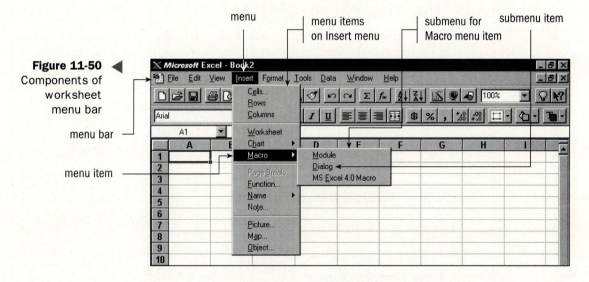

Figure 11-50
Components of worksheet menu bar

Now you will add a new menu, FundRaising, to the worksheet menu bar so that Rotary Club Fund Raising committee members can run their application more easily. The FundRaising menu will appear immediately before the Help menu, and will include several menu items and submenu items. Figure 11-51 shows a sketch of the menu, menu items, and submenu items you will be adding to the worksheet menu. First, modify the worksheet menu to add the new FundRaising menu.

Figure 11-51 ◀
Sketch of FundRaising menu with menu items and submenu items

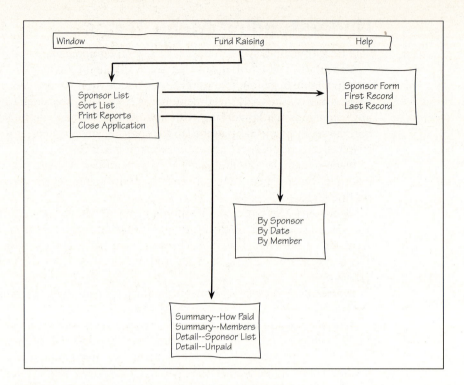

Displaying the Menu Editor

To use the Menu Editor you must first activate a Visual Basic module, or select the Menu Editor button on the Visual Basic toolbar to access the Menu Editor from any type of sheet.

To start the Menu Editor:

1. Click the **modDataEntry** sheet tab.
2. Click **Tools**, then click **Menu Editor** to display the Menu Editor dialog box. See Figure 11-52. Now you are ready to add a menu to the Worksheet menu bar.

Figure 11-52 ◀
Menu Editor dialog box

specify which menu bar

menus for Worksheet menu bar

menu items for File menu

no submenu items for the selected menu item, New

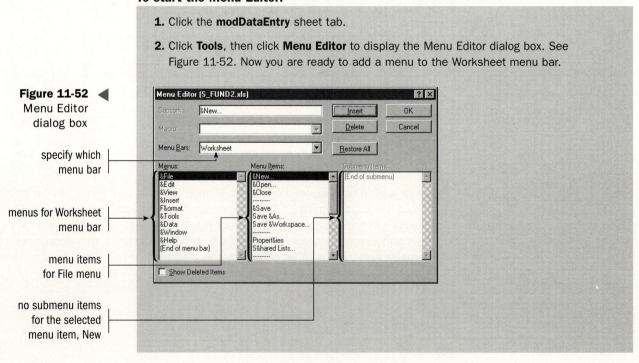

REFERENCE window	**DISPLAYING THE MENU EDITOR**
	▪ Activate an existing Visual Basic module sheet. ▪ Click Tools, then click Menu Editor to display the Menu Editor dialog box. *or* Click the Menu Editor button on the Visual Basic toolbar.

Index

MENU EDITOR

Double-click the Help button to display the Help Topics dialog box, then click the Index tab.

Keyword   **Topic**
Menu Editor
Menu Editor command (Tools Menu)

EXCEL 5.0

Adding a New Menu to an Existing Menu Bar

The Menu Editor enables you to customize any of the Excel menu bars. You can add new menus or delete existing ones. When you add a new menu to a menu bar, you typically add it to the worksheet menu bar. Add the new menu, FundRaising, to the Worksheet menu bar.

To add a new menu to the Worksheet menu bar:

1. Make sure that **Worksheet** appears in the Menu Bars text box.

   Use the Menus list to select the location on the menu bar where you want the menu added. For example, if you select [End of menu bar], your menu will appear at the end of the menu bar.

   Place the new menu to the left of the Help menu.

2. Click **&Help** in the Menus list to place the new menu to the left of the Help menu.

   You are now ready to insert a new menu.

3. Click the **Insert** button. A blank menu line is inserted above the currently selected item in the Menus list and the Caption text box is activated.

   Type the name of the new menu.

4. Type **Fund&Raising** in the Caption text box. See Figure 11-53. Placing the ampersand (&) before the letter R allows the user to press Alt + R to access the FundRaising menu as an alternative to using the mouse to select the menu. The Alt + R combination is called an **access key**.

Figure 11-53
Adding menu to menu bar

caption to appear on menu bar

menu added here

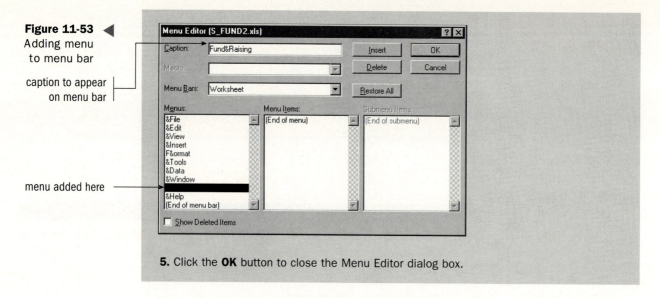

5. Click the **OK** button to close the Menu Editor dialog box.

Now switch to the Sponsors worksheet to see whether the FundRaising menu appears on the Worksheet menu bar.

To see the new menu on the worksheet menu bar:

1. Activate the **Sponsors** worksheet. The menu bar includes the menu FundRaising. See Figure 11-54.

Figure 11-54
Menu added to menu bar

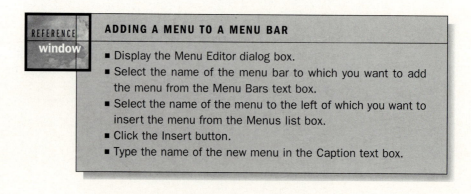

2. Click **FundRaising**. Nothing happens.

Although you have created the menu, you have not yet added menu items to it. Do that next.

REFERENCE window

ADDING A MENU TO A MENU BAR

- Display the Menu Editor dialog box.
- Select the name of the menu bar to which you want to add the menu from the Menu Bars text box.
- Select the name of the menu to the left of which you want to insert the menu from the Menus list box.
- Click the Insert button.
- Type the name of the new menu in the Caption text box.

Adding Menu Items to a Custom Menu

After you have added a menu to the menu bar, you need to add menu items to the menu. Add the menu items Sponsor List, Sort List, Print Reports, a separator, and Close Application to the FundRaising menu.

To add menu items to the FundRaising menu:

1. Switch to the **modDataEntry** module sheet.

2. Click **Tools**, then click **Menu Editor** to display the Menu Editor dialog box.

3. Make sure that **Worksheet** is displayed in the Menu Bars list.

   Identify the menu in the Menus list that you want to add menu items to.

4. Click the **Fund&Raising** menu in the Menus list. When you select a menu from the Menus list box, its menu items appear in the Menu Items list box. Currently, there are no menu items on the FundRaising menu.

   Select the position of the item on the FundRaising menu.

5. Click **[End of menu]** in the Menu Items list to place the item at the bottom of the menu.

6. Click the **Insert** button to add a blank line in the Menu Items list and to activate the Caption text box.

   Enter the name of the menu item you want to add to the menu.

7. Type **Sponsor List** in the Caption text box, then press the **Tab** key. Excel activates the Macro text box, and places the name of the menu item in the Menu Items list box.

   If you want to specify an access key with this menu item, as you did with the FundRaising menu, you can type an ampersand (&) before the character you want to use as the access key.

   If you want to add a separator bar instead of a caption, type a hyphen (-) in the Caption text box. This enables you to group related menu items by drawing a line on the menu to separate them from other menu items.

   If you want a macro to run when the user selects this menu item, you can attach a procedure to the menu item by typing the name of the procedure in the Macro text box.

8. Repeat Steps 5 through 7 to add the **Sort List** menu item to the FundRaising menu.

9. Repeat Steps 5 through 7 to add the **Print Reports** menu item to the FundRaising menu.

10. Repeat Steps 5 through 7 to add a **separator** to the FundRaising menu. In Step 7, type - (hyphen) instead of Sponsor List.

11. Repeat Steps 5 through 7 to add the **Close Application** menu item to the FundRaising menu. Click **CloseFund** in the Macro list box to associate this menu item with the CloseFund macro that saves and closes the application. See Figure 11-55.

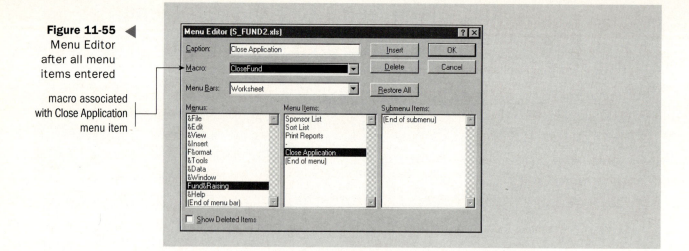

Figure 11-55
Menu Editor after all menu items entered

macro associated with Close Application menu item

Creating a New Submenu

After adding the FundRaising menu and the menu items Sponsor List, Sort List, Print Reports, and Close Application, you can add submenu items to each of the menu items. The submenus appear when the user selects the menu item to which submenu items are attached. Figure 11-56 shows the menu items, the associated submenu items, and the macro that is run when the menu or submenu item is selected.

Figure 11-56
Menu items, submenu items, and macro names for sponsorship tracking

Menu Item	Submenu Item	Macro Name
Sponsor List	Sponsor Form First Record Last Record	DataEntry ViewFirstRecord ViewLastRecord
Sort List	By Sponsor By Date By Member	SortBySponsor SortByDate SortByMember
Print Reports	Summary--How Paid Summary--Members Detail--Sponsor List Detail--Unpaid	PrintHowPaid PrintMember PrintDetail UnpaidRept
Close Application		CloseFund

To add submenu items to the Sponsor menu item:

1. Click **Fund&Raising** in the Menus list.

2. Click **Sponsor List** in the Menu Items list. When you select a menu item from the Menu Items list box, its submenu items display in the Submenu Items list box. Currently, you have no submenu items in the Sponsor List menu item.

3. Click **[End of submenu]** to place the submenu item at the bottom of a group of submenu items.

4. Click the **Insert** button. Excel adds a blank line in the Submenu Items list and activates the Caption text box.

5. Type **Sponsor Form** in the Caption text box, then press the **Tab** key.

   Now attach a macro to the submenu item.

6. Click **DataEntry** in the Macro list or type the name of the macro in the Macro list box to place it in the Macro box.

7. Repeat Steps 3 through 6 to insert **First Record** as a submenu item in the Sponsor List menu item, and select **ViewFirstRecord** in the Macro list.

8. Repeat Steps 3 through 6 to insert **Last Record** as a submenu item in the Sponsor List menu item, and select **ViewLastRecord** in the Macro list. See Figure 11-57.

Figure 11-57 ◀
Submenu items for Sponsor List

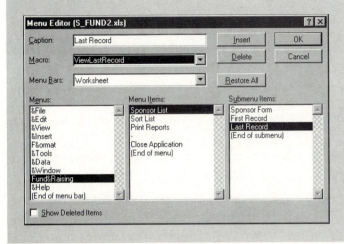

Now add the submenu items to the Sort List menu item.

To add submenu items to the Sort List menu item:

1. Make sure that the menu selected in the Menus list is **Fund&Raising**. Click **Sort List** in the Menu Items list.

2. Click **[End of submenu]** to place the submenu item at the bottom of the submenu.

3. Click the **Insert** button. Excel adds a blank line in the Submenu Items list and activates the Caption text box.

4. Type **By Sponsor** in the Caption text box.

   Attach a macro to the submenu item.

5. Click **SortBySponsor** in the Macro list.

6. Repeat Steps 2 through 5 to insert **By Date** as a submenu item in the Sort List menu item and select **SortByDate** in the Macro list.

7. Repeat Steps 2 through 5 to insert **By Member** as a submenu item in the Sort List menu item and select **SortByMember** in the Macro list. See Figure 11-58.

Figure 11-58 ◀
Submenu items for Sort List

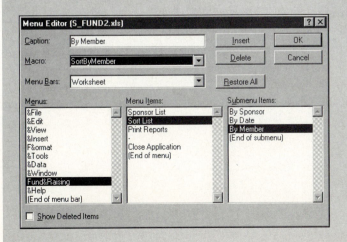

Now add the submenu items to the Print Reports menu item.

To add submenu items to the Print Reports menu item:

1. Make sure that the menu selected in the Menus list is **Fund&Raising**. Click **Print Reports** in the Menu Items list.

2. Click **[End of submenu]** to place the submenu item at the bottom of the submenu.

3. Click the **Insert** button. Excel adds a blank line in the Submenu Items list and activates the Caption text box.

4. Type **Summary--How Paid** in the Caption text box and press the **Tab** key.

   Attach a macro to the menu item.

5. Click **PrintHowPaid** in the Macro list.

6. Repeat Steps 2 through 5 to insert **Summary--Members** as a submenu item in the Print Reports menu item and select **PrintMember** in the Macro list.

7. Repeat Steps 2 through 5 to insert **Detail--Sponsor List** as a submenu item in the Print Reports menu item and select **PrintDetail** in the Macro list.

8. Repeat Steps 2 through 5 to insert **Detail--Unpaid** as a submenu item in the Print Reports menu item and select **UnpaidRept** in the Macro list. See Figure 11-59.

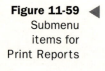

Figure 11-59
Submenu items for Print Reports

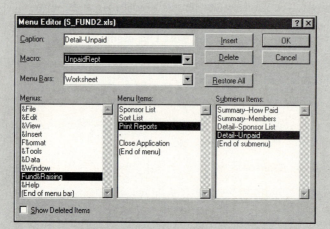

TROUBLE? If you made some mistakes and want to delete the FundRaising menu from the menu bar, a menu item from the menu, or a submenu item from a menu item, open the Menu Editor dialog box, select the item you want to remove, and click the Delete button.

You have inserted all the menu and submenu items.

9. Click the **OK** button to return to the modDataEntry module sheet.

Testing the FundRaising Menu

Now that the FundRaising menu is complete, you can use it to select different options.

To view and test the FundRaising menu:

1. Activate the **Sponsors** worksheet. The worksheet menu bar appears with the FundRaising menu included.

2. Click **FundRaising** to display the menu items. See Figure 11-60.

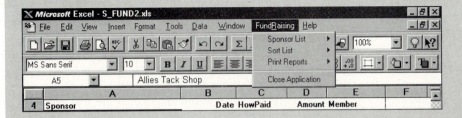

Figure 11-60 ◀ Menu items for the FundRaising menu

TROUBLE? If the menu items are not displayed in the order in which they appear in the menu list, it is most likely *not* because you entered the menu incorrectly. This is a known bug with early versions of Excel 5.0. The problem was corrected with Excel Version 5.0c. To work around the problem, return to the Menu Editor and put separators (-) in between menu items that contain sub-menu items.

Next add a record.

3. Point to **Sponsor List**, then click **Sponsor Form** to display the data entry form.

4. Add your name as a sponsor. You donate **$100** on **8/2/98**, pay by **check**, and **Kenny** is the member. Click the **OK** button. Click the **No** button when asked to enter another sponsor. Was the new sponsor added to the Sponsor list?

5. Click **FundRaising**, point to **Sponsor List**, then click **Last Record** to display the last record in the Sponsor list.

6. Continue to test each of the menu and submenu items. When you are finished testing, click **FundRaising**, then click **Close Application**. The workbook is automatically saved and closed.

7. Exit Excel.

When your workbook is saved, Excel stores your customized menu with the workbook. When you open the S_FUND2.xls workbook again, or any workbook with a custom menu, the custom menu system is activated. When you close the workbook and open a different workbook, the Excel default menus are activated.

You have now completed an Excel application that users will find easy to use, and the application will provide the Garden Grove Rotary Club members with the information they need to track the sponsors for the festival program booklet.

Tutorial Exercises

Open E_FUND1.xls in the Tut11 folder or directory on your Student Disk and immediately save it as S_FUND1.xls.

1. Modify the CloseFund procedure in the modMisc module sheet so that immediately upon executing the CloseFund procedure, users are asked to confirm that they want to close the application. If the user answers Yes, then close the application; otherwise, ignore the statement to close the application and continue running.
2. Recorded print macros often add a number of extraneous lines of code. Examine the PrintDetail macro and reduce it to the fewest number of lines that produce the same result. The macro should
   - display in the print preview window
   - specify the range name Dtabse as the print area
   - remove gridlines from the output

   Eliminate the lines in the macro that are not needed. Test the revised macro. Save the wookbook.
3. Figure 11-61 shows a modified layout of the custom dialog box used in the FundRaising application. Modify the custom dialog box to reflect the changes suggested in Figure 11-61. Add a new sponsor to the Sponsor list. Print the dlgDataEntry dialog sheet. Save the workbook.

Figure 11-61 ◀

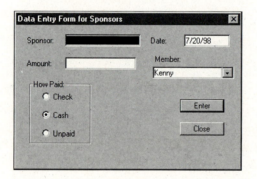

4. Add a new menu item named View Reports to the FundRaising menu. This menu item will have three submenu items: View Summary—HowPaid, View Summary—Members, and Return to Sponsor List. Add the three submenu items. Create macros to go to each report and a third macro to go to cell A1 in the Sponsors worksheet. Attach the macros to the appropriate submenu items.

5. When you click the Close button in the custom dialog box, a subtle logic error occurs. Enter the data for a new sponsor and click the Cancel button, then view the last record in the Sponsor list. Describe the error that occurs. Modify the VBA code to correct the problem. Print the procedure(s) that were modified.

Case Problems

1. Selective Financial Reporting at Grant Corporation Steve Palmer, budget analyst for Grant Corporation, has compiled a workbook that consists of six worksheets: Balance Sheet, Income Statement—Current, 97 Plan, 98 Plan, By Region, and By State. He has found it cumbersome to quickly activate each worksheet. Steve decides to include a menuing system to expedite his access to each worksheet.

Do the following:
1. Open the workbook P_REPORT.xls in the Tut11 folder or directory and immediately save it as S_REPORT.xls.
2. Record macros to activate each worksheet. When finished, you will have six macros—each macro activating a different worksheet.
3. Based on the sketch shown in Figure 11-62, add the Reports menu, associated menu items, and submenu items to the workbook menu bar. Attach each macro created in Question 2 to the appropriate submenu item. For example, selecting Balance Sheet from the Financials menu activates the Balance Sheet worksheet.

Figure 11-62 ◀

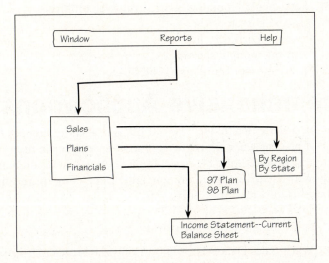

4. Test the Reports menu to make sure you can activate each worksheet using the menu.
5. Print the module sheet.
6. Save the workbook.

2. Employee Phone Directory for Johnson Electric Steven Phillips, office manager at Johnson Electric, is responsible for maintaining and distributing a phone directory for all employees in the building. The directory is distributed to all employees every time an update is printed. He decides to use Excel to maintain this data.

1. Create an Excel list consisting of four columns: Name (last name, first name), Phone Extension, Office Number, and Department. Name the worksheet Directory.
2. Create a custom dialog box to enter the data for the Directory list. You design the layout of the dialog box.
3. Write a macro named DataEntry to display the custom dialog box and transfer the data from the custom dialog box to the Directory list.
4. Develop a macro to sort the Directory list by Name. Name the macro SortByName.
5. Develop a macro to print preview the Directory list. Name the macro PrintDirectory.
6. Add a menu named Directory with three menu items: Data Entry, Sort by Name, and Print Directory. The menu item Data Entry executes the macro DataEntry; the menu item Sort by Name executes the SortByName macro, and the menu item Print Directory executes the PrintDirectory macro.
7. Test each phase of your application. (*Hint:* The VBA code that you use to identify the row in which you add the record will vary depending on whether the database is empty or already contains some records.)
8. Use the custom dialog box to add five employees.
9. Sort the Directory list.
10. Print the Directory list.
11. Print the module sheet(s).
12. Save your workbook as S_DIRECT.xls.

Comprehensive Applications

1. Sales Reports for Health, Inc. Tim Robbins is a sales manager for Health, Inc., a distributor of pharmaceutical products. One of his responsibilities is to track the sales of the company product line. He has compiled a worksheet summarizing sales by product for each month, each quarter, and annually. Depending on the circumstances, Tim needs to output this information in three ways:

- Sales Data Worksheet—This report prints the entire sales data table on one page, using a landscape orientation.

- Yearly Sales Data—This report prints the Product Description (column A) and the Year Total (column R) using portrait orientation, and is centered horizontally.

- Quarterly Sales Data—This report prints the Product Description (column A), Four Quarterly Sales (columns E, I, M, Q), and Year Total (column R) on one page, using portrait orientation, and is centered horizontally. (*Hint:* As part of your macro, you should hide unneeded columns before printing, then unhide the columns when you have finished printing.)

Do the following:

1. Open the workbook P_PRINT.xls and immediately save it as S_PRINT.xls.
2. Record three macros, one for each print report. You decide on the macro names.

3. Create a custom dialog box similar to Figure 11-63 from which a user can select the report to be printed.

Figure 11-63 ◀

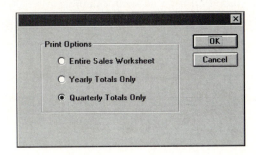

4. Write the VBA code to display the dialog box and execute the selected report based on the option chosen in the custom dialog box. Name this macro PrintOptions.
5. Place a button in the Sales Data worksheet that when clicked runs the PrintOptions macro created in Question 4. Place the button in cells A1:B1 of the Sales Data worksheet and label it Print Options. In other words, when the user clicks the Print Options button, the custom dialog box (Figure 11-63) opens, the user selects a sales report, and the report is printed.
6. Test your application by using the custom dialog box to print each report.
7. Print the module sheet.
8. Save the workbook.

2. Customer Billing for Apex Auto Rental Apex Auto Rental is the only car rental company in a midwest city. The company has been in business two years. John Prescott, founder and president of Apex, has asked you to help him computerize the bills he gives to his customers.

Apex rents two types of cars: compact (Pontiac Sunbird) and luxury (Cadillac Seville). The current rental rates are shown in Figure 11-64.

Figure 11-64 ◀

Type	Charge/Day	Charge/Mile
Pontiac Sunbird	$38	$0.22
Cadillac Seville	$50	$0.32

1. Develop a workbook that calculates and prints customer bills. Divide your workbook into the following sheets:
   - A Documentation sheet that includes a title, your name, date developed, filename, purpose, and table of contents.
   - A custom dialog box to capture the customer billing data (Figure 11-65).

Figure 11-65 ◀

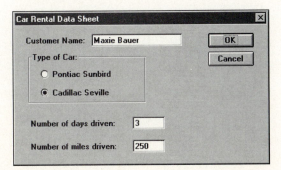

- A worksheet for the customer bill. Name the worksheet CustomerBill. The customer bill should include the information shown in Figure 11-66. *Note:* Amount Due is based on the following calculation:

  (days driven * charge/day) + (miles/driven * charge/mile)

Figure 11-66 ◀

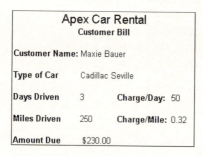

2. Develop the VBA code to display the customer billing dialog box (Figure 11-65) and transfer the data from the dialog box to the CustomerBill worksheet. (*Hint:* As you determine which car was used [option button] in order to transfer the type of car rented to the customer bill, you can also transfer the appropriate charge/day and charge/mile). Name the macro RentalForm.
3. Test the RentalForm macro.
4. Create a macro to print the customer bill with the following specifications: no gridlines; remove page number from footer; include today's date in the right section of the footer; and center horizontally on the page.
5. Test the print macro.
6. Add a new menu, AutoRental, to the worksheet menu bar. The menu will have two items: Data Entry and Print Bill. If a user selects Data Entry, the custom dialog box (Figure 11-65) opens and the bill is prepared. If a user selects Print Bill, the customer bill (Figure 11-66) is printed.
7. Use the data in Figure 11-67 to print a customer bill.
8. Print the module sheet.
9. Save your worksheet as S_RNTCAR.xls.

Figure 11-67 ◀

Fields	Data Values
Name	Jeffrey Kinder
Type of Car	Cadillac Seville
Days driven	4
Miles driven	460

ADDITIONAL CASE 1

OBJECTIVES

In this case you will:

- Create a template worksheet

- Format a worksheet to improve its appearance

- Enhance a worksheet using fonts and borders

- Include a Paintbrush object in a worksheet

- Protect worksheet cells

- Use TODAY, IF, and VLOOKUP functions

- Develop two macros

Sales Invoicing for Island Treasure Chest

CASE Like many entrepreneurs, Kim Howard discovered the old-fashioned way to make money: choose something you like to do, keep costs low and quality high, and make teamwork a priority. This principle has led to the success of her Island Treasure Chest, a gift gallery that features crafts of artists from the Caribbean whose jewelry, paintings, and embroidered giftware capture the spirit of the islands.

Since she opened the gallery two years ago, business has been brisk. At the request of many of her customers, Kim has expanded her business to include mail orders. When customers visit the Treasure Chest, Kim gives them a catalog to take home. Many customers find it more convenient to order items after they return home than to fit extra gifts into an already overstuffed suitcase.

On a good day, Kim receives about a dozen phone calls from customers wanting to place orders. With so few calls, she doesn't need a full-blown order-entry system, but she would like to automate her invoice preparation. She decides to create an Excel workbook with a Documentation sheet and a template worksheet for her sales invoices. After she creates the template, all she needs to do is enter the data for each order and print the invoice.

Kim has recently completed a paper invoice for an order from Nancy Sherwood, shown in Figure 1. Using this invoice as a model to identify the labels, formulas, and format she wants to use in her template worksheet, Kim prepares her planning analysis sheet (Figure 2). The calculations she needs in the template include the current date, the extended price (unit price for each item ordered multiplied by the quantity ordered), the total amount for all items, the sales tax, the shipping amount, and the total amount of the order.

Figure 1
Island Treasure Chest sales invoice

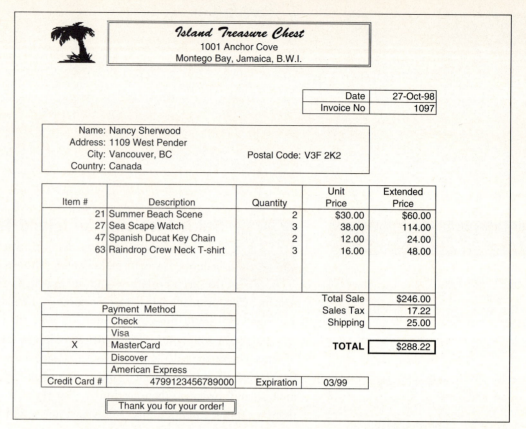

Using her planning analysis sheet and the original paper invoice, Kim sketches the template she wants to create with Excel (Figure 3). For each product ordered, she plans to enter the item number and quantity. Kim wants Excel to automatically look up the description and unit price in the product table when she enters an item number in the sales invoice worksheet. She also wants Excel to perform the calculations described in her planning analysis sheet (Figure 2). The circled numbers are guides to help you relate Kim's sketch to the required calculations.

Figure 2
Kim's planning analysis sheet

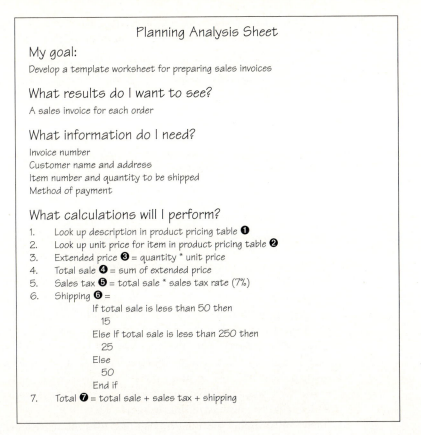

Figure 3
Kim's sketch of her template worksheet

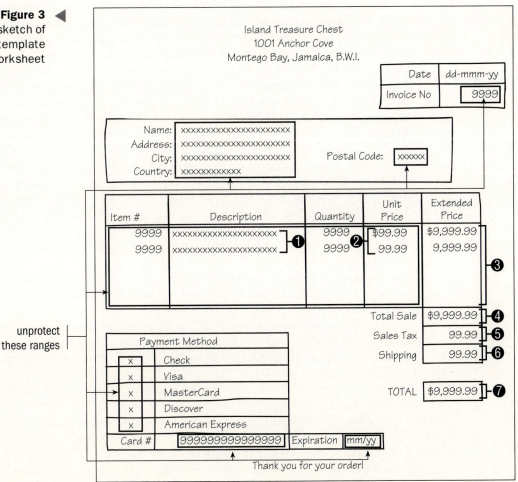

ADVEX 600 ADDITIONAL CASES

Kim also sketches a product pricing table that lists the items that the Island Treasure Chest sells (Figure 4). The table includes the item number, product description, and unit price of each product.

Figure 4 ◄
Product pricing
table

Item	Description	Unit Price
21	Summer Beach Scene	30.00
27	Sea Scape Watch	38.00
31	Victorian Walking Stick	32.00
47	Spanish Ducat Key Chain	12.00
63	Raindrop Crew Neck T-shirt	16.00
67	Stone-washed Twill Jacket	60.00
78	Island Can Coolers	7.00

Help Kim create a sales invoice template worksheet.

1. Enter the data for the product pricing table (Figure 4) into Sheet1 of a new workbook. Name the new sheet "Product." Print a copy of this sheet.

2. In a separate sheet, create the sales invoice for the Island Treasure Chest by entering the labels for the invoice template worksheet. Adjust the column widths as necessary. The placement of the labels should correspond to Kim's sketch, but does not need to match exactly. Name the sheet with the sales invoice "Invoice." Then place the Invoice worksheet before the Product worksheet, since the Invoice worksheet is used most frequently and you want its location to emphasize that usage.

3. Enter the formulas specified by Figure 2 into the worksheet. Obtain the date from the computer's clock, using the appropriate function. Use the Excel VLOOKUP function to automatically look up the description and unit price in the product pricing table when an item number is entered into the Invoice worksheet. If fewer than eight items are entered into the worksheet, the Item # in the unused lines is left blank. If the item # is blank, the Description, Unit Price, and Extended Price columns in that row also remain blank. You accomplish this by nesting the VLOOKUP function within the IF function. The IF function tests for an empty cell in Item #. If the cell is empty, the Description, Unit Price, and Extended Price cells are left blank. The test for an empty cell uses two successive quotation marks (""). A null, or empty, value is displayed in a cell using the same set of quotation marks. The VLOOKUP function uses the item number to obtain the appropriate description and unit price from the product table. Place appropriate formulas in the Description, Unit Price, and Extended Price cells.

4. Format the cells as shown in Figure 3. Remember to format the cell containing the expiration date as a label. Also, note that the first cell in the Unit Price and Extended Price columns is formatted differently than the rest of the cells in those columns.

5. Add fonts and borders as shown in Figure 1. Enhance the appearance of Kim's invoice by choosing additional fonts and borders. Explain why you chose these enhancements.

6. Launch Paintbrush and open the P_ITC1.bmp file in the X_case1 folder or directory on your Student Disk, which contains the Island Treasure Chest logo. Paste the logo into the invoice, as shown in Figure 1. Remove the line that surrounds the logo.

7. Include a Documentation sheet in the sales invoice workbook. Position this as the first sheet in the workbook.

8. Test the Invoice worksheet, using the data from the sales order form (Figure 1).

9. Save your sales invoice workbook as S_ITC1.xls in the X_case1 folder.

10. Create a macro for printing the invoice. Name the macro "PrintInvoice." Attach the macro to a button object. Provide a descriptive label for the button. You determine the best location for the button.

SALES INVOICING FOR ISLAND TREASURE CHEST **ADVEX 601**

11. Create a macro to clear all cells where data may be entered. Name the macro "ClearInvoice." Attach the macro to a button object. Provide a descriptive label for the button. You determine the best location for the button.

12. Test the operation of the worksheet, using realistic data values. Print the sales invoice, using your PrintInvoice macro.

13. Apply protection as indicated in Figure 3 so that only those cells in which data is entered can be changed. Protect the worksheet. If you use a password, make sure you remember it. To help identify cells where data can be entered, apply color to the unprotected cells.

14. Write instructions for operating Kim's sales invoice template and place them in the Documentation sheet. Print the Documentation sheet.

15. Use the ClearInvoice macro to remove all input values from the invoice. Save the revised worksheet as S_ITC2.xlt in the X_case1 folder. This is your invoice template.

16. Intentionally enter item number 76 instead of 67 in the Item # column of the invoice. What appears in the Description column? If it's not blank, use on-line Help from the Function Wizard dialog box to read about the fourth argument of the VLOOKUP function. Modify the VLOOKUP formula to handle entry of an invalid Item #, then test the entry of an invalid Item #. Write a short paragraph describing your test. Clear the invoice of all data, activate the Documentation sheet, then save this worksheet as S_ITC3.xlt in the X_case1 folder. (*Hints:* Use on-line Help from the Function Wizard to read about the ISERROR function; use on-line Help from the system menu to read about *zero values, hiding.*)

17. Kim wants to include an order form, which a customer can complete and return to the Island Treasure Chest, with her catalog. Design this catalog order form. For ideas, you might want to research order forms in catalogs you have received. Create the form using Excel. Save the workbook as S_ITC4.xls, then print a copy of the blank order form.

18. Arrange and clearly identify the printouts and answers for all the problems in this case as your documentation for the case. Also include a printout of your formulas and macros as part of this documentation.

ADDITIONAL CASE 2

OBJECTIVES

In this case you will:

- Create and use a multiple-sheet workbook

- Enhance worksheets with formatting

- Consolidate worksheet files

- Link worksheets

- Create a macro for combining files

- Create charts from summary data

- Create an interactive print macro

- Add a user-defined menu to the worksheet menu bar

- Integrate a word processing document and Excel worksheet

CASE — Performance Reporting for Boston Scientific

Boston Scientific* is on the cutting edge of medical cost reduction. The company develops and manufactures catheters and other products that are used as alternatives to traditional surgery. As described by CEO Peter Nicholas: "We were one of the first companies to articulate the concept of less invasive procedures." Less invasive procedures are possible because current medical imaging techniques allow physicians to see inside the body and manipulate instruments through a natural opening or a tiny incision. Boston Scientific aggressively markets its products for these medical procedures. For example, a traditional coronary bypass operation often costs $50,000 to $70,000, including the hospital stay and weeks of recovery time. By contrast, clearing a clogged artery with one of Boston Scientific's catheters, which is inserted under the skin of a patient's arm, takes just a few hours and costs around $12,000.

Although many of Boston Scientific's products are expensive relative to the cost of a scalpel, they enable a patient to leave the hospital much sooner and avoid huge hospital bills. For this reason, Boston Scientific's products are popular and sales continue to increase rapidly. Another important element in their growth is the company's ability to leverage technology across its four largely autonomous divisions: Medi-Tech (radiology), Mansfield (cardiology), Microvasive Endoscopy (gastroenterology), and Microvasive Urology.

Natalie Reyes joined Boston Scientific last year as a junior accountant. Her responsibilities include preparing the quarterly performance report that consolidates the financial results of the four divisions. Natalie created a template worksheet for reporting quarterly financial results, a copy of which was sent to and completed by the controller at each division. Natalie just received the workbook files from the four divisions. She now needs to prepare the consolidated statement of operation summarizing the division results.

---

*Adapted from: Fortune, "Boston Scientific," April 5, 1993, p. 97.

PERFORMANCE REPORTING FOR BOSTON SCIENTIFIC **ADVEX 603**

You will prepare this statement by completing the following:

1. Read all the problems for this case and develop a planning analysis sheet to plan the consolidation worksheet for Boston Scientific. Use your planning analysis sheet to develop your Excel solution.

2. Open and review the workbook for each division: P_BOSMT.xls (Medi-Tech), P_BOSMF.xls (Mansfield), P_BOSME.xls (Microvasive Endoscopy), and P_BOSMU.xls (Microvasive Urology). These workbooks are all in the X_case2 folder or directory on your Student Disk.

3. Create a multiple-sheet workbook that contains a Documentation sheet, a Consolidated Statement of Operations sheet, and a sheet for each division. Name the Consolidated Statement of Operations sheet "Consolidation." Place the results for each division in the divisions's own sheet in the workbook. Assign appropriate names to the other worksheets. Include formulas in the Consolidation sheet that add the division results to determine the corporate total. Apply appropriate formatting to enhance the title of each sheet. Save the workbook as S_BOS1.xls in the X_case2 folder. Print the Consolidation sheet.

4. Create a macro that lets Natalie print all five statements of operation. Name the macro "PrintConsol." Place the macro in a sheet named "modConsol." Add a "Print Consol" button to the Consolidation sheet to run the macro. Save the workbook as S_BOS2.xls in the X_case2 folder. Run the macro. Print the sheet that contains the macro commands.

5. Create a stacked column chart that compares the operating earnings for each division by quarter. Place this chart in a separate chart sheet. Name the sheet "Charts." Save the workbook. Print the chart. Write a description of the information shown in this chart. (*Hint:* Create a table in the Charts sheet that is linked to the data needed for this chart.)

6. Create a pie chart that compares the operating earnings for the year (the earnings in the total column) for the four divisions. Place this chart in the sheet that contains the stacked column chart. Save the workbook, then print the charts.

7. Create an interactive macro that prints the two charts if you enter "Both," prints the column chart if you enter "Column," or prints the pie chart if you enter "Pie." Name the macro "PrintCharts." Place the macro in a separate module sheet named "modCharts." Add a Print Charts button to the Charts sheet to run the macro. Test the macro. Save the workbook. Print the macro and write a short paragraph describing your test.

8. Create five macros that let Natalie control replacing or updating the consolidation data for a selected division with the data from the individual division workbook files, or that let her redo the entire consolidation for all four divisions. If you used linking formulas in Problem 3, then revise the method used to place the results for each division in the division'61s own worksheet so Natalie can control when the results are included in the muliple-sheet workbook. Place these macros in a separate sheet named "modUpdate." Test the commands that run your macros. Save the workbook as S_BOS3.xls in the X_case2 folder. Print the sheet that contains your macros.

9. Add a menu named "Consol" to the Worksheet menu bar that the user can use to select the options in the Boston Scientific consolidation application. Figure 5 shows the structure of the menu. You will need to create additional macros that allow Natalie to view each sheet. Place these macros in a sheet named "modView." Print these macros. Revise the Documentation sheet to reflect any changes you made to the workbook. Save your workbook.

ADVEX 604 ADDITIONAL CASES

Figure 5 ◀
Structure of
menu

```
View
        Consolidation
        Medi-Tech
        Mansfield
        Microvasive Endoscopy
        Microvasive Urology
        Charts
Print
        Statements
        Charts
Update
        Consolidation
        Medi-Tech
        Mansfield
        Microvasive Endoscopy
        Microvasive Urology
        All Divisions
```

10. Launch your word processor and create a memo to Mr. Nicholas that includes the chart from Problem 5. This memo should include your summary of the results displayed in the chart. Use object linking to include the chart in the memo. Save the word processing document as S_BOS3 in the X_case2 folder. Print the document with the chart.

11. Natalie needs a summary report that contains the product sales and operating earnings data for all quarters and the annual total. She wants the report to list the product sales and operating earnings by division with a corporate total. Prepare a sketch of this report. Create the report as a separate workbook file. Use appropriate fonts and borders to enhance your report title. Use file linking to obtain the necessary data values from each of the individual division workbook files. Include a Documentation sheet. Save the workbook as S_BOS4.xls in the X_case2 folder, then print the summary report.

12. Revise your memo from Problem 10 by adding the summary report from Problem 11 as a table. The memo should now include both the chart from Problem 5 and the summary table from Problem 11. Save the word processor document as S_BOS4 in the X_case2 folder, then print the document. Did you use linking or embedding to place the summary table in the memo? Why?

13. What else could Natalie include in the consolidation workbook to make it more useful? Explain your answer.

14. Write instructions on how to work with the consolidation workbook. Assume that the user knows how to launch and run Excel, but not how to do a consolidation. Place these instructions in a separate worksheet named "Instructions" that immediately follows the Documentation worksheet in the S_BOS2.xls workbook. Print the Instructions sheet.

15. Arrange and clearly identify the printouts and answers for all the problems in this case as your documentation for the case.

ADDITIONAL CASE 3

OBJECTIVES

In this case you will:

- Create a database
- Combine worksheet files
- Create database filter lists
- Create a macro to print a database report
- Use a data form to update a database
- Create a chart from summaries of filter lists
- Create a PivotTable summary
- Create user-defined menu items
- Develop a macro with a loop to selectively change cell properties

CASE — Negotiating Salaries for the National Basketball Association

When Dr. James Naismith nailed a peach basket to a pole, he could not possibly have envisioned the popularity of the sport that he founded. Since those early days of peach baskets and volleyballs, basketball has become one of the most popular sports in the world—certainly in America.

The National Basketball Association (NBA) has become home to some of the greatest athletes in the world. The popularity of the NBA has soared over the last decade, thanks to players like Michael Jordan, Julius Erving, "Magic" Johnson, and Larry Bird. This popularity has resulted in larger attendance at games, larger television viewing audiences, and an increase in advertising sponsorships which, in turn, has led to increased player salaries.

While growing up, Jayson Kassell wanted to be a professional basketball player. However, in his senior year of college, Jayson had reconstructive knee surgery, ending his chances to ever play competitive basketball again. Jayson was still determined to make it into the NBA one way or another. Upon graduation, he was offered a job in the NBA head office in New York, where he works on Commissioner David Stern's staff.

Commissioner Stern and his staff have become concerned about the large number of player salaries being decided through arbitration. Salary arbitration is the process of negotiating a contract when both sides cannot agree to a specific dollar amount. The arbitration process is conducted through an independent third party that listens to arguments from both sides and then makes a final determination as to the terms of the contract. Over the past several years, the number of contracts decided through arbitration has more than tripled.

To help the NBA head office keep track of these arbitration cases, Jayson suggests developing an Excel database that lists the information shown in Figure 6.

Figure 6
Data definition
for a salary
arbitration
database

Field Name	Description
Player	Name of player involved in arbitration
Position	Position player plays (guard, center, forward)
Team	Name of team that is involved in arbitration
Player Bid	Amount that player is asking for
Team Bid	Amount that team is willing to pay
Settle	Amount that arbitrator feels is "fair"

The Commissioner agrees that a database like this would be useful in keeping a watchful eye on the salaries being decided through arbitration. Commissioner Stern asks Jayson to build the database and include a listing of all players who have gone through arbitration during the past five years.

You'll build the salary arbitration database by completing the following:
1. Read through all the problems for this case and develop a planning analysis sheet in preparation for creating, modifying, and manipulating the database. Use your planning analysis sheet to guide the development of your Excel solution.
2. Create the salary arbitration database, using the data definition in Figure 6. List the field names in the same order as in the data definition. Include an appropriate title, centered at the top of your worksheet. Select a typeface and point size for the title. Bold and underline the field names. Include a Documentation sheet.
3. Add the records in Figure 7 to the salary arbitration database. Save the workbook as S_NBA1.xls in the X_case3 folder or directory.

Figure 7
Records for the
salary
arbitration
database

Player	Position	Team	Player Bid	Team Bid	Settle
Miller, Reggie	Guard	Indiana	4450000	3850000	4270000
Smith, Charles	Forward	New York	2350000	1580000	2200000
Perkins, Sam	Center	Seattle	2450000	2100000	2390000
Gamble, Kevin	Forward	Boston	2650000	1950000	1960000

4. Open the P_NBA2.xls workbook in the X_case3 folder and view its contents. The workbook contains a current list of players and teams who have entered into arbitration over the past five years. Make S_NBA1.xls your active worksheet. Combine the contents of the P_NBA2.xls workbook with the salary arbitration database. The fields in the P_NBA2.xls workbook are in the same order as in Figures 6 and 7. Save the combined workbook as S_NBA3.xls in the X_case3 folder.
5. Assign a name to the database range and other appropriate ranges for use with this database. Which ranges did you name? Why?
6. Add a row that contains the averages for the three salary fields between the database field names and the worksheet title. Use functions and range names to calculate these averages. Save the workbook as S_NBA3.xls. Preview and print the salary arbitration database.
7. Create three filtered lists: one each for the guards, forwards, and centers. Arrange each list in alphabetical order by player in a separate sheet. Name each sheet for the appropriate player position. Place an appropriate title above the list. Below each list, add formulas that average the salary fields for that list. Save the workbook as S_NBA3.xls. Preview and print each list separately.
8. Create a column chart in a separate chart sheet that summarizes the averages for each position. This chart should compare the player bid, team bid, and settle contract prices for each position (guard, forward, and center). Include the appropriate headings, labels, and legends. Name the sheet "Column Chart."

9. Create three print macros. One macro should sort the entire database by player and then print it. The second should sort each of the three lists by team and player and then print these reports. The final macro should print the column chart. Save the workbook as S_NBA3.xls. Run the macro that prints the column chart. Print the sheet containing the macros.

10. Jayson wants to be able to update player records in the database. Use a data form to change the data for Otis Thorpe to the following values:

Player Bid   2250000
Team Bid   1710000
Settle   1990000

Save the workbook as S_NBA3.xls. Print the database, using the first print macro. Were all the averages updated? Was the forwards list revised? If not, update this list.

11. Jayson needs to add a new player record to the database. Use a data form to enter the following data:

Player   Chapman, Rex
Position   Guard
Team   Washington
Player Bid   1550000
Team Bid   1200000
Settle   1310000

Save the workbook as S_NBA3.xls. Print the database, using the first print macro. Were the averages updated? If not, which ones were not updated? If necessary, make the required revisions for these average calculations. You may either make any required revisions manually or create a macro for automating them. Describe the method you used.

12. Create a pivot table of positions versus the averages for the player bid, team bid, and settle amounts. Place the pivot table in a separate worksheet after the Column Chart sheet. Save the workbook as S_NBA3.xls.

13. To make the salary arbitration database easier to use, add a user-defined menu named "Database" to the Worksheet menu bar for executing the macros that you have developed. You determine the best arrangement of the menu items on this new menu. Test the menu items. Save the workbook as S_NBA3.xls.

14. Formulate a fourth filter list from the database. Explain why you selected this filter. Create the list for this filter in a separate sheet. Use an appropriate title for this list report. Save the workbook as S_NBA3.xls. Preview and print the list report.

15. Create an Instruction sheet that describes how to operate the workbook and place it immediately after the Documentation worksheet. Assume that the user knows how to access and run Excel, but not how to use the salary arbitration database. Revise the Documentation sheet for these additions to the workbook. Print both the Documentation and Instruction sheets. Save the workbook as S_NBA3.xls.

16. Commissioner Stern wants to know the variance between the team bid and the settle amounts. Add a Variance field to the Excel list and place it immediately to the right of the Settle field. The Variance is calculated by subtracting the Settle amount from the Team Bid (all Variance amounts are positive numbers). Be sure to calculate the Variance for each player. To help the Commissioner spot the salary arbitration cases that he might want to investigate further, create a macro that changes the color property of each Variance amount. A Variance of 200,000 or less is displayed in green, a Variance of 500,000 or more is displayed in red, and the other Variance amounts are displayed in black. Create a macro button for executing this macro and assign the macro to it. Label the button. Place the button in a convenient location in the sheet with the database. Add a menu item to the Database menu created in Problem 13 for running the macro. This allows the macro to be run from either the

button or the menu. Run the macro to change the colors of the Variance amounts. Test the macro by changing a Settle amount for a player so it should be displayed in a different color, then run the macro again. When your test is complete, change the Settle amount back to its original value. Save the workbook as S_NBA4.xls in the X_case3 folder. Print the sheet with the macro that changes the color property of the cells in the Variance field.

17. What else could be included in the database to make it more useful? Explain your answer. Are there other macros or charts that would be beneficial for the database to include? Describe how they would benefit the users of the database.

18. Arrange and clearly identify the printouts and answers for all the problems in this case as your documentation for the case.

ADDITIONAL CASE 4

OBJECTIVES

In this case you will:

- Use Goal Seek

- Create a data table

- Integrate worksheet data into a word processing document

- Create a customized dialog box to add records to an Excel list

- Create a custom menu

- Create macros to sort, filter, and print an Excel list

CASE

Managing Tours for Executive Travel Services

Executive Travel Services (ETS) of San Diego is a travel agency that specializes in selling packaged tours to business executives from Fortune 500 companies. ETS was started in 1982 by Tom Williams, a retired executive from a Fortune 500 company. As an executive, Tom often wished he could socialize with other top executives in an informal setting for several days. Using this idea, Tom founded ETS. ETS schedules tours that last from one to three weeks. The tours are designed to let executives enjoy a variety of activities while becoming acquainted with other executives.

In the last several months, the number of tour requests by executives has nearly doubled. ETS accidentally overbooked several of its more popular tours, such as the Orient Express. Tom discussed the overbooking problem with Melissa Merron, a recently hired travel associate. They agreed that they could use an Excel database to develop a tour management system, which would provide them with the information necessary to avoid future overbooking problems. Tom asked Melissa to analyze the requirements for the database. She worked with Tom and the other ETS associates to develop the data definition shown in Figure 8.

ADVEX 610 ADDITIONAL CASES

Figure 8
Data definition
for the Tours
database

Field Name	Description
Tour	Tour name
Month	Month tour is scheduled to start
Type	Type of tour: Golf, Photo, or Relax
Sold	Number of seats sold for tour
Open	Number of seats still open for sale
Price	Price of tour

Melissa has set up an Excel list to track the Tours database. Tom would like her to make several changes to improve the operation of the tour management system by completing the following:

1. Read all the problems for this case and develop a planning analysis sheet in preparation for creating, modifying, and operating the tour management system. Use your planning analysis sheet to develop your Excel solution.

2. Open the P_ETS1.xls workbook in the X_case4 folder or directory. Review the Tours database. What is missing from the database?

3. Add the appropriate field names in the order in which they are listed in the data definition. Center and bold each field name. Assign the range name Database to the Excel list.

4. Enhance the appearance of the report title and subtitle.

5. Tom wants to know how much revenue the tours are producing. Add a Revenue field to the Excel list and place it immediately to the right of the Price field. Revenue for a tour is calculated as the number of seats sold for the tour multiplied by the price charged for the tour.

6. Add a formula that uses a range name to sum the revenue for all tours. Name the range of the cells being added "Revenue." Place the formula so that additional records can be added easily to the Excel list. Assign the range name "TotalRevenue" to this cell. Use color, shading, or some other formatting enhancement to draw attention to the TotalRevenue cell. (*Hint:* Remember to redefine the definition of the range name Database.)

7. Include a Documentation sheet in the workbook. Save the workbook as S_ETS1.xls in the X_case4 folder. Print the Tours database.

8. Filter the Tours database list to produce a report of all golf tours with a price less than $1,000. Place the list in a separate sheet that you name "GolfSpecial." Adjust the column widths as needed. Place a title describing the list's contents above the list. Sort the list in ascending order by price. Print the list, then save the workbook as S_ETS2.xls in the X_case4 folder.

9. Use the PivotTable feature to produce a report that summarizes tour revenues by month and type of tour. Enhance the appearance of the report. Place the pivot table in a separate sheet that you name "RevenueSummary."

10. Based on the pivot table summary report in Problem 9, construct a chart. You decide the appropriate chart type. Make sure your chart has a title, contains a legend, and that each axis is labeled. Save the workbook as S_ETS2.xls. Print the summary report and chart on one page.

11. Based on the pivot table and chart in Problems 9 and 10, write a memo to Tom summarizing your observations of tour revenue by month and tour type. Incorporate both the pivot table and chart in your memo. Print your memo.

12. In a separate sheet, prepare a professional-looking income statement for ETS, based on the business model in Figure 9. Name the sheet Income Stmt. Include the logo from the P_ETS1.bmp file in the X_case4 folder in the income statement.

Figure 9 ◀
Income
statement
business model

Revenue:
Total Revenue = sum of revenue from all tours (link to total revenue developed in Problem 6)

Expenses:
Commissions = Commission rate * Total Revenue
Administration = Administrative rate * Total Revenue
Reservation System = Reservation system rate * Total Revenue
Supplies = 6000 + Supplies rate * Total Revenue
Rent = 12000
Miscellaneous = 5000
Total Expenses = sum of all expenses

Net Income = Total Revenue - Total Expenses

Input Assumptions:
Commission rate   25%
Reservation system rate   35%
Administrative rate   5%
Supplies rate 3.6%

13. Modify the Documentation sheet to include information describing the pivot table and income statement. Save the workbook as S_ETS3.xls in the X_case4 folder. Print the income statement.

14. Based on the income statement, use the Goal Seek feature to determine how high the commission rate can be raised for ETS to break even (net income zero). Print the input assumptions and income statement on a single page.

15. Formulate a Goal Seek question, using the income statement from Problem 12. Why is this goal seeking? Perform the Goal Seek analysis and print a report of the solution. Save the workbook as S_ETS4.xls in the X_case4 folder. Write a summary interpreting your results. Close the workbook.

16. Formulate an If-Then-Else condition for performing calculations in the income statement. Describe the business situation represented by the If-Then-Else condition. Make these changes beginning with the S_ETS3.xls file from Problem 13. Save this as the S_ETS5.xls workbook in the X_case4 folder, then print the Income Stmt worksheet.

17. Develop high-cost and low-cost scenarios for income statement expenses. Create at least two ranges for these scenarios. Select appropriate expense items and/or key assumptions to include in the scenarios. Print a report with each scenario and circle the values used for each. Save the workbook as S_ETS5.xls. Write a summary comparing the scenarios. Close the workbook.

ADVEX 612 ADDITIONAL CASES

18. Open the S_ETS3.xls workbook. Based on the income statement in Problem 12, prepare a two-input data table to show how net income is affected by varying the Commission rate from 20% to 35% in increments of 2.5% and the Reservation system rate from 20% to 30% in increments of 2%. Place this table in the same sheet as the income statement. Print the two-input data table only. Print the workbook.

19. Create a custom dialog box to capture data for new tours. You decide on the layout of the dialog box. Develop the VBA code to display the Tours dialog box and transfer the data from the dialog box to the Tours list. Name the module sheet that contains these macros "modDataEntry." Remember to include code to update any range names that are based on the Excel list and to copy any formulas used with each record in the list. Print the custom dialog box. Print the VBA code related to this dialog box. Save the workbook as S_ETS3.xls in the X_case4 folder.

20. Figure 10 contains data on two tours. Use the custom dialog box to add these tours to the Excel list.

Figure 10 ◀
New tours

Field	Record 1	Record 2
Tour	Desert Links	Snow Scenes
Month	Jan	Jan
Type	Golf	Photo
Sold	10	2
Open	5	8
Price	1200	750

Problems 21 to 25 involve the creation of several macros. Place all of these macros in the same module sheet, which you name "modETS."

21. Create three macros to sort the Tours database. The macros should sort by
    a. Tour
    b. Type field as the first sort key and Tour field as the second sort key
    c. Revenue (descending order)
    Assign each macro to a button that when clicked performs the desired sort. Place the buttons in a convenient location in the database sheet. Test the macros.

22. Create a macro that will print the Tours database. Assign the macro to a button. Label the button. Place the button in a convenient location in the database sheet. Test the macro.

23. Create an interactive macro to filter the database to produce a list of all tours of a specified type (user enters the type) that are still open. Assign this macro to a button. Label the button "Open tours." Create a second macro that shows all records and removes the filter arrows. Assign this macro to a button. Label the button. Place the buttons in a convenient location in the database sheet. Test the macros.

24. Create a macro to print the income statement and input assumptions. (Omit the two-input data table from Question 18 from this output). Assign the macro to a button. Label the button. Place the button in a convenient location in the Income Stmt sheet. Test the macro.

25. Create a macro to print the pivot table and chart (Problems 9 and 10). As part of the macro, refresh the pivot table. Assign the macro to a button. Label the button. Place the button in a convenient location in the RevenueSummary sheet. Test the macro.

26. Save the workbook as S_ETS3.xls in the X_case4 folder. Print the macros in the modETS sheet.

27. Add a menu, named "Tours," to the Worksheet menu bar that the user can use to select the options in the Tours database application. You decide how to organize the menu and submenu items on the menu. Save the workbook.

28. Arrange and clearly identify the printouts and answers for all the problems in this case as your documentation for the case.

ADDITIONAL CASE 5

OBJECTIVES

In this case you will:

- Use PV and PMT functions

- Print worksheet formulas

- Protect worksheet cells

- Create one-input data tables

- Create a chart

- Create macros to print, clear worksheet cells, use Goal Seek, auto_open, and auto_close

CASE — Retirement Planning Software for McKenzie Investments

As a personal financial planner, Mary Margaret McKenzie wants to increase her customer base. She has a small number of clients and if she wants to stay in business for herself, she must develop a larger base.

Since completing her degrees in economics and finance, she has had some limited success in the field of personal financial planning, focusing mostly on individuals and young families. Her approach has been to develop clients through cold calls and referrals from friends and acquaintances. Mary recently came up with an idea that she thinks will help her meet larger numbers of people than she has been able to meet in the past. She believes that if she can present free seminars to groups of employees at local companies in the region where she lives, she will be able to draw a number of new clients from those companies. She believes the companies will like the idea because they get to provide a free benefit to their employees while encouraging them to save for their retirement.

Her idea involves presenting concepts and concrete data on the need for and methods of saving for retirement. Mary has been surprised at how little people know about the need for saving, how much they will need to retire, and how they will accumulate the money they will need to retire.

Mary needs to develop a retirement planning worksheet that she can use during the seminars at company meetings. Her presentations will include different scenarios that illustrate various planning assumptions to show how much personal savings will be needed at retirement. She plans to give away the retirement planning worksheet free to those attending the seminar. Her hope is that even with the worksheet, these employees will want to become clients so that she can help them set up retirement plans, showing them how and where they could invest for retirement.

Because Mary's retirement planning worksheet will be used by individuals with very diverse backgrounds and abilities, she will need to make it as simple and easy to use as possible. On the other hand, the worksheet must present meaningful information, and it must provide opportunities for the potential clients to do many "what-ifs."

ADVEX 614 ADDITIONAL CASES

As a start, Mary has designed a planning analysis sheet (Figure 11) and sketched a retirement planning report (Figure 12) that will be the basis for the worksheet.

Figure 11 ◀
Retirement
Planning
Analysis Sheet

Planning Analysis Sheet

My goal:
Develop a retirement planning worksheet

What results do I want to see?
Retirement planning report (Figure 12)

What information do I need?
Client name
Current annual salary
Percent of salary at retirement needed for retirement income
Current Age
Age at retirement
Years in retirement
Annual return on investment
Annual salary increase
Current retirement savings (amount currently set aside for retirement)
Annual pension benefit at retirement
Annual Social Security benefit at retirement

What calculations will I perform?

Number of years until retirement=Age at retirement-Current Age
Number of months until retirement=Number of years until retirement * 12
Number of months in retirement=Years in retirement * 12
Salary at retirement
   = Current Salary * (1 + Annual salary increase)$^{\text{Years until retirement}}$
Annual retirement income goal (annual amount to be
received throughout retirement)
   = Salary at retirement * Percent of salary at retirement needed for retirement
Annual retirement income gap (funds needed to be earned by retirement)
   = Annual retirement income goal − (Annual Pension benefits + Annual
   Social Security benefits)
Monthly Retirement income gap
   = Annual income retirement gap/12
Additional dollars needed for retirement (amount still needed by retirement
day so the Annual retirement Income goal can be withdraw)
   =pv(monthly return on investment, months in retirement, monthly retirement
   income gap)*−1
Savings at retirement
   =Current retirement savings * (1 + monthly rate of
   return)$^{\text{Number of months until retirement}}$
Net savings needed for retirement
   = Additional dollars needed for retirement −Savings at retirement
Monthly savings needed to meet retirement goal (amount needed to be saved
each month until retirement in order to reach the Annual retirement income goal)
   = pmt(monthly return on investment, months until retirement, 0, Net savings
   needed for retirement, 1)*−1

Help Mary create her retirement planning worksheet by completing the following:
1. Use the planning analysis sheet (Figure 11) and the sample retirement planning report (Figure 12) to develop the retirement planning worksheet. Remember to assign range names where appropriate. Use the data in Figure 13 to check your results. (*Hint:* To raise a number to a power, use the exponentiation operator (^).) (Check figures: Annual retirement income goal = $74,292 and Monthly savings needed to meet retirement goal = $1,039.) Save the worksheet as S_RETIRE.xls in the X_Case5 folder.

Figure 12
Retirement planning worksheet

Personal Profile		Savings for Retirement	
Name	XXXXX	Annual retirement income goal	XXXXX
Age now	XX	Less: Social Security benefits	XXXXX
Age at retirement	XX	Annual pension benefits	XXXXX
Current annual salary	XXXXX	Annual retirement income gap	XXXXX
Annual percent salary increase	X	Monthly retirement income gap	XXXXX
Percent of salary at retirement	XX		
Current retirement savings	XXXXX	Additional $ needed for retirement	XXXXX
Annual Social Security benefits	XXXXX	Less: savings at retirement	XXXXX
Annual pension benefits	XXX	Net savings needed for retirement	XXXXX
Years in Retirement	XX		
Annual return on investment	XX	Monthly savings needed to meet retirement goal	XXXXX

Figure 13
Sample input data

Personal Profile	
Name	Mike Smith
Age now	45
Age at retirement	65
Current annual salary	35,000
Annual percent salary increase	5%
Percent of salary at retirement	80%
Current retirement savings	5,000
Annual Social Security benefits	10,000
Annual pension benefits	0
Years in retirement	20
Annual return on investment	8%

2. Print the formulas for the retirement planning report. Include the row and column headers in this printout.
3. Create a macro to print the retirement planning worksheet. Assign the macro to a button object. Place a descriptive label on the button. Test the macro.

ADVEX 616 ADDITIONAL CASES

4. Create a macro to clear all cells where data is input. Attach the macro to a button object. Provide a descriptive label for the button.

5. Once the user sees the results of the variable *monthly savings needed to meet retirement goal*, he or she may feel that the saving goal is out of reach and may want to explore other possibilities. One possibility is for you to use the Excel Goal Seek feature to determine the *percent of salary at retirement* one can expect to retire on, based on a change to the variable *net savings needed to meet retirement goal*.

   Create an interactive macro that uses the Excel Goal Seek feature to determine the percent of salary at retirement one can expect to retire on, based on the desired *monthly savings needed to meet retirement goal* that the user enters. (*Hint:* Record the Goal Seek process, then modify the recorded macro to make it interactive.) Assign the macro to a button. Label the button "*What If.*" Test your macro, using $1000 per month as the desired *net monthly savings needed to meet retirement goal*.

   Print the revised retirement planning report. What is the revised *percent of salary at retirement? The revised annual retirement income goal?*

6. Prepare a one-input data table that shows the effect on the variable *monthly savings needed to meet retirement goal* based on annual returns on investment that vary from 5 percent to 15 percent in increments of 1 percent. Place the data table in the same sheet as the retirement worksheet. Use the input data from Figure 13 to develop the data table. Print the data table.

7. Based on the table you created in Problem 6, create a chart to graphically display the results of the data table. You decide on the chart type. Make sure the chart has appropriate title and axis labels.

8. Create a macro to print the data table and chart (do not include the retirement planning report in this printout). Attach the macro to a button object. Provide a descriptive label for the button. Test the macro.

9. Develop an Auto_Open macro that automatically opens the S_RETIRE workbook in full screen view and removes row and column headers. Also, develop an Auto_Close macro that places the workbook in normal view and displays the row and column headers when the workbook is closed.

10. Apply protection to the worksheet so that only cells where the user can enter data can be changed. Apply color to the cells the user can change to help identify the unprotected cells. Test this protection and write a paragraph describing your test.

11. Print the macros.

12. Include a Documentation sheet that includes instructions on how to use the worksheet. Print the Documentation sheet.

13. Save the workbook.

14. What else could be included in the retirement planning worksheet to make it more useful? Suggest ways to enhance the retirement planning model. Describe how these enhancements would benefit the users of the worksheet.

15. Arrange and clearly identify the printouts and answers for all the problems in this case as your documentation for the case.

Index

$, in absolute references, ADVEX 78
* (asterisk) wildcard character, ADVEX 397
? (question mark) wildcard character, ADVEX 397

A

ABS(formula) function, ADVEX 273
absolute references, ADVEX 70, ADVEX 77-79
   adjustment after row deletions, ADVEX 91
   defined, ADVEX 77
access keys, ADVEX 585
activated charts, ADVEX 136-37
active cell, ADVEX 10
active sheet, ADVEX 10
Add Constraint dialog box, ADVEX 245
Add-In dialog box, ADVEX 285-86
Addin object, ADVEX 525
Add Tables dialog box, ADVEX 436, ADVEX 445
Add Table(s) query tool, ADVEX 434
AddToList() macro, ADVEX 567-71, ADVEX 572
adjust cells, ADVEX 215, ADVEX 216
aligning
   text in cell, ADVEX 19
   text headings, ADVEX 98
Analysis ToolPak, ADVEX 300-301
AND logical function, ADVEX 295-97
AND operator, specifying complex criteria
with, ADVEX 440
Answer Reports, ADVEX 251-52, ADVEX 259
   deleting, ADVEX 253
applications, See also custom applications;
Windows applications
   properties, ADVEX 481
area charts, ADVEX 128
arguments, ADVEX 25
arithmetic operators, ADVEX 21
   order of precedence for, ADVEX 23-24
Arrange Windows dialog box, ADVEX 351
array range formulas
   creating, ADVEX 359-60, ADVEX 361-62
   for linked references, ADVEX 361-64
   removing unwanted zeros from,
   ADVEX 362-63
   syntax, ADVEX 359
   using, ADVEX 360-61
array ranges
   defined, ADVEX 358
   linking worksheets with, ADVEX 358-64
arrow objects, adding to worksheets,
ADVEX 111-12
ascending order sorts, ADVEX 390, ADVEX 392,
ADVEX 435
ASCII files, importing, ADVEX 460-65
asset management ratios, ADVEX 53
assigning macros, ADVEX 183-86, ADVEX 190
   to button objects, ADVEX 183-86, ADVEX 192,
   ADVEX 196-97, ADVEX 258
   to shortcut keys, ADVEX 190, ADVEX 191
   to Tools menu, ADVEX 190
assigning range names, ADVEX 92
assigning text labels, ADVEX 94
Assign Macro dialog box, ADVEX 184
asterisk (*) wildcard character, ADVEX 397
Attach Note audit activity, ADVEX 372
auditing
   activities, ADVEX 372
   consolidation workbooks, ADVEX 370-74
AutoCalculate area, ADVEX 11
Auto_Close macro, ADVEX 198
AutoFill
   copying formulas with, ADVEX 71-72
   creating a series with, ADVEX 67-69
   Growth Trends, ADVEX 317
AutoFilters
   filtering lists with, ADVEX 398-401
   specifying complex criteria with,
   ADVEX 402-3
AutoFit, changing column width with, ADVEX 35
Autoformats, for charts, ADVEX 129, ADVEX 134
   variants, ADVEX 134
Auto_Open macro, ADVEX 198
   recording, ADVEX 199
   running, ADVEX 199
Auto Query tool, ADVEX 435, ADVEX 438
AutoSum tool, ADVEX 25
   creating SUM functions with, ADVEX 88
   creating total columns with, ADVEX 74
average collection period, ADVEX 53
AVERAGE(range) function, ADVEX 273,
ADVEX 278
axes
   category axis (x-axis), ADVEX 130
   primary, ADVEX 156
   value axis (y-axis), ADVEX 130
axis number formats, in charts, ADVEX 145
axis scale, in charts, ADVEX 145-46

B

background color, ADVEX 100
backward solving, ADVEX 215, See also goal
seeking
bar charts, ADVEX 128
best-case scenario, ADVEX 233, ADVEX 234-37
Between operator, specifying complex criteria
with, ADVEX 440
binding constraints, ADVEX 252
boldface, applying, ADVEX 39, ADVEX 40
bond interest rates, calculating with YIELD
function, ADVEX 284-86
Book1 workbook window, ADVEX 7
borders
   button palette, ADVEX 98
   in cells, ADVEX 98-99
   for reports, ADVEX 98-99
bottom line, ADVEX 76
break-even solution, ADVEX 217-18
Break mode, ADVEX 532
breakpoints, ADVEX 532, ADVEX 533
budgets, ADVEX 6
business models, ADVEX 6
buttons
   assigning macros to, ADVEX 183-86,
   ADVEX 192, ADVEX 196-97, ADVEX 258
   macro, in templates, ADVEX 324
   running macros with, ADVEX 193
By Category consolidation method, ADVEX 335,
ADVEX 342
By Position consolidation method, ADVEX 335,
ADVEX 342-46
   macro for, ADVEX 378-79

C

calculation, natural order of, ADVEX 24
CAPS, ADVEX 11
category axis (x-axis), for charts, ADVEX 130
category names (labels), in charts, ADVEX 130
Category Shading Options, for maps, ADVEX 169
cell addresses, ADVEX 5
cell contents
   clearing, ADVEX 31-32
   defined, ADVEX 17
   displaying, ADVEX 10
   editing, ADVEX 30-31
   empty, ADVEX 31
   moving with drag and drop, ADVEX 90
cell display, ADVEX 17
cell format, ADVEX 19, See also format
   copying with Format Painter, ADVEX 69
cell names, ADVEX 5
cell pointer, ADVEX 10
cell ranges. See ranges
cell references
   absolute, ADVEX 70, ADVEX 77-79, ADVEX 91
   alternative methods, ADVEX 5
   defined, ADVEX 5
   in linking worksheets, ADVEX 347
   mixed, ADVEX 77
   relative, ADVEX 70, ADVEX 91, ADVEX 406
   specifying by pointing, ADVEX 25-27
cells
   active, ADVEX 10
   adjust, ADVEX 215, ADVEX 216
   alignment of text in, ADVEX 19
   attaching text notes to, ADVEX 222-23
   borders in, ADVEX 98-99
   changing, ADVEX 215
   copying using clipboard, ADVEX 72-73
   defined, ADVEX 4
   protecting, ADVEX 112-14
   set, ADVEX 215
   shading, ADVEX 99-100
   target, ADVEX 215, ADVEX 218
cell width, ADVEX 20
center alignment, ADVEX 19
   center on page option, ADVEX 101
   horizontal, ADVEX 102
   for text in charts, ADVEX 148
   for reports, ADVEX 98
   vertical, for text in charts, ADVEX 148
changing cells
   naming, ADVEX 232
   for scenarios, ADVEX 231
   specifying for optimization problems,
   ADVEX 243-44
ChartDataChoice macro, ADVEX 505-6
chart handles, ADVEX 135
charts, ADVEX 125-70, See also column charts
   activating for editing, ADVEX 136-37
   adding data series to, ADVEX 137-38
   Autoformats, ADVEX 129, ADVEX 134
   axis number formats, ADVEX 145
   axis scale, ADVEX 145-46
   category axis (x-axis), ADVEX 130
   category names (labels), ADVEX 130
   centering text in, ADVEX 148

color of, ADVEX 146-47
creating from pivot tables, ADVEX 424
creating with macro, ADVEX 503-4
data markers, ADVEX 130
data points, ADVEX 130
data series, ADVEX 126, ADVEX 130-31
deleting data series from, ADVEX 138-39
elements of, ADVEX 130
embedded, ADVEX 131, ADVEX 135
fill patterns, ADVEX 146-47
fonts in, ADVEX 144-45
format, ADVEX 128, ADVEX 139, ADVEX 141-42
graphic objects in, ADVEX 147-48,
ADVEX 157-59
legends, ADVEX 130, ADVEX 134
number setting sheet, ADVEX 145
plot area in, ADVEX 154
point size in, ADVEX 144-45
primary axis, ADVEX 156
printing, ADVEX 142-43
Print Preview, ADVEX 142, ADVEX 143
resizing, ADVEX 135-36
reviewing, ADVEX 143-46
saving, ADVEX 142
selecting, ADVEX 135, ADVEX 136
subtitles, ADVEX 130, ADVEX 144-45
tick marks, ADVEX 130
titles, ADVEX 130, ADVEX 144-45
of two-input data tables, ADVEX 229
uses of, ADVEX 126
value axis (y-axis), ADVEX 130
value labels, ADVEX 130
what-if analysis with, ADVEX 151-53
chart sheets, ADVEX 131
chart types, ADVEX 126, ADVEX 128-29
   area, ADVEX 128
   bar, ADVEX 128
   changing, ADVEX 139-42
   column, ADVEX 128, ADVEX 131-38
   combination, ADVEX 128, ADVEX 156-57
   doughnut, ADVEX 128
   line, ADVEX 128, ADVEX 141
   open-high-low-close (OHLC), ADVEX 128
   picture, ADVEX 157-59
   pie, ADVEX 126, ADVEX 128, ADVEX 148-51
   radar, ADVEX 128
   stacked bar, ADVEX 128
   stacked column, ADVEX 128, ADVEX 140
   subtypes, ADVEX 128, ADVEX 140, ADVEX 142
   3-D area, ADVEX 129
   3-D bar, ADVEX 129
   3-D column, ADVEX 129, ADVEX 153-55
   3-D line, ADVEX 129
   3-D pie, ADVEX 129
   3-D surface, ADVEX 129
   XY, ADVEX 128
ChartWizard, ADVEX 129
   charting results of data tables with,
   ADVEX 229
   creating charts from pivot tables with,
   ADVEX 424
   creating column chart with, ADVEX 131-32,
   ADVEX 133-35
   creating combination charts with,
   ADVEX 156
check boxes, in dialog boxes, ADVEX 543-44,
ADVEX 561
circular references, in consolidation workbooks, ADVEX 371-73
Clear method, ADVEX 491, ADVEX 492-93
client programs
   defined, ADVEX 159
   embedding objects in, ADVEX 448
clipboard
   copying cells with, ADVEX 72-73
   copying Excel objects to, ADVEX 450
   defined, ADVEX 72
Code pane, in Debug Window, ADVEX 532
code template, ADVEX 525
coefficients, technical, ADVEX 240
collections, of objects, ADVEX 479
   using VBA to refer to, ADVEX 480
colon (:), in cell ranges, ADVEX 36
color
   background, ADVEX 100
   category shading for maps, ADVEX 169-70
   of charts, ADVEX 146-47
   of data markers, ADVEX 158
column charts, ADVEX 131-38
   activating for editing, ADVEX 136-37
   Autoformats, ADVEX 134
   Autoformat variants, ADVEX 134
   creating with ChartWizard, ADVEX 131-32,
   ADVEX 133-35
   nonadjacent ranges for, ADVEX 132-33
   purpose, ADVEX 128
   resizing, ADVEX 135-36

side-by-side, ADVEX 151-53
    stacked, ADVEX 140
    3-D, ADVEX 153-55
    what-if analysis with, ADVEX 151-53
column fields, in pivot tables, ADVEX 409
Column Input cells, ADVEX 225, ADVEX 227-28
column-oriented data tables, ADVEX 220-24
columns
    hidden, ADVEX 103-4
    inserting, ADVEX 87
    unhiding, ADVEX 104
column width
    resizing with AutoFit, ADVEX 35
    resizing with resize arrow, ADVEX 35-36
combination charts, ADVEX 156-57
combination list-edit boxes, ADVEX 543-44,
ADVEX 555-58
comma format, ADVEX 38
command buttons, in dialog boxes, ADVEX 543-44
commands
    selecting on menu bar, ADVEX 9
    in tutorials, ADVEX 6
comments, in VBA code, ADVEX 188
common fields, in relational databases, ADVEX 433
compile-time errors, ADVEX 527
compiling, ADVEX 527
compound decision tables, logical functions for,
ADVEX 296-97
compound documents
    defined, ADVEX 447
    embedding objects in, ADVEX 448
Consolidate dialog box, ADVEX 343-45,
ADVEX 367-68
consolidation, ADVEX 333-69
    automating with macros, ADVEX 377-79
    By Category method, ADVEX 335, ADVEX 342
    By Position method, ADVEX 335,
    ADVEX 342-46, ADVEX 378-79
    data flow diagram for, ADVEX 338-39
    defined, ADVEX 334
    of multiple workbook files, ADVEX 342-46
    with outline groups, ADVEX 367-70
    overview, ADVEX 334-39
    reviewing results, ADVEX 346
    steps in, ADVEX 344
    SUM function in, ADVEX 335, ADVEX 340,
    ADVEX 342
    3-D Formula method, ADVEX 335,
    ADVEX 347-49
    updating results, ADVEX 346-47
    With Groups method, ADVEX 335
consolidation workbooks
    auditing, ADVEX 370-74
    circular references in, ADVEX 371-73
    expanding, ADVEX 374-77
    Group edit mode, ADVEX 349-51
constants
    defined, ADVEX 214
    in linear regression, ADVEX 302
    shadow prices for, ADVEX 253
constraints
    changing, ADVEX 247-49
    formulas, ADVEX 243-44
    integer, ADVEX 249-51
    in optimization problems, ADVEX 239,
    ADVEX 243, ADVEX 244, ADVEX 245-46
Consumer Price Index (CPI), ADVEX 460
controls, dialog box, ADVEX 543-44
    check boxes, ADVEX 543-44, ADVEX 561
    combination list-edit boxes, ADVEX 543-44,
    ADVEX 555-58
    command buttons, ADVEX 543-44
    drop-down list boxes, ADVEX 543-44,
    ADVEX 561
    edit boxes, ADVEX 543-44, ADVEX 549-51,
    ADVEX 561
    group boxes, ADVEX 543-44, ADVEX 552-53
    labels, ADVEX 543-44, ADVEX 547-49,
    ADVEX 561
    list boxes, ADVEX 543-44, ADVEX 561
    naming, ADVEX 550, ADVEX 551
    option buttons, ADVEX 543-44,
    ADVEX 552-55, ADVEX 561
    placing in custom dialog boxes,
    ADVEX 547-58
    running, ADVEX 552
    scroll bars, ADVEX 543-44, ADVEX 561
    spinners, ADVEX 543-44, ADVEX 561
    viewing, ADVEX 551
control structures
    Do loop statement, ADVEX 501
    For. . .Next statement, ADVEX 501
    If-Then-Else statement, ADVEX 501-7
    Select Case statement, ADVEX 501
Copy button, ADVEX 72, ADVEX 73

copying
    cells using clipboard, ADVEX 72-73
    formulas, ADVEX 69-73, ADVEX 106
    formulas with rounding, ADVEX 80-81
    objects between applications, ADVEX 159-62
Copy method, ADVEX 491, ADVEX 492-93
COST(formula) function, ADVEX 273
COUNT(range) function, ADVEX 273
    in pivot tables, ADVEX 412
CreateChart macro, ADVEX 503-4
Create Links to Source Data option, ADVEX 368
criteria
    custom, specifying with AutoFilters,
    ADVEX 402-3
    exact-match values, ADVEX 439
    specifying values, ADVEX 439-40
Criteria Equals query tool, ADVEX 434
Criteria pane, of Query Window, ADVEX 437,
ADVEX 439-42
currency format, ADVEX 38
Currency Style, ADVEX 145
current ratio, ADVEX 53
cursor movement keys, ADVEX 12
custom applications, ADVEX 737-91
    custom dialog boxes, ADVEX 539,
    ADVEX 543-66
    custom menus, ADVEX 538, ADVEX 582-91
    message boxes, ADVEX 539
    planning, ADVEX 541-43
    reporting options, ADVEX 540
    running, ADVEX 538-41
    sort options, ADVEX 540
Custom AutoFilters, ADVEX 402-3
custom dialog boxes
    building, ADVEX 545-47
    controls, ADVEX 543-44, ADVEX 561
    creating, ADVEX 543-44
    displaying automatically with macro,
    ADVEX 559-60
    inserting dialog sheets for, ADVEX 545-46
    placing controls in, ADVEX 546-58
    processing data entered in, 559, 561-66
    renaming, ADVEX 546-47
    resizing, ADVEX 546-47
    sketch for, ADVEX 545
    testing, ADVEX 558-59
custom footers, ADVEX 102
custom headers, ADVEX 101
custom menus, ADVEX 582-91
    adding menu items to, ADVEX 587-88
    adding to existing menu bar, ADVEX 585-86
    creating, ADVEX 582
    creating submenus for, ADVEX 588-90
    sketching, ADVEX 583
    terms, ADVEX 583
    testing, ADVEX 591
Cycle Thru Total query tool, ADVEX 434

D

data
    categories, for maps, ADVEX 167
    consolidating, ADVEX 342-46
    definition tables, for lists, ADVEX 389
    describing with functions, ADVEX 275-79
    detail, ADVEX 367, ADVEX 368-69
    editing characters, ADVEX 19
    fields, in pivot tables, ADVEX 409
    grouping in pivot tables, ADVEX 421-23
    hiding, ADVEX 103-4
    integrity, in linked workbooks, ADVEX 356-47
    linking, ADVEX 447, ADVEX 449
    pasting, ADVEX 447, ADVEX 448
    points, in charts, ADVEX 130
    sharing, ADVEX 447, ADVEX 448-49
    sharing among Windows programs,
    ADVEX 447
    transferring among Windows programs,
    ADVEX 447
    unhiding, ADVEX 104
Database functions, ADVEX 273
databases, See also lists
    defined, ADVEX 388
    external, ADVEX 432-33
        accessing with MS Query, ADVEX 437
        creating pivot tables for, ADVEX 443-46
Data Consolidate command, ADVEX 342-43,
ADVEX 351, ADVEX 357
    using outline groups, ADVEX 367-70
DataEntry macro, ADVEX 572-75
data flow diagrams (DFDs), for consolidation,
ADVEX 338-39
data forms
    adding records with, ADVEX 394-95
    defined, ADVEX 394
    deleting records with, ADVEX 397-98
    maintaining lists with, ADVEX 394-98
    searching for records with, ADVEX 396-97

Data Map Control dialog box, ADVEX 165,
ADVEX 168-69
Data Map feature, ADVEX 162-70
data markers
    in charts, ADVEX 130
    color for, ADVEX 158
    patterns for, ADVEX 158
    pictures as, ADVEX 157
Data pane
    adding fields on, ADVEX 438-39
    of Query Window, ADVEX 437
data series
    adding to existing charts, ADVEX 137-38
    arranging for charts, ADVEX 130-31
    defined, ADVEX 126, ADVEX 130
    deleting from charts, ADVEX 138-39
    fill patterns, ADVEX 147
Data Source List, ADVEX 438
data sources
    adding, ADVEX 438
    selecting for queries, ADVEX 435-38
data tables, ADVEX 219-30, See also one-input
data tables; two-input data tables
    calculating results, ADVEX 224-26
    charting results, ADVEX 229
    column input cells, ADVEX 224
    column-oriented, ADVEX 220-24
    defined, ADVEX 219
    displaying results, ADVEX 224-25
    one-input, ADVEX 219-25
    row input cells, ADVEX 223
    row-oriented, ADVEX 225
    setting up with drag-and-fill, ADVEX 225-26
    two-input, ADVEX 219, ADVEX 225-28
    what-if analysis on, ADVEX 230
Date & Time functions, ADVEX 273
    Date/Time macro, ADVEX 206-7
    DAY(date) function, ADVEX 273
    TODAY function, ADVEX 97-98
date format, ADVEX 97
debt management ratios, ADVEX 54
debugging macros, ADVEX 532-36
Debug Window
    Code pane, ADVEX 532
    Intermediate pane, ADVEX 532
    Watch pane, ADVEX 532
decimal places, displaying, ADVEX 38, ADVEX 416
Decimal Places spinner, ADVEX 416
decision structure, Select Case statement for,
ADVEX 508-18
decision tables, ADVEX 287-95
    compound, ADVEX 296-97
    IF function, ADVEX 287-92
    modifying, ADVEX 291
    VLOOKUP function, ADVEX 287,
    ADVEX 292-95
    for what-if analysis, ADVEX 290
decision variables, ADVEX 239, ADVEX 246
    specifying integers for, ADVEX 249-50
Decrease Decimal button, ADVEX 38
deleting
    Answer Reports, ADVEX 253
    lines from macros, ADVEX 204
    macros, ADVEX 205
    records from lists, using data forms,
    ADVEX 397-98
    rows, ADVEX 90-91
    worksheets, ADVEX 495-96
delimited text files, ADVEX 461
dependent variables, in linear regression,
ADVEX 301
depreciation, ADVEX 60
descending order sorts, ADVEX 390, ADVEX 435
descriptive statistics, ADVEX 275
destination programs
    defined, ADVEX 159
    embedding objects in, ADVEX 448
    linking objects to, ADVEX 449
    updating linked objects from, ADVEX 454-56
destination workbooks, in linking worksheets,
ADVEX 347
detail data, displaying/hiding, ADVEX 367,
ADVEX 368-69, ADVEX 413
dialog boxes, See also custom dialog boxes
    controls, ADVEX 543-44
    creating with InputBox function,
    ADVEX 497-500
    in custom applications, ADVEX 539
DialogSheet objects, Show method, ADVEX 560
dialog sheets, inserting, ADVEX 545-46
Dim statements, ADVEX 496-97
display, of custom dialog boxes, macro for,
ADVEX 559-60
DisplayForm() macro, ADVEX 564-67,
ADVEX 570-71, ADVEX 572
.doc filename extension, ADVEX 451

MICROSOFT EXCEL FOR WINDOWS ADVANCED INDEX ADVEX 619

Documentation worksheets, ADVEX 76, ADVEX 107
Do. . .Loop statement, ADVEX 501, ADVEX 513, ADVEX 515
doughnut charts, ADVEX 128
Do While. . .Loop statement, ADVEX 513-14
    syntax, ADVEX 514
drag-and-drop
    moving cell contents with, ADVEX 90
    moving data between applications with, ADVEX 159
drag-and-fill, setting up data table with, ADVEX 225-26
Drawing toolbar, ADVEX 110
drop-down list boxes, in dialog boxes, ADVEX 543-44, ADVEX 561
Dynamic Data Exchange (DDE), ADVEX 347, ADVEX 377

E

earnings per share (EPS), ADVEX 54
edit boxes, in dialog boxes, ADVEX 543-44, ADVEX 549-51, ADVEX 561
editing
    Group edit mode, ADVEX 349-51
    macros, ADVEX 203-5
    within a cell, ADVEX 30-31
Edit, Links audit activity, ADVEX 372
electronic spreadsheets, ADVEX 4
elements, of collections, ADVEX 479
elevation, in 3-D column charts, ADVEX 154, ADVEX 155
embedded charts, ADVEX 131, ADVEX 135
    adding and deleting data series, ADVEX 137-39
    resizing, ADVEX 135-36
embedding
    as data sharing method, ADVEX 447, ADVEX 448-49
    vs. linking, ADVEX 456
    maps as embedded objects, ADVEX 165
    objects in word processor documents, ADVEX 457-58
    updating embedded objects, ADVEX 459
EmployeeData dialog box, ADVEX 394
empty cells, ADVEX 31
End Function keywords, ADVEX 477
End Select keyword, ADVEX 508
End Sub keyword, ADVEX 188
Engineering functions, ADVEX 273
errors
    compile-time, ADVEX 527
    logic, ADVEX 531
    minimizing, with range names, ADVEX 93-94
    rounding, ADVEX 78-79
    run-time, ADVEX 529-30
    syntax, ADVEX 527-29
error values, ADVEX 73, ADVEX 74
    #NAME?, ADVEX 94
    #VALUE!, ADVEX 87
exact-match criteria, ADVEX 439
Excel
    exiting, ADVEX 47
    integrating into other Windows applications, ADVEX 431-65
    launching (starting), ADVEX 7-8
Excel 4 Macro language, ADVEX 191
executive information systems (EISs)
    defined, ADVEX 334
    Planning Analysis Worksheet, ADVEX 336
    purpose of, ADVEX 334
    templates for, ADVEX 336
exiting, ADVEX 47
expense analysis, functions for, ADVEX 277, ADVEX 278
Expense Analysis worksheet section, ADVEX 275-76
EXP(formula) function, ADVEX 273
    in regression analysis, ADVEX 310, ADVEX 311, ADVEX 316
exploding pie charts, ADVEX 150
external databases, See also relational databases
    accessing with MS Query, ADVEX 437
    creating pivot tables from, ADVEX 443-46

F

field buttons
    for pivot tables, ADVEX 411-14
    repositioning, ADVEX 414-15
field header rows, in lists, ADVEX 389
field lists, in Table pane of Query Window, ADVEX 437
field names, in lists, ADVEX 389
fields
    adding on Data pane of Query Window, ADVEX 438
    adding to pivot tables, ADVEX 417-18
    common, in relational databases, ADVEX 433
    in lists, ADVEX 388
    removing from pivot tables, ADVEX 418-19

repositioning on pivot table, ADVEX 414-15
filename extensions
    .doc, ADVEX 451
    .wri, ADVEX 451
    .xlt, ADVEX 318
filenames, workbook, ADVEX 9, ADVEX 29-30
fill handle, ADVEX 67
fill patterns
    in charts, ADVEX 146-47
    defined, ADVEX 146
filtering
    with AutoFilters, ADVEX 398-401
    custom options, ADVEX 400
    defined, ADVEX 398
    specifying complex criteria with AutoFilters, ADVEX 402-3
Financial functions, ADVEX 273, ADVEX 279-86
Find Prev button, ADVEX 395
fixed-width text files, ADVEX 461
flow charts
    complex macros, ADVEX 474
    Do While. . .Loop statement, ADVEX 514
    examining object properties, ADVEX 489
    If-Then-Else statement, ADVEX 502
    interactive macros, ADVEX 499
    LoanCalc macro, ADVEX 515
    manipulating worksheet objects, ADVEX 494
    SetColor macro, ADVEX 511
    transferring data between dialog box and holding area, ADVEX 563
    VBA macros, ADVEX 484
fonts
    changing, ADVEX 40-41
    in charts, ADVEX 144-45
    defined, ADVEX 39, ADVEX 40
    for maps, ADVEX 169
    point size, ADVEX 40-41, ADVEX 144-45
    styles, ADVEX 39-40
Font Size list arrow, for charts, ADVEX 144
footers
    custom, ADVEX 102
    defined, ADVEX 100
    specifying, ADVEX 100, ADVEX 101-2
forecast analyses
    growth rate, ADVEX 308-17
    printing, ADVEX 308
    using linear regression, ADVEX 306-17
format
    cell, ADVEX 19, ADVEX 69
    changing, ADVEX 37-41
    for charts, ADVEX 139, ADVEX 141-42
    comma, ADVEX 38
    copying, ADVEX 69
    currency, ADVEX 38
    date, ADVEX 97
    defined, ADVEX 37
    general, ADVEX 23, ADVEX 37
    linking formulas, ADVEX 354
    numbers in pivot tables, ADVEX 416-17
    percent, ADVEX 38-39
    protection, ADVEX 112
Format Column Group menu, ADVEX 139-40
Format Font menu choice, ADVEX 166-67
Format Painter, ADVEX 106, ADVEX 354
    copying cell format with, ADVEX 69
Formatting toolbar, ADVEX 10
formula, optimization, ADVEX 242-43
formula bar, ADVEX 10, ADVEX 22
    adding graphic objects with, ADVEX 147
formulas
    absolute references in, ADVEX 70, ADVEX 77-79
    arithmetic operators in, ADVEX 21
    building by pointing, ADVEX 25-27
    changing key assumptions in, ADVEX 87-88
    characters beginning, ADVEX 21-22
    constraint, ADVEX 243-44
    constructing, ADVEX 21
    copying, ADVEX 69-73, ADVEX 80-81, ADVEX 106
    copying with AutoFill, ADVEX 71-72
    defined, ADVEX 17, ADVEX 21
    display of, ADVEX 22
    entering, ADVEX 21-24, ADVEX 69
    entering in data tables, ADVEX 227
    linking worksheets with, ADVEX 351-58
    order of precedence in, ADVEX 23-24
    range names in, ADVEX 93-96
    readability of, ADVEX 94
    recalculating, ADVEX 22
    referencing values in other worksheets, ADVEX 105-6
    relative references in, ADVEX 70
    with rounding, copying to other cells, ADVEX 80-81
    rounding errors, ADVEX 78-79
    using ROUND function with, ADVEX 79-82
    in what-if analysis, ADVEX 46

For. . .Next Loop statements, ADVEX 509-10
    syntax, ADVEX 510
For. . .Next statement, ADVEX 501
    in macros, ADVEX 510-13
fourth-generation language (4GL), ADVEX 24
F statistic, in linear regression, ADVEX 302, ADVEX 303
Full Screen view, ADVEX 199
function procedures, ADVEX 477
    macros, ADVEX 476
    structure of, ADVEX 477
functions, ADVEX 272-98
    arguments in, ADVEX 25
    defined, ADVEX 17, ADVEX 25
    describing data with, ADVEX 275-79
    entering, ADVEX 25
    entering with Function Wizard, ADVEX 276-77
    entering with range names, ADVEX 278
    names, ADVEX 25
    overview, ADVEX 272-75
    user-defined, ADVEX 477
Function Wizard, ADVEX 243
    displaying PMT function with, ADVEX 281
    entering functions with, ADVEX 276-77
    selecting YIELD function with, ADVEX 285-86
    specifying ROUND function with, ADVEX 79-80

G

general format, ADVEX 23, ADVEX 37
Get External Data dialog box, ADVEX 441
GetProperty macro, ADVEX 490-91
Goal Seek, ADVEX 217-19
Goal Seek dialog box, ADVEX 219
goal-seeking
    defined, ADVEX 215
    split window for, ADVEX 217
    trial-and-error method, ADVEX 215-16
    using Goal Seek, ADVEX 217-19
GoToAssumptions macro, ADVEX 180-87
    assigning to button object, ADVEX 183-86
    recording, ADVEX 180-82
    running, ADVEX 182-83
    viewing VBA code for, ADVEX 186-87
graphic objects, ADVEX 109-12
    adding to charts, ADVEX 147-48, ADVEX 157-59
    positioning, ADVEX 109
    types of, ADVEX 109
GridlinesOff macro, ADVEX 207
gross profit, ADVEX 57, ADVEX 60
group boxes, in dialog boxes, ADVEX 543-44, ADVEX 552-55
Group edit mode, in consolidation worksheets, ADVEX 349-51
grouping, data in pivot tables, ADVEX 421-23
Grouping dialog box, ADVEX 423
groups
    defined, ADVEX 364
    outline, ADVEX 364-70
Group tool, ADVEX 413, ADVEX 423
GROWTH function, in regression analysis, ADVEX 317
growth rate, ADVEX 308-9
    defined, ADVEX 65
    entering formulas for, ADVEX 69
    vs. linear change, ADVEX 309
    negative, ADVEX 65
growth rate forecasts, ADVEX 308-17
    printing, ADVEX 317
    steps in, ADVEX 316
Growth Trends, ADVEX 317
GROWTH(y-range, x-range, new-x-value) function, ADVEX 273

H

HeadCount sheet, ADVEX 450
headers
    custom, ADVEX 101
    defined, ADVEX 100
    specifying, ADVEX 100, ADVEX 101-2
Help
    query tool, ADVEX 435
    VBA, ADVEX 524
Help Desk, for tutorials, ADVEX 33-34
Hide Detail tool, ADVEX 413
hiding/unhiding
    columns, ADVEX 103-4
    criteria query, ADVEX 434
    data, ADVEX 103-4
    data map control, ADVEX 168
    detail data, ADVEX 367, ADVEX 368-69, ADVEX 413
    pivot table items, ADVEX 419-20
    rows, ADVEX 103-4
    worksheets, ADVEX 103-4

ADVEX 620 MICROSOFT EXCEL FOR WINDOWS ADVANCED INDEX

hierarchies
  objects in, ADVEX 478-79
  referencing objects in, with VBA,
    ADVEX 480-81
HLOOKUP function, ADVEX 293
horizontal centering, ADVEX 102
horizontal splitter, ADVEX 85

I

IF function, ADVEX 287-92
  arguments, ADVEX 287
  building in decision tables with, ADVEX 290
  relational operators in, ADVEX 288
If-Then-Else statement, ADVEX 501-7
  in custom dialog box display macros,
    ADVEX 560
  syntax, ADVEX 502
importing, text files, ADVEX 460-65
income before taxes, ADVEX 60
income taxes, ADVEX 61
independent variables, in linear regression,
  ADVEX 301
Information functions, ADVEX 273
In operator, specifying complex criteria with,
  ADVEX 440
input, in planning analysis sheet, ADVEX 14
InputBox function, ADVEX 497-500
  syntax for, ADVEX 498
input cells
  column, ADVEX 223, ADVEX 225-26,
    ADVEX 227-28
  for data tables, ADVEX 220
  row, ADVEX 223, ADVEX 224
  for scenarios, ADVEX 232
input range, in linear regression, ADVEX 301,
  ADVEX 302
inserting
  columns, ADVEX 87
  dialog sheets, ADVEX 545-46
  modules sheets, ADVEX 484-85
  rows, ADVEX 86-89
instructions sheets, for templates, ADVEX 319
integer constraints, in optimization problems,
  ADVEX 249-51
integrating programs, ADVEX 159-62
interactive macros, ADVEX 475, ADVEX 497-500
interactive message boxes, ADVEX 516
Intercept constant, ADVEX 302, ADVEX 311,
  ADVEX 314
INTERCEPT(y-range, x-range) function,
  ADVEX 273, ADVEX 307
interest expense, ADVEX 60
interface, dialog boxes as, ADVEX 543-44
Intermediate pane, in Debug Window, ADVEX 532
Internet, ADVEX 460
intervals, ADVEX 162
INT(formula) function, ADVEX 273
inventory turnover, ADVEX 53
ISERROR(formula), function, ADVEX 273
ISNUMBER(formula) function, ADVEX 273
ISTEXT(formula) function, ADVEX 273
italics, applying, ADVEX 39
items, in collections, ADVEX 479

J

joining tables, ADVEX 443-46

K

key assumptions, changing, ADVEX 87-88
Key Input Assumptions worksheet section,
  ADVEX 75, ADVEX 77
  macro for moving to, ADVEX 180-87

L

labels
  in dialog boxes, ADVEX 543-44, ADVEX 547-49,
    ADVEX 561
  text, entering, ADVEX 17-19
Lagrange multiplier, ADVEX 253
landscape, orientation, ADVEX 101
LARGE(range-list, position) function, ADVEX 274
lease payment, calculating with PMT function,
  ADVEX 282-83
least-squares regression analysis, ADVEX 298,
  ADVEX 309, ADVEX 312-13, ADVEX 317
left-alignment, ADVEX 19
LEFT(text,num-chars) function, ADVEX 274
left-to-right rule, order of precedence, ADVEX 24
legends
  for charts, ADVEX 130, ADVEX 134
  for maps, ADVEX 165, ADVEX 167,
    ADVEX 168-69
LEN(text) function, ADVEX 274
Like operator, specifying complex criteria with,
  ADVEX 440
Limits Reports, ADVEX 251, ADVEX 254-55

linear change, ADVEX 308
  growth rate vs., ADVEX 309
linear programming
  constraints in, ADVEX 239-40
  defined, ADVEX 239
linear regression, See also regression analysis
  dependent variables, ADVEX 301
  forecasted values, ADVEX 306-8
  F statistic, ADVEX 302, ADVEX 303
  general equation, ADVEX 298
  input range, ADVEX 301, ADVEX 302
  interpreting results, ADVEX 303
  Line Fit Plots, ADVEX 302, ADVEX 305
  output range, ADVEX 301-2
  Residuals Plots, ADVEX 302, ADVEX 305
  R-square value, ADVEX 299, ADVEX 302
  steps in, ADVEX 302, ADVEX 307
  summary output, ADVEX 302
line charts, ADVEX 128, ADVEX 141
line continuation characters, ADVEX 500
Line Fit Plots, in linear regression, ADVEX 302,
  ADVEX 305
LINEST(y-range,x-range,constant,stats)
function, ADVEX 274
linking
  as data sharing method, ADVEX 447,
    ADVEX 449
  defined, ADVEX 347
  vs. embedding, ADVEX 456
  to word processing documents, ADVEX 451-53
  updating linked objects, ADVEX 454-56
  worksheets to word processor documents,
    ADVEX 449-50
linking formulas, ADVEX 347, ADVEX 351-58
  creating, ADVEX 353-54
  steps in using, ADVEX 353
  syntax, ADVEX 352
  undoing, ADVEX 357
linking worksheets, ADVEX 347-64
  adding worksheets, ADVEX 374-77
  with array ranges, ADVEX 358-64
  data integrity in, ADVEX 356-57
  destination workbooks, ADVEX 347
  formulas for, ADVEX 351-58
  Group edit mode, ADVEX 349-51
  source workbooks, ADVEX 347
  strategies for, ADVEX 357-58
  3-D SUM function formulas, ADVEX 347-49
liquidity ratios, ADVEX 53
list arrows
  in AutoFilter, ADVEX 399
  removing, ADVEX 403
list boxes, in dialog boxes, ADVEX 543-44,
  ADVEX 561
  drop-down, ADVEX 543-44
list-edit boxes, combination, in dialog boxes,
  ADVEX 543-44, ADVEX 555-58
lists, ADVEX 387-424
  adding records to, ADVEX 394-95
  automating reports with macros,
    ADVEX 406-7
  vs. databases, ADVEX 388
  data definition tables for, ADVEX 389
  defined, ADVEX 388
  field names, ADVEX 389
  fields, ADVEX 388
  filtering with AutoFilters, ADVEX 398-401
  guidelines for creating, ADVEX 389
  inserting subtotals in, ADVEX 404-6
  macro for adding items to, ADVEX 567-71
  maintaining with data forms, ADVEX 394-98
  planning, ADVEX 388-89
  records in, ADVEX 388
  sorting data in, ADVEX 390-93
  sorting on multiple sort fields, ADVEX 391-93
  sorting on one sort field, ADVEX 390-91
  specifying complex criteria with
    AutoFilters, ADVEX 402-3
  summarizing with pivot tables, ADVEX 408-9
LN(formula) function, ADVEX 274
  in regression analysis, ADVEX 310-16
LoanCalc macro, ADVEX 515-17
loan payments, calculating with PMT function,
  ADVEX 279-82
local maximums, ADVEX 250
local minimums, ADVEX 250
locked cells, ADVEX 112-14
logarithmic transformations, in regression
analysis, ADVEX 310-16
LOGEST(y-range,x-range,constant,stats)
function, ADVEX 274
  in regression analysis, ADVEX 317
logical functions, ADVEX 273, ADVEX 295-98
  rules, ADVEX 296
logical operators, specifying complex criteria
with, ADVEX 440

logic errors, VBA, ADVEX 531
Lookup & Reference functions, ADVEX 273
lookup tables, ADVEX 292-95
loop control structure, in macros, ADVEX 509-10
lower limits, in optimization reports, ADVEX 251
LOWER(text) function, ADVEX 274

M

macro buttons
  creating, ADVEX 258
  in templates, ADVEX 324
Macro code, ADVEX 188
Macro dialog box, ADVEX 183
Macro Error dialog box, ADVEX 205
Macro Planning Sheets
  for consolidation updates, ADVEX 378
  for macros in templates, ADVEX 322
  for optimization macros, ADVEX 257
macro recorder, ADVEX 179-83, ADVEX 527
macros, ADVEX 177-205
  adding VBA code to, ADVEX 474-75
  assigning, ADVEX 190
    to button objects, ADVEX 183-86,
    ADVEX 192, ADVEX 196-97, ADVEX 258
    to shortcut keys, ADVEX 190, ADVEX 191
    to Tools menu, ADVEX 190
  automating consolidations with,
    ADVEX 377-79
  automating custom dialog box display
    with, ADVEX 559-60
  automating list reports with, ADVEX 406-7
  complex, building with VBA, ADVEX 473-75
  copying VBA code between, ADVEX 505-6
  creating, ADVEX 179-83
    with macro recorder, ADVEX 179-83
    with VBA, ADVEX 179, ADVEX 483-87
  debugging, ADVEX 532-36
  defined, ADVEX 177, ADVEX 178
  deleting, ADVEX 205
  deleting lines from, ADVEX 204
  describing, ADVEX 180, ADVEX 181
  editing, ADVEX 203-5, ADVEX 570
  Excel 4 Macro language, ADVEX 191
  for executing other macros, ADVEX 572-75
  function procedure, ADVEX 476
  interactive, ADVEX 475, ADVEX 497-500
  logic errors, ADVEX 531
  loop control structures, ADVEX 509-10
  monitoring variable and expression
    values, ADVEX 533-34
  naming, ADVEX 180-82
  planning, ADVEX 180
  printing, ADVEX 200
  for printing reports, ADVEX 579-82
  procedures vs., ADVEX 476-77
  processing data entered in custom dialog
    boxes with, ADVEX 559, ADVEX 561-66
  readability of, ADVEX 485
  recording, ADVEX 180-82, ADVEX 188-89,
    ADVEX 195-97, ADVEX 257-58, ADVEX 323-24,
    ADVEX 406-7, ADVEX 567-69
  regression analysis with, ADVEX 323-26
  reserved names, ADVEX 198
  ResetData, ADVEX 188-94
  running, ADVEX 182-83, ADVEX 487
    automatically, ADVEX 198-99
    samples, ADVEX 178-79
    using buttons, ADVEX 193
    using shortcut keys, ADVEX 193-94
  run-time errors, ADVEX 529-30
  setting recording options, ADVEX 190-91
  shortcut keys for, ADVEX 180
  stepping through, ADVEX 534-36
  stopping during execution, ADVEX 205
  storage locations, ADVEX 190
  sub procedure (subroutines), ADVEX 476
  syntax errors in, ADVEX 527-29
  in templates, ADVEX 322-26
  testing, ADVEX 182, ADVEX 506-7
  VBA code, ADVEX 186-87, ADVEX 191,
    ADVEX 569-70
  viewing, ADVEX 186-87, ADVEX 194
  watch expressions, ADVEX 533-34
  in what-if analysis, ADVEX 255-56
macros (specific)
  AddToList, ADVEX 567-71
  Auto_Close, ADVEX 198
  Auto_Open, ADVEX 198
  ChartDataChoice, ADVEX 505-6
  CreateChart, ADVEX 503-4
  DataEntry, ADVEX 572-75
  Date/Time, ADVEX 206-7
  DisplayForm(), ADVEX 564-67, ADVEX 570-71
  For...Next statements in, ADVEX 510-13
  GetProperty, ADVEX 490-91
  GoToAssumptions, ADVEX 180-87
  GridlinesOff, ADVEX 207

LoanCalc, ADVEX 515-17
MethodDemo, ADVEX 492-93
OpenWorkBook, ADVEX 500
PrintBudget, ADVEX 195-97, ADVEX 474-75
Print Chart, ADVEX 178-79
PrintDetail, ADVEX 579-81
RunSolver, ADVEX 256-60
SelectCase statements in, ADVEX 510-13
SetColor, ADVEX 511-12, ADVEX 532-36
SetRangeName(), ADVEX 571-72
SortBySponsor, ADVEX 576-77
UnpaidRept, ADVEX 581-82
View Chart, ADVEX 178-79
ViewLastRecord, ADVEX 574-75
WorksheetObjects, ADVEX 494-96
Wrap Text, ADVEX 207
maps, ADVEX 162-70
   arranging data for, ADVEX 164
   available, ADVEX 162
   category shading colors, ADVEX 169-70
   creating, ADVEX 165-67
   data categories, ADVEX 167
   as embedded objects, ADVEX 165
   fonts, ADVEX 169
   legends, ADVEX 165, ADVEX 167, ADVEX 168-69
   linking worksheet data to, ADVEX 162
   modifying, ADVEX 168-70
   subtitles, ADVEX 169
   titles, ADVEX 166-67, ADVEX 169
Map toolbar, ADVEX 168
Margins settings, ADVEX 101
market value ratios, ADVEX 54
Math & Trig functions, ADVEX 273
MAX function, ADVEX 276
Maximize button, ADVEX 8
maximums, local, ADVEX 250
MAX(range-list) function, ADVEX 274
MEDIAN(range-list) function, 274, 278
menu bars, ADVEX 9
   adding new menus to, ADVEX 585-86
   components of, ADVEX 583
   defined, ADVEX 583
Menu Editor
   adding menu items to custom menus with, ADVEX 587-88
   adding menus to menu bars with, ADVEX 585-86
   creating submenus with, ADVEX 588-90
   defined, ADVEX 582
   displaying, ADVEX 584-85
Menu Editor dialog box, ADVEX 584, ADVEX 586
menu items, ADVEX 583
   adding to custom menus, ADVEX 587-88
menus, See also custom menus
   custom, ADVEX 538, ADVEX 582-91
   defined, ADVEX 583
   sketching, ADVEX 583
   terms, ADVEX 583-84
message boxes, ADVEX 488, ADVEX 491, ADVEX 495, ADVEX 574
   in custom applications, ADVEX 539
   interactive, ADVEX 516
MethodDemo macro, ADVEX 492-93
methods
   accessing with VBA, ADVEX 491-93
   of objects, ADVEX 482-83
   purposes of, ADVEX 491
   specifying, syntax for, ADVEX 482
Microsoft Query. See Query
Microsoft WordPad. See WordPad
MIN(range-list) function, ADVEX 274, ADVEX 277
Minimize button, ADVEX 8
minimums, local, ADVEX 250
mixed references, ADVEX 77
mode indicators, ADVEX 11
   pointing, ADVEX 26
   when entering text labels, ADVEX 17
models, ADVEX 6
module sheets (modules)
   activating Object Browser through, ADVEX 524
   entering macro in, ADVEX 485-87
   inserting, ADVEX 484-85
   macro code stored in, ADVEX 186, ADVEX 187, ADVEX 477, ADVEX 484
   printing macros on, ADVEX 200
MONTH(date) function, ADVEX 274
monthly payments, calculating with PMT function, ADVEX 270-83
Most likely scenario, ADVEX 233
mouse pointer, shapes, ADVEX 11
moving, cell contents with drag and drop, ADVEX 90
MS Access database, selecting as data source, ADVEX 435-38
MsgBox function, ADVEX 488, ADVEX 531
MS Query. See Query

N

multidimensional worksheet modeling, ADVEX 334
multiple charts, ADVEX 128
Multiple Maps Available dialog box, ADVEX 165
multiple workbook files, consolidation of, ADVEX 342-46

#NAME? error values, ADVEX 94
naming
   changing cells, ADVEX 232-33
   custom dialog boxes, ADVEX 546-47
   dialog box controls, ADVEX 550, ADVEX 551
   fields in lists, ADVEX 389
   macros, ADVEX 180-82, ADVEX 571-72
   ranges, ADVEX 91-92, ADVEX 571-72
   views, ADVEX 102
   worksheets, ADVEX 106-7
natural logarithms, in regression analysis, ADVEX 310-16
natural order of calculation, ADVEX 24
negative numbers, ADVEX 23
net income, ADVEX 61
Netscape Web browser, ADVEX 460
New Query tool, ADVEX 434
nonadjacent selections, for charts, ADVEX 132-33
notes, in text boxes, ADVEX 110-11
NOT logical function, ADVEX 295-98
NOT operator, specifying complex criteria with, ADVEX 440
NPV(interest-rate,range), ADVEX 274
NUM, ADVEX 11
numbers
   entering, ADVEX 19-21
   formatting, in pivot tables, ADVEX 416-17
Number setting sheet, for charts, ADVEX 145

O

Object Browser, ADVEX 524-27
objective function, ADVEX 239-40, ADVEX 247
Object Linking and Embedding (OLE), ADVEX 448-49, See also embedding; linking; objects
   linking vs. embedding in, ADVEX 456
object linking. See linking
object-oriented programming languages, ADVEX 475
objects
   changing properties of, ADVEX 483
   collections of, ADVEX 479
   copying/pasting from one program to another, ADVEX 159-62
   defined, ADVEX 159, ADVEX 478
   embedded, updating, ADVEX 459
   embedding, ADVEX 448-49
   embedding in word processor programs, ADVEX 457-58
   hierarchies of, ADVEX 478-79
     referencing with VBA, ADVEX 480-81
   linked, updating, ADVEX 455
   linking to word processing documents, ADVEX 451-53
   methods, ADVEX 482-83
     accessing with VBA, ADVEX 491-93
   pasting, ADVEX 448
   properties, ADVEX 481-82, ADVEX 483, ADVEX 487-91
   types, ADVEX 478
   worksheet, ADVEX 493-96
Offset method, ADVEX 525, ADVEX 526
one-input data tables, ADVEX 219-25
   entering formulas, ADVEX 222
   entering values, ADVEX 221
   identifying, ADVEX 221
   layout of, ADVEX 220
   worksheet setup for, ADVEX 220
on-line Help, ADVEX 33-34, ADVEX 524
Open dialog box, ADVEX 451
open-high-low-close (OHLC) charts, ADVEX 128
Open Query tool, ADVEX 434
OpenWorkBook macro, ADVEX 500
operating budgets, ADVEX 3-41
operating income, ADVEX 60
operating profit, ADVEX 57
operators
   arithmetic, ADVEX 21, ADVEX 23-24
   logical, ADVEX 440
   relational, ADVEX 288, ADVEX 440
   specifying complex criteria with, ADVEX 440
optimization constraints, ADVEX 239
   technical coefficients of, ADVEX 240, ADVEX 241
optimization problems, ADVEX 239-55
   changing constraints in, ADVEX 247-49
   with different starting values, ADVEX 250
   formulas, ADVEX 242-43
   integer constraints, ADVEX 249-51
   optimal solutions, ADVEX 239, ADVEX 244 47
   parameters for, ADVEX 243

   printing reports, ADVEX 251-52
   problem formulation, ADVEX 239-41
   techniques, ADVEX 238
   understanding results of, ADVEX 253-55
   worksheet setup, ADVEX 242-44
option buttons, in dialog boxes, ADVEX 543-44, ADVEX 561
order of precedence, in formulas, ADVEX 23-24
   overriding, ADVEX 24
orientation
   landscape, ADVEX 101
   portrait, ADVEX 101
OR logical function, ADVEX 295-97
OR operator, specifying complex criteria with, ADVEX 440
outline groups, ADVEX 364-70
   consolidating data with, ADVEX 367-70
   creating automatically, ADVEX 364-67
   detailed data displayed/hidden, ADVEX 367, ADVEX 368-69
outlines
   clearing, ADVEX 367
   defined, ADVEX 364
   symbols, ADVEX 365, ADVEX 366
output, in planning analysis sheet, ADVEX 14
output range, in linear regression, ADVEX 301-2

P

page breaks
   automatic, ADVEX 102
   manual, ADVEX 102-3
   in reports, ADVEX 102-3
page fields, in pivot tables, ADVEX 409
Page Setup, printing worksheets with, ADVEX 100-103
panes, splitting worksheet into, ADVEX 84-86
parameters, for optimization problems, ADVEX 243
parentheses, overriding order of precedence with, ADVEX 24
passwords, for protected worksheets, ADVEX 113, ADVEX 114
Paste button, ADVEX 72, ADVEX 73
Paste Link button, ADVEX 452
Paste Special command, ADVEX 452, ADVEX 457, ADVEX 458
Paste Special dialog box, ADVEX 359-60
pasting
   as data sharing method, ADVEX 447, ADVEX 448
   objects between applications, ADVEX 159-62
patterns
   applying to reports, ADVEX 100
   for data markers, ADVEX 158
percent format, applying, ADVEX 38-39
performance ratios, ADVEX 53-54
Personal Macro Workbook, ADVEX 190
perspective, in 3-D column charts, ADVEX 154
picture charts, ADVEX 157-59
pie charts, ADVEX 126
   changing rotation of, ADVEX 150
   creating, ADVEX 148-51
   exploding, ADVEX 150
   purpose, ADVEX 128
PivotTable Field dialog box, ADVEX 412, ADVEX 419
PivotTable Field tool, ADVEX 413
pivot table items
   hiding and showing, ADVEX 419-20
   rearranging within pivot tables, ADVEX 415-16
pivot tables, ADVEX 408-24
   adding fields to, ADVEX 417-19
   column fields, ADVEX 409
   COUNT function in, ADVEX 412
   creating, ADVEX 409-14
     from external databases, ADVEX 443-46
   creating charts from, ADVEX 424
   data fields, ADVEX 409
   defined, ADVEX 408
   field buttons, ADVEX 411-14
   formatting numbers in, ADVEX 416-17
   grouping data in, ADVEX 421-23
   layout
     changing, ADVEX 414-15
     defining, ADVEX 409-14
   page fields, ADVEX 409
   planning, ADVEX 409
   refreshing, ADVEX 420-21
   removing fields from, ADVEX 418-19
   row fields, ADVEX 409
   SUM function in, ADVEX 412
   for summarizing lists, ADVEX 408-9
   updating, ADVEX 455
   uses of, ADVEX 408
PivotTable Wizard
   adding fields to pivot tables with, ADVEX 417-18

ADVEX 622 MICROSOFT EXCEL FOR WINDOWS ADVANCED INDEX

creating pivot tables with, ADVEX 409-14, ADVEX 422
creating pivot tables from external databases with, ADVEX 443-46
Planning Analysis Sheets, ADVEX 14-15, ADVEX 51, ADVEX 55, ADVEX 58
  charts, ADVEX 127
  custom applications, ADVEX 541
  executive information systems, ADVEX 336
  expense analysis using functions, ADVEX 278
  maps, ADVEX 163, ADVEX 168
  optimization macros, ADVEX 256
  optimization problems, ADVEX 241
  regression analysis, ADVEX 300
  reviewing, ADVEX 82-84
  revising, ADVEX 65
  scenarios, ADVEX 231
plot area, in charts, ADVEX 154
PMT function, ADVEX 274, ADVEX 514
  arguments, ADVEX 280
  calculating lease payments with, ADVEX 282-83
  calculating loan payments with, ADVEX 279-82
pointing, building formulas by, ADVEX 25-27
point size
  changing, ADVEX 40-41
  in chart text objects, ADVEX 144-45
  defined, ADVEX 40
portrait orientation, ADVEX 101
presentation-quality reports, ADVEX 96-100
previews, See also views
  worksheets, ADVEX 41-42
  zooming, ADVEX 42
price/earnings (P/E) ratio, ADVEX 54
prices, shadow, ADVEX 253, ADVEX 254
primary axis, in combination charts, ADVEX 156
primary sort fields, ADVEX 390, ADVEX 391
PrintBudget macro, ADVEX 195-98
  modifying, ADVEX 474-75
  viewing, ADVEX 197-98
PrintChart macro, ADVEX 178-79
PrintDetail macro, ADVEX 579-81
printing
  charts, ADVEX 142-43
  footers, ADVEX 100-102
  headers, ADVEX 100-102
  macros, ADVEX 200
  orientation, ADVEX 101
  ranges, ADVEX 93
  reports, macros for, ADVEX 579-82
  scaling factor, ADVEX 101
  worksheets, ADVEX 41-44
PrintOut method, ADVEX 491, ADVEX 492-93
Print Preview, ADVEX 42, ADVEX 142, ADVEX 143
problem analysis, in worksheet development, ADVEX 13-15
procedures
  defined, ADVEX 476
  function procedure macros, ADVEX 476, ADVEX 477
  macros vs., ADVEX 476-77
  sub procedure macros (subroutines), ADVEX 476
profit
  gross, ADVEX 57, ADVEX 60
  operating, ADVEX 57
profitability ratios, ADVEX 54
program window, ADVEX 8-11, See also windows; worksheet windows
  formula bar, ADVEX 10
  Maximize button, ADVEX 8
  menu bar, ADVEX 9
  Minimize button, ADVEX 8
  title bar, ADVEX 9
  toolbars, ADVEX 10
projections, ADVEX 6
Prompt message, for InputBox function, ADVEX 498
properties
  changing, ADVEX 483
  of objects, ADVEX 481-82, ADVEX 483, ADVEX 487-91
  settings, ADVEX 108, ADVEX 487-91
  syntax, ADVEX 483
protection
  of cells in templates, ADVEX 318-19
  passwords, ADVEX 113, ADVEX 114
  turning off, ADVEX 113-14
  turning on, ADVEX 112-13

Q

queries
  with Criteria pane, ADVEX 439-42
  data sources for, ADVEX 435-38
  defined, ADVEX 432
  guidelines for creating, ADVEX 442

on multiple tables, ADVEX 443-46
on one table, ADVEX 438-39
returning results to Excel, ADVEX 441-42
Query, ADVEX 433-46
  returning results to Excel, ADVEX 441-42
  running, ADVEX 433-34
  toolbar, ADVEX 434-35
  Window, ADVEX 434-35
Query Now tool, ADVEX 435
Query and Pivot Table toolbar, ADVEX 413, ADVEX 423
Query Window, ADVEX 434-35
  Criteria pane, ADVEX 437, ADVEX 439-42
  Data pane, ADVEX 437, ADVEX 438-39
  Table pane, ADVEX 437
question mark (?) wildcard character, ADVEX 397
quick ratio, ADVEX 53

R

radar charts, ADVEX 128
random access memory (RAM), ADVEX 28
range names, ADVEX 91-92
  allowable characters, ADVEX 91
  assigning, ADVEX 92
  for changing cells, ADVEX 232
  entering functions with, ADVEX 278
  in formulas, ADVEX 93-96
  macro for updating, ADVEX 571-72
  using, ADVEX 92
range objects, ADVEX 491-93
ranges
  applying formats to, ADVEX 38
  array, ADVEX 358-64
  copying with AutoFill, ADVEX 71-72
  copying using clipboard, ADVEX 72-73
  defined, ADVEX 25
  inserting rows in, ADVEX 88
  methods, ADVEX 482, ADVEX 491-93
  naming, ADVEX 91-92
  printing, ADVEX 93
  properties, ADVEX 481
  protecting, ADVEX 112-14
  shading, ADVEX 99-100
  specifying, ADVEX 36-37
ratios
  calculations, ADVEX 32
  performance, ADVEX 53-54
read only feature, for saving templates, ADVEX 320-21
recalculation, ADVEX 5, ADVEX 6, ADVEX 11, ADVEX 22
Record New Macro dialog box, ADVEX 180, ADVEX 189, ADVEX 190, ADVEX 257
records
  adding to lists with data forms, ADVEX 394-95
  deleting from lists with data forms, ADVEX 397-98
  in lists, ADVEX 388
  searching for, with data forms, ADVEX 396-97
reference area, ADVEX 10
references
  absolute, ADVEX 70, ADVEX 77-79, ADVEX 91
  mixed, ADVEX 77
  relative, ADVEX 70, ADVEX 91
Reference Windows, ADVEX 7
Refresh Data tool, ADVEX 413, ADVEX 421, ADVEX 455
regression analysis, ADVEX 298-318, See also linear regression
  calculating with macros, ADVEX 323-26
  defined, ADVEX 298
  forecasting with, ADVEX 298-318
  performing, ADVEX 299-308
  steps in, ADVEX 314
Regression dialog box, ADVEX 301, ADVEX 313, ADVEX 323
relational databases, See also external databases
  common fields in, ADVEX 433
  querying, ADVEX 432-33
relational operators, ADVEX 288, ADVEX 440
relative references, ADVEX 70
  adjustment after row deletions, ADVEX 91
  in macros, ADVEX 406
Remove Dependent Arrows audit activity, ADVEX 372
Remove Precedent Arrows audit activity, ADVEX 372
renaming. See naming
reports
  aligning text in, ADVEX 98
  borders in, ADVEX 98-99
  centering horizontally, ADVEX 102
  layout sketches, ADVEX 57, ADVEX 60
  options for custom applications, ADVEX 540
  page breaks in, ADVEX 102-3
  patterns in, ADVEX 99-100
  presentation-quality, ADVEX 96-100

printing with macro, ADVEX 579-82
shading in, ADVEX 99-100
summary, ADVEX 577-79
reserved macros names, ADVEX 198
ResetData macro
  assigning to button object, ADVEX 192
  editing, ADVEX 203-5
  recording, ADVEX 188-89, ADVEX 191
  running, ADVEX 193-94
  viewing code, ADVEX 194
Residuals Plots, in linear regression, ADVEX 302, ADVEX 305
residual value, for PMT function, ADVEX 283
resizing. See sizing
result set, in Data pane of Query Window, ADVEX 437
Return Data button, ADVEX 441
Return Data to Excel query tool, ADVEX 434
return on equity (ROE), ADVEX 54
return on investments (ROI), ADVEX 61
return on sales (ROS), ADVEX 54, ADVEX 57
return on total assets (ROA), ADVEX 54
reviewing, worksheets, ADVEX 82-84
right alignment, ADVEX 19
  for reports, ADVEX 98
RIGHT(text,num-chars) function, ADVEX 274
rotation, in 3-D column charts, ADVEX 154, ADVEX 155
ROUND(formula,decimals) function, ADVEX 79-82, ADVEX 216, ADVEX 218, ADVEX 249, ADVEX 274
  in linear regression, ADVEX 302-3, ADVEX 306
rounding errors, ADVEX 78-79
row fields, in pivot tables, ADVEX 409
Row Input cells, ADVEX 223, ADVEX 225
row-oriented data tables, ADVEX 225
rows
  deleting, ADVEX 90-91
  hidden, ADVEX 103-4
  inserting, ADVEX 86-89
R-square values, ADVEX 299, ADVEX 302
RSQ(y-range,x-range) function, ADVEX 274
Run Dialog button, ADVEX 551-52, ADVEX 556, ADVEX 557, ADVEX 558
RunSolver macro, ADVEX 256-60
runtime errors, VBA, ADVEX 529-30

S

Save As command, ADVEX 28
Save command, ADVEX 28, ADVEX 41
Save File query tool, ADVEX 434
saving
  charts, ADVEX 142
  templates, ADVEX 320, ADVEX 321, ADVEX 324-25
  workbooks, ADVEX 28-29, ADVEX 41
scalar values, in regression analysis, ADVEX 310
Scenario dialog box, ADVEX 234-35
Scenario Manager, ADVEX 231-38
scenarios, ADVEX 231-38
  best-case, ADVEX 235, ADVEX 234-36
  creating, ADVEX 233-38
  defined, ADVEX 231
  displaying, ADVEX 236-37
  most likely, ADVEX 233-34
  naming changing cells for, ADVEX 232-33
  summaries, ADVEX 237-38
  worst-case, ADVEX 233, ADVEX 236-37
Scenario Summary dialog box, ADVEX 238
Scenario Summary worksheet, ADVEX 237
Scenario text box, ADVEX 231
Scenario Values dialog box, ADVEX 235
scroll arrows, ADVEX 10
scroll bars, ADVEX 10, ADVEX 12
  in dialog boxes, ADVEX 543-44, ADVEX 561
scroll boxes, ADVEX 10, ADVEX 12
scrolling
  scroll bar movements, ADVEX 12
  special keys, ADVEX 13
  worksheet, ADVEX 11-13
searching
  for records in lists, using data forms, ADVEX 396-97
  with wildcard characters, ADVEX 397-98
Select Case keyword, ADVEX 508
Select Case statement, ADVEX 501
  in macros, ADVEX 510-13
  making multiple decisions with, ADVEX 508-18
  syntax, ADVEX 508
selected charts, ADVEX 136
Select method, ADVEX 491
Sensitivity Reports, ADVEX 251, ADVEX 260, ADVEX 253-54
serial date number, for YIELD function, ADVEX 284-85

series, creating with AutoFill, ADVEX 67-69
server programs
    defined, ADVEX 159
    embedding objects from, ADVEX 448
set cells, ADVEX 215
SetColor macro, ADVEX 511-12
    debugging, ADVEX 532-36
SetRangeName() macro, ADVEX 571-72
SetValue, ADVEX 487
shading patterns, ADVEX 99-100
shadow prices, ADVEX 253, ADVEX 254
sharing data, ADVEX 447, ADVEX 448-49
    among Windows programs, ADVEX 447
sheet-name, in linking worksheets, ADVEX 347
sheets, See also worksheets
    active, ADVEX 10
Sheets settings, ADVEX 101
sheet tabs, ADVEX 10
shortcut keys, for macros, ADVEX 180,
    ADVEX 190, ADVEX 191, ADVEX 193-94
Show Detail tool, ADVEX 413
Show/Hide Criteria query tool, ADVEX 434
Show/Hide Data Map Control button,
    ADVEX 168
Show Info Windows audit activity, ADVEX 372
Show method, of DialogSheet objects,
    ADVEX 560
Show Pages tool, ADVEX 413
side-by-side column charts, what-if analysis
    with, ADVEX 151-53
SIN(formula) function, ADVEX 274
sizing
    charts, ADVEX 135-36
    column width, ADVEX 35-36
    custom dialog boxes, ADVEX 546-47
slack, ADVEX 252
SLN(cost,salvage,life) function, ADVEX 274
SLOPE(y-range,x-range) function, ADVEX 274
    in linear regression, ADVEX 307
SMALL(range-list,position) function, ADVEX 274
Solver, ADVEX 238-55
    formulating problems for, ADVEX 238-41
    macro for running, ADVEX 256-59
    printing reports, ADVEX 251-52
    reports, ADVEX 251-55
    specifying target cell and changing cells
        for, ADVEX 243
Solver Parameters dialog box, ADVEX 244-46,
    ADVEX 250
Sort Ascending query tool, ADVEX 435
SortBySponsor macro, ADVEX 576-77
Sort Descending query tool, ADVEX 435
sort fields (sort keys), ADVEX 390
    primary, ADVEX 390, ADVEX 391
    secondary, ADVEX 392
sorting
    ascending order, ADVEX 390, ADVEX 392,
        ADVEX 435
    custom order, ADVEX 393
    data in lists, ADVEX 390-93
    descending order, ADVEX 390, ADVEX 435
    macro for, ADVEX 576-77
    on multiple fields, ADVEX 391-93
    options for custom applications, ADVEX 540
    on single field, ADVEX 390-91
source areas, in consolidation, ADVEX 342
source programs
    defined, ADVEX 159
    embedding objects from, ADVEX 448
    linking objects from, ADVEX 449
source workbooks, in linking worksheets,
    ADVEX 347
spell checking, ADVEX 32-33
spinners, in dialog boxes, ADVEX 543-44,
    ADVEX 561
splitting, worksheet window, ADVEX 84-86
spreads, ADVEX 162
spreadsheets, ADVEX 4, See also worksheets
SQRT(formula) function, ADVEX 274
stacked bar charts, ADVEX 128
stacked column charts, ADVEX 140
    activating for editing, ADVEX 136-37
    purpose, ADVEX 128
    resizing, ADVEX 136
Standard toolbar, ADVEX 10
Statistical functions, ADVEX 273
statistics, descriptive, ADVEX 275
status bar, ADVEX 11
STDEV(range-list) function, ADVEX 274,
    ADVEX 279
stepping, through macros, ADVEX 534-36
Sub keyword, in VBA code, ADVEX 188
submenu items, ADVEX 583
    adding to submenus, ADVEX 588-90

submenus, ADVEX 583
    adding submenu items to, ADVEX 588-90
    creating, ADVEX 588-90
sub procedure macros (subroutines), ADVEX 476
subtitles
    for charts, ADVEX 130, ADVEX 144-45
    for maps, ADVEX 169
subtotals, inserting in lists, ADVEX 404-7
Subtotals command, ADVEX 404
SUM(range-list) function, ADVEX 274, See also
3-D SUM function formulas
    in consolidation worksheets, ADVEX 335,
        ADVEX 340, ADVEX 342, ADVEX 348
    copying for across-sheet 3-D
        consolidation, ADVEX 358-59
    creating total columns with, ADVEX 74
    entering with AutoSum button, ADVEX 25
    in pivot tables, ADVEX 412
    revising to include inserted rows,
        ADVEX 88-89
summary reports, ADVEX 577-79
Summary section, of worksheet, ADVEX 76
Summary worksheets, ADVEX 105
SUMPRODUCT function, ADVEX 242-43
syntax, ADVEX 79
    errors, VBA, ADVEX 527-29

T

Table dialog box, ADVEX 223
Table Lookup, ADVEX 292-95
Table pane, of Query Window, ADVEX 437
tables, See also data tables; decision tables;
one-input data tables;
pivot tables; two-input data tables
    joining, ADVEX 443-46
    linking with common fields, ADVEX 433
    multiple, queries on, ADVEX 443-46
    querying on one, ADVEX 438-39
target cells, ADVEX 219
    defined, ADVEX 215
    specifying for optimization problems,
        ADVEX 243-44
Task List, ADVEX 442
technical coefficients, ADVEX 243
    defined, ADVEX 240
    of optimization constraints, ADVEX 240,
        ADVEX 241
templates, ADVEX 318-26
    code, ADVEX 525
    creating, ADVEX 318-21
    defined, ADVEX 318
    for executive information systems,
        ADVEX 336
    instruction sheets for, ADVEX 319
    macros in, ADVEX 322-26
    modifying, ADVEX 318-19
    opening, ADVEX 321
    protecting cells in, ADVEX 318-19
    as read only, ADVEX 320-21
    retrieving, ADVEX 339-40
    saving, ADVEX 320, ADVEX 321, ADVEX 324-25
    testing, ADVEX 325-26
test values, in lookup tables, ADVEX 294
text
    aligning headings, ADVEX 98
    notes, attaching to cells, ADVEX 222-23
    in worksheets, ADVEX 17
text boxes
    adding to worksheet, ADVEX 109-11
    centering text in, ADVEX 148
text files, ADVEX 460-65
    delimited, ADVEX 461
    fixed-width, ADVEX 461
    importing, ADVEX 460-65
Text functions, ADVEX 273
Text Import Wizard, ADVEX 462-64
text labels
    adding in inserted rows, ADVEX 87
    alignment of, ADVEX 19
    assigning to range names, ADVEX 94
    correcting, ADVEX 18
    entering, ADVEX 17-19
    longer than cell width, ADVEX 20
3-D area charts, ADVEX 128
3-D bar charts, ADVEX 128
3-D column charts, ADVEX 129, ADVEX 153-55
    elevation, ADVEX 154, ADVEX 155
    formatting, ADVEX 154-55
    perspective, ADVEX 154
    rotation, ADVEX 154, ADVEX 155
    view, ADVEX 154, ADVEX 155
3-D consolidation, ADVEX 335
    adding worksheets, ADVEX 376-77
    3-D SUM function formulas,
        ADVEX 347-49, ADVEX 358-59
3-D line charts, ADVEX 129
3-D pie charts, ADVEX 129

3-D SUM function formulas, ADVEX 347-49,
    ADVEX 358-59
3-D surface charts, ADVEX 129
tick marks, in charts, ADVEX 130
tiling, windows, ADVEX 351-52, ADVEX 359
times-interest-earned (TIE) ratio, ADVEX 54
title bar, ADVEX 9
titles
    for charts, ADVEX 130, ADVEX 144-45
    entering, ADVEX 68
    for maps, ADVEX 166-67, ADVEX 169
TODAY() function, ADVEX 97-98, ADVEX 274
toolbars, ADVEX 10
    Drawing, ADVEX 110
    Formatting, ADVEX 10
    Map, ADVEX 168
    Query, ADVEX 434-35
    Query and Pivot Table, ADVEX 413,
        ADVEX 423
    Standard, ADVEX 10
    Visual Basic, ADVEX 178-8, ADVEX 484,
        ADVEX 485, ADVEX 487
    WorkGroup, ADVEX 231, ADVEX 233-34
Tools menu, assigning macros to, ADVEX 190
tooltip, ADVEX 10
total asset turnover, ADVEX 53
total columns, creating with SUM function,
    ADVEX 74
Trace Dependents audit activity, ADVEX 372
Trace Error audit activity, ADVEX 372
trace errors, ADVEX 372, ADVEX 373
Trace Precedents audit activity, ADVEX 372
transferring data
    among Windows programs, ADVEX 447
    using copy-and-paste method, ADVEX 449
    using object linking, ADVEX 449-50
transformations
    logarithmic, ADVEX 310-16
    in regression analysis, ADVEX 310,
        ADVEX 312
TREND function, ADVEX 275, ADVEX 307
trial-and-error goal-seeking method,
    ADVEX 215-16
TROUBLE? paragraphs, ADVEX 7
tutorials
    Help Desk for, ADVEX 33-34
    using effectively, ADVEX 6-7
    workbook filenames for, ADVEX 29-30
two-input data tables, ADVEX 219, ADVEX 225-28
    calculating results, ADVEX 227-28
    charting results, ADVEX 229
    displaying results, ADVEX 227-28
    layout, ADVEX 225-26
typefaces, defined, ADVEX 40

U

Unable to Create Map dialog box, ADVEX 165
underline borders, linking formulas, ADVEX 354
underlining, applying, ADVEX 39-40
Undo button, ADVEX 113
    in linked workbooks, ADVEX 357
Ungroup tool, ADVEX 413
unhiding. See hiding/unhiding
unlocked (unprotected) cells, ADVEX 112
UnpaidRept macro, ADVEX 581-82
upper limits, in optimization reports, ADVEX 251
UPPER(text) function, ADVEX 275
user-defined functions, ADVEX 477

V

value axis (y-axis), in charts, ADVEX 130
#VALUE! error value, ADVEX 87
value labels, in charts, ADVEX 130
values
    adding in inserted rows, ADVEX 87
    defined, ADVEX 17, ADVEX 19
    entering, ADVEX 19-21
    repeating, formulas for, ADVEX 69
VALUE(text) function, ADVEX 275
variables, ADVEX 496-97
    decision, ADVEX 239, ADVEX 246,
        ADVEX 249-50
    declaring, ADVEX 496-97
    defined, ADVEX 487, ADVEX 496
    monitoring values of with watch
        expressions, ADVEX 533-34
variance analysis, ADVEX 116
vertical splitter, ADVEX 85
View Chart macro, ADVEX 178-79
ViewLastRecord macro, ADVEX 574-75
View Manager, viewing worksheet with,
    ADVEX 102
views, See also previews
    names, ADVEX 102
    in 3-D column charts, ADVEX 154,
        ADVEX 155

View SQL query tool, ADVEX 434
Visual Basic for Applications (VBA), ADVEX 473-518, See also custom applications
    accessing object's methods with, ADVEX 491-93
    automatic display of custom dialog boxes with, ADVEX 559-60
    building complex macros with, ADVEX 473-75
    control structures, ADVEX 501-7
    creating macros with, ADVEX 179, ADVEX 191, ADVEX 483-87
    custom applications, ADVEX 537-91
    for custom dialog box controls, ADVEX 561
    debugging macros in, ADVEX 532-36
    defined, ADVEX 475
    examining object property settings with, ADVEX 487-91
    macro recorder, ADVEX 527
    making multiple decisions with Select Case statement, ADVEX 508-18
    Object Browser, ADVEX 524-27
    objects, ADVEX 478-79
    on-line Help, ADVEX 524
    overview, ADVEX 475-77
    processing data entered in custom dialog boxes with, ADVEX 559, ADVEX 561-66
    referencing objects in object hierarchy with, ADVEX 480-81
    referring to objects in collections with, ADVEX 480
    uses of, ADVEX 476
Visual Basic for Applications (VBA) code
    components, ADVEX 188
    copying between macros, ADVEX 505-6
    examining, ADVEX 569-70
    logic errors, ADVEX 531
    macro debugging, ADVEX 532-36
    modifying, ADVEX 570
    readability, ADVEX 485
    runtime errors, ADVEX 529-30
    storing, ADVEX 477
    storing values with variables, ADVEX 496-97
    syntax, ADVEX 476
    syntax errors, ADVEX 527-29
    viewing, ADVEX 186-87, ADVEX 194
Visual Basic toolbar, ADVEX 178-8, ADVEX 484, ADVEX 485, ADVEX 487
VLOOKUP function
    arguments, ADVEX 293
    building in decision tables with, ADVEX 295

W

watch expressions, ADVEX 533-34
Watch pane, in Debug Window, ADVEX 532
Web browser, ADVEX 460
what-if analysis, ADVEX 211-59
    built-in decision tables for, ADVEX 290
    charts for, ADVEX 151-53
    constants in, ADVEX 214
    data tables for, ADVEX 219-30
    defined, ADVEX 6
    Goal Seek method, ADVEX 217-19
    macros in, ADVEX 255-56
    performing, ADVEX 46-47
    scenarios, ADVEX 231-38
    Solver, ADVEX 238-55
    trial-and-error method, ADVEX 215-16
what-if tables. See data tables

wildcard characters
    asterisk (*), ADVEX 397
    question marks (?), ADVEX 397
    searching records with, ADVEX 397-98
windows, See also program window; worksheet windows
    tiling, ADVEX 351-52, ADVEX 359
Windows 95, switching among programs in, ADVEX 451
Windows applications
    integrating, ADVEX 159-62
    integrating Excel into, ADVEX 431-65
    opening multiple, ADVEX 451-53
    transferring and sharing data among, ADVEX 447-65
With Groups consolidation method, ADVEX 335
Wizards
    ChartWizard, ADVEX 129, ADVEX 131-32, ADVEX 133-35, ADVEX 154-56, ADVEX 229, ADVEX 424
    defined, ADVEX 79
    Function Wizard, ADVEX 79-80, ADVEX 243, ADVEX 276-77, ADVEX 281, ADVEX 285-86
    PivotTable, ADVEX 409-14, ADVEX 417-18, ADVEX 422, ADVEX 443-46
    Text Import, ADVEX 462-64
WordPad, ADVEX 159, ADVEX 451
WordPad/word processor documents, ADVEX 449-50
    embedding objects in, ADVEX 448, ADVEX 457-58
    linking Excel objects to, ADVEX 451-53
    linking worksheets to, ADVEX 450
    pasting data onto, ADVEX 448
    updating embedded objects in, ADVEX 459
    updating linked objects in, ADVEX 455-56
workbook consolidation. See consolidation
workbooks, See also worksheets
    closing, ADVEX 44
    in collections, ADVEX 480
    defined, ADVEX 7
    filenames, ADVEX 9
    methods, ADVEX 482
    moving worksheets within, ADVEX 108
    multiple worksheets in, ADVEX 104-8
    opening, ADVEX 44-45
    properties, ADVEX 481
    retrieving, ADVEX 214
    saving, ADVEX 28-29, ADVEX 41
    storing macros in, ADVEX 190
    template, ADVEX 318-26
    tutorial files names, ADVEX 29-30
workbooks keyword, ADVEX 480
WorkGroup toolbar
    creating scenarios with, ADVEX 233-35
    Scenario text box, ADVEX 231
worksheet design, ADVEX 15-17
    aesthetic considerations, ADVEX 64
    content considerations, ADVEX 64
    defined, ADVEX 64
    sketches, ADVEX 66, ADVEX 76
WorksheetObjects macro, ADVEX 494-96
worksheets, ADVEX 3-41, See also workbooks
    adding, ADVEX 495
    defined, ADVEX 4
    deleting, ADVEX 495-96
    developing, ADVEX 13-25, ADVEX 63-114
    Documentation, ADVEX 107
    expanding, ADVEX 64-66

frame, ADVEX 10
Full Screen view, ADVEX 199
graphic objects in, ADVEX 109-12
hidden, ADVEX 103-4
linking, ADVEX 347-64
linking data to maps, ADVEX 162
linking to word processor documents, ADVEX 449-50
methods of, ADVEX 482
moving within workbook, ADVEX 108
multidimensional, ADVEX 334
multiple, in workbooks, ADVEX 104-8
names, in cell referencing, ADVEX 5
navigating, ADVEX 11-13
objects, ADVEX 493-96
previewing, ADVEX 41-42
printing, ADVEX 41-44, ADVEX 100-103
problem analysis, ADVEX 13-15
properties, ADVEX 108, ADVEX 481
protecting, ADVEX 112-14
recalculating, ADVEX 5, ADVEX 6, ADVEX 11
renaming, ADVEX 106-7
retrieving, ADVEX 67, ADVEX 214
reviewing, ADVEX 30-33, ADVEX 82-84
revising, ADVEX 84-91
scrolling, ADVEX 11-13
size of, ADVEX 11
spell checking, ADVEX 32-33
Summary, ADVEX 105
viewing with View Manager, ADVEX 102
worksheet sections, ADVEX 76-77
    bottom line, ADVEX 75
    Documentation sheet, ADVEX 76
    Key Input Assumptions, ADVEX 75, ADVEX 77
    Summary, ADVEX 75
worksheet windows, See also program window; windows
    defined, ADVEX 10
    splitting, ADVEX 84-86
    splitting horizontally, ADVEX 85
    splitting vertically, ADVEX 85
    unsplitting, ADVEX 84, ADVEX 85
World Wide Web, ADVEX 460
worst-case scenario, ADVEX 233, ADVEX 234, ADVEX 236
Wrap Text macros, ADVEX 207
.wri filename extension, ADVEX 451
WYSIWYG approach, ADVEX 17

X

XLM macro language, ADVEX 476
.xlt filename extension, ADVEX 318
XY charts, ADVEX 128

Y

y-axis
    changing number format of, ADVEX 145
    scale, ADVEX 145-46
YEAR(date) function, ADVEX 275
YIELD function, ADVEX 275, ADVEX 279
    arguments, ADVEX 284-85
    calculating bond interest rates with, ADVEX 284-86
yield to maturity, ADVEX 284, ADVEX 285

Z

zeros, unwanted, in arrange ranges, ADVEX 362-63
zooming, previews, ADVEX 42

Microsoft Excel for Windows **Task Reference**

TASK	PAGE #	RECOMMENDED METHOD	NOTES
Auditing	ADVEX 370	Click Tools, point to Auditing, click Show Auditing Toolbar	See section "Auditing the Workbook"
AutoFill	ADVEX 67	Enter first value in first cell; click and drag fill handle to select cells to be filled	
AutoFilter, activate	ADVEX 398	Click any cell in the list you want to filter; click Data, click Filter, click AutoFilter	
AutoSum button, activate	ADVEX 25	Select the cells to be summed, including a blank cell to right or below the summed cells; click Σ	See Reference Window "Using the AutoSum Button"
Border, add	ADVEX 98	Select the cells to be bordered, click Borders button list arrow, select border style	See section "Using Borders and Patterns"
Button object, assign to macro	ADVEX 183	Click ▢, position mouse pointer where you want button and draw button; select name of macro to be assigned to button, click OK	See Reference Window "Assigning a Macro to a Button Object on a Worksheet"
Cell contents, clearing	ADVEX 32	Click the cell to be cleared; press Delete	
Cell contents, editing	ADVEX 30	Select cell, press F2 to initiate editing	See Reference Window "Editing Cell contents"
Cell Range, selecting	ADVEX 36	Click the cell that is upper-left corner of range; drag cell pointer to lower-right corner of range, release mouse button	See Reference Window "Selecting a Cell Range"
Chart, activate	ADVEX 136	Double-click anywhere within the chart border	
Chart, add data series	ADVEX 137	Select the data series in worksheet; move pointer to edge of selected range until it changes to ▷; drag selected range until pointer is on top of chart and changes to ▷, release mouse button	
Chart, add graphic object	ADVEX 147	Click ▨, click desired drawing tool, draw graphic object	See section "Adding Graphic Objects to Charts"
Chart, changing chart format	ADVEX 139	Activate chart, right-click to display short-cut menu; click Format, click Subtype tab; select desired chart format	See Reference Window "Selecting A Different Chart Format"
Chart, changing chart type	ADVEX 139	Activate chart, right-click to display short-cut menu; click Chart Type; select desired chart type	
Chart, changing fill patterns	ADVEX 146	Activate chart; double-click area of chart to be filled with pattern, select pattern	See section "Using Colors and Fill Patterns"
Chart, creating	ADVEX 133	Select data to be charted; click ▨ Follow five steps of ChartWizard	
Chart, delete data series	ADVEX 137	Activate chart; click a data marker, press Delete	
Chart, resize	ADVEX 135	Select chart; move mouse pointer over the handles until it changes to ↕, drag to resize	See section "Resizing a Chart"
Chart, select	ADVEX 136	Click anywhere within the chart border	

Microsoft Excel for Windows **Task Reference**

TASK	PAGE #	RECOMMENDED METHOD	NOTES
Chart sheet, insert	ADVEX 149	Click Insert, point to Chart, click As New Sheet	
Chart title, add	ADVEX 144	Activate chart; click Insert, click Titles, check chart title box, click OK; highlight the word "Title" in chart title, press Delete, then type desired title	
ChartWizard, using	ADVEX 133	Click 📊; follow ChartWizard steps	See section "Using the ChartWizard"
Clipboard contents, paste	ADVEX 72	Click 📋	
Close, workbook	ADVEX 44	Click ✕	See Reference Window "Closing a Workbook"
Colors, applying to a range of cells	ADVEX 100	Select range of cells; click 🎨 to display color palette; select color	
Column width, changing	ADVEX 35	Drag right boundary of column in the worksheet border	See Reference Window "Changing Column Width"
Consolidation, by position	ADVEX 343	Click cell in upper corner of destination range, click Data, click Consolidate; enter source filename, then cell reference of incoming data; click Add, click OK	See Reference Window "Consolidating Data using the Position Method with a Data Range"
Copy cells, using absolute reference	ADVEX 77	Place edit cursor anywhere on cell reference in the formula and press F4 to insert the absolute reference	See section "Using Absolute References"
Copy cells, using AutoFill	ADVEX 71	Select cell range for copying; position mouse pointer over the fill handle; drag to outline cell range of desired location	See Reference Window "Copying Cells To An Adjacent Range Using AutoFill"
Copy cells, using clipboard	ADVEX 72	Select range of cells to copy; click 📋 Select the cell range where clipboard content is to be copied; click 📋	See Reference Window "Copying a cell range using the Clipboard"
Custom dialog box, creating	ADVEX 543		See section "Creating a Custom Dialog Box"
Custom menu, creating	ADVEX 582		See section "Creating a Custom Menu"
Data Form, adding a record	ADVEX 394	Click Data, click Form, click New	See Reference Window "Adding a Record Using a Data Form"
Data Form, deleting a record	ADVEX 397	Click Data, click Form, select record, click Delete	See Reference Window "Deleting a Record Using a Data Form"
Data Form, searching for a record	ADVEX 396	Click Data, click Form, click Criteria	See section, "Using the Data Form to Search for Records"
Data list, filter	ADVEX 398	Click Data, click Filter, click AutoFilter	See Reference Window "Filtering a List with AutoFilter"

Microsoft Excel for Windows **Task Reference**

TASK	PAGE #	RECOMMENDED METHOD	NOTES
Data list, retrieving external data	ADVEX 432	Select sheet where new data will be placed; click Data, click Get External Data; select desired data source in Select Data Source dialog box; select desired data file in Add Tables dialog box; click File, click Return Data to Microsoft Excel	See section "Using Microsoft Query"
Data List, sorting rows	ADVEX 390		See Reference Window "Sorting Using a Single Sort Field"
Data table	ADVEX 219		See "One-input data table" and "Two-input data table"
Delete, columns or rows	ADVEX 91	Select columns or rows to be deleted, Click Edit, click Delete	See Reference Window "Deleting Rows and Columns"
Dialog sheets, insert	ADVEX 545	Click Insert, point to Macro, click Dialog sheet	
Edit, Group mode	ADVEX 349		See section "Using Group Edit Mode"
Font, select	ADVEX 40	Select cell or range to format; click Font list arrow, click desired font	
Font, size	ADVEX 40	Select cell or range to format; click Font Size list arrow, click desired font size	
Footer, edit	ADVEX 101	In Page Setup dialog box, click Header/Footer tab, click Footer list arrow, select a pre-set footer or click Custom Footer to edit the existing footer	
Format, bold	ADVEX 40	Select cell or range to format; click **B**	The Bold button toggles on and off
Format, center in cell	ADVEX 41	Select cell or range to format; click ▦	The Center button toggles on and off
Format, comma	ADVEX 37	Select cell or range to format; click ,	
Format, currency	ADVEX 37	Select cell or range to format; click $	
Format, italic	ADVEX 39	Select cell or range to format; click *I*	The Italic button toggles on and off
Format, underline	ADVEX 39	Select cell or range to format; click U	The Underline button toggles on and off
Format Painter button, apply	ADVEX 69	Select cell or range of cells with format to copy; click ✍, select cell or range of cells to format	
Formula, build by pointing	ADVEX 25		See Reference Window "Building Formulas by Pointing"

Microsoft Excel for Windows **Task Reference**

TASK	PAGE #	RECOMMENDED METHOD	NOTES
Functions, enter	ADVEX 276	Click cell where you want function; click Function Wizard, follow steps of Function Wizard	See index or Excel on-line help for individual functions
Goal Seek	ADVEX 217	Click Tools, click Goal Seek; enter target cell reference, goal value, and adjust cell reference; click OK	See Reference Window "Using Goal Seek"
Go To command	ADVEX 182	Press F5 to open the Go To dialog box, click name in the Go To list, click OK	See section, "Recording the GoToAssumptions Macro"
Header, edit	ADVEX 101	In Page Setup dialog box, Header/Footer tab; click Header list arrow to select a pre-set header , or click Custom Header button to edit the existing header	To open the Page Setup dialog box from the worksheet window, click File, click Page Setup
Help, on-line search	ADVEX 34	Double-click Help button, click Index tab; type keyword, click Display, click desired topic, click Display	
Hide, columns	ADVEX 104	Move pointer to column line in worksheet border; click and drag pointer to the left until column disappears; release the mouse button	
Integrate programs, paste	ADVEX 159	Select Excel chart or range. Copy object to clipboard; launch destination program and open document; click where object is to be inserted; click [icon]	See Reference Window "Integrating Programs with Copy and Paste"
Link workbooks, arrays	ADVEX 358		See section "Using Arrays to Link Workbooks"
Link workbooks, formulas	ADVEX 351		See section " Using Formulas to Link Workbooks"
List, insert subtotals	ADVEX 404	Click Data, click Subtotals; in Subtotals dialog box, select column to subtotal on, function to use to summarize, and field to subtotal	See Reference Window "Inserting Subtotals into a List"
Macro, change	ADVEX 205		See Reference Window "Recording Changes to an Existing Macro"
Macro, delete	ADVEX 205	Click Tools, click Macro, select macro to delete, click Delete	See section "Deleting Macros"
Macro, print VBA code	ADVEX 200	Select the module sheet; click File, click Print; click OK	
Macro, record	ADVEX 180	Click Tools, point to Record Macro, click Record New Macro; enter the commands to place in the macro and click [icon] to stop recording	See Reference Window "Recording a Macro"
Macro, run	ADVEX 182	Click Tools, click Macro, click name of macro; click Run	See Reference Window "Running a Macro"
Macro, view VBA code	ADVEX 186	Click Tools, click Macro, select the macro to view, click Edit	See Reference Window "Viewing the Macro Code"

Microsoft Excel for Windows **Task Reference**

TASK	PAGE #	RECOMMENDED METHOD	NOTES
Macro command, add to the Tools menu	ADVEX 190	Click Tools, click Macro, select macro; click Options, enter Menu Item name; click OK, click Close	See section "Setting Recording Options"
Map, change category shading colors	ADVEX 169	Select map, click Map, click Category Shading Options; select desired category; click Color list arrow to select a color	
Map, change legend	ADVEX 169	Double-click map legend; adjust settings in Edit Legend dialog box	
Map, change value shading colors	ADVEX 167	Select map, click Map, click Value Shading Options; click Color list arrow to select a color	
Map, create	ADVEX 164	Select map data, click 🖐; select desired map in Multiple Maps Available dialog box	See Reference Window "Creating a Map"
Menu editor, display	ADVEX 584	Activate module sheet; click Tools, click Menu Editor	
Module sheet, insert	ADVEX 484	Click Insert, point to Macro, click Module	
Move, cell contents	ADVEX 90	Select cell range to be moved; move cell pointer to edge of selected range until it change to ▯; click and drag range outline to new location	See Reference Window "Moving Cell Contents"
Move, worksheet	ADVEX 108	Click and drag tab from initial position to desired position	
MS Query, create a query	ADVEX 434		See Reference Window "Creating a Query"
MS Query, create a query using one table	ADVEX 438	Click ▦, double-click table listed in Add Tables dialog box; drag fields used in query to Table pane	
MS Query, select a data source for	ADVEX 435	Click Data, click Get External Data to start MS Query; double-click Data Source	See Reference Window "Using MS Query to Access an External Data Source"
Non-adjacent ranges, selecting	ADVEX 132	Select initial cell or range, hold down Ctrl key while selecting additional cells	See Reference Window "Selecting Non-adjacent Ranges"
One-input data table, create	ADVEX 219	Set up the one-input table structure, click Data, click Table, enter the column Input Cell, click OK	See section "One-input Data Table"
Open, workbook	ADVEX 44	Click 🖼, select file, click Open	See Reference Window "Opening a Workbook File"
Outline	ADVEX 364	Select range to be outlined, click Data, point to Group and Outline, click Auto Outline	See section "Working with Outline Groups"
Page Breaks	ADVEX 102	Select the row in column to insert page break. Click Insert, click Page Break	See section "Using Page Breaks"
Page setup, open	ADVEX 100	Click File, click Page Setup; change setting sheets as needed	See section "using Page Setup to Print the Worksheet"

Microsoft Excel for Windows **Task Reference**

TASK	PAGE #	RECOMMENDED METHOD	NOTES
Patterns, applying to a range of cells	ADVEX 98		See section "Using Borders and Patterns"
Pivot table, creating from an Excel data list	ADVEX 410		See section "Creating a Pivot Table"
Pivot table, generating from an external data source	ADVEX 443	With all rows in data list displayed, click a cell in the list; click Data, click PivotTable; in PivotTable Step 1 of 4 dialog box, ensure External Data Source option is selected; follow the instructions for activating MS Query and retrieving the external data	
Pivot table, grouping data	ADVEX 421	Select cell containing item you want to group; click the PivotTable toolbar Group button	See section "Grouping Data in the Pivot Table"
Print, worksheet	ADVEX 41	Click 🖨	See Reference Windows "Printing a Worksheet"
Printout, center	ADVEX 102	In Print Preview dialog box, click Setup, click Margins tab, check Horizontally and/or Vertically check boxes	To open the Page Setup dialog box from the worksheet window, click Page Setup on the File menu
Print Preview window, open	ADVEX 42	Click 🔍	
Protection, activating	ADVEX 113	Click Tools, point to Protection, click Protect worksheet	See Reference Window "Turning On Protection"
Protection, deactivating	ADVEX 114	Click Tools, point to Protection, click Unprotect Sheet; if necessary, enter a password	See Reference Window "Turning Off Protection"
Range, paste as a linked Excel worksheet in a destination document	ADVEX 449	Copy the Excel range to paste to the clipboard, activate the destination document, click Edit, click Paste Special; click Paste Link click OK	See section "Linking an Excel Object to a Worksheet Document"
Range, paste as an embedded Excel worksheet in a destination document	ADVEX 457	Copy the Excel range to paste, activate the destination document, click Edit; click Paste Special; click Paste; click OK	See section "Linking an Excel Object to a Worksheet Document"
Range, select nonadjacent range	ADVEX 132	Select range; hold down Ctrl key and select another range	See section "Selecting Nonadjacent Ranges"
Range name, apply to formula	ADVEX 94	Select cell range; click Insert, point to Name, click Apply, select names, click OK	
Range name, assign	ADVEX 92	Select cell range; click Name box, type range name, press Enter	
Regression	ADVEX 301		See Reference Window "Performing a Linear Regression Analysis"
Rounding results	ADVEX 79		See section "Rounding Results"